Python Web Programming

3 - 6 -

Python Web
Programming

Steve Holden

www.newriders.com

201 West 103rd Street, Indianapolis, Indiana 46290

An Imprint of Pearson Education

Boston • Indianapolis • London • Munich • New York • San Francisco

Python Web Programming

Trademarks

Warning and Disclaimer

Publisher
David Dwyer

Associate Publisher
Stephanie Wall

Production Manager
Gina Kanouse

Managing Editor
Kristy Knoop

Senior Development Editor
Lisa Thibault

Product Marketing Manager
Stephanie Layton

Publicity Manager
Susan Nixon

Project Editor
Stacia Mellinger

Copy Editor
Geneil Breeze

Indexer
Joy Dean Lee

Manufacturing Coordinator
Jim Conway

Book Designer
Louisa Klucznik

Cover Designer
Brainstorm Design, Inc.

Cover Production
Aren Howell

Proofreader
Debbie Williams

Composition
Deborah Hudson

❖

To my wife, Dorothy, for her love, support, tolerance,
and understanding.
To my brother, David, for the peace of mind to
undertake this work.
To Dad, who would have been proud of me.
To the cats, Dapple and Paisley, for their continual reminders
that play is a creative activity.

❖

TABLE OF CONTENTS

About the Author

Steve Holden is a consultant, advising on system and network architectures and the design and implementation of programmed web systems for commercial clients. His client base includes GlobalPhone, an international telecommunications company, and the Prometric division of Thomson Learning. He was the technical lead on the major redesign of the National Science Foundation's web site in 1997.

Steve also teaches classes on TCP/IP, UNIX security, web security, intranet technologies, and database topics for Learning Tree International.

Steve has spent time on both sides of the "academic divide" and was an early researcher into the integration of text, graphics, and databases while teaching commercial computing topics at Manchester University. This research led Steve to form Desktop Connection Limited, the first UK reseller of Frame Technology's (now Adobe's) FrameMaker software. His customers included British Telecom, British Aerospace, British Gas, and Sun Microsystems.

Steve was born and raised in the UK, and has traveled throughout Europe and the USA on teaching assignments. He now lives with his wife, Dorothy, in Fairfax, Virginia, where when not consulting, teaching, or writing, he enjoys looking for worthwhile American beers, entertaining friends and family, and reading science fiction.

About the Technical Reviewers

These reviewers contributed their considerable hands-on expertise to the entire development process for *Python Web Programming*. As the book was being written, these dedicated professionals reviewed all the material for technical content, organization, and flow. Their feedback was critical to ensuring that *Python Web Programming* fits our readers' need for the highest-quality technical information.

Alex Martelli is a software developer and writer in Bologna, Italy. After earning a master's degree in Electronic Engineering from Bologna University, he joined IBM Research. Over the years, he has obtained three Outstanding Technical Achievement Awards for contributions on Speech Recognition, Multimedia Frameworks, and statistical processing of Natural Language. Coming back to his native town, he taught then-new ISO Standard C and software development methods in various venues and then taught Numerical Computing as a professor at Ferrara University.

He joined think3, inc, where he is now Senior Software Consultant. For think3, over the years, he has helped develop libraries and frameworks; network protocols for licensing, database access, and file sharing; UI engines; an event framework; and a web access layer for PDM. He is a C++ MVP for Brainbench. His main hobby is bridge; the publication he's proudest of was published in *Bridge World* in Jan/Feb 2000, giving the results of computer research he performed on the foundations of the game of bridge.

John Tobler first programmed a symbolic logic system in Fortran IV for an IBM 1401 computer in 1962. Having started with spaghetti coding, he evolved beyond structured programming and now enjoys designing and engineering complex object-oriented systems with Python, Squeak SmallTalk, Ruby, C++, Java, C#, and whatever other object-oriented language happens to be handy at the moment. He currently strives to imagine (or create) what major software development abstractions will transcend object-orientation. He thinks Linux, XML, .NET (including Mono), Web Services, scripting languages, and open-source software development are good technology bets for today and tomorrow. John is an independent scholar who loves learning everything, sharing cool ideas, and serving humanity in whatever small ways are available each and every day.

Acknowledgments

The author of a technical book as large as this owes a considerable debt to many people. As well as those specifically named here, I would like to thank regular contributors to the `comp.lang.python` newsgroup, for asking and answering many interesting questions. Their discussions enlightened me as well as helped guide the future development of Python, and they exemplify how a newsgroup can act as a supportive community.

Guido van Rossum deserves the gratitude of all Python users. I am certainly glad that he developed, and continues to develop, Python. The language's versatility and elegance are a tribute to his skills as a language designer as well as his determination to choose what he knows to be the right future direction for Python.

Tim Peters, now a colleague of Guido's at Zope (formerly Digital Creations), is a continuous source of information and wisdom, dispensed with a cheerful good humor and a great many fractional winks. I look forward to meeting Tim one day, should he actually turn out not to be a van Rossum Python program.

Many individuals have contributed code to the Python core, as well as important third-party modules, and it is not possible to name them all. However, special thanks go to the authors of several modules I use heavily, both in the book and in my day-to-day tinkering with Python. Marc-André Lemburg authored `mxDateTime` and `mxODBC`, both high-quality modules that many others also find invaluable. Greg Stein wrote the `dtuple` module that makes dealing with database query results both more natural and more comprehensible. Tim O'Malley deserves thanks for the `timeout-socket` and `Cookies` modules, both significant for web programmers and both discussed in this book. Sam Rushing wrote the elegant `asyncore` and `asynchat` modules without which it would be much more difficult to write asynchronous servers in Python. Aaron Watters wrote the `gadfly` database module so useful to those who like to do everything, even SQL database work, in Python. Chuck Esterbrook is the instigator of, and a major contributor to, the Webware environment, another object-oriented web framework from which much can be learned.

Learning Tree International generously gave me permission to use diagrams and examples from their *Relational Databases: Design, Tools, and Techniques* class, a most enjoyable course to teach. I am grateful to them and also to Lynda Whitley, the author of the course.

Andrew Kuchling kindly allowed me to include his descriptions of recent changes to the language as an appendix, and I am grateful to him for this permission.

My ex-colleague and apprentice programmer Dave Beaudoin provided some distinguished graphics for Chapter 18's ("A Web Application—Python.Teach.com") sample web site at short notice. Without his assistance, the site would have done exactly what it does now but would have looked rather less prepossessing.

Stephanie Wall, Associate Publisher for New Riders, has been a source of encouragement and fortitude throughout what (inevitably) turned out to be a longer project than I anticipated. Lisa Thibault, Senior Development Editor, has been my main interface to the publishing process and has cheerfully accepted whatever came in, even if it was sometimes a little late. Geneil Breeze, the principal Copy Editor for the book, improved the book's readability enormously with her eye for stylistic consistency; and Stacia Mellinger, the Project Editor, provided thoughtful questions that led to many clarifications. The whole New Riders team has done an amazing job of turning what regular `comp.lang.python` readers know to be prose full of typographical errors into the seemingly erudite volume you now hold in your hands, and they deserve my thanks. Dealing with a team of such professionals has really helped me to get through the task.

David Beazley, already known to Pythonistas as the author of New Riders' excellent *Python Essential Reference*, kindly provided the XML chapters that make up Part IV, "XML and Python," allowing the book to be published this century when it looked impossible to complete it on time.

Finally, I would like to thank my Technical Editors, John Tobler and Alex Martelli. John's many encouraging remarks gave me the will to continue when sometimes the load seemed too heavy, and all readers should be grateful for his insistence on making the sample code useful and usable. Alex, who is well-known in his own right as an authority on all matters Pythonic, went above and beyond the call of duty by not only providing essential criticism of my text and code, but even adding a couple of necessary sections to crucial chapters.

It strikes me as a measure of how fully electronic communication has changed my life, as I reach the end of this list, that I have only met two of the individuals to whom I have just expressed my thanks. I owe each of them so much I can only hope that this omission will be rectified before too long, and I have already marked the next Python Conference in my diary.

Ultimately, the responsibility for any remaining errors or omissions remains mine. I well know that without the help of each of the individuals named above, my task would have been harder and the resulting book less informative and readable.

Finally, I would like to thank you, the reader. Without readers there could be no writers and I would never have produced this, my first book. You will find my contact details through the New Riders web site at www.newriders.com, and I will always be pleased to receive readers' opinions and suggestions, even when incoming mail volume makes it impossible for me to reply.

Steve Holden
October 2001

Tell Us What You Think

As the reader of this book, you are the most important critic and commentator. We value your opinion and want to know what we're doing right, what we could do better, what areas you'd like to see us publish in, and any other words of wisdom you're willing to pass our way.

As the Associate Publisher for New Riders Publishing, I welcome your comments. You can fax, email, or write me directly to let me know what you did or didn't like about this book—as well as what we can do to make our books stronger.

Please note that I cannot help you with technical problems related to the topic of this book, and that due to the high volume of mail I receive, I might not be able to reply to every message.

When you write, please be sure to include this book's title and author as well as your name and phone or fax number. I will carefully review your comments and share them with the author and editors who worked on the book.

Fax: 317-581-4663
Email: stephanie.wall@newriders.com
Mail: Stephanie Wall
          Associate Publisher
          New Riders Publishing
          201 West 103rd Street
          Indianapolis, IN 46290 USA

Introduction

The Python world has definitely increased its growth rate over the last three years. The primary network newsgroup for the language has seen traffic grow to the point where only some sort of filtering allows the average reader to keep up. The number of questions from new users continues to increase, and the range of application areas with Python solutions is growing daily. Just the same, the programming community at large still manages to resist Python's charms, for reasons often unstated but doubtless including inertia and ignorance. This latter is being addressed by a growing number of books on Python topics, to which I add my own contribution with some trepidation.

The Python language is an interesting contrast with some of the overweight programming products available commercially. Like these other language implementations, Python distributions continue to grow in size. The installer for the ActivePython Windows 2.0 implementation, used to develop much of the code in this book and definitely the largest popular distribution, weighs in at a whopping 7.8 MB—hardly a monster by today's standards. Even so, the Python community is already discussing how to trim some of the fat from the less-used portions of the distribution. My own downloads of the many excellent third-party extensions and applications for Python have probably added another 8 MB, extending the range of the language impressively.

If you do not already know Python, it is worth learning for a number of reasons, including its broad applicability and easy portability. If you are a Python user, I hope to demonstrate in these pages exactly how suitable this fascinating language is for writing web software. I remain continually impressed by the relatively small amount of code required to accomplish some of the tasks you will see tackled by the many sample programs I have included.

Guido van Rossum, Python's originator, has impressed the members of the Python community over the years by steering a careful path through the minefield of possible development directions to retain the language's essential simplicity and purity, while increasing its suitability for an ever-widening range of tasks. Because Python is an open-source project, it has much to teach the interested user about language implementation issues as well as language design. Under Guido's guidance, it seems very unlikely that anyone in the development team will ever be able to sneak a kitchen sink into the language. New features are ruthlessly rejected unless they add real value to the language.

Although it has a few controversial features, most significantly (at least to nonusers) its novel approach to block structure, Python is intentionally not a radical departure from traditional programming practices. Its syntax is simple and therefore easy to understand, and the semantics of the language blend procedural and object-oriented features to allow the most natural expression of algorithms. Although it *is* possible to write obfuscated Python, it is rather more difficult than in other languages, and simplicity (with its attendant advantages, ease of comprehension, and straightforward maintainability) tends to be cultivated as a virtue in the Python world.

This in turn makes Python a very suitable language for beginners. Guido is known to be interested in broadening the scope of computer programming activity, and this goal is quite well-reflected in the attitude of the Python community to new members, who are usually welcomed with friendly advice and encouragement. I hope that in some small way this book too will encourage people, including you, to take up Python and save themselves some time in the process.

Who Is This Book For?

When I first spoke with New Riders about the prospect of writing this book, I was enthusiastic about promoting Python to as wide an audience as possible. If you are browsing this book in a store and wondering whether to part with your hard-earned cash, why should you spend your money on this particular volume?

First, I have tried to include enough material about Python in the early chapters so that if you have any programming experience at all, you should not need any other reference, at least to start with. After you are established as a Python programmer, you will doubtless find many other worthy purchases, but this is intended to be a suitable introductory Python book.

Second, I have tried not to focus too narrowly on any single aspect of web programming but instead to produce a broad coverage of all the important technologies. Building modern web systems requires mastery of several areas that have been the focus of my professional life over the last 30 years. Besides command of a suitable programming language, you need to understand how networked systems operate, how to design and construct relational databases, and how the HTTP protocol works. Rather than simply discuss the mechanics of putting web-based applications together, *Python Web Programming* presents enough background material to help you develop a complete understanding of the underlying technologies.

More and more applications are being web-enabled as the world of the "thin client," with limited desktop maintenance and management, becomes more popular with IT managers. One of Python's strengths is its capability to integrate with other technologies, and so even if your application is programmed in some other language, you may find that you can embed web interfaces in Python more easily than you can extend your existing application code.

You should ideally have a working familiarity with an existing programming language, but it might as easily be Perl as C++ and need not be an object-oriented language. If you are determined to learn, then you might even be a complete beginner to programming, although in that case I would expect you to use the excellent Python tutorial mailing list, `python-help@python.org`. You do not need to understand the principles of object-orientation, although prior exposure to such ideas will make some of the early material easier to follow.

Most of all, you should have an interest in how the web operates in its entirety. If you simply need to write CGI scripts, better books are probably available; although as you will discover, Python excels in the CGI world, too. If you want to understand how several crucial technologies work together to produce focused web systems without a heavyweight infrastructure of existing components, then I hope you will find within these pages all the knowledge you require.

Contents of the Book

Python Web Programming consists of 18 chapters and two appendixes, discussed in the following few sections.

Part I: Why Python, and How?

Chapter 1, "The Python Language," is an overview of Python's history and current role and explains what sort of language Python is, how it compares with other popular languages, and what you can do with it.

Chapter 2, "An Introduction to Python," introduces the syntax of the language and the various control structures and data structures available to the Python programmer. It also explains the role of the Python module and reviews many of the most important built-in functions.

Chapter 3, "Object-Orientation," shows you how to use Python's object-oriented features to define object classes and to create and manipulate instances of those classes.

Part II: Network Programming in Python

Chapter 4, "Client/Server Concepts," deals with the basis of most modern Internet-based distributed computing applications. It discusses the structure and role of the TCP/IP protocol stack and explains how to use the socket library, Python's primary interface to the TCP/IP stack.

Chapter 5, "Available Client Libraries," introduces you to many of the library modules that allow you to write Python programs that use existing network services, such as FTP for file transfer, SMTP and POP for electronic mail, NNTP for network news, and HTTP for web access.

Chapter 6, "A Server Framework Library," introduces you to part of the Python library that you can use to build servers for any TCP- or UDP-based network service. It shows you how the basic server library is successively refined to provide a relatively simple web server that you can use to implement your own web services in very short programs.

Chapter 7, "Asynchronous Services," points out some deficiencies of the server structures you examined in Chapter 6 and explains how to use those modules, as well as the asyncore and asynchat modules, to build more flexible servers to concurrently serve multiple requests.

Part III: Database Programming in Python

Chapter 8, "Relational Database Principles," introduces the principles behind the RDBMS, explains the process of logical database design, demonstrates the value of normalized database structures, and discusses why physical designs ultimately depend on the implementation platform.

Chapter 9, "Client/Server Database Architectures," demonstrates the client/server nature of present-day relational database systems, explains the role of SQL as an interface between applications and the RDBMS, and highlights the value of stored procedures and triggers, as well as some of their pitfalls.

Chapter 10, "The Python Database Interface," discusses the general structure of the API commonly used by Python modules that interface to one or more relational database engines. It also gives details of some real-world Python database modules and explains how Python programs actually interact with the database engine.

Chapter 11, "Adapting the Python Interface to Database Products," discusses how to write applications in such a way as to largely isolate the program code from the specifics of the particular database engine and its SQL implementation. It gives examples with a number of additional database modules, and ends up showing you how you can build a simple database-driven web site entirely in Python.

Part IV: XML and Python

XML is a topic no web professional can afford not to know, and in this part of the book you will learn about the various ways you can process XML in Python.

Chapter 12, "A Bird's-Eye View of XML," provides an appreciation for the role and flexibility of the XML language.

Chapter 13, "XML Processing," explains how to get started with Python XML processing and gives code samples that exemplify the use of the most important Python XML processing modules.

Chapter 14, "SAX: The Simple API for XML," discusses a flexible module that offers an event-driven approach to XML processing.

Part V: Integrated Web Applications in Python

Chapter 15, "Building Small, Efficient Python Web Systems," prepares you to integrate the various technologies that the previous parts have explained. As well as contrasting traditional web systems with the ones you can build for yourself entirely in Python, the chapter discusses approaches to designing and building complex software systems of any kind.

Chapter 16, "Web Application Frameworks," discusses some of the more significant web frameworks written either partially or entirely in Python. It covers the different ways in which Python code can be integrated with an existing web server as well as discussing some of the better-known pure Python web systems.

Chapter 17, "AWeFUL: An Object-Oriented Web Site Framework," shows how you can build a framework for complete web applications using only the Python language.

It concentrates on the most basic functionality, providing an infrastructure that will accept Python applications easily.

Chapter 18, "A Web Application: PythonTeach.com," shows how a fictional company might use a hardened version of Chapter 17's framework to build a production web site, including a limited eCommerce capability, and shows you how to solve many of the practical problems faced by all web application designers.

Part VI: Appendixes

Appendix A, "Changes Since Python 2.0," summarizes the major changes to Python, underlining the fact that Python is a living language that continues to develop and grow. You will find many of the new features to be valuable additions to your python armory.

Appendix B, "Glossary," provides definitions for many of the jargon terms used in the book. This should make it easier to use the book as a reference as well as a learning text, and to allow you to orient yourself more quickly when the index guides you to an unfamiliar part of the book.

Conventions

This book follows a few typographical conventions:

- A new term is set in *italics* the first time it is introduced.
- Program text, functions, variables, and other "computer language" are set in a fixed-pitch font—for example, `class Table`.
- Code continuation characters ➡ appear where the line would not ordinarily break but had to be broken to fit on the printed page.

I

Why Python, and How?

1

The Python Language

PYTHON IS AN OBJECT-ORIENTED SCRIPTING language that is becoming increasingly popular with the web community. There are many reasons for this, not least of which are

- The amazing range of library code that comes with the system or can be obtained from other sources
- The high levels of productivity that can be maintained over large projects
- The wide range of platforms the language supports

I first heard about Python five years ago when I was reviewing languages for server-side web scripting use. I thought it was interesting but eventually opted for Perl on the grounds that more programming staff were available who knew the language. This led to my learning Perl, which I frankly rather wish I had not. True, there is a large Perl programming community, but I never really felt a great affinity for the language. The syntax is deliberately designed so that almost any string has "meaning," and it is not easy to understand an inexperienced programmer's code quickly, which is a requirement in the fast-moving web world.

I followed this experience with Perl by writing web systems in VBScript for Microsoft's Active Server Pages environment. VBScript is an even more frustrating language than Perl because it has much less representational flexibility due to its limited range of data types. Despite this, I managed to build some database-driven sites, which led me to think that with a better language I could extend this framework to be even more useful. At this point I remembered Python and started to use it. One of the things I quickly discovered is that Python is easy to learn.

If you are interested in programming web systems, or simply in programming, then Python is worth learning. Many Python web frameworks have already been developed, and the language is adaptable enough to allow you to develop your own framework if you have special requirements not provided for in existing software.

Where Python Came From

Python has been around for just over a decade now. Although it has academic roots, it has moved fairly rapidly into commercial use, spreading worldwide thanks to the global Internet community. The wide range of applications available in Python is a tribute to its design.

Origins of the Language

Guido van Rossum, who at the time worked for the Mathematisch Centrum in Amsterdam, originally developed Python starting in 1989. Guido had been one of the developers of the ABC language, but its design was limited in its extensibility and unpopular with programmers because of its atypical syntax. Looking for a project to keep him busy over the Christmas vacation, he decided to produce a language that improved on ABC by being more readable and having less unnecessary variability.

He felt that that existing object-oriented languages were too complex, and some used static typing, which forced extra verbiage and increased program complexity. He designed Python to appeal to UNIX/C hackers, building on ABC's extensive usability testing. He also wanted it to be suitable as a programming language for beginners as well as experienced programmers. This led to Python's inheriting, among other things, ABC's indented block structure.

In the mid-1990s Guido moved to the United States to work for the Corporation for National Research Initiatives (CNRI), a nonprofit organization largely funded by the US government. This allowed him to continue his work on Python and to undertake the construction of a number of larger-scale applications. Although he has been discreet about the way the nature of his work changed, it appears that the applications development work eventually started to interfere with the development of the core language.

Whatever the reasons, in 2000, Guido left CNRI and with two other members of the Python team moved to BeOpen.com, a commercial organization active in the development of open-source software. Tim Peters, a long-time Pythonista and a frequent and intelligent contributor to the `comp.lang.python` newsgroup, joined them there. The stated intention was to focus on the development of the core language and its support libraries. Unfortunately, things apparently did not work out with BeOpen. The change was followed, after about three months, by a further move to Digital Creations, now Zope Corporation, a major Python user and the creator of the Zope web system.

The development team is now upbeat about the future direction of language development. Although it seems inevitable that the association with Zope Corporation will emphasize at least some of the features that are important in improving Zope, the core development team is now aligned with an organization with a clear interest in maintaining Python and seeing it move forward.

The Python community is generally happy to have Guido retain the ultimate veto on language changes. He is affectionately referred to as the BDFL, or benevolent dictator for life, and his vote on language changes effectively has the infinite weight of an absolute veto.

Language Features

A small group, who initially helped Guido refine his ideas, enthusiastically took up the first Python implementation and made many suggestions for improvement. This has helped Python to meet the practical needs of both small and large systems. Python has many interesting features that are not always found together in the same language.

Interpreted Language

Python is interpreted rather than compiled, so it is easy to deploy Python programs as a replacement for scripting languages such as Perl, which has become the favored tool of system administrators around the world for file and other system manipulations. The interpreter will, if file permissions allow, produce a compiled bytecode file for imported modules. When you run a program, Python checks the creation times of source and compiled files for each imported module; and, if the compiled file is newer than the source, the inter-preter omits the unnecessary compilation stage. This tends to increase the speed at which library modules load, reducing overall runtimes. This treatment is *not* extended to the main program, however.

Interactive Operation

The Python interpreter is interactive. If you start it without a program file-name, it gives you a prompt and accepts expressions, individual statements, and blocks of code. The value of an expression will be printed out, the statements are executed, and the blocks of code can create definitions of object classes and functions that can be used interactively.

This is a great learning aid and enables interactive testing of new code while programming. Not only that, Python also comes with a multiplatform interactive development environment, *IDLE*. This is a great tool for browsing modules of Python code because it enables you to home in on a particular definition very easily.

In the Windows environment, you can also use a tool called *PythonWin*, which offers a simple interface to most of the important Microsoft Foundation Classes (MFC). PythonWin interacts with you in much the same way as the interpreter but also has great debugging and analysis features.

Flexible Data Representation

Python has a comprehensive set of data types. Numbers can be integer or real, strings are available in ASCII and Unicode, lists can grow and shrink dynami-cally, and dictionaries allow flexible lookup of any data type.

Variables do not have to be declared, and no type is associated with them—the value bound to a variable can be any of the basic Python types, which can include instances of object classes defined in the program. This sometimes causes people to suggest that Python is not a strongly typed language, but it is more correct to say that the data is strongly typed. The variables are dynami-cally typed (by name binding or assignment) rather than statically typed. This is sometimes referred to as *latent typing*.

Object Orientation

The compound data types, such as dictionaries, are objects, which means that they share the definitions of common operations. Most Python operators are extended where practical to the compound data types. For example, it is meaningful to multiply a string by an integer—the result is a new string con-taining the specified number of repetitions of the string operand.

Arbitrarily complex data values can be constructed as simple objects, and more complex objects allow the definition of operations as a part of the object's definitions. This enables programs to be built from objects, which make use of each other in a directed collaboration. Objects provide a simple way to build reusable program components for which the stored data and the algorithms used to operate on it are specified in the definition.

Graphical User Interfaces

Tkinter is a Python-specific interface to the *Tk* toolkit, which provides a range of graphical interface components. Tk is itself an extension of *Tcl*, the Tool Construction Language. If you have Tcl/Tk installed, Tkinter enables you to build Python programs with windowed interfaces. Although Tcl/Tk is multi-platform, its look-and-feel is somewhat different from that of the windows native to the platform. If this is not what you want, consider the wxPython user interface toolkit, which is a Python adaptation of the wxWindows toolkit. This, too, is multiplatform and conforms much more closely to the look-and-feel of the underlying platform. Of course PythonWin is also useful under Windows and offers the platform's native look-and-feel.

Multiplatform

As the preceding paragraph implies, Python is relatively unusual in the open-source world in offering good support for the Windows and Macintosh platforms, as well as many different flavors of UNIX. If you are careful to use only libraries supported on all platforms, or if you are prepared to work around the inevitable interplatform inconsistencies, Python is a very good language for building portable applications. You can also usually access a wide range of platform-specific features from Python, if you do not need your applications to be portable.

Clean Syntax with Indented Block Structure

Unlike conventional languages, Python uses indentation to indicate that statements are to be treated as a group. Bracketing characters often indicate this grouping in other languages, although programmers usually like to use indentation as a visual aid. This can cause problems if the indentation does not match the bracketing, which can happen when code is heavily modified.

Python is a straightforward language and has been kept syntactically simple. Although this may mean that programs are a little more verbose than in other languages, they also are much easier to understand. Because programs are a way of communicating between humans as well as with computers, this has its advantages.

Wide Range of Built-In Functions and Methods

Python includes many built-in functions to perform sometimes quite complex operations. Some of these functions are associated so strongly with particular data types that they are implemented as methods of the type. You can sort lists, apply functions over sequences, discover the data type of the value currently bound to an arbitrary variable, and so on.

Library Support

Finally, Python comes with more than 150 library modules for all kinds of tasks. You get support for network sockets, HTML parsing and analysis, random number generation, zipfile creation and manipulation, database handling, and many other functions. Further, many Python programmers have published their own libraries. Many of them are collected in a web site known as the Vaults of Parnassus, which you can search for modules to satisfy your requirements. Navigate to `http://www.vex.net/parnassus/` to start exploring the vaults.

Comparisons with Other Languages

Every programmer has a different approach to programming, so you might want to remember while you are reading this section that some of this is personal opinion. Opinions, like arteries, tend to harden with the age of the owner. Because of this, your approach to Perl, Java, and C++ may be a little less sclerotic than my own.

You should not, however, interpret my criticisms of other languages as an attempt to deny them the right to existence. Treat them, if you will, as an attempt to elucidate why Python is better for me to use on the particular class of problems in which I am interested.

Perl

Perl—sometimes known as the Pathologically Eclectic Rubbish Lister, but more correctly called the Practical Extraction and Report Language—is a pragmatist's dream or nightmare. It is freely available and freely redistributable. The Perl slogan is "There's More Than One Way To Do It," and Perl's author, Larry Wall, has designed the language to be deceptively simple and yet very rich. It was originally designed as a flexible tool for system programmers and administrators, combining the features of several widely used UNIX utilities. The intended users need quick ways to get systems tasks done, and Perl is undeniably more practical in this respect than UNIX shell command languages or other utilities used to handle text. Not only that, much of the language is portable across UNIX and Windows operating systems.

Like Python, Perl is an interpreted language, but Perl compiles a program each time it runs rather than retaining the compiled code in a separate file. Perl and Python are similarly relaxed about program structure, requiring minimal overhead for simple programs. The "Hello World" program in both languages is precisely one line long, and in fact the same program could be written in a way that would be acceptable to both the Perl and the Python interpreters! In both languages, "simple things are easy and hard things are possible."

When I came to Perl with more than 20 years of programming experience, I found it very difficult to understand other people's programs, which is my preferred way of approaching a new language. My own guess is that this is precisely because of its slogan. Because there is not usually one and only one natural way to perform any given operation, reading other people's code is confusing because the proportion of Perl idioms that are widely used and easily recognizable is lower than in other languages.

Of course, a body of code produced by a competent programming team is likely to be much easier to understand than a collection produced by Perl neophytes. Experienced programmers adopt idioms of their own, or idioms in common use, and consistency leads to comprehension.

A part of my confusion was Perl's insistence on using name prefixes to indicate whether a variable was

- A scalar, in which case its name would begin with a dollar sign
- An array, in which case its name would begin with an "at" sign
- A hash, in which case its name would begin with a percent sign

To compound my confusion, an element of an array called @home is referenced using a dollar sign if the element is a scalar, so its second element would be $home[1]. This leads me to wonder what I should do if the element of an array was itself an array. Now, to be fair to those who would defend Perl, there are rules that you can use to disambiguate such situations. However, this business of *context* seems to me to obfuscate the language unnecessarily.

Perl programmers might claim that context is useful because, for example, it allows you to extract elements from a list in the following way:

```
@home = ("couch", "chair", "table", "stove")
($potato, $lift, $tennis, $pipe) = @home
```

This explanation might fly if it were not possible to write an exactly equivalent assignment in Python without any of Perl's syntactic confusion:

```
home = "couch", "chair", "table", "stove"
potato, lift, tennis, pipe = home
```

In both cases, the `potato` variable ends up holding `"couch"`, the `lift` variable ends up holding `"chair"`, and so on. Given the choice between the two, I'll leave out the "at" signs, dollar signs, and redundant parentheses, thank you very much.

Function and subroutine arguments are less-than-natural to deal with in Perl. Perhaps because of Perl's origins as a replacement for various UNIX utilities, the arguments to a subroutine cannot be referenced by the names of formal parameters. This is because Perl subroutines *have* no formal parameters. Every subroutine call puts the arguments to the call in an array (with the memorable name of @_). To make the argument values accessible by name, the programmer must do so explicitly with a list assignment such as

```
my($key, $value) = @_;
```

Although it is possible to declare a function prototype (and get the benefits of compile-time checking on the type and number of arguments), the method is contrived and still does not name the formal parameters.

My final problem with Perl is its treatment of object-oriented concepts, introduced in the transition from Perl 4 to Perl 5, which seems to me far less natural than Python's. Loosely speaking, a class is defined as a package that contains the methods to deal with objects of that type. Objects are created and then have to be made members of a class using the `bless()` built-in function. Attributes and methods of a class are referred to using a two-character operator, which makes for more typing, as in the following:

```
$circle->draw();
```

This method of creating and handling objects is a tribute to Perl's flexibility (because the transition required no new semantics except the `bless()` function), but it does not make for easy understanding.

Despite all the objections just noted, Perl is still a very useful language for web programming and systems tasks, and its large and easily available collection of library packages and modules makes it easy to apply to a wide range of such tasks. The Python community is generally willing to acknowledge this, while taking occasional sideswipes at its syntax.

C++ and Java

C++ is a fully compiled language with strong static typing. Although derived from the C language, of which it is almost a syntactic superset, C++ includes full-featured object orientation. It supports encapsulation by enabling the programmer to declare exactly which portions of objects are accessible outside the interface and which are available only to the implementation.

Because C++ programs are rendered into machine code after linking, their execution speed is normally considerably higher than that of interpreted languages such as Python and Perl. The price paid for this execution speed is an increased edit-compile-run cycle time, although inroads have been made using incremental compilation techniques in some systems.

Java is also strongly statically typed, and both languages are rather more verbose than Python largely because of this. Rather than producing machine code, Java compilers produce bytecodes similar to Python bytecodes but for the Java virtual machine (JVM). This achieves a high degree of portability because the same bytecodes will run on any JVM. Different virtual machines take different approaches to execution: some interpret the bytecodes in software, and others use a just-in-time compilation technique to turn the bytecodes into machine code immediately before they are executed for the first time.

These execution techniques make Java programs rather slower than their equivalents in C++, which is much faster than Python. A surprising result is that according to results from Glyph Lefkowitz, generally Java is also faster than Python, although the tests should be considered specific to the particular development kit (JDK 1.1.7B versus Python 1.5.2) and operating system (Debian GNU Linux 2.2). These results should not be taken too seriously since they are admittedly subjective and show large variability in the speed ratios of Java and Python.

Glyph Lefkowitz

For more information on Glyph Lefkowitz, visit `http://www.aifb.uni-karlsruhe.de/`
`Lehrangebot/Winter2000-01/E-Shop/Artikel/A%20subjective%20analysis%20`
`of%20two%20high-level.htm`.

Lefkowitz also concluded that a Java program will be approximately three times as long as the equivalent Python and suggests that programming time will be three or four times as long in Java. Clearly, the level of language experience will have an effect on that, but a simple example highlights this. Here's a short Python program:

```
f=open('scratch','wb')
for i in xrange(1000000):
    f.write(str(i))
f.close()
```

Lefkowitz' equivalent Java program follows:

```
import java.io.*;
public class IOTest
{
    public static void main(String[] args) {
        try {
            File f = new File("scratch");
            PrintWriter ps = new PrintWriter(new OutputStreamWriter
                                    (new FileOutputStream(f)));
            for (int i = 0; i < 1000000; i++) {
                ps.print(String.valueOf(i));
            }
            ps.close();
        }
        catch(IOException ioe) {
            ioe.printStackTrace();
        }
    }
}
```

You can see that the necessity of importing the standard libraries and defining a class along with the block structure imposes a high textual overhead on Java. C++ would not suffer quite as badly, particularly on smaller programs, but it too needs declarations and requires similar demarcation of block structure.

According to Guido, in an essay comparing Python with other languages:

Almost everything said for Java also applies for C++, just more so: where Python code is typically 3-5 times shorter than equivalent Java code, it is often 5-10 times shorter than equivalent C++ code! Anecdotal evidence suggests that one Python programmer can finish in two months what two C++ programmers can't complete in a year. Python shines as a glue language, used to combine components written in C++. See http://www.python.org/doc/essays/comparisons.html: *"Comparing Python to Other Languages."*

Both Java and C++ allow the programmer to specify in great detail the interfaces between the various components in a program, allowing some implementation details to be public, some to be shared among a limited range of other components, and still others to be completely private. Python has none of this complexity, making it a simpler language but a more dangerous one. If the programmer wants to deal with the internal implementation of an encapsulated object, this is quite possible.

It is interesting to note that Python is promoted primarily as a scripting language, although many large programs and systems have been written in it. The Jython implementation, built in 100% pure Java, excels at gluing Java components together, as we will discuss briefly in Chapter 3, "Object-Orientation." The preferred strategy for obtaining fast execution in the standard Python implementation is to build a working application and then improve performance as necessary by migrating critical portions of the code into a purpose-built Python extension. The extension typically will be written in C, indicating that Python users tend to be language pragmatists rather than purists.

Is Python Freeware?

With the increased momentum of the open-source movement, licensing terms are receiving more attention. Python was always intended to be a "free" language in the sense that the source code for the interpreter and libraries was publicly available under liberal licensing conditions.

There has been some concern about licensing conditions, although this is probably unnecessary for most readers, because of changes made to the CNRI license with the 1.6 release of Python. This CNRI license is open source and was apparently intended to be compatible with the GNU Public License (GPL). Unfortunately, there was some disagreement as to compatibility with the GPL because of CNRI's insistence that the license should be interpreted under the laws of the state of Virginia. It has, however, received the approval of the Open Source Initiative (see `www.opensource.org`), and more recent licenses are approved as compatible with the GPL.

The Python 2.0 release was produced while the PythonLabs team was working with BeOpen, under what is termed the "BeOpen Python Open Source License Version 1." This license is short and sweet and should cause nobody any real problems. Obviously, corporate lawyers can review any concerns you may have, but the Python licensing terms really are surprisingly liberal and rather simple compared to most. One specific divergence from the

GPL allows the creation and distribution of derivative works without publication of the changes. The GPL allows creation of derived works without restriction, but distribution of a derived work requires the distributor to publish the source. The great advantage of this permission is that you can embed Python in proprietary products as a scripting language without the need to make your proprietary code public.

You may be familiar with the work of Mark Hammond in integrating Python into the Microsoft Windows environment. Mark now works with ActiveState, which produces an ActivePython implementation. In addition to the core binary code, ActivePython currently includes the Python core libraries; commonly used external modules, including *expat* for XML processing and *zlib* for data compression; and a suite of Windows tools developed by Mark Hammond, including the *PythonWin* IDE, the *PythonCOM* system, and more. ActivePython is available for Windows, Linux, and Solaris, and can be freely used for commercial and noncommercial purposes. The distributions are binary, and ActivePython's license forbids redistribution of the binary package even though sources for all components are open. Although it might not be considered open source, ActivePython does provide a convenient package for Python installation.

In summary, Python *is* an open-source project and is likely to remain so. More and more organizations are starting to use open-source software. Some concerns about support and accountability still exist; but because commercial software is usually hedged with limitations of liability, and open-source product developers are often more accessible than commercial support teams, such concerns are slowly disappearing.

Where Python Is Going

The rather nomadic tribulations of the development team generated some uncertainty during the migration from CNRI to Zope Corporation. Now, though, the PythonLabs team appears to have found a new long-term home. This is good news for everyone with an interest in Python.

One recent change has been the introduction of the Python Enhancement Proposal (PEP) process as a means of controlling discussions about the future of the language. PEPs can be informational, intended to shed light on some of the more obscure areas of the language, or they can be standards-track. This latter class of document is usually created as a result of discussions on the `python-dev` mailing list, and each one starts as a draft. After a suitable discussion period, Guido or his delegates review the draft and either reject or accept it.

When accepted, a PEP must be implemented before it is accorded active status, thereby becoming a part of the language.

Recent Developments: Python 2

This book is based on Python 2, which was released in October 2000. Version 2.0 of the language introduced a number of changes, some of them quite significant. At the time of this writing, there are plans for a 2.2 implementation, which will be taken into consideration if it arrives early enough to be included. The major change is to the scoping rules used to determine which namespace a particular variable reference is resolved from. I am reasonably certain that the grasp of Python you obtain from this book will allow you to adapt to any changes not documented in the text or in Appendix A, "Changes Since Pyton 2.0."

The Distant Horizon

As Python has migrated through its several versions to date, the team has exercised great care to try to avoid breaking existing programs. This effort has not always been successful; occasional implementation lapses have found their way into code. One example was the `append()` method for lists, which until version 1.5.2 accepted more than the single argument it originally had been intended to deal with. The 1.6 implementation corrected the fault even though the change broke existing code because the intention had always been to have the method process a single argument. The development team preferred to bring the method in conformance with its documented interface rather than widen the specification to enable existing programs to continue to operate.

It is nevertheless surprising just how far the language has been able to develop without introducing more such problems of backward compatibility. Generally, it has been possible to move Python programs between platforms, and between different versions of Python, with little, if any, change.

For some time now, the Python development team has had a gleam in its collective eye, which has been referred to as *Python 3000*. This was intended as something of a joke about the long-range aspirations of the project, since when it was first envisaged, the computer applications world was going through the tribulations of Y2K adjustment. The intention is to produce a new, Python-like, language that addresses some of the more fundamental issues of efficiency in current implementations (without taking a thousand years about it).

In an interview at the Software Development 2000 conference, Guido said: "Python 3000 is a monumental effort—all the code will be rewritten and the documentation revised. This is my one chance to reimplement Python and fix its efficiency problems. But how incompatible it will be is a very big open question, and I don't have a concrete answer." So clearly, you should not expect guarantees of backward compatibility for the next major release of Python.

There were two significant goals for Python 3000. The first was a unification of the Python types with user-defined object classes. At present (as you will learn in Chapter 3), the object-oriented features of the language do not allow subclassing of the basic Python data types, something that has been a thorn in the language's side for a long time. The second major goal was the introduction of an optional static typing scheme to enable programmers to require that variables hold only values of particular types. This will enable the Python compiler to improve the efficiency of generated code because it will not have to check (at runtime) the type of such variables.

These, and other, changes in Python will cause a radical re-think of many of the language's basic assumptions and will therefore have a correspondingly longer development time frame. Encouragingly, Guido has recently written, "While I've previously said that it might be incompatible, I now expect that there will be a clean migration path for old code, so you don't have to worry about this."

The basis of this book is Python 2.0. As I write, the development team is about to release Python 2.2, and the evolution of Python is now seen as being evolutionary rather than revolutionary. Some interesting new features have appeared in these additional releases, and they are summarized in Appendix A.

Who Maintains Python

The Python team comprises five people: Guido van Rossum, Barry Warsaw, Jeremy Hylton, Fred Drake, and Tim Peters. The project is using the `www.sourceforge.net` open development web site to host the project, and a team of around 30 volunteers is collaborating with Guido's team, each member taking responsibility for specific features.

The SourceForge web site is dedicated to supporting open-source software projects. The Python project moved there when the team left CNRI to move to BeOpen and has remained there even after the relocation to Zope. Although there have been some concerns about response times and the collaboration process, the team seems to feel that progress has been faster after the move to SourceForge because the move opened up the project to a larger number of collaborators. The 2.0 release was originally anticipated late in the year 2000 but actually arrived on October 16. This was in large part due to the participation of other significant contributors, who might not have been able to join the team and contribute so effectively without the SourceForge site.

Guido is very keen to see Python remain open source and to this end has created a body called the *Python Software Foundation*, in which copyrights in the language and its implementations will be vested.

What Use Is Python

Python has been put to an amazing variety of uses and has proven capabilities not simply for scripting (normally thought of as rapidly built or throwaway applications) but also for general-purpose programming. Major web applications are included, as are mathematical programming and database applications.

Major Applications of Python

A list of users is at www.python.org/psa/Users.html, but even this page cannot be kept up to date because Python usage is growing fast! You can learn some of the highlights from the following paragraphs, which focus primarily on web applications.

The best-known application in Python is Zope, a web application server that makes it easy for groups of programmers to collaborate in producing highly dynamic web sites. Zope is the product of Zope Corporation, for whom the Python development team now works, so it has a high degree of Python expertise at its disposal. Zope has an extensive user base, including Verizon Mobile, Red Hat (the producers of possibly the most popular Linux distribution, which also uses Python quite extensively for system configuration and administration), and NASA.

Probably the most highly visible web site written in Python is the Google search engine. This system combines literally thousands of processors (more than 4,000 at the last count), crawls the web continuously, and uses a novel ranking system to select from more than a billion web pages. An additional feature that many users appreciate is the caching of pages, allowing a (sometimes out-of-date) copy of a page to be displayed even when the original site is unavailable due to server or network connectivity problems. The cached copies are presented with your search terms highlighted, allowing easier assessment of their relevance.

Inktomi Search Software is a commercial web search engine, comprising more than 30,000 lines of Python code, which you can buy for incorporation in your own intranet or public web site. A company called Infoseek, which eventually became a part of the Go network, originally produced it, and later the Ultraseek Corporation was acquired by Inktomi to round out its software offerings. The software can handle simple text and HTML files, as well as PostScript, PDF, and Microsoft Office documents.

The Association of American University Presses maintains a web-based catalog of more than 75,000 titles, which you can visit at `aaup.pupress.princeton.edu`. This is implemented in Python, although sadly none of the titles appear to be about Python programming.

The Internet White Pages site at `www.four11.com` uses Python extensively to maintain a huge database of email address and residential telephone listings. This site is now a part of Yahoo.

Thawte Certification, now a subsidiary of Verisign Corporation, is yet another company using Python. Because Thawte issues digital certificates via its web site, it must be highly organized, and yet the site proudly bears the "Python-Powered" logo, linked to the Python web site. Thawte clearly has a high degree of trust in Python!

A Glimpse at the Python 2 Libraries

Just to whet your appetite, Table 1.1 presents a selective list of some of the standard library modules that come as a part of the Python 2 distribution. You will find many more, as well as many third-party offerings, as you read the rest of the book.

Table 1.1 **Selective List of Standard Python Library Modules**

Library Module(s)	Usage
`mmap`	Memory-map the contents of a file, allowing reading and writing as though the file content was a mutable string
`filecmp`	Directory and file comparison functions with time/speed trade-offs
`glob`, `fnmatch`	Filename matching and wildcard expansion
`ftplib`	FTP protocol client
`imaplib`, `poplib`	Mail protocol client
`Queue`	Multiproducer, multiconsumer FIFO queuing
`xml.sax`	SAX-based XML parser support

Library Module(s)	Usage
shutil	High-level file operations
pickle, cPickle	Persistent storage of serialized objects
time, calendar	General time- and date-based support
urlparse	Parse URL into component parts
shlex	Lexical analysis of simple command languages
SocketServer	Network server framework

You can see that the scope of the Python library is wide-ranging and that many network-oriented tasks have support code already available. That is what makes Python so powerful for building web systems. You will be using most of these libraries, and many others, by the time you have finished this book.

Advantages of Object-Oriented Scripting

If you don't have any experience with object-oriented programming languages, you may be wondering what this aspect of the Python language will buy you. An object is, most simply, a collection of data and operations that can be performed on the data. The beauty of object-oriented programming is the capability to define classes of objects. A class definition can contain a specification of operations that can be performed on the instances of that class.

When you have defined a class, you can use that class as the basis of other class definitions, which can inherit behavior from their ancestor class. Thus the class definitions are a hierarchy, and you create specialized classes for specific purposes, keeping their common behavior at the highest level. This capability to build what are sometimes called *inheritance trees* greatly increases code reusability. (Because Python implements multiple inheritance, class inheritance structures are actually acyclic directed graphs.)

You will learn that Python encourages code modularity and that a common use of modules is to define object classes from which you can build your own useful subclasses. Many of the library modules take this approach, so you do not necessarily have to go through the complete learning curve before using object components in Python.

Summary

Python has many features desirable in a modern programming language yet
retains simplicity of design. You can solve problems in many application
domains, frequently with the assistance of a versatile set of library modules. It
is ideal for programming both the client and the server side of web-based
applications, and its object-oriented nature coupled with its easy extensibility
are continually expanding the language's horizons.

In Chapter 2, "An Introduction to Python," you will start to see how easy it
is to learn Python and begin to appreciate why Python use continues to
increase.

2

An Introduction to Python

PYTHON IS AN EXCELLENT FIRST LANGUAGE, but it also appeals to experienced programmers. Its clean syntax, coupled with a lack of static typing, make it ideal for the
pragmatists among us who are primarily interested in programming languages as tools
for getting jobs done. Although Python language-lawyers do exist, the syntax definition of Python is simple enough that you don't need to study it extensively (or even
at all) to be able to use the language effectively.

There is a reason for this: Python is a very permissive language. Other languages
effectively hog-tie you as a programmer with rules and restrictions about what you
can and cannot do. Python (and best-practice advice about programming generally)
suggests what you should and should not do, but leaves it up to you to put the advice
into practice. If you want to ignore the advice, then you can do so in the knowledge
that this might lead to undesirable situations. In brief, Python accepts that the programmer knows best and is the ultimate authority for what should and should not
be done.

Using the Interpreter

The Python interpreter has been designed for interactive use and, when started with
no program file arguments, gives you an interactive prompt. This helps you as a programmer because it is simple to test code snippets by entering them into an interactive

session. Here is what I see when I start the interpreter interactively in a DOS command window on my Windows 98 system:

```
C:\> python
ActivePython 2.0, build 202 (ActiveState Tool Corp.)
based on Python 2.0 (#8, Oct 19 2000, 11:30:05) [MSC 32 bit (Intel)] on➥
win32
Type "copyright", "credits" or "license" for more information.
>>>
```

The prompt indicates that the interpreter is waiting for you to enter code. If you enter a simple expression, the interpreter evaluates it and prints the result. If you enter a simple statement, the interpreter executes it immediately. You also can enter compound statements that have an introductory clause ending in a colon, followed by an indented "suite" of associated code. The interpreter expects such interactive compound statements to be terminated by a blank line. Entering the end-of-file character, which is Ctrl+Z for Windows and Ctrl+D under most versions of UNIX, ends an interactive session.

Learn Python by Using It

If you have no previous Python experience, you are strongly recommended to run the interactive examples as you read the book if you have a Python interpreter available. By entering statements and expressions into the interpreter, you can often answer your own questions far more quickly than by reading a book, and the answers you obtain will be definitive.

You might want to use another environment that gives you more control over the Python development process. *IDLE* (an *Integrated Development Environment for Python*) is a part of the standard distribution and works on any platform that supports the Tkinter GUI. If you are a Windows user, you might consider PythonWin, which also enables you to open Python code in editor windows and run the files you are editing. Both PythonWin and IDLE contain good debugging features.

Many other interactive development environments are either available or in the works. Python users have given ActiveState's Komodo a good write-up, despite the fact that it is multilanguage and also supports Perl and JavaScript! Komodo is based on the Mozilla open-source interface, and the beta release is a little sluggish, but it does have excellent functionality. The open-source Boa Constructor package (at the time of writing still in pre-alpha) is an attempt to produce an IDE for Python with similarities to Borland's Delphi. This software shows some promise as a GUI-builder tool, a class of software eagerly sought by the Python community.

Command-Line Interaction

The examples in the remainder of this book are sometimes complete programs and sometimes snippets of code that you can enter interactively. Because every Python user has the interpreter available, I have chosen to limit the examples to that environment rather than write to a more advanced development environment, which might not be available to all readers. You can tell the difference between complete programs and interactive sessions because in the latter you will see the interpreter's prompts for the interactive snippets. Listing 2.1 shows an example of an interactive Python session.

Listing 2.1   **An Interactive Python Session**

```
>>> s = 'This is a string'         # Comments begin with a pound sign
>>> s1 = "Another string"          # and extend to the end of the line
>>> s
'This is a string'
>>> s1
'Another string'
>>> s + " " + s1
'This is a string Another string'
>>>
```

You can see here that the interpreter has bound two names to string values using assignment statements. One string uses single quotes; the other uses double quotes—in most cases it does not matter which type is used. When the names are entered on their own, the interpreter treats them as expressions (because they are not complete statements) and prints out their values before issuing the next prompt. Finally, an expression that concatenates three strings (the first and the last being variables, the middle one being a literal space) also is printed.

Notice also that Python allows you to use either single or double quotes to delimit strings. This allows you to include single quotes in strings by using double quote delimiters and vice versa.

As your knowledge of Python develops, you will learn that it makes heavy use of *namespaces*. A namespace is just a place in which Python can look up the value associated with a particular name. So when a name is bound to a value, you can think of the name as existing in a namespace, and the value as existing in *object space* (which you can just think of as the area of memory the interpreter uses to store values). After Listing 2.1 is executed, you could think of the situation graphically as shown in Figure 2.1.

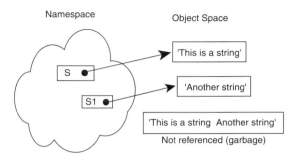

Figure 2.1   The names s and s1 bound to different values in object space.

Note that there is a representation of the string expression in object space, but that no name refers to it. This is because that value was never bound to a name; it was simply created as a by-product of the print statement. Python includes a dynamic garbage collection scheme, which allows it to reclaim the space used by such nonreferenced objects as required.

The more complex example in Listing 2.2 shows treatment of compound statements, which you will be covering in more detail later in this chapter in the section "Compound Statements."

Listing 2.2   **Compound Statements**

```
>>> def f(x):
...     print "Called with", x
...     print "Multiplied by two is:", x*2
...
>>> f(101)
Called with 101
Multiplied by two is: 202
>>> f(2.753)
Called with 2.753
Multiplied by two is: 5.506
>>> f("String!")
Called with String!
Multiplied by two is: String!String!
>>>
```

Here the interpreter is handling a function definition, introduced by the def statement. The function name is f, and it takes a single argument called x. The indented statements following the def statement represent the body of the function, which is terminated by a final blank line (this is not necessary in programs you run from files; it is just a convenience for the interpreter). You can tell when the interpreter is waiting for you to enter the next line of a compound statement because it uses a prompt of three dots rather than three "greater than" symbols as it does when waiting for any statement or expression.

This particular function does not return a value; the output you see is a result of the print statements being executed from inside the function definition. Technically, the function is actually returning a special value, None. The interpreter does not automatically print the values of expressions that yield this result.

You can see that the multiplication operation in Python works just as well on floating-point numbers as on integers. The first call performs pure integer arithmetic. For the second call, because the left-hand operand is a floating-point number, Python converts the right-hand operand to floating-point and returns a floating-point result.

The third call to the function demonstrates that you can multiply a string by an integer, and the result is that many repetitions of the string. This is explained in more detail in the "Sequence Types: Strings" section later in this chapter. You also take a more in-depth look at the def statement in the section "Defining Functions: def" later in the chapter.

Python Syntax

Python syntax is simple. Its simplicity is a design choice: having several ways to syntactically represent the same program construct can lead to difficulties in learning and using the language. Unlike Perl, which absolutely revels in the slogan "there's more than one way to do it," Python's philosophy is more along the lines of "there's usually one obvious way to do it." This does not mean that a simple question will not have several possible solutions because Python users are above all inventive people. Except in rare cases, though, not much will be gained by using a non-obvious solution.

Variables: assignment and typing

The assignment statement is the most common one in nonfunctional programming languages. To keep Python's underlying representation in mind, Python programmers tend to talk about binding a name to a value rather than assigning the value to a variable. Python uses the equal sign to denote an assignment statement.

```
name = expression
```

If the left-hand side of the assignment statement is a name, then Python binds the name to the data value generated by the expression. The expression can be arbitrarily complex, as you will see when you look at the data types available to the Python programmer. If the expression is a reference to a simple value that already exists, then the name is bound to the existing representation of the value. Unlike some other languages, Python does not insist that names can only be bound to particular types of data. Although every value in Python has a well-defined type, no checking needs to be performed before the name is bound because any name can be bound to any type of value.

> **Python Identifiers**
>
> A legal Python name (the documentation sometimes uses the term *identifier*) is made up of letters of either case, digits, and the underscore character. The first character of a name may not be a digit.

If the several different names are to be bound to the same value, this can be done in a single statement:

```
>>> v1 = v2 = v3 = "A text string"
>>> print v1
A text string
>>> print v3
A text string
```

Python Data Types

Each piece of data in Python has an associated type, which determines the operations that can be performed on it. The following sections discuss the various data types built in to Python.

Numeric Types

The basic numeric types you would expect—integer and real (floating-point)—are present in the language. You also can use *long integers*, which allow you to calculate using values whose size is limited only by available memory and complex numbers. Long integer constants are indicated by ending the integer value with a letter "L"— experienced programmers tend to use uppercase rather than lower because a lowercase "l" is far too easily confused with the digit "1."

You can express integers (and long integers) easily in octal using numbers beginning with a leading zero and in hexadecimal by using a leading "0x" or "0X". This can be confusing if you are used to entering decimal numbers with leading zeroes, as this interactive session shows:

```
>>> a = 09345 # illegal non-octal digits
Traceback (  File "<interactive input>", line 1
    a = 09345
          ^
SyntaxError: invalid syntax
>>> a = 9345
>>> a
9345
>>> a = 07345 # note this is an octal number
>>> a # now display it in decimal
3813
>>>
```

Complex numbers are represented as the sum of a real and an imaginary number. *Imaginary numbers* are like floating-point numbers but followed by "j" or "J." There was apparently quite a long discussion about whether to use the letter "i" or "j," and in the end the engineering convention won.

Table 2.1 shows a few examples of values of each type.

Table 2.1   **The Python Numeric Types**

Integer	1, 23, 456, 7890, 01234, 0X1234, 2147483647
Long integer	1L, 23L, 456L, 7890L, 1234567890L, 12345678901234567890L, 0X1234L, 0X12345678901234567890L
Floating-point	0.1, 1.38777878078e-016, .1, 0.000000000000768, 7.6799999999999999e-009
Imaginary	0.1j, 3.2879465J, 7.6799999999999999e-009j

Numeric Literals Are Positive

You have probably noticed that no negative values are shown in Table 2.1. Unary plus and minus operators can be used on any numeric value, so a negative number is actually the result of applying the unary negation operator to a positive number. The unary plus operator leaves all numbers unaltered and is therefore effectively a no-operation on numbers (but it still cannot correctly be applied to values of non-numeric types).

Numeric Operations

Although we are used to using arithmetic operations in our daily lives, computer arithmetic can still hold a few surprises. Python provides all the expected arithmetic operations, as well as a modulo (remainder after division) operator, for which the percent sign is used.

Despite a lot of discussion and some pressure from mathematical Python users, arithmetic expressions involving only integers still always yield integer results. This is sometimes a surprise to new programmers, who expect arithmetic in Python to behave the same way as on a pocket calculator.

```
>>> i = 7
>>> j = 3
>>> k = i / j
>>> print k
2
```

The value of k (due to the fact that integer division *truncates*) is not too surprising when you know to expect an integer result. The modulo operator always yields a result with the same sign as its right operand, which can also lead to unexpected results. The following example shows this:

```
>>> i = -7
>>> j = 3
>>> print i % j
2
```

The result is obtained because -7 is equal to (-3 * 3) + 2, but may seem counter-intuitive if you have used other languages with different definitions. Python 3.0 will see a change to integer division behavior. See Appendix A, "Changes Since Python 2.0," for details.

> **A Note on Floating-Point Numbers**
>
> Programming newcomers are surprised to discover that real numbers expressed as literal decimal values do not always have an exact representation, leading to small rounding errors. The looping constructs are explained later in the chapter, but you should be able to intuit what is going on. Note that your results may differ from those shown here, depending on the particular hardware you are using:
>
> ```
> D:\Python20>python
> Python 2.0 (#8, Oct 16 2000, 17:27:58) [MSC 32 bit (Intel)] on win32
> Type "copyright", "credits" or "license" for more information.
> Alternative ReadLine — Copyright 2001, Chris Gonnerman
> >>> x=1.0
> >>> for i in range(10):
> ...    x -= 0.1
> ...
> >>> x
> 1.3877787807814457e-016
> >>>
> ```
>
> The final value of x often takes people by surprise. A computer's actual binary representations of most decimal floating-point numbers are slightly inaccurate. After 10 iterations (on the computer used for this particular example), x contained something just marginally larger than zero, and so the loop performed a further iteration. Old programming hands are not surprised by slightly different results from the same code on computers of different architectures. They will be prepared for this and always will control loops of this nature using integer arithmetic.

In general, Python converts numeric types by *widening*—if a numeric operation is performed on two numbers of different types, the "narrower" type will be converted to the "wider" type first, and the result of the expression will be of the wider type. Complex is the widest type, then floating-point, then long integer, and finally integer.

Table 2.2 gives the full set of numeric operators. They are presented in descending order of precedence.

> **Operator Precedence**
>
> *Operator precedence* is the way languages specify the order of evaluation of expressions with no parentheses in them. For example in Python, as in standard arithmetic notation, 10*3+4 equals 34 because multiplication has a higher precedence than (or should be performed before) addition. If you aren't familiar with this concept, use parentheses whenever you are in doubt about the exact order of evaluation. In fact, do that even if you *are* familiar with this concept.

Table 2.2 **Python Arithmetic Operators**

Operator	Meaning
**	Power operator, defined for all types of numbers: 2 ** 4 equals 16. 3 ** 2.1 equals approximately 10.04510856630514. (1+1j) ** -1 equals (0.5-0.5j).
unary +	Has no effect on numeric values.
unary —	Negates the value.
unary ~	Applies to integers and long integers only, and yields the bitwise inversion of the integer value (when I is a long integer, this is treated as -(I+1), which agrees with the twos-complement system used by modern CPUs. On my PC, ~-2 equals 1, and ~1234567890L equals -1234567891L.
/, *, and %	Division, multiplication, and modulo, respectively. The modulo operator yields the remainder after dividing the first operand by the second. It can be applied to floating-point and complex numbers, sometimes with confusing results.
+ and —	Addition and subtraction, respectively.
<< and >>	Left and right shift, respectively. This operation can be applied only to integers and long integers, and if either operand is a long integer, then the result is a long integer. Overflow is ignored on integers, which can lead to unexpected sign changes, and the right operand *must* always be positive: 1 << 12 equals 4096, -1 << 12 equals -4096, (255 << 26) >> 26 equals -1 due to overflow and sign extension, and 01234567000 >> 9 equals 342391 (which also equals 01234567).
&, ¦, and ^	Bitwise and, or, and exclusive-or, respectively. These operations can be applied only to integers and long integers, and the usual widening takes place.

Numeric Comparisons and Boolean Operations

Numeric values can be compared in all the expected ways using the operators in Table 2.3. All these operators have the same precedence, lower than that of any of the arithmetic operations. If the types of the operands are different then, as you might expect, widening is performed before the comparison.

Table 2.3 **Python Comparison Operators**

a < b	True if a is less than b.
a <= b	True if a is less than or equal to b.
a == b	True if a is equal to b.
a >= b	True if a is greater than or equal to b.
a > b	True if a is greater than b.

continues

Table 2.3   **Continued**

a != b or a <> b	True if a is not equal to b. This is one of the rare cases where Python was designed specifically to allow two different representations of the same operation. The first form is now preferred, and, according to the documentation, the second should no longer be used.)

All these comparison operators return **0** if the comparison is false and **1** if it is true, but you should realize that Python has no explicit Boolean values. Where a true or false value is required, any numeric zero value is treated as false, even a floating-point or complex zero. Similarly, a nonzero value of any numeric type is treated as true. Non-numeric values can also be interpreted as true or false in Python, but more on that later.

The bitwise operations in Table 2.2 can be applied to some numeric values to evaluate Boolean results. The language also contains explicitly Boolean operators, which are safer and faster since they explicitly treat any nonzero as true, and they do not evaluate operands whose values will make no difference to the result. Tables 2.4 lists these Boolean operators.

Table 2.4   **Python Boolean Operators**

a and b	Logical and: If a is false, b is not evaluated, and the value of the expression is the value of a. If a is true, then b is evaluated, and the value of this expression is the value of b.
a or b	Logical or: If a is true, then b is not evaluated, and the value of the expression is the value of a. If a is false, then b is evaluated, and the value of this expression is the value of b.
not a	Logical negation: If a is true, then this expression is false, and vice versa. This operation always yields either **0** (for false) or **1** (for true).

You can see that the binary Boolean operations are careful to return the value of one of their operands, which makes it easier to handle the multiple representations of true and false, which are discussed as the various types are covered. This occasionally can be useful, but for many purposes can be ignored.

Chained Comparisons

An unusual feature of Python is that comparison operations can be chained together. Consider the following expression:

```
a > b > c
```

This expression will be true if a is greater than b and b is greater than c. You might consider it equivalent to this similar expression:

> `(a > b) and (b > c)`
>
> In this case, however, b must be evaluated twice when it is smaller than or equal to a. In both cases, if a is not greater than b, then expression evaluation will stop there with an immediate false result. This comparison chaining can be extended over as many comparisons as required.

Any Boolean expression can be negated by the not operator. This has a relatively low precedence. So the expression not a < b is evaluated as not (a < b), equivalent to a >= b.

Sequence Types: Strings

Python has three intrinsic sequence types:

- String
- List
- Tuple

Conceptually, a *string* is a sequence of characters, and as you have seen earlier, string constants can be enclosed in either single or double quotes. Rather than having a separate representation for characters, Python represents a single character as a string of length one.

To a large extent, you can choose which quotes you use, but of course if a string contains single quotes, then it is easiest to represent it using double quotes as the delimiter, and vice versa. In yet another notation, you can use three single or double quotes at each end to enclose the string. In this case, the string value can extend over multiple lines and can contain single or double quotes. Such strings are terminated by a second sequence of three single or double quotes. Listing 2.3 shows how to use quotes properly.

Listing 2.3   **Using Quotes**

```
>>> s0 = "Just an ordinary string"
>>> s1 = "string with 'single' quotes"
>>> s2 = 'string with "double" quotes'
>>> s0
'Just an ordinary string'
>>> s1
"string with 'single' quotes"
>>> s2
'string with "double" quotes'
>>> s1+s2
'string with \'single\' quotesstring with "double" quotes'
>>> s3 = """Long string
... with embedded
... newlines"""
```

continues

Listing 2.3   **Continued**

```
>>> s3
'Long string\012with embedded\012newlines'
```

You can see from the output that the interpreter uses the most appropriate type
of quote for the output, regardless of which quotes you use to create the string.
It appears to prefer single quotes when it can use them. The fourth and fifth lines
of output show how it represents strings with both types of quote in them and
characters that cannot be included in normal strings: it uses single quotes and indicates
single quotes and other unusual characters as a sequence of characters beginning with
a backslash.

These sequences are known as *escape sequences*, and you can use these in writing
string literals. The interpreter recognizes the escape sequences shown in Table 2.5.

Table 2.5   **Escape Sequences Recognized in String Literals**

Escape Sequence	Meaning
\newline	Ignored: allows continuation of strings across multiple lines.
\\	Backslash (\)
\'	Single quote (')
\"	Double quote (")
\a	ASCII Bell (BEL)
\b	ASCII Backspace (BS)
\f	ASCII Form Feed (FF)
\n	ASCII Line Feed (LF)
\r	ASCII Carriage Return (CR)
\t	ASCII Horizontal Tab (HT)
\v	ASCII Vertical Tab (VT)
\ooo	ASCII character with octal value ooo
\xhh...	ASCII character with hexadecimal value hh...

Hexadecimal sequences may be of arbitrary length because Python nowadays can
work with larger character sets than can be represented using eight-bit characters.

Treatment of Illegal Escape Sequences
If a backslash occurs in the string but is not followed by one of the recognized escape sequences listed in
Table 2.5, the backslash is retained inside the string. This makes it easier for you to discover mistakes in
your string encoding.

A valid string constant cannot end in a single backslash because that would be interpreted as escaping the quote that was intended to terminate the string constant. You
can see the interpreter's response to this in the next example:

```
>>> s4 = "String ending in backslash\"
SyntaxError: invalid token
```

Interpreter Error Messages

In this and other examples where the interpreter produces error messages, I have removed some of the
output in the interests of brevity. When you try this example yourself, you will see that the missing output contains very little useful information. You will have a chance to see lengthier and more meaningful
error tracebacks later in the book.

The individual elements of a sequence are numbered starting at zero. They can be
accessed using *slicing* notation, which is an extension of the idea of array subscripting
common to many programming languages and uses brackets containing a numeric
expression. The next example shows how you can obtain individual characters from
a string:

```
>>> s3
'Long string\012with embedded\012newlines'
>>> s3[0]
'L'
>>> s3[11]
'\012'
```

The characters in a string can also be accessed using negative indices, and the actual
index used is obtained by adding the length of the string, as you can see from the next
example of accessing a sequence:

```
>>> s4 = "Nineteen characters"
>>> s4[-1]
's'
>>> s4[-19]
'N'
```

For a string of length $L>0$, valid indices for subscripting operations are thus those
between $-L$ and $L-1$, inclusive. For an empty string, any subscripting would raise an
exception.

The same notation is extended to allow the extraction of subsequences (substrings),
using two indexes separated by a colon. The second index indicates the first position
that should *not* be included in the sequence, which means that its maximum legal
value is the sequence length (in which case the last item is included). When the colon
is present, if the first index is omitted, it defaults to zero (the start of the sequence);
and if the second index is omitted, it defaults to the length of the sequence.

```
>>> s4[0:19]
'Nineteen characters'
>>> s4[:]
'Nineteen characters'
>>> s4[:-1]
'Nineteen character'
>>> s4[1:]
'ineteen characters'
```

Remember that the length of the sequence is not valid as a single index. An attempt to use it raises an exception. Sometimes it is useful to think of the string element positions as representing the intercharacter gaps, as shown in Figure 2.2.

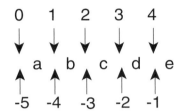

Figure 2.2   Positive and negative character position values.

```
>>> s4[19]
IndexError: string index out of range
```

Unicode

Version 2 of Python also allows you to define *Unicode strings*, which use standard string notation preceded by a letter "U" in either case. This feature's implementation seems clean, but there are still issues to be addressed. For now, my advice is to leave Unicode alone unless you really have to use it. If you do have to use Unicode, then you can take comfort from the fact that these aspects of the language are receiving intense scrutiny, and the support is going to get better with each new release.

Raw Strings

You occasionally need to generate strings with many backslashes in them, and to enable this Python lets you specify a raw string constant by preceding the opening quote (whether single, double, or either of the triple forms) with an "r" or "R". The difference is that backslashes are always retained in the string. Also, the character following a backslash is always copied into the string without change. Even a raw string cannot end in a single backslash, for the same reason that applies to standard strings.

```
>>> s10 = r'\\odd\nstring\b\\'
>>> s10
'\\\\odd\\nstring\\b\\\\'
```

```
>>> print s10
\\odd\nstring\b\\
```

You can probably realize why I added the `print` statement to this example: when the interpreter prints out a string expression, it uses escape sequences. As the first line of output shows, it can be difficult to interpret these, but `print` does not play these tricks and shows you the actual content of the string.

Comparing Strings

The same comparison operators you learned for the numeric values can also be used with characters and strings. The sort order is alphabetic, although case is significant; and in ASCII, all lowercase letters have higher ordinal values than any uppercase letter. The sort order depends on the particular implementation you are working with, so be careful not to build such assumptions into your code.

As with the numeric types, if an 8-bit and a Unicode string need to be compared, then Python will widen the 8-bit string by converting it to Unicode.

Strings as Truth-Values

An empty string is treated as a Boolean false, and a non-empty one as true. In fact, this behavior extends to the other sequence types discussed in the next section. In the following example, the logical `not` operator is used twice to force the interpreter to show the results of considering the strings as Boolean values (the double negation shows the correct truth-values):

```
>>> not not ""
0
>>> not not "non-empty"
1
```

Sequence Types: Lists and Tuples

The remaining two built-in sequence types are similar, and both allow you to aggregate values of any kind. A *list* is represented as a number of expressions separated by commas and surrounded by brackets. A *tuple* is similar but uses parentheses, which in many cases are optional. Because parentheses can also be used in bracketing expressions, you must follow the element value with a comma before the terminating parenthesis to represent a tuple containing a single element.

The same slicing operations that apply to strings also can be applied to lists and tuples, as Listing 2.4 shows.

Listing 2.4   **List and Tuple Slicing Operations**

```
>>> list1 = [1, 4, 'nine', 'sixteen', 25]
>>> list1[0]
1
>>> list1[-1]
```

continues

Listing 2.4 **Continued**

```
25
>>> tpl1=('one', 'four', 'nine', 16, 'twenty-five')
>>> tpl1[0]
'one'
>>> tpl1[4]
'twenty-five'
>>> tpl1[2][2]
'n'
```

The last line of output shows you that if a subscripting operation yields a sequence, a further subscripting operation can be applied to that sequence; as you would expect, the result is the third character of the third item (character two of item two) of the sequence.

An item in a list or tuple can be of any legal data type. It can even be a list or a tuple. The following example shows list-valued list elements:

```
>>> list2 = ['*', ['/', 32, 4], ['+', 3, 10]]
>>> list2[1]
['/', 32, 4]
>>> list2[1][0]
'/'
```

Why does Python have both lists and tuples? The answer to that question is discussed in the section "Mutable and Immutable Types" later in this chapter.

Comparing Lists and Tuples

When a list and a tuple are compared, they will never be equal, even if all elements are the same and in the same order, because they are of different types, and no implicit conversion or widening takes place. The rules for comparing tuples and lists with other tuples and lists, respectively, however, are the same. They are compared lexicographically, which is to say in the same way that strings are.

The first element in each sequence is examined; and if they differ, then the sequence containing the lower value (however Python works that out since the elements need not be of the same type) is considered the lower. Otherwise, the next element in each sequence is considered, and so on until the elements of one of the sequences have been exhausted. At that point, if the elements of the other sequence have also been exhausted, then the two sequences are equal; otherwise, the shorter sequence is the smaller.

Lists and Tuples as Truth-Values

In the same way as strings, lists and tuples can be used as truth-values, and the empty sequence is regarded as false, as Listing 2.5 demonstrates.

Listing 2.5   **A False Empty Sequence**

```
>>> not not []
0
>>> not not [1, 2]
1
>>> not not ()
0
>>> not not (1, )
1
```

Testing for Sequence Membership

You can use the in and not in operators to determine whether a particular value is a member of a sequence. This allows you to discover whether a particular character occurs in a string, or whether an arbitrary value is a member of a list or tuple. Both operators return 0 if the condition is false and 1 if it is true, as the example in Listing 2.6 demonstrates.

Listing 2.6   **Using *in* and *not***

```
>>> "a" in "Python"
0
>>> "h" in "Python"
1
>>> 4 in [1, 4, 9, 16]
1
>>> 12 not in [1, 4, 9, 16]
1
>>> (1, 2) in ((0, 1), (1, 2), (2, 3))
1
```

Mapping Types

Python has only one built-in mapping type, the *dictionary*, although other mappings are defined in various extension modules. A dictionary is an associative array, which holds values stored against keys. The literal representation of a dictionary is a set of braces enclosing a comma-separated list of key-value pairs, where each key is separated from the associated value with a colon. An empty dictionary can be represented as an empty pair of braces.

Access to the values is by *subscripting*, with the key value inside square brackets, as you can see in Listing 2.7.

Listing 2.7   **An Example of Dictionary Subscripting**

```
>>> d1 = {'one': 1, 'two': 2, 'three': 3}
>>> d1["one"]
1
>>> d1["three"]
3
>>> d1["non-existent"]
KeyError: non-existent
```

There is no default value for entries not found in the dictionary. Although the preceding example shows the use of string keys, numbers and tuples can also be used, as you see in Listing 2.8.

Listing 2.8   **Numbers and Tuples as Dictionary Keys**

```
>>> d2 = { (1, 2, 3): "tuple", 1: "integer", 3.7: "floating point",
...        (3+2j): "complex" }
>>> d2[(1, 2, 3)]
'tuple'
>>> d2[1]
'integer'
>>> d2[(1.0+0j)]|
'integer'
```

Listing 2.8 contains a couple of other instructive points:

- You can see, from the code that creates the table, that the interpreter detects when a braced (or bracketed or parenthesized) expression is incomplete at the end of a line and prompts you for further input for the same statement or expression. You also can use this feature to continue lines in your program: The interpreter assumes that the next line of your program is a continuation of the previous one if there are any outstanding unmatched braces, brackets, or parentheses.

- When numeric keys are involved, Python simply uses numeric widening, treating the integer 1 and the complex value (1.0+0j) as equivalent for this purpose.

Comparing Dictionaries

Two dictionaries are considered equal if they contain the same set of keys and if the values for each key are equal in both tables. Remember, though, that because widening takes place on numeric key values before they are compared, a floating-point key is considered equal to an integer key of the same value and so on.

```
>>> {1: "one"} == {1.0: 'one'}                    # equal
1
>>> {1: "one", 2: "two"} == {1: "one", 2: "three"}    # unequal
0
```

The only comparisons that really make sense for mapping types are equality and inequality. If you compare two dictionaries using any of the other operators, Python generates a list of (key-value) pairs for each dictionary, sorts the two lists, and compares them. This is an expensive operation and is infrequently used because the comparisons often don't have much meaning.

Dictionaries as Truth-Values

Just like the sequence types, dictionaries can be interpreted as being true or false. Just like the sequences, a dictionary is considered false when it is empty; otherwise, it is considered true.

```
>>> not not {}
0
>>> not not {1: "something"}
1
```

Files

Files are relatively simple in Python. To open a file, you use the built-in `open()` function, which you call with a file path argument, optionally followed by a mode argument to say whether you want to read, write, or append, and a buffer size argument you can use to control how much buffering is performed. The return value of this function is a *file object* which you can use to access the file from your program by calling its methods. You will learn more about file object methods in the section "File Functions and Methods" later in this chapter.

A file object is always considered true if evaluated in a Boolean context.

A Special Type: *None*

Python has a type that can be used to indicate that no specific value can be, or has been, provided. The type is known as `None`, and there is only one value of this type, for which the name `None` is used. Be careful, though, to understand that this is *not* a reserved word in the language and that it is possible to bind the name to another value. This would be confusing in the extreme, however, and should only be used in obfuscated Python contests!

`None` always evaluates false in a Boolean context. Also note that the interpreter does not print out the result of any operation that evaluates to `None`, which is why some expressions apparently produce no output:

```
>>> None
>>> x = None
>>> x
>>>
```

Mutable and Immutable Types

Remember that in Python it is usual to talk about binding a name to a value rather than assigning a value to a variable. The names bound to the values actually hold pointers to the values rather than the values themselves.

The *dereferencing* of the names (to yield the appropriate value when the name is used in expressions) is automatic, so in any expression a name always stands for the value to which it is currently bound.

The left-hand side of an assignment, however, need not be a name. Assignment can also be used to bind an element of a list, or of a dictionary to a value, and can even be used to replace complete sublists by binding a slice to a new value.

The values to which names or other values (such as list and dictionary elements) are bound may be *mutable* (in which case they may be changed) or *immutable* (in which case they are guaranteed to remain the same forever).

Assignment to List and Dictionary Elements

Subscripted names can be used in assignments to indicate that an element of a list or a dictionary rather than a simple name should be bound to a value. See Listing 2.9 for an example.

Listing 2.9   **Using Subscripted Names**

```
>>> lst2 = ['*', ['/', 32, 4], ['+', 3, 10]]
>>> lst2
['*', ['/', 32, 4], ['+', 3, 10]]
>>> lst2[1] = 8        # Bind list element to value
>>> lst2
['*', 8, ['+', 3, 10]]
>>> dct1
{'one': 1, 'three': 3, 'two': 2}
>>> dct1["one"] = "Have a banana"      # Bind dictionary element to value
>>> dct1
{'one': 'Have a banana', 'two': 2, 'three': 3}
```

Because you can change the value of elements in data items, you can be surprised to find that a change to the data item to which one name is bound can result in apparent changes to other names bound to the same value. Really, of course, all that is happening is the mutable value to which both names are bound has mutated (been changed) in-place. In the next example, the name d1 is bound to a dictionary, and an assignment binds the name d2 to the same dictionary (see Figure 2.3). When a change is made to the dictionary using the second name, the same change is seen in the dictionary when it is accessed by the first name.

```
>>> dct2 = dct1
>>> dct2
```

```
{'one': 'Have a banana', 'two': 2, 'three': 3}
>>> dct2["one"] = "Zipfile"
>>> dct1
{'one': 'Zipfile', 'two': 2, 'three': 3}
```

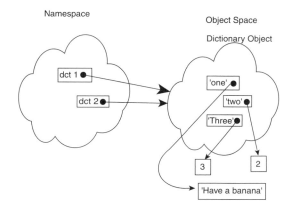

Figure 2.3 Python store after the assignment `dct2 = dct1`.

After the first assignment, both names are bound to the same dictionary (see Figure 2.4).

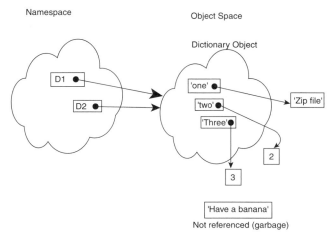

Figure 2.4 Python store after the assignment `dct2["one"] = "Zipfile"`.

Consequently, when one of the dictionary items is changed, the updated value is seen whether you use the name dct1 or dct2 to access the dictionary. Both names are still bound to the same (mutable) data value, and the underlying value has changed.

Mutability

Because assignments can be made to individual elements of these composite types, lists and dictionaries are known as *mutable* types. Types that cannot be changed in this way are unsurprisingly called *immutable*. The immutable types you have come across so far are the numeric types, strings, and tuples.

As well as assigning to a list element, replacing a single value with another one, you can assign to a slice of a list to replace several elements with a new list of the same or different length. The final statement in Listing 2.10 shows that by replacing a null sublist, you can append items to the end of a list, although there are more efficient ways to do this as you will see when list methods are covered later in the section "List and Tuple Operations, Functions, and Methods."

Listing 2.10   **Simple List Operations**

```
>>> l = [0, 1, 2, 3, 4, 5, 6, 7, 8, 9]
>>> l[2:4]
[2, 3]
>>> l[2:4] = ["two", "three"]
>>> l
[0, 1, 'two', 'three', 4, 5, 6, 7, 8, 9]
>>> l[2:3] = [7, 7, 7, 7, 7]
>>> l
[0, 1, 7, 7, 7, 7, 7, 'three', 4, 5, 6, 7, 8, 9]
>>> l[14:14]
[]
>>> l[14:14] = ["extra", "elements"]
>>> l
[0, 1, 7, 7, 7, 7, 7, 'three', 4, 5, 6, 7, 8, 9, 'extra', 'elements']
```

Note that the expression assigned to a slice of a list must itself be a list, as Listing 2.11 shows. If it is the empty list, then you are effectively deleting the slice to which you made the assignment.

Listing 2.11   **Assignment to List Slices**

```
>>> l[5:16] = "Wrong"
TypeError: must assign list (not "string") to slice
>>> l[6:16] = ["Right"]
>>> l
[0, 1, 7, 7, 7, 7, 'Right']
>>> l[2:4] = []
>>> l
[0, 1, 7, 7, 'Right']
```

The difference between lists and tuples is precisely that tuples are immutable. If you try the same tricks with a tuple, the interpreter will quickly point out the error of your ways, as you see in this example:

```
>>> t = (0, 1, 2, 3)
>>> t[2] = "two"          # Assign to tuple element
TypeError: object doesn't support item assignment
```

So why does Python have these two types, which appear to differ only in their mutability? The answer is that keys in a dictionary should be immutable, so tuples can be used as keys whereas lists cannot. Python seeks for keys in a dictionary using a hashing algorithm. If the value of the key were to be changed after an entry had been made in a dictionary, the key would no longer hash to the same value, making it impossible to locate elements reliably and quickly. This is clearly shown in the following example:

```
>>> d4 = {(1, 2, 3): "tuple"}   # Create dictionary with tuple key
>>> d5 = {[1, 2, 3]: "list"}    # Create dictionary with list key
TypeError: unhashable type
```

Dictionaries are also mutable, and you can change the value of existing entries, as well as adding new ones using assignment, which Listing 2.12 shows.

Listing 2.12   **Adding New Entries to Dictionaries**

```
>>> d = {}
>>> d["one"] = 1.0
>>> d["two"] = 2.0
>>> d
{'one': 1.0, 'two': 2.0}
>>> d["one"] = (1+0j)
>>> d
{'one': (1+0j), 'two': 2.0}
>>> d["pi"] = 3.141549
>>> d
{'one': (1+0j), 'two': 2.0, 'pi': 3.1415489999999999}
```

This should also suffice to remind you that floating-point representations are not exact.

Comparing Arbitrary Data Types

The comparison operators you learned when looking at numeric values also work for the other data types, although no conversions are performed on non-numeric types. Two non-numeric values of different types will consistently compare unequal. This might seem arbitrary, but it helps in the sorting of lists, which can hold values of many different types. In such a case, it clearly helps if all numeric values appear together, all strings appear together, all lists appear together, and so on. You can find out the ordering of the types using the interpreter.

continues

Comparing Arbitrary Data Types (Continued)

```
>>> {} < [] < ""
1
>>> 1 == "1"
0
```

The first expression shows that, in Python 2.0 on the Windows platform, dictionaries sort lower than lists, which sort lower than strings. The relative order of the different types is not guaranteed to be the same among different releases, and so should not be relied on to determine program behavior. The second comparison acts as a notification that, although Python is capable of converting between numeric and string representations, it often does not do so unless explicitly instructed.

Augmented Assignment

Suppose that you have a complicated list structure and you want to add one to a value stored in element three of a list, which in turn, is stored in element two of another list. You could use standard assignment as follows:

```
result[2][3] = result[2][3] + 1
```

This involves some unnecessary work, however, since both sides of the assignment require the same expression, result[2][3], to be evaluated. Even if you put up with this unnecessary calculation, the more complicated the element specification becomes, the higher the probability that you will make a typing mistake and introduce an error into the statement.

Python 2.0 introduced a set of *augmented assignment* operators. You can appreciate the increased simplicity of augmented assignment by looking at the following statement:

```
result[2][3] += 1
```

This is *almost* exactly equivalent to the preceding example, but there are a couple of points to bite the careless. First, the expression receiving the assignment is evaluated only once, which makes a difference if it involves any side effects. Second, the methods that implement the augmented operations are at liberty to modify the data value of mutable types *in place* if that is what their implementor chooses to do.

If other names or data elements are bound to the same mutable data, this can lead to results similar to the ones you saw earlier, when multiple names were bound to a single dictionary. The in-place change is an optimization, and there would be no problem with the previous statement, because numeric types are not mutable.

The augmented assignment operations available are as follows:

```
+=,  -=,  *=,  /=,  %=,  **=,  >>=,  <<=,  &=,  ^=,  ¦=
```

Each implements the same operation as the nonassignment operator using the same symbol.

Python Statements

Python is designed to include as few statements as possible, to encourage programmers to do the simplest thing wherever possible. You have already seen many assignment statements, but a program with only assignments in it will not be interesting or practical.

Any expression is a valid Python statement; the interpreter evaluates the expression and then throws away the result. This is mostly used when you want to call functions whose side effects are more important than the returned result.

Although it is usual for Python programs to contain one statement per line, this is not invariably the case. If statements are short enough, several can usually be placed on the same line, separated by semicolons (but this is not considered good style in Python; it's never really necessary to do so). You have already seen that a statement can be extended across multiple lines (and this may indeed be necessary, if a statement is textually long).

Simple Statements

The simplest statements in Python stand by themselves, usually on a single line. They are not all listed in this section because some of them belong more naturally in the next section, which discusses the compound statements.

pass

This is the simplest statement of all and does nothing! You will find an occasional use for a no-operation statement in Python, and when you need it, you just use the single word `pass`.

print

The `print` statement by default writes to the standard output file object. It takes a comma-separated list of values, converts each value to a string if necessary, and sends the strings to the output file separated by single spaces. If the list ends in a comma, then no line terminator is output; otherwise, it then sends a line terminator to the output file.

In Python 2, you can follow the word `print` with a right-shift operator (>>), a file object (or something with similar behavior), and a comma, followed by the usual list of values. In this case, the output representing the list of values goes to the specified file. This is one of Python's rare syntactic oddities. It caused a great deal of discussion on the Python newsgroup but was adopted anyway.

```
>>> temperature = 37
>>> print "The temperature is:", temperature
The temperature is: 37
>>> outf = open("Newfile.txt", "w")
>>> print >> outf, "The temperature is:", temperature
>>> outf.close()
```

del

The del statement deletes things: names, list elements, dictionary entries, and more.
When an object has no more references to it, Python is at liberty to reclaim the space
it occupied. del is one way you can remove references, as shown in Listing 2.13.

Listing 2.13   **Using *del***

```
>>> list1 = [1, 2, 3, 4]
>>> del list1[2]
>>> list1
[1, 2, 4]
>>> dict1 = {1: "one", 2: "two", 3: "three" }
>>> del dict1[2]
>>> dict1
{3: 'three', 1: 'one'}
>>> temp = 37
>>> del temp
>>> temp
NameError: There is no variable named 'temp'
```

break **and** *continue*

These statements should be used only inside loops. break causes early termination of
its containing loop, whereas continue terminates the current iteration and proceeds
immediately to the next one. They are described in more detail in the section
"Looping: for and while" later in the chapter.

return **and** *global*

The return statement is used to return a value from a function, and the global statement declares that certain names belong to the global namespace. Both are described
in the section "Defining Functions" later in the chapter.

exec

The exec statement is where Python reveals its true colors as an interpreted language.
Avoid using it wherever possible!

In its simplest form, the keyword exec is followed by a string expression, whose
value is code in Python. The interpreter compiles the Python into bytecodes and then
executes it.

Compound Statements

The compound statements are where Python shows its most obvious differences from
other languages. These statements are generally concerned with the flow of control of
a program: pieces of code are either executed or not executed, or executed repeatedly

in loops. In Python terminology, these pieces of code are *suites*, subordinate to clauses that control them. Every compound statement begins with a clause that ends with a colon.

Block Structure by Indentation

If the suite is a single statement (and not itself compound), then it can follow the compound statement on the same line. For multiline suites, it is mandatory (and for single-line suites it is desirable) to put the suite on the line(s) following the compound statement. In this latter case, the suite must be indented, which you might consider a bizarre way of showing program structure if you are coming to Python from a more conventional language.

Every year, many new Python users suggest that this feature be modified, and every year the feature remains as it is. If you persevere, you will find that this aspect of the language leads to desirable results. No more braces or begin/end pairs; no more worrying about whether the indentation matches the block structure: the indentation *is* the block structure.

The indentation you use is up to you, but there are a number of clear style guidelines. It is possible (though foolhardy) to mix tabs and spaces. The interpreter always behaves as though tab stops were set every eight spaces. Much modern code seems to use four spaces per indentation level, and this gives a good compromise between readability and space utilization. Tab-indented code has a tendency to migrate off past the right margin in complex logic.

def

The def compound statement is so important that it has a section to itself under "Defining Functions" later in the chapter.

Conditional Execution: *if ... elif ... else*

You have already learned about the comparison operators and how they operate on the common data types, which also can be regarded as Boolean values. The if statement makes use of this by enabling your programs to take different actions depending on truth-values. Consider this simple example, where you want to print out a message if a particular list is empty:

```
>>> if not mylst:
...     print "List is empty"
...
List is empty
```

The if statement in the preceding example has a simple one-statement suite, so you could have entered the same example on a single line as follows:

```
>>> if not mylst: print "List is empty"
...
List is empty
```

The interpreter cannot work out that the compound statement terminates after the single line, however. To do this, it would have to be psychic because there is the possibility that you might want to perform some alternative action if the list is not empty, such as printing it. That would require an `else` portion, as shown in Listing 2.14.

Listing 2.14   **Using** *else*

```
>>> mylst = [1, 2, 3, "bananas"]
>>> if not mylst: print "List is empty"
... else: print "List contents:", mylst
...
List contents: [1, 2, 3, 'bananas']
```

Although the single-line format of compound statements can save time when you are entering commands interactively, it does not improve readability and is not good style. Because the multiline form can always be used, most experienced Python programmers would expect to see the same example written in a program as follows:

```
if not mylst:
    print "List is empty"
else:
    print "List contents:", mylst
```

When there are multiple possibilities, rather than use nested `if` statements, you can elide an `else` and an `if` into a single `elif`. Suppose that you wanted to take different actions depending on whether the list was empty or had one element or more. In that case, you might write the following:

```
if not mylst:
    print "List is empty"
elif len(mylst) == 1:
    print "List contains a single element:", mylst[0]
else
    print "List contents:", mylst
```

You might feel that the absence of a `case` statement in Python is a serious omission, but in fact the best it could do would be to abbreviate the preceding form somewhat. The underlying logic would be the same. Presumably on the grounds of simplicity, there is no such statement.

Looping: *for* and *while*

In line with its generally minimalist philosophy, Python contains only two looping constructs. The first iterates over a sequence, and the second executes repeatedly until a condition becomes false. Listing 2.15 shows a simple example of the first type of loop.

Listing 2.15   **Iterating over a Sequence**

```
>>> for w in ["this", "is", "a", "python", "program"]:
...     print w
...
this
is
a
python
program
```

Be careful not to modify the sequence you are iterating over inside the loop suite in a `for` statement. Doing so can lead to unpredictable results that may vary from release to release, as the semantics are stated to be undefined in the language specification. Listing 2.16 shows a loop of the second kind, the `while` statement, for which sequence modifications are all right.

Listing 2.16   **Executing Repeatedly Until a Condition Is False**

```
>>> lst = ["this", "is", "a", "python", "program"]
>>> while lst:
...     print lst
...     del lst[0]
...
['this', 'is', 'a', 'python', 'program']
['is', 'a', 'python', 'program']
['a', 'python', 'program']
['python', 'program']
['program']
```

Loop Control: *break*, *continue*, and *else*

It is possible to terminate either type of loop early by use of the `break` statement. When the `break` is executed, control passes to the statement immediately following the entire loop construct. The code in the `loop-suite` also may be terminated prematurely *for the current iteration only* by the `continue` statement, in which case control passes back to the looping clause at the head, and the next iteration begins immediately.

To allow for the possibility of taking different action in the case of normal termination, both kinds of loops may be followed by an `else` clause. The suite subordinate to this clause will be executed only in the case where the loop ends normally. Listing 2.17 summarizes the syntax of the loops.

Listing 2.17   **Syntax of *loop-suite***

```
for name in sequence:
    loop-suite
else:
    termination-suite

while condition:
    loop-suite
else:
    termination-suite
```

Listing 2.18 shows a simple program that reads in lists of words separated by spaces and prints out a comment if the word "Python" is not found. It uses the raw_input() function, which is discussed later, to read interactive input.

Listing 2.18   ***PyDetect.py:* A Python Detector**

```
while 1:
    line = raw_input("Sentence: ")
    if line == "":
        break
    words = line.split()
    for w in words:
        if w == "Python":
            break          # Python detected!
    else:
        print 'Does not contain "Python"'
```

The outer loop is essentially infinite because 1 is always true. If its suite did not contain a break statement, there would be no way for it to terminate other than a program exception. This usage is common in Python.

The inner loop iterates over all the words in the line. Each time around the loop, the name w is bound to the next word from the list bound to words, and the loop terminates with a break if the word "Python" is found. Otherwise, after the for-loop terminates normally, the else suite is executed and prints a message. There is no else suite for the outer loop because it can only ever terminate abnormally.

Listing 2.19 shows the output from a Windows command-line session, where the interpreter is told to run the program, and four lines of input are provided (an empty line must be input to indicate that input is terminated).

Listing 2.19   **Running the Python Detector**

```
D:\Code\Ch2>python PyDetect.py
Sentence: Elvis is the greatest
Does not contain "Python"
Sentence: Who's learning Python then?
```

```
Sentence: Monty Python's Flying Circus
Does not contain "Python"
Sentence: There's a Python in my soup
Sentence:
```

The third sentence does not trigger the Python detector because the `split()` string method is breaking only at spaces, and so the second word is `"Python's"` rather than `"Python"`.

Iterating Over Integer Sequences

You may be surprised at the apparent lack of any form to allow iterating over sequences of numbers. The `range()` function is designed specifically to produce lists of integers. So the usual technique is to have `range()` produce the desired list of values, using a `for` loop to iterate over them. The following list of numeric powers for the integers from 0 through 9 shows this.

```
for i in range(10):
    print i, i**2, i**3, i**4
```

The output from this example, shown in Listing 2.20, shows that with a single argument `range()` produces the integers from 0 to one less than the argument. This is because a frequent use of the function is to generate indexes for a list or tuple, and such indexing starts at zero.

Listing 2.20   **Output from *PowerList.py***

```
0 0 0 0
1 1 1 1
2 4 8 16
3 9 27 81
4 16 64 256
5 25 125 625
6 36 216 1296
7 49 343 2401
8 64 512 4096
9 81 729 6561
```

The `range()` function and its `xrange()` equivalent (provided for efficiency reasons) are more versatile than this simple example makes them appear. These functions are described more fully in the "Major Built-in Functions and Methods" section later in this chapter. After you have installed Python, you can also consult the documentation. This is rarely a bad idea.

Exception Handling: *try*

Although the `try` statement is compound, it is treated later in this chapter in the "Exception Handling" section.

Defining Functions

You have become familiar with some of Python's built-in functions already, and you will read more about them in the next section. Python enables you to define your own functions as well.

A Simple Function Definition

The `def` statement is the compound statement used to define functions. The keyword is followed by the name of the function and a parenthesized argument list. If the function takes no arguments, then the list will be empty; but it must be present, as you see in Listing 2.21.

Listing 2.21   **An Argument List Is Needed with** *def*

```
>>> def f:
Traceback (  File "<interactive input>", line 1
    def f:
         ^
SyntaxError: invalid syntax
```

The full error message from the interpreter, which has been abbreviated in previous examples, does its best to show you where syntax errors are detected by indicating the line position where the problem was detected.

Suppose you wanted to write a function to read lines of the form *name value* and store them in a dictionary. It could go something like the code shown in Listing 2.22.

Listing 2.22   **A Function to Read an Options File**

```
 1 def readoptions():
 2     opdict = {}
 3     f = open("options.ini")
 4     lines = f.readlines()
 5     for line in lines:
 6         if line == "\n":
 7             continue
 8         s = line[:-1].split(None, 1)
 9         opdict[s[0]] = s[1]
10     return opdict
```

The most interesting statement in this function is the one at line 8, which extracts the required values from the input file line. First, it applies the `split()` method to the expression `line[:-1]`—the slicing operation removes the trailing line terminator. The first argument to `split()` tells it to split wherever it sees a run of white space of any length. Usually a literal string is used here, but such an argument only allows you to split on exact chunks of white space. The second argument tells it to perform no more than one split operation, which ensures that it will always return a list of at most two elements. The `readoptions()` function assumes that every line will have at least one separator in it.

The first element is used as the key, and the second as the value stored against that key in the `opdict` dictionary.

Functions Return Values: *return*

The last statement of the `readoptions()` function in Listing 2.22 passes the generated dictionary back as the result of the function. Without the last statement, there would have been no way for the calling program to know what the function had read.

A `return` statement terminates the execution of the function immediately and need not appear at the end of the function. If `return` is not followed by a value, or if there is no `return` statement in a function, what gets returned is the special value `None`.

Functions Are *Values*

The `def` statement is not a declaration. It is executed, and the function name is bound to the function definition from the subordinate suite. This name can be used as a value just like any other name, and in particular other names can be bound to the same value to which it refers. With the previous definition of `myfunc()` in place, the following code shows function assignment in operation:

```
>>> myfunc = readoptions  # bind myfunc to the same function
>>> d = myfunc()  # call the function
>>> print d
{'author': 'Steve Holden', 'tech-ed': 'martellibot',
 'editor': 'Stephanie Wall', 'timing': 'slow'}
```

Using the function name as a value does *not* cause the function to be called; like a function definition, a function call must always have parentheses after the function name. After a function is assigned to another name, it is just as though the function had been defined under both names. You can get the interpreter to print the function's string representation to confirm this.

```
>>> readoptions
<function readoptions at 016DEF7C>
>>> myfunc
<function readoptions at 016DEF7C>
```

Function Calls Create Namespaces

When a value is assigned to a name, if that name has not previously been assigned, then it is created in the current namespace. In this sense, namespaces are similar to dictionaries, in which entries are created as new keys are used. The examples of assignment you have seen so far have defined names in a global namespace, associated with the program (or, as you will learn later, with the module from which code is currently executing).

Every function call, however, creates a new namespace in which bound names are created during execution of the function. The initial members of this namespace are the argument values to the call. When Python looks for a name to retrieve the associated value, it looks in three places:

1. First it searches the *local* namespace, which will exist if a function is being executed.

2. Then it looks in the *global* namespace.

3. Finally, if the name still has not been found, Python looks in the *built-in* namespace in which the names bound to the system functions and objects are predefined.

Changes to Namespace Searching Rules

One of the major recent changes to Python is the introduction of *nested scopes*. This modifies the rules slightly, but you will probably not notice the difference unless you are defining functions inside other functions. Appendix A, "Changes Since Python 2.0," gives the details if you need to understand the exact scoping rules, which were introduced in Python 2.1 and became the default behavior in Python 2.2.

When the interpreter encounters a `def` statement, it processes the subordinate suite, storing the code as the value of the function. Because it has processed the suite, the interpreter knows which names are bound to values as a result of assignments in the function code. All these names are regarded as being local to the function—even if their values are accessed before any binding takes place. As Listing 2.23 demonstrates, a name defined inside a function as a local variable effectively makes it impossible to access the global name.

Listing 2.23   **A Name Defined Inside a Function as a Local Variable**

```
>>> def f(a):
...     x = a
...     print "Local x:", x
...     print "Local y:", y
...
>>> y = 265
>>> x = 128
>>> f(64)
Local x: 64
Local y: 265
>>> print "Global x:", x
Global x: 128
```

You can see that the function f() treats x as a local variable because of the assignment to it. The global y is used because that name is not assigned inside the function suite.

The *global* Statement

The rule for determining which variables are local has a desirable side effect: it makes it difficult to assign to a global variable from inside the function body because the interpreter assumes that a name is local when it sees an assignment to it inside a function body. The only way to work around this is to use the only declaration in Python: the global statement. This declaration tells Python that names bound in the global namespace should be used, despite the fact that they are re-bound inside the function suite. Contrast the previous example with the one shown in Listing 2.24, which differs only in the addition of a single global statement inside the function body.

Listing 2.24   **Adding a Single Global Statement Inside a Function**

```
>>> def f(a):
...     global x
...     x = a
...     print "Local x:", x
...     print "Local y:", y
...
>>> y = 265
>>> x = 128
>>> f(64)
Local x: 64
Local y: 265
>>> print "Global x:", x
Global x: 64
```

In this case, the assignment to the name x inside the function also affects the value of x defined outside it because the global declaration overrides the interpreter's ideas about which name lives in which namespace.

Function Arguments

The most common way of passing arguments into a function is simply to list them inside the parentheses following the function name. The functions in the previous two examples use a single argument to pass a value through from the caller. Inside the function, you access the arguments by the names corresponding to their positions in the list. Listing 2.25 shows three arguments.

Listing 2.25 **Three Arguments**

```
>>> def prf(a, b, c):
...     print "First:", a, "second:", b, "third:", c
...
>>> prf("one", 2, 3.00001)
First: one second: 2 third: 3.00001
```

If you provide too many arguments, or too few, Python tells you:

```
>>> prf(1, 2)
TypeError: not enough arguments; expected 3, got 2
>>> prf(1, 2, 3, 4)
TypeError: too many arguments; expected 3, got 4
```

The arguments can be of any type, and there is no way for Python to restrict the types of argument used with a particular function. This can work to your advantage, of course, because Python is flexible about doing the right thing under varied circumstances. If the correct type is crucially important then you have to check it, but as you see in Listing 2.26, you can write code that will work with *any* type of sequence.

Listing 2.26 **A Function to Handle Any Sequence**

```
>>> def prf2(s):
...     for e in s:
...         print e,
...     print
...
>>> prf2("string")
s t r i n g
>>> prf2([1, 2, 3, 4])
1 2 3 4
>>> prf2((4, 3, 2, 1))
4 3 2 1
```

Here, each of the different sequence types is handled correctly without any problems. Even Python has its limits, however, and you see that it cannot iterate over something other than a sequence type:

```
>>> prf2(123)
Traceback (innermost last):
  File "<interactive input>", line 1, in ?
  File "<interactive input>", line 2, in prf2
TypeError: loop over non-sequence
```

Keyword Arguments

There is another way to provide arguments: by keyword. In a function call, you can put the argument name, and follow it with an equal sign and the value you want assigned to that argument. This call method means that you are no longer forced to give arguments in a particular order. You can even mix positional and keyword arguments in the same call, as long as all the positionals come first. Consider the `prf()` function, shown in Listing 2.27, which was defined in the preceding section and takes three arguments.

Listing 2.27   *prf()*

```
>>> prf(c=3, b=2, a=1)
First: 1 second: 2 third: 3
>>> prf('one', 'two', c=3)
First: one second: two third: 3
>>> prf('one', b=2, 'three')
Traceback (SyntaxError: non-keyword arg after keyword arg
```

Providing Defaults

Sometimes it is convenient for a particular argument to default to a certain value if no value is supplied in the call. You might have noticed that the `strip()` string method does this, defaulting its first argument to `None` (split on runs of white space) and its second to `0` (split on all separators with no limit). You can do the same with your functions by using the keyword notation in your definitions. In this case, the expression on the right-hand side of the equal sign is the value to be used if the argument is not provided in a call. You still have to provide the values for arguments without defaults, as the last line in Listing 2.28 shows.

Listing 2.28   **Keyword Arguments Provide Default Values**

```
>>> def prf(a, b=2, c="three"):
...     print "a:", a, "b:", b, "c:", c
...
>>> prf ('one')
a: one b: 2 c: three
>>> prf ('one', 'two')
a: one b: two c: three
>>> prf('one', c=3)
a: one b: 2 c: 3
>>> prf(1, 2, 3)
a: 1 b: 2 c: 3
>>> prf(b="b", c="c")
TypeError: not enough arguments; expected 1, got 0
```

In the same way that you have to give all the positional arguments to a call before any keyword arguments are given, you cannot follow a defaulted argument with one that has no default value, or Python will complain:

```
>>> def zzz(a, b=1, c):
...     print "a:", a, "b:", b, "c:", c
Traceback (SyntaxError: non-default argument follows default argument
```

Also understand that the default values are evaluated, and the arguments bound to them, when the function definition is processed. These bindings initialize the local namespace for each call. If you supply a default value for an argument as a name, and later re-bind that name, the default value for the argument remains bound to the value it was assigned when the function definition was processed. Listing 2.29 shows this.

Listing 2.29 **A Default That Is Bound to Its Assigned Value**

```
>>> default = "Original value"
>>> def f1(a=default):
...     print "a:", a
...
>>> f1()
a: Original value
>>> default = "Some new value"
>>> f1()
a: Original value
```

When the default value is mutable, however, if the function (or some other code) mutates the default by changing it in-place, then this mutated value becomes the new default. Suppose that you want to define a function that takes a list as an argument and adds a new value to it using the append() list method. You might want to provide an empty list as a default argument. The obvious way to do this is best avoided, as you see in Listing 2.30.

Listing 2.30 **Defining a Function Using *append()***

```
>>> def lapnd(v, lst=[]):
...     lst.append(v)
...     return l
...
>>> lapnd(1)
[1]
>>> lapnd(2)
[1, 2]
>>> ll = []
>>> lapnd(3, ll)
[3]
>>> lapnd(4, ll)
[3, 4]
>>> ll
[3, 4]
```

You can see that whether you use the default list or provide a list, that list is modified. The standard solution to this is to use None as a default value and test inside the function to see whether the argument was provided, creating a new list if required. Listing 2.31 shows this solution in action.

Listing 2.31   *None* **as a Default Value**

```
>>> def lapnd2(v, lst=None):
...     if lst is None:
            return [v]
        else:
...             lst.append(v)
...             return lst
...
>>> lapnd2(1)
[1]
>>> lapnd2(2)
[2]
>>> ll = ["lapnd2"]
>>> lapnd2(3, ll)
['lapnd2', 3]
>>> lapnd2(4, ll)
['lapnd2', 3, 4]
>>> ll
['lapnd2', 3, 4]
```

Handling Arbitrary Arguments

All this is well and good if you always know how many arguments a function requires. Sometimes it is better to be able to deal with an arbitrary number of arguments. In a function definition, you can specify that arbitrary additional arguments are accepted by adding an argument of the form *name at the end of the argument list. The asterisk specifies that this argument's value is set to a tuple of all excess positional parameters. If there are none, of course, it is the empty tuple (see Listing 2.32).

Listing 2.32   **Handling a Variable Number of Positional Arguments**

```
>>> def var1(a, *t):
...     print "a:", a, "t:", t
...
>>> var1(1)
a: 1 t: ()
>>> var1(1, 2, 3, 4)
a: 1 t: (2, 3, 4)
```

A similar feature allows you to collect any excess keyword arguments, but in this case a double asterisk is used; and, because the names are as important as the data values, they are collected in a dictionary. The names become the keys to the corresponding values. The double-asterisked argument (see Listing 2.33) must be after all normal (non-defaulted and defaulted) arguments, and it must also follow the single-asterisked one if both are present.

Listing 2.33   **Handling a Variable Number of Keyword Arguments**

```
>>> def var2(a, *t, **d):
...     print "a:", a, "t:", t, "d:", d
...
>>> var2('first', 'second', 'third', fourth=4, fifth=5)
a: first t: ('second', 'third') d: {'fourth': 4, 'fifth': 5}
```

Major Built-in Functions and Methods

Python has a very large range of built-in functions, and this section covers only the most important ones. Also note that as the language develops, more of the behavior formerly specified by simple functions is being provided as *methods* of the built-in data types. Methods calls are easy to spot because they use qualified names: a dot, the method name, and a parenthesized list of arguments follow a value of a type that supports the method. You have already read about file methods, and the more general example in Listing 2.34 should make this clearer.

Listing 2.34   *WordCount.py:* **A Simple Counting Program**

```
 1  counter = {}                    # create empty directory
 2  file = open("walrus.txt")       # open file for input
 3  while 1:                        # forever ...
 4      line = file.readline()      # read the next line
 5      if line == "":              # end of file?
 6          break                   # yes: terminate loop
 7      for w in line.split():      # for each word in the line
 8          if counter.has_key(w):  # have we seen this word before?
 9              counter[w] += 1     # yes: add one to its count
10          else:
11              counter[w] = 1      # no:  establish count of one
12  file.close()                    # tidy up
13
14  words = counter.keys()          # extract a list of words found
15  words.sort()                    # sort the list
16  for w in words:                 # for each word in the list
17      print w, counter[w]         # print the word and its count
```

If the file `walrus.txt` contains the following text:

```
the time has come the walrus said
to speak of many things
of sailing ships and sealing wax
of cabbages and kings
```

The output of the program will be

```
and 2
cabbages 1
come 1
has 1
kings 1
many 1
of 3
said 1
sailing 1
sealing 1
ships 1
speak 1
the 2
things 1
time 1
to 1
walrus 1
wax 1
```

Because the comments explain how the program works, few details are necessary. Remember that Python indicates statement groupings by *indentation*—the first `while` loop runs from lines 3 through 11 because only at line 12 does the indentation return to the same level as the controlling `while` keyword. The inner loop runs from lines 7 through 11 for the same reason, and the `if` statement executes line 9 if the condition is true and line 11 if the condition is false.

There is little difference, from the programmer's point of view, between a function and a method. A method call looks like a function call but implicitly provides an additional parameter, which is the object whose method is being called.

Line 4 uses the `readline()` method of the `file` object created in line 2. Line 7 uses the `split()` method of a string object, which returns a list of the individual words in the line. Line 8 uses the `has_key()` method of the `counter` dictionary, which returns true or false according to whether the current word already exists in the dictionary. Line 14 uses another dictionary method, `keys()`, which returns a list of all the keys in counter, and line 15 uses the `sort()` method of the resulting list to sort it (in-place) into alphabetical order.

> **Optional Arguments**
> In the following sections, optional arguments are shown in brackets. The brackets are not to be used in the code and are present only to indicate that the arguments they enclose are optional.

Numeric Functions

Numeric types have no methods. Although it would be possible to extend the runtime system to include them, they would be confusing syntactically because the dot that separates the object from the method name might be taken to be a part of the number. Table 2.6 shows the principal numeric functions.

Table 2.6 **Principal Numeric Functions**

Function	Description
abs(x)	Returns the absolute value of its argument.
cmp(x, y)	Compares x and y, returning an integer that is negative when x < y, zero when x == y, and positive when x > y.
complex(real[, imag])	Returns a complex number made up of the given real and imaginary components.
divmod(a, b)	Returns the two-element tuple (a / b, a % b).
float(x)	Converts the string or number x to a floating-point number.
int(x[, radix])	Converts the number or string x to an integer. If radix is given, its value must be between 2 and 36, and x must be a string.
long(x)	Converts a string or number x to a long integer.
min(s[, args...]) and max(s[, args...])	Operates over a sequence given a single argument; otherwise over all arguments, returning the lowest or the highest value, respectively.
pow(x, y[, z])	Raises x to the power y and, if z is given, reduces the result modulo z.
round(x[, n])	Rounds the number x to n decimal places. If n is omitted, it defaults to zero.

String Functions and Methods

Since version 2, much of Python's string functionality resides in methods rather than functions. There are, however, a few functions with string results that should not, logically, be string methods. Table 2.7 describes these functions.

Table 2.7   **Simple String Functions**

Function	Description
chr(i)	Returns a single-character string, in which the character has the ordinal value i.
hex(x)	Returns a string containing the hexadecimal representation of the integer or long integer argument.
len(s)	Returns the length of the string argument.
oct(x)	Returns the string containing the octal representation of the integer or long integer argument.
repr(s)	Returns a string representation of the argument, which is for many types Python code that could be evaluated to yield the original value.
str(x)	Returns a string representation of the argument usable for printing purposes.

Because there are now so many string methods, I have split them into logically related groups in Tables 2.8 through 2.12.

Table 2.8   **Case Alteration String Methods**

Method	Description
s.capitalize()	Returns a copy of s with its first letter converted to uppercase.
s.lower()	Returns a copy of s converted to lowercase.
s.swapcase()	Returns a copy of s in which all lowercase characters are uppercase and all uppercase characters are lowercase.
s.title()	Returns a copy of string s, in which words start with uppercase characters and all other characters are lowercase.
s.upper()	Returns a copy of s converted to uppercase.

The group of methods in Table 2.9, which take no arguments, answer simple questions about the content of a string, and all return a Boolean result. If there are no characters in the string to which the method is applied, it returns false. The term *cased character* means a character having both an uppercase and a lowercase version.

Table 2.9   **Content Analysis String Methods**

Method	Description
s.isalnum()	True if all characters are alphanumeric.
s.isalpha()	True if all characters are alphabetic.
s.isdigit()	True if all characters in the string are digits.
s.islower()	True if all cased characters are lowercase. False if the string contains no cased characters.

continues

Table 2.9 **Continued**

Method	Description
s.isspace()	True if s contains only white space characters.
s.istitle()	True if the string is "title cased": uppercase characters may only follow uncased ones, and lowercase characters may only follow cased characters.
s.isupper()	True if all cased characters are uppercase. False if s contains no cased characters.

Many of the methods in Table 2.10 have optional start and end arguments. If these arguments are both omitted, then the whole of the string is scanned. If only the end is omitted, then start specifies the leftmost character to be scanned, and the remainder of the string is scanned. When both arguments are present, the string scanned is s[start:end].

Table 2.10 **String Searching Methods**

Method	Description
s.count(sub [,start[, end]])	Returns the number of (non-overlapping) occurrences of sub in the scanned string.
s.startswith(sub [, start[, end]])	Returns true if the scanned string begins with string sub.
s.endswith(sub [, start[, end]])	Returns true if the scanned string ends with string sub.
s.find(sub [,start[, end]])	Returns the leftmost index in the scanned string where sub occurs. Returns –1 if sub is not found.
s.index(sub [,start[, end]])	Same as find(), but raises an IndexError exception if sub is not found.
s.rfind(sub [,start[, end]])	Returns the rightmost index in the scanned string where sub occurs. Returns –1 if sub is not found.
s.rindex(sub [,start[, end]])	Same as rfind(), but raises an IndexError exception if sub is not found.

The methods in Table 2.11 return a modified copy of the string they operate on.

Table 2.11 **String Transformation Methods**

Method	Description
s.expandtabs ([tabsize])	Returns a copy of s with tabs replaced by spaces. Uses a default tabsize of 8.
s.lstrip()	Returns a copy of s with leading white space removed.

Method	Description
s.replace(old, new [, maxsplit])	Returns a copy of string s with occurrences of old replaced by new a maximum of maxsplit times. If maxsplit is omitted, replaces all occurrences.
s.rstrip()	Returns a copy of s with trailing white space removed.
s.strip()	Returns a copy of s with leading and trailing white space removed.
s.translate(table [, deletechars])	Returns a copy of s where all characters in deletechars (if present) have been removed, and all others have been translated using table, which must be a string of 256 characters.

The methods in Table 2.12 can split a string up into a list of substrings and join a list of strings back into a simple string.

Table 2.12   **String Splitting and Joining Methods**

Method	Description
s.split([sep[, maxsplit]])	Returns a list of strings between successive occurrences of sep. If sep is not given, or is None, any run of white space is treated as a separator. If maxsplit is given, no more than maxsplit splits are performed.
s.join(seq)	Returns a string generated by concatenating the strings in the sequence seq, putting the string s between each pair of sequence members.

List and Tuple Operations, Functions, and Methods

Tuples and lists share fundamental similarities: the tuple is immutable, the list is mutable, but otherwise they are alike. It should not be surprising that most operators and functions are common to them both, and that they also have something in common with strings, the third sequence type. The operations shown in Table 2.13 apply to all.

Table 2.13   **Sequence Operations**

Operation	Description
s1 + s2	Concatenates the two sequences, generating a new sequence containing the elements of the first followed by the elements of the second.
s * n, n * s	Where n is an integer or long integer, generates a new sequence equal to n concatenated copies of the original.
s[i]	Returns the element numbered i from the sequence where i is an integer or long integer.

continues

Table 2.13 **Continued**

Operation	Description
s[i:j]	Returns the subsequence specified by the slice arguments.
x in s, x not in s	Returns true (1) or false (0) according to whether the sequence contains the value x.
len(s)	Returns the length of the sequence.
min(x), max(x)	Returns the smallest or largest value from the sequence.

The string methods have already been covered, but lists have a set of methods that cannot be applied to strings or tuples because they are immutable. In Table 2.14, lst is assumed to be a list.

Table 2.14 **List Methods**

Method	Description
lst.append(x)	Adds a new element x to the end of the list.
lst.extend(l)	Equivalent to the statement s = s + l, where l is also a list.
lst.index(x)	Returns the smallest value i such that lst[i] == x.
lst.remove(x)	Removes the first x in the list.
lst.sort()	Sorts the list in place. Note that this function returns the value None, *not* the sorted list.

File Functions and Methods

As you learned previously, the built-in open() function is used to open a file. It takes one or two arguments and returns a file object. The first argument is a string containing the name of the file to be opened, and the second, optional argument is the mode—a string with three basic values as shown in Table 2.15.

Table 2.15 **Basic File Modes**

"r"	read (the default)
"w"	write
"a"	append

Adding a "b" to the mode causes the file input and output to be in binary. Without this, Python treats the file as text and ensures that input lines always end with just a line feed. Adding a "+" to the mode tells Python you will be updating the file. Be careful because using "w+" will cause an existing file to be truncated to zero length.

Supposing the name f is bound to a file object, the most useful of the file methods are shown in Table 2.16.

Table 2.16   **Basic File Methods**

Method	Description
`f.read([size])`	Returns the next `size` bytes from the file. If the `size` argument is omitted, returns the content of the file up to its end.
`f.readline([size])`	Returns the next `size` bytes from the file, or the next line including its line terminator if this is less than `size` bytes long. If `size` is omitted, just returns the next line with its line terminator. Returns the empty string if the file is already at the end.
`f.readlines ([sizehint])`	Returns a list of lines read from the file, each one including its line terminator, of approximate total size `sizehint` bytes. If `sizehint` is omitted, returns all lines up to the end of the file.
`f.write(str)`	Writes string `str` to the file. Does *not* append a line terminator, for compatibility with the reading methods that do not remove it.
`f.writelines(list)`	Writes each member of the list to the file, again without appending line terminators.
`f.close()`	Closes the file, flushing any partially written buffers.

The standard idioms in Python for processing each line of a file are shown in Listings 2.35 and 2.36, as code snippets that print each line of the file `Myfile.txt`.

Listing 2.35   **Line-by-Line Reading and Processing of a File**

```
1 f = open("Myfile.txt")
2 while 1:
3     l = f.read()
4     if l == "": break
5     print l
6 f.close()
```

Listing 2.36   **Reading a Whole File and Processing Each Line**

```
1 f = open("Myfile.txt")
2 for l in f.readlines():
3     print l
4 f.close()
```

Python newcomers, who expect a more elegant looping form, often question the first idiom. There are sound reasons for its structure. If you do not like it, investigate the description of iterators in Appendix A.

Modules in Python

Despite Python's capability to express algorithms compactly, you may need to write a Python application that is too large to be comfortably constructed as a single unit of source code. Alternatively, you might feel that some of the code you have written is so useful you would like to be able to reuse it in other programs. At this point, the tool you need is the module.

It is also necessary to understand modules because some really useful parts of Python—the libraries—are distributed as modules. Without an understanding of how they operate, you will not get the most from these valuable contributions.

Using Modules: The *import* Statement

Any valid Python program is a module. You can use its code by importing the contents into another program, which makes the names bound in the module available to the importing program. It may be that several different components in an application require the same module, and in that case the import will be repeated several times. However, the first import is special.

When the interpreter imports a module for the first time, it executes the code in the module. On subsequent imports, it does not because it now has all the information it needs to effect the import without further execution. In Listing 2.37, you see two files. One is a module to be imported, which prints a comment and assigns to a variable. The other is a program that imports it twice, printing out what it is doing.

Listing 2.37   **A Simple Module and an Application That Imports It Twice**

```
# mod1.py
print "Mod1 executing"
x = 1

# app1.py
print "Importing the first time"
import mod1
print "Importing the second time"
import mod1
```

Notice that the application that imports the module does not use the full filename. It refers to the module by name, omitting the `.py` extension. The module name is not a string, but a simple Python name just like all the others you have seen. Because the name must correspond to the name of the file containing the module code, module filenames must also be valid Python names.

The following session trace shows what happens when you run `app1.py`. You can see that the first `import` causes the `print` statement in the module to be executed, but the second does not.

```
D:\Code\Ch2> python app1.py
Importing the first time
Mod1 executing
Importing the second time
```

Why Import Only Once?

Python operates this way for efficiency reasons. The code and data in a module might be imported by several other components of an application. If the module contains lengthy initialization code, it does not make sense to repeat the execution of this code. So, on the first import it executes the code in the module file, which will typically have side effects inside the module, such as name bindings. On second and subsequent imports, Python just makes available the information it generated on the first import.

Interactive Imports

You can use `import` statements in interactive sessions as well. Listing 2.38 tries to access the variable that is set during the module's import.

Listing 2.38   **Where Are the Module's Variables?**

```
>>> import mod1
Mod1 executing
>>> print x
NameError: There is no variable named 'x'
```

Clearly the module code doesn't put the names it binds into the same namespace that your top-level code, typed directly into the interpreter, does. The same thing would have happened even if you had run these two statements from a program file. So, where is the elusive x?

Modules Are Namespaces

In the same way that calling a function creates a namespace, so does importing a module for the first time. Unlike the function's local namespace, which ceases to exist when the function returns, the module namespace continues to exist throughout the execution of the program. When you define a function, execution of the `def` statement assigns the code of the function to the function name in the current namespace. When you import a module, execution of the `import` statement assigns the module namespace to the module name.

The module namespace is where names bound inside the module are stored. Because you can access that namespace by using the module name, you can access names bound inside the module by prefixing the name you want with the module name and a dot. The syntax is essentially the same as is used to access methods of the built-in types. Here you see how we finally access the value of x defined in module mod1:

```
>>> import mod1
>>> mod1.x
1
```

Remembering the action of the `def` statement, you will readily understand that when you define a function inside a module, its name also is stored in the module namespace and can be accessed using the same naming technique. Listing 2.39 shows a slightly more complex module that defines two functions along with an application that calls one of them.

Listing 2.39 **A Module That Defines a Function and an Application That Calls It**

```
# mod2.py
print "Mod2 executing"

def samecase(s):
    return s.islower() or s.isupper()

 def allsame(s):
    if samecase(s):
        print s, "has no case variations"
    else:
        print s, "has mixed case"
#-------------------

# app2.py

import mod2

mod2.allsame("Hello")
mod2.allsame("hello")
mod2.allsame("HELLO")
#-------------------
```

The `samecase()` function is fairly simple one. It returns true if the string passed as an argument is *either* all lowercase *or* all uppercase. The module defines a further function, `allsame()`, to print out one message if mixed case is detected and another if not. From within the application, this latter function is called by using the module name to qualify the function name.

How does this work? When the module is imported, the module name `mod2` in the current local namespace (which is the one associated with the application) is bound to a reference to the module, and in particular its namespace. The interpreter resolves the reference to `mod2.allsame` by looking up `mod2` in the local namespace and then looking up `allsame` in the namespace to which `mod2` has been bound. Figure 2.5, which illustrates this, helps to make things clearer.

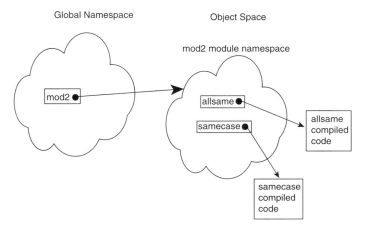

Figure 2.5 Namespace relationship between an application and an imported module.

Within the mod2 module, there is no need to qualify a reference to the samecase function because code within the module runs in the module's namespace, and therefore unqualified names are sought first in that namespace. Just to confirm that this all works as expected, Listing 2.40 shows the application being run.

Listing 2.40 **The Application Being Run**

```
D:\Code\Ch2> python app2.py
Mod2 executing
Hello has mixed case
hello has no case variations
HELLO has no case variations
```

Changing the Module Name: *import … as*

On occasion, you may want to import a module under a different name. You can do this by using a slightly extended form of the import statement, as shown in this example:

```
>>> import mod2 as steve
Mod2 executing
>>> steve.allsame("Hi there!")
Hi there! has mixed case
```

The module mod2 is imported but is referenced as steve in the remainder of the code. This can be very useful if you want to import a module whose name is inconveniently long to type, and also if a module's name conflicts with something you have already defined in your program before realizing you needed to import the module.

Selective Imports: the *from ... import ...* Statement

If you only want to access a few items from a module, it may be more convenient to be able to access them directly in the current namespace than to use compound names. You can do this by importing those specific names from the module, using a statement that binds names from a module in the current namespace rather than in the module's:

```
from module import a, b, c
```

In this selective form, the module code is executed as usual if this is the first time the module has been imported; otherwise, the previously imported copy is used. The module name is not bound to the module in the current namespace, however. Instead, each name in the list is copied into the current namespace, where it gives access to whatever value the name was bound to during the import. The net result is that names bound in the module end up bound directly in the namespace of the caller.

The previous statement is roughly equivalent to the following series of statements, with the *caveat* that the module name binding does not really take place, not even transiently:

```
import module      # bind the module to its name
a = module.a       # bind "a" to the module's "a"
b = module.b       # bind "b" to the module's "b"
c = module.c       # bind "c" to the module's "c"
del module         # remove the binding of the module name
```

Importing All Names from a Module

To import all the names from a module, you can use an asterisk rather than a list of names. This format can be dangerous, however, because unless great care has been used to construct the module, it is difficult to be sure that there will be no conflicts between the names you import and the names you create in your own code. Generally, you should avoid the `from module import *` form unless the module's documentation gives a specific assurance that this is safe (and documents the names that it binds to values).

The value of this feature is that, because the names defined in the module are imported into the local namespace, there is no need to qualify them with the module name. Some well-known modules such as Tkinter have been designed to be safe, defining only an easily identifiable set of names.

Telling Python Where to Find Modules

The `import` statement tells the interpreter to load a module of code. This clearly has to come from some point in the filestore, so you might wonder what determines where the interpreter looks. In a system module called `sys`, the name `path` is a list of directories, which the interpreter searches in sequence. So, if you want to add your own directory to the path, the following statement shows you how:

```
sys.path.append("/home/steve/pythonlib")
```

You should never assign directly to `sys.path` unless you know exactly what you are doing. If you delete the directories containing the standard library modules, your programs will no longer be able to import them!

Running Programs

If you give a program name as an argument to the interpreter when you start it, the interpreter reads the code and executes it almost as though you had typed the text contained in the program file into an interactive session. When it executes the final statement in the file, or when an exception occurs, it terminates.

Modules Are Programs Too: Python's Execution Environment

When the Python interpreter runs (either interactively or reading a program file), the environment is simple. Although Python has many built-in modules, only two, named `sys` and `__builtin__`, are initialized by execution before code is read from the appropriate source.

The `sys` module provides access to various system services and is fully documented, so it is not discussed further at this stage. The `__builtin__` module is where built-in functions, exceptions (discussed in the later section "Exception Handling"), and `None` are defined. Immediately before beginning code execution, the interpreter creates a namespace called `__main__`, which provides a namespace to hold the names that the top-level code binds.

Until you start to work with object-oriented code (in the next chapter), or deal with nested functions, there are at most three places where the Python interpreter looks to resolve a name before retrieving the value associated with it:

- The first is the *local namespace*, which is created dynamically when a function is invoked. If no local namespace is active (global module-level code is being executed), then obviously the interpreter cannot look in it.

- Next it looks in the *global namespace*, but be aware that this name is a little misleading. It might be easier to think of it as the *module namespace* because it is associated with the module whose code is currently being executed. When you run a Python program, the global namespace initially is that of the `__main__` module, but for code in other modules, it is the namespace of that module.

- Finally the interpreter looks in the `__builtin__` namespace, where it finds the predefined objects that are built-in to the language.

If the name resolved is the first component of a *qualified name* (a sequence of dot-separated names), the value to which the name is bound is expected to include a namespace. If such a namespace is found, then the next component of that name is looked up in it, and so on until all components of the name are resolved. An *exception* (the final topic of this chapter) is raised if any component of the name is not found, or if no namespace is found.

Consider a statement such as the following, where `mod` is some module you have imported into whatever module currently is executing:

```
result = mod.func()
```

The name `mod` must first be resolved. This could happen in the local namespace, if a function that imported the module happens to be executing. It is much more usual, however, to import modules at the top level of other modules, so it is likely that the name will be resolved in the current global namespace. If the name really does have a module bound to it, then that module will have an associated namespace. Assuming that the `mod` module contains a `def` statement defining `func`, then this second component of the name will be resolved, yielding as its value the compiled code corresponding to the function's suite.

When the function code is called, the interpreter creates a new local namespace for the call, and it makes the `mod` module's namespace the global namespace. To ensure consistency for the calling environment, the previous local (if any) and global namespaces will be saved before the call is made and restored when the call terminates.

How Modular Is a Module?

In Python it is easy, using modules, to isolate code in easily reusable chunks. Unlike some other languages, however, there is little protection that the author of a module can impose to stop other code, which imports the module, from accessing its namespace. Python is deliberately designed to lay bare most of its internals, and as always the temptations to the adventurous can lead to foot-shooting behavior.

The namespaces associated with modules are completely accessible, for both reading and writing. Given the name of a module, you not only can access names from it but also bind new values to them. This means that to program effectively, you need to exercise a certain maturity and discipline to get the most effective coupling between the components of your program. Listing 2.41 shows you the complete abandon with which you can override Python's module boundaries. It binds a function from the importing module to a function name defined inside the module.

Listing 2.41   **Crossing Module Boundaries in a Confusing Way**

```
#
# mod3.py
#
def m3f(a,b):
    print "m3f called:", a, b


#
# app3.py
#
```

```
import mod3

def mainf(x, y):
    print "mainf called:", x, y

mod3.m3f("one", "two")
# rebind module function name
mod3.m3f = mainf
mod3.m3f("three", "four")
```

The output from running `app3.py` is shown here:

```
D:\Code\Ch2 python app3.py
m3f called: one two
mainf called: three four
```

Running Programs Interactively: *reload()*

Whether you have written a complete Python program or a module intended for use by many different programs, you need to repeatedly execute it during testing. Even an experienced programmer, faced with the interactive Python interpreter for the first time, can find it difficult to understand how to run a program.

All you need to remember is that the code in a module is executed when it is imported for the first time. So to execute your program in the interpreter, simply enter an `import` statement on the module containing the program. But, of course, this does not work a second time, because even if you use an editor to change the source code, the interpreter will simply refer to the previously loaded copy. Here is an attempt to run the `mod1` module you saw a little while ago twice:

```
>>> import mod1
Mod1 executing
>>> import mod1
```

To tell the interpreter to go through the whole process of executing the module code again, you have to use the `reload()` built-in function. This function takes the module object (which is normally bound to the module name) as its argument. Listing 2.42 is an example, entered into a newly started copy of the interpreter.

Listing 2.42 **Reloading a Module Forces Re-Execution**

```
>>> import mod1
Mod1 executing
>>> reload(mod1)
Mod1 executing
<module 'mod1' from '/home/steve/projects/python/mod1.pyc'>
```

Notice, by the way, that reload() returns the re-imported module (the interpreter prints as much detail as it reasonably can).

Testing Modules Interactively

When Python imports a module, it binds the variable __name__ in the module's name-space to a string containing the module's name. Every module can therefore gain access to its own name. When the interpreter starts running, either interactively or with a program file as an argument, it is not importing a module, and the special global namespace is active. In this namespace, the interpreter binds the value "__main__" to __name__. The code in a module can use this fact to determine whether it has been run as a program or imported from some other module. To make your modules self-testing, it is a good idea to include some test code at the end, which only executes if the module is run as a program.

```
if __name__ == '__main__':
    # do some tests to verify module works
```

A common technique is to define a function and call that function if the module is being run as a program. Some people like this function to receive the command-line arguments, if any. These are accessible as a list from the sys module, so a typical piece of testing code might look like this:

```
if __name__ == '__main__':
    main( sys.argv[1:] )
```

It is good practice, when you start to write significant modules intended for reuse, to make them self-testing in this way. This makes it easy to check that changes to the code do not affect the function of the module without having to import and test it interactively.

If you want to go further, Release 2.1 of Python integrates the pyunit and doctest modules. pyunit is a Python implementation of a unit-testing framework originally built for the Java language, but now ported to several other environments. doctest is a system that allows you to specify tests in the documentation strings of your code, and it executes them and reports back for you. If you believe, like Extreme Programming (XP) devotees, that no code should be written until after you have tests for it, these modules are for you.

Exception Handling

One of the most difficult tasks in program design is creating programs that respond correctly to abnormal inputs and other conditions where it is no longer possible to continue execution along the lines intended. Despite the fact that they have been used to construct many major pieces of software, C programs using UNIX system calls are particularly pernicious, for two reasons. They are, however, typical rather than exceptional:

- System calls and library functions in UNIX generally return results, which the programmer must remember to check for exceptional conditions. It is easy to write code that "works" in the normal case and forget to go back and retrofit the error checks. Only when the unusual conditions occur after deployment is the shortcut noticed, and sometimes not even then.

- Even when all tests are correctly incorporated, it may not be convenient to build the program logic. When a system call is performed and an error is detected, a function might need to terminate immediately, itself returning an error code. The caller that sees the abnormal return must also have similarly contorted logic. Often, the normal case becomes buried deep in nested or sequenced conditionals, most of which exist to allow cancellation of several layers of function calls as a result of diverse errors that may have occurred.

Program logic is much easier to understand when the main focus of the code is the desired functionality, not the error handling. From this point of view, it makes much more sense to have a mechanism that breaks the flow of control when exceptional conditions occur. When you are writing a function, you do not want to have to code for every possible error condition that could occur. Often the only action the function could take is to return an error to its caller, and this complicates the logic. To avoid this complication, Python uses exceptions to report abnormal conditions that cannot be processed as anticipated.

As you write your programs, you write your code to handle the normal cases; if exceptions occur, then you catch them and handle them outside the flow of the normal logic. If you have not previously worked in a language, such as Java or C++, with exception handling mechanisms, you will appreciate the simplicity that this approach allows for error-handling in your programs.

Built-in Exceptions

Python has many exceptions that, because they can be raised by the interpreter itself, must be built in. You will more fully appreciate Python exceptions after covering the material about object orientation in Chapter 3, "Object Orientation." For now, it is sufficient to say that exceptions can be related to one another: all the built-in exceptions are children of a single parent, known as `Exception`. Without detailing the family tree, Table 2.17 shows all the built-in exceptions that might be raised.

Table 2.17   **Python Built-in Exceptions**

Exception	Description
AssertionError	An assert statement has failed.
AttributeError	A qualified name was not found in the namespace of the qualified object.
EOFError	Signals termination of console input.
FloatingPointError	Floating-point arithmetic error—configuration of the interpreter is required to enable this.
IOError	I/O operation failed.
ImportError	Problem executing an import or from ... import statement.
IndexError	Sequence subscript out of range.
KeyError	Dictionary key not found.
KeyboardInterrupt	User has hit interrupt key.
MemoryError	Python has run out of memory.
NameError	Unqualified local or global name not found.
NotImplementedError	Usually raised by user code to indicate incomplete implementation of functionality.
OSError	Operating system call failed.
OverflowError	Arithmetic result is too large to be represented.
RuntimeError	Catchall exception raised when no other category appears to apply.
SyntaxError	Python code with incorrect syntax was presented to the eval() function or exec statement.
SystemError	Internal error occurred in interpreter.
SystemExit	Program has called sys.exit().
TypeError	Operation or function has been attempted on data of an inappropriate type.
UnboundLocalError	Name has been referenced inside a function before a value has been bound to it.
UnicodeError	Encoding or decoding problem with Unicode string.
ValueError	Built-in operation or function has been applied to data of the correct types but inappropriate value.
WindowsError	Windows-specific error.
ZeroDivisionError	Division by zero is mathematically undefined.

Code expected to raise exceptions is written as a suite subordinate to a try clause. This establishes a framework for dealing with any exceptions. The suite may itself contain further try clauses, which will establish further frameworks inside the first one, and so on. Naturally, try statements can be nested to any level, both statically according to the program's structure and dynamically as functions are called.

When an exception occurs, the framework of the most recently executed active `try` is examined to see whether it can handle the current exception. If it cannot, the framework of the next most recently executed active `try` is examined, and so on until there are no more possible frameworks. At this stage, the interpreter must deal with the exception, which it does by printing a traceback and terminating the program's execution.

There are two major variant forms of exception handling in Python. The first allows special actions to be taken when exceptions occur, and the second ensures that required finalization is executed before the exception is passed to the relevant handler.

The *try ... except ... else* Statement

The `try` statement is compound, and the suite that follows is executed to the end unless an exception is raised. One or more `except` clauses follow this first suite, each with its own suite that specifies the actions to be taken when particular exceptions are raised. The `except` clauses may optionally be followed by an `else` clause, whose suite will only be executed if no exceptions were raised in the `try` suite. Listing 2.43 shows the various possibilities for the `except` clauses.

Listing 2.43   *except* **Clause Possibilities**

```
 1 try:
 2     some actions
 3 except NameError, duffname:
 4     actions to take on NameError: duffname is bound
 5     to a string holding the name that was not found
 6 except IOError:
 7     actions to take on IOError: no additional data
 8 except (FloatingPointError, ZeroDivideError):
 9     actions to be taken when any error in the tuple is raised
10 except:
11     actions to be taken for any other error
12 else:
13     actions to be taken if no error occurred
```

The last `except` clause (at line 10) in Listing 2.43 is dangerous because it will catch absolutely any error that occurs. Such an `except` clause should be used extremely sparingly, because it will catch even unexpected errors. If you use an empty `except` on the assumption that only a `KeyError` can be raised, for example, you might take completely the wrong action if a `ValueError` is raised because you have made some silly programming mistake. The real danger is that your testing may never reveal that the `ValueError` was raised.

A common mistake is to include too much code in the `try` suite. If you really are concerned about only one statement raising a `KeyError`, but this statement is followed by another, which you do not realize can also raise a `KeyError`, you might mistakenly write the following:

```
try:
    statement 1
    statement 2
except KeyError:
    handles an error in either statement
```

It would be better to write

```
try:
    statement 1
except KeyError:
    handle error in statement 1
else:
    statement 2
```

In this latter example, if `statement 2` raises a `KeyError`, then it will not be trapped by the `except` clause, and so is more likely to be detected as a programming error.

The *try ... finally* Statement

Sometimes a program allocates resources that must be released in the event of an exception. In this case, the allocation and subsequent code should be the suite of a `try` clause, and the release code should be the suite subordinate to a `finally` clause, as shown in Listing 2.44.

Listing 2.44   **Using *finally* to Ensure Execution**

```
try:
    allocate resources
    work with resources,
    possibly raising exceptions
finally:
    release resources
```

If an exception is raised by the `try` clause's suite, then the interpreter passes control to the `finally` suite immediately. After this executes (and the resources are released), the exception will be re-raised, hopefully to be handled by some surrounding exception handler. If no exception is raised in the `try` suite, then the `finally` suite is executed after the `try` suite; thus, the finalization is always executed. Note that a `break` or `return` statement inside the `try` suite also will cause the `finally` suite to be executed (a `continue` inside the `try` suite, on the other hand, currently gives a syntax error at compile time).

The `finally` clause cannot be used under the same `try` statement as the `except` or `else` clauses. This is not such a limitation as it might at first seem because if an exception is raised to trigger the `finally` clause, it will be passed upward to any surrounding try statement. By nesting a `try ... finally` inside a `try ... except ... else` statement, you can have the best of both worlds (see Listing 2.45).

Listing 2.45   **Nesting a *try … finally* Inside a *try … except***

```
>>> try:
...     try:
...         a = 8/0
...         print "Never gets here"
...     finally:
...         print "finally processed"
... except ZeroDivisionError:
...     print "You cannot divide anything by zero!"
...
finally processed
You cannot divide anything by zero!
```

User-Defined Exceptions

Although you have not yet learned the object-oriented aspects of Python that allow you to do so, it might be reassuring to know at this point that you can define your own exceptions. They are treated just like built-in exceptions and handled in exactly the same way. Your applications code can benefit from the structural advantages of exception handling, resulting in cleaner and more maintainable code.

Raising Exceptions: The *raise* Statement

Even before you can define your own exceptions, you can subvert the ones built in to Python for your own purposes. As a trivial example, suppose you are writing a stock control system, and the product codes use a check digit scheme to validate the part numbers. Let's say that part numbers are five digits plus the check digit. The idea behind such schemes is that you perform a computation on the first five digits, yielding a single-digit result. If this result is equal to the sixth digit that the user entered, then the odds are high that no data entry error was made. A good check digit scheme guarantees to catch all digit transpositions and many other errors as well.

If you choose to separate the validation from the data entry, then your top-level logic has to call the input routine and then call the validation routine. It must break out of sequence, if an error is detected, and otherwise perform its processing (with the possibility that later errors may need to be detected and handled). Instead of this, why not have the entry routine do the checking itself and raise appropriate exceptions when it detects conditions that require processing to be terminated? Nothing is easier, as Listing 2.46 shows.

Listing 2.46   **A Parts Processing Program with Check Digit Validation**

```
1 #
2 # CheckDigit.py
3 #
```

continues

Listing 2.46 **Continued**

```
 4 def check(s):
 5     if len(s) != 6:
 6         raise TypeError
 7     if not s[5].isdigit():
 8         raise ValueError
 9     c = 0
10     for digit, weight in zip(s[:5], [3, 5, 7, 11, 13]):
11         if not digit.isdigit():
12             raise ValueError
13         c += int(digit) * weight
14     if (c % 10) != int(s[5]):
15         raise ValueError
16
17 try:
18     while 1:
19         try:
20             s = raw_input("Part #: ")
21             if s == "":
22                 break
23             check(s)
24             #
25             # Here we would process the part
26             #
27             print "Part", s, "processed"
28         except ValueError:
29             print "Invalid check digit"
30         except TypeError:
31             print "Not a part number"
32     print "\n\nProgram Terminated"
33 finally:
34     print "\n\nThank you for your input"
```

This is what the program looks like in action (an empty line must be input to indicate that input is terminated):

```
D:\Code\Ch2> python CheckDigit.py
Part #: 123453
Part 123453 processed
Part #: 123543
Invalid check digit
Part #: rhubarb
Not a part number
Part #: 364759
Part 364759 processed
Part #:
```

```
Program Terminated
```

```
Thank you for your input
```

Notice that if the user enters an end-of-file character, this raises an `EOFError`. After the `finally` clause has been executed, the error is re-raised and causes the interpreter to give a traceback because there is no handler to catch it. You can see this error occurring in Listing 2.47.

Listing 2.47   **Incorrect EOF Handling**

```
D:\Code\Ch2> python CheckDigit.py
Part #: 123453
Part 123453 processed
Part #: [user enters ^Z]
Thank you for your input
Traceback (most recent call last):
  File "CheckDigit.py", line 20, in ?
    s = raw_input("Part #: ")
EOFError

D:\Code\Ch2>
```

This structural error in the code would be relatively simple to remedy: catch the `EOFError` with an `except` clause and `break` from the loop in response to the end of file, just as in response to an empty input line.

Re-raising an Exception

Occasionally, you will find that during exception processing the particular exception you are dealing with needs to be handled by a surrounding exception handler even though you have already caught the exception. Because exceptions can actually be complicated in their structure, you do not want to have to completely analyze the error to duplicate it.

The `raise` statement, when the keyword is used on its own, does exactly this: re-raises the specific exception that was last caught, identical in all its detail, and propagates it outwards toward surrounding exception handlers, if any.

Summary

Your knowledge of Python, although not complete, should now enable you to read other people's Python code proficiently even if you are as yet a little hesitant about writing your own. You have covered all the major topics and have an understanding of the significance of namespaces to Python.

3

Object-Orientation

So far you have seen the more conventional aspects of the Python language. But how do you build and manipulate the data structures your application will need? To answer this question, you have to look a little deeper into the language and start to take an *object-oriented* view of programming.

Object-orientation is not a new idea. It essentially sprang out of simulation work in the late 1960s and got a huge boost from Alan Kay, then of Xerox PARC, in the 1970s with his work on the SmallTalk language. In the simulation world, you can take a number of different approaches, depending on what you want to simulate. Discrete-event simulation deals with the cases where things interact periodically and relatively large amounts of time go by in which nothing happens.

Much of the work of writing programs (and especially simulation programs) is really information modeling. You build a model of some subset of the universe that is of significance to you by describing the characteristics of interest with data. Then you look at the model for information instead of the real world because it's easier and faster to do so.

Accounting systems, for example, build a representation of the accounting structure of an organization and its accounting relationships with suppliers, customers, and so on. This allows staff to retrieve the current balances for supplier accounts, print a list of transactions between particular dates, produce invoices and statements, and so on.

The reason for *maintaining* the model is to be able to deduce information about the real word from the state of your model. In most commercial information systems, the updates to the data model take place more or less in step with the real world, so the model continues to be accurate in the dimensions of importance. Many of the parallels with discrete-event simulation are obvious: An account balance will not change by itself; some transaction must occur to trigger the change. Real-world events need to trigger updates to the data model. If the data model is up-to-date, information from the model will tell you accurately about those aspects of the real world you are modeling.

Object-oriented languages allow you to build active models: You can specify what data is held about objects of a particular type; you can also specify the operations that can be performed on each type of object.

For example, many of us maintain multiple accounts with banks and credit card companies. All accounts are updated by processing one or more transactions. So an account is a set of data (each account has a name, a balance, and a transaction history unique to the account) and some operations that can be performed on that data (such as "process a transaction," "print current balance," or "list transaction history since June 1, 2000"). The same operations (in Python called the *methods*) can be performed on all accounts, regardless of the different individual data they contain.

Objects for Database Developers

If you have done any relational database design, you may be familiar with the process of establishing a logical schema. If not, you can read about it in Chapter 8, "Relational Database Principles," and it might make more sense to read this sidebar after you have absorbed that material.

In the schema design process, you identify types of *entities* (things) about which the user requirements tell you information is required—for example, customers, orders, products, and so on. You then identify the important *attributes* of each entity type, which are the things you need to know about them to perform your business functions. Typical attributes of a customer might be name, address, credit limit, and so on.

Each *entity set* (collection of things all of the same type) appears in the logical schema as a relation or *table*. Each row in a table represents a particular occurrence of that type, and each column represents an attribute. Relationships can be declared between the different entity sets, resulting in the entities of one type containing references to entities of another type.

A real-world object of some type is modeled as a set of data—for example, a row in the appropriate table. Application programs implement a set of operations over the data, using arguments provided by users that may represent new information or may be just parameters, such as reporting periods, which do not add anything new to the database contents but condition the outputs.

The logical schema for a complete application is a map of all the different types of things that the system must represent. It tells you what data (or *attributes*) you must maintain for each entity, and what the relationships are between the different entity types. The logical schema is, to all intents and purposes, the blueprint for a data model of a subset of the real world.

Traditional relational systems have no way to represent the behavior specifications that, in the object-oriented world, are implemented as methods.

Data in Python

Python is an object-oriented language. The difference between an object-oriented logical schema and a database logical schema is the scope of the definitions. In Python, the definitions of new types of objects are *classes*, and the objects created from the classes are *instances* of the class they are created from. Defining a class is similar to defining an entity type for a logical schema, but you also provide definitions of the operations that you want to perform on the instances of that particular class.

You have already come across some built-in types, such as lists, tuples, and dictionaries, which have a certain amount of structure. They are aggregates of other types, and you can access the individual elements, and subsets of them, using subscripting and slicing operations.

Certain operations (methods) are common to all objects of a given type. You invoke the methods of an object using a functional style, following the name of the variable bound to the object with a dot and the name of the particular method. You probably remember, for example, that you can test for the presence of a particular key in a dictionary using

```
dict.has_key("KeyVal")
```

This is because dictionaries all share a has_key() method, which returns a Boolean result. Even when you construct an object in the code, or use a literal representation rather than a variable bound to an object, you can invoke the methods of the object's type. So you might join a list of objects with a particular string using

```
print ", ".join(["spam","spam","egg","chips","spam"])
spam, spam, egg, chips, spam
```

Here we are invoking the join() method of a literal string ", " and giving it a list (of other strings) as an argument. You can create objects (instances of a particular type) for use in your programs either by using literal representations:

```
s = "This is a string"           # string
u = u"This is a Unicode string"   # Unicode string
l = [1, 2, 3]                     # list
t = ('a', 'b', 'c', 'd')          # tuple
d = {"bad": 'andy', "good": 'pizza'}  # dictionary
```

or by calling some function that returns a value of a particular type:

```
import string
l = string.split("spam spam eggs chips spam")# returns a list
t = tuple("spam")                            # returns ("s", "p", "a", "m")
```

The functions can be built-in, but equally you might have defined them yourself. With your present knowledge of Python, you can write functions that operate on arguments and return values of any of the built-in types you already know about. These values are *objects*, and objects of a given type have certain shared characteristics, even though they may have different values.

For example, if you access any of the sequence types (strings, lists, and tuples) with a subscript greater than or equal to its length, you would expect to see an `IndexError` exception raised. All dictionaries share a `has_key()` method, and all strings share a `join()` method.

The point is that a type in Python can specify more than just a data value or a set of data values. The type of an object determines what operations you can perform on it. For the moment, however, forget the operational side of things, and simply learn how to use Python to build data structures.

Data Structures in Python

Data structures are the simplest objects that we can create for ourselves. They are collections of data items often called *members*, *fields*, or *attributes*. Because each different attribute in a structure has its own use, Python allows you to use names with some mnemonic significance.

For this purpose, every object you create contains a namespace in which attributes can be found. Just like the methods of the built-in types, you access attributes by qualifying the name of the variable with a dot and an attribute name, writing

```
object.attribute
```

You can assign a value to the attribute of an object in exactly the same way you would expect from your existing Python knowledge: You use an assignment statement with a qualified name on the left-hand side:

```
object.attribute = value
```

The expression representing the value can be any legal Python expression. Python uses its usual trick of creating the value in object space if necessary; what actually gets stored in the attribute is a reference to the value (in object space) rather than the representation of the value itself. As always, this is largely transparent to you as a programmer, but you should keep it in the back of your mind for those occasions when you need to understand exactly what is going on.

Before starting to look at the uses of attributes, you should understand why the Python you already know, although sufficient for the purpose, isn't the most convenient way of building data structures.

Suppose you want to represent bank and credit card accounts in a Python program and that each account will have four attributes:

- A *name*, used in printed headings and other output, for identification purposes
- An opening date
- A *balance* showing current indebtedness
- A *history* of the transactions posted to the account

This detail of an account is not intended to be complete, but it captures enough of the properties for you to determine how useful a particular representation might be. After you have mastered the techniques, you will find it quite natural to extend whatever definition you may start with.

List Representations of Data Structures

If you chose to represent an account as a list, a literal expression representing an account might be

```
Amex = ["American Express", "2000-11-18", 0.0, []]
```

In this case, each attribute of the account is represented by a different integer subscript value, starting (as usual) with 0. So the expression

```
Amex[0]
```

would retrieve the account name. This works, but it is not very mnemonic. You would like the ability to reference each attribute by name, as well as the advantages of aggregating the attributes under a common name.

One way to provide a measure of symbolic access to the structure would be to define the offset of each attribute as a numeric variable:

```
AcName = 0
OpenDate = 1
Balance = 2
History = 3
```

This would provide a little more mnemonic significance, because you could now access the name of the account by writing

```
Amex[AcName]
```

This is rather a lot of trouble to go to, and using these names across module boundaries would introduce further complexity. If you imported the preceding code from module accts, for example, then you would have to refer to the account name of the Amex account as

```
Amex[accts.AcName]
```

Dictionary Representations of Data Structures

Losing confidence in the list representation, you might choose to use a dictionary to hold the fields, and write

```
Amex = {'AcName': 'American Express',
    'OpenDate': '2000-11-08',
    'Balance': 0.0,
    'History': []}
```

You could then use the expression

```
Amex["AcName"]
```

to refer to the account name in code. Similarly, you could add an item to the transaction history for the account with

```
Amex["History"].append(('2000-11-20', 'Laptop Computer', 3896.99))
```

This gives you symbolic reference to each of the attributes and makes your code more readable. It is also easier to understand the literal representation of the account because each attribute's name appears as a literal string.

The string quotes and the square brackets, however, are there only because you have chosen to represent the data as a dictionary. You are effectively using the dictionary like a namespace, with string subscripts naming the various values you want to store about the account. You could reduce the amount of typing somewhat by again defining symbolic values; this time they would be the string subscripts needed to access the individual attributes:

```
AcName = "AcName"
OpenDate = "OpenDate"
Balance = "Balance"
History = "History"
```

This would allow you to use a slightly simpler subscripted representation for the individual fields because the string quotes would no longer be necessary, and you could write

```
Amex[AcName]
```

and

```
Amex[History].append(('2000-11-20', 'Laptop Computer', 3896.99))
```

Again, though, if you put the code into a module, then each of the subscript-valued variables would need to qualify the module name. This would again increase the length of representation and make your programs more complex.

Defining Classes

To represent the data structures that you define yourself, you would probably prefer a simpler, and therefore more usable and more readable, way to aggregate values that belong together.

Really you need a true namespace, similar to a module, in which you can find the attribute names as symbols rather than having to create variables to refer to them as numeric or string values, possibly qualified by module names. The *class*, a Python type you have not come across yet, provides this for you and a lot more.

A class in Python (as in other object-oriented languages) is a specification that you can use to create objects, referred to as *instances of the class*. To define a class, you use the `class` compound statement, which (like the `def` statement used to define functions) is executable and not simply declarative. The name of the class follows the keyword which, like all compound statement headers, ends with a colon.

The indented suite that represents the class definition follows the `class` statement. The Python interpreter executes that definition and saves the resulting objects in a namespace associated with the class, which is stored under the class name given in the `class` statement. Because an `Account` as presently conceived is a simple class, you can make do with the simplest possible class definition, which in Python is

```
class Account:
    pass
```

The definition suite of this particular class is a single `pass` statement, which does nothing, underlining the fact that you are dealing with a simple class of objects indeed. The objects defined have no data attributes as a part of their definition, and there are no methods specific to the class. We'll look at these aspects of class definitions in "The *class* Statement" later in the chapter, but they are not necessary for now.

You can create *ad hoc* data structures by

1. Defining a class
2. Creating instances of the class
3. Assigning values to attributes of those instances

Classes Are Callable

After you have defined a class by executing a `class` statement, you create instances by calling the class as though it were a function. You can think of the class as a factory function for creating objects. The result of each call is a new object, which is an instance of the class from which it was created. You will see in section, "A Special Method: *__init__()*" (found later in this chapter), that it is possible, and even useful, to provide arguments to the class calls.

For now, though, be satisfied without this refinement. Simply be aware that classes are, like functions, an example of what Python refers to as *callables*.

Creating Instances

When you know how to define simple classes, you can treat them like special home-built types and create instances of those classes by calling the class as though it were a function. If you defined the class `Account` as shown previously, you would create an instance of the class by writing

```
Amex = Account()    # Create an instance of the Account class
```

This new instance has its own namespace, individual to that particular instance. Here you have bound to the `Amex` variable the result of calling the class, using zero-argument function-call syntax. `Amex` refers to a new object, whose type is an *instance* of the class `Account`. You would usually simplify things by saying that "`Amex` is an `Account`". This closely parallels the operation of the built-in types. In the same way, when you write

```
S = string.join(words)
```

you could say that you are telling Python to *create an instance of type string,* since the result of the `string.join()` method is a string. Informally, however, it's more common to just say you have "created a string." This represents a kind of programmer's shorthand—when you are familiar with strings and the operations on them, you tend to take their creation and usage as given. The same applies to the classes you define for yourself.

If you had forgotten to define the `Account` class, you would see an error message:

```
NameError: There is no variable named 'Account'
```

when Python tried to evaluate the expression on the right-hand side of the assignment to `Amex`. This is completely usual behavior. When it encounters the call to the class at runtime, Python searches the usual namespaces for the name `Account`. That name appears in the local namespace only once the `class` statement is executed. Before that time, there is no such name to be called, and so Python raises the `NameError` exception. This makes sense when you remember that Python does not use declarations: All this is really saying is that *you can't create instances of a class before you've defined the class* (that is, executed its defining `class` statement).

After you have your object (an instance of class `Account`) in the `Amex` variable, you can assign values to its attributes using Python's standard assignment syntax:

```
Amex.AcName = "American Express"
Amex.OpenDate = '2000-11-18'
Amex.Balance = 0.0
Amex.History = []
```

Attributes are referenced, just like the methods of built-in types, by following the name of the reference to the object with a dot and the name of the attribute. Each instance contains a namespace, and when it encounters the expression

```
instance.attribute
```

in code, Python looks up the `attribute` variable inside the namespace associated with the `instance` object. This notation is certainly more direct and easier to use in referring to the attributes of the `Account` than the list or dictionary representations you looked at previously. The built-in `dir()` function is a useful way to discover which attributes have been defined for any particular instance:

```
print dir(Amex)
['AcName', 'Balance', 'History', 'OpenDate']
```

You will probably not be surprised to learn that a reference to an attribute that has not been created by assignment will raise an exception:

```
print Amex.NoSuch
AttributeError: 'Amex' instance has no attribute 'NoSuch'
```

This is another standard action of the Python system at runtime. The expression `Amex.NoSuch` is an instruction to Python to look for the name `NoSuch` inside the namespace associated with the `Amex` variable (which happens to be an instance rather than a module). Because there is no such attribute name, an `AttributeError` exception is raised. You have already seen the same thing happen when you tried to access an undefined name from a module, although in this case the error message is a little more meaningful.

The possibility of `AttributeError` exceptions makes it important to ensure, as far as possible, that standard code is always used to perform the operations on objects. The code you have seen so far to set attributes of an instance is independent of the creation of the instance. If you forget to create a certain attribute, then this might cause `AttributeError` exceptions later. Scattering the code to maintain the attributes of instances around your program is asking for trouble. It's a bit like using global variables—it isn't that you necessarily shouldn't do it, just that you should expect trouble if you do it too much, or unwisely. You need to take an organized approach to objects to get maximum value from them.

Defining Operations on Instances

Given that you now know how to set attribute values, the next obvious question is "How can I make sure that the attributes of my instances are set in a standardized way, according to the operations I want to perform on the instances?"

When an operation is required repeatedly at many different places in a program, it's usual to write a function to perform that operation. As you saw in Chapter 2, "An Introduction to Python," if the function is likely to be useful for several programs, you can put it in a module, which you can import into different programs or into other modules. So functions look like a good candidate for specifying operations on the instances you create.

If you want to create many instances of a particular class, you might well define a function that creates a new instance and initializes the attributes from the arguments of the function call. This would give you a simple way to communicate the required initial attribute values to the instance creation process. You could improve readability and utility by using keyword arguments, possibly with default values.

Listing 3.1 shows a function that creates a new `Account` object, taking mandatory `AcName` and `OpenDate` arguments and an optional `Balance` keyword argument whose default value is zero.

Listing 3.1   **A Function to Create a New *Account* Object**

```
1 def newAccount(AcName, OpenDate, Balance=0.0):
2     a = Account()
3     a.OpenDate = OpenDate
4     a.AcName = AcName
5     a.Balance = Balance
6     a.History = []
7     return a
8 Amex = newAccount("American Express", "2000-11-18")
```

This "factory function" idiom is a neat and flexible way to encapsulate the creation of a new instance. As long as you always create `Account` objects with the `newAccount()` function, your instances will be created with a predictable set of values in the required attributes.

Of course this isn't the only way to organize instance creation and initialization. You might decide to separate the creation of the instance completely from the initialization of the attributes. In that case you would also have to pass to the function the instance you wanted to initialize. Listing 3.2 shows a function that organizes the creation and initialization in that way.

Listing 3.2   **A Function That Initializes an Instance**

```
1 def initAccount(acct, AcName, OpenDate, Balance=0.0):
2     acct.OpenDate = OpenDate
3     acct.AcName = AcName
4     acct.Balance = Balance
5     acct.History = []
6 Amex = Account()
7 initAccount(Amex, "American Express", "2000-11-18")
```

Thinking again of each `Account` as an object, the operations you can perform on `Account` objects are shared across all the different instances. There is no need for each `Account` object to carry its own implementation of them. So when you are defining the `Account` class, specify the operations (methods) once only, in a way that allows them to easily operate on any account object. When you revisit the `class` statement, you'll see this all start to fit together.

Instances Are Namespaces

You can see from Listing 3.2 that the attribute names of an instance are available even when you pass that instance as an argument. When it is compiling the `initAccount()` function, the Python interpreter does not know whether the `acct` argument will have a `Balance` attribute. It simply produces bytecode to look up the attribute in the namespace provided at runtime.

The interpreter checks for attribute presence dynamically, when the attribute is needed in the program. As you saw previously, when an attribute is not found, Python raises an `AttributeError` exception. In the object-oriented world, this approach is referred to as *late binding* of names.

This approach contrasts with that of some other object-oriented programming languages, such as C++, which can pretty much predict the presence of the attribute names and methods, whose addresses are therefore computable at compile-time. This contrasting approach is called *early binding*. It has strengths and weaknesses, which we need not discuss in a Python book since it is not available. The important thing is that each instance of a class is a namespace, in which the interpreter can look up attributes used as qualifiers to the name of the variable or argument representing the object.

Notice also that the `initAccount()` function does not return a value, since it simply operates on an existing instance. As you learned in Chapter 2, a function with no `return` statement actually returns the value `None` when it drops off the bottom of the function definition. Here this behavior is irrelevant, since the result of the function is not used and so the result is silently discarded.

You would probably write other, similar, functions to implement common operations on `Account` instances. For example, Listing 3.3 shows a simple function that processes a transaction against an `Account` that is again passed as the first argument to the function call. For now, the transaction is represented as individual data values passed as arguments to the function.

Listing 3.3   **A Function That Processes a Transaction**

```
1 def processTransaction(acct, date, amount, reason):
2     acct.Balance = acct.Balance + amount
3     acct.History.append((date, amount, reason))
```

The *class* Statement

When you took your first look at the `class` statement, I mentioned that an indented suite, which represented the definition of the class, followed it. The suite we used was a simple `pass` statement, which is Python's no-operation code.

You also have observed that instances of a class are effectively namespaces, in which attributes can be stored. As with all stored values in Python, the values themselves are stored in object space, and the names in the namespaces are associated with references to the values in object space.

In fact, the `class` statement has a number of additional features that you have not seen in the code presented so far. To get the most from Python's object-oriented features, you now need to look in a little more detail at the class type.

Classes Are Namespaces Too

When the `class` statement is executed, what actually happens is that a namespace is created. Names created during the execution of the suite associated with the `class` statement are stored in the new namespace (which effectively becomes the local namespace for the duration of the suite). Finally, the new namespace is stored in the current local namespace under the name given in the `class` statement. It becomes the *value* of the class.

Of course there are different ways to create names; as you've seen with instances, assignment is the simplest. This fact comes in handy when you start to look at the broader compass of classes. Just as creating a name in an instance's namespace creates an instance attribute, so creating a name in the namespace of a class creates a *class attribute*. This is a value associated with the class rather than with a particular instance.

Class Attributes

Attributes such as default values should ideally be shared among all instances of a class. It clearly is more efficient to store shared data once instead of creating separate copies for each instance. You can arrange this by using the namespace features of classes.

As you already know, Python looks in several namespaces when trying to find a value for a particular name. When you start to look at class inheritance, you will see that a whole chain of namespaces can be involved. Confusion is easily possible, though, even when you only have instances and the class itself to consider.

For now it's enough for you to focus on the fact that classes also can have attributes. Following is another simple class definition:

```
class AttributeProblem:
    mysterious= "default"
```

Here again the suite associated with the definition of the `AttributeProblem` class consists of a single statement, but in this case that statement associates a value with the name `mysterious`. The value then is stored under that name in the class namespace. You can verify this with a simple `print` statement:

```
print AttributeProblem.mysterious
default
```

Now create three instances of this class, and in the first two alter the value of the `mysterious` attribute:

```
i1 = AttributeProblem ()
i2 = AttributeProblem ()
i3 = AttributeProblem ()
i2.mysterious= "Spam"
```

```
i1.mysterious= "Eggs"
print "i1:", i1.mysterious, dir(i1)
print "i2:", i2.mysterious, dir(i2)
print "i3:", i3. mysterious, dir(i3)
i1: Eggs ['mysterious']
i2: Spam ['mysterious']
i3: default []
```

You are probably wondering why i3 is so suspiciously different from i1 and i2. The answer is that in setting the attribute values explicitly for i1 and i2, you create *instance variables*, local to the particular instances in which they were set. You can see this by examining the dir() results printed after the attribute values.

In the case of i3, however, there is no such instance variable—as you can clearly see from the empty output of the dir(i3) call—and yet no AttributeError is raised, and a value is printed for the attribute! What's going on here?

The answer is that after it looked in the instance's namespace and failed to find mysterious, Python went on to look in the class namespace for the attribute. Because the class itself does indeed have a mysterious attribute, *which is shared between all instances*, Python returns the value it finds in the class namespace for mysterious. You can verify this with the dir() function:

```
print "CLASS:", AttributeProblem. mysterious, dir(AttributeProblem)
CLASS: default ['__doc__', '__module__', 'mysterious']
```

For now, ignore those two (even more mysterious?) names __doc__ and __module__, which are a part of Python's class-handling mechanism. You can see that the class AttributeProblem does indeed have a mysterious attribute, whose value was established when the class definition was executed. The value used when retrieving the attribute for instance i3 is the value of the class attribute. You can easily test this empirically by changing the value of the class attribute. You would expect to see a corresponding change in the attribute value of the i3 instance:

```
AttributeProblem.mysterious= "NewDefault"
print "i3:", i3.mysterious, dir(i3)
i3: NewDefault []
```

Sure enough, i3 shows up as having the same value for its mysterious attribute as the new value for the class, and the i3 instance still has no instance mysterious attribute. Therefore, both classes and instances are Python namespaces, and if Python is told to look for an attribute of an instance, failure to find it causes Python to look for the attribute in the corresponding class.

Classes Also Specify Behavior

You now know a lot about how Python classes can be used to define data structures. You have seen functions defined that can act as standard operations on instances of the classes, but these functions were not in any way integrated with the class definition. Any function that acts on a data structure requires some knowledge of the structure. It would make sense to centralize the definitions of the class operations as a part of the `class` suite. Fortunately, this can be done easily, with the bonus that it's easier to define class methods than it is to define arbitrary functions.

The Methods of a Class Are Functions

Earlier, you saw how to define functions that operate on class instances. You can now put the final part of the jigsaw puzzle into place if you remember that function definitions also create names in a namespace. A *method* is an operation that should be performed in the context of, and particularly using the namespace of, some object representing an instance of a particular class. The previous functions, to create and maintain accounts, were able to accept `Account` objects as arguments. One of them, `newAccount()`, returned an `Account` object as its result. However, their definitions were entirely separate from the rather restricted `Account` class definition. Because you already know how to create functions in Python, you have all the tools you need to write methods by expanding the class statement to include method definitions.

Because the methods are associated with the definition of a class rather than with the individual instances, it makes sense to define them as a part of the suite following the class statement. Remember that when you define a function (using the `def` statement), the definition of the function is stored in the local namespace. In the same way, when the interpreter encounters a `def` statement in the suite subordinate to a class statement, it stores the function definition in the class namespace, as shown in Listing 3.4.

Listing 3.4   **Defining Class Methods with the *def* Statement**

```
 1 class Account:
 2
 3     def initAccount(acct, AcName, OpenDate, Balance=0.0):
 4         acct.OpenDate = OpenDate
 5         acct.AcName = AcName
 6         acct.Balance = Balance
 7         acct.History = []
 8
 9     def processTransaction(acct, date, amount, reason):
10         acct.Balance = acct.Balance + amount
11         acct.History.append((date, amount, reason))
```

You can examine the names that have been stored in the class namespace, to verify that the method names are now included, in the usual way:

```
print dir(Account)
['__doc__', '__module__', 'initAccount', 'processTransaction']
```

If you create a new `Account`, you can call the methods on it, accessing the methods from the namespace of the class and providing the instance as an argument to the method (see Listing 3.5).

Listing 3.5   **Calling the Methods of an *Account***

```
Current = Account()
Account.initAccount(Current, "Checking Account", "2000-11-26", 1234.56)
Account.processTransaction(Current, "2000-11-26", -1000.00, "Cash Withdrawal")
print "%8.2f" % Current.Balance
234.56
```

You saw earlier that if Python cannot find an attribute in the namespace of an instance, it will look for it in the namespace of the associated class. Is the same true for methods? One way to test this is to replace the class method calls in Listing 3.5 with *instance* method calls (instead of qualifying the name of the class with the name of the method, qualify the name of the instance), as shown in Listing 3.6.

Listing 3.6   **Replacing Class Method Calls with *Instance* Method Calls**

```
Current = Account()
Current.initAccount(Current, "Checking Account", "2000-11-26", 1234.56)
Current.processTransaction(Current, "2000-11-26", -1000.00, "Cash
Withdrawal")
print "%8.2f" % Current.Balance
    Traceback (most recent call last):
     File "exectest.py", line xx, in ?
        Current.initAccount(Current, "Checking Account", "2000-11-26", 1234.56)
    TypeError: too many arguments; expected 4, got 5
```

What has happened here? Python appears to have done as expected and located the `initAccount()` method, even though it was qualifying the instance name rather than the class name. However, it then complains that you have provided too many arguments. This is something of a surprise given that both the source code and the traceback clearly show that the offending call to `initAccount()` has exactly the four arguments Python is insisting are required!

The problem here is Python's special treatment of instance method calls. In the code as written, both method calls qualify the instance with the method name. Both calls also have the instance as the first argument to the method. This is at best unnecessary typing; at worst it allows error to creep in by allowing the programmer to pass the wrong instance to the method.

It seems obvious that methods should almost always refer to attributes and methods of the instance that was used to invoke them. Consequently, *when an instance method is called, Python automatically adds the instance as the first argument to the call.* This explains the incorrect argument count that Python is now complaining about. You can easily check this, and fix the code, by omitting the explicit first arguments to both method calls:

```
Current = Account()
Current.initAccount("Checking Account", "2000-11-26", 1234.56)
Current.processTransaction("2000-11-26", -1000.00, "Cash Withdrawal")
print "%8.2f" % Current.Balance
  234.56
```

Selfishness: Talking to Yourself

The special behavior of Python described in the preceding section occurs only when the method name is qualifying an instance. You saw that no error occurred in the preceding example, where the method name qualified the class name. When class methods were used, you had to explicitly pass the instance as the first argument.

We call a method invoked by qualifying an instance rather than the class a *bound method*, because the context of the call binds it to a particular instance of the class for which it is a method (or, as you will see later, one of its subclasses). The methods are still stored in the class namespace, of course.

The convention among Python programmers is to name the first method argument `self`, as a reminder that it refers to the instance whose name was qualified when the method was invoked. As you can tell, this is purely a convention. Otherwise, the previous example, which used the name `acct`, would have failed. Remember that although this is purely a convention, it is almost universal, and therefore you ignore it at your peril. At the very least, others will find it difficult to understand your class code. Worse, however, other programs designed to operate on Python programs may not properly modify or understand your code.

A Special Method: *__init__()*

Consider briefly the `initAccount()` method used in the last example. This represents a common idiom in Python programs, where we often want to create a new instance and then set certain attribute values. In fact, this requirement is so common that Python builds still further automation around it.

When calling a class creates an instance, Python looks in the class definition for a method with the special name `__init__()`. If it finds such a method, the interpreter calls the method with (as usual for a bound method) the new instance as the first argument. Further, if there are any arguments to the class call that created the instance, *they too are appended to the call of the* `__init__()` *method*.

This allows you to abbreviate your instance creation code still further. Up until now, you have created an instance by calling the class with no arguments and then calling `initAccount()` with the arguments to initialize the instance variables to the required values. Now, by renaming `initAccount()` as `__init__()`, you can combine these two purposes into one and pass `AcName` and `OpenDate` arguments to the call of the class. They then become the remaining arguments to `__init__()` along with `Balance`, which defaults to zero if not provided when the class is called.

The new class definition isn't actually that different, although the first argument has been renamed to acknowledge its special role, as shown in Listing 3.7.

Listing 3.7 **Automatic Instance Initialization**

```
 1 class Account:
 2
 3    def __init__(self, AcName, OpenDate, Balance=0.0):
 4        self.OpenDate = OpenDate
 5        self.AcName = AcName
 6        self.Balance = Balance
 7        self.History = []
 8
 9    def processTransaction(self, date, amount, reason):
10        self.Balance = self.Balance + amount
11        self.History.append((date, amount, reason))
```

Please note carefully that the `__init__()` method does not return a value. By the time it is called, the object in question has been created, and all that is required is to set the necessary attributes to the required values. Any value returned by the method is ignored. Under this new definition, you create an account simply by writing

```
Amex = Account("American Express", "2000-11-18")
```

The call to the class creates the object. This triggers the call on the class definition's `__init__()` method, with the new object as the first argument, `"American Express"` as its second argument, and `"2000-11-18"` as its third and final argument. Because there is no `Balance` argument, it defaults to `0.0` in the usual way. This initializes the object by setting the attribute values according to the arguments provided to the call on the class.

Protection by Convention, not Legislation

One of the nice things about Python (if you happen to like it) is the open access you get to the data structures used to represent the data model. Python lays bare almost all its inner workings for those who know enough about the language and its implementation. For better or worse, Python has few ways to prevent the programmer from adding attributes to an instance, or modifying the values of existing attributes, anywhere in the program. If an instance is accessible, then so are its attributes, whether you like it or not. This aspect of the language can be used in some advanced ways to provide *introspection*—programs can develop arcane knowledge about their class and module structures. It can be a mixed blessing, of course. The more you mess with internals, the easier it is to make a fatal mistake.

Do bear in mind that just because something is possible doesn't necessarily make it desirable. It would be poor programming practice to write a class definition that assumed the programmer was going to change class attributes from outside the class methods. The same goes for instance attributes. Ideally, everything that performs operations on the internal data of the class and its instances should be a part of the class definitions.

The early work on object-orientation specified three desirable properties for programming languages:

- Encapsulation
- Polymorphism
- Inheritance

You are already in a position to understand the first two of these principles.

So far you have learned how to define simple classes, create instances of those classes, and define class methods, which can be used to manipulate the instances. The programmer who uses an object need not know the implementation details of the methods of an object. Nor should details of the data structures used inside the instances be required. Indeed it is cleanest and least error-prone to write classes so that instances are manipulated solely by calling their methods. This property is usually referred to as *encapsulation*.

You have also seen that Python uses late binding when looking for attributes and methods. This means that the checks for the presence of the attributes and methods do not take place until runtime. One of the implications of late binding is that the type of an object passed in to a function need not be known. The object simply has to possess the required members (attributes and methods) when references to those members occur in the code. This property is known as *polymorphism*, which means "of multiple shapes" or "of many forms."

Polymorphism is the second side of the object-orientation triangle, and its essence is the capability to write code to handle many different types of objects, as long as they all have the required attributes and methods. Of course, if you have correctly observed the encapsulation requirement, then nothing outside your class definitions will refer to the attributes anyway, meaning objects will only be required to implement the required methods.

There is only one great secret left to reveal. This third secret explains how you can start by building general objects and successively refine them for specific purposes.

Inheritance allows you to program by saying that one class of objects is "like another class, but different." The primary advantage of inheritance is that the definitions of the similarities apply across all classes, allowing you to concentrate only on the differences when you define the more specialized classes.

More About Inheritance

You have already seen a definition of the Account class, which maintained four attributes and had only two methods: One initialized the instances, and the other processed transactions. If you wanted to define several different account-handling classes, it would be wasteful to have to repeat the same method definitions for each class. If you decided to change the way accounts worked, such a program organization would also make the changes long-drawn-out and error-prone.

Because inheritance is best seen in action when objects exhibit complex behavior, the first thing to do is to enhance the definition of the Account class. I will do this by adding a couple of methods: one that prints the transaction history and the other that prints out the current balance and returns it. Listing 3.8 shows the revised class definition.

Listing 3.8   *AccountClass.py:* **Designed as an Inheritance Model**

```
class Account:

    def __init__(self, AcName, OpenDate, Balance=0.0):
        self.OpenDate = OpenDate
        self.AcName = AcName
        self.Balance = self.OpenBal = Balance
        self.History = []

    def processTransaction(self, date, amount, reason):
        self.Balance = self.Balance + amount
        self.History.append((date, amount, reason))

    def printHistory(self):
        print "%10s  %-28s %10.2f" % (self.OpenDate, "Opening Balance",➡
        self.OpenBal)
        bal = self.OpenBal
        for date, amount, reason in self.History:
            bal = bal + amount
            print "%10s  %-15s  %10.2f  %10.2f" % (date, reason, amount, bal)

    def printBalance(self):
        print "%-15s: %10.2f" % (self.AcName, self.Balance)
        return self.Balance

if __name__ == "__main__":
    Current = Account("Checking Account", "2000-11-18", 1234.56)
    Current.processTransaction("2000-11-20", -200.00, "Cash Withdrawal")
    Current.processTransaction("2000-11-21", -300.00, "Cash Withdrawal")
    Current.processTransaction("2000-11-23", -400.00, "Cash Withdrawal")
    Current.processTransaction("2000-11-26", 1400.00, "Royalties")
    Current.printHistory()
    print "=" * 51
    Current.printBalance()
```

continues

Listing 3.8   **Continued**

```
    print "-" * 51
2000-11-18  Opening Balance                 1234.56
2000-11-20  Cash Withdrawal      -200.00    1034.56
2000-11-21  Cash Withdrawal      -300.00     734.56
2000-11-23  Cash Withdrawal      -400.00     334.56
2000-11-26  Royalties            1400.00    1734.56
=====================================================
Checking Account:     1734.56
-----------------------------------------------------
```

This code appears in a module, `AccountClass.py`, since things are getting to the point where some modularity is required as protection against the complexity starting to appear. It uses the usual trick of testing the value of the __name__ variable, ensuring that an instance is created and manipulated only when the module runs as a main program. This allows you to verify that the `Account` class works and gives you a basis for regression testing should you choose later to change the implementation.

Python allows you to minimize the programming work required by defining classes in a hierarchy. Instead of each class standing on its own, you can tell Python that a new class is like an existing one, except for the differences specified in the new class definition. You do this by giving the name of the existing class in parentheses after the name of the new one in the `class` statement.

It would be relatively easy to alter the way that the history was printed. All you have to do is define a new class that inherits from `Account` but defines its own `printHistory()` method. An instance of this class would then inherit all the methods of `Account` not a part of its own class definition. At this stage, you are approaching the complexity level where modules are useful. You could define the new class as shown in Listing 3.9, importing the previous example to gain access to the `Account` class definition.

Listing 3.9   *QuickAccount.py:* **Inheriting from the Account Class in the *AccountClass* Module**

```
import AccountClass

class QuickAccount(AccountClass.Account):

    def printHistory(self):
        for h in self.History:
            print "%12s %10.2f" % (h[0], h[1])

if __name__ == "__main__":
    Current = QuickAccount("Checking Account", "2000-11-18", 1234.56)
    Current.processTransaction("2000-11-20", -200.00, "Cash Withdrawal")
    Current.processTransaction("2000-11-21", -300.00, "Cash Withdrawal")
    Current.processTransaction("2000-11-23", -400.00, "Cash Withdrawal")
```

```
        Current.processTransaction("2000-11-26", 1400.00, "Royalties")
        Current.printHistory()
        print "=" * 51
        Current.printBalance()
        print "-" * 51
        print "QuickAccount:", dir(QuickAccount)
   2000-11-20    -200.00
   2000-11-21    -300.00
   2000-11-23    -400.00
   2000-11-26    1400.00
   ===================================================
   Checking Account:    1734.56
   -------------------------------------------------
   QuickAccount: ['__doc__', '__module__', 'printHistory']
```

Notice the last line of output. The `QuickAccount` class has only one method, which overrides the method inherited from its parent `Account` class. Just the same, the `processTransaction()` and `printBalance()` methods of the `Account` class can be called just as though they were methods of the `QuickAccount` class.

This is the magic of inheritance. When searching for a method or an attribute of an object, Python first looks in the instance, then it looks in the class definition, then in the definition of the superclass, and so on all the way up the inheritance tree.

Things You Want to Know About Classes

You may think, having read all this about classes, that there isn't much difference between using a Python type such as a dictionary and using your own objects created from a user-defined class. Current Python implementations, unfortunately, maintain a distinction between built-in types and user-defined classes.

Classes are actually instances of the built-in Python class type, and class instances are actually instances of the Python instance type. The specialized behavior you have just learned about keeps them separate from the other built-in Python types.

You might like to be able to define subclasses of the basic types (a specialized dictionary, for example), but this currently isn't possible (although the early stages of the transition are close at hand: see Appendix A, "Changes Since Python 2.0," for details of Python 2.2). In earlier versions, an attempt to subclass a Python type raises an error:

```
import types
class SpecialDict(types.DictionaryType):
    pass
```

   TypeError: base is not a class object

Clearly, Python is expecting to find an instance of type class in the list (or possibly a list of such types, although you haven't yet seen that possibility). This does not imply that you can't define classes that are a specialization of the basic types, though. It just means you can't do it by subclassing. Take a look at the `UserDict` module, and you will see that it defines a class with all the methods of the dictionary type. These methods are mostly just calls to the corresponding methods of an underlying dictionary object, which `UserDict` creates in its `__init__()` method and stores as an instance variable.

We call such a class a *wrapper class* because it wraps up the behavior of the Python type inside a user-defined class that your own classes can then inherit from. You also will find `UserList` and `UserString` modules in the standard library, which wrap the *list* and *string* types, respectively. Wrapper classes allow you to access the functionality of the built-in types and alter it by inheritance. Remember, though, that they carry a certain amount of overhead because they add a Python method call to the code, which must be executed to access the type's methods.

The Python class hierarchy is a powerful way of reusing existing code. Because classes and instances are both namespaces, there is a lot of flexibility for methods and attributes to be defined at any point in the hierarchy. As you will see later, a Python class can actually inherit from multiple base classes. This allows you, for example, to define `mixin` classes, which specify a set of behaviors for inheritance by many different classes.

Jython: A Unique Blend of Two Languages

As an object-oriented scripting language, Python shares many characteristics with the Java language, although it also has several distinctions. The parallels between the two languages, together with their complementary strengths, led Jim Hugunin to reimplement the Python language in certified 100 percent pure Java.

The original implementation was known as JPython and was licensed by CNRI along the same liberal lines as the original Python implementation, which is usually called *CPython* ("Classic Python") when the two implementations are being discussed. Since the move of the Python team away from CNRI, the system has been renamed *Jython*, to avoid infringement of CNRI's rights to the original name. Hugunin now has moved to Xerox PARC to work on the AspectJ language, and the primary maintainers are now Barry Warsaw and Finn Bock (with the assistance of the usual "cast of thousands").

Similarities Between Python and Java

Both languages are object-oriented, and both use pretty much the same model of assignment, where a variable is effectively a pointer to an object. Both languages were intended for compilation into an intermediate code form, although it turned out that the Java virtual machine's operations weren't always a comfortable fit for compiling Python.

Strangely enough, Java also has basic types that aren't comfortable members of the class hierarchy. In Java, you have type *integer*, which cannot be subclassed, and type *Integer*, which can. This is done for execution efficiency, as in Python.

Both languages also allow introspection, which gives programmers the ability to delve into the object structures to dynamically determine the available behavior (although the introspection mechanisms of the two languages differ radically).

Differences Between Jython and Python

With all these similarities, you might feel that the two languages were a natural fit, but they also differ in many important ways that had to be taken into account during the original JPython implementation.

Python is a scripting language, whereas Java is a system language. This means that productivity is much higher in Python, where it's easy to run an interactive interpreter session to test some basic ideas and then copy your code into a script for live use in a program. Scripting languages are less demanding than programming languages, and Jython excels as a framework in which to make use of already-developed Java classes. Rick Hightower, in the Java Developer's Journal, cites the following uses of scripting languages (see `http://www.sys-con.com/java/archives/0503/hightower/`):

- Extending existing applications
- Debugging applications
- Learning and experimenting with the Java API
- Rapid system prototyping
- Gluing together subsystems and components
- Automation of testing and regression testing

Python is a much more liberal language than Java in many ways, reflecting the development philosophy. This gives Java much greater declarative complexity than Python, since the declarations are required to allow the Java compiler to perform the tasks that Python defers until runtime. Python has only one declaration, the `global` statement, and all this does is point the compiler to a different namespace to resolve the names declared.

Python variables can refer to values of any type, whereas Java requires variables to be declared with a type, and only values of that type can be assigned. This static typing mechanism allows many more programming errors to be detected at compile-time and also makes for more efficient code generation.

Python allows multiple inheritance (so object classes can be subclasses of multiple superclasses), but Java was designed to avoid some of the pitfalls of this approach. There are parallels between Python's *mixin* classes and Java's interfaces. Interfaces allow multiple classes to exhibit the same behavior, with a specification that the compiler can check (but it does not support the ease of code reuse that mixins afford; Java's "nested classes" do recover some of that, but at a substantial price in terms of conceptual complexity).

In Java, the same method can be declared with different *signatures* (types and numbers of arguments), and the compiler determines which method implementation the call signature requires. The Python programmer does not have this ability to overload class methods. In Python, however, much of the implementation mechanism is evident to the programmer, and so certain operators can be extended to operate on programmer-defined classes by the implementation of methods with specific names such as __add__() for the + operator. This allows the Python programmer to use programmer-defined classes in a natural way in many expressions. Java does not allow operator overloading of this nature.

In general, many requirements that Java enforces are simply a matter of convention in Python, not a requirement of the language. This increased freedom gives programmers more rope with which to hang themselves. It also makes Python programming more productive.

For a more thorough discussion of Jython, take a look at *Jython* (New Riders Publishing, 0-7357-1111-9).

Jython's Implementation Strategy

Jython works by compiling Python code into bytecodes for the Java virtual machine (rather than into the Python bytecodes produced, and later interpreted, by CPython). Jython programs are therefore executed in the same environment as Java ones, and the interplay between the two languages is tremendous: Jython can import any Java library as a module and can create instances of Java classes in Python and *vice versa*. Not only that, but Python classes can be subclasses of Java classes.

The Jython system uses a complex type-inference system, using the introspection features, to determine which one of a number of possible overloaded methods of a Java class should be called. It performs necessary conversions where possible to provide arguments that conform to a method signature. This allows the Jython programmer to call methods without having to spend too much time considering which signature will be used.

Jython also includes a compiler, which translates Python into Java and then compiles the Java into a class file (normally the Jython system produces Java bytecodes directly). These compiled class files can be used just like those produced from Java with no initial Jython compilation step, allowing complete freedom of mixing and matching the language features to perform any task in the most appropriate language. This means you can use Jython to create applets, servlets, even Java Beans.

The Jython implementation uses the underlying features of the Java language to make the implementation task easier. Because Java already has a garbage collector, for example, this automatically comes into play to collect Jython garbage. Unlike the C implementation, no complex reference counting scheme is required. Java's binary portability, thread-safety, and existing exception-handling all make the task of mixing Java and Python code much easier than mixing, say, C and Python.

The only drawback is that Python extension modules written in C are no longer available, although the majority of the pure Python library modules have now been ported to Jython. This is a relatively small price to pay and one Java programmers do not find troublesome since they do not in any case rely on these features in their native language.

Summary

When you start to use Python, much of the language remains below the surface. In Chapter 2 you learned about the standard procedure-oriented features of Python, which allow you to write code without using any of the language's object-oriented features. Those features, however, allow you to write programs that create and manipulate instance objects that carry their own data about with them as instance attributes. The class used to create a given instance can provide further attributes, the class attributes that are shared among all instances. The class also holds the method definitions, which are again common to all instances.

Object-oriented programming can help to make programs simpler. Encapsulation makes objects self-contained, polymorphism allows you to deal with many different types of object in the same code, and inheritance allows you to specialize objects for your own specific purposes by building on the capabilities of an existing base class that provides some of the functionality you want.

Web systems can make good use of object-oriented techniques. They are, of course, primarily distributed computing systems, in which a central server handles requests from outlying clients. In the next chapter you will study the basics of client/server computing.

II

Network Programming
in Python

4

Client/Server Concepts

BEFORE PLUNGING INTO NETWORKING CODE, you might find an introduction to the whole idea of network computing useful. If you already are familiar with client/server computing, understand the concept of a networking API such as the socket library, and don't feel any need for revision, then you can move on to Chapter 5, "Available Client Libraries." You should not really start using the Python client libraries, however, before reading the sidebar "A Note on Time-Outs" later in this chapter, which describes a useful module to help keep your networked applications responsive.

Client/server is by far the most widespread approach to distributed computing. Most network services are structured so that a *server process* gains access to a particular network access point and waits for requests to arrive from *client processes*. It is thus an event-driven model: the server sits around until a client connects to it, and the two processes then undertake interactions whose nature is defined by some *application protocol*.

Functions of the Four Internet Protocol Layers

In network-based systems, it is important that application code (as far as possible) should have to handle only the application protocol. For example, it would be completely inappropriate, and result in a lot of wasted time and duplicated effort, for an application to have to determine whether its client had connected over an ethernet or a token ring and take different actions accordingly.

The OSI Seven-Layer Model

To try and define the best way to partition networking applications, the International Standards Organization specified an idealized layered model of networking systems. Because the model was intended to encourage open systems interconnection, it is usually called the *Open Systems Interconnection (OSI) model*. It is outlined in Table 4.1.

Table 4.1 **The ISO OSI Seven-Layer Model for Networking Applications**

Layer Name	Layer Functions
Application	Specifies the syntax to be used between sending and receiving processes
Presentation	Converts between native and network data representations, allowing machines of different architectures to communicate in a common "network-neutral" format
Session	Handles login, restart, checkpointing, and other session state maintenance issues
Transport	Provides reliability where appropriate
Network	Handles point-to-point routing across the network, fragments data into chunks appropriate to the datalink technology to be used, and reassembles on receipt
Datalink	Takes network-layer datagrams and frames them for transmission
Physical	Converts datalink frames into bitstreams for transmission over some medium

The OSI model is good for discussing network architectures and comparing them but is overcomplicated for many purposes. Few practical systems actually define all seven layers and have software components operating at those levels. Just the same, it provides a common standard for comparison of different protocol sets.

The Internet family of protocols (usually just called *TCP/IP*) is a conceptually simpler four-layer model. If a particular application needs the functions described in the OSI session and presentation layers, they must be specified as a part of the application protocol. The TCP/IP model does not look too closely at physical intercommunication and groups the OSI datalink and physical layers into a single "subnetwork" layer. This is shown in Table 4.2.

Table 4.2 **The TCP/IP Layering Model**

OSI Layer	Sample TCP/IP Protocols	TCP/IP Layer	Data Unit
Application			
Presentation	DNS, FTP, Telnet, SMTP, SNMP, NTP, HTTP, NFS	Application	Message
Session			
Transport	TCP, UDP	Host-to-host	Segment
Network	IP	Internetwork	Datagram
Datalink	Ethernet, IEEE 802.3, IEEE 802.5, HDLC, PPP	Subnetwork	Frame
Physical			

We often call the collection of software components that implement communications protocols a *stack* to reflect the layered nature of the communications processing. The sending application process passes a message to the transport layer, which passes data down to the network layer, which uses the subnetwork layer to relay the data to another machine. In a complex network, IP datagrams may be relayed across several subnetwork links, and each intermediate router does the following:

1. Strips off the incoming datalink framing
2. Examines the destination address
3. Makes a routing decision about where to send it next
4. Encapsulates the IP datagram in appropriate datalink framing
5. Sends the datagram off to the next router on its way to its destination

When (if) the datagram arrives at its intended destination, the IP headers are examined to determine whether the datagram is carrying TCP or UDP (or some other transport protocol); and when the IP headers have been stripped off, the resulting segment is handed up to the appropriate transport layer. The transport layer determines which application process finally receives the segment (less the transport layer headers) as a message.

Application Layer

The purpose of an application layer protocol is to allow processes at opposite ends of a network communication path to collaborate on a common task. The nature of the task depends on the application, so each application has its own protocol specification. Application layer programs on the Internet generally use either the Transmission Control Protocol (TCP) or the User Datagram Protocol (UDP) transport layer. The choice between them depends on whether the application requires automatic reliability, which TCP provides at the cost of some complexity.

Transport Layer

The transport layer, whether TCP, UDP, or some other protocol, allows parallel communications between multiple processes on the same pair of hosts without confusion. The transport layer acts as a multiplexing and demultiplexing mechanism, and both TCP and UDP use a software identifier called a *port number* to identify the sending and receiving processes. In the Internet world, services most usually are identified with fixed port numbers under 1024, called *well-known* ports. A Telnet client by default connects to TCP port 23 on the server, a web browser by default connects to TCP port 80 on the server, and so on.

Servers for a particular service will therefore open a connection to the particular port associated with their service and listen for incoming requests from clients. If the service task is short, the server might simply handle each request and then listen for the next incoming connection, relying on the transport layer to queue incoming connection requests as necessary. A more complex server might start a new process for each request, passing the open client connection, then continue to listen on its port for further incoming requests.

In the latter case, several clients potentially may be on the same host, connected to different server processes using the same port number. How does the server transport layer know which server process should receive particular incoming segments? This relies on the behavior of the transport layer at the client side: When a client program opens a connection to a server, it (usually) does not care which port number it uses, and so it requests an *ephemeral port*, which has an arbitrary number above 1023. The transport layer guarantees when it allocates ephemeral ports that no two processes simultaneously receive the same port number.

This means that when the server-side transport layer sees incoming data from one of the client processes, even though the source and destination IP addresses are the same from both clients, as are the destination port numbers, the *source* port numbers will differ. So as long as the transport layer maintains a record of four pieces of data for each connection (local and remote IP address, local and remote port number), at least one of these is guaranteed to be different for each connection.

Network Layer

Every 32-bit IP address contains two portions, one specifying the network number containing a host and the other specifying which host is being addressed on that network. The sending IP network layer receives segments from the transport layer above, which may be buffering to even out the flow of data and avoid sending too many small segments. It examines the destination address, and first tries to match the network number with that of each of its local interfaces.

If a match is found with a local interface, then LAN techniques are used to translate the IP address into a datalink (ethernet, token ring, and so on) address, and the destination host receives the datagram directly, wrapped in an appropriate datalink layer frame.

When the network number does not match any local interface, routing tables are consulted, which specify a "next-hop" destination for each known destination network. The routing tables associate the IP address of a connected router with each known destination network. For unknown networks, the IP address of a *default route* is used if available. Ultimately, an IP address on some local interface is chosen for the next hop, and the datagram is transmitted as described previously.

The datagram is treated in the same way at each intermediate node's network layer, until it arrives at its destination network, where it can be delivered to the specified host. If any intermediate node cannot determine where to send the datagram, or if it is simply too busy to handle the traffic, it may disregard the datagram. The IP network layer is therefore a "best efforts" service, with no guarantee of delivery. Furthermore, routing decisions are made independently for each packet, so there is no guarantee that datagrams will arrive in the sequence they were transmitted, or even over the same route.

Because network-layer addressing is always in terms of 32-bit IP addresses, the transport and application layers do not need to know which type of datalink layer will be used in any particular case. This is a powerful logical abstraction, enabling any application to connect to any reachable IP network no matter what datalink technology may be in use there.

The network layer also can split a datagram into fragments if it reaches a network that is unable to transmit it in one piece. These fragments may, in turn, be fragmented again if they must cross a network that handles even smaller datagrams. To avoid delay and conserve buffer space, reassembly of the fragments only takes place at the destination host.

The Loopback Interface

IP addresses are normally quoted in *dotted decimal* notation to make the numbers easier to handle. Each byte of the 4-byte address is given as a decimal number, and the four bytes are separated by dots. Addresses whose first byte is 127 are special: They force the use of the *loopback* datalink layer, which does not involve any physical hardware at all. A datagram sent to 127.0.0.1 is immediately received as an incoming datagram on the same host it was sent on. This loopback interface is convenient for testing when only one computer is available: Both client and server can run on the same host and in the absence of any networking hardware.

Although the standards require the network layer to treat any address beginning with 127 as local, some stacks only respond to 127.0.0.1.

Subnetwork Layer

This layer exists to pass datagrams between the network layers on different hosts. At this level, the addressing specifics of each datalink type must be handled, and the appropriate device drivers must be utilized for transmission to a particular host. Note that the datalink layer does not know (nor does it care) whether it is transmitting IP datagrams to their eventual destination or simply to an intermediate hop along the way. In fact, it does not care whether it is dealing with IP datagrams or some other type of network traffic.

When a frame is received from some other host on a connected subnetwork, if it contains an IP datagram, then the subnetwork layer passes it up the stack to the IP network layer component, which makes exactly the same routing decisions as it does with datagrams built locally from transport layer segments. The subnetwork layer performs no routing functions: the destination host is directly connected to the same network.

Connectionless Versus Connection-Oriented Networking

The choice of transport protocol is left to the application programmer (or application protocol designer) and depends on several factors. First, is there an extended dialog between a single client process and a single server process, in which data transfer needs to be reliable? If the answer to this question is "yes" (as in, for example, FTP, Telnet, SMTP, and HTTP), then the transport protocol required is definitely going to be TCP.

The TCP transport protocol uses complex mechanisms to allow the client process to connect to a server on a particular IP host and to transfer streams of information in both directions simultaneously. The details of the protocol are more complex than you need to know, but it is important to note that when two hosts communicate using TCP, if information is received at all, it can be relied on. The TCP transport layer does not deliver data that is out of sequence or incorrect to the application layer.

If communications must be one-to-many (or even many-to-many), then TCP is not a suitable transport layer, because TCP expects to create a *virtual circuit* between a single process at each end. This makes it a *connection-oriented* protocol. UDP, however, is prepared to allow broadcast addresses as destinations and therefore will deliver messages to single or multiple recipients without any formal setup at all. Hence, UDP is a *connectionless* protocol and transmits datagrams one at a time, independently of each other. UDP does not include the complex error correction mechanisms of TCP and so is essentially a "best efforts" service.

Applications that use UDP at the transport layer must therefore be prepared to cope with packet loss. In the simplest case, protocol malfunctions can be recovered by requiring that the user try again; but in more complex cases, this might mean applications having to build-in their own error-correction mechanisms.

There is a general, but mistaken, belief that UDP-based (connectionless) applications tend to be faster than TCP-based (connection-oriented) ones by nature of their simplicity. This is not necessarily true: TCP uses a so-called *sliding window* mechanism to allow multiple sends before acknowledgment is received and has also added an improved acknowledgment system to reduce unnecessary retransmissions. In the absence of network errors or application protocol synchronization requirements, this is likely to provide much faster data transmission than a UDP application, which requires acknowledgment round-trips for each block of data transmitted. If you doubt this, time FTP (TCP-based) and TFTP (UDP-based) transfers of a large file and see which one is faster.

The Concept of a Network Socket

You can think of a connection between two hosts across a network as connecting to a process at each end. Five pieces of data uniquely identify any connection and allow the various protocol layers to successfully multiplex and demultiplex information streams across a network. Each end of the connection keeps the same information, although obviously what is remote at one end will be local at the other. The five pieces of data are

- Transport protocol (UDP, TCP)
- Remote IP address
- Remote port number
- Local IP address
- Local port number

The pathway connecting the remote and local endpoints is what the client and the server use to transmit data between them. One way of looking at this is to say that the pathway offers a "socket" at either end, into which client and server programs can be "plugged." By far the most common way to handle networked communications between processes (and the only one considered in this book) is the so-called *socket API*, which specifies a way for programmers to create a network connection and transmit information across it.

What Is an API?

An API, or Application Programming Interface, specifies which routines must be called, and in what sequence, to use the features of a particular program component. Usually, an API describes the interface to a program library. Object definitions also specify an API, which describes how to construct instances, which methods can be called, and with what arguments.

Network Programming Concepts

The socket API was originally developed for the BSD implementation of UNIX but has proved so popular, it is now in wide use on many operating systems. Despite implementation variations, it is a good platform for network applications. The socket library, which is a part of every Python implementation, does a good job of hiding the differences between platforms. The following sections explain how you can use sockets for server and client programs.

Server Structure

Listing 4.1 is a slightly modified copy of an example server from the socket library documentation. It is a simple server that echoes back anything sent to it and is small enough to study for an understanding of the socket library.

Listing 4.1   *Server.py:* **A Simple TCP Socket Server**

```
 1 # Echo server program
 2 import socket
 3
 4 HOST = '127.0.0.1'          # The local host's loopback interface
 5 PORT = 50007                # Arbitrary non-privileged port
 6 s = socket.socket(socket.AF_INET, socket.SOCK_STREAM)
 7 s.bind((HOST, PORT))
 8 s.listen(1)
 9 conn, addr = s.accept()
10 print 'Connected by', addr
11 while 1:
12     data = conn.recv(1024)
13     if not data: break
14     conn.send(data)
15 conn.close()
```

The library is used for the first time when the name s is bound to a new socket object on line 6. The socket.AF_INET argument to the socket.socket() creation call specifies that Internet family protocols are to be used, and the socket.SOCK_STREAM argument requests the use of TCP (stream, connection-oriented) rather than UDP (datagram, connectionless) services. Both these constants are defined in the library module, along with several others. In case you had not realized it, socket.socket is a class, so the call on line 6 creates an instance that the program can use.

The program next binds the socket to an address and a port number, passed as a tuple to the bind() socket method. The address 127.0.0.1 indicates that the loopback interface should be used, and the client and the server will be running on the same host. After these two arguments are bound, the program tells the transport layer to listen at that IP address and port number, queuing a maximum of one connection, by calling the listen() method.

The accept() call in the next statement effectively blocks the program, which therefore uses no further CPU time until a connection is received from a client. When such a connection occurs, the name conn is bound to a new socket, already connected to the client side, and addr is bound to the remote client's address. This is because `accept()` returns a two-element tuple, so each name is bound to an element of the tuple. Line 9 is therefore an example of an *unpacking assignment*: the components of the tuple on the right of the equal sign are individually bound to the names on the left.

After printing the client's address, the server then goes into a loop, requesting blocks of data from the connected socket of up to 1024 bytes at a time and sending the same data back to the client. When the socket returns a zero-length block, this indicates that the client has closed its end of the connection, and so the server breaks its loop and does the same.

Note that this simple server does not then attempt to handle a further connection request, which a production server would need to, nor does it attempt to start another process to handle the incoming request. Despite these omissions, it is typical of the server-side handling of socket connections.

Client Structure

Listing 4.2 shows a simple client program, also taken from the Python documentation and even simpler than the server.

Listing 4.2 *Client.py:* **A Simple TCP Socket Client**

```
 1 # Echo client program
 2 import socket
 3
 4 HOST = '127.0.0.1'        # The server host
 5 PORT = 50007              # The same port as used by the server
 6 s = socket.socket(socket.AF_INET, socket.SOCK_STREAM)
 7 s.connect((HOST, PORT))
 8 s.send('Hello, world')
 9 data = s.recv(1024)
10 s.close()
11 print 'Received', `data`
```

The client program creates the same type of socket as the server. Because TCP ports are entirely separate from UDP ports, this makes sense: A UDP client could not talk to a TCP server and *vice versa*. Then, rather than prepare its socket for incoming connections, it tells it to make a connection to a listening socket.

After making the connection, it sends a string to the process at the other end, receives a single reply, closes its socket, and prints out what it has received (using back-quotes to ensure a printable representation). The `close()` call on the client end of the socket causes the server to receive a zero-length input, indicating the end of the network dialog.

Running the Client and the Server

Figure 4.1 shows what happens when you run a server and then run the client twice. The listings are adjusted to show the relative timings of events on the server side and the client side.

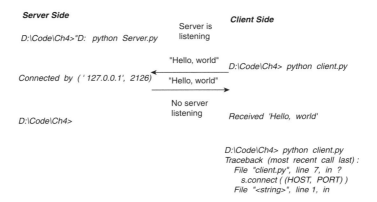

Figure 4.1 The client and the server interact.

The server and client activities appear side-by-side on the same timeline, showing you the order in which events occurred at the user interface. After the server starts, it waits until a client is started. The client then connects to it, which is reported by the server. After the connection is opened, the client sends a string, which the server returns. The client then closes the connection, terminating the server and reporting the string it received. Finally, the client is run again, this time with no server process running. The client-side socket routines raise an exception because the connection attempt finds no process listening at the specified IP address and port number.

The *socket* Library

The library module offers the capability to handle two address families, each identified by names in the module. You will find no further references to socket.AF_UNIX in the remainder of this book. See Table 4.3 for a list and explanation of the socket address families.

Table 4.3 *socket* **Address Families**

Address	Description
socket.AF_UNIX	These sockets connect to UNIX named pipes, which unfortunately are not the same thing as NetBEUI named pipes, do not interoperate with them, and are only available on UNIX platforms.

| socket.AF_INET | These are Internet-style (TCP/IP) sockets, giving access to the Internet family of protocols. |

Within the Internet address family, five socket types are available, of which only the first two shown in Table 4.4 are generally useful. SOCK_SEQPACKET and SOCK_RDM types, not listed, can be ignored.

Table 4.4   **Socket Types**

Socket	Description
socket.SOCK_STREAM	Defines a stream-oriented socket, which uses TCP as a transport-layer protocol.
socket.SOCK_DGRAM	Defines a datagram-oriented socket, which uses UDP as a transport-layer protocol
socket.SOCK_RAW	Defines a socket that gives raw access to the subnetwork layer, allowing you to formulate your own network layer datagrams

Most of the code you will see in the rest of the book uses libraries other than socket. This does not mean that the socket library is not used; quite the contrary. Almost all Python networking code uses the socket library. It is rather low level, however, for real-world purposes, and so the libraries you will use are layered over the socket library.

To get a better idea of how to use the socket library in practice, consider reading the source of the library modules you will be using in Chapter 5, "Available Client Libraries." This is not an activity for the faint-hearted, however, and you are advised to defer this until you have some solid experience under your belt.

Connections: Needed or Not?

You already have seen a comparison of the features and facilities offered by the two major socket types, which you can think of as corresponding with the two major choices of transport protocol. If your application requires reliable process-to-process data transfer, then a SOCK_STREAM socket is useful. If your application wants mostly just to pass blocks of data back and forth, and if the occasional network error will not be disastrous, consider SOCK_DGRAM sockets.

Socket Operations

Table 4.5 outlines the *major* methods of the socket library. There are others that you might find useful should you ever start programming at the socket level. For those, consult the Python online library documentation. In Table 4.5, s is assumed to be a socket object, created by a call on socket.socket() or some other method.

Where an address argument is required, for Internet sockets, it must be a two-element tuple containing a remote host address and port number. Several methods take an optional `flags` argument, which allows finer control over socket operations.

Table 4.5 **Principal Socket Methods**

Method	Description
`s.accept()`	`s` must be bound to an address and listening for connections. Returns a tuple (`conn`, `address`), where `conn` is a new socket and `address` is the address of the host at the other end. The `conn` socket will transmit data to, and receive data from, the connected process.
`s.bind(address)`	Binds `s` to the given address(es): for Internet family sockets. Null string specifies all available addresses.
`s.close()`	Closes the socket, causing any future operations to fail.
`s.connect(address)`	Connects to a remote socket at `address`.
`s.listen(backlog)`	Listens for connections to the socket, allowing a maximum of `backlog` queued connections. This should always be at least 1.
`s.recv(bufsize [, flags])`	Receives at most `bufsize` bytes from the socket, returning a string composed of the bytes actually received.
`s.recvfrom(bufsize [, flags])`	Receives data from the socket, returning a tuple (`string`, `address`) where `string` is the data received, and `address` is the address of the socket sending the data.
`s.send(string [, flags])`	Sends data to the socket, which must already be connected. Returns the number of bytes sent.
`s.sendto(string [, flags], address)`	Sends data to the socket, which should not be connected because the destination is provided. Returns the number of bytes sent.

A Note on Time-Outs

A problem with any kind of network programming is precisely that the Internet network layer is a "best efforts" service. Thus, there is no guarantee of delivery or sequencing. It appears that many platforms will allow a client connection request to retry many times before finally timing out the connection request and raising an error: two hours might not be unusual!

If you want your network software to be usable, this is clearly not a good idea. Fortunately, there is a third-party library called timeoutsocket, written by Timothy O'Malley, which does a fine job. It effectively displaces the standard socket library, using its facilities but offering a slightly modified interface to the programmer.

Because it replaces the standard socket library, any application that uses this library can be transparently adapted to time out its sockets in a sensible fashion. This avoids the knotty problem of an application that cannot make a connection, and therefore hangs for up to two hours in the attempt.

To use the timeoutsocket module, you need to import both socket and timeoutsocket into your application. If you want connection attempts to time out, you must set a default time-out (in seconds) before any connections are attempted. Because the connections are often made inside library code called by your application, you should ensure that the following call is made before you call any library routines that open socket connections:

```
timeoutsocket.setDefaultSocketTimeout(delay)
```

The delay argument should be a floating-point expression (naturally, integers will be widened as necessary) specifying the number of seconds an operation will be allowed to proceed before raising a timeoutsocket.Timeout exception. If your library code gives you access to the socket it uses, you also can set time-out values on a socket-by-socket basis using the following (assuming sock is a socket):

```
sock.set_timeout(delay)
```

You can download this useful module from http://www.timo-tasi.org/python/timeout➥socket.py.

Connectionless Client Structures

Figure 4.2 shows the structures of connectionless client and server programs and the interactions between them. This should give you some idea of the sequence of operations both ends of a connectionless transaction need to perform.

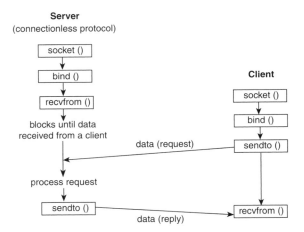

Figure 4.2   Connectionless socket system calls.

The detail of server processing, including whether to create a new process to handle each request or to loop around handling queued requests, is deliberately omitted here because the main purpose of the diagram is to show how the various socket calls are used over UDP.

Message-Oriented Services

There is a trend toward systems that can operate in the face of only partial connectivity: Sometimes the client and server will be able to establish a connection, but at other times they will not. In such cases, a messaging system is sometimes used, and the client-side system buffers request until connectivity can be established.

Although it might seem natural to think about implementing such messaging systems using connectionless protocols, in fact, reliability may still be required when the messages pass from client to server. Therefore, the important factor in choosing a suitable transport layer is the requirement for reliability *when network connectivity is available*. Messaging systems, despite their name, are not inherently better suited to either UDP or TCP.

Typical Connectionless Applications

The *Trivial File Transfer Protocol (TFTP)* is a simplistic, block-oriented file transfer scheme with application-level end-to-end acknowledgments. It runs over UDP principally because it is often used in an environment where no operating system support is available (for example, at bootstrap time). The UDP transport layer is simple enough to implement in ROM, whereas TCP would be more difficult.

The *domain name system (DNS)* is a hierarchical, distributed database that often operates over UDP (although the application is designed to use either TCP or UDP). The nature of the application protocol is such that several servers might answer a particular query; so if no reply is received from one due to traffic loss, the answer is usually obtained from another source.

Connection-Oriented Client Structures

Figure 4.3 illustrates typical connection-oriented client and server program structures and the interactions between them. This should give you some idea of the sequence of operations both ends of a connection-oriented dialog need to perform.

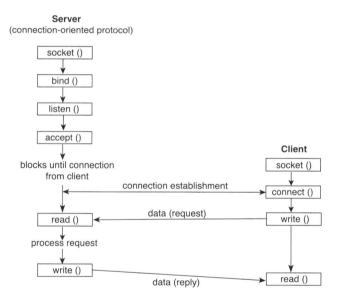

Figure 4.3 Connection-oriented socket system calls.

The detail of server processing, including whether to create a new process to handle each request or to loop around handling queued requests, is deliberately omitted here because the main purpose of the diagram is to show how the various socket calls are used over TCP.

Typical Connection-Oriented Applications

FTP, the *File Transfer Protocol*, is a stream-oriented bidirectional platform-independent system for transferring both text and binary files between the client and the server. It uses a control connection to allow the client to send commands to the server and dynamically creates additional connections for data transfer as required. Error detection and recovery are essential to the protocol, which is complex enough without adding such features to it.

SMTP, the *Simple Mail Transfer Protocol*, passes electronic mail messages across the Internet. For email to be effective, its users must be confident in the integrity of the transmissions, so once again TCP's reliability keeps the application protocol simple while ensuring messages are neither lost nor modified in transmission.

Advantages and Disadvantages of TCP

The major feature of TCP is the transmission reliability it offers, and this often makes it the obvious transfer protocol for network applications. At the same time, this reliability does add some complexity and requires the transport layer components to maintain state about currently open virtual circuits. The memory pool used to hold this state information can become a critical resource allowing denial-of-service attacks (for example, SYN flood attacks) to divert resources or make them unavailable.

Furthermore, the establishment of a virtual circuit requires three datagrams be exchanged between the client and the server, requiring two network turnarounds before the circuit is completely set up. By that time, an efficient UDP-based application protocol could (often) have completed its task.

Summary

Client/server computing is how the majority of distributed computing systems work, although so-called *peer-to-peer* systems are slowly assuming greater significance. All web-based systems use client/server principles, so this chapter has laid the foundations for a better understanding of the web as a whole.

Python provides libraries for both client-side and server-side use. Because servers are readily available on the Internet, it is easier to start by building network client software. The next chapter explains how to use the many Python client libraries to interact with various types of Internet servers.

5

Available Client Libraries

O NE OF THE JOYS OF PYTHON is the lack of the need to "reinvent the wheel."
Because Python has targeted Internet tasks for a long time, the standard library contains much code to help with the things you commonly want to do. Although the
library includes code for both server-side and client-side tasks, you are starting with
the client-side because these are usually simpler and easier to understand.

Client-side modules are relatively simple, primarily due to the uncomplicated
nature of the protocols they implement. For a complete understanding, read the source
code: none of the modules is longer than about 1000 lines, and most are much
shorter. After you understand the principles behind them, the code is not that difficult
to comprehend.

The client libraries usually define one or more classes, instances of which can be
used to connect to the server. Often the connection parameters can be specified as
arguments to the object's creation. The object encapsulates the state of the connection
as well as provides methods to manipulate it by interacting with the server. Many also
provide debug output if requested, which can make it easier to understand why the
protocol is not giving you the desired activity in difficult cases.

In the TCP-based application protocols you will study in this chapter, the client
usually makes requests by sending command lines beginning with an alphabetic
command. The server in turn replies with one or more lines, the first of which begins
with a three-digit response code. A one-line reply is referred to as a *short* response, a

multiline reply as a long response. The library modules for the different protocols end up having a lot of code in common because they need to parse replies, but nobody has as yet refactored them to put the common code into a "base client" module.

Your Testing Environment

The examples that follow in this chapter and the matching test code from the web site require access to the following servers for testing:

- FTP (File Transfer)

- SMTP (Email transmission)

- POP (Email collection)

- NNTP (Network News)

- HTTP (web)

Modify the test programs to access the particular servers you plan to use. *I cannot guarantee that running software against live data will retain the integrity of the data.* I can, however, report that my own general experience has been good.

- **FTP and HTTP**—Xitami provides a readily configurable FTP and web server whether your system is Windows or UNIX. In my lab, I have NT, Windows 95 and 98 systems, and Linux, plus cable modem access to Internet servers, so finding a server isn't usually a problem. Because much of this book had to be written while traveling, however, I really needed a portable server. Alex Martelli pointed me to Xitami, with which Python interacts well, and it is now my web server of choice on my laptop. Follow the Xitami link from `http://www.imatix.com` for download and installation notes.

- **SMTP and POP**—You should be able to get SMTP and POP from the same server you access with your standard mail software. That way, you can try to send mail to your own mailbox and collect mail from it. If you have an unused mail account available, so much the better.

- **NNTP**—For network news services, your ISP is normally the most promising initial point of contact, and many ISPs do offer NNTP service. If you are unlucky, then consider using a paid or free subscription service after a web search.

File Transfer

A number of different protocols can be used to transfer files between two systems. The FTP protocol has a long and respected history and is the transfer method of choice on the Internet, even though file transfers using HTTP are now also possible. A file transfer protocol also is implemented as a part of the BSD UNIX distribution to support the `rcp` command, but this is a fairly esoteric system with known security problems and probably best left alone. Recently, the scp protocol, a part of the secure shell suite, has started to see some use in collaborative environments, such as sourceforge. Perhaps its increasing popularity is due to its availability on Windows.

FTP is not a difficult protocol to understand, but several complexities have been added as refinements since the original definition. It is also made more complex by requiring separate connections between the client and the server for protocol commands and data transfer. In fact, there are many complexities that it is best to ignore when only simple data transfer is required: if you want to know about these, read RFC 959 for the complete specification.

Trivial File Transfer Protocol (TFTP), a much simpler protocol, is based on the UDP (User Data Protocol) transport layer, whereas FTP and HTTP are TCP-based. This means that there is no guarantee of reliable data transfer, and each block transferred must be acknowledged at application level before the next is sent. TFTP is mostly used by low-level code such as the bootstrap PROM (Programmable Read-Only Memory) of network-based computing devices, where little support code is available and slower speeds are acceptable for the relatively infrequent transfers required.

ftplib: **Batch Data Transfer**

The client makes an initial connection to the server's control process, typically on Port 21, and the client's first action is usually to authenticate itself. As with most client/server protocols, the server's authentication database is used (that is, the client-side user must have an account on the server). This *control connection* uses the FTP protocol, but from time to time data transfers are required. It is important to remember that either direction of data transfer is possible: from the client to the server (a *put* transfer) or from server to client (a *get* transfer). In either case, the client initiates the transfer. To make these transfers, a separate *data connection* is used, normally involving an ephemeral port on the client and Port 20 on the server.

File transfer normally is in ASCII or binary mode (although the defining standard also allows EBCDIC and byte modes, which are esoteric enough to ignore for most practical purposes). In binary mode, the file is transferred as a binary image and therefore will be exactly the same on the receiving system as on the sending system. In ASCII mode, transfers occur one line at a time, and the receiving system (whether it be client or server) thus has the chance to insert appropriate line terminators. When text files are transferred in binary mode between a client and a server using different line-ending conventions, trouble can ensue. If it is difficult to repeat the transfer in ASCII mode, then some local processing will usually bring about the required change.

How the Module Works

Authenticated Access Needed

Some examples in this section may require you to have authenticated access to the FTP server concerned. You can use Xitami as outlined earlier in the "Your Testing Environment" sidebar.

The first task you must perform is to create an FTP object, which you manipulate to give you access to an FTP session. Under most circumstances, you can specify the site you want to connect to along with the username and password, using optional arguments to the creation call `ftplib.FTP()`.

`f = ftplib.FTP ([host[, user[, passwd[, acct]]]])`

Creates an FTP class instance, which can be used to interact with an FTP server. If the `host` argument is given, a connection is attempted to Port 21 at that host. The `user`, `passwd`, and `acct` arguments, if given, specify the login details to be used. Most servers do not require an `acct` to be specified.

If no arguments are given, then the connection must be established by calling the `connect()` method, and authentication must be performed with the `login()` method.

Following is a simple example of making a connection to a server:

```
PythonWin 2.1 (#15, Apr 19 2001, 10:28:27) [MSC 32 bit (Intel)] on win32.
Portions Copyright 1994-2001 Mark Hammond (MarkH@ActiveState.com) - see➡
'Help/About
PythonWin' for further copyright information.
>>> import ftplib
>>> ftp = ftplib.FTP('ftp.cdrom.com', 'username', 'email@address.com')
>>> ftp.getwelcome()
'220 wcarchive.cdrom.com FTP server (Version DG-4.1.73 983302105) ready.'
>>> ftp.dir()
total 12
-rw-r—r— 1 root  wheel   480 May  1 16:59 RATECARD.TXT
-rw-rw-r— 1 root  wheel   696 Nov 19 1997 README
-rw-r—r— 1 root  wheel  3344 Sep  1 2000 UPLOADS.TXT
drwxrwxr-x 2 root  wheel   512 Oct  5 1998 archive-info
lrwxr-xr-x 1 root  wheel    21 Nov 22 1998 catalog.txt -> pub/cdrom/catalog.txt
lrwxr-xr-x 1 root  wheel    26 Nov 22 1998 config.txt -> archive-➡
info/wcarchive.txt
drwxr-xr-x 2 root  wheel   512 May  2 1999 etc
drwxrwxr-x 2 root  wheel  2048 May  1 22:38 pub
>>>
```

This shows you that `ftp` is an object you can use for FTP activities. Because the `FTP` class call does not return the message supplied by the server, FTP objects provide a method to allow you to access it: some servers do actually provide useful information!

`f.getwelcome()`

Returns the welcome message sent by the server on receipt of a client connection.

```
>>> ftp.getwelcome()
'220 Xitami FTP 2.4d7 (c) 1991-98 iMatix <http://www.imatix.com>'
```

If the host is using a nonstandard port number, then you need to create an FTP object providing no arguments and use further methods to connect to the relevant port and authenticate yourself.

```
f.connect(host, port=21)
```

Connects to the given host and port number. This method can be called only on FTP objects created without connection parameters and can be called only once. Returns the welcome banner from the server.

```
f.login(user='anonymous', password='user@hostname'[, acct])
```

Authenticates a connected FTP object with the server. When no password argument is given, the username in the default value is obtained from the environment, and the hostname is obtained from the socket module. This method should be called at most once, after a connection is made, and not at all if authentication parameters were provided when the FTP object was created. Most servers do not require an acct argument.

A lengthier way to connect to an FTP server, with no real advantages, is as follows:

```
>>> ftp = ftplib.FTP()
>>> ftp.connect('127.0.0.1')
'220 Xitami FTP 2.4d7 (c) 1991-98 iMatix <http://www.imatix.com>'
>>> ftp.login('book', 'bookpw')
'230 User book logged-in'
```

What Is in the Site?

After you have created a connected and authenticated FTP instance, what can you do with it? One simple method allows you to take directory listings, although these listings are by default sent direct to the *standard output*. You can do this with the dir() method.

Callbacks: Event–Driven Software

The next example method is one of several to which you can present a callback argument, to which a call will be made for each of several pieces of information. Instances of objects can be called like functions (if they implement the semimagical __call__() method), and this can be a good way to process data in complex ways.

`f.dir([argument, ...])`

Takes a listing of the current server directory or the directory named by the argument. Additional arguments can be used to pass nonstandard arguments to the FTP server. If the final argument is callable, then it is used as a *callback* and is called once for each line of directory listing, with the line as an argument. The default callback prints the lines to standard output.

```
>>> ftp.dir()
drw-------   1 user     user            0 Feb  5 21:45 BookDir
-rw-------   1 user     user          194 Oct 25  1997 index.txt
-rw-------   1 user     user           57 Feb  5 21:07 rhubarb.txt
```

If you want to capture the output from this method, you must provide a callback function. One easy way to do this is to create an empty list and then provide the list's `append()` method as a callback. Each time a line of listing is produced, it is appended to the list:

```
>>> lst = []
>>> ftp.dir(lst.append)
>>> for l in lst:
...     print "<<", l, ">>"
...
<< drw-------   1 user     user            0 Feb  5 21:45 BookDir >>
<< -rw-------   1 user     user          194 Oct 25  1997 index.txt >>
<< -rw-------   1 user     user           57 Feb  5 21:07 rhubarb.txt >>
```

This appears to be the only easy way to determine which entries are files and which are directories. You might need to do this to scan an FTP file system, copying files at all levels, for example. Of course, you can parse the entries in the list to break out the individual pieces of information. Note that this particular listing style shows a time for dates in the current year but shows a year for dates more than a year ago, which you must take into account if you intend to parse the dates for comparison purposes.

File and Directory Manipulations

You can cause the client to change the working directory on the server with the `cwd()` method.

`f.cwd(path)`

Changes current working directory on the server to `path`.

`f.pwd()`

Returns the pathname of the current working directory on the server.

There also are methods to manipulate the directory structures on the server by creating and deleting them. Removing a directory uses a different method from the one used to remove a file.

---

f.mkd(*pathname*)   f.rmd(*pathname*)

Creates or removes the directory identified by *pathname*, which can be an absolute or relative directory path on the server.

You can rename files with the rename() method. Note, however, some servers will not allow you to rename directories.

---

f.rename(*oldname*, *newname*)

Renames the file (or directory, on some servers) named oldname to newname.

```
>>> ftp.rename('rhubarb.txt', 'junk.txt')
'250 Requested file action okay, completed'
>>> ftp.dir()
drw-------   1 user      user              0 Feb  5 21:45 BookDir
-rw-------   1 user      user            194 Oct 25  1997 index.txt
-rw-------   1 user      user             57 Feb  5 21:07 junk.txt
```

Finally, you can remove files from the server with the delete() method.

---

f.delete(*filename*)

Deletes the file *filename* from the server, returning the server's response.

Transferring Files

Transfers can be made either in active or passive mode. In active mode, the server is told (by a PORT protocol command) which IP address and port number the other process will be using, and it connects from its data transfer port (by default, Port 20). In passive mode, the client requests (by a PASV protocol command) that the server listen on an ephemeral port, which it reports in its reply. This allows firewall restrictions to be overcome and is nowadays so useful that from Python 2.1 onwards ftplib uses passive mode by default. Fortunately, this complexity is hidden by a simple API call that tells the library which mode to use.

---

f.set_pasv(boolean)

Enables passive mode if the boolean argument is true; otherwise, enables active mode.

The module's transfer methods are available in two flavors: names ending in `lines` indicate a text mode transfer, whereas names ending in `binary` indicate a binary mode transfer. The `storlines()` and `storbinary()` methods perform a transfer to the server, whereas `retrlines()` and `retrbinary()` perform a transfer to the client.

`f.storbinary(command, file[, blocksize])`

Stores a file in binary transfer mode, returning the server's response. The `command` argument should be an FTP protocol command such as `"STOR filename"`, *file* is the open file object whose contents are to be transferred, and *blocksize* is the number of bytes that will be taken from the file with each call to its `read()` method.

Here is a simple example of transferring a file to a remote server:

```
>>> ftp = ftplib.FTP('127.0.0.1', 'book', 'bookpw')
>>> f = open("AutoIndent.pyc", "rb")
>>> ftp.storbinary("STOR AutoIndent.pyc", f, 1024)
'226 Closing data connection'
>>> ftp.dir()
-rw-------   1 user     user          19171 Feb 12 11:27 AutoIndent.pyc
-rw-------   1 user     user            194 Oct 25  1997 index.txt
```

Note that the `open()` call specified binary mode: in text mode under Windows, Python replaces carriage return–line feed (CR-LF) pairs with a single line feed and treats the Ctrl+Z character as an end-of-file. In general, these sequences might appear in a binary file, and so it is necessary to make sure that they do not cause trouble.

`f.storlines(command, file)`

Stores a file in ASCII transfer mode, returning the server's response. The `command` argument should be an FTP protocol command such as `"STOR filename"`, and *file* is the open file object whose contents are to be transferred. Lines are read from *file* using its `readlines()` method, until EOF is returned.

This simple text transfer uses passive mode to check that the server can communicate in this way. As you can see, no problems are encountered:

```
>>> ftp = ftplib.FTP('127.0.0.1', 'book', 'bookpw')
>>> ftp.set_pasv(1)
>>> f = open("AutoIndent.py", "r")
>>> ftp.storlines("STOR AutoIndent.py", f)
'226 Closing data connection'
>>> ftp.dir()
-rw-------   1 user     user          20529 Feb 12 11:45 AutoIndent.py
-rw-------   1 user     user          19171 Feb 12 11:27 AutoIndent.pyc
-rw-------   1 user     user            194 Oct 25  1997 index.txt
```

Retrieving files is a little more complicated because the library does not assume that you want to make a local copy in your filestore and therefore gives you the option of processing the data as a text or binary information stream as it is received from the server. The retrieval processing routines use callback functions that process each portion received.

`f.retrbinary(`*command*`,` *callback*`[,` *maxblocksize*`[,` *rest*`]])`

Retrieves a file in binary transfer mode. *command* should be an appropriate command such as `"RETR `*filename*`"`. For each block of data received, the *callback* argument (which should be a function) is called with the received data block as a single argument. If a *maxblocksize* argument is given, it limits the size of block transferred on the underlying network socket. If a *rest* argument is given, it is a byte offset into the file at which the transfer will start, which is useful for recovery but may not be accepted by all servers.

This does make it easy to transfer a binary file from an FTP server to local filestore. In such a case, the function used as a callback can simply be the `write()` method of a file opened for binary output.

```
>>> ftp = ftplib.FTP('127.0.0.1', 'book', 'bookpw')
>>> f = open("MyPycFile.pyc", "wb")
>>> ftp.retrbinary("RETR AutoIndent.pyc", f.write)
'226 Closing data connection'
>>> f.close()
```

You can see that the optional arguments are not used here, allowing the socket layer to choose whatever block size seems appropriate and transferring the whole file.

`f.retrlines(`*command*`[,` *callback*`])`

Retrieves a file in ASCII transfer mode. `command` should be an appropriate command such as `"RETR `*filename*`"`. For each line of data received, the *callback* argument (which should be a function) is called with the received line (less line terminator) as a single argument. When no *callback* argument is provided, the lines are printed to standard output.

Downloading a text file is hardly more difficult than downloading a binary file: you are simply dealing with text lines rather than data blocks. Listing 5.1 provides a callback that is a callable instance created to write a particular file (the same one being read from the server).

Listing 5.1   **Using an Object Instance as an FTP Callback**

```
1 class Writer:
2
```

continues

Listing 5.1 **Continued**

```
 3     def __init__(self, file):
 4         self.f = open(file, "w")
 5
 6     def __call__(self, data):
 7         self.f.write(data)
 8         self.f.write('\n')
 9         print data
10
11 FILENAME = "AutoIndent.py"
12 writer = Writer(FILENAME)
13
14 import ftplib
15 ftp = ftplib.FTP('127.0.0.1', 'book', 'bookpw')
16 ftp.retrlines("RETR %s" % FILENAME, writer)
```

FTP Commands

You can see from the description of the methods in the preceding section that you do need a simple understanding of the FTP protocol commands to achieve file transfers. The RFC that defines the standard gives a huge list of possible commands, most of them not connected with transfers at all. For practical purposes, you can restrict yourself to the STOR protocol command for sending files to the server and the RETR protocol command for receiving them from the server. Both need to be followed by a space and a filename, which is the filename *on the server*.

If you want more control over your interactions with the server, two methods allow you to send arbitrary commands.

`f.sendcmd(command)`

Sends a simple command string to the server and returns the server's response.

`f.voidcmd(command)`

Sends a simple command to the server and handles the response. If the return code is in the range 200–299, returns None. Otherwise, raises an exception.

Debugging FTP Connections

Occasionally, things will not go quite as you expect. In such cases, you can often gain useful information by examining the interactions between the client and the server. A method is provided to enable debug output from the FTP object methods.

> `f.set_debuglevel(`*`level`*`)`
>
> Sets the debug level to the value given by the level argument. Level 1 debug output generally produces a single line per request. Level 2 or higher logs each line sent and received over the control connection.

Listing 5.2 shows an example of a debugged transfer.

Listing 5.2 **Debug Output from an FTP Transfer**

```
>>> ftp = ftplib.FTP('127.0.0.1', 'book', 'bookpw')
>>> f = open("MyPycFile.pyc", "wb")
>>> ftp.set_pasv(1)>>> ftp.set_debuglevel(1)
>>> ftp.retrbinary("RETR AutoIndent.pyc", f.write)
*cmd* 'TYPE I'
*resp* '200 Command okay'
*cmd* 'PASV'
*resp* '227 Entering Passive Mode (127,0,0,1,0,200)'
*cmd* 'RETR AutoIndent.pyc'
*resp* '150 Preparing to transfer binary file'
*resp* '226 Closing data connection'
'226 Closing data connection'
```

At Debug Level 2 (see Listing 5.3), there is a little more output, and you see the action of the library in more detail because debug lines now show the exact interaction across the control channel. You still get only a sketchy idea of the interaction between the data transfer modules, however.

Listing 5.3 **An FTP Transfer with Debug Level 2 Output**

```
>>> ftp.set_pasv(1)
>>> ftp.set_debuglevel(2)
¦>>> ftp.retrbinary("RETR AutoIndent.pyc", f.write)
*cmd* 'TYPE I'
*put* 'TYPE I\015\012'
*get* '200 Command okay\015\012'
*resp* '200 Command okay'
*cmd* 'PASV'
*put* 'PASV\015\012'
*get* '227 Entering Passive Mode (127,0,0,1,0,200)\015\012'
*resp* '227 Entering Passive Mode (127,0,0,1,0,200)'
*cmd* 'RETR AutoIndent.pyc'
*put* 'RETR AutoIndent.pyc\015\012'
*get* '150 Preparing to transfer binary file 15\012'
*resp* '150 Preparing to transfer binary file'
*get* '226 Closing data connection\015\012'
*resp* '226 Closing data connection'
'226 Closing data connection'
```

Closing the Connection

The "polite" way to close an FTP connection is for the client to send a QUIT protocol command to the server, which you can do using the quit() method. It is possible, but unlikely, that the server will raise an exception. If it does, then the close() method tears down the socket connection unilaterally.

`f.quit()`

Sends a QUIT protocol command to the server and, unless an exception is raised, closes the socket connection.

`f.close()`

Unilaterally closes the socket connection to the server. Not required (and should not be used) if the quit() method succeeds.

FTP Programming Examples

With your existing knowledge of the FTP protocol transfer commands, you can use the FTP module to perform transfers by sending transfer commands. One of the attractions of this approach is that it gives you access to the socket objects used to communicate with the server. You can use these sockets directly to use the FTP server as a data source and sink.

`f.transfercmd(command[, rest])`

Initiates a transfer using the given *command* over a data connection, whether active or passive. Returns a socket over which data can be sent or received, depending on the command. The optional *rest* argument, if given, is a byte offset at which the transfer should begin. This allows restart of partially completed transfers, for example. An exception is raised if this option is unacceptable to the server.

`f.ntransfercmd(command[, rest])`

Like transfercmd() but returns a two-element tuple consisting of the socket and the expected size of the data. If the expected size cannot be computed, the returned data size will be None. The optional *rest* argument has the same meaning as for the transfercmd() method.

Listing 5.4 is a sample program in which a client transfers a file from one server to another, changing its name as it performs the transfer. Note that this is *not* code-intended for production, so you are warned that it does not handle exceptions that might occur.

Listing 5.4   *ftpxfer.py:* **An FTP-to-FTP Transfer Program**

```
 1 import ftplib, sys
 2 # Establish ftp connections
 3 ftp1 = ftplib.FTP("127.0.0.1", "book", "bookpw")
 4 ftp1.cwd("/BookDir")
 5 ftp2 = ftplib.FTP("www.holdenweb.com", "bookuser", "bookpw")
 6 ftp2.cwd("/public")
 7 # Prepare sockets for transfer
 8 sock1 = ftp1.transfercmd("RETR bigfile.tgz")
 9 sock2 = ftp2.transfercmd("STOR newfile.tgz")
10 # Loop through transfers until done
11 flen = 0                           # track data length
12 while 1:
13     block = sock1.recv(1024)       # read up to a kilobyte
14     if len(block) == 0:            # handle end of file
15         break
16     flen += len(block)             # update data length
17     while len(block) > 0:          # until all handled
18         sentlen = sock2.send(block) # write some data
19         block = block[sentlen:]    # and delete from block
20 print "Transferred", flen, "bytes"
21 sock1.close()
22 sock2.close()
23 ftp1.quit()
24 ftp2.quit()
```

The program opens a reading socket to the source FTP server in line 8, and a writing socket to the sink FTP server in line 9. It then just performs a socket-to-socket transfer in lines 12 through 19. This logic is a little more complex than for a simple file-to-file transfer for two reasons. First, a zero-length data block indicates the end of data when reading a socket, so line 14 tests for this condition. Second, there is no absolute guarantee that a socket will be able to handle all the data written to it in a single block, so lines 17 through 19 repeatedly try to write data, deleting whatever has already been written, until none is left. Lines 21 through 24 simply close the sockets and terminate the FTP connections.

Of course, if anything goes wrong during the process, the interpreter handles the exceptions raised to indicate the problem by terminating the program with a stack trace. If such behavior offends you, then it would be relatively easy to dress up the code to catch the various possible exceptions and handle them appropriately. For the moment, however, let's pretend nothing is going to go wrong. The best part about the code in Listing 5.4 is that it shows you how to read and write data streams from an FTP server.

Since Chapter 3, "Object Orientation," of course, you've known how to build objects in Python, and you are probably wondering when you get to see one built. Python newcomers might mistrust a module of the complexity of Listing 5.4, which requires some knowledge of the FTP protocol and an understanding of a complex interface. What they need is an easily usable `FTPStream` class. Suppose that an `ftpStream` object allowed you to connect to a server, read and write files from that server, and then disconnect. How could an object offer all the features of the `FTP` object and these additional facilities?

One possibility is inheritance, defining a subclass of `ftplib.FTP`, but there are some reasons why you might want to avoid this. For example, the `FTP` object has a `close()` method: if we want to be able to `open()` and `close()` files over a single connection, this would mean overriding the `FTP.close()` method, which would then be awkward to use.

Better is the creation of a new class that creates and uses an `FTP` object to perform the connection and transfer. Your class can use all the methods of its `FTP` object for its own purposes. Our object must be able to delegate these operations to its `FTP` object. This class is called `ftpStream`.

Annotated Listing of *ftpStream.py*

This section presents an annotated listing of a module designed to make FTP transfers easier. Rather than presenting the whole module in one indigestible chunk, I follow each logical portion with a brief description.

```
 1 """ftpStream: Enhanced FTP with enhanced usability.
 2
 3     Features:    server connect
 4                  [FTP operations]
 5                  open
 6                  close
 7
 8     $Revision: 10 $
 9     Released into the public domain $Date: 3/04/01 11:42a $
10     Steve Holden    http://www.holdenweb.com/
11 """
12
```

This is about a minimum file header, although (for example) I forgot to document the server disconnection capability. The date and revision number are inserted courtesy of my source control system, and the code is in the public domain to maximize its utility and help me not to expect money for a feat of programming orders of magnitude less than those of others who give their code away. The URL is the easiest way for people to contact me should they feel the need.

Stylistically, it might be better to document the class as a part of this "docstring," but you are about to read a discussion of the interface, and you should not have to read things twice.

```
13 import ftplib
14
15 class ftpStreamError(ftplib.Error):
16     pass
17
18 class InvalidModeError(ftpStreamError):
19     pass
20
21 class StreamOpenError(ftpStreamError):
22     pass
23
```

Clearly, you need to import the `ftplib` module to use it, so that is done here. A base error class is declared as a subclass of the error class used by `ftplib`. The specific error classes of an `ftpStream` are subclasses of this `ftpStreamError` class. Users of the `ftpStream` can therefore trap all exceptions as `ftplib.FTP` exceptions but also can trap exceptions specific to `ftpStream` as a separate subclass if necessary.

```
24 class ftpStream:
25     "Specialised FTP with file-like interface."
26
```

A documentation string follows the class definition header, at least pointing the way to how documentation should be constructed.

```
27     def __init__(self, host='', name='', passwd='', acct=''):
28         "Create FTP object and set stream socket inactive."
29         self.ftp = ftplib.FTP(host, name, passwd, acct)
30         self.strsock = None
31
```

When an `ftpStream` is initialized, it creates an FTP object and records the fact that no socket is currently open for this stream. This little piece of state information is used later to make the object behave more sensibly if users decide to abuse the interface.

```
32     def __getattr__(self, attrname):
33         "Delegate unrecognised methods/attributes to the FTP object."
34         return getattr(self.ftp, attrname)
35
```

The `__getattr()__` method is one of Python's pieces of magic (the double-underlines are a reliable guide that some under-the-hood knowledge is being applied). Whenever the interpreter tries to access a method or an attribute of an object and fails to find it, it gives the object one last chance to provide it by calling this method and giving the name of the method or attribute being sought. The `ftpStream` simply chooses to hand these requests on to the FTP object that was created at the same time, by calling its `getattr()` method. This technique is known as *delegation*—the `FTPStream` object delegates methods it knows nothing about to the `FTP` object.

```
36     def open(self, file, mode="r"):
37         "Open an input or output socket on a remote file."
38         if self.strsock:
```

```
39              raise StreamOpenError
40          self.mode = mode
41          if mode == "r":
42              self.strsock = self.ftp.transfercmd("RETR " + file)
43          elif mode == "w":
44              self.strsock = self.ftp.transfercmd("STOR " + file)
45          else:
46              raise InvalidModeError
47
```

Before allowing an open(), this method checks that no file is currently open on the stream. It then records the mode (for use as a check when the other methods are called) and initiates either retrieval or storage of the named file with an appropriate FTP protocol command.

```
48      def read(self, size=1024):
49          "read a block from the stream socket."
50          if self.mode != "r":
51              raise InvalidModeError
52          block = self.strsock.recv(size)
53          return block
54
```

The read() method first checks that the request matches the current transfer direction, and if this check succeeds, it returns whatever comes in from the socket. Because a socket only ever returns a zero-length block when the socket is closed, read() uses this condition to indicate end-of-file by returning the empty block in turn to its caller.

```
55      def write(self, block):
56          "write a block to the stream socket."
57          if self.mode != "w":
58              raise InvalidModeError
59          while len(block) > 0:
60              sentlen = self.strsock.send(block)
61              block = block[sentlen:]
62
```

The write() method adapts the socket interface to a more file-like style. Unlike sockets, files are expected to be capable of writing arbitrarily large chunks of data at a single gulp.

```
63      def close(self):
64          "Close stream socket but retain FTP connectivity."
65          if self.strsock:
66              self.strsock.close()
67              self.strsock = None
68              return self.ftp.voidresp() # Handle expected response
69          else:
70              raise ftpStreamOpenError
71
```

The `close()` method must terminate only the data connection and ask the `FTP` object to handle the response from the server. The `ftp.voidresp()` method call accepts any response code beginning with 2, indicating success. `close()` should only be called if it really is closing a socket. If this is not the case, an exception reports the abuse, which is intended to be helpful during debugging.

```
72    def quit(self):
73        "Close stream socket and quit underlying FTP object."
74        if self.strsock:
75            self.close()
76        self.ftp.quit()
77
```

The `quit()` method actually tears down the connection with the FTP server, making the object unusable. If the user has forgotten to close a stream socket, `quit()` tries to help by doing this. There is nothing to stop you from trying to reuse this object, but the documentation for `ftplib.FTP` suggests such attempts will fail.

That is the complete `ftpStream` class. The tradition of the Python community is that modules should be self-testing, and the remaining 60 or so lines of code do just that.

```
78 #
79 # Simple test if called as main routine
80 #
81 if __name__ == "__main__":
```

This statement ensures that the tests are run only when the module is run directly by the interpreter, and not when imported.

```
82    INHOST = "127.0.0.1"
83    INPATH = "/BookDir"
84    INFILE = "bigfile.tgz"
85    OUTHOST = www.holdenweb.com
86    OUTPATH = "/public"
87    OUTFILE = "newfile.tgz"
88    INUSER = OUTUSER = "anonymous"
89    INPASS = OUTPASS = user@site
90
```

Clearly, you need to modify the data presets before testing in your own environment. Perhaps if my testing has been successful, you can take the module on trust, but at least you can see how to test using your own sites if necessary.

```
91    print "<<<File per stream>>>"
92    # Test streams at various blocksizes
93    for size in [2**x for x in range(10,16)]:
94        # Establish ftp connections
95        instream = ftpStream(INHOST, INUSER, INPASS)
96        outstream = ftpStream(OUTHOST, OUTUSER, OUTPASS)
97        instream.cwd(INPATH)
98        outstream.cwd(OUTPATH)
99        # Prepare sockets for transfer
```

```
100          instream.open(INFILE)
101          outstream.open(OUTFILE, "w")
102          # Loop through transfers until done
103          flen = 0
104          while 1:
105              block = instream.read(size)      # read next block
106              if len(block) == 0:              # handle end of file
107                  break
108              flen += len(block)               # update data length
109              outstream.write(block)
110          instream.quit()
111          outstream.quit()
112          print "Transferred", flen, "bytes in blocks of", size
113
```

The preceding lines repeatedly perform a transfer by establishing a connection to the two FTP servers and performing a single transfer using a given block size. A variety of block sizes is used, ranging from 1,024 to 32,768. These are generated using a *list comprehension* on line 93. The construct was introduced in Python 2.0 to enable easier creation of dynamic lists.

```
114          print "<<<Multiple files on one stream>>>"
115          # Test multiple transfers via a single stream
116          instream = ftpStream(INHOST, INUSER, INPASS)
117          outstream = ftpStream(OUTHOST, OUTUSER, OUTPASS)
118          instream.cwd(INPATH)
119          outstream.cwd(OUTPATH)
120          for size in [10**i for i in 1,2,3,4]:
121              # Prepare sockets for transfer
122              instream.open(INFILE)
123              outstream.open(OUTFILE, "w")
124              # Loop through transfers until done
125              flen = 0
126              while 1:
127                  block = instream.read(size)      # read next block
128                  if len(block) == 0:              # handle end of file
129                      break
130                  flen += len(block)               # update data length
131                  outstream.write(block)
132              instream.close()
133              outstream.close()
134              print "Transferred", flen, "bytes in chunks of", size
135          instream.quit()
136          outstream.quit()
```

This block of code is primarily to test that a single connection can handle a sequence of transfers. During development, this test block highlighted the need to handle the server response in the close() method. Because a looping structure is used, the test uses a range of block sizes (10, 100, 1000, and 10,000). These are created on-the-fly by the specification on line 121 using a further list comprehension.

The `ftpStream` class is useful because it does everything that a standard FTP object does, allowing you to request passive mode, connect to a server, and change directories, for example. It also has its own methods, however, which allow you to make a connection to an FTP server and then use files on that server as input or output streams. It would perhaps be nice to be able to set the connection to run in either block or stream mode because the latter would allow conversion of line-endings between clients and servers with different conventions, but overall the code is sound and reasonably well-tested. Listing 5.5 shows the output from running the module on local servers with correct account details.

Listing 5.5   **Output from a Test of the *ftpStream* Module**

```
D:\Code\Ch5>"D:\python20\python" ftpStream.py
<<<File per stream>>>
Transferred 12266 bytes in blocks of 1024
Transferred 12266 bytes in blocks of 2048
Transferred 12266 bytes in blocks of 4096
Transferred 12266 bytes in blocks of 8192
Transferred 12266 bytes in blocks of 16384
Transferred 12266 bytes in blocks of 32768
<<<Multiple files on one stream>>>
Transferred 12266 bytes in chunks of 10
Transferred 12266 bytes in chunks of 100
Transferred 12266 bytes in chunks of 1000
Transferred 12266 bytes in chunks of 10000
```

The *ftpmirror* Tool

Python includes a tool that is instructive about how to use the `ftplib` module and performs a useful set of tasks as well. Look in the `Tools/Scripts` directory in your Python distribution. Listing 5.6 shows the script's doc string, which tells you succinctly what to expect.

Listing 5.6   **The *ftpmirror* Doc String**

```
 1 """Mirror a remote ftp subtree into a local directory tree.
 2
 3 usage: ftpmirror [-v] [-q] [-i] [-m] [-n] [-r] [-s pat]
 4                  [-l username [-p passwd [-a account]]]
 5           hostname [remotedir [localdir]]
 6 -v: verbose
 7 -q: quiet
 8 -i: interactive mode
 9 -m: macintosh server (NCSA telnet 2.4) (implies -n -s '*.o')
10 -n: don't log in
11 -r: remove local files/directories no longer pertinent
```

continues

Listing 5.6 **Continued**

```
12 -l username [-p passwd [-a account]]: login info (default anonymous ftp)
14 -s pat: skip files matching pattern
15 hostname: remote host
16 remotedir: remote directory (default initial)
17 localdir: local directory (default current)
18 """
```

Using this tool alone it is practical to mirror various FTP sites of interest. With a permanently connected Internet, it is more efficient to mirror remote sites nightly and use your local copies for day-to-day work. Unless you need minute-by-minute replication of changes, this will be adequate.

Dealing with Mail

Before the advent of the web, email was the primary reason for many organizations to connect to the Internet. It remains one of the most popular applications. Three different protocols are in active use for handling email, and it helps to be able to distinguish them:

- SMTP
- POP3
- IMAP4

In dealing with mail systems, remember that in many environments (such as a UNIX or Windows NT server) the email functions are separated into a *mail user agent* (MUA) and a *mail transfer agent* (MTA). The MUA is responsible for showing users the contents of their mailbox, allowing them to compose messages, and so on: it is the user interface to the email system. The MTA, on the other hand, tries to deliver messages across the Internet autonomously, possibly over multiple hops. The MUA (a program such as Netscape Messenger or Microsoft Outlook Express) typically passes outgoing messages to a local or remote MTA for further handling.

The first major mail protocol of the Internet was SMTP, the Simple Mail Transfer Protocol. In "the old days," mail hosts were expected to handle messages on demand. SMTP therefore has the sender as the client: it triggers message transfer by connecting to the server (normally on TCP port 25). The server validates the message addresses and, if they are acceptable, reinterprets the recipient address(es) locally. This may in turn require delivery to one or more local mailbox(es) and/or onward transmission to one or more further remote email addresses, depending on mail aliases in force at the receiving server.

Although SMTP works well between permanently connected servers, it is not ideal when a recipient's computer is connected only intermittently, such as when using dial-up connectivity. In such a case, the sending system must store messages until it can connect to the next destination for the message, or some time-out or retry count forces it to raise an error.

With intermittent connectivity, it makes more sense for the recipient to trigger the final transfer from mail server to desktop machine. Under such a regime, mail is delivered to a nominated server, where it waits until the recipient can connect and retrieve it. This gives the end-user more control and avoids clogging up the Internet with failed attempts to deliver mail to systems that are not even online.

Two further protocols offer this kind of interface to email servers: Post Office Protocol (POP3) and Internet Message Access Protocol (IMAP4). An MUA almost invariably will use SMTP to send mail, usually via a server whose name or address is configured into the MUA software.

POP3 is the older protocol and is less capable than IMAP4 but also simpler to program. It uses an offline mail reading model, where the client system connects to the server and downloads messages to the user's personal machine for reading and possible reply. IMAP4 allows users to adopt either an online or an offline model: they may transfer messages down to their personal computer if they want, but they may equally retain messages in folders on the server. The MUA in this case generally allows copying or moving of messages between folders on the server or on the client. Unfortunately, IMAP is so complex that it would be difficult to do it justice in the space of this chapter.

All Internet mail assumes that messages comply with the format described in RFC 822. For a long time, this specification was the only standard that dictated the structure of email messages. An RFC 822-compliant message comprises an arbitrary number of headers, followed by a blank line, followed by the message body.

Each header begins on a new line with a keyword followed after optional white space by a colon, further optional white space, and finally the value or list of values associated with the keyword. The value may extend over multiple lines, provided that continuation lines begin with white space. The specification of individual header formats is beyond the scope of this book, so you may want to consult RFC 822 if these details interest you. The message body is simply the text following the blank line after the headers.

Creating Mail Messages

It is easier to *create* mail messages than it is to parse them and split out the contents. You can read messages in and handle them using `rfc822` and various other related modules, but these libraries cannot create messages. The simplest way to do so is to use the `MimeWriter` module. The module defines a simple object capable of creating both simple mail messages and the more complex MIME-compliant multipart messages with attachments you will learn about later in this section. You may need to bring other modules into play to create content suitably encoded for transmission over the character-based email network.

MimeWriter: A Recursive Mail Generator

The module defines only one type of object, `MimeWriter.MimeWriter`. You call the class with a single argument, which should be either a file opened for writing or some other object that offers both `write()` and `writelines()` methods. The `StringIO` and `cStringIO` modules create such objects, allowing you to build messages in strings rather than files. Listing 5.7 shows a simple example of a `MimeWriter` creating a plain message in a file.

Listing 5.7 *mailwrite.py:* **Creating a Simple RFC 822-Compliant Mail Message**

```
 1 import MimeWriter
 2
 3 mfile = "mailmsg.txt"
 4 f = open(mfile, "w")
 5
 6 w = MimeWriter.MimeWriter(f)
 7 w.addheader("From", "Steve Holden <sholden@holdenweb.com>")
 8 w.addheader("To", """Gentle Reader <bookuser@holdenweb.com>,
 9     Steve Holden <sholden@holdenweb.com>""")
10 w.addheader("Received", """from thinker [64.134.121.94] by mail.holdenweb.com
11    (SMTPD32-6.04) id A244C78500BA; Thu, 08 Mar 2001 01:10:12 - 0500""")
12 f = w.startbody("text/plain", prefix=0)
13 f.write("""
14 Here we have a simple message. The lack of attachments means that the message
15 is simple to process, as the body can simply be read from the file after the
16 headers have been processed into an rfc822.Message object.
17
18 Regards
19   Steve
20 """)
21 f.close()
```

The program simply creates a `MimeWriter`, adds a few headers, and then starts the body (which adds a `Content-Type` header) and writes it. The `prefix=0` argument to `startbody()`, which also can be used with `addheader()`, puts the `Content-Type:` header at the end of the current header list rather than at the beginning. Listing 5.8 shows the resulting mail message.

Listing 5.8 **Output from *mailwrite.py***

```
From: Steve Holden <sholden@holdenweb.com>
To: Gentle Reader <bookuser@holdenweb.com>,
    Steve Holden <sholden@holdenweb.com>
Received: from thinker [64.134.121.94] by mail.holdenweb.com
    (SMTPD32-6.04) id A244C78500BA; Thu, 08 Mar 2001 01:10:12 -0500
Content-Type: text/plain
```

Here we have a simple message. The lack of attachments means that the Message
is simple to process, as the body can simply be read from the file after the
headers have been processed into an rfc822.Message object.

Regards
Steve

MIME: The Body Becomes an Envelope

Eventually the requirement to carry more complex data across the mail network led to
a realization that the message body could itself be structured. This led to the development of the MIME (Multipurpose Internet Mail Extension) standard, described in
RFC 1521, which is also a significant component of web-based systems. A MIME-
compliant message is recursively structured: each portion may itself be MIME-
compliant, holding multiple parts, or it may be a single piece of content formatted
according to RFC 822.

To allow binary as well as textual components, the standards specify how data may
be encoded in formats suitable for transmission over email channels. This generally
means that lines are of 72 characters or less, with a 7-bit character set. With the
introduction of MIME, email was freed from the onerous restrictions of being a
text-only medium. Listing 5.9 shows a program that produces a multipart/mixed
message in a file. Because the program is naturally sequential in nature, commentary
explains each section.

Listing 5.9   *multiwrite.py:* **Writing a Multipart MIME Message**

```
1 import MimeWriter, base64
2 #
3 # Writes a multipart mail message: text plus associated graphic
4 #
5 mfile = "multimsg.eml"
```

The two key modules are imported, and a name is set for the output to be produced.

```
6 f = open(mfile, "w")
7 # Create a MimeWriter
8 mail = MimeWriter.MimeWriter(f)
```

A MimeWriter is created from an already-open output file.

```
9 mail.addheader("From", "Steve Holden <sholden@holdenweb.com>")
10 mail.addheader("To", """Gentle Reader <bookuser@holdenweb.com>,
11     Steve Holden <sholden@holdenweb.com>""")
12 mail.addheader("Subject", "The Python You Wanted")
```

```
13 mail.addheader("Received", """from thinker [64.134.121.94] by➡
   mail.holdenweb.com
14    (SMTPD32-6.04) id A244C78500BA; Fri, 09 Mar 2001 07:33:38 - 0500""")
```

A number of headers are added to the RFC 822 headers of the envelope containing the message.

```
15 # Mail will be multi-part: First part explains format
16 part1 = mail.startmultipartbody ("mixed")
```

The `multipart/mixed` type selected for `startmultipartbody()` is by far the most common. You might want to look into other types in the RFC 1521 standard.

```
17 part1.write("This is a MIME-encoded message, with attachments. "
18 "If you are seeing this message your mail program probably cannot "
19 "show you the attachments. Please try another program, or read "
20 'Python Web Programming' to see the attached picture."
21 """
22 Sorry ...
23 Steve Holden
24 """)
```

The initial portion of a multipart message should bring the nature of the message to the attention of an unwary reader not blessed with a MIME-compliant mail user agent.

```
25 # Second part is intended to be read
26 part2 = mail.nextpart()
27 f = part2.startbody("text/plain")
28 f.write("Here we have a multipart message. This "
29 "means that the message body must be processed "
30 "as MIME-encoded content where possible [which "
31 "it clearly is in Outlook Express]."
32 """
33
34 regards
35 Your Humble Author
36 """)
```

The next part is a simple text message such as you might type to a friend or acquaintance. Think of it as the cover note if you're looking (for example) to implement electronic billing.

```
37 # Third part is a graphic, which we encode in base64
38 part3 = mail.nextpart()
39 part3.addheader("Content-Transfer-Encoding", "base64")
40 f = part3.startbody("image/gif", [["Name", "python.gif"]])
41 b64 = base64.encodestring(open("pythonwin.gif", "rb").read())
42 f.write(b64)
```

The preceding section shows the expressive power of Python. Line 38 creates a third body part, and line 39 indicates the data will be base-64 encoded (a common way of ensuring easy text transfer of binary data). Line 40 indicates that the attachment will be a GIF graphic whose name should (where possible) be represented as `python.gif`.

```
43 # Never forget to call lastpart!
44 mail.lastpart()
```

This is a traditional reminder that unless the final part of the body is correctly terminated (by the boundary parameter value of the `Content-Separator:` header, which the `MimeWriter` has conveniently generated automatically for you), your message is not MIME-compliant. On double-clicking the output of this program in Windows Explorer, imagine the author's pleasant surprise to be presented with the window shown in Figure 5.1.

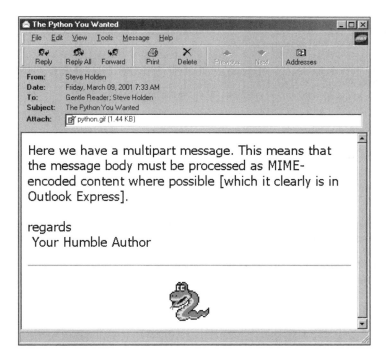

Figure 5.1   *multimsg.eml*, created by *multiwrite.py* and viewed in Outlook Express.

The output from the program is shown in textual form in Listing 5.10.

Listing 5.10   ***multimsg.eml* Shown as a Text File**

```
Content-Type: multipart/mixed;
    boundary="10.1.1.111.1.-16442665.985148107.930.30685"
From: Steve Holden <sholden@holdenweb.com>
To: Gentle Reader <bookuser@holdenweb.com>,
```

continues

Listing 5.10 **Continued**

```
        Steve Holden sholden@holdenweb.com
Subject: The Python You Wanted
Received: from thinker [64.134.121.94] by mail.holdenweb.com
    (SMTPD32-6.04) id A244C78500BA; Fri, 09 Mar 2001 07:33:38 -0500

This is a MIME-encoded message, with attachments. If you are seeing this➡
message your
mail program probably cannot show you the attachments. Please try another➡
program, or
read 'Python Web Programming' to see the attached picture.
Sorry ...
Steve Holden

--10.1.1.111.1.-16442665.985148107.930.30685
Content-Type: text/plain

Here we have a multipart message. This means that the message body must➡
be processed
as MIME-encoded content where possible [which it clearly is in Outlook Express].

Regards
Your Humble Author

--10.1.1.111.1.-16442665.985148107.930.30685
Content-Type: image/gif;
    Name="python.gif"
Content-Transfer-Encoding: base64

R0lGODlhQABAAPcAAAAAAIAAAACAAICAAAAAgIAAgACAgMDAwMDcwKbK8AD/AP//AAAA//8A/wD/
/////wAAAIAAAACAAICAAAAAgIAAgACAgICAgMDAwP8AAAD/AP//AAAA//8A/wD//////wAAAIAA
[    AND LOTS MORE, SIMILAR LINES    ]
1GGg0IVYGXx15lciiLqK6Bag116I1LNwqpltqrHGmxW6beZKKbwmBSupt4lCpK2MCL3Y7XhowvvYXUJuaW
KxDhsQEAA7

--10.1.1.111.1.-16442665.985148107.930.30685--
```

Message Handling: *rfc822* and Friends

Many modules are useful for creating and dealing with mail messages, up to and including complex multipart messages with attachments containing attachments. The rfc822 module can parse message headers, and the mailbox module allows you to access existing mail folders for a variety of open-format mail systems (although, sadly, proprietary formats, such as those used by modern Microsoft products, currently are lacking). Just as MimeWriter is useful for the creation of MIME-encoded messages, the MultiFile module allows the reading of the individual parts of multipart messages. It maintains a stack of separators, so if the current component is itself a multipart document, the individual components can be read by a suitably recursive program. The `mimetools` module is primarily for parsing existing MIME messages, a rather more difficult task than creating them. It defines a subclass of `rfc822.Message`, with additional methods useful in dealing with more complex content types.

rfc822: **Reading and Deciphering Headers and Bodies**

The `rfc822` library module allows you to read and parse the header portion of mail messages (or other information with a similar structure) from files (or from other objects that are sufficiently file-like, such as the `ftpStream` class defined previously). If you have a mail message in file `mailmsg.txt`, Listing 5.11 shows some of the possibilities for processing it.

Listing 5.11   *message.py:* **Simple Message Handling with the** *rfc822* **Module**

```
 1 import rfc822
 2
 3 f = open("mailmsg.txt")
 4 m = rfc822.Message(f)
 5 b = m.fp.readlines()
 6 f.close()
 7
 8 addrs = m.getaddrlist("to")
 9 print "%-15s %s" % ("Recipient", "Email Address")
10 for rcpt, addr in addrs:
11     print "%-15s %s" % (rcpt, addr)
12
13 print
14 rcvd = m.getheader("received")
15 print "Received:", rcvd
16
17 print
18 for bl in b:
19     print bl[:-1]
20
```

Lines 3 and 4 open the file containing the message and process the headers. This leaves the file positioned just before the message body. Line 5 reads the body using the `fp` property of the `rfc822.Message` object, and then closes the file. This is not strictly necessary in this case but is generally good practice. Line 8 retrieves the content of all the `To:` headers as a list of addresses—each address is represented as a (name, address) pair. Lines 9 through 11 print the list, with some formatting. Lines 13 through 15 retrieve and print the `"Received:"` header, and lines 17 through 19 simply print the message body.

Notice that the lines of the body have the trailing line feed trimmed in line 19 because the `print` statement adds line feeds. If you feel slightly awkward with this and want to avoid the creation of lots of temporary trimmed strings, you always can opt for the following form, which shows a little more Pythonicity than the original loop:

```
for bl in b:
    sys.stdout.write(bl)
```

Yet another alternative is the following code, which uses the trailing comma on the `print` statement to suppress the usual line terminator:

```
for bl in b:
    print bl,
```

The `write()` file method, unlike the `print` statement, does not append a line terminator to what is written and is therefore preferable where the data already contains newlines, as it often will. Listing 5.12 shows the output from the script. Obviously, you will see different output from your messages. Most mail clients have a way of storing messages as ASCII, which should be suitable for this program's purposes. Beware, though, that not all mail clients include attachments when they save a file as text.

Listing 5.12   **How** *message.py* **Reports the** *mailmsg.txt* **File**

```
D:\Code\Ch5> python message.py
Recipient        Email Address
Gentle Reader    bookuser@holdenweb.com
Steve Holden     sholden@holdenweb.com

Received: from thinker [64.134.121.94] by mail.holdenweb.com
  (SMTPD32-6.04) id A244C78500BA; Thu, 08 Mar 2001 01:10:12 -0500

Here we have a simple message. The lack of attachments means that the Message
is simple to process, as the body can simply be read from the file after the
headers have been processed into an rfc822.Message object.

regards
 Steve
```

There is a slight misfit between the `mimetools` and `mailbox` modules. Although the latter makes it easy to retrieve messages sequentially from a mailbox, it returns the messages as `rfc822.Message` objects when it would be more convenient to have `mimetools.Message` objects. A module shown in Listing 5.13 defines a subclass of `mailbox.UnixMailbox`. It replaces the original `next()` method with a similar one that returns the required object type.

Listing 5.13   *mailhandler.py:* **A Slightly Enhanced** *Mailbox* **Class**

```
1 import mailbox
2 import mimetools
3
4 class MimeMailbox(mailbox.UnixMailbox):
```

```
 5
 6    def next(self):
 7        while 1:
 8            self.fp.seek(self.seekp)
 9            try:
10                self._search_start()
11            except EOFError:
12                self.seekp = self.fp.tell()
13                return None
14            start = self.fp.tell()
15            self._search_end()
16            self.seekp = stop = self.fp.tell()
17            if start <> stop:
18                self.fp.seek(start)
19                return mimetools.Message(self.fp)
20            else:
21                return None
```

The details of the next() method are unimportant: to understand them, you can read
the mailbox module source from the library. The difference from the standard method
of mailbox.UnixMailbox is that this method returns a mimetools.Message object rather
than an rfc822.Message allowing a broader range of functionality to be used. To
demonstrate how this small and simple module can be used, Listing 5.14 is a program
that uses it. (Of course it is only small and simple because it inherits almost everything
from the class on which it is based, completely unchanged.)

Listing 5.14   *mailshow.py:* **Analyzing the Contents of MIME Messages**

```
 1    import mailhandler
 2    import multifile, mimetools, sys
 3
 4    MFILE = "mailbox.txt"
 5
 6
 7    class mailStream:
 8
 9        def __init__(self, filename):
10            try:
11                self.fp = open(filename, "r")
12                print "+++Opened", filename
13            except IOError:
14                sys.exit("Could not open mailfile '%s'" % filename)
15            self.mb = mailhandler.MimeMailbox(self.fp)
16
17        def next(self):
18            ptr = self.fp.tell()           # save start point
19            msg = self.msg = self.mb.next()   # read next from mailbox
20            atts = self.atts = []
```

continues

Listing 5.14 **Continued**

```
21        if msg:
22            boundary = msg.getparam("boundary")
23            if boundary:
24                mf = multifile.MultiFile(self.fp)
25                                    # create Multifile
26                mf.push(boundary)   # save for recognition
27                self.fp.seek(ptr)   # point to multifile start
28                while mf.next():    # each message
29                    atts.append(mimetools.Message(mf))
30                                    # read up to next boundary
31                mf.pop()            # restore previous
32            return msg, atts        # return message and attachments
33        else:
34            return None, None       # no message
35
36 m = 0
37 ms = mailStream(MFILE)        # create the message stream
38
39 while 1:                      # forever
40     msg, atts = ms.next()     # get next message
41     if msg is None:           # quit if there's nothing
42         break
43     m += 1                    # bump count
44     if atts:
45         a = 0
46         print "Mail %d: multipart with %d attachments" % (m, len(atts))
47         for att in atts:
48             a += 1
49             print "Att", a, "Type: ", att.gettype(),➡
50                   "encoding:", att.getencoding(),
51             print "File:", att.getparam("name")
52     else:
53         print "Mail %d: plain message" % m, "from", msg['from']
54     print "----------------------------------------------"
```

Line 4 identifies a mail file that happens to contain four messages, all being MIME-encoded with embedded attachments. Starting at line 7, you see the declaration of a class, which deals with all the administration of the mailbox, helping to keep the main program shorter and easier to understand. You create a mailStream by passing it the path of a UNIX mailbox file (Netscape creates these very nicely, even on Windows). The next() method returns a two-element tuple consisting of the original message and a list of attachments (which is empty if none are present). Both elements are None when the mail content is exhausted. For multipart messages, it uses the multifile module to handle separate content items as individual pieces.

Lines 36 and 37 initialize a counter and create the mailStream object. The remainder of the code is a loop, which reads the next message and terminates the loop if no message is found; otherwise, the message count is incremented.

If it has to deal with a MIME-structured body, the program loops over the attachments, printing out some identifying information. Listing 5.15 shows the output from
this program.

Listing 5.15   *mailbox.txt* **as Reported by** *mailshow.py*

```
+++Opened mailbox.txt
Mail 1: multipart with 2 attachments
Att 1 Type:  text/plain encoding: quoted-printable File: None
Att 2 Type:  text/html encoding: quoted-printable File: CALLBA~1.HTM
-----------------------------------------------
Mail 2: multipart with 2 attachments
Att 1 Type:  text/plain encoding: 7bit File: None
Att 2 Type:  application/rtf encoding: base64 File: INV0008.rtf
-----------------------------------------------
Mail 3: multipart with 6 attachments
Att 1 Type:  text/plain encoding: 7bit File: None
Att 2 Type:  image/png encoding: base64 File: billpie.png
Att 3 Type:  image/png encoding: base64 File: Sbill013.png
Att 4 Type:  image/png encoding: base64 File: SBillLinux.png
Att 5 Type:  image/png encoding: base64 File: Sbillsor.png
Att 6 Type:  image/png encoding: base64 File: Sbilltmp.png
-----------------------------------------------
Mail 4: multipart with 4 attachments
Att 1 Type:  text/plain encoding: 7bit File: None
Att 2 Type:  image/jpeg encoding: base64 File: christmas.jpg
Att 3 Type:  image/gif encoding: base64 File: Office Assistant.gif
Att 4 Type:  text/plain encoding: 7bit File: PersonalDeployment.txt
-----------------------------------------------
```

You can see from the output that each compound message begins with a component
in plain 7-bit ASCII text. This is the usual message that explains the bizarre-looking
mail structure to users of mail readers that do not handle MIME-compliant messages,
and who therefore see the whole multipart content as a single text.

mimecntl: **Reading and Writing Messages**

Another library, `mimecntl`, was developed to integrate a set of features that make mail
handling easier, but this is not a part of the standard library. It can be downloaded
from the Vaults of Parnassus: search for `mimecntl` at `http://www.vex.net/parnassus/`,
and you should go straight there.

   This module was written to provide what its author, Michael P. Reilly
(`arcege@shore.net`), describes as "a clear merge between `mimetools.Message` and
`MimeWriter.MimeWriter`." What has resulted is a complex object that, in earlier incarnations, was not well-documented. Fortunately, later releases remedied this defect, and
`mimecntl` has been used to analyze 60 MB of email into a relational database.

A simple application of the library is shown in Listing 5.16, an extract from a program the author wrote to inform address book contacts of a change of email address.

Listing 5.16   **I'm Not in the Spam Business (Am I?)**

```
 1 #
 2 # Create the base message the user will read in the mail
 3 #
 4 #
 5 # Wrap the message, and its attachment, in a single MIME envelope
 6 #
 7 g = mimecntl.MIME_document("", type='text/plain',
 8         From="sholden@holdenweb.com",
 9         To="Contact List <sholden@holdenweb.com>",
10         Subject = 'Email address change notification')
11 g['message-id'] = MsgIdBase % msgcount
12 g['reply-to'] = g['errors-to'] = sholden@holdenweb.com
13 g.write("""Dear Contact,
14
15 This message is to inform you that the email address
16
17     sholden@bellatlantic.net
18
19 is no longer valid.  You are being notified as a
20 recorded contact of that address.  Could you please update
21 your records to show the following address instead:
22
23     sholden@holdenweb.com
24
25 This is an automatic mailing, but does not mean that you
26 will receive further automatic mailings.  I'm not in the
27 spam business!
28
29 regards
30 Steve Holden
31
32 http://www.holdenweb.com/              +1 (703) 967 0887
33 """)
```

The `mimecntl` library, as you might be able to tell from Listing 5.16, gives you a little more flexibility in the way you deal with messages. You might observe that headers can be added as keyword arguments when a `MIME_document` is created as well as later in the style of dictionary entries. If a keyword contains a hyphen, you must add it separately because Python names cannot contain hyphens. You might just find that `mimecntl` suits your programming style better than the standard library modules.

smtplib: **Sending Mail Using SMTP**

Now that you can create and analyze mail messages, it might be time to start thinking about sending and receiving them. In the same way as creating a message is easier than analyzing it, so sending a message is easier than receiving one. You may remember that SMTP is almost invariably used to send Internet mail from modern mail clients, and the next example shows you this is not a complicated process.

It does, however, need an SMTP server to operate against. If you do not have such a server on-site, you will probably find that you can use the same server as your standard mail client. Look in its configuration parameters for the server's DNS name or IP address.

How the Module Works

The `smtplib` module is strictly for use as an SMTP (or extended SMTP) client, which limits you to the role of sending mail. You should not be concerned; the `poplib` module you will be meeting next can receive mail. As usual, you create an object (an `smtplib.SMTP` object, to be precise) that you can use to connect to an appropriate server. When connected, that single object can send as many mails as you want. For the next server, create another object.

`smtplib` is a simple library to use. The complexities usually arise when you need to format complex mail messages, or use several servers and use the DNS to look up mail exchanger systems for the domains to which you are sending.

Simple Mail Programming with *smptlib*

Just as a simple test, the script shown in Listing 5.17 sends the `multimsg.eml` file used earlier to a couple of recipients. You should realize that the recipients are not extracted from the mail message's headers but provided separately. This means that you can send blind copies to recipients by providing their addresses as arguments to the `SMTP` object's `sendmail()` method without putting them in the mail message.

Listing 5.17   *mailsend.py:* **Sending Mail over an SMTP Connection**

```
 1  import smtplib, socket
 2
 3  fromaddr = sholden@holdenweb.com
 4  toaddrs  = ["bookuser@holdenweb.com",
 5              "nosuchuser@holdenweb.com",
 6              "sholden@holdenweb.com"]
 7
 8  msg = open("multimsg.eml", "r").read()
 9
10  try:
11      server = smtplib.SMTP('10.0.0.1')
12      result = server.sendmail(fromaddr, toaddrs, msg)
13      server.quit()
```

continues

Listing 5.17 **Continued**

```
14      if result:
15          for r in result.keys():
16              print "Error sending to", r
17              rt = result[r]
18              print "Code", rt[0], ":", rt[1]
19      else:
20          print "Sent to all recipients without errors"
21  except (smtplib.SMTPException, socket.error), arg:
22      print "SMTP Server could not send mail", arg
```

Mail sending, as you can see, is not too complex if you know how to formulate messages. This particular message is read from the file produced earlier, and the From: and list of To: addresses are hard-coded. After an SMTP object has been created, the object's sendmail() method is used to send the message to the connected server host. If the message is not sent to *any* recipient, then sendmail() raises an exception, which for simplicity's sake is not caught in this program. The SMTP object's connection normally will still be open for other sendmail() calls.

If the server accepts the message for at least one recipient, the method returns a dictionary, each of whose keys is a recipient to whom the message was *not* sent. The entries are two-element tuples, the first of which is the numeric completion code, and the second is the message with which the receiving system returned. The program returned the following output:

```
D:\Book1\Code\Ch5> python" mailsend.py
Error sending to nosuchuser@holdenweb.com
Code 550 : <nosuchuser@holdenweb.com>... User unknown
```

The sendmail() method accepts two optional arguments not used in the preceding code. These are both lists of extended service options, which are specified in RFC 1869 and not supported by all servers. The first set is for use with the sending addresses, the second with the receiving addresses.

poplib: Receiving Mail

Reading mail from files is all very well, but of course most mail is downloaded from a server, received over some network connection. The POP protocol originally was devised for use when a personal computer was only intermittently connected to the network. It also is convenient when workstations are inside a firewall. Because POP is an offline protocol, the messages can be read only when they have been downloaded to the mail user agent software at the user's workstation. This can be tedious when using dial-in connectivity because most user agents indiscriminately collect all messages irrespective of length, which sometimes means that you have a long wait before you can start reading your messages.

The Structure of a POP Session

The client system connects to the server, usually using the well-known TCP port number 110, and the server responds with a greeting. Interaction then proceeds with the client issuing commands consisting of a keyword followed by zero or more arguments, and the server responds with single- or multiline responses.

A response from the server begins with +OK for a positive response or -ERR for a negative one. A line containing a single period terminates multiline responses. For example, here is an extract from RFC 1725 showing the client (C) requesting a mailbox status listing from the server (S):

```
C: LIST
S: +OK 2 messages (320 octets)
S: 1 120
S: 2 200
S: .
```

The session proceeds through a number of states, starting in the AUTHORIZATION state. The client moves the session state to TRANSACTION by providing authentication data, using USER and PASS protocol commands from the client to the server. The mail account then is locked, and transactions against it are processed. Finally, the client issues the QUIT protocol command, and the server enters the UPDATE state. In this state, it updates the mail account and unlocks it, issuing a confirmation message and closing the TCP connection. If the TCP connection is lost during the session, then the server usually times out after at least 10 minutes, and in that case the account is not updated with the transactions.

How the Module Works

As usual, you start by creating an object (in this case a poplib.POP3 object), giving the name or IP address of the host to which you want to connect, and optionally a port number. You then call the various methods of the object to interact with the server to which the connection was made.

Presumably for efficiency reasons, all debugging statements in the poplib module have been commented out. Because the current module has only five debugging statements, it is a relatively simple matter to remove the comment marks. The debugging level can be set by the set_debuglevel() method. The stat() and putcmd() methods give debugging output for any nonzero level, and three internal methods give debug output for a level greater than 1.

Table 5.1 summarizes the creation of POP3 objects and the methods you will need to use to authenticate the session before processing starts.

Table 5.1 **Connecting to a POP Server and Performing Authentication**

`p = poplib.POP3(host[, port])`	Creates a POP3 class instance, which can be used to interact with an POP server. The `host` argument specifies which server to connect to. If the optional `port` argument is not specified, then TCP Port 110 is the port to which the object connects.
`p.getwelcome()`	Returns the welcome string from the server's connection response.
`p.user(username)`	Sends the given username to the server for authentication.
`p.pass_(password)`	Note the underscore at the end of the method name, to avoid conflict with a Python reserved word. Sends the given password to the server for authentication.
`p.apop(user, secret)`	Logs in to the server using the more secure APOP-style authentication.
`p.rpop(user)`	Logs in to the server using UNIX rsh-style authentication.

Note that any given mail account requires the use of either one authentication style or the other: you cannot choose which to use. The methods, if they succeed, return the server response. Note that for security reasons, most modern POP servers accept the username from `user()` even if it is nonexistent and fail when the password is given with `pass_()`. This avoids leaking information about which accounts exist on the server.

The POP3 object reports problems by raising an `error_proto` exception, with the server's response as an argument. The response of a server to an incorrect interactive login is shown here:

```
>>> p = poplib.POP3("10.0.0.1")
>>> p.user("nosuch")
'+OK User name accepted, password please'
>>> p.pass_("banana")
Traceback (innermost last):
  File "<interactive input>", line 1, in ?
  File "d:\python20\lib\poplib.py", line 186, in pass_
    return self._shortcmd('PASS %s' % pswd)
  File "d:\python20\lib\poplib.py", line 149, in _shortcmd
    return self._getresp()
  File "d:\python20\lib\poplib.py", line 125, in _getresp
    raise error_proto(resp)
error_proto: -ERR Bad login>
```

The methods shown in Table 5.2 are those used most frequently to interact with a server which is running in TRANSACTION state. Please remember that if you fail for whatever reason to use the `quit()` method before the connection is dropped, then the mailbox is likely to be locked for a significant period of time.

Table 5.2 **Methods for Interaction with a TRANSACTION-State POP Server**

p.stat()	Returns a tuple (*count*, *size*) where count is the number of messages in the mailbox, and *size* is the total number of bytes it contains.
p.list([*msgnum*])	Returns a tuple whose first component is the server response and whose second component is a list of strings. Each string is of the form *msg octets*, where *msg* is the message number, and *octets* is the size, in bytes, of the message. If the optional *msgnum* argument is given, the server reports only on that message.
p.retr(*msgnum*)	Returns a three-element tuple whose first element is the server's response. The second element is a list of strings representing the message identified by the *msgnum* argument, with no trailing line terminators. The third element is the number of bytes in the message, which will include line terminators and therefore will be greater than the sum of the lengths of the lines.
p.dele(*msgnum*)	Marks the given message number for deletion at the end of the session. Returns the server's response.
p.rset()	Removes all deletion marks from messages on the server. Returns the server's response.
p.quit()	Puts the session into UPDATE state and returns the server's response after it has finished updating the mailbox. The TCP connection between the client and the server is closed at that point.

Other methods that you may want to know about for more advanced POP programming are covered in the standard Python module documentation.

Simple POP Programming

To show you the library in action, Listing 5.18 is a program that scans a POP mailbox and summarizes it by displaying the recipients and number of body lines for each of the messages it contains. You will come across a new library here, StringIO, which is used to create a filelike object from the message. The purpose of this is to allow use of the rfc822 library to analyze the message content.

Listing 5.18 *popsum.py:* **Summarizing a POP Mailbox**

```
1  import poplib
2  import rfc822, sys, StringIO
3
4  SRVR = "mymailserver.com"
5  USER = "user"
6  PASS = "password"
7  try:
8      p = poplib.POP3(SRVR)
9  except:
```

continues

Listing 5.18 **Continued**

```
10      print "Unable to contact server %s" % SRVR
11      sys.exit(-1)
12
13 try:
14      print p.user(USER)
15      print p.pass_(PASS)
16 except:
17      print "Authentication failure"
18      sys.exit(-2)
19
20 msglst = p.list()[1]
21 for m in msglst:
22      mno, size = m.split()
23      lines = p.retr(mno)[1]
24      print "--- Message %s -------------" % mno
25      file = StringIO.StringIO("\r\n".join(lines))
26      msg = rfc822.Message(file)
27      body = file.readlines()
28      addrs = msg.getaddrlist("to")
29      print "%-15s %s" % ("Recipient", "Email Address")
30      for rcpt, addr in addrs:
31          print "%-15s %s" % (rcpt, addr)
32      print len(body), "lines in message body"
33 print "----------------------------"
34 p.quit()
35 sys.exit()
```

Lines 1 through 6 import the necessary libraries and set up the account details. Lines 7 through 18 connect to the POP server and authenticate the account, handling exceptions appropriately. Line 20 uses the list() method to retrieve the list of messages.

Lines 21 through 32 loop over this list. Line 22 extracts the message number and size, and line 23 retrieves the message from the server; only the message lines from the second element of the response are saved. Line 25 creates a StringIO object from the message, inserting a carriage return and a line feed between each line to provide the contents of the filelike object, which is now ready for reading by the rfc822 library.

Line 26 creates an rfc822.Message object from the headers, and line 27 reads the remainder of the message (the body) into a list. Lines 27 through 31 build and print a list of recipients from the message headers, and line 32 terminates processing of the current message by indicating the length of the message body.

As you can see, interacting with a POP server is not difficult, particularly since Python provides so many supporting libraries to handle commonly required tasks. The capability of the StringIO object (and its speedier but more limited cousin, the cStringIO object) to mimic file behavior is extremely useful. It allows file-processing libraries such as rfc822 to access data that has already been read from other sources.

nntplib: **Receiving Network News**

The network news system is a distributed service based on the Network News Transfer Protocol (NNTP) that allows articles for a newsgroup to be posted on any server and eventually distributed to every server handling that newsgroup. Interactions between servers are complex because each has to advertise the articles present in its newsgroups and the connecting server must then say which articles it would like to transfer.

Usenet and UUCP Transfers

Although Internet users often refer to network news as Usenet News, in fact Usenet was originally a separate network, based on UUCP transfer of articles over dial-up telephone lines. This ingenious scheme would use free local calls in the United States if the hop distances were not too great. The result was that an article might take 24 hours to travel from one side of the country to the other, but it would do so without increasing anybody's telephone bill. NNTP was introduced as local area networking became more popular, making sense of the idea of a central repository that LAN clients could access. As the Internet grew, there was less need for UUCP transfers.

News has many advantages over electronic mail:

- By having the servers exchange articles over the Internet backbone and then make them available for reading locally, there is a considerable saving in network bandwidth.

- You can "drop in and out" of a newsgroup: unlike a mailing list, if you go on vacation, articles will expire while you are away rather than facing you threateningly when you return.

- Each individual can manage his own subscriptions relatively easily by interacting with a local server.

The `nntplib` library module implements the NNTP client-side protocol, but because news servers also act as clients to other servers, it contains features that could be used to program partial server-side functionality. The library does not allow your code to accept connections from other news clients, however, and so is primarily useful for keeping up with particular newsgroups in an automated way.

Servers allow clients to refer to articles in two ways: either by an article number within a particular newsgroup or by their unique identifiers. Because both are often represented as strings, article identifiers are denoted by the angle brackets that surround them. A typical article identifier would be something like the following example:

```
<KmJy6.93927$m04.3450360@e420r-atl1.usenetserver.com>
```

News articles are structured in exactly the same way as mail messages, meaning that you can use the `rfc822` library module to process them. Please remember, though, that in most newsgroups, postings are expected to be exclusively textual; resist the temptation to attach binary files.

How the Module Works

As usual, you create an object, which connects to the server on your program's behalf, and then you call object's methods to effect the required server interactions.

```
n = nntplib.NNTP(host, port=119, user=None, password=None, readermode=None)
```

Creates an NNTP object connected to the given host by default to the standard NNTP port. If the `user` argument is given, then the `password` argument also must be given, and they will be used to authenticate the session at the server. The `readermode` argument is not usually required, but may need to be set to true if you are connecting to a local server and issuing certain reader-specific commands.

```
n.quit()
```

Terminates interaction with the news server, returning its final response before the TCP connection is closed.

```
n.getwelcome()
```

Returns the welcome string from the server's connection response, which may contain useful information.

```
n.set_debuglevel(level)
```

Sets the object's debug level. A `level` argument of zero suppresses debugging output, 1 produces summarized debug outputs, and 2 or higher produces output that includes each command and response passing between the client and the server.

After you have a connected `NNTP` object, you can use it to find out what groups are available. News clients generally keep some state information between sessions because downloading information about the available newsgroups, or reading data about all messages on a newsgroup, can be time-consuming even over a relatively fast network link.

```
n.list()
```

Retrieves a list of groups available on the server. Returns a tuple (*response, list*) where *response* is the server's response string and *list* is a list of tuples. Each tuple describes a newsgroup and is of the form *(group, last, first, flag)*. *group* is the name of the newsgroup; *last* and *first* are numbers (in string form) of the available articles; and *flag* is "y" (posting allowed), "n" (no posting allowed), or "m" (postings are moderated).

```
n.newgroups(date, time)
```

Retrieves a list of groups created on the server since the given *date* (formatted as *yymmdd*) and *time* (formatted as *hhmmss*). Returns a tuple *(response, groups)* where *response* is the server's response string, and *groups* is a list of newsgroup names.

```
n.newnews(groups, date, time)
```

Retrieves a list of articles created on the server in the given *groups* since the given *date* (formatted as *yymmdd*) and *time* (formatted as *hhmmss*). The *groups* argument can be as simple as a single group name or a comma-separated list of groups, including asterisks to act as wildcards. Returns a tuple *(response, articles)* where *response* is the server's response string, and *articles* is a list of unique message identifiers, which you can use to retrieve messages from the server.

The `list()` method is likely to take a significant amount of time and is intended for infrequent use, principally at a client's initial connection. Obviously one of the things you should cache is the last date and time your client made a `newgroups()` and/or `newnews()` call. That helps your code to download minimal information at each connection.

The `newnews()` call is primarily useful when you are tracking news articles by their unique identifiers and can save you downloading duplicates. If you use wildcard group names, then you will have to examine the article headers to see the group(s) to which each message was posted. Some servers will disable the `NEWNEWS` protocol command used by this method, particularly for newsreader clients. Presumably, this limits bandwidth consumption by individual users. Unless you are writing a comprehensive client program, or a program to generate a local server feed, you probably will find it most convenient to access the messages by number within a particular newsgroup and accept the inefficiency of downloading articles cross-posted to different groups several times.

`n.group(`*`name`*`)`

Sets the server's current group to the given group *name*, returning a tuple of strings *(response, count, first, last, name)*. The server's response is a string, usually containing the other four items. If *count* is zero, there are no messages in the group; otherwise, it is an estimate of the number of messages. The first and last article numbers are given by *first* and *last* respectively, and *name* is the name of the newsgroup.

This method establishes *name* as the current newsgroup, used when accessing articles by number rather than identifier. If no current newsgroup is specified, then attempts to access articles by number will fail.

In the following method descriptions, the *art* argument may be either an article number within the current group or a unique identifier. In the latter case, the *number* returned may be meaningless.

`n.stat(`*`art`*`)`

Returns *(response, number, id)*, where *number* is a string containing the article's number within the current group, and *id* is its unique identifier. The article becomes the current article.

`n.next()`

Moves the current newsgroup to the article following the current article. Returns *(response, number, id)*, as for the `stat()` method.

`n.last()`

Moves the current newsgroup to the article preceding the current article. Returns *(response, number, id)*, as for the `stat()` method.

`n.head(`*`art`*`)`   `n.body(`*`art`*`)`   `n.article(`*`art`*`)`

Returns *(response, number, id, list)*, where *number* is a string containing the article's number within the current group, and *id* is its unique identifier. *response*, *number*, and *id* are as for the `stat()` method. *list* contains either just the article's headers, just the lines of its body, or the whole article, depending on which method is called. The lines returned have no trailing line terminator.

There are a number of common extensions to news servers that you should be aware of because they can save you some time. Because they may not be available on all servers, check the help message to determine whether your server supports them. The two you are most likely to find useful are shown here.

---

n.xhdr(*hdr, range*)

The *hdr* argument is a header keyword such as `"subject"`, and *range* is a string defining a message range in the form *first-last*. The method returns a tuple whose first member is the server's response, and whose second member is a list of header values, one for each article from the current newsgroup in the range. Note that the last item in the message is, with unusual lack of Pythonicity, included in the message numbers, which have to be checked on the server. Unfortunately, the protocol was invented before Python, so we just have to put up with it.

n.date()

Returns *(response, date, time)*, where *date* and *time* are suitable for use in the `newgroups()` and `newnews()` methods.

The remaining methods can be found, as always, in the Python library documentation. You should understand that `nntplib` is not as well-structured as some other modules and does not use Python features that might provide a more convenient interface for interaction with the server. This will become a little more obvious in the next section.

Programming Interaction with a Network News Server

Network news management can be a complex business if multiple groups are to be managed without duplication of cross-posted articles. Listing 5.19 connects to a news server, establishes the right starting point in the `comp.lang.python` article stream, and downloads the headers for a maximum of 10 articles.

Listing 5.19   *newscheck.py:* **Extract Articles from a Newsgroup**

```
 1   import nntplib, cStringIO, rfc822, sys
 2
 3   SRVR = "news.demon.co.uk"           # Your news server
 4   USER ="username"                    # Your account name
 5   PASS = "xyzzy"                       # Your password
 6   newsgroup = "comp.lang.python"      # Group of your choice
 7
 8   news = nntplib.NNTP(SRVR, user=USER, password=PASS)
 9   resp, estimate, first, last, name = news.group(newsgroup)
10
```

continues

Listing 5.19   **Continued**

```
11  if estimate == '0':
12      print "No messages in ", newsgroup
13      sys.exit(-1)
14
15  first = int(first)
16  last = int(last)
17
18  artnum = first # better: cached from the previous run
19
20  # establish first available article
21  while artnum <= last:
22      try:
23          news.stat(str(artnum))
24          break
25      except nntplib.NNTPError, err:
26          if err.response[:3] != '423':
27              raise
28          else:
29              artnum += 1
30  else:
31      print "No messages available in ", newsgroup
32      sys.exit(-2)
33
34  # loop through articles, extracting headers
35  artnum = str(artnum)
36  count = 0
37  while count < 10:
38      try:
39          hdrs = news.head(artnum)[3]
40          mesg = rfc822.Message(cStringIO.StringIO("\r\n".join(hdrs)))
41          print '%s\n   +++%s' % (mesg.getheader("from"),
42                                  mesg.getheader("subject"))
43          count += 1
44      except nntplib.NNTPError:
45          pass
46      try:
47          artnum = news.next()[1]
48      except nntplib.NNTPError, err:
49          if err.response[:3] != '421':
50              raise
51          else:
52              break
53  news.quit()
```

Lines 8 and 9 establish a connection to the server and set a current newsgroup. Lines 11 through 13 exit if the server definitely has no articles in the group. Because not all articles within the range returned need exist, lines 18 through 32 locate the first article number.

This startup logic repeatedly increments the article number until a `stat()` call succeeds, which is why lines 15 and 16 convert the string values from the server to integers. If an error occurs, the `except` clause starting at line 25 analyzes the cause. A server response of `423` indicates that the requested article does not exist, and so the article number is incremented, and the loop continues. Otherwise, the error is re-raised because it is outside the scope of the code. If the loop's `else` clause is executed at line 30, then no `stat()` call succeeded, and the program again exits.

Now the program has an article number that definitely exists. The `head()` method requires article numbers as strings, and the `next()` call returns string article numbers, so the integer article number obtained from the startup code is converted to a string on line 35. The main logic of the program is contained in the loop at lines 37 through 52, which limits the maximum number of articles retrieved.

The first `try`/`except` group ignores any errors because it is possible that an article will not be available for some reason. If the error is real, then the attempt to access the next message also gives an error. Line 39 extracts the headers from the result of the `head()` method call. It would be better if the responses were instances of some class, to allow attribute references such as `news.head(artnum).data` rather than indexed list elements, but this is not the case. Line 40 joins the headers with carriage return/line feed terminators and puts them into `rfc822.Message` format to assist header processing. The `From:` and `Subject:` headers are then printed, and the message count is incremented.

Line 47 moves the server to the next article in the newsgroup. The article number (as a string) is extracted from the returned tuple; again this access would be clearer were the return value an instance rather than a tuple. The exception processing handles server response `421` (no further messages in this group) by terminating the loop early. Any other errors are re-raised, so the user will become aware of the problem.

The Difference Between NNTP Clients and Servers

There are some similarities between the client and server functions for network news. A client and a server both maintain a local collection of articles, each associated with one or more newsgroups. The NNTP protocol includes a `SLAVE` protocol command to allow a server to identify itself as such when it contacts another server. The standard carefully refrains from defining any actions that should be taken in response to this command.

Whereas the client simply contacts servers to add to its collection, expiring them locally according to user-expressed rules, the server will periodically advertise its new articles to other servers (using the `IHAVE` protocol command). This operation has to be somewhat selective to avoid articles looping around the Internet, and so a server is usually careful to ensure that it does not advertise articles to other servers known to have processed them already.

httplib: **Writing Web Clients**

HTTP is the protocol of the World Wide Web. Although HTTP was designed to carry HTML between the web server and the browser, it has many other possible applications. Most web clients are currently browsers, but with the emergence of SOAP and XML-RPC there will be an increasingly wide range of HTTP clients, using the protocol as a medium for interchange of many types of structured information.

Browsers are rapidly becoming XML-capable, with the capability to present the same (XML) data in many different ways. Because XML is much more tightly structured than HTML, it is more useful as a general medium for data exchange. Thus HTTP, which can carry XML just as easily as HTML, is likely to become one of the principal media for exchange of data between organizations. Microsoft's BizTalk represents one effort to standardize the description of interchange data, to allow a general interoperability among diverse business systems. For more information, see Sams Publishing's book *XML and SOAP Programming for BizTalk Servers.*

A Brief Introduction to HTTP

The HTTP protocol (version 1.1) is specified in RFC 2616, which is almost 200 pages long. This might give you a false impression of the protocol's complexity. Although it is true that HTTP involves some complex semantics (which concern the interpretation of the protocol), the syntax of HTTP is easy to understand. In fact, having coped with email and network news already, you have acquired the tools to understand most of the HTTP syntax.

HTTP is yet another client-server protocol, which defines the syntax and semantics of *requests* and *responses*. Both requests and responses may transfer a data item, known in RFC 2616 as an *entity.* When no entity is transferred, an HTTP message consists of a single-line *method specification* for a request, or a single status line for a response, followed by a set of RFC822-compliant request or response headers. If an entity is included, then there also will be *entity headers*, then a blank line, and finally the *entity body*.

The interchanges between web clients and servers are therefore syntactically exactly like a one-line request or response specification followed by a mail message whose body portion is optional. Unlike mail messages, the data channel used to communicate the request is not assumed to be 7-bit, text-only. Binary transmission is therefore a possibility, and the entity body is not constrained to be in textual form as it is in an RFC822-compliant mail message.

Methods: *GET, PUT, POST,* and Friends

The defining RFC specifies eight different request methods, but in practice most of these can be ignored. I would guess that more than 99 percent of HTTP requests use the GET, HEAD, or POST methods. An HTTP request contains three components, with a space between each, and its structure is shown in Figure 5.2.

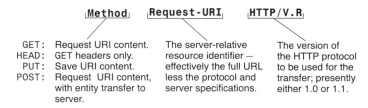

Method	Request-URI	HTTP/V.R

GET: Request URI content.
HEAD: GET headers only.
PUT: Save URI content.
POST: Request URI content,
        with entity transfer to
        server.
	The server-relative
	resource identifier —
	effectively the full URL
	less the protocol and
	server specifications.
		The version of
		the HTTP protocol
		to be used for the
		transfer; presently
		either 1.0 or 1.1.

Figure 5.2   Structure of an HTTP request method specification.

The only difference between a GET and a POST request is that POST transmits an entity (most usually the content of a form filled out in the browser window) along with the request, whereas with a GET the only way to include data is as a part of the URI. Listing 5.20 shows the GET request that a browser sends to TCP Port 80 for the simple URL http://10.0.0.131/cgi-bin/image.py. The Accept: header has been wrapped for printing to keep the listing's width within bounds, although the browser sent it as a single line.

Listing 5.20   **A Simple HTTP *GET* Request**

```
GET /cgi-bin/image.py HTTP/1.1
Accept: application/vnd.ms-excel, application/msword,
     application/vnd.ms-powerpoint, image/gif,
     image/x-xbitmap, image/jpeg, image/pjpeg, */*
Accept-Language: en-us
Accept-Encoding: gzip, deflate
User-Agent: Mozilla/4.0 (compatible; MSIE 5.5; MSNIA; Windows 98)
Host: 10.0.0.131
Connection: Keep-Alive
```

No entity is transmitted as a part of the GET request, so all the headers you see are request headers. As a contrast, Listing 5.21 shows the POST request generated by filling in the web form shown in Figure 5.3.

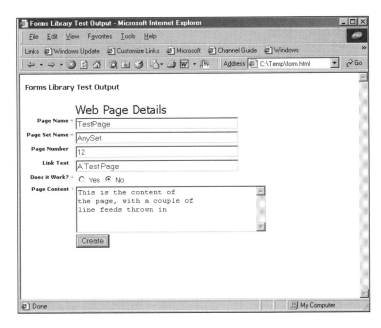

Figure 5.3   A web form used to generate a POST request.

Listing 5.21   **A Simple HTTP *POST* Request**

```
POST /cgi-bin/process-form.py HTTP/1.1
Accept: application/vnd.ms-excel, application/msword,
     application/vnd.ms-powerpoint, image/gif,
     image/x-xbitmap, image/jpeg, image/pjpeg, */*
Accept-Language: en-us
Content-Type: application/x-www-form-urlencoded
Accept-Encoding: gzip, deflate
User-Agent: Mozilla/4.0 (compatible; MSIE 5.5; MSNIA; Windows 98)
Host: 10.0.0.131
Content-Length: 172
Connection: Keep-Alive
Cache-Control: no-cache

Name=TestPage&PageSet=AnySet&Num=12&LinkText=A+Test+Page&
Answer=OFF&Content=This+is+the+content+of%0D%0Athe+page%2C
+with+a+couple+of%0D%0Aline+feeds+thrown+in&Submit=Create
```

In Listing 5.21, the Accept: header has again been wrapped. For printing purposes, the single line of entity data also has been broken at arbitrary points. No line feeds were included in the entity as it was transmitted because the HTTP protocol specification defines certain encodings: space characters are represented as plus signs, and certain other characters (carriage return, line feed, and comma) are represented as a percent sign followed by the character value as two hexadecimal digits. (Care is required in handling forms submitted in Unicode character sets, where characters can be larger than 8 bits each.) As you can see, the entity is a list of form fields separated by ampersand characters, and each form field is passed as a `name=value` pair.

The Headers Can Be Involved

The `POST` request includes some additional headers not transmitted with the `GET` request. These are entity headers (the `GET` request did not include an entity, so it had no need of them). They are

```
Content-Type: application/x-www-form-urlencoded
Content-Length: 172
Cache-Control: no-cache
```

These headers tell the server what type of content the entity represents, how much of it there is, and ensures that no device along the chain of communication caches the content. Table 5.3 summarizes the more significant headers that relate to the entity transferred with a request or response. You might notice that `Cache-Control:` is not listed among the entity headers; it is a *general header field*, which applies to all transfers of the content at HTTP level.

Table 5.3 **Common HTTP Entity Headers**

Header	Description
Allow	Specifies which methods may be used with a particular resource.
Content-Encoding	Specifies encodings that have been applied to the entity's content, and hence the decodings that must be used by the recipient to retrieve the content.
Content-Language	Describes the natural languages of the intended audience.
Content-Length	Specifies the number of bytes of data in the entity, as encoded for transmission.
Content-Location	In a multipart entity, specifies a URI that can be accessed for the content of a particular component.
Content-MD5	A message digest, computed on the entity content before any `Content-Encoding` was applied, which can be used to check the integrity of the received data.
Content-Range	For a partial entity, specifies where in the entity the particular portion being transmitted is located.
Content-Type	Allows specification of the media type and character set of the entity.
Expires	Gives the date and time after which the content of the entity should be considered stale, and therefore unusable.
Last-Modified	The date and time the entity content was last modified.

The `Content-Type:` header may, just as in email, indicate that the entity comprises several different portions, and each of these may also be multipart. Thus the structure of an HTTP entity is theoretically recursive in the same way as that of a MIME-compliant electronic mail message.

Interacting with a Web (FTP, gopher) server: *urllib*

The Python library contains many modules that handle interactions with various server types a web browser can contact through a URL. Mostly, however, these modules are not intended for direct use because the `urllib` module packages them all together in a form that effectively gives you similar reading capabilities to a web browser. `urllib` can handle URL types `http:`, `ftp:`, `gopher:`, and `file:`.

The module makes it easy to use such network sources by providing a `urlopen()` function that returns a filelike object. This object provides the usual methods available for reading files. There are no facilities to write network data sources.

`u = urllib.urlopen(url, data=None)`

Creates a connection object (normally a `urllib.FancyURLOpener`, but this can be modified) that allows a program to read data from network or file sources described by the `url` argument. The `data` argument is used only for `http:` scheme URLs, and if present causes the server to be accessed using a `POST` protocol request rather than the usual `GET`. The data must be encoded in the standard form required, which is `application/x-www-form-urlencoded`. The library's `urllib.urlencode()` function can be used to perform this encoding.

`u.read(), u.readline(), u.readlines(), u.fileno(), u.close()`

These methods allow the network connection to be treated similarly to built-in files.

The module makes reading web pages easy, even from the interactive command prompt, as the following example shows:

```
>>> u = urllib.urlopen("http://www.holdenweb.com")
>>> content = u.readlines()
>>> content[1:3]
['<html>\015\012', '<head>\015\012']
>>> content[-1]
'</html>\015\012'
```

You can access through proxy servers if your environment requires this, although the code *does not support authentication to the proxy*. The Macintosh implementations will pick up the proxy details from Internet Config data. In Windows or UNIX environments, set the appropriate environment variables from the following list:

```
http_proxy
ftp_proxy
gopher_proxy
```

There are other methods of the connection object you can use to get more information about the connection used to access the URL.

---

u.info()

Returns a `mimetools.Message` object containing data in RFC822-compliant headers, whose content depends on the scheme used.

Http:

Returns all headers transmitted by the HTTP server. The two most useful will probably be `Content-Length:` and `Content-Type:`, depending on your application.

Ftp:

A `Content-Length:` header will be present if the server passed a file length back in response to the file retrieval request.

File:

Returned headers normally will include `Content-Length:`, `Date:` (representing the file's last-modified date), and `Content-Type:`, which usually will be a guess based on the filename's extension.

Gopher:

No useful headers normally are available from gopher accesses.

---

u.geturl()

Returns the actual URL used to access the resource. This is usually the same as the `url` argument to `urllib.urlopen()`, but if the server redirected the request, then the method will return the redirected URL.

This can be useful for web pages but tends to be less so for others. HTTP uses encoded content rather more frequently than the other schemes, so client software has to know how to decode it before putting it to use.

```
>>> h = u.info()
>>> h.getheader("date")
'Mon, 09 Apr 2001 16:27:32 GMT'
>>> h.getdate("date") # easy to use with time module
```

```
(2001, 4, 9, 16, 27, 32, 0, 0, 0)
>>> u.geturl()
'http://www.holdenweb.com'
>>> h.getheader("Content-Encoding") # none this page
>>> h.getheader("Content-Type")
'text/html'
```

If what you require is a local copy of the remote resource, urllib contains a function you can use to achieve this.

Fn, h = urllib.urlretrieve(url, filename=None, hook=None, data=None)

Copies the network resource referred to by url into a local file, if necessary. It will not be necessary if the url argument uses the file: scheme, or if the module has cached the resource.

Returns the tuple (*filename, headers*), where *filename* is the local filename in which the content is stored, and *headers* is *None* if the resource is local or the value returned by the *info()* method otherwise.

If the *filename* argument is absent, then a unique name will be generated for the local copy. If the hook argument is given, then it should be a function, which will be called when the transfer connection is established and after each block is read. The arguments to the call will be a count of blocks transferred so far, a block size in bytes, and the total size of the file (or −1 if the size cannot be established).

The usage of the data argument is the same as for urlopen().

A number of utility functions are also provided, which you can use to ensure that your URLs and data arguments are correctly encoded for network use.

---

quote(string, safe="/")   quote_plus(string, safe="/")

Returns the string argument with special characters replaced by appropriate "%xx" hexadecimal escape sequences (and, in the case of quote_plus, with spaces replaced by plus signs). If the safe argument is given, it should be a string containing characters that should not be quoted.

---

unquote(string)   unquote_plus(string)

Returns the string argument with "%xx" escape sequences replaced by the characters they encode (and, in the case of unquote_plus, with plus signs replaced by spaces).

---

urlencode(dict)

Returns a "URL-encoded" string suitable for use as a data argument to urlopen() or urlretrieve(). The string returned contains an ampersand-separated list of key=value strings for each key/value pair in the dict argument. Both key and value will be encoded by quote_plus() to ensure correct decoding at the web server.

You now have at your disposal everything you need to be able to submit queries to web sites and retrieve the HTML results. Displaying the results is often best left to a browser, of course. You may, however, want to analyze the resulting HTML yourself, and you will learn how to do that in the next section, "Parsing the Received HTML." For now, take a look at the HTML code in Listing 5.22, which is extracted from the web resource `http://www.newriders.com/` (the home page of this book's publisher). Figure 5.4 shows the form's appearance in the browser window.

Listing 5.22   **Search Form HTML Code from the New Riders Home Page**

```
 1 <FORM action="/search/results.cfm" method=post>
 2 <font size="3" face="arial">
 3 site search
 4 </font>
 5 <br>
 6 <INPUT name="criteria" size="13">
 7 <br>
 8 <input type="hidden" name="MaxRows" value="20">
 9 <input type="hidden" name="StartRow" value="1">
10 <input type="image" border="0" src="/images/buttons/search_go.gif">
11 </FORM>
```

Figure 5.4   The New Riders home page, including search form.

This form allows you to enter search terms. The page that processes the input from the form searches the publication's database and returns a page of HTML showing any

books matching the search term(s) you entered. When you enter **COM** in the criteria
input field and click on the GO button, the following data is transmitted in an HTTP
request:

```
criteria=COM&MaxRows=20&StartRow=1&x=10&y=13
```

The values for x and y are the pixel coordinates of the mouse-hit in the unnamed
button image input and are not necessary for the operation of the search script. It is
therefore relatively easy to write code that searches the New Riders site for books
about COM:

```
>>> import urllib
>>> u = urllib.urlopen("http://www.newriders.com/search/results.cfm",
...     "criteria=COM&MaxRows=20&StartRow=1")
>>> f = open("C:/Temp/searchout.htm", "w")
>>> f.write(u.read())
>>> f.close()
```

You would want to apply the `urlencode()` function to the form data had you
accepted it as user input rather than typing it directly into an interactive session. This
code creates a file containing the server's HTML response which, when loaded in a
browser window, looks like Figure 5.5.

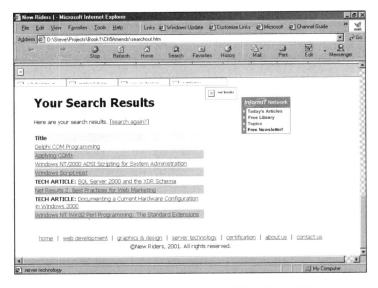

Figure 5.5   Search results displayed from local disk.

The graphics in the page are all broken links because the content has been loaded
from local disk and the URLs defining the graphics are relative to the Internet site's
root, but you can clearly see that the search output has been successfully captured. In

the next section, you will learn some of the options for dealing with HTML content in a more intelligent way.

You also may be interested to know that urllib contains ways to extend the capabilities of the existing module—although the techniques are not the most elegant. You rebind the module's _urlopener variable to a subclass of the classes used by urlopen() and urlretrieve() to open URLs. You can consider those beyond the scope of this text, however. A much more extensible urllib2 library was introduced with release 2.1, but urllib continues to be available, and is by far the simplest way to interact with web servers.

Parsing the Received HTML: *htmllib* and *sgmllib*

Now that you know how to retrieve data from a web server, you are probably wondering how it is possible to extract portions of the retrieved data for use in other programs. The htmllib and sgmllib modules provide these facilities.

The support for HTML is not complete: the library documentation claims, "It supports all entity names required by the HTML 2.0 specification (RFC 1866). It also defines handlers for all HTML 2.0 and many HTML 3.0 and 3.2 elements." Because the current specification is HTML 4.01, and the XHTML specification also has been released, this may not be good enough for your requirements, particularly since the parser does not handle table elements. You will learn one way to fix this shortly.

HTML, however, is really just one application of a much more comprehensive language called SGML, the Standard Generalized Markup Language. If the web output you have to deal with is more complex than htmllib can handle, you can always fall back to treating it as SGML with sgmllib. The structure of the SGML and HTML parsers is similar—the latter simply extends the former, with predefined methods for the tags encountered in HTML.

The principal object offered by these two libraries is a *parser*, which is fed with data by calling its feed() method as many times as you want with successive portions of the source as the argument to the calls. The parser responds to these calls by analyzing the source and calling other methods. The methods called depend on the types of tag the parser encounters in the source.

Using *htmllib*

You use the module by creating a parser object (an instance of class htmllib.HTMLParser). When you create this object, you must provide a formatter object. The formatters use a writer object to create output. A formatter library module contains a couple of ready-made formatters and writers you can use.

HTML tags such as <P>, which have no corresponding closing tag, will trigger a call on a *tag method* of the parser whose method name begins with do_—in this particular case, the do_p() method would be called. Tags that come in opening and closing pairs will result in the parser calling a starting tag method when the opening tag is encountered and an ending tag method for the closing tag. In the case of the `<H1>` tag, for example, the methods called would be `start_h1()` and `end_h1()`, respectively.

By default, if no method is defined for a particular tag, then no error is generated. This means that you can process HTML streams containing illegal or nonhandled tags without having to patch up the code. However, it also means that text surrounded by unknown tags will be processed as though it were untagged. You may therefore want to use fairly aggressive tag checks, at least as an option when puzzling output appears.

The tag methods of the parser provided in `htmllib` make appropriate calls to methods of the formatter provided when the parser was created. The formatter methods in turn call writer methods to produce output. If you are more interested in handling the structure of the document than in seeing it (for which it is usually easier to use a browser anyway), then use no argument when you create your parser. It will then use `formatter.NullFormatter`, which never calls any writer methods, and therefore produces no output.

Listing 5.23 shows a simple HTML parser that accepts up to two command-line arguments. An optional first argument of `-s` causes it to use the null formatter. Otherwise, it will use an `AbstractFormatter` driving a `DumbWriter`, which produces simple text output wrapped at 72 characters per line. The second argument is the URL whose content is to be scanned.

Listing 5.23 *webparse.py:* **Parsing the HTML of a Web Page**

```
 1  import htmllib, urllib, formatter, sys
 2
 3  def Usage():
 4      print """
 5  Usage: python webparse.py [-s] URL
 6  """
 7
 8  def parse(url, formatter):
 9      f = urllib.urlopen(url)
10      data = f.read()
11      f.close()
12      p = htmllib.HTMLParser(formatter)
13      p.feed(data)
14      p.close()
15
16  if len(sys.argv) < 2:
17      Usage()
18  else:
19      if sys.argv[1] == "-s":
20          fmt  = formatter.NullFormatter()
21          del sys.argv[1]
22      else:
23          fmt = formatter.AbstractFormatter(
24                  formatter.DumbWriter(sys.stdout))
25      parse(sys.argv[1], fmt)
```

The `parse()` function starting on line 8 is the core of this program. It opens the URL passed in as its `url` argument and reads all the output in to the `data` variable. It then creates an `HTMLParser` using whichever `formatter` was passed in as its formatter argument, feeds all the data in to the parser, and closes it. When this program is called with the command line

```
python webparse.py -s http://www.holdenweb.com/
```

it produces no output. When the `-s` option is removed, the output is essentially the text of my home page, as shown in Listing 5.24.

Listing 5.24 **Partial Output from** *webparse.py http://www.holdenweb.com/*

```
P {font-family:'Arial', 'Helvetica', 'sans-serif'; font-size: 8pt}

Steve
Holden

My good friend Steve Hughes took this picture while we were setting up
classrooms. Thanks, Steve! Click here if you'd like to animate this
graphic[1]

Making Web Sites Work to Communicate

My main professional focus is building web sites with programming behind
them. I try to avoid the "code bloat" of automatic generators such as
FrontPage and NetObjects Fusion. I am currently doing a lot of work with
the Python[2] programming language. You can find my public domain Python
code[3] here.

etc ...
```

The first line shows that the parser does not understand style tags: this output came from a section early in the web page that reads

```
<STYLE>
P {font-family:'Arial', 'Helvetica', 'sans-serif'; font-size: 8pt}
</STYLE>
```

It would have been better if the text had not been treated as printable! Also note in the output in Listing 5.24 there are numbers in brackets. Each of these represents an anchor tag (hypertext link) in the original page. The parser's default `<A>` tag processing method calls another method, which adds the URL to a list maintained for the whole page and adds its number to the output stream.

Subclassing the *HTMLParser*

The `do_*()`, `start_*()`, and `end_*()` tag methods provided by the default parser are mostly simplistic, which is good because you can override them easily in your own parser subclass. When the parser calls the `do_*()` and `start_*()` methods, it passes a list of tuples, containing the attributes of the tag, as an argument. The first tuple elements are the names of the attributes, and the second elements are the given attribute values.

You easily can create a parser subclass to demonstrate this, overriding the tag methods from the base `HTMLParser`, and even handle tags not currently handled by the library by adding new methods. As an example, suppose that you wanted to see the table structure of a page more clearly. You can use the standard `HTMLParser` writing the to the `NullFormatter` to parse the HTML without producing output.

To make your parser process the `<table>` ... `</table>` tags, you will need to define `start_table()` and `end_table()` methods. Because tables can be nested, you need to have the tag methods keep track of the nesting level. A simple program to do this, and also show only the `width` and `cellspacing` attributes of each table, is given in Listing 5.25.

Listing 5.25 *showtbls.py:* **List the Table Structure of a Web Page**

```
1   import htmllib, urllib, formatter, sys
2
3   def Usage():
4       print """
5   Usage: python showtbls.py URL
6   """
7
8   class myHTMLParser(htmllib.HTMLParser):
9
10      def __init__(self, f):
11          htmllib.HTMLParser.__init__(self, f)
12          self.tblindent = 0
13
14      def start_table(self, attrs):
15          sys.stdout.write("%s<table" % ("    " * self.tblindent, ))
16          for k, v in attrs:
17              if k in ("width", "cellspacing"):
18                  sys.stdout.write(' %s="%s"' % (k, v),)
19          print ">"
20          self.tblindent += 1
21
22      def end_table(self):
23          self.tblindent -= 1
24          print "%s</table>" % ("    " * self.tblindent, )
25
26  def parse(url, formatter):
27      f = urllib.urlopen(url)
28      data = f.read()
29      f.close()
30      p = myHTMLParser(formatter)
31      p.feed(data)
32      p.close()
```

```
33
34  if len(sys.argv) != 2:
35      Usage()
36  else:
37      fmt  = formatter.NullFormatter()
38      parse(sys.argv[1], fmt)
```

The major difference between showtbls.py and webparse.py is that a parser subclass is declared on lines 8 through 24. The __init__() method for this class simply extends the standard parser's __init__() by setting a table indent variable to zero.

When a <table> tag is encountered, the start_table() method at line 14 is called. This prints out a summary of the table tag at the current indentation level, processing the attributes but only taking action when one of interest is detected. The method terminates after incrementing the indentation level, so nested tables will be indented further. When a </table> tag is processed, the end_table() method is called. It decrements the indentation level and prints a closing tag.

The remainder of the code is similar to that for webparse.py but simpler because there is no need to select a particular formatter depending on an optional argument.

When showtbls.py is run on my home page, it prints the following structural analysis.

```
<table cellspacing="2" width="595">
    <table width="100%" cellspacing="5">
    </table>
</table>
<table>
</table>
```

You can see that, true to my philosophy of minimizing HTML "code bloat," I have tried to keep the structure of my page simple. The program gives a more comprehensive output for a more complex page, such as that at http://www.cnet.com/, for example. (At the time of writing, CNet was using a complex page structure with tables nested to several levels.)

Example: Crawling a Web Site

To round off the chapter, here is an annotated copy of spider.py, a simple program that crawls the web from a URL, reading the web page and following the links in that page to other pages, and so on. The code has several limitations, so if you want a more complete job, take a look at the webchecker.py program in the Tools directory of your Python distribution. spider.py is complex enough to give you more ideas about how you might use htmllib, though. Also remember that the code is written for clarity rather than efficiency, so you may well be able to spot better ways to achieve the same ends. Use the robotparser module to only crawl the areas so designated by the site management.

```
1  import htmllib
2  from urllib import basejoin
3
```

The `basejoin()` function from `urllib` is used to apply defaults to incomplete URLs.

```
4  MAXDIST = 3
5
```

This global variable is used to stop the spider from crawling forever. It will stop checking pages when it has followed this many links from the URL it was started at.

```
6  class myHTMLParser(htmllib.HTMLParser):
7      """Modified to return URL references as a list after parsing."""
8
```

The major modification in this particular parser is to post-process the information the standard `HTMLParser` collects from the anchor tags it finds in the HTML. These are collected in a list during HTML processing. When the page scan is complete, the list is split into "interesting" and "uninteresting" links; the interesting ones are within the site whose base URL is given as an argument to the program.

```
9      def __init__(self, formatter, URL, site):
10         htmllib.HTMLParser.__init__(self, formatter)
11         self.rootURL = basejoin("http://",URL)
12         self.URLstore = [self.rootURL]
13         self.ignored = []
14         self.site = site
15
```

Initialization starts by calling the parser's standard `__init__()` method. A number of instance variables are then bound. `rootURL` is forced to use the `http:` scheme if it does not already, and a list of URLs is initialized with that. `ignored` will be a list of uninteresting URLs, and `site` is the URL used to start the scan.

```
16     def build_hrefs(self):
17         """Build the list of unique references from the anchor list."""
18         # XXX need to treat http://hostname
19         #     and http://hostname/ as equivalent;
20         #     should also process "." and ".."
21         if self.base is None:
22             base = self.rootURL
23         else:
24             base = basejoin(self.rootURL, self.base)
25         for href in self.anchorlist:
26             ref = basejoin(base,href)
27             if ref.startswith(self.site):
28                 if ref not in self.URLstore:
29                     self.URLstore.append(ref)
30             else:
31                 if ref not in self.ignored:
32                     self.ignored.append(ref)
33
```

The `build_hrefs()` method is used when the HTML has been processed. By this time, the parser has set its base instance variable if a `<BASE>` tag has been seen. This tag sets the default portions for relative URLs encountered within the HTML. If no `<BASE>` tag was found, then the URL base is the URL of the page being scanned.

The loop at line 25 scans the list of hypertext references, at line 26 turning relative links into absolute ones. If the link is inside the site, then it will start with the site URL, and in that case, it is added to the interesting links in `URLstore`. Otherwise, it is added to the uninteresting links list in `ignored`.

```
34      def close(self):
35          """Terminate parse and return unique URL list."""
36          htmllib.HTMLParser.close(self)
37          self.build_hrefs()
38          return self.URLstore, self.ignored
39
```

When the parser is closed (indicating all input has been received), it calls the `close()` method of the standard parser to ensure that everything is correctly shut down and fully processed. It then builds the lists of interesting and uninteresting links and returns those two lists to its caller as a tuple.

```
40  class Link:
41      """Stores information about a URL discovered by web crawling.
42
43      distance specifies number of hops from the root page.
44      good indicates whether the page is available.
45      refs is a list of URLs which refer to this page.
46
47      """
```

The `Link` object is used to store interesting links. One feature of the object that the current code does not take advantage of is storing a list of referring pages in the `refs` instance variable.

```
48      def __init__(self,distance):
49          self.good= None;
50          self.distance = distance
51          self.refs = []
52
```

The `__init__()` method simply initializes the instance variables.

```
53      def addref(self, ref):
54          self.refs.append(ref)
55
```

The `addref()` method simply accumulates references to this page. No attempt is made to avoid storing duplicates. This feature could easily (if inefficiently) be added by testing for the presence of the reference in the existing list, but the calling code is reasonably careful to ensure that this is not necessary.

```
56      def setgood(self):
57              self.good = 1
58
```

Links are initialized as bad. After they have been successfully accessed, this method is used to show that they are in fact acceptable.

```
59  def CheckPresent(URL):
60      """Returns true if a page can be opened.
61      Only used at distance limit."""
62      try:
63          f = urllib.open(URL)
64          f.close()
65          return 1
66      except:
67          return 0
68
```

When the spider reaches its distance limit, the CheckPresent() function is used to verify that links in the "edge" pages are not broken.

```
69  def check(site):
70      """Checks a whole site from a base URL."""
71      import sys, formatter, urllib
72
```

The check() function is effectively the main portion of the program, the glue logic used to connect all the other parts together.

```
73      # initialize links and visited lists
74      known={site: Link(0)}
75      pages=[[site]]
76
```

It starts by building a dictionary of known links, which initially contains only the site URL the program is being asked to check. The pages list contains a separate entry for each distance and starts out with only the element for distance zero in it. This is naturally enough a link containing only the root page. As links are found in successive pages, they will be added to the list at the appropriate distance. Because this is the root page, its distance is set to zero.

```
77      fmt = formatter.NullFormatter()
78
```

Because the code analyzes web pages instead of printing them, this code uses the null formatter and produces no output during its page scans.

```
79      ignored = []
80      distance = 1
```

The list of ignored links is initially empty, and the distance of the pages about to be scanned is one greater than that of the root page.

```
81          while distance < MAXDIST:
82              pages.append([])
```

The function loops, checking links to increasingly distant pages, until it reaches as far away from the root as it may go. Although in this implementation MAXDIST is a global variable, it could easily be made a program argument. A new element is added to the pages list to store the new links, which will be found in the pages at the previous distance.

```
83              for URL in pages[distance-1]:
84                  try:
85                      f = urllib.urlopen(URL)
86                      data = f.read()
87                      f.close()
88
```

The function then loops over all the URLs from the previous distance. It tries to open each (if it cannot, then the URL will be marked bad by default, and an error will be reported by the exception-handling code further down).

```
89                      p = myHTMLParser(fmt, URL, site)
90                      p.feed(data)
91                      links, rubbish = p.close()
92                      known[URL].setgood()
93
```

The parser is then created and called on the page content, and the sets of interesting and uninteresting links are extracted from the close() method. Because the page was read and the parse completed without any exceptions, the Link object for this URL is tagged as a good link in the known dictionary.

```
94                      for r in links:
95                          if not known.has_key(r):
96                              pages[distance].append(r)
97                              known[r] = Link(distance)
98                          known[r].addref(URL)
99
```

Next, the interesting links are scanned. If a link is already known, then either it has been scanned or it is due to be scanned because it has already been encountered. Otherwise, it is added to the pages list of pages found at the current distance, and a Link is created as the known entry, with the current URL as the *referrer*.

```
100                     for r in rubbish:
101                         if not r in ignored:
102                             ignored.append(r)
103
```

A simple technique is used to keep track of ignored links. This probably will not be terribly interesting for most sites. This is one of those parts of the code where efficiency could be improved by using a dictionary rather than a list.

```
104                    except IOError, msg:
105                        print "Error:", URL, ":", msg
106
```

If an exception occurs during reading of the page, then it is recorded here. The exception handling is probably the weakest part of this program, but in practice few exceptions have occurred in some large site scans. Any uncaught exceptions would, therefore, really be exceptional.

```
107              print "Round", distance, len(pages[distance]), "outstanding"
108
```

A summary is printed at the end of the iteration, so you can check on progress as the distance increases. It is interesting to see how the number of unprocessed pages varies with distance from a site's root URL.

```
109              distance = distance+1
110
```

Finally the distance is increased, and the next iteration starts to scan new links found in the previous iteration.

```
111        for URL in pages[distance-1]:
112            if CheckPresent(URL):
113                known[URL].setgood()
114
```

When the program reaches its distance limit, iteration ceases. It makes a final check on pages not so far scanned. If they are accessible, it tags them as good.

```
115        # XXX Need more intelligent sorting and output options here
116
117        ignored.sort()
118        for r in ignored:
119            print "Ignored:", r
120
121        print "\n\n\n"
122
```

The list of uninteresting links is sorted and printed. This code also could easily be omitted if this information is really not of interest.

```
123        reflist = known.keys()
124        reflist.sort()
125        for k in reflist:
126            kk = known[k]
127            print "%3d : %s" % (kk.distance, k)
128 #          for l in kk.refs:
129 #          print "  <== %s" % l
130
```

Finally the list of known URLs is generated: this is simply the set of keys of the known dictionary. After sorting, it is used to access the information about the link. As you can see, the code to print out the list of referrers is commented out. For most sites this will be too voluminous.

```
131   import sys
132   if len(sys.argv) == 1:
133       check("http://www.python.org/")
134   else:
135       check(sys.argv[1])
```

By default, the program checks our favorite web site. Otherwise, it checks whatever you tell it to on the command line.

Summary

In this chapter, you have seen the variety and flexibility of the Python client-side libraries and learned how to handle a variety of protocols and data formats with little coding. This can surprise programmers who have worked in Java, C, or C++.

You should, if you have been working even a few of the examples, be confident in your ability to write client-side code in Python. There are many areas in which your knowledge can be expanded by a small amount of reading in the Python documentation.

So now we are going to move on and take a look at the server side.

6

A Server Framework Library

WHAT DOES THE SERVER HAVE TO do to make sure that it finds out when a connection or service request arrives, and what needs to happen then to make sure that the request receives proper service? A client requests a network service by connecting to a particular port at a particular IP address. How can you offer service on particular network ports? These are some of the questions that this chapter answers.

Server Structures

First, remember that to listen for connections, the server program calls `bind()` to bind the socket to a port number on one, more, or all IP addresses of the host it runs on. Each incoming TCP connection creates a new socket connected to the client process that initiated the connection. Each incoming UDP request returns the datagram contents and a return address.

A TCP server, then, indicates its willingness to accept incoming traffic by issuing a `listen()` call on its socket. When the `listen()` call succeeds, the server then uses the `accept()` call to retrieve a new socket it can use to talk to the connected client process using `send()` and `recv()`. A UDP server, after it has bound its socket, simply issues a `recvfrom()` call, which returns data when incoming UDP datagrams arrive addressed to its port. The reply uses one or more `sendto()` calls to the source address of the incoming datagrams. The process of handling requests is largely separate from the communication process, and the core Python library contains modules designed to provide useful frameworks for creating servers.

Synchronous Services

The `SocketServer` module you use in this chapter is the basis for a whole range of services, both connectionless and connection-oriented. If service is fast and does not require extended resources that might pause the server process, the server can handle requests as they arrive. In the event of congestion, more clients see rejected connections because of limits in the transport layer's queuing capacity.

The server responds to requests by creating a *request handler* object of a type you specify. After the request handler's `__init__()` method returns, the server goes back to servicing the next request. `SocketServer` comes with HTTP service layer components offering both `GET` and `POST` protocol method processing, with ordinary file service and CGI scripting capabilities. It is therefore of prime interest to you.

Asynchronous Services

In Chapter 7, "Asynchronous Services," you will see how, using `SocketServer`, each request or connection can trigger the creation of a new process or Python thread in which the request-handling code runs. When service is more long-drawn-out (think of a Telnet login session, for example), then it makes sense to use these `SocketServer` features. This frees the server process or thread to go back and start handling another incoming connection or service request concurrently. At the expense of a certain amount of additional overhead, your servers will be able to handle greater loads by servicing multiple simultaneous TCP connections.

The `asyncore/asynchat` modules take a different approach to providing network services. This TCP framework treats each active connection as a *channel* whose methods the server calls when events occur at the network interface. Python's `socket` module makes it easy for the process to sleep when no network events are outstanding, giving a single-process server that handles service requests efficiently. These modules are the basis of a high-performance server architecture, which again provides HTTP service (although in this case CGI services are absent).

SocketServer Libraries

You have already seen that the core Python library has a wonderful range of modules to help you handle client-side functions. In this chapter, you will learn that the library also provides a server framework, which makes it just as simple to build network servers. The server framework uses network sockets.

All you have to do is add suitable components to handle the requests coming in from the clients. The basic framework is synchronous, serving one request at a time. After you understand how to implement network services, you can extend them relatively easily using additional features of the library.

Connectionless Versus Connection-Oriented Servers

You may remember from Chapter 4, "Client/Server Concepts," which started Part II, "Network Programming in Python," that you have a choice of transport layer protocol. UDP is simple but does not provide reliability, whereas TCP (which does) is more complicated and makes virtual circuit connections between the client and the server processes. In this section, we examine the differences in structure for the two protocols from a programming point of view.

The SocketServer library provides both TCPServer and UDPServer classes, and both offer a similar framework for writing the server program. UDP-based services normally are much simpler than TCP-based ones, and mostly involve the client sending a single message to the server and receiving a single reply from it. This type of interaction is ideally suited to the SocketServer model because serving one request is a limited operation, easily encapsulated as a method definition.

Some TCP services use a similar interaction model—a typical and notable example being HTTP protocol interactions between web browsers and servers. Originally, each browser request established a separate TCP connection to the server. Since the introduction of Keep-Alive: headers and HTTP 1.1, however, the client has the option of retaining the TCP connection for further interactions with the server. A sequence of interactions over a socket is not as easy to encapsulate inside a simple method, and such protocols offer more of a challenge to your programming skills.

The server needs to know when the client has transmitted a complete request, and this is not always as easy as you might think. With message-based protocols, it is usually relatively simple to parse the client input from a single datagram and ensure that a whole request has been received. With stream-based, connection-oriented protocols, the question is usually less clear-cut, and it is more probable that the process of obtaining the whole of a request might span a number of recv() calls on the connecting socket.

Writing Servers with the *SocketServer* Module

The SocketServer module tries to simplify creating a network server by standardizing the tasks involved. When you create a server, you pass it a *request handler* class. Each time a new connection arrives, the server framework creates an instance of the request handler class (resulting in a call to its __init__() method). You define your request handler class as a subclass of a prototype class, BaseRequestHandler. The simplest subclass just overrides the handle() method, which is ultimately called to handle the request after the framework performs various housekeeping tasks.

SocketServer is Synchronous

The base classes provided with the SocketServer library are synchronous: they wait for a client request on a particular network port and when it arrives, they create an appropriate RequestHandler object to handle the request. The server does not handle other requests concurrently. If additional client connections arrive while the server is handling a request, they either are queued in the transport layer or, if the permitted queue length is exceeded, rejected at the network interface.

The servers provide two methods to activate the service they implement. Calling the `handle_request()` method has the server service a single request and then terminate. To handle requests one after the other, you call the server's `serve_forever()` method. This is simply an infinite loop, which repeatedly calls the `handle_request()` method. In Chapter 7, you will learn how to extend the basic synchronous framework to improve service scalability and performance.

The Structure of a Synchronous Server

A synchronous server receives a request from the transport layer, serves its result, and loops around for the next request. It relies on the transport layer to queue requests, and because it only serves one request at a time, this places limits on performance and scalability. It is easy to understand, which makes it a good place to start your server-writing experiences.

Define a request handler class (based on `BaseRequestHandler`), create a server to listen on the desired IP address(es) and port number, and call its `handle_request()` or `serve_forever()` method. That is all you need to do. The rest is a matter of adding more complexity to improve performance, and the rule is "first, make it work; then, if it doesn't work fast enough, make it work faster." For simple services, you may well find that a synchronous server provides all you need in the way of performance.

By default, the `TCPServer` and `UDPServer` classes ask the transport layer to handle a queue of five requests. If this is inadequate, you can create simple subclasses that set the value of the `request_queue_size` instance variable to some higher value, although you might find that your transport layer is not prepared to accept long request queues.

Netstrings: Unambiguous Communication of Variable-Length Data

If you are designing your own application protocol, you want to ensure deterministic communication between the client and the server. If you are trying to implement an existing protocol, then you might find it a little trickier and need to provide some way to ensure the receipt of a complete request.

In 1997, D. J. Bernstein (djb@pobox.com) published a description of a way that network components can represent strings so as to make them easy to communicate. The representation of a string for transmission over a network connection is

    Length:<STRING>,

Length is the decimal representation in ASCII of the number of characters in the string. A colon follows the length, then come the bytes comprising the actual string value, and then a terminating comma that serves as a simple check for correct reception.

In this representation, the 12-byte string

```
"hello world!"
```

would actually be transmitted as the 16-byte string

```
"12:hello world!,"
```

Because the length of the string appears at the start of its representation, you can program the socket to read the whole string, even over a network connection that delivers variable-length chunks of data. Further, it is possible to use a set of netstrings as the body of a single netstring and extract the individual netstrings from the transmission. You can find Bernstein's complete description at http://cr.yp.to/proto/netstrings.txt.

Handling TCP and UDP Requests

You probably want to see how you can build a server. Using the `SocketServer` library, it is straightforward. At this stage, you can take some liberties with network communication and assume that a server will receive a small request in one chunk. All you need to do is define a request handler class with an appropriate `handle()` method and pass the class (not an instance) as an argument to the creation of an appropriate server. The server framework creates a request handler automatically for each incoming request.

The simple example shown in Listing 6.1 does just that, serving TCP port 8080. If that port is already in use, you easily can use some other port number. Use a port number greater than 1023 just to be on the safe side—many low-numbered ports are reserved as "well-known ports" for standard services; and, on some operating systems, the system will not allow a user program to serve on such a port, unless the user has appropriate privileges.

Listing 6.1   *server1.py:* **A Simple Server to Capture Single Short Requests**

```
1  import SocketServer
2
3  class MyRequestHandler(SocketServer.BaseRequestHandler):
4      def handle(self):
5          print "--------------------"
6          print "From:", self.client_address
7          print "--------------------"
8          input = self.request.recv(10240)
9          print input.replace('\r', '')
10         print "--------------------"
11         self.request.send("HTTP/1.1 200 OK\r\n")
12         self.request.send("Content-Type: text/html\n\n")
13         self.request.send("<HTML><BODY><H2>Hello!</H2></BODY></HTML>")
14         self.request.close()
15
```

continues

Listing 6.1 **Continued**

```
16  myServer = SocketServer.TCPServer(('', 8080),
17              MyRequestHandler)
18  myServer.handle_request()
```

The class definition starting at line 3 defines a simple subclass of `BaseRequestHandler`, whose `handle()` method makes a single large `recv()` call on the `self.request` instance variable. This is where the code takes liberties: in the case of a `TCPServer`, `self.request` is the network socket on which the request arrived, and the code assumes that the whole request will arrive as the result of a single `recv()` call. The provision of a socket is specific to TCP servers. You will see later that UDP handles things differently.

Each time a new connection arrives, the server creates a new `MyRequestHandler` object, whose `handle()` method will be called at the right point in the service process. When the `handle()` method is called, it prints the request to standard output with carriage returns stripped. It then sends an HTTP response back down the socket. This is to make testing easier: you can use a web browser as the client and actually see a result in the browser window.

Line 16 creates a `TCPServer` instance, indicating the network port on which to listen for incoming requests. Because no IP address is given, the server binds to all network addresses. The `TCPServer` call passes in the `MyRequestHandler` class, so the server creates a `MyRequestHandler` instance when a request comes in. Request handlers are slightly unusual classes in that creating the handler (which is to say calling its `__init__()` method) should do everything needed to handle the request as soon as the server creates it. Fortunately, the default `__init__()` method does everything needed to ensure that `handle()` is correctly called. This makes `SocketServer` over-complex for simple test cases like Listing 6.1 but also allows you to encapsulate a long-term interactive client/server session within an object instance. If you examine the server class code in the library, you will see that `BaseRequestHandler` does indeed trigger all necessary actions from its `__init__()` method. This feature becomes more valuable as you move up to asynchronous services: it allows the server to create several request handlers concurrently.

Line 18 tells the server to handle a single request, after which the program stops. You can test this module easily. Run the server in a command window and then use your web browser on the same computer to navigate to

`http://127.0.0.1:8080/try/this/for/size.html`

If you have another computer, you can test the server from that too, using a URL with the server's external IP address instead of the loopback address. Obviously, the port number in the URL should agree with the port number in your server code! You should see a browser window similar to Figure 6.1, and the output you see from the server should look something like the following:

```
---------------------
From: ('127.0.0.1', 1226)
---------------------
GET /try/this/for/size.html HTTP/1.1
Accept: */*
Accept-Language: en-us
Accept-Encoding: gzip, deflate
User-Agent: Mozilla/4.0 (compatible; MSIE 5.5; MSNIA; Windows 98)
Host: 127.0.0.1:8080
Connection: Keep-Alive


---------------------
```

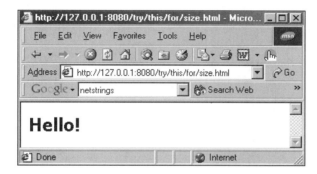

Figure 6.1   Internet Explorer displays the HTTP response.

See whether you can run the command

```
netstat -an
```

on the server host while the server is running (it may not be available, or you may not have permission to run it). Your server should be listed among the current network sockets, represented by a line that reads (depending on your platform) something like

```
TCP     0.0.0.0:8080          0.0.0.0:0                    LISTENING
```

The console output from the server displays the address and port number of the other end of the socket and the HTTP GET request details. You can see that the browser has included the path from the URL as the URI in the first line and that this particular test ran on Internet Explorer 5.5 on a Windows 98 computer. If this does nothing else, it should convince you that building a simple server does not require that you write much code.

Of course, the server is indeed simple. It serves a single request and then terminates, so if you tell your browser to reload the URL, it will spin its wheels for a while and then announce that it sees no response from the server. If you replace the call to handle_request() with a call to serve_forever(), you should be able to reload without any trouble. If you feel confident, you can modify the code to send a different HTML output back to the browser. You are writing web servers!

A Module to Handle Netstrings

The code in Listing 6.1 is all very well, but it does rely on receiving the whole browser request in one chunk. Netstrings, mentioned previously, are a useful way of transmitting content so that the receiver can be sure that it has the whole string. Listing 6.2 shows a netstring module, which you can use in your client and server code.

Listing 6.2   *netstring.py:* **A Module for Handling Netstrings**

```
1  def readns(sock):
2      """read a netstring from a socket."""
3      size = ""
4      while 1:
5          c = sock.recv(1)
6          if c == ":":
7              break
8          elif not c:
9              raise IOError, "short netstring read"
10         size = size + c
11     size = sz = int(size)
12     s = ""
13     while sz:
14         ss = sock.recv(sz)
15         if not ss:
16             raise IOError, "short netstring read"
17         s += ss
18         sz -= len(ss)
19     if len(s) != size:
20         raise IOError, "short netstring read"
21     if sock.recv(1) != ",":
22         raise IOError, "missing netstring terminator"
23     return s
24
25  def writens(sock, s):
26      """write a netstring to a socket."""
27      s = encode(s)
28      while len(s):
29          l = sock.send(s)
30          s = s[l:]
31
32  def encode(s):
33      return "%d:%s," % (len(s), s)
34
35  def decode(s):
36      try:
37          if s[-1] != ",":
```

```
38        raise ValueError
39      p = s.index(":")
40      l = int(s[0:p])
41      if len(s) != p + l + 2:
42        raise ValueError
43      return s[p+1:-1]
44    except ValueError:
45      raise ValueError, "netstring format error: " + s
```

The readns() function is careful to ensure, even if a netstring is broken into several segments received separately, that the string reconstruction will be correct. The loop starting at line 4 builds the length of the string, which is bound to both sz and size in line 11. The sz variable is used as an upper limit on the number of bytes to be received and is used to control the receive loop at line 13, which raises an exception if the socket is closed early. Line 19 is a sanity check, and line 21 ensures that the final comma is present to terminate the string.

The writens() function also handles the case where it is not able to pass all the bytes to the transport layer at the same time (although most modern transport layers can handle large segments). After testing with 1-megabyte netstrings, the code seems to be robust.

The encode() function was split out to make it easy to build netstrings containing other netstrings, and decode() does as much checking as is feasible to make sure that it really is dealing with a netstring, raising an exception message if any of the checks fail. Note that the index() function call on line 39 also raises a ValueError, caught by the except clause at the end of the routine, if it does not find a colon.

A Netstring-Based Persistent Server

You will see in the upcoming section "The *SimpleHTTPServer* Module" that a special library module provides many of the features required in an HTTP server. There is little point developing your own code to parse HTTP requests. That module already includes such code, and so knows when it is in possession of a complete request.

Listing 6.3, however, shows a server that uses the netstring module. It differs from the one in Listing 6.1 because each connection to the server engages in an extended dialog with the client, returning the uppercase value of each string the client sends to it until the client requests termination.

Listing 6.3   *server2.py:* **A Persistent Uppercase Server Using TCP**

```
1    import SocketServer
2    import netstring
3
4    class MyRequestHandler(SocketServer.BaseRequestHandler):
5      def handle(self):
6          print "----------------------"
```

continues

Listing 6.3   **Continued**

```
 7          print "From:", self.client_address
 8          print "--------------------"
 9          while 1:
10              rq = netstring.readns(self.request)
11              print rq
12              netstring.writens(self.request, rq.upper())
13              if rq.lower() == "end":
14                  break
15
16  myServer = SocketServer.TCPServer(('', 8081),
17                  MyRequestHandler)
18  myServer.handle_request()
```

Listing 6.4 shows a complementary client program. This client simply reads strings from the user, sends them to the server, and prints the reply on standard output. When the user presses Return, the program sends the termination request and then closes its socket.

Listing 6.4   *client2.py:* **An Uppercase Client Using TCP**

```
 1  import socket
 2  import netstring
 3
 4  s = socket.socket(socket.AF_INET, socket.SOCK_STREAM)
 5  s.connect(('127.0.0.1', 8081))
 6  while 1:
 7      arg = raw_input("Send: ")
 8      if not arg:
 9          netstring.writens(s, "end")
10          break
11      netstring.writens(s, arg)
12      ret = netstring.readns(s)
13      print "Returned:", ret
14  s.close()
```

This seems like a lot of work just to convert strings into uppercase. It does represent a good first introduction to writing server processes in Python, and the server could easily do more than simply translate its input into uppercase. Think of it as a framework, into which you can plug your own server function.

You easily can see the synchronous nature of this service by trying to connect with a second client during the dialog with a first client. You should find that the connection request is accepted, but then nothing happens until the first client terminates its session. That is because the server does not check its socket for new connections until after the handle() method (and hence the request handler __init__() method) is terminated.

It also exposes one of the problems of protocol design: the client is designed to detect the end of the dialog by an empty input and pass the indication to the server by sending a "sentinel" value. Unfortunately, you will find that the client sends exactly the same sequence if the user types in the word "end" as input. The client will then experience a failure on its next attempt to use the socket because by that time the server will have closed its end of the connection.

A UDP Server Based on Netstrings

The framework so far, although adequate for use with the TCP transport layer, will not work if you simply replace TCPServer with UDPServer in the server program and use a SOCK_DGRAM socket on the client. For datagram services, the server hands a tuple comprising the received string and an output socket to the request handler, rather than a socket. Tuples do not have send() and recv() methods (which should not be used on UDP sockets anyway).

Furthermore, with UDP there is no concept of a connection, so the server has to be listening for the client requests, and the client has to listen for the server responses. You can see a UDP version of the server developed so far in Listing 6.5.

Listing 6.5   *server3.py:* **A UDP Uppercase Server**

```
1   import SocketServer
2   import netstring
3   import sys
4
5   class MyRequestHandler(SocketServer.BaseRequestHandler):
6       def handle(self):
7           global Done
8           request, socket = self.request
9           rq = netstring.decode(request)
10          print "From:", self.client_address, ":", rq
11          print "---------------------"
12          sys.stdout.flush()
13          result = netstring.encode(rq.upper())
14          if result == "END":
15              Done = 1
16              return
17          socket.sendto(result, self.client_address)
18
19  myServer = SocketServer.UDPServer(('', 8081),
20                  MyRequestHandler)
21  Done = None
22  while not Done:
23      myServer.handle_request()
```

You will notice in the MyRequestHandler class definition that the handle() method uses a global flag called Done to indicate when it has received a termination request from a client. This would not normally be a feature of a UDP server: servers normally terminate only under instruction from the system manager. The `handle()` method receives a request tuple, and line 8 binds the components to separate variables. The `request` variable holds the string received from the client, and the `socket` variable is the server's socket, which the handler can use to reply to the client. After decoding and displaying the request (and flushing the standard output stream to make sure that it is seen even if the server is killed), the handler checks for the special sentinel value. It sets the `Done` flag and exits if it finds the sentinel value; otherwise, it encodes the result as a netstring and shoots it back to the client on the socket that the server provided as a part of the request.

Line 19 creates a server in just the same way as the previous example, except that this is a `UDPServer`. A loop calls its `handle_request()` method until the `Done` flag is set. In a production server, you would simply call the `serve_forever()` method, but then `handle()` would have no way to terminate the server as a result of client input—any exceptions raised in `handle()` are trapped by the request handler infrastructure. This is sensible: normally you probably would want a production server to continue despite possibly transient errors in request-handling code.

Because there is no connection between the client and the server, it makes no sense for a single request to involve multiple interactions between the client and the server such as the TCP server. There is no easy way to associate successive incoming transmissions with the same client.

A Common Framework for TCP and UDP

The differences in handler class interfaces for different transport layer protocols would make it more complicated than it needs to be to write a server to handle both. Fortunately, the library provides two request handler classes to simplify the job. By choosing the appropriate class for your server and handler at runtime, you can implement the same logic over whichever transport layer the user chooses.

You have to adopt a different interface to the server if you do this: the new classes, `StreamRequestHandler` and `DatagramRequestHandler` provide a uniform interface to the handler through `self.rfile` and `self.wfile` instance attributes. These are filelike objects that you can read and write, respectively. You can see a simple dual-protocol server in Listing 6.6.

Listing 6.6   *server4.py:* **A Dual-Protocol Uppercase Server**

```
1  import SocketServer
2  import sys
3
4  def freadns(f):
5      """read a netstring from a file."""
6      size = ""
7      while 1:
8          c = f.read(1)
```

```
 9              if c == ":":
10                  break
11              elif not c:
12                  raise IOError, "short netstring read"
13              size = size + c
14      size = sz = int(size)
15      s = ""
16      while sz:
17          ss = f.read(sz)
18          if not ss:
19              raise IOError, "short netstring read"
20          s += ss
21          sz -= len(ss)
22      if len(s) != size:
23          raise IOError, "short netstring read"
24      if f.read(1) != ",":
25          raise IOError, "missing netstring terminator"
26      return s
27
28  def fwritens(f, s):
29      """write a netstring to a file."""
30      s = encode(s)
31      f.write(s)
32
33  def encode(s):
34      """return a string's netstring."""
35      return "%d:%s," % (len(s), s)
36
37  handlerClass = SocketServer.StreamRequestHandler
38  serverClass = SocketServer.TCPServer
39  if len(sys.argv) > 1:
40      if sys.argv[1] == "-u":
41          handlerClass = SocketServer.DatagramRequestHandler
42          serverClass = SocketServer.UDPServer
43      elif sys.argv[1] != "-t":
44          sys.exit("Unknown option: "+sys.argv[1])
45
46  class MyRequestHandler(handlerClass):
47      def handle(self):
48          rq = freadns(self.rfile)
49          print "From:", self.client_address, ":", rq
50          print "---------------------"
51          sys.stdout.flush()
52          result = rq.upper()
53          fwritens(self.wfile, result)
54
55  myServer = serverClass(('', 8081),
56                  MyRequestHandler)
57  myServer.serve_forever()
```

Lines 4 through 35 are similar to the code shown in the `nestrings` module in Listing 6.2 but adapted to the file inerface provided by the request handlers. Lines 37 through 44 are simple option processing code. The server can be run with either a -u or a -t option, the latter being the default. According to the option, two variables are bound to the appropriate server class and request handler base class.

Line 46 begins the request handler code and shows how dyamic Python's inheritance mechanisms are. The base class, whose `handle()` method the `MyRequestHandler` class overrides, is chosen according to the option value! Whichever class ends up as the base class for the handler, `MyRequestHandler` ovrrides its `handle()` method to read a string from the client using instance variable `self.rfile` and write its uppercase equivalent back using `self.wfile`. Line 55 instantiates whichever server class the `serverClass` variable is bound to, providing the newly defined handler class to be instantiated when requests are received. At line 57, the server then runs forever.

The client side is a little more complex because there is no socket implementation readily available here to help you unify the code. In the end, it seemed more instructive to use two separate branches to implement the TCP and UDP logic, and this allows you to see them clearly in the same program. Listing 6.7 shows the client program.

Listing 6.7   *client4.py:* **A Dual-Protocol Uppercase Client Program**

```
1  import socket
2  import sys
3  import netstring
4
5  sockType = socket.SOCK_STREAM
6  if len(sys.argv) > 1:
7      if sys.argv[1] == "-u":
8          sockType = socket.SOCK_DGRAM
9      elif sys.argv[1] != "-t":
10         sys.exit("Unknown option: "+sys.argv[1])
11
12 while 1:
13     arg = raw_input("Send: ")
14     if not arg:
15         break
16     s = socket.socket(socket.AF_INET, sockType)
17     if sockType == socket.SOCK_STREAM:
18         addr = ('127.0.0.1', 8081)
19         s.connect(addr)
20         netstring.writens(s, arg)
21         ret = netstring.readns(s)
22     else:
23         s.sendto(netstring.encode(arg), ('127.0.0.1', 8081))
24         ret, addr = s.recvfrom(1024)
25         ret = netstring.decode(ret)
26     print "Address:", addr, "Returned:", ret
27     s.close()
```

As with the server, the client first determines (in lines 5 through 10) from command-line options (if any) which mode to work in, and sets the `sockType` variable accordingly.

A loop starting at line 12 continually reads strings from the user, terminating when the user enters a blank line, and creates sockets of the required type. If the user selected TCP, then the client uses the netstring module. A `connect()` call connects to the server, the `sendns()` function sends the input to the server, and the `readns()` function receives the response. For UDP, a `sendto()` call on the socket sends a netstring containing the user's input to the server, and a `recvfrom()` call receives the response, which the netstring `decode()` function validates.

In both cases, the client program prints the result at line 26 and closes the socket, implying a separate connection for each input when using TCP. The loop then resumes by asking for another input.

SocketServer Summary

The `SocketServer` library is a versatile module. You can implement your own application protocols using either TCP or UDP as the transport layer, and implement the same services over both transport layers relatively easily. If you are designing your own protocols, then netstrings add a useful measure of determinism over a sometimes uncertain transport layer. Handling requests is as easy as defining a subclass of a class defined in the library and overriding its `handle()` method.

You also know that care is needed when designing your own protocols. Try to ensure that the client's transmissions to the server are unambiguous, to avoid loss of synchronization between the two processes. Fortunately, for web systems, the protocol design is fixed and embedded into readily available server modules.

HTTP Server Modules

The first server you saw in this chapter was an HTTP server, albeit a simple one. Although it did not do anything terribly exciting, you probably realized that it could be the basis of a special-purpose web server. Because HTTP is a popular protocol, the library includes three modules especially designed to make the task of building HTTP servers easier. The first module, `BaseHTTPServer`, is not for direct use. It does define the base class for the `SimpleHTTPServer` and `CGIHTTPServer` modules, however, each of which defines a more capable request handler in its own separate module.

The latter two modules both use the server framework established in `BaseHTTPServer`, but each provides its own request handler class. `SimpleHTTPServer` responds only to `GET` and `HEAD` HTTP requests, and treats its working directory as the server root. It will happily follow symbolic links in a UNIX system outside the bounds of the directory subtree, so you should not regard it as secure for production purposes. It does provide a flexible test bed for checking out new ideas, though.

The *SimpleHTTPServer* Module

The server reads the HTTP request and interprets the URI as a path relative to its working directory. If the URI maps to a directory, it tries the following actions in order:

1. If the directory contains an `index.html` file, it serves that file as described after step 3.

2. If it cannot find an `index.html` file, it lists the contents of the directory if it can.

3. Otherwise, it returns an HTTP error (404, no permission to list directory).

If the server cannot read the file to which the URI maps, which typically raises an `IOError` exception, it returns a different HTTP error (404, file not found). Otherwise, the server makes a guess at the type of the file based on its extension and outputs a `Content-Type:` header containing the appropriate MIME type, followed by a blank line, followed by the content of the file, which it reads in binary mode.

The `BaseHTTPServer` module defines the framework for request handling in a `BaseHTTPRequestHandler` class, which is a subclass of `SocketHandler.StreamRequestHandler`. When the `handle()` method receives a request, it calls a `parse_request()` method to validate the incoming HTTP. Assuming that `handle()` detects no errors, it then extracts the HTTP method (`GET`, `PUT`, or whatever) from the request and validates it by checking for an instance method named `do_<method>()`. If `handle()` finds such a method, it calls that method with no arguments. Otherwise, it returns an HTTP error (501, unsupported method).

BaseRequestHandler Methods

The two HTTP server modules you will look at both use the same server object: this is the `HTTPServer` class defined in the `BaseHTTPServer` module. Each server module defines its own request handler. As you might imagine, `BaseHTTPRequestHandler` implements most of the common functionality. Table 6.1 shows a list of its methods with a brief description of what they do.

Table 6.1   *BaseRequestHandler* **Methods**

Method	Description
`address_string(self)`	Returns the client address, formatted for logging.
`date_time_string(self)`	Returns the current date and time, formatted for use in a message header.
`end_headers(self)`	Sends a blank line to terminate the HTTP headers.
`handle(self)`	Looks for a method named `do_XXX()` (where *XXX* is the HTTP method in the request) and calls it or, if no method is found, raises an error.

Method	Description
Log_date_time_string(self)	Returns the current time formatted for logging.
Log_error(self, *args)	Logs an error.
Log_message(self, format, *args)	Logs a message, interpolating `args` into the string provided as the `format`.
Log_request(self, code="-", size="-")	Logs an accepted request.
Parse_request(self)	Splits the HTTP request into several instance variables, validating it in the process.
Send_error(self, code, message=None)	Sends and logs an error reply.
Send_header(self, keyword, value)	Sends an HTTP header of the form `keyword: value`.
Send_response(self, code, message=None)	Sends the response header and logs the response code.
Version_string(self)	Returns a server version string.

You will see that no do_XXX() methods are defined, which means that the base request handler cannot handle any HTTP requests. It provides an exceedingly useful framework, however, for request handlers that do perform useful work.

SimpleHTTPRequestHandler Methods

SimpleHTTPRequestHandler, which has only file serving functionality, extends the base request handler framework. It implements the additional request handling methods found in Table 6.2.

Table 6.2 *SimpleHTTPRequestHandler* **Methods**

Method	Description
copyfile(self, source, outputfile)	Copies the contents of an open file `src` to an open file `outputfile`.
do_GET(self)	Serves an HTTP GET method request.
do_HEAD(self)	Serves an HTTP HEAD method request.
guess_type(self, path)	Guesses the MIME type of a file from its name—the default set of MIME types is defined in the class variable extensions_map, which you can modify or override in a subclass.
list_directory(self)	Produces a directory listing when the URL specifies a directory that does not contain an index.html file.

continues

Table 6.2   **Continued**

Send_head(self)	Sends the HTTP response code and a `Content-Type:` header back to the client.
Translate_path(self, path)	Translates the path from the URI to a path in the local filestore.

The `SimpleHTTPRequestHandler` object therefore has enough functionality to respond to `GET` and `HEAD` HTTP protocol requests, serving the content of a file store just like any other HTTP server. It has no way to handle `POST` HTTP protocol requests because they explicitly require that more be executed, using the CGI interface.

The *CGIHTTPServer* Module

The `CGIHTTPServer` module defines an even more specialized request handler than that defined in `SimpleHTTPServer`. Naturally, rather than reimplement everything the simple server does, it subclasses the request handler from that module so that it starts with all the file-serving capabilities present and correct. To understand more clearly the differences between `CGIHTTPServer` and `SimpleHTTPServer`, you need a little more insight into how a web server interacts with its clients.

The Common Gateway Interface (CGI)

Data are usually communicated to a web script as a result of the user submitting a form. You may remember that submission can use either the `GET` or the `POST` method, and that the browser (or other web client) uses the appropriate HTTP protocol request to transmit the form contents. For a `GET` HTTP protocol request, the parameters to the script are located at the end of the URL, following a question mark. Each parameter is coded as

```
name=value
```

and multiple parameters are separated by ampersand (&) characters. Clearly, this makes it problematic to include ampersands and equal signs (and some other characters) as a part of a parameter value, so an encoding scheme is used. "Troublesome" ASCII characters are encoded as a percent sign followed by two hexadecimal digits representing the ordinal value of the character.

So, for example, the URL

```
http://server/charmap.py?amp=%26&string=hello,%20world
```

should result in the script `charmap.py` being run from the root directory of the server, with the parameter `amp` having the value "&" and the parameter `string` having the value "hello, world."

There is, of course, nothing to stop you from writing URLs yourself that include parameters in this way. When a database is in use, it actually is convenient to do this, as such URLs can be constructed from database content and thereby tailored to the database content. This is also a convenient way of ensuring that the URLs generated in your code contain correct references to database fields.

The POST protocol request, normally preferred for large forms because it does not have GET's restriction on data length, uses a similar encoding scheme but sends the encoded data after the HTTP headers for the request.

The *Common Gateway Interface (CGI)* is a standardized way of having the web server present such data, plus additional information that provides a context to the request, to whatever script ends up running as a result of the request. The value of CGI is that most web servers use this technique, so it is possible to write standard routines that are of use to all web CGI scripts. The CGI standard specifies what information is passed to an executable web method, and there are three categories of such information:

- **CGI environment variables**—The Python web script can access these from the os.environ dictionary. It includes such useful variables as REQUEST_METHOD, whose value will be the HTTP method, such as GET or POST used to make the request, and QUERY_STRING, whose value is the untranslated parameter string that followed the question mark in the URL. The CONTENT_TYPE variable describes how input is encoded, and browsers usually send the contents of a form as type "application/x-www-form-urlencoded."

- **Command-line options**—These are infrequently used nowadays and can be ignored for most practical purposes.

- **Standard input**—This usually will be the contents of a form. By the time the web script executes, the HTTP server will have stripped off the headers and the blank line that follows them (these headers are available as environment variables whose names begin with HTTP).

The standard output of the script should be the HTTP response, including any relevant headers. Your scripts should usually send a Content-Type: header and may provide others. Most servers will add a number of headers to the script's response before forwarding it to the requesting client. Unfortunately you cannot check this with your browser, since it will only show you the HTML source.

Extending the Server to Programmed Requests

Until Python 2.0, the core library offered no way to implement CGI functions on the Windows platform. CGI calls usually require a separate program, possibly in a different language, to be run externally to the server. Because older versions of the module used the fork() library function (only available on UNIX) to create the external process, the library was not portable to Windows. The development team updated the module for Python 2.0 to use `fork()` if it can, but otherwise to use the Windows-compatible `popen2()` if that function is present. If neither of these is available, CGI functionality is limited to Python scripts, which are run inside the server process. This gives about the maximum possible scripting utility.

You might think that because the `CGIRequestHandler` object has to cope with `GET` requests for both files *and* CGI scripts, it would provide its own `do_GET()` method. The architects of the module have had `CGIRequestHandler` inherit the `do_GET()` method from `SimpleHTTPRequestHandler`. That method in turn calls the `send_head()` method, which `CGIRequestHandler` overrides with its own version. If the URL does not identify a CGI script, the CGI version of `send_head()` simply delegates to the `SimpleHTTPServer`'s `send_head()` method. Otherwise, `send_head()` runs the CGI script, as this is the only way to generate the headers. It also means that for CGI scripts, the whole output from the script goes back out to the client, and `send_head()` then returns `None` to indicate to `do_GET()` that there is nothing left to do.

What Extras Are Required?

Table 6.3 shows the methods implemented in `CGIHTTPRequestHandler`, most of which are new. Only `send_head()` overrides the equivalent method in `SimpleHTTPRequestHandler`, as described previously.

Table 6.3 *CGIHTTPRequestHandler* **Methods**

Method	Description
`do_POST(self)`	Checks that a CGI script is being run and, if so, calls the `run_cgi()` method to respond to the request.
`is_cgi(self)`	Tests whether the request path specifies a file in one of the CGI script directories (by default this list is stored in class variable `cgi_directories`).
`is_executable(self, path)`	Uses a module-local `executable()` function and tests whether the script identified by path is an executable file.
`is_python(self, path)`	Tests if `path` identifies a file whose extension is `.py` or `.pyw`.
`run_cgi(self)`	Establishes the correct environment to run a CGI script and uses either `fork()`, `popen2()`, or `execfile()` to run the requested script in a CGI environment. This method is the heart of the request handler.
`send_head(self)`	Described in previous text—sends header and file content for CGI scripts; otherwise, sends header only.

If you are not used to working with object-oriented programming systems, the development of a sequence of increasingly complex and capable servers, starting with SocketServer and running through to CGIHTTPServer is a great example of their power. A BaseHTTPServer is a TCPServer with basic HTTP handling capabilities added to the TCPStreamHandler features. A SimpleHTTPServer is a BaseHTTPServer with a more complex request handler. A CGIHTTPServer is a SimpleHTTPServer with still further extensions to the request handling. With each class inheriting the capabilities of its ancestors, the source of each is comprehensibly small, as Table 6.4 indicates.

Table 6.4   **Lines of Source Code for Server Modules (includes blank lines)**

Module	Total Code Lines	Blanks, Comments, and Docstrings	Code Only
SocketServer.py	447	295	152
BaseHTTPServer.py	482	305	177
SimpleHTTPServer.py	198	92	106
CGIHTTPServer.py	305	95	212

Adding HTTP server capabilities to the socket server roughly doubles the code size. Methods to serve files bring the code total up to 1,000 lines. A further 30-percent increase adds CGI capability. You are dealing with a powerful language here.

Given the 1,300 lines of program text (only 647 of which are true code) to support you, how many more lines of code must you write to actually implement a CGI server? Very few, as you can see from Listing 6.8, which creates an HTTP server using the CGI request handler and then tells it to serve forever. There are five lines of code in all, if you count the continued line as two. If you regard lines of code as a significant measure of program size, you could compress the two import statements into one (import CGIHTTPServer, BaseHTTPServer) and omit the line break in the assignment statement for a 40-percent reduction in size to three lines.

Listing 6.8   *cgiserver.py:* **A CGI-Capable Synchronous Server**

```
1  import CGIHTTPServer
2  import BaseHTTPServer
3  httpd = BaseHTTPServer.HTTPServer(('', 8000),
4              CGIHTTPServer.CGIHTTPRequestHandler)
5  httpd.serve_forever()
```

Testing the CGI Server

This server takes the current directory as its web root. If you have downloaded the material from the book's web site, navigate to the ... /Code/Ch6 directory and run cgiserver.py. Then (on the same machine) direct your browser to

    http://127.0.0.1:8000/

If all is working well, your browser will show you the content of the index.html file from the Ch6 directory. You can examine the code files by clicking on their names, which are hypertext links. Two further links at the bottom of the page refer to CGI scripts. Clicking the topmost of these two should give you a browser window similar to Figure 6.2. You should ensure, by editing as necessary, that the scripts in the cgi-bin directory correctly identify your Python interpreter on their first line.

Figure 6.2 CGI server serves the Chapter 6 home page.

If you click on the bottom link, your output should be similar to Figure 6.3.

Figure 6.3 A CGI script displays the server environment.

Summary

Part of Python's power comes from its object-oriented nature. In this chapter, you saw how this power allows the developers of the language to provide powerful library modules by layering complexity using the inheritance model. When you understand the library modules well, complex functionality is sometimes just a matter of writing a few lines of code.

The server structures you examined in this chapter are all based on the `SocketServer` module. The examples should have helped you understand how you can build your own special-purpose services and given you an idea of the appropriate modules on which to build the functions your services should provide. You also saw the power of inheritance in Python's object-oriented model, as successively more complex servers were defined using subclasses of (and subclasses of subclasses of) `SocketServer` objects. In the next chapter, you will see how to write services that handle requests asynchronously, increasing their versatility still further.

7

Asynchronous Services

Y OU SHOULD NOW HAVE ENOUGH CONFIDENCE to tackle the client/server software environment with some zest. If processes need to communicate with each other, then there is no reason why they should not do so. You have seen that the programming to make them communicate is not black magic. Now you need to think about how multiple requests might interact.

Synchronous Limitations

So far, you have worked with server processes that handle one client at a time. As loads increase, you will find that this becomes less satisfactory: a server cannot start to process a request from a new client until it has completely processed all preceding requests. Given that request handling might involve file transfers, or other activities that cause a substantial amount of idle time during processing, it would be better if several requests could proceed concurrently. The server could use the idle time of one request to process other requests. There are always different approaches to any problem. Overcoming the limitations of synchronous service is no exception.

You could create a separate process to handle each request. This has the advantage that the operating system will create an entirely separate address space for each request handler, minimizing interference between requests. Process creation can be an expensive operation, however, since the operating system needs to perform a lot of preparatory work to set up a new process's operating environment.

Apache and similar web servers take the trouble to spawn child processes in advance to avoid real-time startup overhead. This scales reasonably well until the number of users exceeds the number of processes, after which some requests have to wait.

Alternatively, you could write your server to handle multiple requests on its own inside a single process. This requires some discipline but is likely to reduce the per-request resources considerably. Furthermore, it makes it easier to maintain state information from one request to the next, which is always a problem in web systems where each interaction between the client and the server effectively stands alone.

Some server single-process asynchronous architectures work by creating a new thread for each request. A *thread* is similar to a lightweight process: a threaded model tracks several concurrent execution paths within a single address space. This approach can bring other problems with it, however; multithreaded programs are difficult to write and maintain, and there has to be some way to schedule the different threads within the single process that houses them.

Extending the *SocketServer* Approach

You can extend the HTTP server you used in Chapter 6, "A Server Framework Library," by giving it the capability to fork a new subprocess or a new thread for each request. The SocketServer architecture has this capability built in, and therefore automatically extends the enhancement to the HTTP servers, which layer on top of it. The SocketServer library provides two mixin classes, ForkingMixIn and ThreadingMixIn, and these redefine the process_request() method used by the TCPServer class. When you define your own request handler to use multiple base classes, putting the appropriate mixin class first in the list of base classes, you automatically make it an asynchronous handler.

To help you develop confidence in the approach, it would be a good idea to make sure that it works with a simple server such as the uppercase server of the last chapter. The first TCP server was a good model because each incoming request became a session, terminated when the client sent a sentinel value to the server. Listing 7.1 shows a threading version of that server, with slight differences in the diagnostic output and session logic.

Listing 7.1   *threadserver.py:* **A Multithreaded Uppercase Server**

```
1   import SocketServer
2   import netstring
3   import sys
4   import string
5
6   class MyRequestHandler(SocketServer.BaseRequestHandler):
7       def handle(self):
```

```
 8            print "Connected:", self.client_address
 9            while 1:
10                rq = netstring.readns(self.request)
11                print "From:", self.client_address, rq
12                sys.stdout.flush()
13                if rq == "":
14                    break
15                netstring.writens(self.request, string.upper(rq))
16
17  myServer = SocketServer.ThreadingTCPServer(('', 8081),
18                  MyRequestHandler)
19  myServer.serve_forever()
```

The code is simple. Each TCP connection from a client initiates a new request, which triggers the creation of a MyRequestHandler object and an eventual call to its handle() method, whose definition starts on line 7. handle() loops, reading a netstring from the client and returning the result in uppercase until the client sends an empty string. Termination of the method automatically closes the socket to the client.

Line 17 creates a ThreadingTCPServer rather than a TCPServer. This simple modification causes the server to create a new thread for each request (session), and therefore means that the requests (sessions) can proceed concurrently. Also be aware that the SocketServer model does not define a ThreadingUDPServer or a ForkingUDPServer. Datagram services should not require this level of complexity.

Forking and Threading in Python

The threading and forking servers presented in this chapter rely on certain features being present in the operating environment. The forking servers should work with Python 2.0 and later in Windows and UNIX environments because the server structures were updated to use platform-dependent features. The Macintosh does not, however, support forking servers (although there is no reason why forking support should not be possible under OSX).

The threading servers should work in Windows and UNIX environments, but until version 2.1 you had to explicitly compile the interpreter with thread support. The prebuilt versions that many Windows users rely on typically did not include support for threads until the 2.1 release. Even after this, support for threads is not possible with the Cygwin support libraries, which have recently done so much to improve cross-platform portability and helped in the migration of many UNIX utilities to Windows. At the time of writing, this issue is still outstanding, although a solution should appear before too long.

To test this new server, you need a client program. The client shown in Listing 7.2 uses the getopt module to make it a little more flexible. When the client is called, a -h option can be followed by a hostname or address, and a -p option can be followed by a port number. This makes testing from other hosts a little easier because no rewriting is required. Apart from that modification, there are no changes from the first client in the previous chapter.

Listing 7.2   *client.py:* **An Uppercase Client with Option Processing**

```
 1  import socket
 2  import netstring
 3  import sys
 4  import getopt
 5
 6  parms = {'-h': '127.0.0.1', '-p': 8081}
 7  try:
 8      opts, pargs = getopt.getopt(sys.argv[1:], "h:p:")
 9  except getopt.GetoptError, msg:
10      sys.exit(msg)
11
12  for o, v in opts:
13      print o,v
14      parms[o] = v
15  host = parms['-h']
16  port = int(parms['-p'])
17
18  print "Host:", host, "port:", port
19
20  s = socket.socket(socket.AF_INET, socket.SOCK_STREAM)
21  s.connect((host, port))
22  while 1:
23      arg = raw_input("Send: ")
24      netstring.writens(s, arg)
25      if not arg:
26          break
27      ret = netstring.readns(s)
28      print "Returned:", ret
29  s.close()
```

The option processing starting at line 7 is simple. The `getopt.getopt()` function takes a first argument containing the command-line options (the first element of `sys.argv`, the program name, is omitted). The second argument is a string of letters representing valid options. If the option takes a value, then a colon follows its letter. An optional third argument, omitted here, allows you to specify extended arguments such as `--host=hostname`. The return value is a tuple, whose first element (assigned to opts in line 8) is a list of (`option, value`) tuples and whose second element (unused in this example) contains any remaining command-line arguments. The loop at line 12 overwrites the default values established in the `parms` dictionary by line 6.

The main body of the client begins at line 20, where the server connection is established. The client then sends each string the user enters as a netstring to the server, looping around until the user enters an empty string. The server converts nonempty strings into uppercase and returns the result to the client, which prints it. The client closes the socket after sending an empty netstring as a terminator.

Output from a multisession run of the threading server appears in Listing 7.3 and clearly shows that several different connections were concurrently active.

Listing 7.3   **Output from** *ThreadServer* **with Multiple Clients**

```
Connected: ('127.0.0.1', 1528)
From: ('127.0.0.1', 1528) Yes?
From: ('127.0.0.1', 1528) Really?
From: ('127.0.0.1', 1528)
Connected: ('127.0.0.1', 1529)
Connected: ('127.0.0.1', 1530)
From: ('127.0.0.1', 1530) Thinko!
From: ('127.0.0.1', 1529) What do you think?
From: ('127.0.0.1', 1529)
Connected: ('10.0.0.1', 1038)
From: ('10.0.0.1', 1038) Remote client connection!
From: ('10.0.0.1', 1038) Just checking
From: ('10.0.0.1', 1038)
From: ('127.0.0.1', 1530)
```

The web site code for this chapter also contains a forking server. Because the `fork()` calls on which `ForkingTCPServer` relies are UNIX-only, do not expect them to work under Windows. Unlike the CGI code, there is no attempt to accommodate Windows in this particular variation of the code. The forking server has been tested on a UNIX machine, and works fine. The only difference between the forking server and the threading server shown in Listing 7.1 are lines 17 and 18, which read

```
17 myServer = SocketServer.ForkingTCPServer(('', 8081),
18                 MyRequestHandler)
```

It is possible to have the appropriate server class selected by option, similarly to the protocol selection in Chapter 6's dual-protocol server. You could try this as an exercise.

An Asynchronous *CGIHTTPServer*

Moving right along, you were probably pleasantly surprised in Chapter 6 to learn that you could write a CGI HTTP server in five lines of code. How easy would it be to convert this into a threading or forking server? It turns out to be simple and neatly displays the power of Python's multiple inheritance.

`HTTPServer` is a subclass of `TCPServer` and overrides its `server_bind()` method. You want your threading CGI server to inherit its behavior from an `HTTPServer`, but you want it to use threading behavior, to start a new thread for each request. You might think this would require duplication of the `HTTPServer` declaration using `ThreadingTCPServer` as the base class instead of `TCPServer`. Although this approach would work, it is unnecessary.

The definition of the `ThreadingTCPServer` is simple, as you see from its complete source, listed here:

```
class ThreadingTCPServer(ThreadingMixIn, TCPServer): pass
```

The class inherits from two superclasses, and because of Python's method search algorithm, methods common to both superclasses are effectively inherited from ThreadingMixIn. So, the threading CGI server can use a server class that uses multiple inheritance, first from the ThreadingMixIn class and then from the TCPServer class. In this way, ThreadingMixin overrides methods also defined in TCPServer, and the server exhibits threading behavior! Listing 7.4 shows the source code of the threading CGI server.

Listing 7.4   *threadCGI.py:* **A Threading CGI HTTP Server**

```
1   import SocketServer
2   import BaseHTTPServer
3   import CGIHTTPServer
4
5   class ThreadingCGIServer(SocketServer.ThreadingMixIn,
6                     BaseHTTPServer.HTTPServer):
7       pass
8
9   import sys
10
11  server = ThreadingCGIServer(('', 8080), CGIHTTPServer.CGIHTTPRequestHandler)
12  #
13  try:
14      while 1:
15          sys.stdout.flush()
16          server.handle_request()
17  except KeyboardInterrupt:
18      print "Finished"
```

The server has the further refinement of trapping the KeyboardInterrupt exception and exiting quietly, although you may find you need to "wake up" the server by sending it a network request before it sees the interrupt.

A Forking CGI Server

Having read the source of the threading CGI server in Listing 7.4, you will not be surprised to learn that you can implement a forking CGI server simply by replacing all occurrences of the string Threading with Forking. The web site contains such a file, called forkCGI.py. Because the structure of the server is such that it will anyway fork (or on Windows, spawn) a new process in which to run the CGI script, the whole exercise is unnecessary except for the intellectual satisfaction of it.

The *asyncore* Module

Network servers are often *I/O-bound*, which means that there is an interesting alternative to forking or threading to get asynchronous service. Because network connections are usually relatively slow, a server process spends most of its time waiting for network data transmissions to complete. A single process can therefore handle many connections if it can effectively multiplex them, keeping the details of each connection separate.

A general-purpose web server tends to rely on cookies to maintain state information across a number of interactions with a web browser, because a separate process will probably handle each request. You easily can overlook the fact that for special purposes it is often easier to implement persistent behavior in a single process. A single process also can more easily coordinate actions where a number of clients need to access common state, such as in multiplayer games. As more systems become web-based, this will give further emphasis to special-purpose asynchronous servers.

Sam Rushing, of Nightmare Software, developed the `asyncore` module, which entered the Python core library at Release 1.6. This module, with its partner `asynchat`, is the basis of Rushing's high-performance Medusa TCP/IP server architecture. `asyncore` relies on an asynchronous processing loop using the `select()` call and gives you the advantages of threading without actually having to use threads. The advantage of using `select()` is that it effectively puts the program to sleep until a time-out expires or any one of a number of sockets changes status. The `asyncore` documentation is sketchy at the time of this writing, and the `asynchat` module comes without any documentation whatsoever.

Multiplexing Socket Activities with *select()*

`select()` takes as arguments three lists (of sockets) and a (floating-point) time-out period in seconds. It returns when any of the following conditions become true:

- A socket in the first list becomes readable.
- A socket in the second list becomes writable.
- An "exceptional condition" occurs on a socket in the third list.
- The time-out period expires.

The value returned by `select()` is a tuple containing three lists: the first is a list of readable sockets, the second a list of writable sockets, and the third a list of sockets on which exceptional conditions have been detected. These lists are subsets of the lists provided as arguments. When the function returns because of a time-out, all three lists are empty.

Event-Driven Socket Programming

When using `asyncore`, your main program adopts an event-driven structure. It creates one or more `dispatcher` objects, each of which is a thinly wrapped network socket, and then calls the `asyncore.loop()` function. This function repeatedly calls `select()`, and the process sleeps until the time-out expires or one or more of the dispatchers requires attention. The loop terminates when no more `dispatcher` objects exist.

The `asyncore` loop carefully analyzes the conditions under which the sockets become readable and/or writable, and makes calls to appropriate methods of the socket objects.

Each `dispatcher` can hold all the state information required to handle network interactions with a remote process. The asynchronous event loop interacts with `dispatcher` objects by calling their methods when socket events occur, so a single program can handle many interactions in parallel, consuming CPU only when there is work to do. A `dispatcher` object serviced by the asynchronous loop is sometimes called a *channel*.

To program asynchronous network communications, you create subclasses of the `asyncore.dispatcher` class, which you then instantiate to create your clients or servers. Your subclasses should override some subset of the methods listed in Table 7.1, most of which `asyncore.loop()` treats as callbacks. The loop uses changes in socket status to determine the appropriate method to call.

Table 7.1   *asyncore.dispatcher* **Object Methods**

Method	Description
`handle_accept()`	Called on listening sockets when a new connection arrives.
`handle_connect()`	Called when a client socket makes a connection to its server.
`handle_close()`	Called when the socket is closed.
`handle_read()`	Called when there is new data that the socket can read.
`handle_write()`	Called when a socket can write data if required.
`handle_expt()`	Called when out-of-band data is available on the socket. This facility should be used sparingly and is difficult to program correctly.
`readable()` `writable()`	Called to determine whether a dispatcher is interested in readable and writable events. When these methods return `true` (as the default implementations always do), then the dispatcher's socket will be included in the appropriate set in the `select()` call made inside the asynchronous loop.
`create_socket` `(family, type)`	Creates a socket of address family `family` and type `type`, adding it to the asynchronous loop. Normally, you will use a family value of `socket.AF_INET`, and a type of either `socket.SOCK_STREAM` or `socket.SOCK_DGRAM`.

The `dispatcher` object also has a complete set of socket methods, which operate on the socket held by the `dispatcher` object (whether that socket was created by the `create_socket()` method, or passed to the dispatcher's `__init__()` method). You use these socket methods to deal with communications when the event processor triggers your dispatcher's entry-points as callback routines.

An Asynchronous Client

When you start to deal with asynchronous communications, it is perhaps easier to understand client-side code. Listing 7.5 shows a simple test program, adapted from a sample by Sam Rushing. It accesses any number of web pages in parallel, displaying information when it receives data from the channel associated with the request.

Listing 7.5 *ashttpcli.py:* **An Asynchronous HTTP Client**

```
1   import asyncore
2   import socket
3
4   class http_client (asyncore.dispatcher):
5
6       def __init__ (self, host, path, cnum):
7           asyncore.dispatcher.__init__ (self)
8           self.path = path
9           self.cnum = cnum
10          self.host = host
11          self.wflag = 1
12          self.create_socket (socket.AF_INET, socket.SOCK_STREAM)
13          self.connect ((self.host, 80))
14
15      def handle_connect (self):
16          self.send ('GET %s HTTP/1.0\r\n\r\n' % self.path)
17          print "Channel:", self.cnum,➡
18                  "Sent request for", self.path, "to", self.host
19          self.wflag = 0
20
21      def handle_read (self):
22          data = self.recv (8192)
23          print "Channel:", self.cnum, "Received", len(data), "bytes"
24
25      def handle_write (self):
26          print "Channel:", self.cnum, "was writable"
27
28      def writable(self):
29          return self.wflag
30
31  import sys
32  import urlparse
33  cnum = 0
34  for url in sys.argv[1:]:
35      parts = urlparse.urlparse (url)
36      if parts[0] != 'http':
37          raise ValueError, "HTTP URL's only, please"
38      else:
39          cnum += 1
40          host = parts[1]
41          path = parts[2]
42          http_client(host, path, cnum)
43  asyncore.loop()
```

The __init__() method of the http_client class, starting at line 6, takes three arguments: a hostname, a path, and a channel number used for logging. It initializes itself as a dispatcher, records its arguments in instance variables, sets a write flag to ensure that the handle_connect() method will be called, creates a TCP Internet socket, and attempts to connect to the requested host.

The asynchronous loop calls the handle_connect() method at line 15 when the connection is established. This method sends a request to the server for the identified path and logs the send. It never sends any more data and therefore is not interested in writable events, so it clears the write flag. This stops the asynchronous control loop from including the socket in its writability checks, conserving processor time.

The handle_read() method at line 21 simply logs the amount of data received. The handle_write() method at line 25 logs the call but takes no other actions. The writable() method returns whatever value is stored in the write flag, allowing the http_client object to declare itself uninterested in writable events. If you want to convince yourself of the value of the writability optimization, comment out line 19 (where the write flag is cleared after the connection is handled), and you will see the asynchronous control loop continually activating the sockets' handle_write() method.

The main program starting at line 31 simply loops over the program arguments, splitting out the server name and path (under the simplifying assumption that the standard port 80 should be used). It creates an http_client object (a subclass, you will remember, of asyncore.dispatcher) for each URL, which initiates the TCP connection. Finally, it calls the asynchronous loop function. The loop, and hence the program, terminates when all dispatcher objects have closed their connections.

To test this client program, simply run the server and then run the client from the command line with as many URLs as you feel like passing as arguments. It is chatty enough to give you a clear idea of how it proceeds. It helps if the servers respond at different speeds and with different amounts of data.

Listing 7.6 **Output as *ashttpcli.py* Handles Four Connections Asynchronously**

```
D:\Book1\Code\Ch7> python ashttpcli1.py http://holden/
                  http://www.python.org/ http://www.holdenweb.com
                  http://wwwnightmare.com
Channel: 1 Sent request for / to holden
Channel: 1 was writable
Channel: 1 Received 2746 bytes
warning: unhandled close event
Channel: 1 Received 0 bytes
Channel: 3 Sent request for / to www.holdenweb.com
Channel: 3 was writable
Channel: 2 Sent request for / to www.python.org
Channel: 2 was writable
Channel: 4 Sent request for / to www.nightmare.com
Channel: 4 was writable
Channel: 2 Received 1460 bytes
Channel: 4 Received 452 bytes
```

```
warning: unhandled close event
Channel: 4 Received 0 bytes
Channel: 3 Received 4824 bytes
Channel: 3 Received 1763 bytes
warning: unhandled close event
Channel: 3 Received 0 bytes
Channel: 2 Received 2920 bytes
Channel: 2 Received 4380 bytes
Channel: 2 Received 2898 bytes
warning: unhandled close event
Channel: 2 Received 0 bytes
```

You can see from Listing 7.6 that this program handles asynchronous communications nicely. The first URL is a small page from a local server on the same LAN as the client, and its transfer completes quickly—even before the program has made a connection to any other server. The connections to the three other servers arrive at more or less the same time, and data arrives unpredictably thereafter.

The warning messages you see come from each channel's `handle_close()` method, which `http_client` does not override and which is therefore inherited from the base `dispatcher` object. This is a useful reminder that the object is using a default method. The `recv()` method called from `handle_read()` calls `handle_close()` when it sees zero bytes of data, the usual socket end-of-file indication. Hence, each warning is immediately followed by a receive notification for zero bytes of data.

An Asynchronous Server

Server objects are a little more complex to create than client objects. You must bind a socket to accept connections from clients. When a connection arrives, a new socket is returned by the `accept()` call. You have to make sure that this new socket becomes a part of the asynchronous loop, handles the request, and (when service is complete) removes itself from the loop. When the server is quiescent, a single non-writable server channel waits for connections.

Listing 7.7 shows a very simple HTTP server, which serves a simple canned response to whatever protocol commands it receives. As connections arrive, the server creates handler objects, each of which is an additional socket channel, to deal with them. To make it easier to see the asynchronous nature of the software, the handlers are time-delayed to respond only after at least 10 seconds. The `close()` call removes the channel from the asynchronous loop after it has handled its request.

Listing 7.7   *ashttpsrv.py:* **A Simple Asynchronous HTTP Server**

```
1  import socket
2  import syncope
3  import time
4
```

continues

Listing 7.7 **Continued**

```
5   class http_server(asyncore.dispatcher):
6
7       def __init__(self, ip, port):
8           self.ip= ip
9           self.port = port
10          self.count = 0
11          asyncore.dispatcher.__init__(self)
12          self.create_socket(socket.AF_INET, socket.SOCK_STREAM)
13          self.bind((ip, port))
14          self.listen(5)
15
16      def writable(self):
17          return 0
18
19      def handle_read(self):
20          pass
21
22      def readable(self):
23          return self.accepting
24
25      def handle_connect(self):
26          pass
27
28      def handle_accept(self):
29          try:
30              conn, addr = self.accept()
31          except socket.error: # rare Linux error
32              print "Socket error on server accept()"
33              return
34          except TypeError: # rare FreeBSD3 error
35              print "EWOULDBLOCK exception on server accept()"
36              return
37          self.count += 1
38          handler = http_handler(conn, addr, self, self.count)
39
40      def decrement(self):
41          self.count -= 1
42
43  class http_handler(asyncore.dispatcher):
44
45      def __init__(self, conn, addr, server, count):
46          asyncore.dispatcher.__init__(self, sock=conn)
47          self.addr = addr
48          self.buffer = ""
49          self.time = time.time()
50          self.count = count
51          self.server = server
52
53      def handle_read(self):
54          rq = self.recv(1024)
```

```
55              self.buffer = """"HTTP/1.0 200 OK Canned Response Follows
56   Content-Type: text/html
57
58   <HTML>
59   <HEAD>
60      <TITLE>Response from server</TITLE>
61   </HEAD>
62   <BODY>
63   <P>This is socket number %d
64   </BODY>
65   """ % self.count
66
67      def writable(self):
68          if time.time()-self.time > 10:
69              return len(self.buffer) > 0
70          else:
71              return 0
72
73      def handle_write(self):
74          sent = self.send(self.buffer)
75          self.buffer = self.buffer[sent:]
76          if len(self.buffer) == 0:
77              self.close()
78          self.server.decrement()
79
80   server = http_server('', 8080)
81
82   asyncore.loop(timeout=4.0)
```

The server defines two subclasses of `asyncore.dispatcher`: the first is a server object, whose code starts at line 5. The server has only two interesting methods. The `__init__()` method establishes a listening socket, monitored by the asynchronous loop, which simply accepts connections. When a connection arrives, the `handle_accept()` method uses the socket `accept()` call to retrieve the connection's socket. It then creates an `http_handler` object to deal with the request.

The server's `readable()` method, on lines 22 and 23, tells the asynchronous control loop to look for input on the server's main dispatcher socket if it is accepting connections. Because only one main server socket is created in this program and because the call to the `listen()` method on line 14 sets the dispatcher's accepting flag, this only saves the socket from being read-polled once or perhaps twice. It is good practice, however, in programs where server sockets are created dynamically and may exist for arbitrary periods of time before they are started up.

The `http_handler` definition starts at line 43. Its `__init__()` method receives the socket, the remote address, the server object, and a count as arguments. It stores most of these values, along with the start time, in instance variables. The dispatcher's `__init__()` method receives the socket passed in from the server, rather than having the handler create a new one as a client would. The asynchronous loop calls the handler's `handle_read()` method when the request arrives, which establishes a response that includes the socket channel number. However, the handler's `writable()` method only indicates that the channel has data when 10 seconds have elapsed since the request arrived (and only when data is still available). This gives you time to start several clients in parallel.

After the handler acknowledges that it is interested in its counterpart becoming writable, its `handle_write()` method is finally called from the asynchronous loop, and it writes a chunk of the data, removing the written data from the buffer, each time the asynchronous loop activates it. When the buffer is empty, `handle_write()` calls the dispatcher `close()` method (removing the channel from the asynchronous loop) and tells the server to decrement its channel count.

After the class definitions, the main program is simplicity itself and consists of precisely two lines. Line 80 creates a server object serving port 8080 on any available address, and line 82 starts the asynchronous loop. Because there is no provision to remove the server object from the asynchronous loop, this program will run forever, as a proper server should, so you will need to interrupt it to terminate its operation. Figure 7.1 shows six browser windows that have all made parallel requests to the server, and you will observe that each shows a different socket number.

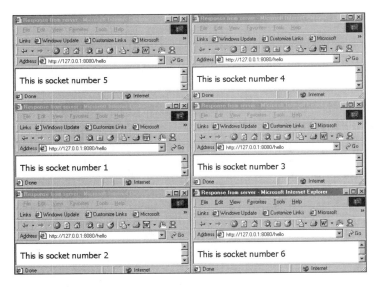

Figure 7.1 *ashttpsrv.py* output from six concurrent requests.

asynchat: **Handling Structured Conversations**

Useful as the `asyncore` module is, it cannot easily handle conversations where specific character sequences terminate a communication in an interprocess interaction. Although you might overcome this limitation using solutions based on the netstrings you saw in earlier chapters, this is not possible for many existing protocols. FTP, SMTP, NNTP, and HTTP along with many other TCP/IP application protocols all use a structured conversation (the relevant application protocol) in which commands and responses are terminated by particular character sequences.

The `asynchat` module is an extension of `asyncore` that can deal with terminated strings as well as inputs of a given length. It is included in the standard Python distribution but (as of Release 2.1) comes with no documentation. This is a pity because more people would use it if they could appreciate its benefits. The primary class it defines is the `async_chat` object, a subclass of `dispatcher` that defines the additional methods listed in Table 7.2.

Table 7.2   *async_chat* **Additional Methods**

Method	Description
`set_terminator(self, terminator)`	Set the string or character count used to identify end-of-request. For most Internet protocols, this is the string `'\r\n'` (a carriage return followed by a line feed); to turn off input scanning, use `None` as a terminator.
`collect_incoming_ data(self, data)`	Called whenever data is available from a socket; your code usually accumulates this data into a buffer of some kind.
`found_terminator(self)`	Called whenever an end-of-request marker has been seen; typically your code processes and clears the input buffer.
`push(data)`	This is a buffered version of `send()`; it places the data in an outgoing buffer queue.

Listing 7.8 shows a simple asynchronous uppercase server based on the `asynchat` module.

Listing 7.8   *asucsrv.py:* **An Asynchronous Uppercase Server**

```
1   import asyncore, asynchat, socket, sys
2
3   class uc_server(asyncore.dispatcher):
4
5       def __init__(self, host, port):
6           asyncore.dispatcher.__init__(self)
7           self.create_socket(socket.AF_INET, socket.SOCK_STREAM)
8           self.bind((host, port))
9           self.listen(5)
10
```

continues

Listing 7.8   **Continued**

```
11      def handle_accept(self):
12          uc_handler(self, self.accept())
13
14  class uc_handler(asynchat.async_chat):
15
16      def __init__(self, server, (conn, addr)):
17          print "Connection from", addr
18          sys.stdout.flush()
19          self.addr = addr
20          self.server = server
21          self.buffer = ''
22          self.outbuffer = ''
23          asynchat.async_chat.__init__(self, conn)
24          self.set_terminator('\n')
25
26      def collect_incoming_data(self, data):
27          self.buffer += data.replace('\r', '')
28
29      def found_terminator(self):
30          data = self.buffer.upper()
31          if data == '':
32              print "Disconnect:", self.addr
33              sys.stdout.flush()
34              self.close()
35              return
36          self.buffer = ''
37          self.push(data + '\r\n')
38
39  server = uc_server('', 9999)
40
41  asyncore.loop()
```

The program has a now-familiar structure: it declares a server object, whose purpose is to accept connections and create handlers. The interesting code is that for the uc_handler class, starting on line 14, which is a subclass of the asynchat.async_chat class. When a new connection arrives, the server creates a uc_handler object, which calls the set_terminator() method to request debuffering of network input when a line feed character is received. In the general case, the terminator could be any string, or an integer would indicate the need for a fixed number of input bytes.

The send and receive interfaces of the async_chat object are rather different from dispatcher. As data comes in, the default handle_read() method makes calls to the collect_incoming_data() method, until it detects termination of the input stream. At this point, handle_read() calls the found_terminator() method. This method therefore knows that the object has now accumulated all the data for a single request.

This particular server's found_terminator() method checks whether the user entered a blank line, terminating the connection if so. Otherwise, it sends a response back to the client by translating the input into uppercase and calling the `push()` method with the result data as its argument.

After all the definitions are complete, it is again a simple matter of creating a server and starting the asynchronous loop, in this case at lines 39 and 41, respectively. You can test this particular server using any number of telnet client programs, and Listing 7.9 shows the output from a typical test session. Most telnet clients let you connect to an arbitrary port if you give the port number as a second argument (after the hostname or IP address) on the command line. So the clients shown connecting in Listing 7.9 would be started with a command line like the following:

```
telnet 127.0.0.1 9999
```

You can see that the server is handling three sessions in parallel before the clients start to disconnect. Depending on your particular telnet client software settings, you might not see your input echoed as you type it.

Listing 7.9 **Output from *asucsrv.py***

```
D:\Book1\Code\Ch7> python asucsrv.py
Connection from ('127.0.0.1', 2563)
Connection from ('10.0.0.1', 1061)
Connection from ('10.0.0.131', 1238)
Disconnect: ('10.0.0.131', 1238)
Disconnect: ('10.0.0.1', 1061)
Disconnect: ('127.0.0.1', 2563)
```

async_chat Output Queuing

Although Listing 7.8 again shows that server creation is not difficult in Python, it does not allow you to appreciate the flexibility of the output side. All you have seen so far is the program pushing strings on to a *FIFO* (a first-in first-out queue), which the default `handle_write()` method consumes as it transmits the data to the other end of the socket. The queuing mechanism allows you to do rather more than this, however. As well as pushing data on to the output FIFO, you can use the `push_with_producer()` method to push a *producer*, a simple object requiring only one method: `more()`. If you can produce your output by computation, you can use the `more()` method to produce chunks of output at a time.

There are a number of advantages to this approach. First, `async_chat` objects only call the producer for output when the output socket indicates its readiness to receive data. Because producers are typically small objects, `async_chat` objects require less memory than objects that produce output as soon as they receive their input. Second, you can wrap producers around each other to create arbitrarily complex behaviors. Because you push producers on to a FIFO, you can write other producers to use that FIFO as a data source and modify it in some way.

medusa: An Asynchronous Server Framework

To complete this chapter, you get to look at a program that acts as a low-level proxy server. Its function is really closer to a circuit-level gateway because it works with any application protocol. The sample code comes, with permission, from Sam Rushing's Medusa web pages. Medusa is a server framework Sam has built on top of the `asyncore` and `asynchat` modules. It includes a web server (although without CGI), an FTP server, and an Internet Relay Chat server, all in a single package. You can monitor Medusa using a special client program, which communicates with a *monitor* server that comes as yet another part of Medusa. You actually can use the monitor client to execute Python statements in the context of the running server! If your server has failed in some catastrophic way, you can shut down your servers and restart them in-process using different port numbers. Then you can start up another production server and continue to use the monitor channel to debug the problem on the original server.

Medusa is an extremely flexible system with not too much in the way of documentation. If you are prepared to read the source code, then visit `http://www.nightmare.com/medusa/` to download the software. The source code repays study.

Figure 7.2 shows the proxy in operation, relaying traffic between a client and a server. You start the program giving it an IP address and a port number of a (possibly remote) service that you want to monitor. The proxy starts to listen on a local port number 8000 higher than that of the remote service. When it receives a connection, it starts two handler objects. The `proxy_receiver` relays incoming data from the client to the server, and the `proxy_sender` relays server responses back to the client. Because the whole point of the program is to help analyze network interactions, both proxy objects use a line feed separator and log each line to standard output as it passes through.

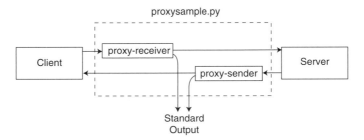

Figure 7.2   An `asynchat`-based proxy relays data between a client and a server.

The program appears in Listing 7.9. Because the program is inherently capable of handling multiple connections, the proxy objects tag each line with an identifying connection number. This program is remarkably small considering its scope, although you could add other refinements.

Listing 7.9 *proxysample.py:* **An asynchat-Based Logging Proxy Program**

```
1   import asynchat
2   import syncope
3   import socket
4   import string
5
6   class proxy_server(asyncore.dispatcher):
7
8       def __init__(self, host, port):
9           asyncore.dispatcher.__init__(self)
10          self.create_socket(socket.AF_INET, socket.SOCK_STREAM)
11          self.set_reuse_addr()
12          self.there =(host, port)
13          here =('', port + 8000)
14          self.bind(here)
15          self.listen(5)
16
17      def handle_accept(self):
18          proxy_receiver(self, self.accept())
19
20  class proxy_sender(asynchat.async_chat):
21
22      def __init__(self, receiver, address):
23          asynchat.async_chat.__init__(self)
24          self.receiver = receiver
25          self.set_terminator(None)
26          self.create_socket(socket.AF_INET, socket.SOCK_STREAM)
27          self.buffer = ''
28          self.set_terminator('\n')
29          self.connect(address)
30
31      def handle_connect(self):
32          print 'Connected'
33
34      def collect_incoming_data(self, data):
35          self.buffer = self.buffer + data
36
37      def found_terminator(self):
38          data = self.buffer
39          self.buffer = ''
40          print '==>(%d) %s' %(self.id, repr(data))
41          self.receiver.push(data + '\n')
42
43      def handle_close(self):
44          self.receiver.close()
45          self.close()
46
47  class proxy_receiver(asynchat.async_chat):
48
49      channel_counter = 0
```

continues

Listing 7.9 **Continued**

```
50
51      def __init__(self, server,(conn, addr)):
52          asynchat.async_chat.__init__(self, conn)
53          self.set_terminator('\n')
54          self.server = server
55          self.id = proxy_receiver.channel_counter
56          proxy_receiver.channel_counter = proxy_receiver.channel_counter + 1
57          self.sender = proxy_sender(self, server.there)
58          self.sender.id = self.id
59          self.buffer = ''
60
61      def collect_incoming_data(self, data):
62          self.buffer = self.buffer + data
63
64      def found_terminator(self):
65          data = self.buffer
66          self.buffer = ''
67          print '<==(%d) %s' %(self.id, repr(data))
68          self.sender.push(data + '\n')
69
70      def handle_close(self):
71          print 'Closing'
72          self.sender.close()
73          self.close()
74
75  if __name__ == '__main__':
76      import sys
77      import string
78      if len(sys.argv) < 3:
79          print 'Usage: %s <server-host> <server-port>' % sys.argv[0]
80      else:
81          ps = proxy_server(sys.argv[1], string.atoi(sys.argv[2]))
82          asyncore.loop()
```

The heart of the program is the proxy_server object defined starting at line 6, a subclass of dispatcher. This object, when created, records the address and port number of the server and starts listening on all interfaces to a port number 8000 higher. When it accepts a connection, it creates a proxy_receiver object, which in turn creates a proxy_sender object. These last two objects are subclasses of the asyncore.async_chat class.

The proxy_receiver object sets a line feed terminator, establishes its identity from a channel counter maintained as a class variable (shared by all instances), creates the proxy_sender object, and clears its buffer. From then on, it simply accumulates data from the client until it finds a line feed, at which point it logs the line and calls push() to send the data to the server. When the connection is closed, the receiver closes both itself and the sender. The proxy_sender uses similar logic to transfer data from the server to the client, closing both objects when the connection is closed. This shuts things down correctly whether the server or the client eventually terminates the network connection.

To use `proxysample.py`, simply run it on your own machine (using the `-u` command-line option to ensure unbuffered output), giving the IP address and port number of the web site of your choice. Supposing that you wanted to debug interactions with the Python language site, your command line might look like this:

```
python -u proxysample.py www.python.org 80
```

Then browse to `http://127.0.0.1:8080/`, and you should see the Python site in your browser. As a bonus, the standard output from the proxy server shows the conversation between your browser and the server. You probably will find that graphics do not always appear as you expect them. This is usually because the graphic data, sent in binary, does not end in a line feed, and therefore some data remains unsent when the channel is closed. This same "feature" can cause your browser to hang waiting for the final characters of the graphic.

Summary

Asynchronous service provision is not as difficult as it might appear and can be very useful when the server can directly compute the required output from the input. The `asyncore` and `asynchat` modules make it easy to write servers to use a single process to handle many simultaneous requests, with a very low overhead per connection. They are also useful for asynchronous client programs.

When the process of computing the server output is more complex, using file or database access, for example, the scheme may be less successful. The operating system will not return to the asynchronous loop until the output computation has completed, even though the process may block waiting for something other than network I/O.

Part III, "Database Programming in Python," moves on to considering database services, without which many web servers would require a considerable amount of additional programming.

Database Programming in Python

8

Relational Database Principles

MODERN WEB SITES CAN MAKE EXTENSIVE USE of databases, and so a thorough understanding of database technology can be crucial in making a web system easy to code and reasonably efficient in operation. Modern database systems are almost all based on relational technology, which you should therefore understand to some degree. A modest insight into relational principles can help you make sure that your database is sensibly structured and therefore easy to use and maintain.

The normal process of building a database system requires you to produce a *logical design*, which is a conceptual representation of the way data is represented in your system. This chapter introduces the principles behind relational systems through a technique called *entity-relationship modeling*, just one particular form of logical design.

After you have a logical design that appears to satisfy the needs of your application, you can turn it into a *physical design*, which is an implementation of the logical design in some relational database management system (RDBMS).

If you are new to relational systems, the terminology might be a little different from what you are used to. Despite the fact that relational technology is built on mathematical foundations, there is no need for a deep understanding of the underlying mathematical theories to make effective use of the technologies, although an appreciation of set theory can be useful. One reason for this is that modern relational systems implement the *Structured Query Language* (SQL), which allows you to specify your retrievals and updates without detailing the exact sequence of operations required. For this reason, SQL is sometimes called a *non-procedural* language.

If you are careful about your system design, you can build applications to be more or less independent of any particular database management system. This chapter concentrates on the design tasks that you need to undertake before you move to a physical design.

What Is a Database?

Simply, a *database* is a collection of related data, designed for a known group of users, to be used in particular applications. There are three key phrases in this definition:

- **Related data**—A database is normally designed with specific purposes in mind, and the data are stored and manipulated to reflect those purposes. Although a modern RDBMS is multipurpose, unrelated data normally will be kept in separate databases, and possibly even managed by separate instances of the database management system.

- **A known group of users**—If you do not know who the users are, you cannot know the requirements that the database must satisfy; this would make it impossible to ensure that the database met all users' needs.

- **Specific applications**—The applications for which the data are required ultimately determines the requirements of the users; you must know the scope of the application as well as the user community to be sure that the users' needs are met.

Note that nothing in the definition implies that you must use a relational system (or any other particular mechanism) to store your database. Early information systems used file storage as a database repository, and many simpler applications still do. More recently, vendors have built *hierarchical* and *network* database management systems. These were more suitable, but both suffered from the need to structure the data according to the processing that the application performed on it. Relational technology now dominates the database world.

Data Modeling and Database Design

Chapter 3, "Object-Orientation," pointed out that most information systems are built to provide information about the real world, and they do so by storing data about selected aspects of it. Some applications (games and simulations, for example) explicitly deal with constructed worlds. You can use relational technology to model those worlds too, if you choose. Each system has a different scope and stores different data about different aspects of the world. You can think of the data stored in a system as a *model* of those aspects of the real world of interest to the system's users.

The intention behind this is to improve convenience and efficiency. With a well-designed application, it is usually much easier and simpler to consult a data model using a computer interface than it is to check on the real world. When order-entry clerks take calls from customers, they cannot visit the warehouse and examine the inventory on the shelves to determine whether particular items are in stock. Even if they did, this would not tell them whether the stock had already been allocated to orders from other customers. Of course, for a model to be useful, there has to be some sensible correspondence between its data and the state of the real world.

This in turn means that a system must update the model when the real world changes—for example, by reducing the available stock quantity when an order is received for a particular product. If the inventory data is not updated by lowering the stock levels each time an order is taken, customers eventually will be disappointed because they have placed orders for out-of-stock items without being told about it. A data model is only useful as long as it is sufficiently accurate, where the application dictates the meaning of "sufficiently accurate."

At the same time, you do not want unnecessary complexity in your data model: although a human resources system may well find it necessary to record, for example, the name, address, and social security number of each employee, few such systems will concern themselves about the color of the employees' hair or the type of car they drive. Such data are not relevant to the purposes of the application. This puts the onus on the designer to carefully evaluate the information needs of the application as summarized by the users' statements of requirements.

Modeling the Real World

The users' requirements are, in fact, the key to sound systems design whatever type of database is used. When you start to plan an application, you have to collect as much information as possible about user requirements: what do users want it to do, who should be able to perform which actions, what real-world events must trigger changes in the model, and so on. This requirements information is invaluable in determining the scope of the data model because with enough information from the users, you will know exactly what information they expect to see coming out of the application.

Any information the application produces must obviously either be stored in the data model or computable from it. For a large system, you typically will have to talk to many different types of user, each with his own concerns and knowledge of the organization, and possibly you will have to talk to some people several times. At this stage, you are concerned with finding out what kinds of things users need to store data about, what data they need to store about them, and which real-world events need to trigger changes to the data.

A Book Sales Example

Suppose that you have been asked by a bookstore's owners to design and build a system to sell books over the Internet. An initial conversation with the principals of the bookstore tells you they want **customers** visiting the web site to be able to place **sales orders** for **books**. Ideally, the customer will be able to search for books by author's name, by title, by ISBN (international standard book number, a worldwide numbering scheme that gives each volume its own unique number), or by entering words from the title. When an order is entered, the system should check that it is currently in stock. If not, at the end of the day it will be put on a **purchase order** to the appropriate **publisher**, and the customer will be sent an email explaining that the book is currently out of stock, but that it will be delivered as soon as possible. In-stock books will be sent to the customer in a single **shipment**, usually consigned to a carrier the same day as the sales order is placed (up to a certain cutoff time).

This information is not detailed enough to allow anything like a complete specification of the system. Already, though, it provides a certain amount of information about things important to the system, as well as describes some of the data you have to store about them. The process of logical database design can start.

Entities

The words highlighted in boldface in the preceding sidebar, "A Book Sales Example," are all things significant to the application about which information must be stored. In formal database parlance, these names are *entity types*, and an item of a particular entity type is an *occurrence* of that entity. What you would refer to in normal conversation as "a sales order," for example, should formally be thought of as *an occurrence of entity type sales order*.

The significant entities are the first things you need to identify for your database design. Often they will be identified in conversation with users by nouns and noun phrases such as *customer* and *purchase order*. By focusing on the entities, you identify the basic items that must appear in the data model and about which information must be stored. As your discussions become more detailed, you will learn about an increasing number of pieces of data associated with each occurrence of an entity type: these are the *attributes* of the entity.

Concrete, Conceptual, and Event Entities

Entities are easiest to understand (at least for this author—your experience may be different) when they correspond with something physical in the real world, such as a person or a computer. Because they relate to tangible objects, these often are called *concrete entities*. Usually, it is easy to decide what attributes the concrete entities in a system must possess.

Sometimes you need to record data about things that do not have a tangible real-world equivalent but that are nevertheless significant from the point of view of the application. An example of such an entity might be a special offer in a sales database, whose attributes might include the product identity, a percentage price reduction, and a range of valid dates. These are called *conceptual entities*. Information needs to be stored about them even though they do not correspond with objects in the real world, which can be picked up or moved about.

The third type of entity is an *event entity*. These can be the most difficult because they are really just interactions taking place at a specific point in time. For example, when a shipment of stock is consigned to a customer, a delivery takes place at the point when the carrier hands the shipment to the customer and gets a signature for it. A carrier such as UPS or FedEx needs to record relevant attributes of the delivery entity—for example, the date and time, the name of the recipient, and the identity of the courier's representative—to be able to prove that they have met their service obligations to their customers.

Relational Entity Representation: Relations and Attributes

In a relational database, a *relation* represents each entity. Mathematically speaking, a relation is a mapping, or function, from a set of key values to a set of *tuples*. Each key corresponds to exactly one occurrence of an entity, and the tuple to which the relation maps the key is the set of attributes for the occurrence. This is similar in concept to a Python dictionary (which you may recall is described as a mapping type) whose values are tuples, with the exception that the keys also are contained within the tuples.

In practice, you can most easily visualize relations as tables with named columns, which is how they appear to be stored in a relational database (the physical storage varies with the platform and is transparent to the user). The rows of the table correspond with the occurrences of the entity type, and the columns correspond to the *attributes* of that entity. Table 8.1 shows a sample BOOK relation, in which each of the four occurrences of entity type BOOK has five attributes: *ISBN, Author, Title, Publisher,* and *Date*.

Table 8.1 **A Simple *BOOK* Relation with Five Attributes**

ISBN	Author	Title	Publisher	Date
0735710910	Beazley	*Python Essential Reference, 2E*	New Riders	2001
0735710902	Holden	*Python Web Programming*	New Riders	2001
1565924649	Lutz and Ascher	*Learning Python*	O'Reilly	1999
1565926218	Hammond and Robinson	*Python Programming on Win32*	O'Reilly	1999

If you felt so inclined, you could model this BOOK relation as a Python dictionary, as shown in Listing 8.1.

Listing 8.1 **Code to Represent the *BOOK* Relation as Python Data**

```
 1  BOOK = {
 2        "0735710910": ("07357109109",
 3                        "Beazley",
 4                        "Python Essential Reference",
 5                        "New Riders", 2001),
 6        "0735710902": ("0735710902:,
 7                        "Holden",
 8                        "Python Web Programming",
 9                        "New Riders",
10                        2001),
11        "1565924649": ("1565924649",
12                        "Lutz and Ascher",
13                        "Learning Python",
14                        "O'Reilly",
15                        1999),
16        "1565926218": ("1565926218",
17                        "Hammond and Robinson",
18                        "Python Programming on Win32",
19                        "O'Reilly",
20                        1999)
21        }
```

It would not be strictly necessary to include the key values as a part of the tuples, but relational systems normally store the key as a part of the data, whereas Python dictionaries do not usually do so. Relations have several properties you should bear in mind:

- Each tuple in the relation is unique. The same combination of attribute values can occur only once. The formal foundation of relational theory is relational algebra, which is based on set theory, and a relation is a set of tuples. Something can only be a member of a set or not a member; it cannot occur in a set more than once.

- Each column is named.

- The values in a given column are all of the same type.

- The ordering of the rows in the relation is not significant: two relations are equivalent if they contain the same set of tuples, no matter what order they occur in.

- The ordering of the attributes in the relation is not significant; the attributes are identified by name.

- Each cell contains a single (atomic) value. Sets or lists are not allowed as attribute values in relational structures.

Clearly the Python dictionary representation shown in Listing 8.1 does not in itself enforce most of these criteria. Of course, you could design objects that allow you to do this, but the coding effort would be considerable. It usually makes more sense simply to interface your Python applications to a relational database.

The NULL Value

In relational systems, it is sometimes convenient to record the fact that an attribute value for a particular occurrence of an entity is either unknown or irrelevant. Just as Python has None, so relational systems have the special value NULL, which is used for precisely the purpose just outlined.

When you are new to relational systems, it is easy to overlook that the use of NULL introduces three-valued logic because a Boolean expression may evaluate to True, False, or NULL. Because NULL is neither True nor False, our usual logical assumptions are violated. This can cause problems, so I would advise you to hold off using NULL until you meet a situation that really requires it.

The usual indication that NULL values are required is when you start to feel the temptation to use *sentinel values*—data values inserted with some special semantic significance. This was typical in older programs, where you would often see date fields holding "impossible" values such as December 31, 2099, to indicate that no actual date was associated. In such circumstances, the use of NULL values is far more desirable than the complex special coding that has to be inserted to deal with the sentinel values (and that often is overlooked during program maintenance).

The RDBMS will most often allow you to specify whether a column may store NULL values.

Primary Keys: Uniquely Identifying Rows

There must be a way to identify one tuple in a relation among all the others. Normally one attribute, or a small number of attributes taken together, can be guaranteed unique for each tuple in a relation. The unique identifier (or *primary key*) of the BOOK relation in Table 8.1 is ISBN, which is why the attribute name is underlined. In general, the unique identifier can be either a single attribute or a collection of attributes taken together (usually referred to as a *composite key*). Because the primary key must be unique for each tuple, this also guarantees that no tuple occurs more than once.

Sometimes the data will be such that several different attributes or sets of attributes might be used as the primary key. You must then choose one of these so-called *candidate keys* as the primary key (often simply referred to as the key), the one normally used to select rows. The other candidates are sometimes called *secondary keys*, and most databases have a way for you to ensure that these values also remain unique.

As you will understand better when you learn about relationships in the next section, it is highly desirable that primary key values are *stable*—they do not change during normal operation of the system. For this reason, many designers today prefer to have the database system assign primary keys directly rather than use one of the entity's natural attributes as the key. Most RDBMSs can assign key values automatically when tuples are created, although with a less-capable RDBMS, it can be tricky to establish what value the system has assigned.

Relationships Between Entities

When a number of entities are used to build a data model, you have to represent *relationships* between them. For a model containing books, authors, publishers, sales orders, and customers, Figure 8.1 lists a few of the relationships that you might need to record.

subject *relationship* object
author *wrote* book
book *was-written-by* author
publisher *published* book
book *was-published-by* publisher
customer *places* order
order *is-placed-by* customer
order *requests* book
book *is-requested-by* order

Figure 8.1 Possible relationships in a bookselling application.

These relationships are shown in pairs because relationships have a natural duality, depending on which of the related entities is treated as the subject of the relationship. Thus *author wrote book* is the dual of *book was-written-by author.* Whether you use the name "wrote" or "was-written-by," you are talking about the same relationship but from the point of view of one or other of the entities involved.

Relations and Relationships

Remember that the relationships exist between the relations. The similarity of the two words makes it important to separate them clearly in your mind. If it's any consolation, apparently they are even easier to confuse in Italian.

Relationship Cardinality: One-to-Many, Many-to-Many

The simple book relation in Table 8.1 treated the publisher and author as simple attributes of the book. If the application required that data be stored about publishers and authors, then it would be more sensible for them to be entities. In that case, Figure 8.2 shows how the relationships between the book, publisher, and author entities would be expressed as an *entity-relationship diagram* (ERD) in which entities are represented by rounded rectangles, and relationships are lines between the entities.

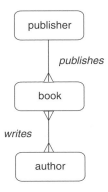

Figure 8.2   Three entities, with two relationships.

As you can see, the book entity takes part in relationships with both the author and the publisher entities. The difference between *author writes book* and *publisher publishes book* in Figure 8.2 is one of *cardinality*—a single publisher can publish many books, and so book is attached to publisher using a crow's foot symbol on the book side. Because a single publisher will publish any given book, then a single line is used on the publisher side. Formally, you would say that the relationship between book and publisher is *many-to-one* (or equivalently that the relationship between publisher and book is *one-to-many*). Because a single author may write several books, and a single book might have many authors, the relationship between book and author is said to be *many-to-many*, and the crow's foot symbol is used at both ends of the relationship.

Reading Relationships

How do you know from Figure 8.2 that *author writes book* and not *book writes author*? This may not be a serious question for an ERD with only two relationships in it. However, when you are faced with a design containing several hundred entities and as many or more relationships, not all of which you are familiar with, it helps to know which way around a relationship should be read.

Most designers who use ERDs adopt the *clockwise rule* (see Figure 8.3). If the relationship is read from one entity to the other, the name that applies is the one on the same side of the relationship as the clockwise arc from the first entity to the second. Using this simple rule, you can tell that the relationship in Figure 8.3 is newsworthy—as the old editorial adage says, "when a dog bites a man, that's nothing; when a man bites a dog, that's news"! By the clockwise rule, *man bites dog*, and *dog is-bitten-by man*.

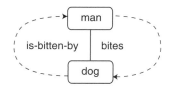

Figure 8.3   Who's biting whom in this relationship?

Foreign Keys: Implementing Relationships

Suppose that the information held about the publishers and authors is as shown in Tables 8.2 and 8.3.

Table 8.2   **Publisher Entity Data**

PubId	Name	URL
1	New Riders	www.newriders.com
2	O'Reilly	www.ora.com

Table 8.3   **Author Entity Data**

AuthId	FirstName	LastName	Location
1	David	Beazley	USA
2	Steve	Holden	USA
3	Mark	Lutz	USA
4	David	Ascher	USA
5	Mark	Hammond	Australia
6	Andy	Robinson	UK

The information in Tables 8.2 and 8.3 also could be represented as Python dictionaries, as shown in Listing 8.2.

Listing 8.2   **Establishing the Publisher and Author Entities as Python Data**

```
1  PUBLISHER = {
2    1: (1, "New Riders", "www.newriders.com"),
3    2: (2, "O'Reilly", "www.ora.com")
4  }
5
6  AUTHOR = {
7    1: (1, "David", "Beazley", "USA"),
```

```
 8     2: (2, "Steve", "Holden", "USA"),
 9     3: (3, "Mark", "Lutz", "USA"),
10     4: (4, "David", "Ascher", "USA"),
11     5: (5, "Mark", "Hammond", "Australia"),
12     6: (6, "Andy", "Robinson", "UK")
13   }
```

An integer primary key now identifies the data for each author and publisher. You
could represent the relationship between a book and its publisher by storing the
publisher's key value as an attribute of the book. Inside the book relation, the publisher
number is known as a *foreign* key—it identifies an occurrence of some other entity
type by the primary key value of the related occurrence. In relational terminology,
foreign keys on the many side implement a one-to-many relationship.

You could perform a similar trick with the authors and books, but this relationship
is fundamentally different: although each book has exactly one publisher, it may have
one or several authors. You might therefore adopt the expedient of storing a *tuple* of
author keys in the book data, which would then be represented in Python as shown
in Listing 8.3.

Listing 8.3   **Book Data Including Relationships with Publisher and Author**

```
 1   BOOK = {
 2     "0735710910": ("0735710910",
 3             (1, ),
 4             "Python Essential Reference",
 5             1,
 6             2001),
 7     "0735710902": ("0735710902:,
 8             (2, ),
 9             "Python Web Programming",
10             1,
11             2001),
12     "1565924649": ("1565924649",
13             (3, 4),
14             "Learning Python",
15             2,
16             1999),
17     "1565926218": ("1565926218",
18             (5, 6),
19             "Python Programming on Win32",
20             2,
21             1999)
22   }
```

Note that representing a many-to-many relationship using a tuple for the author
attribute violates relational requirements. A tuple used as an attribute has multiple
values, and attributes must be single-valued in relational systems. Ignoring this for the

present, you could easily use the data structures from Listing 8.3 in a Python program to reproduce the book data listed in Table 8.1, as the code in Listing 8.4 shows.

Listing 8.4   *booklist1.py:* **Reproducing Book Data from Dictionaries (Showing Output)**

```
#
# AUTHOR, BOOK and PUBLISHER are dictionaries,
# defined as shown in the preceding text
#
for b in BOOK.keys():
    print "%12s %-20s  %-30s %-12s %d" % (
        BOOK[b][0],                    # ISBN
        " and ".join([AUTHOR[i][2] for i in BOOK[b][1]]),
        BOOK[b][2],
        PUBLISHER[BOOK[b][3]][1],
        BOOK[b][4])
1565926218 Hammond and Robinson   Python Programming on Win32   O'Reilly     1999
0735710910 Beazley                Python Essential Reference    New Riders   2001
1565924649 Lutz and Ascher        Learning Python               O'Reilly     1999
0735710902 Holden                 Python Web Programming        New Riders   2001
```

The code in Listing 8.4 could be clearer, however. Python dictionaries are representing relations, and the only way to iterate over the dictionary is by extracting a list of keys. Furthermore, indexing must be used to access the elements of the tuples held in the relations. For example, the expression

```
PUBLISHER[BOOK[b][3]][1]
```

actually means "the name of the publisher of the book whose key is b," but you have to be well-versed in the details of the structures to understand this instinctively. I wrote the code, and it took me a while to write the description you just read!

Some of this complexity can be mitigated by the use of Python's tuple-unpacking assignment to break out each book's individual fields into named variables while using the same data structures. This gets rid of the more complex multiply subscripted names, as you can see in Listing 8.5, which shows only the amended loop code.

Listing 8.5   *booklst1a.py:* **Tuple-Unpacking Gives Names to Book Fields**

```
38  for b in BOOK.keys():
39      Bookid, authids, booktitle, pubid, bookyear = BOOK[b]
40      print "%12s %-20s  %-30s %-12s %d" % (
41          Bookid,                    # ISBN
42          " and ".join([AUTHOR[i][2] for i in authids]),
43          booktitle,
44          PUBLISHER[pubid][1],
45          bookyear)
```

The approach in Listing 8.5 makes the loop code easier to comprehend, but it would be difficult to extend it to the AUTHOR and PUBLISHER data because they are components in an expression. Furthermore, each tuple-unpacking assignment relies on the fields being stored in a specific order. If this order were changed, then every such assignment would also have to be changed, with a high probability that some would be missed in a large program.

Another implementation is shown, this time in its entirety, in Listing 8.6. This allows the individual attributes to be accessed as attributes of the Python objects used to store them.

Listing 8.6 *booklst2.py:* **Implementing Attribute Names**

```
1   class Table:
2
3       def __init__(self, *columnames):
4           """Creates table definition: assumes first column is key."""
5           self.columnames = columnames
6           self.key = self.columnames[0]
7           self.records = {}
8
9       def addrec(self, **kwargs):
10          """Adds a record to a table."""
11          if not kwargs.has_key(self.key):
12              raise ValueError, "record must have value for key column➡
                "+self.key
13          newrec = Record(self.columnames, **kwargs)
14          self.records[kwargs[self.key]] = newrec
15
16      def getrec(self, k):
17          return self.records[k]
18
19      def values(self):
20          return self.records.values()
21
22  class Record:
23      def __init__(self, columnames, **kwargs):
24          for k in kwargs.keys():
25              if k not in columnames:
26                  raise NameError, "table has no column named "+k
27              setattr(self, k, kwargs[k])
28
29  PUBLISHER = Table("PubNo", "PubName", "PubWebSite")
30  PUBLISHER.addrec(PubNo=1, PubName="New Riders",➡
    PubWebSite="www.newriders.com")
31  PUBLISHER.addrec(PubNo=2, PubName="O'Reilly", PubWebSite="www.ora.com")
32
33  AUTHOR = Table("AutNo", "AutLast", "AutFirst", "AutLoc")
34  AUTHOR.addrec(AutNo=1, AutFirst="David", AutLast="Beazley", AutLoc="USA"),
35  AUTHOR.addrec(AutNo=2, AutFirst="Steve", AutLast="Holden", AutLoc="USA"),
```

continues

Listing 8.6 **Continued**

```
36  AUTHOR.addrec(AutNo=3, AutFirst="Mark", AutLast="Lutz", AutLoc="USA"),
37  AUTHOR.addrec(AutNo=4, AutFirst="David", AutLast="Ascher", AutLoc="USA"),
38  AUTHOR.addrec(AutNo=5, AutFirst="Mark", AutLast="Hammond",➥
    AutLoc="Australia"),
39  AUTHOR.addrec(AutNo=6, AutFirst="Andy", AutLast="Robinson", AutLoc="UK")
40
41  BOOK = Table("BkISBN", "AutNo", "BkName", "PubNo", "BkYear")
42  BOOK.addrec(BkISBN="1565924649",
43              AutNo=(1, ),
44              BkName="Python Essential Reference",
45              PubNo=1,
46              BkYear=2001),
47  BOOK.addrec(BkISBN="0735710902",
48              AutNo=(2, ),
49              BkName="Python Web Programming",
50              PubNo=1,
51              BkYear=2001),
52  BOOK.addrec(BkISBN="0735710910",
53              AutNo=(3, 4),
54              BkName="Learning Python",
55              PubNo=2,
56              BkYear=1999),
57  BOOK.addrec(BkISBN="1565926218",
58              AutNo=(5, 6),
59              BkName="Python Programming on Win32",
60              PubNo=2,
61              BkYear=1999)
62
63  for b in BOOK.values():
64      print "%12s %-20s  %-30s %-12s %d" % (
65          b.BkISBN,                      # ISBN
66          " and ".join([AUTHOR.getrec(i).AutLast for i in b.AutNo]),
67          b.BkName,
68          PUBLISHER.getrec(b.PubNo).PubName,
69          b.BkYear)
```

At the expense of a rather more complicated setup, the tabulation code in Listing 8.6 is somewhat more readable. In this model, a relation is modeled by a `Table` object, which stores `Record` objects against their primary keys in a private dictionary. When a `Table` is created, a list of permissible column names is passed to the `__init__()` method defined at line 3. Because there is no set number of columns in a table, the `*columnames` argument collects them all as a list, which is stored for future use at line 5. The first one given is taken to be the primary key (a simplifying assumption), and an empty `records` dictionary is created.

A `Record` is added to the `Table` by calling its `addrec()` method (starting at line 9), which expects each column value to be passed as a keyword argument. The `**kwargs` notation collects all keyword arguments as a dictionary, and line 11 ensures that the user has provided a primary key value for the `Record`. The creation of the `Record` object requires the permitted column names to be passed in by the creating `Table` at line 13, and line 14 adds this new `Record` under its primary key. This particular implementation will happily "add" (overwrite) some other record with the same primary key. The `getrec()` method at line 16 simply returns the appropriate `Record` for the given primary key value.

The `Record` class is simple. During creation, it iterates over the keys from the `**kwargs` argument, again a dictionary of keyword arguments. If the argument's name is a valid column name, then the `setattr()` method stores the column value as an instance variable under the name of the column. This means that column values can be retrieved from `Record` objects as simple attributes, which is syntactically convenient.

Most of the rest of the program builds the `Table` objects required. Line 63 then iterates over each `Record` in the `BOOK` table, printing out the ISBN, a list of authors whose last names are retrieved from the appropriate `AUTHOR` `Record`, the book's name, the publisher name retrieved from the appropriate `PUBLISHER` `Record`, and the book's year of publication.

This object-oriented approach works, as you can see by running the program, but again there are several defects in the code. First, there is no check when a record is created to make sure that all necessary column values are added. Attempts to access a missing column would give rise to `KeyError` exceptions, which the code makes no attempt to handle. This could be fixed by adding a `__getattr__()` method to the `Record` class that returned `None` if the requested attribute was absent.

Second, there is no indication of whether a particular column is required. It would be more rigorous (and therefore better design practice) to extend the `Table` class so that when a `Table` was created, each column had an indication of whether it was required. The `addrec()` method already checks that the key field is present, and it could extend this checking by iterating over a list of required columns (which would be provided when the `Table` was created).

Implementing Many-to-Many Relationships

The structures used in Listings 8.5 and 8.6 are a simple analog of relational systems. The major violation of relational principles was to store a tuple of author keys as the value of each book's `Author` column, which we can do only because Python's data structures are more flexible.

In a relational database management system, all data has to be represented as tuples of single values, requiring a different way to implement many-to-many relationships. In practice, these relationships must be resolved into two relationships between the original entities and a new *linking* or *associative* entity created explicitly for this purpose. You can see this in Figure 8.4 with a linking entity called *authorship*. Sometimes the most difficult part of the resolution process is thinking up convincing names for the entities and relationships.

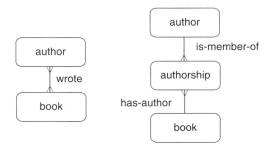

Figure 8.4   Resolving a many-to-many relationship into two one-to-many relationships.

The linking entity will have a composite primary key, comprising the primary keys of both original entities. In Figure 8.4, that makes the primary key of *authorship* the composite (BkISBN,AutNo). Note that neither component could be used on its own as the primary because this would prohibit the duplication of values required when either a book has multiple authors or an author has multiple authorships.

Besides being a part of the primary key, each component is a foreign key into one of the tables that the original many-to-many relationship joined. You might have noticed that a one-to-many relationship is always represented as a foreign key on the many side, and this is true even when the relationship is the result of resolving a many-to-many.

Database Integrity: Referential and Entity Integrity

Relational integrity is maintained as far as possible in industrial-strength databases by the database engine itself, to ensure that the data model accurately represents the required subset of the real world under as wide a variety of circumstances as possible.

In a relational database system, foreign keys implement relationships. *Referential integrity* requires that in each occurrence of every entity, foreign key attribute values *must* either

- Be NULL, indicating that this particular occurrence does not take part in the relationship, or
- Occur as a primary key value in the related table

All this really says is that an occurrence of one entity must relate to an occurrence of another entity and cannot reference a nonexistent occurrence. In less capable systems, you may have to write application code to maintain referential integrity.

Entity integrity simply requires that no part of the foreign key can take the NULL value. Because the primary key uniquely identifies each row in the relation, you must be able to say whether it has a particular value. Because the NULL value would yield a "don't know" value in any comparison, it must be forbidden as an element of a primary key.

Every relational database system can enforce this requirement without external programming.

Normalization: Avoiding Update Anomalies

The point of having each relation record data about only one entity type is to ensure that the relational structures are easy to update and can accurately model the real world in all its variety. Consider the relation in Table 8.4, which stores information about parts and suppliers.

Table 8.4 **A Non-Normalized Relation**

PartNo	Description	Price	Supplier	Address
PK321	Widget, Green	21.65	Smithson	214 Hotton Creek
PK321	Widget, Green	21.65	Tompkins	239 Bingley Road
PK734	Widget Holder	17.46	Smithson	214 Hotton Creek
PK374	Widget Holder	17.46	Allen	18 Bradley Drive
PK891	Widget Cup	12.75	Smithson	214 Hotton Creek
PK973	Desk	315.90	Smithson	214 Hotton Creek

Although this representation might seem suitable at first glance, it poses a number of problems, which quickly become clear when you consider how the world (and your need to model it) might change:

- **Delete anomaly**—Suppose that Widget Holder PK374 was deleted from the inventory as no longer required. Because this is the only part supplied by Allen, deleting the part details also deletes the details of the supplier as a side effect.

- **Insert anomaly**—Conversely, if you want to add a new supplier's details, there is nowhere to store the information unless the new supplier supplies an existing part.

- **Update anomaly**—If Smithson's address were to change, three different rows will have to be updated for the records to remain correct. Multiple rows also would need to be updated if the price of Widget Holders increased, also.

To normalize this structure, you need to ensure that the information is only stored against keys it actually depends on in some functional sense. The concept of *functional dependency* is a tricky one mathematically, but you are already familiar with it from Python. The items in a dictionary have a functional dependency on the keys: given a key, Python can look up the associated value. Note particularly that the same value can be stored against several keys, so you cannot necessarily say which key produced a given value.

This information would be more easily stored in three relations, as shown in Figure 8.5. Here the primary keys are underlined, and you should be able to see that each piece of data in each table depends on the primary key, the whole primary key, and nothing but the primary key.

PART

PartNo	Description	Price
PK321	Widget, Green	21.65
PK734	Widget Holder	17.46
PK891	Widget Cup	12.75
PK973	Desk	315.90

SUPPLIER

Supplier	Address
Smithson	214 Hotton Creek
Tompkins	239 Bingley road
Allen	18 Bradley Drive

PART/SUPPLIER

PartNo	Supplier
PK321	Smithson
PK321	Tompkins
PK734	Smithson
PK734	Allen
PK891	Smithson
PK973	Smithson

Figure 8.5 A normalized version of the part/supplier data.

Notice the effect of this transformation on the anomalies discussed previously. Deleting part PK734 no longer removes information about supplier Allen because that data is held in a separate relation. A new supplier who supplies no parts can be added simply by adding a row to the supplier relation, and if a supplier's address or a part's price changes, then the change can be affected by modifying a single piece of information.

The Rules of Normalization

The example in Figure 8.5 described a many-to-many relationship between `part` and `supplier`. If you have a moderate degree of experience at building data structures, you might have looked at it and thought this was the obvious implementation. If so, then the notion of functional dependency has probably become ingrained in your thinking, and you will not find it difficult to design normalized structures.

Otherwise, you might require some assistance, in which case, you should learn *Codd's Rules* for normalization. These rules, applied to relational data structures, allow you to produce your designs in *third normal form*. Although there are normalized forms beyond this, they handle special cases, which are unlikely to arise in your early uses of relational systems and can therefore be ignored until you *know* you need them.

Normalization is useful if you have existing data structures, perhaps from a legacy application, that need to be reconciled with a design for a new or updated system using relational technology. The discussion you are about to read refers to Figure 8.6, which describes a file layout typical of magnetic tape files from the applications of yesteryear. After you have normalized the structure, it fits naturally into a relational data store and can also easily be compared with and reconciled to a new design based on entity-relationship diagrams.

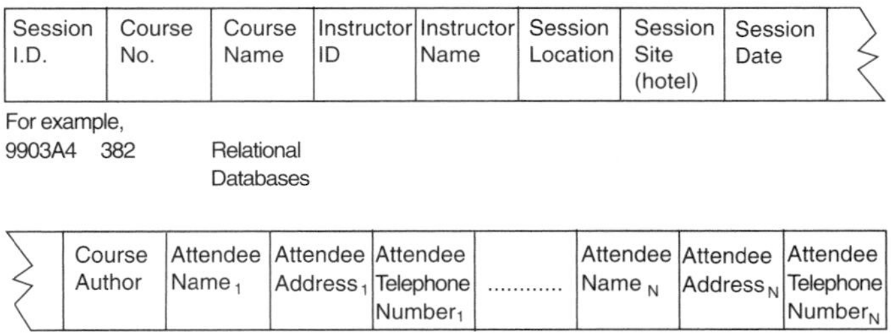

Session I.D.	Course No.	Course Name	Instructor ID	Instructor Name	Session Location	Session Site (hotel)	Session Date

For example,
9903A4   382   Relational Databases

	Course Author	Attendee Name$_1$	Attendee Address$_1$	Attendee Telephone Number$_1$	....	Attendee Name$_N$	Attendee Address$_N$	Attendee Telephone Number$_N$

Figure 8.6   A seminar attendance legacy data store format for normalization.

The records shown in Figure 8.6 describe sessions held by a training company, which presents various courses in seminar sessions around the world. Several instructors are available to teach each course, and attendees normally attend a series of seminars (although some attend just one).

First Normal Form: Remove Repeating Groups

First normal form requires that there be no repeating groups. This is logical because each entity can have only a fixed number of single-valued attributes. When splitting out the repeating group, you also must include the primary key of the entity from which it is being removed. This becomes a foreign key in the relation holding the repeating group's data, maintaining a many-to-one relationship between the new and the original entities.

Figure 8.6 has one repeating group:

```
(AttendeeName, AttendeeAddress, AttendeeTelephoneNumber)
```

In splitting this out as a separate entity, you have to choose a key. It is pretty obvious in this case that `AttendeeName` is the only candidate key. Our single entity has now become two, as shown in Figure 8.7.

Session

Session ID	Course No.	Course Name	Instructor ID	Instructor Name	Session Location	Session Site	Session Date	Course Author

Attendance

Session ID	Attendee Name	Attendee Address	Attendee Telephone

Figure 8.7   The seminar attendee data store in first normal form.

Second Normal Form: Remove Partial Dependencies

The new entity created by the transformation into first normal form, `Attendance`, has two key elements. The `SessionID` relates it back to the `Session`; and the second, `AttendeeName`, acts as a key for the particular attendee. Second normal form requires that each attribute in every relation depend on the whole key and not just a part of it.

If you think about it, the `AttendeeAddress` and `AttendeeTelephone` attributes cannot depend on the `SessionID`: if they did, then the attendee's address and telephone number might be different for each of the seminars he attended. So these two attributes properly depend only on the `AttendeeName` key. To put the data into second normal form, you create a separate `Attendee` entity to hold these attributes and the key element they depend on.

This `Attendee` entity also leaves its key in the original `Attendance` entity because the relationship between the old and the new entities must be retained to preserve the integrity of the data structure. Figure 8.8 shows the second normal form, in which the `Attendance` entity has been truncated by the removal of all the attributes that do not depend on all elements of the primary key to a separate `Attendee` entity. The composite primary key is all that remains.

Session

Session ID	Course No.	Course Name	Instructor ID	Instructor Name	Session Location	Session Site	Session Date	Course Author

Attendee

Attendee Name	Attendee Address	Attendee Telephone

Attendance

Session ID	Attendee Name

Figure 8.8   The seminar attendee data store in second normal form.

At this stage, you might think that `AttendeeName` is not a perfect choice for the key of the `Attendee` relation because it is conceivable that several attendees might have the same name. You would be correct. In the original data this did not appear to matter because the attendee data was repeated for each seminar attended.

In normalized relations, however, one goal is to avoid redundancy. Any particular piece of data should be stored only once, so there will only be one copy of each attendee's information, and each attendee must be uniquely identifiable. This avoids the update anomalies discussed earlier.

Clearly it is possible, and increasingly probable as the customer base grows, that several attendees will have the same name. Therefore at this stage, it is a good idea to add a further attribute to the `Attendee` entity, which acts as a reliable primary key on which all other attributes depend. Figure 8.9 shows this revision, and you can see that the new key also is used as the foreign key in the `Attendance` entity.

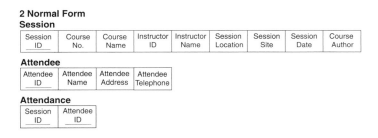

Figure 8.9   The second normal form with a revised attendee primary key.

Third Normal Form: Remove Attributes Wholly Dependent on Non-Keys

The revised second normal form in Figure 8.9 has three entities and appears to have satisfactory keys for each. When you examine the `Session` entity, however, you will see that some of the attributes are not determined by the primary key at all but by other attributes in the relation.

The `CourseNumber` and `CourseName` attributes for a given session depend directly on the `CourseNo` attribute, and only indirectly on the `SessionID` (because the `CourseNo` depends on the `SessionID`). In other words, course 367 will always be called "Introduction to TCP/IP" and written by a particular author, no matter which session presents it. Consequently, this data should be broken out into a new `Course` entity, leaving behind only the `CourseNo` key value to relate it back to the `Session`.

Similarly, the instructor retains his or her name no matter which session he or she presents, and therefore the `InstructorName` attribute depends directly on `InstructorID` and only indirectly on `SessionID`, so again a new entity is broken out leaving the key attribute behind to mark the relationship. At this stage, the original structure has been translated into third normal form, as shown in Figure 8.10, and now contains five entities.

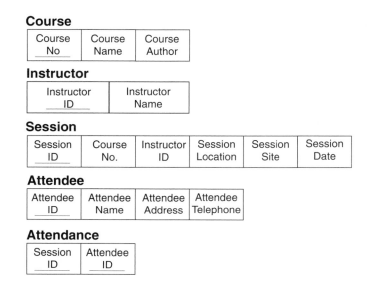

Figure 8.10 The seminar attendee data store in third normal form.

This might seem more complicated than the original representation, but it is a much cleaner design. As a by-product of the transformation, it is now apparent that there are five entities of interest. Instructor and Attendee are concrete entities, whereas Session and Course are conceptual. Attendance is an event, which occurs when a particular student attends a particular session, presumably with the intention of learning the material from the course that the session presents.

The same design is presented as an entity relationship diagram in Figure 8.11. From the graphical representation, it is easier to see that Session encapsulates a many-to-many relationship between courses and instructors and that Attendance encapsulates a many-to-many relationship between sessions and attendees.

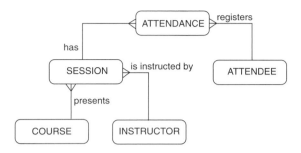

Figure 8.11 Entity relationship diagram of the normalized seminar attendee data.

Semantic Integrity: Applying Business Rules

Every organization is constrained in many ways. Some of the constraints are legislative; some are a matter of organizational policy. But the upshot is that certain states of the database can be allowed, and certain others cannot. For example, a sales organization usually maintains a credit limit for each of its customers and requires that the total of their outstanding orders plus their current account balance be less than that credit limit.

This is usually called a *business rule*. Database workers talk about "maintaining the semantic integrity of the database," which is another way to say that the application that maintains the data model must ensure that the database content always observes all business rules. The database engine can usually handle entity and referential integrity without assistance, but these alone will not suffice.

Constraining the Database Contents

The database engine enforces *declarative constraints*—the range of values for a specific attribute can, for example, be limited with a CHECK constraint, which the engine evaluates whenever updates and insertions take place. Constraints of this nature usually involve single attributes—salaries must be positive numbers, start dates must be valid dates, and so on. Primary key uniqueness, and foreign key referential integrity are usually the most complex declarative constraints available. You also can declare that any attribute may or may not hold the NULL value.

More complex constraints might involve several attributes in a row, or even several rows in the same table. As an example of the first kind, it might be illegal to employ people below, say, the age of 16, in which case an employee's date of birth must be at least 16 years before her start date. In the second case, if each employee's department and manager are recorded, perhaps an employee's department must be the same as his manager's (whose data will not be recorded in the same row).

The more complex the business rule is, the less likely you will be able to find a declarative constraint to enforce it. In that case, you may have to code the rules as a part of your application logic, which in a large application can lead to the likelihood that different programs will contain the same logic. This can lead to maintenance difficulties, because if the rule changes, there will be several different places where the code must be changed, and any inconsistency might violate the semantic integrity of the data.

You will discover a better solution when you read about stored procedures and triggers in Chapter 9, "Client/Server Database Architectures." These techniques allow you to use the database as a repository for code to enforce the rules automatically, without each individual program having to incorporate them.

Cascaded Updates and Deletes

With two related tables, you normally expect the database engine to enforce the relational integrity rules. If it does, what should it do when you try to delete a row whose primary key is used as a foreign key value in related tables? There are three alternatives, and you choose the required alternative for each relationship when you apply the relationship constraint.

Delete Restriction

The simplest, and usually the default, case is that the engine simply raises an error. Deletion is only acceptable when the primary key of the record to be deleted is not in use as a foreign key; otherwise, the RDBMS restricts you from performing the deletion, raising an error. Often the message provided by the database engine itself is not terribly meaningful to end-users, so you should ensure that users understand why the operation they have requested is not allowed by producing a suitable message in the application. In other words, tell them "There are current orders against this supplier, so you cannot delete the supplier details," not "This operation would violate referential integrity."

Cascading Delete

Sometimes you want the database engine to proceed with the deletion and enforce referential integrity by also deleting related rows in another table. This is a good option to choose when the related data provide supporting information, which will no longer be relevant when the related item is deleted. In an inventory system where suppliers are recorded, it makes sense when deleting a supplier to delete all records of the parts they supplied.

Even then you sometimes will want to code the application to warn the user that related data also will disappear, rather than simply letting the deletion cascade over another table. This requires a message such as "This company is recorded as supplier of 15 parts. Please confirm the deletion request."

Nullification

The third option for deletion still maintains referential integrity, but it does so by setting any related foreign key values to NULL (obviously, this has to be permissible under the declarative constraints). This last option is appropriate when you do not want to lose the data to which the deleted primary key is related. Such a policy might be appropriate if your organization ran a mentoring scheme. Your Human Resources Department might record who mentors whom as a relationship between Employee and Employee—an example of a *recursive relationship*, where the same entity is involved at both ends.

In this case, restriction would be inappropriate because mentors cannot be prohibited from leaving the organization, and cascading would be inappropriate because it would delete the details about the employees who were being mentored. So you would choose nullification, which might leave some employees without a mentor but nevertheless retains the referential (and semantic) integrity of the database.

Physical Design Considerations

The usual way to proceed in the implementation of database applications is to produce a normalized logical data model, using either or both normalization and entity relationship diagramming. Before application testing can begin, you must implement the data model within the RDBMS of your choice. At this stage you, or preferably your database administrator (DBA), will become involved in *physical* design: the data model ceases to be a theoretical abstraction and becomes a real object that can store real data.

Up to this point, you will have been mostly concerned with *correctness*: does the logical data model accurately represent the real world for the application, and are the required constraints correctly maintained over all changes? Now the implementation team starts to worry about *efficiency*: does the system work fast enough so that performance goals can be met? Physical database design targets both performance and manageability issues.

Platform-Dependence of Physical Design

It is impossible to give too many rules for physical design without referring to the specifics of the database engine used to implement a relational system. Performance is a key competitive discriminator among the database vendors, who expend great efforts to excel at transaction processing benchmarks. They each have their own techniques and often provide extensions to the SQL language to allow their use. This is one of the reasons why a DBA is invaluable: she will know the details of your RDBMS and will be able to bring the specific features of the engine into play to increase the efficiency of the system's operation for the processing performed by the application.

An important feature of any modern RDBMS is that changes can be made to the physical representation used without affecting the application code, which continues to work in terms of the logical data model. Efficiency goals are usually met by minimizing disk input and output, and so physical design decisions must be based on data volumes, frequency of access, and so on. A good DBA will change the physical design as usage patterns change and as hardware and software updates become available. None of this should affect the logical data model, so program changes will not be needed.

Indexing and Its Impact on Performance

The most common technique for improving performance is to have the RDBMS maintain indexes. These are like subsidiary tables, held separately from the main data tables and automatically updated by the RDBMS as the data changes. The index may cover one or several columns from a table; and besides containing copies of the table data from those columns, it will record a pointer to the data from the corresponding table row. If a table has many columns, an index will be much smaller, frequently small enough for the RDBMS to retain it in memory.

Indexes are special structures, and they are stored in such a way that random access to a single key is fast, but it is also efficient to process the index sequentially. Because each index row points directly to the corresponding data table row, this in turn speeds up sequential access to the table.

The only downside is that the indexes have to be maintained as the underlying tables are updated. Consequently, although retrieval performance improves, there is a corresponding degradation in update performance. The index update load makes performance become worse as the number of indexes increases.

Rather than degrade regular operations to speed up one program in an application, sometimes a DBA will have the RDBMS create an index just before the program starts and remove it after the program completes. In this case, the update performance degradation is only temporary, but of course there is an extra wait for the index to be created. Indexing a moderately sized table with, say, two million rows is not an insignificant operation, and testing is usually needed to determine whether there is an overall improvement.

One further indexing benefit is when a particular column or set of columns must hold unique values. In this case, it is much more efficient for the RDBMS to check an index for the existence of a value than it is to have to scan the whole table, and so indexing such columns usually is beneficial.

Denormalization: Risks, Rewards, and Alternatives

As you have learned in this chapter, normalized data structures offer huge benefits, including

- The elimination of update anomalies
- Minimization of redundant storage
- Simplification of program logic

In addition, the database design becomes much less dependent on the initial application, so new functions can be added relatively easily, without modifying existing logic. This encourages separate applications to share data, because the data is structured in such a way as to be easily processed in whatever way the application may require.

You may sometimes encounter an application where, despite the best efforts of the designers and DBAs, performance is still not satisfactory. Then, and *only* then, you might want to consider moving away from a normalized design. Because such a move involves changes to the *logical* data model, however, it requires changes to the programs that process the data. The denormalization approach is therefore most useful where the data is read-only or infrequently changed because this minimizes the impact of the various update anomalies.

Denormalization should be undertaken as a last resort and most frequently involves producing tables by joining together two or more tables from the original normalized design across defined relationships. Of course, if the data has to be updated, then your programs have to cope with the update anomalies you read about earlier. This is a significant change in some circumstances.

The major alternative to denormalization is to *fragment* the tables. This involves partitioning them into disjoint sets of rows or columns.

The first approach (*horizontal fragmentation*) takes a table from the normalized design and splits it into a number of tables each containing some rows from the original table. This is most useful if there are users who only require access to a subset of the rows but need access to all attributes of the rows they use. The application can then be parameterized as to which of the fragment tables the user running the program should access.

The second approach (not surprisingly called *vertical fragmentation*) is useful if the majority of programs only need access to a limited set of attributes for an entity. The designer splits up the relevant table into a set of frequently accessed columns and a set of less-frequently accessed columns. The original entity effectively becomes two entities with a *one-to-one* relationship between them, and the primary key field is the same in both. If each row of the original table contained many columns, then speed-up will occur in the dominant programs because they will have to process a greatly reduced amount of data.

You can hide these denormalizations to a certain extent by providing database *views* that make the data appear like the original tables. For horizontal fragmentation, the view would provide the union of all the fragments, whereas for horizontal fragmentation, you would have to join rows of each table for equal primary key values. This will have a negative effect on performance but will allow you to make code changes in a more controlled way, tackling the most significant performance requirements first.

Both denormalization and fragmentation have the disadvantage that they change the logical data model and so require changes to the application logic. This is why they must be considered only after all other changes to the physical model have failed to yield adequate performance.

Summary

This chapter explained *why* relational database systems are structured the way they are and gave you an understanding of sound design rules. Correct application of design principles yields a database design that might *seem* complex, but in fact actually yields much simpler programming logic. Ultimately, this is a big win because program defects have a much higher cost in the long term than performance issues.

If the performance of your design turns out to be inadequate, you can take action by changing the physical implementation of the logical model, which will not require code changes. Your DBA might be able to adjust the location of your data to avoid device conflicts, for example; and most modern RDBMSs, when heavily loaded, respond to the addition of more memory with huge increases in performance. Indexing techniques, some of which will be specific to your chosen RDBMS, can give you yet another increment in performance. It is sometimes even worth creating temporary indexes just to speed up a batch operation and allow a faster return to online operations. Finally, and as a last resort, you can change your logical data model. This brings with it changes to your program code, which might include the need to cope with update anomalies.

In the next chapter, you will see how database architectures have evolved, largely as a result of the growth in client/server applications, so that they can support the web operations of the present day and, hopefully, the future.

9

Client/Server Database Architectures

THE MAIN FUNCTION OF AN RDBMS (relational database management system) is to allow for the management and use of one or more databases. The RDBMS should make it easy to construct new databases, evolve the structure of the databases it manages, and manipulate the user data contained in the databases. It should provide one or more standard interfaces so that tools of many kinds from different vendors can perform the required functions. A good RDBMS allows concurrent access by many users, provides security features to protect the data from unauthorized access or manipulation, and maintains the integrity of the data.

In this chapter, you will learn how modern database systems have evolved to support distributed computing architectures, which have become more common over the last 15 years. After reading this chapter, you will better understand how applications communicate with the database server. You also will have a basic familiarity with the Structured Query Language (SQL), which has become an almost universal interface to relational systems at the application level.

The Client/Server Nature of Modern Relational Databases

Relational database systems today tend to separate the database engine from the other system components, to the extent that these components can run on separate machines. The RDBMS has become a server component in a client/server architecture.

The Role of the Database Engine

The engine is the heart of the RDBMS, providing data management services to a wide range of client application processes such as

- Backup and restore tools
- Database design tools
- Report writers
- Form-driven, natural-language, and query-by-example query tools
- Application development packages
- Spreadsheets
- Custom applications code

The structure of the application data (the user tables, the attributes of each table, the primary and foreign key constraints, and so on) is held in predefined system tables collectively referred to as the *data dictionary*. The data dictionary stores data about the user data, sometimes referred to as *metadata*. The RDBMS updates the system tables as the structure of the database changes and uses them to provide access to the data when applications need to manipulate it. A further use of the data dictionary is to record access controls, allowing the RDBMS to ensure that users may only access and change the subsets of the data for which they have authorization. There are no standards for the data dictionary—vendors each have their own proprietary formats, and interoperability is nonexistent at this level.

It is the engine's responsibility to efficiently implement data storage and access, and to do this, most database systems use proprietary technology to optimize query processing. This optimization uses the data dictionary, statistical information concerning the actual contents of the tables, and information about available indexes that could help to speed up particular queries. Because performance is so important, this is another area of competitive research and development.

The database engine must, to allow safe concurrent processing, support *transaction processing*. A transaction is a logical unit of work that might involve several accesses to the database, which moves the database from one consistent state to another. A transaction must be treated as atomic: it either executes in its entirety, or the database is left as though nothing happened. This involves maintaining a log of completed transactions, which is also useful for recovery purposes.

If the database system fails and has to be restarted, the transaction log is examined, and any incomplete transactions are rolled back to leave the database consistent. The log is also useful in the case of media failure. Then a backup copy of the database must be loaded, and the transactions processed since the backup was taken are replayed from the log to bring the database back up-to-date.

SQL as a Standard Interface

As distributed computing systems became a reality in the 1980s and early 1990s, tools emerged to enable communication between clients and servers. You have already looked at the Internet family of protocols that allow the construction of heterogeneous systems—those built from different kinds of computers. The same problems had to be solved at a higher level to allow communication across networks between database components.

At the application level, the common ground for all database systems is ANSI SQL, a standardized version of the Structured Query Language. Unfortunately, RDBMSs do not fully implement ANSI SQL, which makes portability across engines somewhat problematic. Further, most vendors have introduced proprietary extensions to SQL, and use of these extensions will have a further negative effect on portability. This may or may not be important for your applications, but you should be aware of it. In the section "SQL and Its Subsets" later in the chapter, you will have a chance to become more familiar with this fascinating language.

Platform Independence

Some database driver software is smart enough to take ANSI SQL and adapt it (by translating it on-the-fly) to the particular engine in use. Vendors normally make the features of their database available via a *call level interface* (CLI). This is an API used by programmers to request the database engine to take actions. Usually the primary goal is to pass SQL queries to the database, although some CLIs allow the programmer to manipulate the structures more directly. You will greatly increase the effort of migrating to another engine by using a specialized CLI.

Fortunately, there has been wide agreement in the industry that database products should provide a high level of interoperability. Accordingly, there are several ways that you can avoid having to adapt your applications to the vagaries of a specific RDBMS, although the SQL extensions are always lurking on the side to tempt you into a proprietary solution. Because databases now operate in a client/server environment, the drivers naturally accommodate the capability for the consumer of database services to run on a different host from the provider, the RDBMS.

Originally the database client and server would run on the same machine. The client program called routines in the CLI, either directly or by having a preprocessor translate a program with SQL statements embedded in it into a program that used the RDBMS CLI. When the program was executed, the CLI library routines would access the database and return results as required to the application program. You can see the setup in Figure 9.1. The solution is *homogeneous* because all code is compiled for the same architecture. This follows from its *monolithic* nature: everything runs on the same machine.

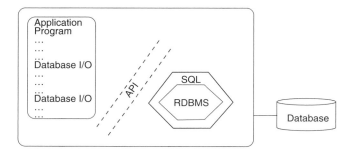

Figure 9.1   A traditional database application using the database API.

One disadvantage of this technique is that it makes it difficult to distribute an application such as a spreadsheet and have it communicate with any required database. Because the preprocessor inserts engine-specific calls into the code, you would have to compile one version with an Oracle preprocessor, another with a Sybase preprocessor, and so on. As for operating against multiple database products, this would simply be impossible.

Client/server systems are obviously not monolithic, and given the right technology, they do not have to be homogeneous either: a PC client can easily access a mainframe server if the right API is available on the client. Even better, the networking aspects of the client/server systems can be transparent to the programmer. If the API is the same in Figure 9.2 as it is in Figure 9.1, then no changes would be required to the application program.

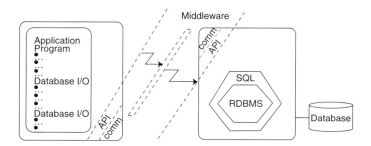

Figure 9.2   Transparent networking in a distributed database application.

Driver Structures

Many different driver structures are likely to be available with whatever database engine you adopt. Using a proprietary call-level interface may be necessary if you have to extract the last ounce of speed out of your system, but this is the worst solution in terms of portability. Various multiplatform solutions have been proposed in the past, but few have captured the market as effectively as ODBC, discussed in the next section. Your applications will be linked to drivers in various ways: either statically, if you choose a CLI, or dynamically by other methods.

The disadvantage of CLIs, as well as embedded SQL, is the impossibility of integrating multiple data sources from different vendors in a single program. Python has standardized an API for databases, and most of the contributed drivers have made efforts to comply with this standard. Python programmers are luckier than many others who do not have language-specific database bindings. You will meet the Python database interface (more formally known as the DB-API specification, version 2.0) in Chapter 10, "The Python Database Interface."

ODBC: The Jewel in the Crown

Some time ago a group called the SQL Access Group specified a call-level interface intended to be easy to implement for a wide range of data sources—even non-relational ones. Microsoft implemented the CLI and named its implementation *Open Database Connectivity* (ODBC). The original design makes it easy to interface to any data source for which there is a driver, and three different levels of SQL compliance are defined. ODBC is now the most widely supported API of its kind. Most commercial database vendors include ODBC drivers for their engines as a part of the product, and there is an active market in third-party ODBC products as well as a few open-source implementations. ODBC uses a four-layer architecture as shown in Figure 9.3.

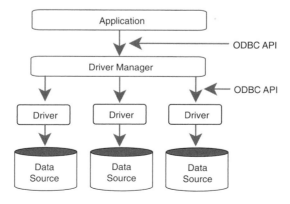

Figure 9.3   ODBC architecture.

The application code makes calls to the ODBC driver manager, which provides a uniform API independent of any particular back end. The driver manager in turn makes calls (using the same API) to one or more ODBC drivers, specific to a particular back-end database. Drivers are registered when they are installed on a machine, and each driver can be used to access any number of different data sources of the same type. These data sources are also registered, and referenced by name from within an application.

When an application accesses a data source, the driver manager dynamically loads the correct driver and uses it to connect with the back end. Data sources can be parameterized to include authentication details, or they can be left open, in which case the user is prompted to provide the details when the database connection is made. Many of the drivers include middleware to communicate across the network with the back end, making client/server database applications practical. Ultimately, of course, the drivers will use the vendor's proprietary CLI, but this is completely transparent to the application, which only interacts with the driver manager.

Why Not OLEDB?

You might have heard that Microsoft has developed a more generic approach still to accessing data sources and calls it OLEDB. Microsoft now encourages customers to write for OLEDB rather than ODBC, claiming greater efficiency and better data source integration. Although these claims may be true, remember that unlike ODBC, OLEDB is built on Microsoft's proprietary COM technology, which is still fairly limited in its interoperability with non-Microsoft platforms.

OLEDB may be a better solution if you are committed to a Microsoft-only network, as many are. Although vendors are now supplying OLEDB drivers for the Microsoft environment, the huge installed base of ODBC applications makes it improbable that vendors will desert ODBC *en masse*, so you are probably safe in continuing to use it.

Be aware, however, that Microsoft's determined promotion of OLEDB has definitely led to a lack of focus on ODBC, with the result that ODBC drivers are not being maintained as aggressively as the newer OLEDB drivers. Therefore you may need to migrate to OLEDB to use the newer functionality introduced in more recent products, or simply to avoid known long-standing bugs in ODBC-based products.

SQL and Its Subsets

The Structured Query Language is the common interface between databases and their applications, no matter what communications technique is used between the client and the server. The primary benefits of SQL have been twofold. First, there is no longer any need, when designing program logic, to know anything about the physical representation of the data on storage media. Second, SQL implementations do all the grunt work of query optimization and do not require programmers to specify the sequence of relational algebra operations required to implement a query.

SQL has gone through the standardization process a number of times, most recently in 1999. The original 1986 standard specified the syntax of the language but did not define how database systems were supposed to respond to SQL statements, leading to patchy interoperability and confusion about the meaning of the language. The 1989 standard introduced bindings for the C and ADA languages and added ways to specify declarative constraints for uniqueness of values, referential integrity, value checking, and the provision of default values.

In 1992, a third standard, much revised and about four times longer, specified four different levels of compliance. A standard for call level interfaces appeared in 1995, and this and other work has now been integrated in the 1999 standard, usually referred to as SQL3. This standard has five parts at the time of this writing:

- The framework is described in 85 pages.

- An 1147-page section provides the foundation of the specification.

- A 421-page section describes the call level interface.

- A 170-page section describes features of persistent stored modules, discussed briefly in the later sections on stored procedures and triggers.

- Language bindings are discussed in a 261-page section.

Further work is proceeding on the standard framework, and further sections are likely to be added in the near future discussing the management of external data and changes to the language to better support *online analytical processing* (OLAP), which is typically used on the high-volume, read-only databases known as *data warehouses*. Although OLAP systems have much in common with standard relational databases, there is a much stronger emphasis on denormalization to achieve high performance levels on queries over huge volumes of data.

SQL is in the process of becoming a much broader language than it was in its earlier incarnations, to the extent that it will support user-defined data types and an object-oriented model in the future. This is a book on Python, not SQL, though, so although the next sections will get you started, do not regard this exposition as complete. Traditionally, SQL is regarded as three sub-languages serving three different functions, each with its own commands, and this is a good approach for learning purposes.

SQL Syntax and Sample Code

As you will see, from the examples in this chapter, SQL is a free-format language. Its syntax is not case-sensitive, though comparisons of string values are normally sensitive to case unless a DBA switches off this feature. In the examples, SQL-reserved words are in uppercase to help draw attention to the user-defined elements, such as table and column names. When the syntax of SQL statements is discussed, brackets imply the component is optional, and an ellipsis (...) implies the preceding element may be repeated.

Despite the best efforts of the ANSI and ISO standards organizations, you will almost inevitably have to adapt your SQL to the idiosyncrasies of the particular product you use. Some vendors come close to

continues

> **SQL Syntax and Sample Code (Continued)**
>
> implementing the 1992 standard at the highest level (four compliance levels are defined). Others come less close. The 1999 standard will affect product development for years to come. Most of the examples in this chapter work on both Microsoft SQL Server 7.0 and Access 2000 (technically the Jet engine, to which Access is a front end and which can be freely downloaded from Microsoft's web site), which are the database systems most readily available to the author.
>
> A semicolon terminates each SQL statement. Not all systems require such a terminator, and some systems allow the use of other terminators, but the format used is most likely to be universally acceptable. In Access, the statements have to be entered one by one because the Query window will not accept multiple statements. The SQL samples are intended to be close enough to standard SQL that you should be able to adapt them readily to whichever platform you must use.
>
> The sizes of the columns in the examples are deliberately small to make it easier for the publisher to typeset printed output from retrieval queries. Normally much wider fields would be required in production applications.

DDL: Defining the Data Model

After you have produced a logical data model, you have to implement it in an RDBMS as a physical model, a realization of the logical model that can actually be used to store data. The subset of SQL that allows you to do this and to maintain the model by changing its structure and tuning it as requirements and usage changes, is called the *Data Definition Language* (DDL). There are three principal DDL verbs:

- **CREATE**—Used to insert new definitions (table, indexes, constraints, and so on) into the data dictionary
- **DROP**—Used to remove definitions from the data dictionary
- **ALTER**—Used to modify definitions already present in the data dictionary

Simple examples of the **CREATE** verb being used to create tables are shown in Listing 9.1, where definitions compatible with the earlier book sales example are given.

Listing 9.1   *create1.sql:* **The *CREATE* Verb Used to Build a Simple Physical Model**

```
 1   CREATE TABLE Publisher   (
 2          PubNo             INT              NOT NULL,
 3          PubName           VARCHAR (12)     NOT NULL,
 4          PubWebSIte        VARCHAR (50)
 5   );
 6
 7   CREATE TABLE Author      (
 8          AutNo             INT              NOT NULL,
 9          AutFirst          VARCHAR (10)     NOT NULL,
10          AutLast           VARCHAR (10)     NOT NULL,
11          AutLoc            VARCHAR (10)
```

```
12  );
13
14  CREATE TABLE Book       (
15         BkISBN      CHAR    (12)     NOT NULL,
16         BkName      VARCHAR (30)     NOT NULL,
17         PubNo       INT              NOT NULL,
18         BkYear      INT
19  );
20
21  CREATE TABLE Authorship (
22         AutNo       INT              NOT NULL,
23         BkISBN      CHAR    (12)     NOT NULL
24  );
```

This is straightforward. CREATE TABLE precedes the name of the table to be created and a parenthesized list of attribute (column) specifications. Each column specification names the column and associates a data type with it. You can include constraints in the column specification if you want, and the example in Listing 9.1 includes NOT NULL constraints to limit the RDBMS to creating NULL values only in the following columns:

- Publisher.PubWebSite
- Author.AutLoc
- Book.BkYear

The preceding list of columns uses qualified names, in which the table name precedes the column name and is separated from it by a dot. SQL allows you to use non-qualified names where there is no ambiguity. The columns in Listing 9.1 all take either integer or character string values. Although the ANSI standard has for a long time specified the permissible data types for SQL, the standard is more honored in the breach than the observance. Table 9.1 lists some of the more common types you are likely to come across.

Table 9.1 **Common SQL Data Types (consult your documentation…)**

Type	Description
CHARACTER(N)	Fixed-length ASCII string of length N.
CHAR(N)	
VARCHAR(N)	Variable-length ASCII string of maximum length N.
DEC (P,S)	Numeric values with a fixed-point representation giving P digits of precision and S decimal places.
DECIMAL (P,S)	
NUMERIC(P,S)	

continues

Table 9.1   **Continued**

Type	Description
DOUBLE PRECISION	Floating-point number with high precision.
FLOAT	Floating-point number with standard precision.
REAL	
INT	Integer.
INTEGER	
NCHAR(*N*)	Unicode character string of length *N*. The encoding used is generally determined when the database is installed.
NATIONAL CHAR(*N*)	
NATIONAL CHARACTER(*N*)	
NCHAR VARYING	Unicode character string of maximum length *N*. The encoding used is generally determined when the database is installed.
NATIONAL CHAR VARYING	
NATIONAL CHARACTER VARYING	
SMALLINT	Integer values with a smaller range than the standard type.

In practice, constraints are frequently not included in the table definitions when first implementing a data model. The main reason is to make the data easier to load. After the RDBMS starts to monitor constraints, data must be loaded into table in a sequence that maintains referential integrity. To add a constraint to an existing table, use the ALTER TABLE statement. Listing 9.2 adds primary and foreign key constraints to the tables defined in Listing 9.1.

Listing 9.2   *alter1.sql:* **Adding Primary and Foreign Key Constraints**

```
 1  ALTER TABLE Author
 2        ADD CONSTRAINT Aut_PK
 3        PRIMARY KEY (AutNo);
 4
 5  ALTER TABLE Book
 6        ADD CONSTRAINT Bk_PK
 7        PRIMARY KEY (BkISBN);
 8
 9  ALTER TABLE Publisher
10        ADD CONSTRAINT Pub_PK
11        PRIMARY KEY (PubNo);
12
13  ALTER TABLE Authorship
14        ADD CONSTRAINT Ashp_PK
15        PRIMARY KEY (AutNo, BkISBN);
16
17  ALTER TABLE Book
```

```
18          ADD CONSTRAINT BkPub_FK
19          FOREIGN KEY (PubNo) REFERENCES Publisher;
20
21   ALTER TABLE Authorship
22          ADD CONSTRAINT AshpBk_FK
23          FOREIGN KEY (BkISBN) REFERENCES Book;
24
25   ALTER TABLE Authorship
26          ADD CONSTRAINT AshpAut_FK
27          FOREIGN KEY (AutNo) REFERENCES Author;
```

Listing 9.2 adds the primary key constraints first, then the foreign key constraints. You are not required to include a name for constraints as this example does, but it *is* convenient: otherwise, the database system uses its own names for the constraints, which you have to discover before you can drop the constraint.

As a check that the DDL has produced the required structures, the statements were entered into SQL Server, which has the helpful ability to produce entity-relationship diagrams from the table structures and constraints it finds in a database. Figure 9.4 shows the result, which verifies that this design is indeed what is required.

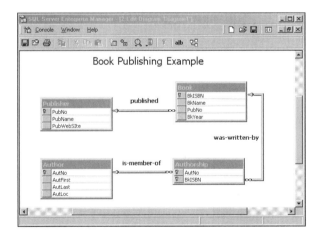

Figure 9.4 SQL Server 7.0 maps relational structures.

The ALTER TABLE statement is one of the more syntactically complex in SQL, with many options not specified in the standard having been added by various RDBMS suppliers to support proprietary extensions. ALTER TABLE also can be used for purposes as varied as adding new columns, dropping existing columns, and modifying the characteristics of columns (changing the length of a character field, for example). Because of the wide variations, you would be well advised to consult your system's manuals to find out what is valid.

The DROP verb removes objects from the database. To drop a column or a constraint from a table, use a DROP clause in an ALTER TABLE statement. To drop a table from a database, you need the DROP TABLE statement. Listing 9.3 shows how to drop the tables and constraints created in the previous two examples, ensuring that the constraints on a table are dropped before the table itself. Strictly, there is no need to drop the primary key constraints. Because there are no external dependencies, dropping the table drops the primary key as well, but the example underlines that you can drop the constraint while retaining the table. Attempting to drop the tables without deleting the *foreign* key constraints would result in an error, though, since the relationship makes the related tables interdependent.

Listing 9.3   *drop1.sql:* **Dropping Constraints and Tables**

```
 1  ALTER TABLE Authorship DROP CONSTRAINT AshpBk_FK;
 2  ALTER TABLE Authorship DROP CONSTRAINT AshpAut_FK;
 3  ALTER TABLE Authorship DROP CONSTRAINT Ashp_PK;
 4  DROP TABLE Authorship;
 5  ALTER TABLE Book DROP CONSTRAINT Bk_PK;
 6  ALTER TABLE Book DROP CONSTRAINT BkPub_FK;
 7  DROP TABLE Book;
 8  ALTER TABLE Publisher DROP CONSTRAINT Pub_PK;
 9  DROP TABLE Publisher;
10  ALTER TABLE Author DROP CONSTRAINT Aut_PK;
11  DROP TABLE Author;
```

Deletion and Update: Referential Integrity Alternatives

Some databases allow you to specify automatic actions to be taken on foreign key columns when the related primary key is deleted or modified. The declaration of these constraints is made with the foreign key because there can be several different foreign keys related to the same primary, and they may require different actions:

- **RESTRICT**—The default action is as described previously: the RDBMS raises an error rather than allow changes to violate referential integrity.

- **CASCADE**—For a deletion, the rows containing the related foreign keys are also deleted; for an update, the foreign key values are automatically updated to the new primary value, retaining referential integrity in either case.

- **NULLIFY**—If a relationship is optional, its foreign keys may hold null values because not all occurrences of the related entity take part in the relationship. Nullification sets the foreign keys relating to a deleted primary key to NULL.

DML: Dealing with the Data

The data manipulation language (DML) portion of SQL uses four verbs:

- **INSERT**—Creates new rows in user tables

- **SELECT**—Retrieves information from one or more tables in the database (including data dictionary tables if required)
- **UPDATE**—Allows changes to be made to existing rows in the user tables
- **DELETE**—Removes rows from the user tables

Note that you should only retrieve data from the built-in tables in the data dictionary with SELECT, and never use the UPDATE, INSERT, or DELETE verbs on them. The DDL verbs covered in the preceding section make changes to their contents in a defined manner. Trying to update the data dictionary using DML statements is likely to lead to disaster because the data dictionary's contents determine the processing of all SQL statements.

INSERT

Insertion of data normally happens one row per INSERT statement, although there are variant forms of INSERT and SELECT that allow you to selectively copy data between tables. The simplest form has the syntax

```
INSERT INTO table VALUES(value1, value2, ...)
```

Try not to use this syntax because it assumes a particular column order, which you cannot depend on if something later changes the table structures. It is much safer and hardly more complicated to use the complete syntax:

```
INSERT INTO table (colname1, colname2, ...) VALUES (value1, value2, ...)
```

This method removes any ambiguity. If not all columns are given values, then columns with a DEFAULT VALUE constraint will be set to the specified default, and other columns will be set to the NULL value (unless this is prohibited by a NOT NULL constraint). In either case, a new row appears in the target table (unless the insertion would violate RDBMS declarative constraints). Listing 9.4 shows an example that uses INSERT to populate the tables created in Listings 9.1 and 9.2.

Listing 9.4   *insert1.sql:* **Inserting the Book, Publisher, Author, and Authorship Data**

```
 1   INSERT INTO Author (AutNo, AutFirst, AutLast, AutLoc)
 2         VALUES (1, 'David', 'Beazley', 'USA');
 3   INSERT INTO Author (AutNo, AutFirst, AutLast, AutLoc)
 4         VALUES (2, 'Steve', 'Holden', 'USA');
 5   INSERT INTO Author (AutNo, AutFirst, AutLast, AutLoc)
 6         VALUES (3, 'Mark', 'Lutz', 'USA');
 7   INSERT INTO Author (AutNo, AutFirst, AutLast, AutLoc)
 8         VALUES (4, 'David', 'Ascher', 'USA');
 9   INSERT INTO Author (AutNo, AutFirst, AutLast, AutLoc)
10         VALUES (5, 'Mark', 'Hammond', 'Australia');
11   INSERT INTO Author (AutNo, AutFirst, AutLast, AutLoc)
12         VALUES (6, 'Andy', 'Robinson', 'UK');
13
14   INSERT INTO Publisher (PubNo, PubName, PubWebSite)
```

continues

Listing 9.4 **Continued**

```
15          VALUES (1, 'New Riders', 'www.newriders.com');
16  INSERT INTO Publisher (PubNo, PubName, PubWebSite)
17          VALUES (2, 'O''Reilly', 'www.ora.com');
18
19  INSERT INTO Book (BkISBN, BkName, PubNo, BkYear)
20          VALUES ('0735710910', 'Python Essential Reference', 1, 2001);
21  INSERT INTO Book (BkISBN, BkName, PubNo, BkYear)
22          VALUES ('0735710902', 'Python Web Programming', 1, 2001);
23  INSERT INTO Book (BkISBN, BkName, PubNo, BkYear)
24          VALUES ('1565924649', 'Learning Python', 2, 1999);
25  INSERT INTO Book (BkISBN, BkName, PubNo, BkYear)
26          VALUES ('1565926218', 'Python Programming on Win32', 2, 1999);
27
28  INSERT INTO Authorship (AutNo, BkISBN) VALUES(1, '0735710910');
29  INSERT INTO Authorship (AutNo, BkISBN) VALUES(2, '0735710902');
30  INSERT INTO Authorship (AutNo, BkISBN) VALUES(3, '1565924649');
31  INSERT INTO Authorship (AutNo, BkISBN) VALUES(4, '1565924649');
32  INSERT INTO Authorship (AutNo, BkISBN) VALUES(5, '1565926218');
33  INSERT INTO Authorship (AutNo, BkISBN) VALUES(6, '1565926218');
```

You can see that single quotes delimit literal strings, and that you can escape a single quote by doubling it (as in `'O''Reilly'`, the second publisher's name, on line 17). An additional flavor of the INSERT syntax allows you to insert the result of a SELECT query, covered in the next section, into a table. The general syntax is as follows:

```
INSERT INTO table [(column-list)]
    SELECT-statement;
```

Here the number and type of the columns retrieved in the SELECT statement must agree with those of the optional `column-list` if it is given, and omitting the `column-list` again leaves the statement vulnerable to structural changes in the database.

SELECT

Now that the tables are populated with data, you can start to learn about retrieval, for which you use the SELECT statement. This is powerful, and therefore potentially complex in its syntax. Simple statements are easy to understand, though, with a relatively simple syntax:

```
SELECT column [,column...]
    FROM table [,table ...]
    [WHERE condition]
    [ORDER BY column {ASC ¦ DESC] ...]
```

The simplest statements can even omit the WHERE clause usually used to restrict the retrieved values to those of interest. Unless an ORDER BY clause appears, the database will spit out the data in whatever sequence is most convenient, so your outputs from a different database will not necessarily appear in the order shown in this chapter's examples. A special column name of * is used to indicate all columns (this name, like others, can be qualified by a table name if required). Therefore, to see all the data from the Book table, you would use the following statement:

```
SELECT * FROM Book;
```

BkISBN	BkName	PubNo	BkYear
0735710910	Python Essential Reference	1	2001
0735710902	Python Web Programming	1	2001
1565924649	Learning Python	2	1999
1565926218	Python Programming on Win32	2	1999

If you want to retrieve data from multiple tables, you must be careful to specify how the data are joined together. Suppose that you wanted to retrieve the title and publisher for each book. You might think at first glance that the following query would suffice:

```
SELECT Book.BkName, Publisher.PubName
    FROM Book, Publisher;
```

BkName	PubName
Python Essential Reference	New Riders
Python Web Programming	New Riders
Learning Python	New Riders
Python Programming on Win32	New Riders
Python Essential Reference	O'Reilly
Python Web Programming	O'Reilly
Learning Python	O'Reilly
Python Programming on Win32	O'Reilly

The output from this query might surprise you, but when you understand the problem it is easy to fix. By default, the database joins each row in the first table with each row of the second. The solution is to include a *join condition*, which tells it to include only those pairings of interest. A better query for this purpose would be this one:

```
SELECT Book.BkName, Publisher.PubName
    FROM Book, Publisher
    WHERE Book.PubNo = Publisher.PubNo;
```

BkName	PubName
Python Essential Reference	New Riders
Python Web Programming	New Riders
Learning Python	O'Reilly
Python Programming on Win32	O'Reilly

Now the system only joins two rows together when the publisher's publisher number is the same as the book's, giving a much more sensible (and useful) output. Queries can get complex, and it is often useful to use some sort of visual query builder to create the trickier ones. Many such products are available. When designing queries, you get used to "thinking along the relationships." Suppose you wanted to know the publisher for whom each author wrote. In that case, you need "the publisher who published the book(s) written by an authorship including the author" (honestly). This would come out in SQL as shown in Listing 9.5.

Listing 9.5 *select1.sql:* **Which Author Writes for Which Publisher?**

```
SELECT AutFirst, AutLast, Publisher.PubName
    FROM Author, Authorship, Book, Publisher
    WHERE Author.AutNo = Authorship.Autno
      AND Authorship.BkISBN = Book.BkISBN
      AND Book.PubNo = Publisher.PubNo;

AutFirst    AutLast     PubName
----------  ----------  ----------
David       Beazley     New Riders
Steve       Holden      New Riders
Mark        Lutz        O'Reilly
David       Ascher      O'Reilly
Mark        Hammond     O'Reilly
Andy        Robinson    O'Reilly
```

You can see now why it is a good idea for RDBMS products to include a query optimizer. Although it is easy to compute these results from the given data (which is one reason why such a limited data set was used), imagine the complexity of having to perform such a query over hundreds of thousands of books and authors. Personally I am happy to leave all the strategy to the query optimizer and simply tell it, using SQL, what I want it to produce for me.

Conditions in the WHERE clause need not be join conditions. They also can restrict output where not all rows are of interest. Supposing you wanted to list the books produced by authors located in the United States, the following query would provide the desired output:

```
SELECT AutFirst, AutLast, BkName
    FROM Author, Authorship, Book
    WHERE Author.AutNo = Authorship.Autno
      AND Authorship.BkISBN = Book.BkISBN
      AND AutLoc = 'USA';

AutFirst    AutLast     BkName
----------  ----------  --------------------------
David       Beazley     Python Essential Reference
Steve       Holden      Python Web Programming
Mark        Lutz        Learning Python
David       Ascher      Learning Python
```

Another way to achieve similar ends is to use subqueries. Here one query appears inside another to provide results for use in the outer query, as in Listing 9.6, which shows a query that returns the details of books written by UK authors.

Listing 9.6   *select2.sql:* Which Books Were Written by UK Authors?

```
SELECT BkName, BkYear, PubName
    FROM Book, Publisher
    WHERE Book.PubNo = Publisher.PubNo
      AND BkISBN IN (
        SELECT Book.BkISBN
            FROM Book, Authorship, Author
            WHERE Book.BkISBN = Authorship.BkISBN
              AND Authorship.Autno = Author.Autno
              AND AutLoc = 'UK');


BkName                           BkYear      PubName
----------------------------     ----------  --------
Python Programming on Win32      1999        O'Reilly
```

Here the action of the SQL interpreter is to first evaluate the parenthesized subquery, much as Python does when evaluating expressions, and then to use the values it produces as a set in the outer query. As it happens, the nested subquery only yields one value, and so we could have used `WHERE BkISBN = (...)` rather than `WHERE BkISBN IN (...)`, but defensive design principles suggest that this would have been less sound in the general case.

This section has given you a flavor of data retrieval in SQL. A good textbook will be a valuable reference if you need to learn SQL in detail. It is a complex subject, and getting more complex as the standards move forward. For simple web applications, you can usually get away with either a visual query builder or crafting the required SQL by hand. You will see more queries as we move on to using databases, and additional features will be explained as required.

UPDATE

The `UPDATE` statement allows you to selectively modify one or more columns in a selected set of rows in one table. The general syntax is as follows:

```
UPDATE table
    SET column = value [, column = value ...]
    [WHERE condition]
```

As a simple example, suppose Mark Hammond moves to Toronto; you might perform the following update:

```
UPDATE Author
    SET AutLoc = 'Canada'
    WHERE AutNo = 5;
```

There are other ways to perform this update. For example, you might have referred to Mark by name rather than by primary key, as shown here:

```
UPDATE Author
    SET AutLoc = 'Canada'
    WHERE AutFirst = 'Mark' and AutLast = 'Hammond';
```

There is always the danger when not selecting by primary key that you will update more rows than intended. Common sense requires that if you intend to update only a single row, you should use a WHERE clause that specifies a value for a set of columns with a uniqueness constraint on them, and the primary key is always guaranteed to be unique. There is nothing to stop you from updating all the rows in a table with a single statement, except your own good sense and the presence of a WHERE clause specifying the rows to be modified.

The values assigned to the columns actually can use column values from the row before update. To change all publisher names to uppercase, you could use this statement, which uses the SQL UPPER() function (similar to Python's string.upper() function). It does not have a WHERE clause, and so changes all rows in the table:

```
UPDATE Publisher
    SET PubName = UPPER(PubName)
```

The UPDATE statement is actually flexible, although most uses of it tend to change one or more column values in a single row. Such UPDATE statements are relatively easy to construct dynamically from user input, a feature you will see in Chapter 10.

DELETE

Like the UPDATE statement, DELETE by default (without a WHERE clause) operates on all rows in a table. Because it deletes the rows you select, it is a fine way to remove all the data from a table, but this is most often something you want to avoid. The general syntax is as follows:

```
DELETE FROM table
    [WHERE condition]
```

The DELETE statement may fail if it attempts to remove a row referenced by data in another table with a FOREIGN KEY constraint. If the DELETE attempts to remove multiple rows, and any one of the removed rows violates a constraint, the table will not be modified. This makes it generally necessary, when working with related data, to remove related foreign key references before removing a row in the parent table. Of course if you are working with a system that supports cascaded deletes and the relationship has deletion cascading included in its specification, you will not need to take this precaution.

The practical implications of the restrictions just described for the sample data model in this chapter are the following:

- You cannot delete an author or a book while relevant authorships remain
- You cannot delete a publisher without first deleting all the books it publishes.

You might have observed similar requirements in the order of insertion—referential integrity requires that the primary keys exist before you can insert related foreign keys, and those foreign keys must be deleted before the related primary.

So, to remove the details of the book you are reading from the database, you could use the following statement:

```
DELETE FROM Book
    WHERE BkISBN = "0735710910"
```

Because this volume is so far your author's only recorded book, the author record would no longer have any foreign key dependencies, and either of the following two statements would delete his record:

```
DELETE FROM Author
    WHERE AutNo = 2

DELETE FROM Author
    WHERE AutFirst = 'Steve'
      AND AutLast = 'Holden'
```

The first form would be preferred because it avoids the problems raised by the existence of two authors named Steve Holden. Even after these last two deletions, the following statement would fail:

```
DELETE FROM Publisher
    WHERE PubNo = 1
```

This is because New Riders also is the publisher of Beazley's *Python Essential Reference*, so to delete New Riders would violate the referential integrity of the Books table.

COMMIT *and* ROLLBACK: *Transaction Control*

Each connection with the RDBMS can process transactions independently of the other connections. The idea is that each transaction should obey the *ACID* rules for transactions:

- **Atomicity**—Each transaction should be an all-or-nothing set of interactions with the database, which either completes in its entirety or returns the database to its original state.

- **Consistency**—The transaction, starting with a database that obeys all semantic integrity constraints, should leave the database in a similarly consistent state.

- **Isolation**—Changes made during the course of a transaction on one connection should not become visible to other connections until the transaction is successfully completed.

- **Durability**—After the transaction has amended the database and completed its changes, it will continue in effect with no way to erase it except further transactions reversing its effect.

So that programmers can group SQL statements into transactions, the language provides the COMMIT and ROLLBACK verbs. Use COMMIT when you successfully complete the

final changes of the transaction to ensure its durability. Use ROLLBACK if your program
detects conditions that make it impossible to complete the transaction; this returns
the database to its state before you started the transaction. As long as the database
begins a transaction in a consistent state, it should still be consistent after either
a COMMIT or a ROLLBACK.

SQL in Summary

SQL is a complex language, whose standardization has resulted in excellent interoperability between products from competing vendors. It is easy to learn, though the
subtleties can take much longer to appreciate. You can develop a reading familiarity
with the language in a relatively short time. Because SQL is non-procedural, it is often
easier to solve database manipulation problems in SQL than it is by explicit programming in an application, and this approach has two advantages. First, no Python code
has to be developed; and second, if the RDBMS performs all manipulations, this limits
the traffic between the client and the server to the transmission of a SQL statement to
the server and the server's response back to the client.

Stored Procedures

Traditional client/server systems used two tiers. The back-end system was typically a
database engine that handled data management tasks; and the front end was a desktop
system incorporating presentation (user interface) logic, application logic, such as help
systems, and code to enforce the business rules. The hope in the 1980s and early 1990s
was that distributed computing structures of this kind would lead to a clean separation
between a central data store and an outlying application base.

The major problem turned out to be client-side software maintenance. In these
so-called *thick client* systems, the logic on the client side contained significant assumptions about, and knowledge of, the structure of the database. If the structures were
changed, or if the business rules changed, this mandated new versions of the client-side
applications for the desktop machines, and their deployment had to be synchronous
with the deployment of the new database structures. This might be practical in small
organizations with maybe 20 desktop systems all in one place, but multinational
organizations with a worldwide desktop count in the thousands found the task all
but impossible to manage.

This in turn led to ways to reduce client dependency on the database structure and
reduced inclusion of business rule support in the desktop computers. At the same
time, the emergence of web-based systems led to a push for *thin client* architectures
where the desktop code would either be minimal or dynamically updateable, avoiding
the maintenance problems so prevalent on early systems.

The web browser hosted on a PC is an ideal thin client, perhaps even better than
the network PCs proposed by Oracle and Sun Microsystems. Network PCs have the
advantage of being able to interact with Microsoft Terminal Server (MTS)-based

systems, providing user interaction services for remote Windows applications. Windows applications have a better-looking and more usable set of interface elements than traditional form-based web CGI interfaces, but this advantage is being eroded by the capabilities of Java applets and ActiveX controls to interact with the user.

The requirement to remove structural dependencies from the desktop has led to a general move toward *three-tier* architectures. In such systems, the desktop computer handles the user interaction and possibly some of the application logic. A middle tier, running *business objects*, interacts with the desktop client and applies business rules. The middle tier communicates with the database engine, which continues to handle data management tasks.

The Database as a Code Store

A stored procedure is simply a named module of code, stored in the database. An RDBMS client can invoke a stored procedure by name, passing arguments and receiving results, in much the same way that a Python program can call functions. One stored procedure can use another, so there is the chance to layer procedures up to any desired level of abstraction. Listing 9.7 shows a SQL Server 7.0 procedure to implement a takeover in the publishing world.

Listing 9.7   *proc1.sql:* **Allowing Publishing Takeovers Under SQL Server 7.0**

```
1   CREATE PROCEDURE PubTakeOver
2       @Acquirer  varchar(12),
3       @Target varchar(12)
4   AS
5   DECLARE @acquirerNo int
6   DECLARE @targetNo int
7   SET @acquirerNo = (
8       SELECT PubNo
9           FROM Publisher WHERE PubName = @Acquirer)
10  SET @targetNo = (
11      SELECT  PubNo
12          FROM Publisher WHERE PubName = @Target)
13  IF @acquirerNo IS NULL OR @targetNo IS NULL
14  BEGIN
15      RAISERROR('Takeover requires two valid publisher names', 15, 1)
16  END
17  ELSE
18  BEGIN
19      UPDATE Book Set PubNo = @AcquirerNo
20          WHERE PubNo = @TargetNo
21      DELETE FROM Publisher
22          WHERE PubNo = @TargetNo
23  END
```

When this procedure is called with valid arguments, one publisher's books are automatically transferred to the acquiring publisher, as shown in the next example:

```
EXEC PubTakeOver 'New Riders', 'O''Reilly';
```

If you run the query from Listing 9.5 after such a procedure call, you would see the following output:

```
AutFirst    AutLast    PubName
----------  ---------- ----------
David       Beazley    New Riders
Steve       Holden     New Riders
Mark        Lutz       New Riders
David       Ascher     New Riders
Mark        Hammond    New Riders
Andy        Robinson   New Riders
```

Although not clear from the preceding output, there would no longer be a row in the Publisher table for O'Reilly.

Advantages of Stored Procedures

The RDBMS vendors realized early on that there would be advantages in storing code in the database itself and allowing clients to request its execution. The RDBMS can optimize queries in the stored code in advance, improving performance, and network traffic reduces because the client now transmits a simple call request rather than the complete SQL content. Furthermore, procedures can implement common application tasks in a uniform way without the programmers of client-side applications needing to know any details of how the procedures' manipulations affect the content of the database. Procedures *encapsulate* such manipulations behind a documented interface, allowing representations to change if necessary.

Disadvantages of Stored Procedures

SQL standards have only recently addressed the representation of and syntax for stored procedures, so at present, be wary of depending on them too heavily if you are likely to want to migrate from one RDBMS to another. All use of stored procedures depends on the use of proprietary procedural extensions to the essentially non-procedural SQL language.

The 1999 standard raises hopes that this situation will improve as time goes by, but you must commit to one vendor's architecture if you want to use stored procedures today.

Triggers

A *trigger* is a stored procedure run automatically by the RDBMS when certain changes occur. The changes that fire the trigger are specified when the trigger is installed. The syntax for trigger specifications is just as varied as that for stored procedures, and systems vary about the firing conditions that they allow. For this reason, an example would not be terribly helpful.

Oracle 8 allows separate triggers to fire either before or after an insertion, a deletion, or the update of one or more specified columns. In contrast, SQL Server 7 triggers fire on insertion, deletion, or update of any column or columns. Inside the trigger code, there is a way to access the information that will be (or has been) inserted or deleted. In SQL Server 7.0, for example, you use pseudo-tables called `inserted` and `deleted`. Usually the code associated with a trigger ensures that the changes do not violate the semantic integrity of the database and, if they do, rolls back the transaction of which the firing operation is a part.

The real significance of triggers is that they allow the RDBMS to centralize the enforcement of business rules rather than require the application's code to enforce them. This enhances all applications: because the database will fire triggers to check any significant changes before they are made, it will not be possible for a naïve programmer to write code that violates the business rules. The utility of triggers and stored procedures has accelerated the migration of data manipulation code back toward the center of distributed systems. Triggers centrally maintain the semantic integrity of the database, and stored procedures provide reusable code, which frees application programmers of the need to understand the database structures, and reduces network loading by doing more of the computation in the engine.

Summary

Modern relational systems can support large numbers of users and varied applications. They are also moving toward the support of user-defined data types. If the database vendors realize their vision, the database will become the repository of application code as well as data, and will play an increasingly important role in maintaining the semantic integrity of applications data.

There is an interesting parallel between an entity type in a relational system and a class definition in Python. The rows of the table representing an entity type correspond with the instances of the class, and each has state information stored as attributes. The principal difference between relational and object systems is that the former do not associate methods with entity types.

When this becomes possible, an RDBMS will allow the creation of systems much more like the object-oriented systems Python programmers are used to building. The capability of triggers to ensure that no changes can violate the semantic integrity of the model is a powerful incentive to use them in an ever-wider range of applications.

10

The Python Database Interface

T HIS CHAPTER SHOWS HOW TO USE THE SQL you have learned inside Python programs, using modules that ideally conform to the accepted Python standard for code to drive databases. After a discussion of the Python standard API, you will see how a simple but complete database-driven web server can be written in about 150 lines of Python.

Database Interfaces

In the early days of relational databases, each vendor would provide a *call level interface* (CLI) to allow programmers to access the features of their system. As relational systems became more popular, the user base clamored for better interoperability at an application level in much the same way as they had for network communications.

One result of this pressure from the user community was SQL, the Structured Query Language. Another was the *Open Database Connectivity (ODBC) interface*, now widely adopted by database vendors. ODBC provides a standard set of functions with which the database programmer can interact using any database system with an ODBC-compliant driver. The ODBC API is low-level and can be unforgiving. It is therefore not suitable unless you know exactly what you are doing.

Microsoft has also developed a number of proprietary data access standards over the years, including Data Access Objects (DAO), Remote Data Objects (RDO), and

ActiveX Data Objects (ADO). This latter technology operates over OLEDB, discussed in Chapter 9, "Client/Server Database Architectures." Because of Microsoft's market dominance, the ADO approach can be useful, but for maximum interoperability, the ODBC route is preferred. Fortunately, OLEDB can use ODBC drivers where appropriate, but this, however, limits the functionality offered by ADO.

To try to avoid involvement in particular technologies, the Python DB SIG has developed a standard API, now in its second revision, to which Python database modules should conform. Although it is fair to say that implementations are at present a little uneven around the fringes, the DB API does offer a good level of compatibility across different database engines, making it practical to write multiplatform and cross-platform database client code with sometimes startling ease.

The Underlying Interface Model

The DB API assumes that programs will make one or more *connections* to one or more databases. Each connection should be independently capable of supporting database I/O, and transactions in one connection are independent of transactions in another connection. Applications create *cursors* associated with a connection to implement SQL operations on the database. After you establish a connection to a database, you can use the connection to create cursors. You use cursors to execute SQL statements (with their `execute()` method), and if the SQL returns a result set (usually this will be a `SELECT` statement) then you access those results using the cursors' `fetchone()`, `fetchmany()`, or `fetchall()` methods.

The various `fetch*()` methods return lists of tuples, each tuple in the list representing a row from the query output, and each row element corresponding to a particular column. Because cursors write data in the same format, it is easy to perform database updates by reading data in, modifying the list of tuples and writing it out again by using it as an argument to an `execute()` call on an `UPDATE` or `INSERT` statement.

Simple examples can be misleading about the value of database cursors, as it is difficult to get a true picture of their power when you see them created and deleted one at a time. By running several cursors across the same connection (effectively making them a part of the same transaction), you can often speed up your code. In this sense, read cursors represent an in-program caching of data retrieved from the database, although the underlying mechanism does not necessarily read all the data at once—there are methods you can call to control the size of transfer between the database engine and your program.

There is no reason why a program cannot have several concurrent connections to a database, or to different databases. In the same way, many database modules support several cursors on a single connection. Remember that such multiple cursors will all be a part of the same transaction.

A hierarchy of exception classes is defined to allow error detection with as much specificity as possible. The DB API specification uses the exception inheritance model shown in Figure 10.1. The standard does not specify exact meanings for any of the exceptions, but the hierarchy is supposed to be descriptive enough to give you a reasonable idea what went wrong.

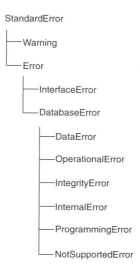

Figure 10.1   The DB API exception classes.

Depending on the particular interface module you are using, you may well see additional information from the database system, delivered back through the driver. A typical error message (wrapped for easier readability) follows:

```
Traceback (innermost last):
  File "<interactive input>", line 1, in ?
ProgrammingError: ('S0002', -1305, "[Microsoft]
  [ODBC Microsoft Access Driver]
  The Microsoft Jet database engine cannot find
  the input table or query 'MFILE'.  Make sure it
  exists and that its name is spelled correctly.", 4513)
```

Each module must provide a connect() function to create connections and must implement the following module variables, which programs can read to modify their behavior if they want to adapt to modules of varying capability:

- **apilevel**—A string constant that records the supported DB API level. Currently must contain either '1.0' or '2.0', as these are the only currently defined levels. You should work with DB API v2.0 implementations as far as possible, and this chapter discusses only this level.

- **threadlevel**—An integer constant indicating the level of thread-safety the module provides. May contain one of the following values:

- **0**—Threads may not share the module.
- **1**—Threads may share the module but may not share connections.
- **2**—Threads may share both the module and connections it creates.
- **3**—Threads may share the module, connections, and cursors.
- **paramstyle**—A string constant stating how parameters are marked in prepared statements (discussed in the section "SQL Statement Parameterization" later in the chapter).

Connection Objects

Creating a connection object requires you to call the `connect()` function of the database module. All modules compliant with the DB API v2.0 must provide such a method, although the parameters may be specific to the particular database with which you are dealing.

The `connect()` function should take keyword arguments, and those shown in Table 10.1 are typical, though not necessarily universally valid.

Table 10.1   **Typical *connect()* Keyword Arguments**

dsn	Data source name as a string.
user	Username as a string.
password	Password as a string.
host	Optional hostname for remote data sources.
database	Database name.

Thus a typical `connect()` call, to create a connection through an imaginary module called `mydb`, might look like the following:

```
import mydb
conn = mydb.connect(dsn="HoldenWeb", username="Steve", password="secret")
```

If no errors occur, then the `connect()` function returns a connection object, which you can use to create cursors and hence perform database operations. Connection objects should support the methods shown in Table 10.2.

Table 10.2   **DB API Connection Methods**

close()	Closes the connection immediately rather than waiting for the garbage collector to reclaim the connection and call its __del__() method.
commit()	Commits any pending transactions to the database, making their results visible to other transactions. The module will disable auto-commit (where each interaction through a connection is automatically committed to the database) initially if it is supported, but may provide a method to enable it.

`rollback()`	If a database supports transactions, then calling this method on a connection causes the database to return to the state it was in before any changes relating to the current transaction were performed.
`cursor()`	Returns a new cursor object using the connection.

After you create a connection object, you can start to operate on the connected database using cursors.

Cursor Objects

A cursor associated to a particular connection uses that connection to execute operations on the database. The cursor receives a query as a (possibly parameterized) SQL statement, passed as a string argument to the `execute()` method. If a cursor executes a retrieval statement, there are several different ways you can interact with it to access the retrieved data. Database modules may optimize repeated executions of the same statement if the underlying relational engine has this capability. The programmer does not need to take any particular action to have this happen, except to correctly parameterize the SQL statements.

Of course, you are at liberty to create SQL statements dynamically in your program before passing them to the cursor's `execute()` method. Remember that it is more efficient to `execute()` a single parameterized SQL query many times (with varying parameters) than it is to dynamically create several similar but different SQL statements and `execute()` them individually. You can read more about this feature, and the `paramstyle` cursor attribute, in the section "SQL Statement Parameterization" later in this chapter.

Executing SQL Statements

Database cursors have three methods you can use to execute SQL statements, shown in Table 10.3.

Table 10.3 **Methods Implementing DB API Cursor Operations**

`c.execute(operation[, parameters])`	Prepare a SQL statement and execute it. For a parameterized statement, the `parameters` argument must be either a sequence or a mapping, as required by the module's `paramstyle` setting. Parameter values must be in the format required by the particular database.
`c.executemany(operation, parameter_sequence)`	Prepare a SQL statement and execute it with each of the parameter sets in the `parameter_sequence`, which is a list or tuple of sequences or mappings as required by the module's `paramstyle` setting.

continues

Table 10.3   **Continued**

`c.callproc(procname[, parameters])`	This method is optional: it requires stored procedure support, which is not available with all database engines. Calls the stored procedure named `procname`. The `parameters` argument, if given, should be a sequence object. Note that you can usually make stored procedure calls from SQL using `execute()` or `executemany()` if your database module does not implement `callproc()`.

The `execute()` and `executemany()` methods do not define a return value, although some modules provide one. You access the results, if the operation produced any, using other cursor methods. For the `callproc()` method, the result of the call is a modified copy of the `parameters` sequence provided to the call. Input parameters are unchanged; the call will have replaced output and input/output parameters with the values returned by the stored procedure.

Retrieving Results from a Cursor

After a cursor has executed a SQL operation, you can use two read-only attributes to discover information about the returned result set:

- **description**—A sequence of seven-item sequences, each one of which corresponds to one column of the result. The elements of each sequence contain the following values:

`name`	A string containing the name of the column.
`type_code`	A code indicating the column type. The code might compare equal with several column types if several different Python data types can yield a particular column type, see "SQL/Python Communication" later in the chapter.
`display_size`	Size of item's string representation. May be `None`.
`internal_size`	Size of item's internal representation. May be `None`.
`precision`	Length of the data.
`scale`	Scale factor (usually zero for non-numeric types).
`null_ok`	1 if `NULL` values can be stored in the column; otherwise, 0.

- **rowcount**—The number of rows returned by the operation. If you have not yet executed an operation on the cursor, or if the interface cannot determine the number of rows, it may return -1. Some database modules cannot generate a `rowcount` until you have retrieved all results from the cursor; some modules simply do not offer the feature.

Because most modern database systems operate in client/server mode, you can affect the efficiency of your database operations radically by choosing whether to retrieve one or many rows at a time. The DB API provides three different methods to retrieve results from a cursor, shown in Table 10.4. If the cursor has not yet executed an operation, or if that operation returned no data, any attempt to retrieve data raises an exception. As Table 10.4 mentions, a cursor's `arraysize` attribute (which you are free to modify) can affect the efficiency of operations.

Table 10.4   **Cursor Result Retrieval Methods**

`c.fetchone()`	Returns a sequence containing the next row of the cursor's current result set, or `None` if no more data is available.
`c.fetchmany(` `[size=c.`➡ `arraysize])`	Returns a number of rows from the result set as a sequence of sequences. Each cursor has a read/write attribute, `arraysize`, with a default value of one, which determines by default how many rows the method returns. For best efficiency, all calls should use the same value for `size`. Setting the `arraysize` attribute is the best way to specify the return set size.
	The return set may contain fewer rows if a call exhausts the data from the cursor's last operation.
`c.fetchall()`	Fetch all remaining rows from the result set as a sequence of sequences. Note that the `arraysize` cursor attribute can affect the efficiency of this operation and that the default value of one typically results in low efficiency on operations that produce large result sets.

The data returned by all these methods represents a result row as a tuple. The `fetchone()` method therefore returns a single tuple; the other two each return a list of tuples. When you are dealing with large result sets, remember two factors that can have a crucial effect on performance:

- Avoid retrieving data for client-side operations that it would be better to perform on the server. For example, avoid retrieving all the rows in a table just to count them, when it would be easier and much quicker to use a `"SELECT COUNT(*) FROM <table>"` query and have the server deliver a single result.
- Try to avoid transferring the result rows from the server one at a time. This saves memory, but at the expense of slowing down network operations. The `array-size` cursor attribute can help here because it makes it easy to test with various chunk sizes to decide the best number of rows to transfer with each client request.

Implied Versus Explicit Commit

Many database systems operate in *auto-commit* mode, where each interaction with the database implicitly forms a transaction. The DB API requires that compliant modules initially switch off auto-commit mode. Although the specifications permit modules to provide some way to switch it back on again, it does not specify the API to perform this action. Therefore, use of auto-commit mode is non-standard. It is more satisfactory to explicitly commit your transactions anyway (or, of course, roll them back in the event of some program error being discovered).

Consider an example where a bank transfers $1,000 from one account to the other. From an accounting control point of view, the bank would have to require that the sum of the account balances be the same before and after the transaction. If the programmer simply uses the following SQL, there is no such guarantee:

```
UPDATE ACCOUNTS SET balance = balance-1000
    WHERE accountno = 31243564
UPDATE ACCOUNTS SET balance = balance+1000
    WHERE accountno = 98675429
```

Problems would arise under several circumstances. Suppose the program were to fail after executing the first statement but not the second. In that case, the money would have been removed from the first account but not deposited in the second, and $1,000 would have gone missing. If the database connection is using transaction controls, the programmer can add a COMMIT statement at the end of the transaction:

```
UPDATE ACCOUNTS SET balance = balance-1000
    WHERE accountno = 31243564
UPDATE ACCOUNTS SET balance = balance+1000
    WHERE accountno = 98675429
COMMIT
```

Before the COMMIT statement was executed, other database connections would continue to see the old account balances when they read them, and the database would probably lock these rows to prevent conflicting writes. After the COMMIT executes, the database guarantees that both changes have been made and will be visible to reads on other database connections.

If you are new to database work, you will probably find yourself wondering at some stage why changes you have made to the database do not appear. This is especially true if you have been used to working with a system such as Access 2000, whose graphical user interface uses auto-commit mode. Hopefully, this paragraph will cause little alarm bells to ring, reminding you of the need to explicitly commit changes to the database.

Memory Optimizations

Where performance is important, there is an API you can use to condition the database modules to expect data of particular sizes. The DB API specifications explicitly state that modules need not implement anything except a no-operation, so there is no guarantee these optimizations will improve performance. It is worth trying with the more complex modules, however. You can use two cursor methods for these optimizations, as shown in Table 10.5.

Table 10.5   **Cursor Optimization Methods**

`c.setinputsizes(sizes)`	Before you pass parameters to SQL statements in the `execute*()` methods, you can call this method with a `sizes` argument containing a sequence. The sequence should contain one item for each parameter, and the items can be either
	▪ A `Type` object corresponding to the data type that will be passed (see the section "SQL/Python Communication" for a discussion of `Type` objects).
	▪ An integer specifying the maximum string size.
	▪ `None`, in which case no memory will be reserved for the corresponding parameter.
`c.setoutputsize(size[, column])`	When you are fetching large objects (such as `LONG` or `BLOB`) from the database, you can use this method to tell the cursor how much space to reserve for each long object. Without a `column` argument, the method reserves size bytes for each long object. If you use a `column` argument, then the method reserves `size` bytes for the result set column indexed by `column`.

Some Database Modules

Python users are lucky. A wide range of database interface modules are available for the language, all written by third-party developers and mostly available for download at no cost. It is therefore easy to use all the major databases from Python, even if not from your platform of choice—driver availability can affect module portability. The UNIX world still awaits a good open-source ODBC driver set, although apparently good drivers are commercially available.

The next two sections discuss three database modules. The first, `odbc` from Mark Hammond's Win32 extensions, is minimal, but it is nevertheless possible to work with it. It is donated software, from a company called EShop, which no longer offers support. The second, `mx.ODBC` from Marc-André Lemburg, is at the opposite end of the spectrum, with many bells and whistles that extend the DB API specification considerably. The third, `gadfly` from Aaron Watters, is a database module written entirely in Python. `gadfly` allows Python programs a convenient way to store, retrieve, and query tabular data without having to rely on any external database engine or package. The file formats it uses are portable across operating systems, but it lacks the advanced concurrency control and indexing features of mature commercial products.

The Python world has other good reasons to be grateful to all these authors. Mark Hammond determinedly dragged Python into the Windows world, creating a huge set of Windows extensions as well as PythonWin, the first flexible Python integrated development environment (IDE). Marc-André Lemburg has written a number of excellent Python extension modules, including `mxDateTime`, now recommended by the DB-SIG as the preferred way to handle dates in Python. You can find `mxDateTime`, along with a number of other useful modules, by following links from `http://www.egenix.com`. Aaron Watters also has produced the `pysimplex` module (see `http://www.chordate.com/pysimplex/`) for basic symbolic programming, and a number of other useful modules.

Table 10.6 shows a comparison of the features of the three packages.

Table 10.6 **Database Module Feature Comparison**

Feature	*odbc*	*mx.ODBC*	*gadfly*
Apilevel	x[1]	2.0	x[1]
Threadlevel	x	1	x[8]
Paramstyle	x[2]	'qmark'	x[2]
Connect()	x[3]	u	x[5]
Close() connection	u	u	u
Close() cursor	u	u	u
Commit()	u	u	u
Rollback()	u	u	u
Cursor()	u	u	u
Execute()	u	u	u
executemany()	x[4]	u	x[4]
callproc()	x	x	x
description	x	u	u
rowcount	x	u[6]	x
fetchone()	u	u	u
fetchmany()	u	u	u
fetchall()	u	u	u
Setinputsizes()	u	u	u
Setoutputsize()	u	u	u
Setautocommit()	u	x[7]	x[7]

[1] odbc implements a subset of DB API version 1.0, and `gadfly` a subset of DB API version 2.0. Neither implements the `apilevel` module attribute.

[2] Will work with `'qmark'` style parameters but does not set the `paramstyle` module attribute.

[3] Use `conn = odbc.odbc("connectstring")` to create a connection.

[4] The effect of executemany() can be obtained by calling execute() with a list of tuples as the second argument. This is generally true of DB API modules, but executemany() is preferred when it is available.

[5] Use conn = gadfly.gadfly("*database*", "*directory*") to create a connection to an existing database. To create a database, use conn = gadfly.gadfly() and then conn.startup("*database*", "*directory*").

[6] The rowcount attribute is dynamic and updates as result rows are fetched from the cursor.

[7] mxODBC offers a clear_auto_commit keyword argument to connect(), which defaults to one. gadfly offers an autocheckpoint keyword argument to gadfly.gadfly(), which defaults to zero.

[8] gadfly databases are specifically intended for update by a single process. It does offer the capability for several clients to connect to a single server process using TCP/IP, and with such mediation, the clients may each update the same database.

Although Mark Hammond's Win32 extensions are exceptionally reliable, the third-party odbc module included with them is a little fragile at the time of writing (but is likely to improve in the future). During testing, several examples caused the Python interpreter to crash. As usual, although your mileage may vary there is no substitute for careful testing.

Test Data Sources

Because the Python core contains no database support, you will have to install at least one database module of your choice to run the programs in this chapter. Although ODBC and engine-specific database are available for both Windows and UNIX, gadfly is the best choice for portability because it is a pure Python solution.

The web site directory for this chapter contains a gadfly directory with a prebuilt gadfly database in it, and an Access 2000 database WebData.mdb. The program gfbuild.py, which shows how one program can access two databases and transfer data between them, built the gadfly database from the Access database. You therefore have several ways to establish a data source for the programs:

- Install gadfly on your system and use the ready-made gadfly database.

- Install the Access database as ODBC source WebData, and use either the odbc module that comes with the Win32 extensions, mxODBC, or some other driver.

- Import the Access database into SQL Server using Data Transformation Services and establish the resulting SQL Server database as ODBC source WebData with odbc or mxODBC.

The sample code is programmed to use gadfly, odbc, or mxODBC according to user choice. If you must use some other database driver, you will have to create your own database. You can use the gfbuild.py program as a model of how to transfer the simple data into your preferred database. Otherwise, you will need to manually create the required table. The data is not complicated, and a comma-separated value file for each table also is included.

A Simple Database-Driven Web

Finally, you are in possession of all the information to build a database application. Because you are roughly halfway through the book, a web server with database content would seem to be appropriate. The usual way of approaching this task is to build an infrastructure using a web server such as Apache. By now you should realize that for testing purposes that is not necessary, as you have all the tools you require to craft the server from whole cloth. The server shown in Listing 10.1 should hold few mysteries by now.

Listing 10.1   *dbwebsrv.py:* **A Simple Data-Driven Asynchronous Web Server**

```
1  #!/usr/bin/env python
2  #
3  # A simple database-driven web server
4  #
5  import dbpages
6  import asyncore, asynchat, socket, sys
7
8  class http_server(asyncore.dispatcher):
9
10     def __init__(self, ip, port, dbsource):
11         self.ip= ip
12         self.port = port
13         self.dbsource = dbsource
14         asyncore.dispatcher.__init__(self)
15         self.create_socket(socket.AF_INET, socket.SOCK_STREAM)
16         self.bind((ip, port))
17         self.listen(5)
18
19     def readable(self):
20         return self.accepting
21
22     def handle_accept(self):
23         try:
24             conn, addr = self.accept()
25         except socket.error: # rare Linux error
26             print "Socket error on server accept()"
27             return
28         except TypeError: # rare FreeBSD3 error
29             print "EWOULDBLOCK exception on server accept()"
30             return
31         http_handler(conn, addr, self.dbsource)
32
33  class http_handler(asynchat.async_chat):
34
35     def __init__(self, conn, addr, dbsource):
36         asynchat.async_chat.__init__(self, conn=conn)
37         self.addr = addr
38         self.dbsource = dbsource
```

```
39              self.ibuffer = ""
40              self.obuffer = ""
41              self.set_terminator("\r\n\r\n")
42
43          def collect_incoming_data(self, data):
44              self.ibuffer += data.replace('\r', '')
45
46          def found_terminator(self):
47              request = self.ibuffer.split("\n")[0]
48              op, path, protocol = request.split()
49              path = path[1:]
50              if not path:
51                  path = "Home"
52              self.ibuffer = ""
53              self.obuffer = dbsource.page(op, path)
54
55          def writable(self):
56              return len(self.obuffer) > 0
57
58          def handle_write(self):
59              sent = self.send(self.obuffer)
60              self.obuffer = self.obuffer[sent:]
61              if len(self.obuffer) == 0:
62                  self.close()
63  if __name__ == "__main__":
64      if len(sys.argv) < 2:
65          type = "mx"
66      else:
67          type = sys.argv[1].lower()
68          if type not in ('mx', 'gf', 'odbc'):
69              sys.exit("USAGE: %s mx ¦ gf ¦ odbc\n" % sys.argv[0])
70      dbsource = dbpages.dbsource("WebData", type)
71      server = http_server('', 8080, dbsource)
72      try:
73          asyncore.loop(4.0) # Frequent checks for interrupt
74      except KeyboardInterrupt:
75          dbsource.close()
76          print "Finished"
```

Of course, all the database mechanics hide inside the dpbages module, which you will examine next. The http_server now takes an additional dbsource argument to its __init__() method. This should be a dbpages.dbsource object; line 70 creates such an object. As usual, the server creates a handler object for each incoming request, and the handler's __init__() method takes a dbsource argument.

The handler collects data in self.ibuffer until it sees the end of the HTTP headers. It splits out the operation and the path from the HTTP command, and calls the page() method of the dbsource to generate the HTTP response, which is stored in the output buffer self.obuffer. In the program's body, there is some argument checking; and assuming everything checks out, an `http_server` is created serving port 8080 using the generated `dbsource`. You also will observe that the program runs the asynchronous loop more frequently than happens by default, so you can terminate your server cleanly with a keyboard interrupt without having to wait too long.

Listing 10.2 shows the `dbpages` module that generates pages from database content.

Listing 10.2   *dbpages.py:* **Generating Simple HTML from a Database**

```
 1  #
 2  # This object creates pages from a small database
 3  #
 4  class dbsource:
 5      def __init__(self, source, type):
 6          if type == 'mx':
 7              import mx.ODBC.Windows as odbc
 8              self.conn = odbc.connect(source)
 9          elif type == 'odbc':
10              import dbi, odbc
11              self.conn = odbc.odbc(source)
12          elif type == 'gf':
13              import gadfly
14              self.conn = gadfly.gadfly(source, "gadfly")
15          else:
16              raise ValueError, "Illegal data source type %s" % type
17          self.cursor = self.conn.cursor()
18  #
19  # Build the navigation links
20  #
21      def navlinks(self):
22          self.cursor.execute("SELECT PgName, PgNum from PgData ORDER BY PgNum")
23          lnkLst = []
24          for row in self.cursor.fetchall():
25              lnkLst.append('<a href="/%s">%s</a><br>' % (row[0], row[0]))
26          return "\r\n".join(lnkLst)
27
28  #
29  # Build the main page content
30  #
31      def page(self, op, path):
32          if op.upper() == "GET":
33              self.cursor.execute("SELECT PgText FROM PgData WHERE PgName=?", ➡
                  (path, ))
34              result = self.cursor.fetchall() # only one, we hope!
35              if result:
36                  text = result[0][0]
37              else:
38                  text = "Sorry. No page '%s' in the database" % path
39          else:
40              text = "Sorry. The '%s' operation you requested is invalid." % op
```

```
41              return➥
42  """HTTP/1.0 200 OK Response Follows
43  Content-Type: text/html
44  Cache-Control: no-cache
45
46  <HTML>
47  <HEAD>
48      <TITLE>Operation %s %s</TITLE>
49  </HEAD>
50  <BODY>
51  <TABLE>
52    <tr>
53      <td valign="TOP" width="80">%s</td>
54      <td valign="TOP" width="150"><b>Page <i>%s</i></b><br>%s</td>
55    </tr>
56  </TABLE>
57  </BODY>
58  """ % (op, path, self.navlinks(), path, text)
59
60  #
61  # Tidy up
62  #
63      def close(self):
64          self.cursor.close()
65          self.conn.close()
```

The `dbpages.dbsource` object's __init__() method creates a database connection
according to the requested type and generates a cursor from it. This particular version
is coded to adapt to a number of database modules and has been tested with each of
the three discussed in the previous section (with mixed results using the `odbc` module).

A Note on gadfly to Python 2.1 Users

Checks with Python 2.1 reveal that `gadfly` uses the deprecated `regex` module for its regular expression
handling. This currently results in warning messages being generated as the code is executed. The code
should nevertheless work, but the messages will not disappear until a little more work is done on the
`gadfly` module.

There does not appear to be any current schedule for this desirable revision. The Win32 `odbc` module is
apparently not yet ready for prime time under Python 2.1.

The `navlinks()` method retrieves each page name and generates an HTML string
where each page appears on a separate line as a hypertext link. The `page()` method
takes an operation and a path, and generates a complete, albeit simple, HTTP response.
The output includes an HTTP header that instructs browsers (and any caching prox-
ies) not to cache the pages. This saves you from having to refresh when you update the
database. The HTML is just a one-row two-column table with the navigation bar in
the left-hand cell and the (slightly embellished) page text in the right-hand cell.

Figure 10.2 shows a browser displaying this little site's home page. In testing, the server handled requests from several simultaneous browsers on different computers without any problems.

Figure 10.2   Your first database/web server in action.

SQL/Python Communication

The database engine usually needs to use particular data formats to bind to an operation's input parameters. For example, if you are providing a parameter the database will use as a DATE, a particular string format will be required. The parameters to the execute*() methods are not typed, however. When you pass a string in as an argument to a cursor operation, Python does not know whether to bind the value as a CHAR column, a MEMO column or a DATE.

To allow for implementation differences between different databases, each DB API module must implement a number of constructor functions, which produce objects that can be stored in particular field types. They also must provide Type Objects, which you can compare against the type codes returned as a part of a cursor's description attribute.

Conversion Functions

The standard specifies module-level functions to convert other representations into dates and timestamps. There is a potential problem with UNIX ticks because of a 32-bit overflow that will occur in the year 2038. Avoidance of this problem is easy: Marc-André Lemburg has written the mxDateTime module, which almost certainly will do everything you want and more with dates and times. Indeed the DB API specifications recommend `mxDateTime` as the preferred date and time object types. Table 10.7 lists the conversion functions available, and you can download the code via `http://www.egenix.com`.

Table 10.7   **DB API Conversion Functions**

`Date(yr, mon, day)`	Constructs a date object for the given day, month, and year.
`Time(hr, min, sec)`	Constructs a time object for the given hour, minute, and second.
`Timestamp(yr, mon, day, hr, min, sec)`	Constructs a timestamp from the given arguments.
`DateFromTicks(ticks)`	Constructs a date value from the given UNIX ticks value.
`TimeFromTicks(ticks)`	Constructs a time value from the given UNIX ticks value.
`TimeStampFromTicks(ticks)`	Constructs a timestamp value from the given UNIX ticks value.
`Binary(string)`	Constructs an object capable of holding a (binary) string value of arbitrary length.

Type Codes

The cursor description attribute, described earlier in the section "Retrieving Results from a Cursor," returns a type code for each column of a retrieval operation. The DB API specifies a number of Type Objects, which implement an unusual version of comparison. For example, `DATETIME` Type Objects might compare equal to any of the type codes for date, time, and timestamp columns.

In this way, database modules can be reasonably sure how to convert the data you provide into a representation that the database engine will accept. You probably will not need to use Type Codes unless you start dealing with some esoteric data types. Table 10.8 shows the available codes.

Table 10.8   **DB API Type Objects**

`STRING`	Describes string-based columns such as `CHAR` and `VARCHAR`.
`BINARY`	Describes (long) binary columns such as `BLOB`s, `LONG`, or `RAW`.
`NUMBER`	Describes numeric columns.
`DATETIME`	Describes date, time, and timestamp columns.
`ROWID`	For databases that have such values, describes row identifier columns (these are not a part of the SQL standard).

A conformant database module represents SQL `NULL` values by `None` on both input and output. Not all database modules have yet implemented a complete type code scheme, so you should check your module's cursor `description` attribute before assuming type codes are present.

Parameter Styles and Substitutions

Inexperienced Python database programmers often make the mistake of generating each SQL statement in its entirety as a string before passing it to the cursor `execute()` method. This is sometimes necessary (for example, when you cannot predict the number of parameters a given statement will need), but you should avoid it when you can. It can greatly reduce the efficiency of the SQL implementation, which loses the chance to pre-optimize a number of queries that use the same template. It also passes up the opportunity to use the `executemany()` method with a list of tuples, putting unnecessary looping constructs into your code.

Instead you should consider separating the SQL from the actual data, by parameterizing your statements as described in the following section and providing a second argument to the `execute()` method containing a tuple of the data to be substituted for the parameters in the SQL statement. Among other things, this gives the database driver the chance to optimize multiple executions of the same statement.

SQL Statement Parameterization

You indicate where parameter substitutions should take place inside a SQL statement by including parameter markers. The DB API allows five different styles of parameter markers, and each module can choose which technique to use. Some modules extend the DB API to allow you a choice, but for full generality, you should write programs to be able to handle any of the available parameter styles. Table 10.9 lists the values of the `paramstyle` module attribute that you might have to work with.

Table 10.9 **Database Module *paramstyle* Values**

Paramstyle	Meaning
`'qmark'`	Question marks indicate the location of each parameter: `"SELECT Dept FROM Employee WHERE FirstName=? AND LastName=?"`
`'numeric'`	Numeric codes preceded by a colon indicate the location of each parameter: `"SELECT Dept FROM Employee WHERE FirstName=:1 AND LastName=:2"`
`'named'`	Named codes preceded by a colon indicate the location of each parameter: `"SELECT Dept FROM Employee WHERE FirstName=:fn AND LastName=:ln"`
`'format'`	Format codes, as used in string substitutions, indicate the location of each parameter: `"SELECT Dept FROM Employee WHERE FirstName=%s AND LastName=%s"`
`'pyformat'`	Extended Python format codes indicate the location of each parameter: `"SELECT Dept FROM Employee WHERE FirstName=%(fn)s AND LastName=%(ln)s"`

When a parameterized SQL statement is used, the `'named'` and `'pyformat'` parameter styles will expect a mapping (typically a dictionary) to provide the parameter values. The other three styles require a sequence. For example, assume you want to insert the following data into columns `drinker`, `bar`, and `visits` in table `regulars`:

```
vlst = [
    ('norm', 'cheers', 3),
    ('cliff', 'cheers', 5),
    ('steve', "nag's head", 4)
]
```

The inefficient way to do this would be as follows:

```
for r in vlst:
    sql = """INSERT INTO regulars (drinker, bar, visits)
                VALUES ('%s', '%s', %d)""" % r
    cursor.execute(sql)
```

Worse than the inefficiency is the problem that the apostrophe in the third bar's name will cause the generated SQL statement to be ill-formed. This will lead to an exception from the database module. Although it is possible to write a function to double up the single quotes as required by the SQL syntax, this takes time, adds complexity, and leaves the possibility of error when you forget to apply the function in one case. A more efficient way to perform the same task uses SQL parameter markers:

```
for r in vlst:
    cursor.execute("""INSERT INTO regulars (drinker, bar, visits)
                VALUES (?, ?, ?)""", r)
```

This uses the optional second argument to `execute()` to pass a tuple of parameters, which the database package substitutes inside the SQL string. There is no need to treat strings and numbers differently, and all escaping happens automatically. An even more efficient way to perform the same task is to use the `executemany()` method. The task now becomes a single statement:

```
cursor.executemany("""INSERT INTO regulars (drinker, bar, visits)
                VALUES (?, ?, ?)""", vlst)
```

Not only is this Python simpler and hence less error-prone, it also gives the database module the best chance to optimize performance over the whole set of insertions. The preceding examples used the `'qmark'` parameter substitution style. The other styles are slightly different. You could insert the same data using a package operating in `'numeric'` style this way:

```
cursor.executemany("""INSERT INTO regulars (drinker, bar, visits)
                VALUES (:1, :2, :3)""", vlst)
```

Using the `'format'` style, the statement would need to be as follows:

```
cursor.executemany("""INSERT INTO regulars (drinker, bar, visits)
                VALUES (%s, %s, %s)""", vlst)
```

To use the 'named' or 'pyformat' styles, the data would need to be in a different form, as a list of dictionaries. Such a list appears with the appropriate execute() calls as follows:

```
vlst = [
    {'drinker':'norm', 'bar':'cheers', 'visits':3},
    {'drinker':'cliff', 'bar':'cheers', 'visits':5},
    {'drinker':'steve', 'bar':"nag's head", 'visits':4}
]
# named style
cursor.executemany("""INSERT INTO regulars (drinker, bar, visits)
        VALUES (:drinker, :bar, :visits)""", vlst)
# pyformat style
cursor.executemany("""INSERT INTO regulars (drinker, bar, visits)
        VALUES (%(drinker)s, %(bar)s, %(visits)s)""", vlst)
```

Summary

You still have much to learn about the integration of web and database technologies in Python. You have now seen the two technologies working together, however, and if you have taken the trouble to download and install gadfly, you have seen that Python is all you need for simple data-driven web sites.

Your knowledge of database usage from Python is up-to-speed, and you should find it natural to use both database code and socket programming in the same program. Although this does not stop you from using the industrial-strength infrastructure components such as IIS and Apache, you can probably appreciate that this is not always necessary in simple applications.

In the next chapter, you will look at the specifics of certain database modules, with a view to keeping your programs as portable as possible over a range of database engines.

11

Adapting the Python Interface to Database Products

I N THIS CHAPTER, YOU WILL SEE serious interaction between database and web code. If you want to test the code, you will therefore require both a functioning database interface and a web server to support the CGI scripts used in the latter half. The first half of the chapter examines various ways of supporting as wide a range of databases as possible. The second half shows you how you can use the web for simple data entry and maintenance tasks.

Now that you are familiar with some of the ways that Python can interact with database products, you will want to put this knowledge to use by writing more database interaction code than you saw in the preceding chapter. Because there are many database modules, it is important to understand that not all these modules are 100 percent compliant with the DBI specification. You should also realize that SQL implementation varies between different database engines. If code portability is important to your project (and if you think it is not, remember that good projects often far outlive original expectations), you are likely to have to adapt your code to be able to deal with different back ends. There are therefore two levels at which you will want to consider portability.

First, you have to ensure (as the simple example in Chapter 10, "The Python Database Interface," attempted to) that your Python code is compatible with each of the modules it uses. This typically involves writing a "shim" layer, which provides a uniform interface to your code and adapts to whichever modules you are using to support the database operations. In Chapter 10, you saw that the `__init__()` method of the `dbpages` module took a type argument, allowing the user to select the `ODBC`, `mxODBC`, or `gadfly` modules for database support. The particular code used was not elegant, but the remainder of the code was identical for each of the modules.

A second issue arises because of engine incompatibilities. No matter which modules you may use to access your database, and remembering that some modules will interface to several engines, you must allow for different engines implementing different subsets of SQL, sometimes with slight syntax variations. If you want your applications to support multiple engines, you may also need to adapt the SQL handling portions of your code. This affects your implementation in two ways: you might have to cope with unsupported features, and you might need to handle syntax differences.

What Help Are Standards?

Unfortunately, standards in many areas (database and HTML being no exceptions) are more honored in the breach than the observance. For example, if you use SQL *views* in your code, this bars you from using the Jet database engine, which comes as a part of Microsoft Access. That engine simply does not support the `CREATE VIEW` and related statements. Certain other SQL features have variations in syntax between different vendors' implementations, and that can require that your implementation adapt by modifying the SQL that your program presents to the database, according to the engine it uses. This is particularly true of features such as stored procedures and triggers, which SQL standards did not cover until 1999. You also will need to handle variations in data typing—for example, long textual fields need to be of type `MEMO` in Access, type `TEXT` in SQL Server, and so on.

It would be rather ambitious (although possible) to adapt for the total lack of a statement such as `CREATE VIEW`. Such a solution might work out for a single session, but views are supposed to persist in the database and be available in later sessions. The best solution here is to raise an exception: the platform is simply not up to the task being demanded of it. Adaptation to SQL syntax variations is relatively easy, however.

Summarizing, you can treat the two portability requirements as *module adaptations* and *SQL adaptations*. Each different module requires its own adaptations no matter which engine it is driving, and each different engine requires its own SQL adaptations. Because you can access the same engine using different modules, the two sets of adaptations should ideally be independent of each other. Module adaptation is less likely to be required: you are much more likely to want your application to operate against a range of database engines than you are to adapt your program to use different modules with the same engine, and so the former situation is addressed in this chapter.

Of course, this is all very annoying when you consider that the whole point of the standardization process is to make such contortions unnecessary. This is an imperfect world, in which we must adapt to survive. After the finalization of the SQL-99 standard, you might hope that the vendors will improve to conformance of their SQL implementations in future releases, but do not hold your breath. The current lack of conformance simply underlines the complexity of SQL and the difficulty of implementing database engines, and the same will be true in the future. You can, of course, vote with your wallet and spend your money with vendors committed to supporting published standards. This still leaves you with the problem of how to handle multiple database engines.

Available Database Modules

The best source of information about Python database modules is the DB Special Interest Group (SIG). Visit its page at `http://www.python.org/sigs/db-sig/`, for the latest information about what is available. At the time of this writing, it listed the modules shown in Table 11.1.

Table 11.1 **Available Python Database Modules**

Database	DB API driver module(s)	DB API level	Author(s)	Platform(s)
DB/2 (IBM)	DB2	2.0	Man-Yong (Bryan) Lee	UNIX, Windows
Gadfly	gadfly	2.0	Aaron Watters	UNIX, Windows
Informix	Informixdb	1.0	Stephen J. Turner,	UNIX, Windows?
	Kinfxdb[1]	1.0	Alexander Kuznetsov	UNIX
Interbase 4.0/5.0	Kinterbasdb	2.0	Alexander Kuznetsov	UNIX, Windows
Ingres	?	?	Holger Meyer	?
JDBC	ZxJDBC	2.0	B. Zimmer	Jython
MySQL	MySQLdb	2.0	Andy Dustman	UNIX, Windows
ODBC	MxODBC	2.0	Marc-André Lemburg	UNIX, Windows
ODBC	ODBC	1.0	unsupported	Windows
PostgreSQL	PyGreSQL	2.0	D'Arcy	UNIX
	PoPy	2.0	J.M. Cain,	UNIX
	psycopg	2.0	Thierry Michel, Michel Comitini	UNIX
Sybase	Sybase[2]	2.0	Dave Cole	UNIX

[1] *This module is incomplete and has apparently received no maintenance since 1998. It appears that a revised version may be published by the time you read this book.*

[2] *Cursor* execute() *method supports only* SELECT *statements; others must use a non-standard connection* execute() *method. This module is under revision now, so the restriction may have been removed by the time you read this.*

The database SIG list does not seem to be updated to include newer modules. Specifically, a couple of Oracle modules (DCOracle2 and cx_Oracle) are not included. So be aware that it is always worth a web search to see what else has been contributed. A good place to start your search is http://dmoz.org/Computers/Programming/Languages/Python/Modules/Database/.

SQL Adaptation Layer Tasks

Because each RDBMS has subtle and not-so-subtle variations in its SQL implementation, it is desirable to adapt your logic to the engine you want it to deal with. The idea is to ensure that each engine only sees SQL statements with appropriate syntax.

Alternative Statement Sources

One way to avoid engine dependencies is to keep a separate representation of each statement for each engine, or to provide a default value with some way of indicating modified statements for use with engines that will not accept the default value. Listing 11.1 shows how you might represent each statement as a SQLstmt object for this purpose.

Listing 11.1 **Providing SQL Adaptation Using RDBMS-Specific Statement Variants**

```
1 class SQLstmt:
2     def __init__(self, stmt, alts):
3         self.stmt = stmt    # default statement
4         self.alts = alts    # list of variants
5     def get(self, engine):
6         if self.alts.has_key(engine):
7             return self.alts[engine]
8         else:
9             return self.stmt
```

There is a base statement, with noted variations saved in the alts dictionary. When you retrieve the statement, you tell the get() method which engine you are using, and if there is an engine-specific variant, then get() returns it. Otherwise, it simply returns the default statement. This approach has the advantage of simplicity, but it does mean that adding a new RDBMS requires you to examine all the SQL statements in your application and add a new variant to each if the RDBMS requires it.

You could extend this approach to indicate that certain SQL statements (such as `CREATE VIEW` in the Jet engine) are unavailable, using some value such as `None` in the `alts` dictionary to indicate that the particular engine cannot run the statement concerned.

An Internationalization Approach

A second possible method of adapting to SQL syntax variations is to use Python's standard localization features, which are based on the architecture defined by the GNU `gettext` package. A `gettext` module is available in Python, though unfortunately, the documentation seems a little opaque. This is largely because the interface is extensively described before you get to the section that explains practical use of the module.

The essence of this approach is that you replace your message strings, such as "This is a message," with calls on the `_()` function that use the original message string as an argument. You then run the `pygettext.py` program (found in your Python distribution's `/Tools/i18n` directory) with your script as input. This creates files that can be used by the runtime function `_()` to translate to the appropriate language.

If you are already using `gettext` for natural-language issues, it might be appropriate to use it for SQL as well, effectively specifying each SQL dialect as a different language.

An Object-Oriented Dynamic SQL Adaptation Layer

A third method of avoiding SQL dependencies is to use program logic to generate the SQL rather than present it as string literals. You might use this technique to generate the alternatives for the first method, or you could use it in your program dynamically to generate statements according to the engine your program must use. Because most SQL implementations have a lot in common, this is a natural application for object-oriented techniques.

You can provide an adaptation layer as a base class to implement behavior common to all RDBMS engines and then subclass that class to handle the non-standard specifics of a particular engine. The adaptation layer should provide the capability to generate SQL statements so that variations in grammar can be provided by specializing the relevant methods. In this way, you can accommodate a range of requirements in a single program. Because the cursor object executes SQL statements in the Python DB API, this seems like a natural class to extend with SQL capabilities. Because the connection object implements certain operations (principally database commit), the adapter object might retain a reference to both a cursor and the connection that created it, centralizing database operations around a single object.

This approach has the disadvantage of making SQL statement generation a little more complex. It offers the compensating advantage, however, of being able to adapt to new database engines by simply designing a new adapter subclass. As long as the

SQL generation technique is sufficiently general to accommodate the different engines, you can provide the adaptation by programming.

This is a work in progress, so the code is relatively skeletal. Despite this, it has hosted some interesting experiments in database portability and seems to offer an interesting approach. For that reason, you see here an annotated listing of parts of an early version of `basecursor.py`. Be aware that code that appears later in this chapter is based on an updated version of the `basecursor` code with slightly increased functionality. That is the version you will find on the web site.

Cursor Initialization

The whole scheme is built around a `baseCursor` class, which acts as a kind of combination of a connection and a cursor.

```
1   #
2   # baseCursor.py: base class for database adaptation layer
3   #
4
5   # XXX Add DATE/TIME/TIMESTAMP, maybe others?
6
7   from types import StringType
8
9   class baseCursor:
10
11      def __init__(self, cursor, conn):
12          self.cursor = cursor
13          self.conn = conn
14
```

Because it emulates the behavior of both, and because several cursors can share the same connection, it seems easiest to pass both the connection and the cursor to the _init_() method of `baseCursor`. The cursor and connection are saved as instance variables for later use. The XXX comment underlines the experimental nature of the code.

```
15   #
16   # Connection operations
17   #
18      def commit(self):
19          return self.conn.commit()
20
21      def rollback(self):
22          return self.conn.rollback()
23
```

The two key connection operations might be required within the class (although they are currently unused), so they are delegated to the connection inside these methods. The creation of the cursor and the closing of the connection should be performed outside the class, so those methods are not delegated. Cursor creation, as you saw in Chapter 10, can require different arguments in different modules anyway, so it is easier not to try and standardize it.

DELETE

This is the first of a number of methods that construct SQL statements. They are intended (roughly) to handle ANSI SQL, but the experimental nature of the code might mean that non-standard SQL occasionally appears.

```
24  #
25  # Data Manipulation language SQL statement generators
26  #
27      def DELETE(self, tname, WHERE=None):
28          result = "DELETE FROM %s" % tname
29          if WHERE:
30              result += " WHERE %s" % WHERE
31          return result
32
```

The approach for DELETE is fairly typical of the other statements, taking the table name as a positional argument and using a keyword argument to nominate the (possibly empty) WHERE clause.

The following call:

```
c.DELETE("workt", WHERE="SSN='222-33-4444'")
```

gives the following result:

```
DELETE FROM workt WHERE SSN='222-33-44'
```

This is undeniably less convenient than simply writing the SQL statement, but that is the cost of portability.

INSERT

The INSERT method is more complex than DELETE(), reflecting the greater complexity of the underlying SQL statement. The VALUE list is essential: without it there would be nothing to insert! The field names, however, are optional—you will remember that the standard allows you to assume a particular order for the fields, although this is generally bad practice.

```
33      def INSERT(self, tname, fnames=None, VALUES=None):
34          if VALUES is None:
35              raise ValueError, "Value list not provided for INSERT"
36          if fnames is not None:
37              if isinstance(fnames, StringType):
38                  fnames = [fnames]
39              flist = "(%s) " % ", ".join(fnames)
40          else:
41              flist = ""
42          if isinstance(VALUES, StringType):
43              values = VALUES
44          else:
45              values = ", ".join(map(str,VALUES))
46          return "INSERT INTO %s %sVALUES(%s)" % (tname, flist, values)
47
```

A list is created if a single field is given, offering the caller the convenience of specifying a single field without using list notation, and the list is joined together as a comma-separated string. Similar concessions are made with the VALUES argument, which again becomes a comma-separated string.

After everything has been reduced into string form, the final generation of the INSERT statement is simply a case of string formatting.

The following call:

```
c.INSERT("workt", ["worker", "time"], ["'Norman'", 1.5])
```

gives the following result:

```
INSERT INTO workt (worker, time) VALUES('Norman', 1.5)
```

One of the disadvantages of this scheme is that you have to quote the field names to provide them as string arguments to the method calls. In practice, however, such lists are easily constructed using an expression like "field1 field2 field3 field4".split(), and you often find that the field lists are required in enough different places for this to be a worthwhile approach.

SELECT

The SELECT statement takes a list of fields as positional arguments and the following keyword arguments:

- A FROM clause
- A WHERE clause
- A catchall REST

```
48      def SELECT(self, fields, FROM=None, WHERE=None, REST=None):
49          if isinstance(fields, StringType):
50              result = "SELECT " + fields
51          else:
52              ff = []
53              for f in fields:
54                  if isinstance(f, StringType):
55                      ff.append(f)
56                  else:
57                      ff.append(self.fldalias(f))
58              result = "SELECT " + ", ".join(ff)
59          if FROM:
60              result += "\n    FROM %s" % self.tables(FROM)
61          if WHERE:
62              result += "\n    WHERE %s" % WHERE
63          if REST:
64              result += "\n    %s" % REST
65          return result
66
```

The call

```
c.SELECT(["mnth", ["sum(hits)", "totalhits"]],
        FROM="accesses",
        WHERE="mnth<>1",
        REST="""group by mnth
            ORDER BY 2""")
```

returns the result

```
SELECT mnth, sum(hits) AS totalhits
    FROM accesses
    WHERE mnth<>1
    group by mnth
                ORDER BY 2
```

This method also optimizes the single-field case. If the `fields` argument is a list, then each element may be a string. Fields aliased with a local name are represented as a two-element list containing the field name and its alias. Because field alias syntax can differ, the alias clause is computed by another method, which can be overridden independently of the statement syntax.

The `FROM` argument may specify either a single table name or a list, and again the table names can have aliases. Once more the alias syntax is generated by another method to allow for syntax variations. The `WHERE` and `REST` arguments are handled just as the `WHERE` argument to the `DELETE()` method. As the development becomes more intimately involved with the implementation details of a number of database systems, it may prove necessary to add arguments for other clauses currently bundled together under the `REST` argument.

UNION

The next example shows how statements can themselves be arguments to the creation of more complex statements. You can do a similar thing with `SELECT()` when you need to use subqueries.

```
67      def UNION(self, *stmts, **kywds):
68          union = "UNION"
69          if kywds.has_key("DISTINCT") and kywds["DISTINCT"]:
70              union += " DISTINCT"
71          union = "\n    %s\n" % union
72          result = union.join(stmts)
73          if kywds.has_key("REST"):
74              result = "%s\n    %s" % (result, kywds["REST"])
75          return result
76
```

The call

```
c.UNION(c.SELECT([["drinker", "x"]], FROM="likes"),
        c.SELECT([["beer", "x"]], FROM="serves"),
        c.SELECT([["drinker","x"]], FROM="frequents"))
```

results in

```
SELECT drinker AS x
    FROM likes
    UNION
SELECT beer AS x
    FROM serves
    UNION
SELECT drinker AS x
    FROM frequents
```

UNION is used in SQL to build a result set by adding several result sets from different queries together. The SQL syntax requires a list of statements each separated by the keyword UNION, and these statements are collected under the *arg argument. Because a DISTINCT keyword argument also is required, keyword arguments are picked up in the **kywds argument.

Why Not Just Use a DISTINCT Keyword Argument?

The primary argument to the UNION method is a list of SELECT statements, and as you saw in Chapter 2, "An Introduction to Python," the *arg form is used to collect these arguments together under one name. The UNION() method, however, also requires an optional DISTINCT argument, which is treated as a Boolean. Unfortunately, if this keyword argument were put in the method definition as an initial keyword definition of the form

```
def UNION(self, DISTINCT=0, *args)
```

Python would associate it with the first positional argument. To allow the list to be presented as positional arguments, the DISTINCT keyword therefore has to be extracted from a dictionary of keyword arguments, as you were shown in Listing 2.33. Technically, the code should examine the keyword argument list for additional keywords and complain if any are found. The approach adopted tends to work reasonably well in practice, however, and a caller who provides additional keywords should soon discover that they have no effect.

```
77    def UPDATE(self, table, cols, vals, WHERE=None):
78        if len(cols) != len(vals):
79            raise ValueError, "UPDATE column count differs from  value count"
80        result = "UPDATE %s SET %s" % (table, ", ".join(map(lambda x,y:➡
          x+"="+y, cols, vals)))
81        if WHERE:
82            result += " WHERE " + WHERE
83        return result
```

CREATE INDEX

The examples you have seen so far show how to create data manipulation language statements. The data definition language also has its variants, and so portability techniques can be useful here as well.

```
84    #
85    # Data definition language SQL statement generators
```

```
86    #
87        def CREATE_INDEX(self, ixname, tbl, fields, UNIQUE=0):
88            if isinstance(fields, StringType):
89                fields = [fields]
90            if UNIQUE:
91                unique = "UNIQUE "
92            else:
93                unique = ""
94            return "CREATE %sINDEX %s ON %s(%s)" % (unique, ixname, tbl, ",➥
              ".join(fields))
95
```

The call

```
c.CREATE_INDEX("wname", "workt", "name", UNIQUE=1)
```

results in

```
CREATE UNIQUE INDEX wname ON workt(name)
```

Strictly speaking, the CREATE INDEX statement is a performance optimization. A null statement would therefore be an acceptable result for a purist SQL implementation, but indexing is widely used, and it is therefore desirable to support it. Many implementations use indexing to verify uniqueness constraints, but an occasional system does not support UNIQUE indexes.

CREATE TABLE

Creating tables is a major area where portability can be a problem, especially because data types can vary so much from engine to engine. You will see the definitions of some simple field data type declarations later in the listing.

```
96        def CREATE_TABLE(self, tname, *fields):
97            ff = []
98            for f in fields:
99                ff.append("%s %s" % (f[0], f[1]))
100           return "CREATE TABLE %s (\n    %s)" % (tname, ",\n    ".join(ff))
101
```

The call

```
c.CREATE_TABLE("accesses",
   ['page', c.VARCHAR(14)],
   ['hits', c.INTEGER],
   ['mnth', c.INTEGER])
```

results in

```
CREATE TABLE accesses (
    page VARCHAR(14),
    hits INTEGER,
    mnth INTEGER)
```

CREATE VIEW

Creating views requires a SELECT statement, and this example shows how a nested SELECT() call generates a subquery. Otherwise, the basic syntax is straightforward.

```
102      def CREATE_VIEW(self, vname, fields, select):
103          return "CREATE VIEW %s (%s) AS\n    %s" % (vname, ", ".join(fields),➡
             select)
104
```

The call

```
c.CREATE_VIEW("nondrinkers", ("d", "b"),
     c.SELECT(["drinker", "bar"],
         FROM="frequents",
         WHERE="drinker not in (%s)" %
             c.SELECT("drinker", FROM="likes")))
```

results in

```
CREATE VIEW nondrinkers (d, b) AS
    SELECT drinker, bar
    FROM frequents
    WHERE drinker not in (SELECT drinker
    FROM likes)
```

DROP INDEX/TABLE/VIEW

The DROP statements are very straightforward.

```
105      def DROP_INDEX(self, i, t):
106          return "DROP INDEX %s" % I
107
108      def DROP_TABLE(self, t):
109          return "DROP TABLE %s" % t
110
111      def DROP_VIEW(self, v):
112          return "DROP VIEW %s" % v
113
```

The calls

```
c.DROP_INDEX("wname", "workt")
c.DROP_TABLE("workt")
c.DROP_VIEW("nondrinkers")
```

result in

```
DROP INDEX wname
DROP TABLE workt
DROP VIEW nondrinkers
```

Data Type Declarations

This part of the code is currently the least developed, but you should be able to clearly see the principle at work. The data types you declare at application level need not directly correspond with the engine data types, and you can use logic to choose different types depending on parameters. As a simple example, the Jet engine handles TEXT fields up to 255 characters, but MEMO fields can be up to 64 KB long, albeit at some cost in performance. The Jet adapter could declare a VARCHAR(200) column as TEXT(200), but a CHAR(1000) column as MEMO.

```
114  #
115  # Datatype generation statements and constants
116  #
117      def VARCHAR(self, n):
118          return "VARCHAR(%d)" % n
119
120      INTEGER = "INTEGER"
121      FLOAT = "FLOAT"
122
```

Cursor Methods

This baseCursor object is, when all else is said, a database cursor. It must therefore be able to do all the normal cursor things. You can easily arrange this using the _getattr_() method to delegate any unrecognized method calls to the cursor provided by the client when the BaseCursor was created. This so-called *blind delegation* also allows you to use any methods and data attributes that your chosen cursor implements, although you should be careful to use non-standard features only as a conscious decision.

```
123  #
124  # Local cursor operations.
125  # Other cursor operations are delegated to
126  # the cursor supplied as an argument
127  #
128      def __getattr__(self, attrname):
129          "Delegate unrecognised methods/attributes to the cursor object."
130          return getattr(self.cursor, attrname)
131
```

Delegation Alternatives

Some cursor method attributes could be explicitly delegated using

```
    setattr(self, attrname, self.cursor.attrname)
```

in the _init_() method. This explicit delegation would optimize the more general technique used by _getattr_(), which would only be called when the attribute was not found in the baseCursor's namespace. This approach works only for methods, and not data attributes; however, a data attribute *must* be retrieved from the cursor each time it is used, so delegation is still necessary to retrieve (for example) the cursor description attribute that holds the descriptions of the columns returned by a SELECT statement.

You could, of course, limit the attributes made available by checking their names in getattr() before delegation and raising an error if the attribute name were not in some list or dictionary of approved names. This technique can afford useful protection when a range of different object classes and/or types is being accessed polymorphically (using methods that they all implement) to ensure that only "approved" method calls are delegated.

Support for Syntax Variations

As mentioned when discussing the SELECT() method previously, certain database engines require or forbid the use of the keyword AS between a table name or a column specification and its alias. To allow such variations to be easily accommodated, table aliases are generated by methods that can be overridden in a particular case.

```
132  #
133  # Utility functions: may be overridden to modify SQL grammar
134  #
135      def fldalias(self, f):
136          if len(f) != 2:
137              raise ValueError, "Field alias should be exactly two elements"
138          else:
139              return " AS ".join(f)
140
141      def tables(self, FROM):
142          if isinstance(FROM[0], StringType):
143              FROM = [FROM]
144          result = []
145          for t in FROM:
146              if isinstance(t, StringType):
147                  result.append(t)
148              else:
149                  result.append(self.tblalias(t))
150          return ", ".join(result)
151
152      def tblalias(self, t):
153          if len(t) != 2:
154              raise ValueError, "Table alias should be exactly two elements"
155          else:
156              return " AS ".join(t)
```

The tables() method creates a list from a single table name if necessary and uses the tblalias() method to handle tables known inside the query by an alias. The fldalias() method builds the representation for an aliased column. This allows the adaptation layer for a specific database to override the syntax for table and column aliases.

Tailoring the Adaptation Layer

There are two easy ways to tailor the `BaseCursor` object to deal with the real database you want to use:

- Define a subclass and override the methods for which the `BaseCursor` generates incorrect SQL.

- Develop a `mixin` class, which can be used by several different cursor types that require common behavior.

The next section, "Adapting Specific DB Modules and Engines," shows some classes to adapt to specific products. The example in Listing 11.2 modifies baseCursor to use a plus sign instead of the "¦¦" string concatenation operator. Both Gadfly and SQL Server use this syntax, so it was simpler to develop the ccCursor class as the inheritance parent for both cursors.

Listing 11.2   *ccCursor.py:* **Modifications to** *BaseCursor* **Replacing "¦¦" with "+"**

```
 1   #
 2   # ccCursor.py: baseCursor to handle "+" instead of "¦¦"
 3   #
 4   from baseCursor import baseCursor
 5
 6   def gfs(s):
 7       if s:
 8           return s.replace("¦¦", "+")
 9
10   def gft(x):
11       if x:
12           if type(x) == type(""):
13               return gfs(x)
14           else:
15               return [gft(e) for e in x]
16
17   class ccCursor(baseCursor):
18       """Subclass replacing ANSI concatenation with "+"."""
19
20       def DELETE(self, tname, WHERE=None):
21           return baseCursor.DELETE(self, tname, gft(WHERE))
22
23       def INSERT(self, tname, fnames=None, VALUES=None):
24           return baseCursor.INSERT(self, tname, fnames, VALUES=gft(VALUES))
25
26       def SELECT(self, fields, FROM=None, WHERE=None, REST=None):
27           return baseCursor.SELECT(self, gft(fields), FROM=FROM,➨
             WHERE=gft(WHERE), REST=gft(REST))
```

The `gfs()` function replaces the standard concatenation operator with a plus sign. The `gft()` function uses `gfs()` to operate on either strings or lists. The functions are carefully composed to handle `None` correctly. The `ccCursor` class is a subclass of the `baseCursor` class that uses `gft()` to replace concatenation operators in any DML method argument that might contain them. Of course it would be more rigorous to parse the SQL clauses to ensure that no changes are made to string literals (for example) that happen to contain the concatenation operator. So far this has not been an issue, but it will probably become necessary as the software develops.

Adapting Specific DB Modules and Engines

As you saw in Table 11.1 there really is quite a large selection of database modules to choose from. In practice, as you read in Chapter 10, ODBC is (currently) often the most satisfactory connectivity option, and the `mx.ODBC` module can communicate with Adabas, IBM DB2, DBMaker, Informix, MySQL, PostgreSQL, Oracle, Solid, Sybase, Windows ODBC Manager, the UNIX iODBC Driver Manager, the UNIX unixODBC Driver Manager, EasySoft ODBC Bridge, and others. It also can be adapted to communicate with some other ODBC driver if you are prepared to read the source and recompile the module, which is freely available in source form.

Using a single ODBC-based module also means that you have to contend with SQL adaptation only because the module interface will be the same no matter which database you use. It may be that mxODBC's licensing terms are unsatisfactory from your point of view, however (the software is free for personal use but must be licensed for commercial use), so you may want to explore other alternatives. It still might be important, then, to know the wrinkles of particular database packages, and this section looks at some specific products, with a view to helping you formulate your own ideas about database module and engine independence.

Microsoft Access (Jet)

Although many people regard Access as a standalone database, it is actually better thought of as a GUI front end with a separate database engine, properly referred to as the Jet engine. The front end is perfectly capable of using other engines via a linking mechanism that allows you to specify the data source containing the tables you want to use. This front end is a commercial product, however, whereas the engine may be freely downloaded from Microsoft's web site.

The Jet engine is an acceptable development platform, but you must realize that it is not optimized for multiuser access. When multiple users access a Jet database in the Windows environment using an Access front end, they are usually simply sharing the database file. An ODBC driver also is available for the Jet engine, but the driver will simply be a further user of the database file. A further limitation, which may or may not be significant, is the restriction of database size to 2 GB. Jet also has quite severe restrictions on the SQL it accepts and does not allow the creation or use of views, stored procedures, or triggers.

Microsoft suggests that you do not use Jet when the total number of users exceeds 20, although in theory the engine can accept up to 255 concurrent users. The engine did not provide transaction logging until release 4.0 (so recovery after hardware failure was impossible, and transaction processing was not supported), and cannot support symmetric multiprocessing.

Given all the restrictions, you may wonder why anyone would ever consider using the Jet engine as the data source for a web site. The primary answer to this question is Jet's ubiquity. More than 70 percent of all desktop computers have Microsoft Office components installed, so it is tempting to use the software's database component. Jet databases are freely distributable as part of solutions created with Office and Visual Studio, and Jet drivers are available on Windows NT Server, for example. Indeed, until the release of SQL Server 7.0 (which would run under Windows 95 and 98), I often used Jet to support the initial development of customer web sites, so I could continue development while traveling. This led to the understanding that it is indeed possible to develop databases on one engine and migrate them to another for production. The trick is to ensure that you test your migration process before becoming too heavily involved in database development.

Microsoft originally designed Access as a single-user database, and it has served that class of user extremely well. When it comes to support of industrial-strength processes, however, its deficiencies become more relevant. You can do more with Access from the built-in Visual Basic for Applications (VBA) interpreter than you can in plain SQL across an ODBC connection.

The `jetCursor`, shown in Listing 11.3, required very few adaptations. It inherits from `ccCursor` to use a plus sign for concatenation and provides its own `DROP_INDEX` method to accommodate Jet's syntax discrepancy.

Listing 11.3 *jetCursor.py:* **An Adaptive Cursor for the Jet Engine**

```
 1  #
 2  # jetCursor.py: jet variant on ANSI cursor
 3  #
 4  from ccCursor import ccCursor
 5
 6  class jetCursor(ccCursor):
 7      """Jet cursor using "+" for concatenation and specialized DROP_INDEX."""
 8
 9      def DROP_INDEX(self, index, table):
10          return "DROP INDEX %s ON %s" % (index, table)
```

Microsoft SQL Server and MSDE

Microsoft's industrial-strength database engine is SQL Server 2000, although many sites are still currently working with its predecessor, SQL Server 7.0. The version of

SQL implemented in these products is *Transact-SQL* (or T-SQL for short). In common with other "enterprise-level" products, this perverts SQL into becoming a procedural language and allows you to process cursors similar in concept to the cursors implemented by the Python DB API.

Any SQL variant that allows stored procedures and triggers must extend the language with procedural features. The procedural language features are currently outside the scope of the adaptation layer.

Although there is a good awareness of the SQL Server product, far fewer people know about the Microsoft Database Engine (MSDE), which comes as a part of certain Microsoft products. It can be downloaded from Microsoft's web site for those who have not purchased the relevant products, although without a product purchase you have no rights to redistribute the software. MSDE is 100-percent compatible with T-SQL and, according to Microsoft's literature, is "optimized for up to five simultaneous users." It is a useful development choice if you want to avoid Jet, and if you need something you can distribute, it has a small footprint. The only difference between MSDE and the SQL Server delivered as part of such products as the Small Business Edition appears to be the lack of certain GUI-based tools.

SQL Server, like Jet, uses the plus sign for concatenations. It also requires slight variations for indexing, again for the `DROP INDEX` statement. This gives a relatively small `ssCursor` module, shown in Listing 11.4.

Listing 11.4   *ssCursor.py:* **An Adaptive Cursor for SQL Server and MSDE**

```
 1 #
 2 # sscursor.py: SQL Server variant on ANSI cursor
 3 #
 4 from ccCursor import ccCursor
 5
 6 class sscursor(ccCursor):
 7     """Slightly modified cursor for SQL Server with "+" for concatenation."""
 8
 9     def DROP_INDEX(self, i, t):
10         return "DROP INDEX %s.%s" % (t,, i)
```

Oracle

The Oracle RDBMS is one of the most widely used database management systems in the world. It is, however, sold under some rather restrictive terms and conditions that can make comparisons with other systems quite difficult. Python users can use Oracle with an ODBC interface, or they can use the `DCOracle2` module built and maintained by Digital Creations, or the newer `cx_Oracle` module from Computronix.

These latter two modules make a fair job of compatibility with the DB API, and both claim UNIX and Windows operability. Like several third-party modules, the assumption tends to be that you will be able to compile the modules for yourself, and UNIX tends to be favored for the build. If this is not the case, then you might have to hunt around for a precompiled binary distribution appropriate to your particular version of Windows and/or Python. cx_Oracle, an open-source product from Computronix, is available as a binary distribution consisting of a single file.

In terms of SQL compatibility, the Oracle SQL adaptation layer requires very little code, as shown in Listing 11.5. The only requirement seems to be for column aliases and table aliases to be introduced without the AS keyword.

Listing 11.5 *oracleCursor.py:* **An Adaptive Cursor for Oracle**

```
 1  #
 2  # oraclecursor.py: Oracle 8 variant on ANSI cursor
 3  #
 4  from baseCursor import baseCursor
 5
 6  class oracleCursor(baseCursor):
 7      """Specialized cursor."""
 8
 9      def fldalias(self, f):
10          if len(f) != 2:
11              raise ValueError, "Field alias should be exactly two elements"
12          else:
13              return " ".join(f)
14
15      def tblalias(self, t):
16          if len(t) != 2:
17              raise ValueError, "Table alias should be exactly two elements"
18          else:
19              return " ".join(t)
```

Web Server Interaction with Database Programs

In Chapter 10 you saw a simple database web server that ran as a standalone program. For certain simple applications such a "Python mini-web server" might be adequate, but most programmed web services are actually built around an existing web server. Several popular web servers (if you haven't already chosen one, then http://serverwatch.internet.com/webservers.html is a good place to look) provide a ready-made framework to support web services written in Python or any other language. If you use the Windows platform with Microsoft's IIS server, then your web pages will run in the Active Server Pages (ASP) environment, which is rather different from most other web servers. Windows supports a number of other web servers, including the popular Apache and the less well-known Xitami, so you do have a choice in this matter.

The database code you have already seen could run under the control of a web server, except that it does not produce the required HTML output. If you remember the material on HTTP communications, you will remember that either a GET or a POST HTTP protocol request can result in the running of an executable. Before you start writing too much database code, however, make sure that you understand the communication conventions, as they are usually handled by web servers.

Maintaining Data in Python CGI Scripts

The acronym CRUD often used in database training refers to the create, read, update, and delete database activities handled by the SQL verbs INSERT, SELECT, UPDATE and DELETE, respectively. Reading the database tends to dominate almost every production application, and web databases are no different. Even so, there is a definite need for create, update, and delete operations, if only for maintenance. This section shows how simple data management code can be applied to maintaining a single table in an RDBMS.

Inevitably, a large proportion of the code in the following sections concerns generation of HTML. Such code is usually straightforward, mostly involving the substitution of parameters into long strings. The database code is the main focus, so if your understanding of HTML is less than thorough, you should simply run the code and let the browser show you how it renders the HTML.

Listing Data for Selection

Listing 11.6 shows a simple CGI script that does not take any inputs. Its purpose is to produce a list of links, each of which should bring up the data for a particular mini-web page in a form suitable for editing and resubmission to the database. The form of the URLs it generates is

```
wdform.py?PgName=XXX
```

It also adds a final URL, which calls the wdform.py script without any parameters. This link is intended for the creation of new pages.

Listing 11.6 *wdlist.py:* List Mini-Web Pages with Editing Links

```
 1  #!C:/Python20/python.exe
 2  #
 3  import mx.ODBC.Windows as odbc
 4  from jetCursor import jetCursor
 5  import urllib
 6
 7  print """Content-Type: text/html\n
 8  <HTML>
 9    <HEAD>
10      <TITLE>Min-Web Page List</TITLE>
11    </HEAD>
12    <BODY>"""
```

```
13
14   cn = odbc.connect("WebData")
15   cr = jetCursor(cn.cursor(), cn)
16   sql = cr.SELECT("PgName", FROM="PgData")
17   cr.execute(sql)
18   data = cr.fetchall()
19   cr.close()
20   cn.close()
21   print """<H2>Page List for Mini-Web Database</H2>
22   <P>Click the page name to show data in an edit form<BR>"""
23   for d in data:
24       PgName = d[0]
25       print """
26          <A HREF="wdform.py?PgName=%s">%s</A><BR>""" %➡
27                        (urllib.quote(PgName), PgName)
28   print """<BR>
29          <A HREF="wdform.py">Create New Page</A><BR>
30      </BODY>
31   </HTML>
32   """
```

Line 1 tells the web server that this script should be run by the Python interpreter.
You may need to change this line if your web server requires such identification and
you have your Python interpreter at a different location. The only other point of note
is the use of the `urllib.quote()` function on line 27 to ensure that even if the page
name contains "dangerous" characters (such as space and question mark), they will be
correctly encoded in the HREF attribute of the anchor. Such encoding is not required
in the text of the link. The output from this script looks something like Figure 11.1,
with links for each of the pages in your mini-web database.

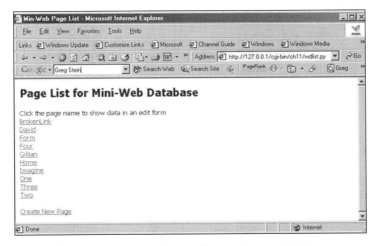

Figure 11.1   Output from *wdlist.py* in Internet Explorer.

Editing Data: HTML Form Generation

The listing script you just saw allows the user to easily select any existing page for editing or to request creation of a new one. The former case results in the transmission of the page name as a part of the URL that triggers the form generator.

The cgi module is designed to simplify the task of accessing parameters provided as a part of the URL, or in form data. The primary object it defines is the FieldStorage, which allows access to fields from the URL or form input by name. The FieldStorage object, when created, queries the environment to determine whether it should use the query string (for GET protocol methods) or the standard input (for POST), and establishes the received values internally after decoding as necessary.

Parameter values can be obtained from the FieldStorage object using the value attribute of the entry accessed like a dictionary, indexing by parameter name. If you had bound a FieldStorage object to the variable form (a traditional name), you could access the value of the PgName parameter as

```
PgName = form["PgData"].value
```

Alternatively, you can use the FieldStorage's getvalue() method with the parameter name as an argument. Be careful not to create more than one FieldStorage object because in the case of a POST HTTP protocol method, its creation will consume the CGI script's standard input.

With this in mind, you should be able to understand the Python CGI script in Listing 11.7. When invoked from a sensible URL, such as those generated by wdlist.py, it generates a form that presents either the contents of one row from the database table, or an empty form into which the data for a new page can be entered.

Listing 11.7   *wdform.py:* **Data Edit/Entry Form for Mini-Web Pages**

```
 1  #!C:/Python20/python.exe
 2  #
 3  import cgi
 4  import mx.ODBC.Windows as odbc
 5  from jetCursor import jetCursor
 6
 7  class NoSuchPage:    # Exception
 8      pass
 9
10  form = cgi.FieldStorage()
11  print """Content-Type: text/html\n
12  <HTML>
13    <HEAD>
14      <TITLE>Mini-Web Data Entry/Edit Form</TITLE>
15    </HEAD>
16    <BODY>"""
17  try:
18      if form.has_key("PgName"):  # edit existing page
19          PgName = form["PgName"].value
20          cn = odbc.connect("WebData")
```

```
21              cr = jetCursor(cn.cursor(), cn)
22              sql = cr.SELECT(["PgNum", "PgText"], FROM="PgData",
23                  WHERE="PgName=?")
24              cr.execute(sql, (PgName,))
25              data = cr.fetchall()
26              if len(data) == 0:
27                  raise NoSuchPage
28              op = "Update"
29              it = "HIDDEN"
30              cr.close()
31              cn.close()
32              button2 = """
33              <INPUT NAME="op" TYPE="SUBMIT" VALUE="Delete"
34                      OnClick="return(confirm('Do you REALLY""" """ want to➥
                        delete this record?'))">"""
35          else:                           # create new page
36              op = "Create"
37              it = "TEXT"
38              data = ( (0, ''), )
39              PgName = ''
40              button2 = ''
41          PgNum, PgText = data[0]       # common logic
42          print """
43              <H2>%s Mini-Web Page Data</h2>
44              <FORM METHOD="POST" ACTION="wdupdt.py">
45              Page Name: %s<BR>
46              <INPUT NAME="PgName" TYPE="%s" LENGTH="25" VALUE="%s"><BR>
47              Page Number:<BR>
48              <INPUT NAME="PgNum" TYPE="TEXT" VALUE="%d"><BR>
49              Page Text:<BR>
50              <TEXTAREA COLS="50" ROWS="7" NAME="PgText">%s</TEXTAREA><BR>
51              <INPUT NAME="op" TYPE="SUBMIT" VALUE="%s">
52              %s
53              </FORM>""" % (op, PgName, it, PgName, PgNum, PgText, op, button2)
54      except NoSuchPage:
55          print """<H2>Page %s Not Found</H2>
56          <P><A HREF="wdlist.py">Return to page list</A>""" % PgName
57      print """
58        </BODY>
59      </HTML>
60      """
```

Most of the logic is concerned with handling the differences between updating an existing page and creating a new one. In the logic for existing pages, the form field type for the PgName input is set to HIDDEN. The value must be transmitted to the update script because it is the primary key for the table, but the user must not be allowed to edit it. For a new page, the user must be able to enter a new value, and so the form field type is set to TEXT. The button used to submit the form is differently captioned in each case, which makes the user interface friendlier.

A second button is only included for the update case—it does not make sense to try to update a record that has not yet been created. Some simple JavaScript is used to force the user to confirm her intention to delete a page. I have never liked allowing a single incorrect user action to result in loss of data, and this trick has stood me in good stead over the years.

It is important to ensure that the HTML your CGI scripts generate is as well-formed as possible, and for this reason an exception class is defined to detect whether a user attempts to generate a form for a nonexistent page. This exception is used to break the regular flow of control and insert a message as the main page content. Figure 11.2 shows a page generated by this program.

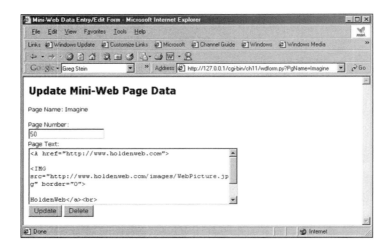

Figure 11.2   An edit form produced by *wdform.py*.

`wdlist.py` and `wdform.py` together solve the first part of the database update problem: the user can see the web pages listed by name, and selecting a page shows its data in a form, where the user can change it. Of course the final action required is to update the database, and two different sets of logic are required here.

For new pages, a new row must be inserted into the `PgData` table using a SQL `INSERT` statement. To edit an existing row, the relevant row must be updated with `UPDATE`, and a `DELETE` statement must be used to remove a row from the table. This is a second reason why the primary `SUBMIT` button's value varies between update and creation: the button's value is used in the script that processes the form data to select the appropriate database logic.

Creating, Updating, and Deleting Data: Forms Handling

You can see that the same CGI script, `wdupdt.py`, is always used as the action for the form. The required action is indicated by the value of the button on which the user clicks to submit the form. Three other items are present in the data sent by the browser when the form is submitted:

- The page number (which determines the sequence in which it is listed in the mini-web)
- The page name (input by the user for a new page, or retrieved from the form script's URL and transmitted in a hidden field for an existing page)
- The page text, which is the HTML to be displayed by the mini-web server

To simplify the HTML generation logic, the update script, shown in Listing 11.8, uses two functions. The first reads the form data, returning None if an error occurs, and the second establishes the correct SQL statement and data tuple according to the operation that has been requested, again returning None if an invalid operation was requested. Dynamic parameterization is used in the SQL.

The nested try blocks ensure that the database connection is properly closed down no matter what errors may occur and that database exceptions are correctly caught and handled. This really shows the power of exception handling to simplify program logic. If you try to recast the script as simple sequential logic with error detection using if/then, you will find its structure becomes surprisingly opaque.

Listing 11.8   *wdupdt.py:* **Creating, Updating, and Deleting Records**

```
1  #!C:/Python20/python.exe
2  #
3  import cgi
4  import mx.ODBC.Windows as odbc
5  from jetCursor import jetCursor
6
7  def formRead():
8      form = cgi.FieldStorage()
9      try:
10         num = int(form["PgNum"].value)
11         name = form["PgName"].value
12         text = form["PgText"].value
13         op = form["op"].value
14         return num, name, text, op
15     except (KeyError, ValueError):
16         return None
17
18 def opSetup(formdata, cr):
19     PgNum, PgName, PgText, op = formdata
20     if op == "Update":
21         return (
22         cr.UPDATE("PgData", ["PgNum", "PgText"], ["?", "?"],➡
           WHERE="PgName=?"),
23         (PgNum, PgText, PgName))
24     elif op == "Create":
25         return (
```

continues

Listing 11.8 **Continued**

```
26          cr.INSERT("PgData", ["PgNum", "PgText", "PgName"], ["?", "?", "?"]),
27          (PgNum, PgText, PgName))
28      elif op == "Delete":
29          return (
30          cr.DELETE("PgData", WHERE="PgName=?"),
31          (PgName, ))
32
33  print """Content-Type: text/html\n
34  <HTML>
35    <HEAD>
36      <TITLE>Mini-Web Data Update</TITLE>
37    </HEAD>
38    <BODY>"""
39
40  formdata = formRead()
41  if formdata:
42      PgNum, PgName, PgText, op = formdata
43      cn = odbc.connect("WebData")
44      cr = jetCursor(cn.cursor(), cn)
45      try:
46          try:
47              opstuff = opSetup(formdata, cr)
48              if opstuff:
49                  sql, data = opstuff
50                  cr.execute(sql, data)
51                  cr.commit() # ensure persistence
52                  print """
53                  <H2>Mini-Web Page %sd</h2>""" % op
54              else:
55                  print "<H2>Illegal Operation Requested</H2>"
56          except odbc.Error:
57              print """<H2>Database %s Failed</H2>""" % op
58      finally:
59          cr.close()
60          cn.close()
61  else:
62      print "<H2>Missing or Illegal Forms Data</H2>"
63  print """
64    <P><A HREF="wdlist.py">Return to page list</A>
65    </BODY>
66  </HTML>
67  """
```

Error checking is reasonably scrupulous in this script, although the reporting is sketchy. The script's output contains a link back to the listing script, as a user convenience. The output after a successful update should look like Figure 11.3.

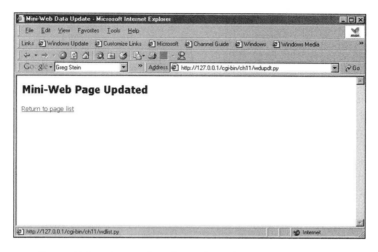

Figure 11.3 Output from *formupdt.py* after a successful update.

Deceptive Simplicity

The scripts you have just examined are really simple. Do not be fooled, if you have done no previous web development, into thinking that is all there is to data maintenance. The austere appearance of the web pages produced by the scripts would only be acceptable for in-house use. A major part of the complexity of web development is imposing a consistent look-and-feel on all pages in a web. This is a major part of the role of the web frameworks described in Chapter 16, "Web Application Frameworks," and the skeletal web server you will read about in Chapter 15, "Building Small, Efficient Python Web Systems."

However, these scripts do present the basis of most data-maintenance tasks. Sometimes the picture is complicated by the need to maintain several tables in a coordinated fashion, but the principles remain the same:

1. Present links to the appropriate data for user selection.
2. Display the selected data in a form (or a blank form to create new data).
3. Process the form content by updating the database.

Generalizing Data Maintenance

After you have written several table maintenance programs such as the preceding ones, you will begin to see a sameness about them all. Certainly my own experience was that I started to generalize the logic into a form that could be used for different tables simply by changing the data passed into a number of functions. Much of the data-maintenance logic can be parameterized if you can write the code so that it is driven by descriptions of the data to be edited.

The problem with generalizing in this way is that the devil is in the details, and the code becomes more complex as the number of low-probability special cases that have to be handled increases. A module of real utility in simplifying database code is Greg Stein's `dtuple` module, which you can download from `http://www.lyra.org/greg/python/dtuple.py`.

The library lets you treat the tuples returned as results of database retrievals in a much more natural way than simply indexing them numerically: you can use nominated field names as dictionary-style indexes or (assuming they are syntactically valid Python names) as attribute names. The next section shows you how you can use `dtuple` to generalize the task of generating data-maintenance forms such as the `wdform.py` page in the previous section. The same principles can be extended to the listing and update routines as well.

A Simple, General GUI Structure

The `dtuple` library defines two types of objects: the `TupleDescriptor` and the `DatabaseTuple`. When you initialize a `TupleDescriptor`, you pass a sequence of element descriptors, which are themselves tuples or lists. The first member of each sequence is the name of the field described. Various aspects of the fields of a form are significant, so let's decide to store the following information about each form field:

- **FieldName**—The name of the corresponding database field.

- **Description**—A more descriptive name to be used in the form to describe it to the user.

- **Key**—A flag that tells you whether this is a key field (remember that keys are treated differently in update forms).

- **Size**—The maximum number of characters allowed in data entry for the field.

You could describe the data from the Chapter 10 mini-web with the following simple `TupleDescriptor`:

```
mwRec = dtuple.TupleDescriptor((
    ("PgName", "Page Name",    1, 25),
    ("PgNum",  "Page Sequence", 0, 5),
    ("PgText", "Page Content",  0, (4, 40))
))
```

The `Size` entry for the page text is itself a tuple, since `<TEXTAREA>` HTML form elements can be given a height in rows and a width in columns. The second class defined in the `dtuple` module is the `DatabaseTuple`, which you construct using a `TupleDescriptor` and a data tuple, usually (but not necessarily) retrieved from a database. Supposing that you had retrieved one or more rows from the mini-web page database into a tuple name `dbrows`, you could now process each row to list the pages' names and sequence numbers using the following code:

```
for row in dbrows:
    row = dtuple.DatabaseTuple(mwRec, row)
    print "%3d: %s" % (row.PgNum, row.PgName)
```

The output from your database would look something like mine, shown here:

```
 0: Home
10: One
20: Two
30: Three
40: Four
50: Imagine
75: BrokenLink
99: Form
```

The second statement in the `for` loop could equally well have been

```
print "%3d: %s" % (row["PgNum"], row["PgName"])
```

In this case, the mapping-style field addressing is used. In either case, you can see that the names associated with the fields are those given as element zero of each row of the `TupleDescriptor`. Of course, so far you have not used any other fields of the tuple. To construct a form, you will need access to this information, iterating over each column to generate the appropriate form field for it. An easy way to gain attribute and mapping access to the fields of the `mwRec` structure is to describe them using a `TupleDescriptor` consisting of just names!

   This technique is used in `dtform.py`, shown in Listing 11.9. The script uses a tuple of the names of each field in the tuples describing the database record, and it constructs a `TupleDescriptor` from them. This produces much more readable programs than using indexing to select the data from the raw tuple.

Listing 11.9   *dtform.py:* **An Automated Data Maintenance Form Generator**

```
 1  #!C:/Python20/python.exe
 2  #
 3  import cgi
 4  import dtuple
 5  import mx.ODBC.Windows as odbc
 6  from jetCursor import jetCursor
 7
 8  class NoSuchPage:    # Exception
 9      pass
10
11  cn = odbc.connect("WebData")
12  cr = jetCursor(cn.cursor(), cn)
13
14  fldDsc = dtuple.TupleDescriptor((
15          ("name", ), ("description", ), ("key", ), ("size", )
16      ))
17
```

continues

Listing 11.9 **Continued**

```
18  cols = (
19          ("PgName", "Page Name",     1, 25),
20          ("PgNum",  "Page Sequence", 0, 5),
21          ("PgText", "Page Content",  0, (4, 40)))
22      )
23  colDsc = dtuple.TupleDescriptor(cols)
24
25  # Iterate over cols to get name of key field (1 only,
26  # not a textarea, assumed) and list of field names
27  fieldnames = []
28  for rec in cols:
29      rec = dtuple.DatabaseTuple(fldDsc, rec)
30      if rec.key:
31          keyname = rec.name
32      fieldnames.append(rec.name)
33
34  form = cgi.FieldStorage()
35  print """Content-Type: text/html\n
36  <HTML>
37    <HEAD>
38      <TITLE>Mini-Web Data Entry/Edit Form</TITLE>
39    </HEAD>
40    <BODY>
41    <H2>Automated Edit Form</H2>
42    <TABLE>"""
43  try:
44      if form.has_key(keyname):  # edit existing page
45          keyval = form[keyname].value
46          sql = cr.SELECT(fieldnames, FROM="PgData",
47                  WHERE=keyname+"=?")
48          newpage = 0
49          cr.execute(sql, (keyval,))
50          data = cr.fetchall()[0] # assume one row!
51          if len(data) == 0:
52              raise NoSuchPage
53          data = dtuple.DatabaseTuple(colDsc, data)
54          op = "Update"
55      else:                        # create new page
56          newpage = 1
57          op = "Create"
58      print """
59          <H2>%s Mini-Web Page Data</h2>
60          <FORM METHOD="POST" ACTION="wdupdt.py">
61          """ % op
62          # generate form field for each database column
63      for col in cols:
64          col = dtuple.DatabaseTuple(fldDsc, col)
65          ff = """<TR><TD VALIGN="TOP">%s:</TD><TD>""" % col.description
66          if newpage:
```

```
 67                  dval = ""
 68             else:
 69                  dval = data[col.name]
 70            if col.key and not newpage:
 71                  ff += data[col.name]
 72                  ftype = "HIDDEN"
 73            else:
 74                  ftype = "TEXT"
 75            if type(col.size) == type(1):
 76                  ff += """<INPUT NAME="%s" TYPE="%s" """➡
 77                      """LENGTH="25" VALUE="%s">"""➡
 78                      % (col.name, ftype, dval)
 79            else:
 80                  ff +="""<TEXTAREA COLS="50" ROWS="7" """➡
 81                      """NAME="PgText">%s</TEXTAREA><BR>""" % dval
 82            ff += "</TD><TR>"
 83            print ff
 84      print """
 85      <TR><TD></TD><TD><INPUT NAME="op" TYPE="SUBMIT" VALUE="%s">""" % op
 86      if not newpage:
 87          print """
 88      <INPUT NAME="op" TYPE="SUBMIT" VALUE="Delete"
 89                  OnClick="return(confirm('Do you REALLY"""➡
 90                  """ want to delete this record?'))">"""
 91      print """
 92      </FORM></TD></TR>
 93      </TABLE>
 94  """
 95  except NoSuchPage:
 96      print """<H2>Page %s Not Found</H2>
 97      <P><A HREF="wdlist.py">Return to page list</A>""" % PgName
 98  cr.close()
 99  cn.close()
100  print """
101      </BODY>
102  </HTML>
103  """
```

This more (but still not completely) general script is slightly more than 100 lines of code, compared with wdform's 67. Some of the additional code relates to the use of HTML tables to make the presentation a little more attractive, and the extra functionality has been provided at a reasonable cost. Other considerations have been ignored, though, such as how to handle composite (multicolumn) keys, how to perform client-side (in the browser) data validation, and how to take data typing into account.

Although this particular script still has the table name built in to it, it is reasonably general. It uses the name of the key field to look for the CGI argument defining which record to edit. The names of the data columns retrieved from the database are extracted from the cols tuple. You can see that the script could easily accommodate additional fields in the underlying table, with the simple addition of elements to the `cols` tuple. The use of the `dtuple` module makes the internal logic (particularly expressions such as `data[col.name]`, in which a `dtuple` is indexed by an attribute of another `dtuple`) easier to understand without requiring the definition of particular classes to represent to structural information. Without `dtuple`, the same expression would have had to be written using numeric indexes, or each row would have had to be converted into a mapping or some special-purpose object.

The listing and update scripts could be similarly modified, and parameterized as to the table to operate on as well as the fields to be included. In a completely general design, the data for the `TupleDescriptions` could itself be retrieved from a database. The whole data-editing subsystem might eventually become data-driven.

Advantages of Generalized Editing

Even at this intermediate level of generalization, much has been gained. Data-driven code of this nature is useful because it allows you to modify the functionality of the code merely by modifying data structures. The code is effectively being driven by *metadata*, which describes the structure of the data to be edited.

It also makes your applications easier to deliver and (to some extent) maintain, since the same piece of code is able to handle more of the system's needs. Ultimately, providing forms to edit the metadata and allowing the users some freedom to define their own data-editing process could bootstrap the whole process.

Not only that, but a change to the application logic, once made, is immediately available for use in all areas of the system. It may take more effort to upgrade the functionality, but such changes need be made only once rather than in every similar program. This reduces the likelihood that an error will be made in one of several programs that have been updated for the same change. When properly tested, the program will be tested for all uses.

Disadvantages of General Editing

Of course the code to handle the greater level of generality is of necessity more complex and therefore more difficult to test. Its production and maintenance requires a higher level of skill because its control structures are driven by the data rather than being hard-wired into the code. That means more expense if you are hiring programmers.

Would you rather have your programming staff delivering and maintaining many simple programs, or a few complex ones? This is an important question as the competitive pressures of software development force compensation upwards, making it more difficult to compete for high-caliber staff.

Summary

You have seen how it is possible to write code that is to a large degree independent of the syntax variations among different database engines. If you want your systems to be as portable as possible, this is a valuable asset.

You also have seen a simplistic approach to data maintenance on the web, using three programs to allow you to maintain any single table. You have had the opportunity to compare this with a more general approach, which has both advantages and disadvantages. You should have at least a rudimentary understanding of how to write scripts that conform to the CGI interface and that will therefore run under many different web servers.

In the next section (Part IV, "XML and Python"), you will look at Python technologies to handle XML, which is a fairly recent standard for data interchange that promises to revolutionize the web world.

IV

XML and Python

12

A Bird's-Eye View of XML

THIS CHAPTER PROVIDES A HIGH-LEVEL OVERVIEW of XML (eXtensible Markup Language), an increasingly popular document and data-encoding standard used on the Internet and in many other areas of computation. Although a comprehensive discussion of XML is far beyond the scope of a single chapter, the essential features of XML are described with an emphasis on the structure of XML documents. Consult the references listed in the sidebar for more detailed coverage of XML and related technologies.

Useful XML References

Because this chapter only gives you enough information to understand the material on Python XML processing in the next two chapters, it is necessarily abbreviated. One readable source of more information about XML is S. Holzner's *Inside XML*, New Riders Publishing. The World Wide Web Consortium's web site, www.w3c.org, contains the latest information on XML standards and should be regarded as the ultimate authority. As with many standards documents, however, much of the material you will find there is dense and difficult to understand because it has to be complete enough to guide implementers.

Background

XML is a standard that specifies how to define customized markup languages for various types of documents. Developed by the World Wide Web Consortium (W3C) and first published in 1998, XML is most often described as a solution to various shortcomings in HTML. However, XML is in fact a simplification and extension of SGML (Standard Generalized Markup Language)—a standard for defining structured documents that long predates the development of the World Wide Web.

Given the amount of hype that surrounds XML, it is easy to be overwhelmed with acronyms and terminology such as XML, XSL, XSLT, XLinks, XPointers, XHTML, RDF, CDF, DTDs, schemas, CSS, SAX, DOM, XML-RPC, SOAP, and so forth. To make sense of this mess, keep in mind that most of these refer to specific XML-related technologies rather than XML itself. The XML standard itself, although nontrivial, is relatively simple and self-contained.

Much of the excitement that surrounds XML is due to its ability to represent almost any kind of structured data ranging from documents to system configuration files. By storing such data in a highly standardized way, you can more easily transfer data between applications and process that data using a common set of tools and libraries (contrast this to creating a customized or proprietary data format for each application).

Shortcomings of HTML

Much of XML's popularity has been driven by perceived shortcomings of HTML. For example, consider the following HTML document for a delicious recipe:

```
<html>
<body>
<h1>Famous Guacamole</h1>

<p>
A southwest favorite!

<h2>Ingredients</h2>
<ul>
<li>4 Large avocados, chopped
<li>1 Tomato, chopped
<li>1/2 C. White onion, chopped
<li>2 tbl. Fresh squeezed lemon juice
<li>1 Jalapeno pepper, diced
<li>1 tbl. Fresh cilantro, minced
<li>1 tbl. Minced garlic
<li>3 tsp. Salt
<li>12 bottles ice-cold beer
</ul>

<h2>Directions</h2>

<p>
Combine all ingredients and hand whisk to desired consistency.
Serve and enjoy with ice-cold beers.
</body>
</html>
```

Although this document generates a perfectly viewable web page, it also contains information that might be useful in other contexts. For example, you might want to make an easily searchable database of recipes. Or perhaps you want to be able to easily change the formatting so that you could include the recipe on other types of web pages (or to produce a printed book). Maybe you want to make it easy to export the ingredient list to other applications such as a shopping list or online ordering system.

Unfortunately, these sorts of tasks are difficult to implement because HTML documents are confined to a relatively small number of generic formatting elements such as <h1>, <h2>, <ul>, <li>, and so forth. Although it is theoretically possible to dissect a document based on the information enclosed within each type of tag, this tends to be rather *ad hoc* and error-prone. For instance, no predefined structure defines how the tags are supposed to be arranged. Furthermore, documents may use the tags in a wildly inconsistent manner (for example, another recipe page might use a different set of HTML tags depending on the author). Clearly this makes it difficult to write scripts that both manage and extract data from raw HTML files.

The main problem with HTML is that it really only serves as a low-level formatting language for defining how a document is supposed to appear in a browser. Thus, even though it provides a collection of document elements such as paragraphs, headings, tables, and bulleted lists, none of these things really capture the underlying semantic structure of the document. As an analogy, you might compare the presentation of the preceding recipe to one formatted in PostScript for printing. Although the PostScript document clearly contains all the recipe information, it is even more deeply embedded in a bunch of formatting instructions related to page placement, fonts, and so forth. Like HTML, this makes it difficult to extract specific document information such as the list of ingredients or even the name of the recipe.

XML

XML differs from HTML in that it allows you to create a user-definable markup language customized for your specific application. In fact, XML is not a markup language like HTML, but a set of rules that describe how to create new markup languages in a highly standardized manner. For instance, instead of describing a recipe in terms of HTML tags, XML allows you to use a much more descriptive document such as this:

```
<?xml version="1.0" encoding="utf-8"?>
<recipe>
   <title>Famous Guacamole</title>
   <description>
   A southwest favorite!
   </description>
   <ingredients>
       <item num="4"> Large avocados, chopped </item>
       <item num="1"> Tomato, chopped </item>
       <item num="1/2" units="C"> White onion, chopped </item>
       <item num="2" units="tbl"> Fresh squeezed lemon juice </item>
```

```
        <item num="1"> Jalapeno pepper, diced </item>
        <item num="1" units="tbl"> Fresh cilantro, minced </item>
        <item num="1" units="tbl"> Garlic, minced </item>
        <item num="3" units="tsp"> Salt </item>
        <item num="12" units="bottles"> Ice-cold beer </item>
    </ingredients>
    <directions>
    Combine all ingredients and hand whisk to desired consistency.
    Serve and enjoy with ice-cold beers.
    </directions>
</recipe>
```

In this example, user-definable elements such as <description> and <ingredients> precisely describe different parts of the document. Because different sections of the recipe are identified by unique element names, such as the recipe description, the ingredient list, and directions, it is much easier to write software for transforming or extracting information.

By allowing user-definable elements, XML lets you encode documents in a manner that preserves the underlying semantic structure. For instance, the <ingredients> element in the XML version precisely describes that part of the document, whereas the <ul> element in HTML really only describes formatting and is vague about the content actually being formatted.

Because XML allows user-definable elements, you can apply it in any domain that involves structured data. For example, a book written in XML would include elements such as chapters, sections, subsections, paragraphs, quotations, tables, figures, and so forth. Similarly, XML can be used in settings not normally associated with documents. For example, a program with a graphical user interface might use XML as a convenient format for specifying the structure of windows, menu bars, and pull-down menus. Microsoft, for example, chose an XML-based representation of the "channels" it introduced in Internet Explorer 4.

Similarly, a compiler could use XML to export a parse tree to a code generation tool. A scientific simulation could use XML to store information about simulation parameters or as a highly structured output format. Naturally, you also can use XML to generate web pages.

The Structure of XML Documents

Most XML documents start with a standard header that looks like this:

```
<?xml version="1.0" encoding="utf-8" standalone="yes"?>
```

This header defines the XML version and the document encoding. Because XML documents may be encoded in Unicode, the encoding attribute specifies the document encoding to use. Many text editors support only 7-bit ASCII characters, so utf-8 tends to be the most common encoding (the ASCII character set is a subset of UTF-8). However, general-purpose XML processing tools should be written to anticipate other encodings, such as utf-16, utf-16-le, utf-16-be, and so forth. If the version number is omitted, the XML version is assumed to be 1.0. If the encoding is omitted, utf-8 is used.

Unicode Character Encodings Oversimplified

The information technology world has had to come to grips with the wide range of character sets used by humans. The 7-bit ASCII character set is simply not sufficient to represent the possible range of characters that must be distinguished from each other. The Unicode Consortium, a nonprofit organization founded explicitly to address these issues, solves the problem by defining a widely adopted standard for the representation of text in computer programs. This standard gives each unique character its own number, called a *code point*, although what users think of as a single character may actually be encoded as a sequence of code points.

You should realize that this has little to do with the printable representation of characters. For legibility reasons, for example, many publication processes replace the two characters "f" and "i" appearing consecutively with a single *glyph*, the *fi ligature*. This does not affect the representation of the character string inside a program, which should still represent the string as an "f" followed by an "i."

The significant aspect from a programming point of view is that character strings are represented using an *encoding form*. The encoding form states how each code point in the *repertoire* (the set of all characters to be handled) is represented as sequences of Unicode *code units*. The code units are integers (of up to 24 bits) that can be held in computer memory. They are represented in storage using *encoding schemes*, which specify sequences of one or more bytes for each represented code unit.

Because XML is required to handle Unicode characters, each XML document should contain the name of the encoding scheme that it uses. The names of the encoding schemes are chosen so that they are represented the same way in all encodings. This feature allows document-processing software to determine how to translate between the encoding scheme of an external document and the representation it uses internally.

If two encoding forms are each capable of representing all characters in the repertoire, then loss-less transformation between them is possible. The two most widely used encoding schemes in the Western world are

- UTF-8, which uses a mix of one to four 8-bit code units to represent each character

- UTF-16, which uses one or two 16-bit code units to represent each character

These issues are extremely complex, and this explanation only skims the surface. To understand representational issues more thoroughly, start by visiting the Unicode Consortium's web site at www.unicode.org. The Unicode character-encoding model actually uses five different representational layers!

The optional standalone attribute, if supplied, specifies whether the document requires an external Document Type Definition (DTD) to be processed. This topic is described in the next section.

Following the `<?xml ...?>` header, many XML documents contain a collection of XML *markup declarations* denoted by the following syntax:

```
<! ... >
```

Although not shown in our earlier example, these declarations control the behavior of XML processing itself. Typically, a markup declaration is used to include a DTD that defines the set of allowable document elements and attributes. For example:

```
<?xml version="1.0" encoding="utf-8"?>
<!DOCTYPE RECIPE SYSTEM "Recipe.DTD">
```

The following XML syntax is used to denote a comment:

```
<!-- Some comment -->
```

Comments may appear anywhere in a document following the initial XML header.

In some cases, additional processing instructions are supplied. These are always enclosed in `<? ... ?>` just like the `<?xml ... ?>` header. Typically, these are used to control the behavior of programs that process XML documents. For example, an XML document that is going to be processed using XSLT (a formatting application) might include a declaration like this:

```
<?xml-stylesheet type="text/xml" href="recipe.xsl"?>
```

Following the XML header, markup declarations, and processing instructions, the rest of the document must be contained within a *single* top-level element. For instance, in our recipe example, the entire document is enclosed by a pair of tags like this:

```
<recipe>
...
</recipe>
```

This structure is analogous to HTML where everything in the document has to be enclosed by a single pair of `<html>` tags:

```
<html>
...
</html>
```

It is important to note that only one top-level element is allowed. Therefore, an XML document does not allow the following:

```
<?xml version="1.0"?>
<recipe>
  ...
</recipe>
<recipe>    <!-- Illegal -->
  ...
</recipe>
```

Within the document, elements are defined by surrounding sections of text with a pair of opening and closing tags. For example,

```
<title>Famous Guacamole</title>
```

defines a "title" element. XML always requires both an opening and a closing tag for an element. This differs from HTML, which is somewhat *ad hoc* in its handling of tags (for example, in HTML it is common to omit certain closing tags for elements such as `</p>` or `</li>`). This is not allowed in XML—every opening tag must have a matching closed tag.

Elements may be nested, but the opening and closing tags of inner elements must be wholly contained within any enclosing element. For example, this is legal:

```
<foo><bar>Blah</bar></foo>
```

whereas this is not:

```
<foo><bar>Blah</foo></bar>        <!-- Bad XML -->
```

Again, this differs from HTML, which is rather permissive in how tags may be nested. For instance, most browsers have no trouble dealing with text such as `<b><i>Bold italics</b></i>` even though this is illegal in XML.

The nesting restriction ensures that all XML documents define a tree of elements. For example, the recipe example defines the tree shown in Figure 12.1.

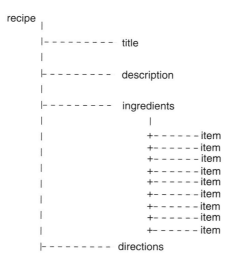

Figure 12.1 XML document tree.

If an element contains no data, you can use the following syntax:

```
<foo></foo>
```

To specify elements that accept no data, you can abbreviate this, compressing the opening and closing tags into a single item:

```
<foo/>
```

XML places a number of restrictions on element names. Specifically, element names must start with a letter or underscore (_) and may contain only letters, digits, periods, hyphens, and underscores thereafter. There is no length limitation, although you probably don't want to use extremely long names unless your intent is to annoy users. In addition, element names are case-sensitive. Therefore, `<title>` is different from `<TITLE>` or `<Title>`.

Because the special characters < and > are used to denote tags, they cannot appear in an XML document. Instead, special sequences called *entity references* must be used to denote these characters. The references for the less than and greater than characters are `&lt;` and `&gt;`, respectively. For example:

```
<para>The &lt;BLINK&gt; tag rulez man!</para>
```

A similar syntax of `&#nnnn;` where nnnn is a decimal number is used to specify an arbitrary Unicode character. For example:

```
Jalape&#241;o pepper
```

Hexadecimal characters can be specified using `&#xhhhh` as follows:

```
Jalape&#xf1;o pepper
```

Because trying to remember numeric character codes is somewhat inconvenient, common characters are sometimes referenced using entity references with special names. For example:

```
Jalape&ntilde;o pepper
```

In certain cases, using the special character codes is awkward or inconvenient. For instance, if you wanted to include an interactive Python session in a document, you might have to write the following:

```
&gt;&gt;&gt; import xml.sax
```

Every XML processor is required to recognize the entities for less than (`&lt;`), greater than (`&gt;`), ampersand (`&amp;`), apostrophe (`&apos;`) and quote (`&quot;`). As you will discover in the "Physical Structures and Entities" section, you also can declare your own entities. However, you do not *always* need to use entity references: XML allows raw character data to be inserted into a document as follows:

```
<![CDATA[>>> import xml.sax]]>
```

In general, repeated white space such as newlines and extra spaces are not regarded as significant in XML documents. However, documents may specify alternate white space handling rules in a number of ways. For instance, a CDATA section described previously can be used to include preformatted text. Similarly, a document element can indicate that spacing should be preserved by including the `xml:space` attribute as follows:

```
<code xml:space="preserve">
for i in range(0,10):
    print i
</code>
```

`xml:space` is a reserved attribute that is either `"default"` or `"preserve"`.

Just as XML allows user-definable elements, elements can have an arbitrary number of user-definable attributes. Attributes are additional properties of an element. For example:

```
<item num="1"> Jalapeno pepper, diced </item>
<item num="12" units="bottles"> Ice-cold beer </item>
```

Attributes are always defined by a `name=value` pair as shown. Like element names, attribute names must start with a letter or underscore and are case-sensitive. The value is always a string enclosed within double quotes (") or single quotes ('). Unlike HTML, an attribute value must always be supplied, and it must always be enclosed in quotes.

If an attribute value contains quotes, it should be enclosed by the other type of quote. For example:

```
<expletive type="d'oh">
<door height='84"'>
```

If both kinds of quotes appear, they need to be escaped using an entity reference such as `&quot;` (") or `&apos;` (').

DTDs

One of XML's greatest strengths is that it allows you to create highly customized documents by defining new types of elements and attributes. However, doing this in a completely haphazard manner may lead to chaos. To keep things under control, many XML documents are written according to a specification known as a *document type definition* (DTD).

A DTD is a formal specification that enumerates all the allowable elements, attributes, and values that may appear in a document. Not only that, a DTD precisely defines how these elements are supposed to be used in relation to each other within the document tree structure. For instance, in the recipe example, a DTD would specify that `<recipe>` is supposed to be the top-level element, `<item>` can only appear inside `<ingredients>`, `"num"` and `"units"` are the only allowable attributes of `<item>`, the `"num"` attribute has to be a number, and so forth.

DTD information is specified using XML markup declarations, as denoted by the special `<!....>` syntax previously defined. The declaration of a DTD usually looks like this:

```
<!DOCTYPE recipe [
<!-- The RECIPE DTD appears here -->
<!......>
<!......>
...
]>
```

Each declaration within the DTD then defines additional information about the document. For example, if the recipe document were to include a DTD, it might look like this:

```
<?xml version="1.0" encoding="utf-8"?>

<!DOCTYPE recipe [
<!-- The RECIPE DTD appears here -->
    <!ELEMENT recipe (title, description?, ingredients, directions)>
    <!ELEMENT ingredients (item+)>
    <!ELEMENT title (#PCDATA)>
    <!ELEMENT description (#PCDATA)>
    <!ELEMENT item (#PCDATA)>
    <!ELEMENT directions (#PCDATA)>
    <!ATTLIST item num     CDATA     #REQUIRED
                   units  (C ¦ tsp ¦ tbl ¦ bottles ¦ none)  "none">
]>
<!-- End of DTD -->

<recipe>
    ...
</recipe>
```

In words, this DTD defines the following properties:

- The <recipe> element must include a <title> element, an optional <description> element, an <ingredients> element, and a <directions> element in that order. No element may appear more than once. Furthermore, a <recipe> may not contain any additional text (it can only contain those four elements).

- The <ingredients> element must contain one or more <item> elements.

- The <title>, <description>, <item>, and <directions> elements can contain arbitrary parsable character data (#PCDATA). However, they may not contain any other elements.

- The <item> element has two allowable attributes: "num" and "units". The "num" attribute is required. The "units" attribute is optional and is restricted to specific values such as "C", "tsp", "tbl", and so forth. It has a default value of "none".

When a DTD appears directly in the XML document file as shown, it is known as an internal DTD—meaning that the DTD only applies to that document. However, because it is usually more useful to apply a DTD to a whole collection of XML documents, it is more common to include the DTD from a separate location using a reference to the external representation:

```
<?xml version="1.0" encoding="utf-8"?>
<!DOCTYPE recipe SYSTEM "recipe.dtd">
<recipe>
  ...
</recipe>
```

In this case, the DOCTYPE element specifies that the recipe DTD is in a file, `recipe.dtd`. The contents of this file include the same DTD as before except that the enclosing `<!DOCTYPE [ ... ]>` text is not included. For example:

```
<!-- recipe.dtd -->
<!ELEMENT recipe (title, description?, ingredients, directions)>
<!ELEMENT ingredients (item+)>
<!ELEMENT title (#PCDATA)>
<!ELEMENT description (#PCDATA)>
<!ELEMENT item (#PCDATA)>
<!ELEMENT directions (#PCDATA)>
<!ATTLIST item num    CDATA     #REQUIRED
        units  (C ¦ tsp ¦ tbl ¦ bottles ¦ none)  "none">
```

When a DTD is read from an external location, it is known as an *external DTD*. However, in some cases, a document may define DTD elements both externally and internally. For example:

```
<?xml version="1.0" encoding="utf-8"?>
<!DOCTYPE recipe SYSTEM "recipe.dtd" [
    <!-- Internal DTD subset -->
    <!ENTITY GuacImage SYSTEM "guac.gif" NDATA GIF>
    ...
]>
<recipe>
   ...
</recipe>
```

In this case, the external DTD is used to define general document structure, whereas the internal DTD subset is used to define features specific to the document. In this case, the internal DTD is defining a reference to an unparsed entity `guac.gif` (described shortly).

The topic of writing DTDs is advanced, and this chapter has only provided a high-level view of what a DTD actually looks like when it is included in a document. Because many XML documents do not include DTDs, and DTDs generally do not play a central role in most XML processing applications (other than document validation), no further details are provided here. Consult an XML book for the gory details of DTD design and creation.

Physical Structure and Entities

Complicated XML documents are rarely created as in a single file. Instead, different pieces of the document tend to be included from other files or public URLs. For example, in the previous section, a declaration was used to include a DTD from a separate file:

```
<?xml version="1.0" encoding="utf-8"?>
<!DOCTYPE recipe SYSTEM "recipe.dtd">
<recipe>
  ...
</recipe>
```

More formally, when an XML document is composed from multiple pieces like this, each "piece" is known as an *entity*. In simple terms, you might think of entities as being files. For example, the external DTD `recipe.dtd` is an entity, and the XML document itself is an entity. If you were composing a very large XML document such as a book, you might divide it up into a collection of smaller files for each chapter like this:

```
Book.xml
|
|-------> Book.dtd
|-------> chap1.xml
|-------> chap2.xml
...
|-------> chap37.xml
|-------> index.sml
```

In this case, each file is an entity. One reason for using the "entity" terminology is that entities are really more general than simple files. For example, you could also compose a document by linking to documents elsewhere on the Internet (as specified by a URL). For example:

```
Book.xml
|
|------> http://www.newriders.com/Book.dtd
|------> chap1.xml
|------> chap2.xml
|------> http://www.dead.com/book/draft/chap3.xml
...
```

XML also allows entities to be defined internally. Entities are always declared in a DTD using an `<!ENTITY ...>` declaration. The simplest kind of entity is an internal general entity, which is defined like this:

```
<!DOCTYPE recipe [
...
<!ENTITY guac "Guacamole">
]>
```

In this case, the entity works exactly like a simple macro. To use it, simply use & like this:

```
<title>Famous &guac;</title>
```

In this case, the `&guac;` sequence is simply replaced with the text "Guacamole." XML provides a few predefined entities already described in a previous section:

```
&lt;        <
&gt;        >
&amp;       &
&quot;      "
&apos;      '
```

By defining new internal entities, you can create new substitutions of your own. For example:

```
<!ENTITY ntilde "&#xf1">
...
Jalape&ntilde;o pepper
...
```

When an entity refers to another file or location, it is known as an *external general entity*. For example, if you composed a book in several parts, you might do this:

```
<!DOCTYPE Book SYSTEM "book.dtd" [
   <!ENTITY chap1 SYSTEM "chap1.xml">
   <!ENTITY chap2 SYSTEM "chap2.xml">
   <!ENTITY chap3 SYSTEM "http://www.dead.com/book/draft/chap3.xml">
   ...
]>

<Book>
  ...

  &chap1;
  &chap2;
  &chap3;
  ...

</Book>
```

In this case, each entity is replaced by the entire contents of the location specified in the DTD. For example, &chap1; is replaced by all the text in the file `chap1.xml`. When this substitution occurs, it is exactly the same as if you inserted `chap1.xml` into the file at that location.

When specifying an external entity, the SYSTEM keyword is used to specify a location on the local machine (a file or a URI). For example:

```
<!ENTITY chap1 SYSTEM "chap1.xml">
```

The name used is formally known as a *system identifier*.

In certain cases, an entity may use a formal public identifier (FPI). This is most commonly used when referring to entities that are highly standardized or in wide public use. For example, if you were to create an XHTML document, you would start with a declaration like this:

```
<!DOCTYPE html
     PUBLIC "-//W3C//DTD XHTML 1.0 Strict//EN"
     "http://www.w3.org/TR/xhtml1/DTD/xhtml1-strict.dtd">
```

In this case, the PUBLIC keyword provides a formal name for the XHTML DTD and a URI where the DTD can be obtained. The reason for using a public identifier is that XML processing tools might decide to create local copies of commonly used public entities. For instance, if a copy of the XHTML DTD was already located on the local machine, an XML processor could use the public identifier to perform a lookup and use the local copy instead of actually fetching data from the URI given in the `<!DOCTYPE ... >` declaration.

In some cases, an external entity refers to data that is not in XML format as with images, typesetting, and so forth. This type of entity is called an *external unparsed entity*. To create an unparsed entity, you first need to include a `<!NOTATION>` declaration like this:

```
<!DOCTYPE ... [
    <!NOTATION GIF SYSTEM "image/gif">
    ...
]>
```

The `NOTATION` declaration gives a name to a specific type of data. In this case, we are declaring the name `"GIF"` to refer to the MIME type `"image/gif"`. Next, to declare an entity in this format, you use a declaration like this:

```
<!ENTITY photo SYSTEM "photo.gif" NDATA GIF>
```

This declares the entity `"photo"` to be unparsed data of type `GIF`.

When declared, you cannot simply include the entity in the usual manner. For example, it is illegal to do this:

```
&photo;      <!-- Illegal: photo is unparsed data  -->
```

Instead, the entity must be associated with an element attribute like this:

```
<!DOCTYPE ... [
    <!ELEMENT image EMPTY>
    <!ATTRLIST image name ENTITY #REQUIRED>
    ...
    <!NOTATION GIF SYSTEM "image/gif">
    ...
    <!ENTITY photo SYSTEM "photo.gif" NDATA GIF>
]>
```

Then the entity is included in a document as follows:

```
<image name="photo"/>
```

In addition to general entities, XML allows entities to be defined for use in DTD definitions. These are known as *parameter entities* and are not described here because they are of little practical importance to the XML processing topics covered in the next two chapters. Consult an XML book for details on DTD entity definitions.

XML Namespaces

An issue that sometimes arises when working with XML documents is how to deal with conflicts between element names. For example, two entirely different XML documents may use similar or the same element names, though those elements in each document mean different things. In isolation, this isn't a problem. However, there are many situations where it is desirable to embed XML content from one document definition into another document. For example, if you wanted to allow HTML code to be embedded in our recipe code, you might consider having a document like this:

```
<?xml version="1.0" encoding="utf-8"?>
<recipe>
    <title>Famous Guacamole</title>
    <description>
    A <em>southwest</em> favorite!
    </description>
    ...
</recipe>
```

However, this now raises a number of questions. First, is the `<em>` element used in the description part of the recipe document, or is it HTML markup? Also, how is `<title>` supposed to be handled? Is that HTML, or is it part of a recipe? Or is it both?

To deal with this, XML provides support for namespaces. A *namespace* simply allows a set of document tags to be referenced by prepending them with a specific prefix to distinguish them from other tags. To use a namespace, you simply include a namespace declaration using `xmlns` like this:

```
<recipe xmlns:html="http://www.w3.org/1999/xhtml">
```

Now, in the document, if you wanted to use HTML tags, you would write

```
<description>
A <html:em>southwest</html:em> favorite!
</description>
```

The general form of a namespace declaration is

```
< ... xmlns:prefix="identifier" ...>
```

The `prefix` field is the name of the namespace that you will use in your document. The identifier is simply a unique identifier that is the actual name of the namespace. Typically, this is a URI (Uniform Resource Identifier) that refers to a DTD for the namespace. However, this is not a strict requirement (you can pick any unique name if you really want).

The choice of a prefix is arbitrary. For example, you could also write

```
<recipe xmlns:HTML="http://www.w3.org/1999/xhtml">
<description>
A <HTML:em>southwest</HTML:em> favorite!
</description>
```

or

```
<recipe xmlns:h="http://www.w3.org/1999/xhtml">
<description>
A <h:em>southwest</h:em> favorite!
</description>
```

It also is possible to include more than one namespace in a document. For example:

```
<document xmlns:foo="http://www.dead.com/foo.dtd"
          xmlns:bar="http://www.alive.com/bar.dtd">

    <foo:section>
        ...
    </foo:section>
    <bar:section>
    </bar:section>
```

Namespace declarations also can be attached to any document element—not just the root node. For example, in the recipe example, if you only wanted HTML to be used in the description part, you might do this:

```
<recipe>
<description xmlns:html="http://www.w3.org/1999/xhtml">
A <html:em>southwest</html:em> favorite!
</description>
```

Documents also define a default namespace by omitting the namespace prefix. For example:

```
<recipe xmlns="http://www.dead.com/recipe.dtd">
<description>
...
</description>
...
</recipe>
```

When elements are in the default namespace, the prefix can be omitted. For example, no prefix is attached to recipe elements. If you wanted to flip the example around and make HTML the default namespace, you might write this:

```
<recipe:recipe xmlns:recipe="http://www.dead.com/recipe.dtd"
               xmlns="http://www.w3.org/1999/xhtml">
<recipe:description>
A <em>southwest</em> favorite!
</recipe:description>
...
</recipe:recipe>
```

Finally, when working with namespaces, it is important to note that the namespace prefix also is prepended to attribute names. Therefore, if you put a recipe into a recipe namespace as shown previously, attributes would be specified like this:

```
<recipe:item recipe:num="1"> Jalapeno pepper, diced </recipe:item>
```

That is all you need to know about XML namespaces. For the most part, it amounts to nothing more than prepending element and attribute names with a prefix to identify which of several possible meanings should be associated with an element or attribute name.

Validating Versus Nonvalidating XML Parsing

When processing XML documents, you often hear about "validating" parsers and "nonvalidating" parsers. This distinction primarily pertains to the amount of error checking performed by an XML parser. Nonvalidating parsers only require that an XML document be well formed. An XML document is well formed if it conforms to the following rules:

- There is only one root document element.
- All document elements have starting and ending tags.
- Document elements are nested properly.
- There are no unresolved parsed entities (for example, all expansions of the form &name; can be resolved).

A validating parser requires that a document not only be well formed but also that it conforms to a DTD or XML schema. This means that all elements, attributes, and entities must be formally defined in the DTD. It also means that all document elements must be properly structured according to the DTD specification.

Although validating parsers can be useful for debugging and verification, they are difficult to write, slow, and generally not needed in most XML applications. Many processing applications really only require the use of a nonvalidating parser.

Summary

This high-level overview introduced the most important parts of XML without going into too much detail. XML is important because it allows you to specify the permissible structure of a document and unambiguously define content in a way that programs can easily manipulate. This is why many people regard XML as the *lingua franca* of the future for complex data interchange.

In the next chapter, you learn how you can use XML in Python programs.

13

XML Processing

THIS CHAPTER PROVIDES A GENERAL OVERVIEW of XML processing topics in Python. Particular attention is given to the PyXML toolkit developed by the Python XML-SIG, available at `http://www.python.org`. However, readers should be aware that a wide variety of other XML processing tools has been developed (a fairly complete list is available at `http://pyxml.sourceforge.net/topics/software.html`). Also, this chapter is not intended to be a comprehensive reference. More details about the SAX interface are provided in Chapter 14, "SAX: The Simple API for XML," but consult the Python library reference documentation for further details of other topics.

Installing the Software

Starting with Python 2.0, the Python standard library includes a number of modules related to XML processing (`xml.sax`, `xml.dom`, `xmllib`, and so on). However, most of these modules are only high-level interfaces that are useless unless you also install a suitable XML parsing module. Unfortunately, no such module is included in a standard Python source distribution. Therefore, to enable this capability, you may need to either download a binary distribution that includes XML support or install a common XML parser such as expat on your machine prior to building Python.

For the most trouble-free results, you can download and install the PyXML package. Information about this package is available at `http://www.python.org/`

sigs/xml-sig/. The version used for the examples in this book is 0.6.6. The PyXML package includes a number of useful features, such as the xmlproc validating XML parser, SAX and DOM interfaces, and a variety of utility modules.

Installing the PyXML package on UNIX-like platforms is easy. Simply download the software and type the following (make sure you have permission to write to the Python library directory first):

```
$ tar -xf PyXML-0.6.6.tar
$ cd PyXML-0.6.6
$ python setup.py build          # Build the package
$ python setup.py install        # Install the package
```

On Windows, prebuilt versions of PyXML are available for Python 1.5.2, 2.0, and 2.1 by following download links from http://sourceforge.net/projects/pyxml. These distributions are executable installers, so setting up the package is usually straightforward.

In addition, for some of the examples presented in this chapter, you may need to download the expat XML parser, which is available at http://www.jclark.com/xml/expat.html. To see whether you need expat, simply type the following:

```
$ python
>>> from xml.parsers import expat
```

If you get an ImportError exception, then expat needs to be installed. If you built Python from source, you can enable the expat module by first installing the expat libraries and headers in a common location (for example, /usr/local on UNIX). Then go to the Python source directory and type the following:

```
$ cd Python-2.1
$ python setup.py build
$ python setup.py install
```

Creating XML Documents

To create an XML document, simply use any standard text editor, such as vi or emacs. Although XML documents may contain wide Unicode characters, using a normal ASCII editor is usually fine. If you are working with 8-bit data, you will probably want to include specific encoding information in the document. For example:

```
<?xml version="1.0" encoding="utf-8"?>
```

or

```
<?xml version="1.0" encoding="iso-8859-1"?>
```

If an XML document is encoded with wide characters such as UTF-16, it may be difficult to view or edit in certain editors. However, Python 2.0 and all newer releases support Unicode text, as does the PyXML toolkit.

It is also simple to generate XML from a program by outputting text that includes an appropriate set of XML tags, as shown in Listing 13.1.

Listing 13.1 *makexml.py:* **Generating XML in Python**

```python
1   # Python program that outputs XML
2   recipe = {
3       'title' : 'Famous Guacamole',
4       'description' : 'A southwest favorite!',
5       'ingredients' : [ ('4',None,'Large avocados, chopped'),
6                         ('1',None,'Tomato, chopped'),
7                         ('1/2', 'C', 'White onion, chopped'),
8                         ('2','tbl','Fresh squeezed lemon juice'),
9                         ('1',None,'Jalapeno pepper, diced'),
10                        ('1','tbl','Fresh cilantro, minced'),
11                        ('1','tbl','Garlic, minced'),
12                        ('3','tsp','Salt'),
13                        ('12','bottles','Ice-cold beer')
14                      ],
15      'directions'  : 'Combine all ingredients and hand whisk to desired '
16                      'consistency. Serve and enjoy with ice-cold beers'
17      }
18
19  # Turn a recipe into XML
20  def make_xml(r,f):
21
22      # Utility function to format an item
23      def make_item(num,units,desc):
24          if units:
25              return '<item num="%s" units="%s">%s</item>\n' % (num,units,desc)
26          else:
27              return '<item num="%s">%s</item>\n' % (num,desc)
28
29      # Make ingredient item list
30      ingr_str = "".join([make_item(*i) for i in r["ingredients"]])
31
32      f.write(
33  """
34  <recipe>
35  <title>%(title)s</title>
36  <description>
37  %(description)s
38  </description>
39  """ % recipe)
40
41      f.write(
42  """
43  <ingredients>
44  %s
45  </ingredients>
```

continues

Listing 13.1 **Continued**

```
46   """ % ingr_str)
47
48      f.write(
49   """
50   <directions>
51   %(directions)s
52   </directions>
53   </recipe>
54   """ % recipe)
55
56   # Try it out
57   f = open("foo.xml","w")
58   f.write('<?xml version="1.0" encoding="iso-8859-1"?>\n')
59   make_xml(recipe,f)
60   f.close()
```

XML documents may contain Unicode characters, and it is common for programs that produce XML to work with Unicode strings. Remember that in Python, Unicode strings are specified by preceding a string with a u prefix. In addition, arbitrary Unicode characters are specified using the \uxxxx escape sequence as shown for the "ñ" in "Jalapeño":

```
s = u'Jalape\u00f1o Pepper'
```

One problem with Unicode strings is that you cannot just print them out using the standard print or file write() method statement, because attempting to do so may raise an exception. For example:

```
>>> print s

Traceback (most recent call last):
  File "<stdin>", line 1, in ?
UnicodeError: ASCII encoding error: ordinal not in range(128)
>>>
```

To work around this problem, you need to write Unicode data using a special data encoder that converts Unicode characters into a standard encoding format such as UTF-8 or UTF-16. The Python codecs module contains functions for dealing with this problem. Here is a simple example that shows how you would write a Unicode string in UTF-8 format:

```
import codecs
f = codecs.open("foo","w","utf-8")
s = u'Jalape\u00f1o Pepper'
f.write(s)
f.close()
```

To modify the earlier example to work properly with Unicode, you might modify the last part of it to read like this:

```
import codecs
f = codecs.open("foo.xml","w","utf-8")
f.write('<?xml version="1.0" encoding="utf-8"?>\n')
make_xml(recipe,f)
f.close()
```

For further details about Unicode strings and I/O, consult *Python Essential Reference, Second Edition* (New Riders, ISBN 0-73-571091-0).

Validating XML Documents

After you create a few XML documents, it is useful to validate them for proper syntax and structure. When you install the PyXML toolkit, you get two command-line tools (both written in Python) for this purpose. These tools appear in the `Scripts` directory of the Python installation after a Windows install. The `xmlproc_parse` command can be used to see whether an XML document is well-formed. For example:

```
$ xmlproc_parse guac.xml
xmlproc version 0.70

Parsing 'guac.xml'
Parse complete, 0 error(s) and 0 warning(s)
$
```

If you make a mistake, such as misspelling a tag, you will see one or more error messages. For example, suppose that `<ingredients>` was closed with `</ingredient>` by accident:

```
<?xml version="1.0" encoding="utf-8"?>

<recipe>
    <title> Famous Guacamole </title>
    <description>
    A southwest favorite!
    </description>
    <ingredients>
        <item num="4"> Large avocados, chopped </item>
        ...

    </ingredient>
    <directions>
    Combine all ingredients and hand whisk to desired consistency.
    Serve and enjoy with ice-cold beers.
    </directions>
</recipe>
```

Then the `xmlproc_parse` tool will report the following:

```
$ xmlproc_parse guac.xml
xmlproc version 0.70

Parsing 'guac.xml'
```

```
E:guac.xml:18:17: End tag for 'ingredient' seen, but 'ingredients' expected
E:guac.xml:23:10: End tag for 'recipe' seen, but 'ingredients' expected
Parse complete, 2 error(s) and 0 warning(s)
$
```

xmlproc_parse only checks the structure of the XML document. If you want to validate the document against a DTD, the xmlproc_val tool can be used. If you run xmlproc_val on a document without supplying a DTD, you will see many errors. For example:

```
$xmlproc_val guac.xml
xmlproc version 0.70

Parsing 'guac.xml'
E:guac.xml:3:9: Element 'recipe' not declared
E:guac.xml:4:11: Element 'title' not declared
E:guac.xml:5:17: Element 'description' not declared
E:guac.xml:8:17: Element 'ingredients' not declared
E:guac.xml:9:23: Element 'item' not declared
...
E:guac.xml:19:16: Element 'directions' not declared

Parse complete, 14 error(s) and 0 warning(s)
$
```

Therefore, your document needs to either include a DTD directly or import one from elsewhere. For example, consider the simple recipe DTD from the previous chapter:

```
<!DOCTYPE recipe [
<!-- The recipe DTD appears here -->
   <!ELEMENT recipe (title, description?, ingredients, directions)>
   <!ELEMENT ingredients (item+)>
   <!ELEMENT title (#PCDATA)>
   <!ELEMENT description (#PCDATA)>
   <!ELEMENT item (#PCDATA)>
   <!ELEMENT directions (#PCDATA)>
   <!ATTLIST item num    CDATA    #REQUIRED
          units  (C ¦ tsp ¦ tbl ¦ bottles ¦ none)  "none">
]>
<!-- End of DTD -->
```

Now, see the effect of making a few mistakes in the XML file by reordering two elements and changing one of the attribute names:

```
<recipe>
   <description>
   A southwest favorite!
   </description>

   <title> Famous Guacamole </title>

   <ingredients>
```

```
        <item num="4"> Large avocados, chopped </item>
        ...
        <item quantity="12" units="bottles"> Ice-cold beer </item>
    </ingredient>
    <directions>
    Combine all ingredients and hand whisk to desired consistency.
    Serve and enjoy with ice-cold beers.
    </directions>
</recipe>
```

Look at the output of xmlproc_val:

```
$ xmlproc_val guac1.xml
xmlproc version 0.70

Parsing 'guac1.xml'
E:guac1.xml:17:17: Element 'description' not allowed here
E:guac1.xml:31:45: Attribute 'quantity' not declared

Parse complete, 2 error(s) and 0 warning(s)
$
```

Although you probably won't use xmlproc_parse and xmlproc_val directly in your own XML programs, they are useful debugging tools to make sure your XML documents are valid before you start work on them with your own software.

XML Parsing with Regular Expressions

If you only need to extract a few simple pieces of information from an XML document, you might consider using of Python regular expression pattern matching, a feature you have not seen before in this book. For example, if you only wanted to extract a recipe title, you might write a short script like Listing 13.2.

Listing 13.2   *xmlre1.py:* **Processing XML with Regular Expressions**

```
1  #!/usr/local/bin/python
2  import sys, re
3
4  pat = r'<title>(.*?)</title>'
5  data = open(sys.argv[1]).read()
6
7  # Search for a match
8  m = re.search(pat,data)
9  if m:
10     print m.group(1)
```

Now running it will produce the following output:

```
$ title.py guac.xml
 Famous Guacamole
$
```

Even if you are unfamiliar with regular expressions, the simple example of Listing 13.2 is easy to understand. The Python library documentation on the re module is relatively complex, but it is essential reading if you intend to make serious use of regular expressions. Listing 13.3 shows a more complicated script that extracts the ingredient list from a document.

Listing 13.3   *xmlre2.py:* **Extracting the Ingredients from a Recipe with Regular Expressions**

```
 1  #!/usr/local/bin/python
 2  import sys
 3  import re
 4
 5  pat = r'<ingredients>((.|\n)*?)</ingredients>'
 6  filename = sys.argv[1]
 7
 8  data = open(filename).read()
 9
10  m = re.search(pat,data)
11  if not m:
12      print "No ingredients found"
13      print sys.exit(1)
14
14  ingredients = m.group(1)
15
16  pat = r'<item\s.*?>(.*?)</item>'
17  all = re.findall(pat,ingredients)
18
19  for item in all:
20      print item
```

Although such techniques work in simple cases, XML's treatment of white space and formatting often presents problems, increasing the complexity of the regular expressions to cope with the many different possibilities. For instance, in the first example, the pattern for matching a title was specified as this:

```
pat = r'<title>(.*?)</title>'
```

However, the <title> element might appear in a variety of formats. For example:

```
<title>
Famous Guacamole
</title>

<title >
Famous Guacamole
```

```
</title >

<title xml:lang="en">Famous Guacamole
</title>

<title
    xml:lang="en">
Famous Guacamole
</title>
```

To deal with these many variations properly, regular expressions start to get complicated quickly. For instance, you might rewrite the pattern as follows, making it even more difficult to understand:

```
pat = r'<title\s*(.|\n)*?>((.|\n)*?)</title\s*(.|\n)*?>
```

In addition to this, you have to be careful when trying to match up starting and ending tags. For instance, if you write a pattern like this:

```
pat = r'<item>(.|\n)*</item>'
```

and apply it to this text:

```
<item>Large avocado</item>
<item>Tomato</item>
```

it finds the longest possible match. In this case, it matches the entire text instead of just the first item. To prevent this, you need to use special modifiers such as **?** to force shortest-length matching. For example:

```
pay = r'<item>(.|\n)*?</item>
```

Other issues with regular expressions can cause problems. For instance, text in XML comments or CDATA sections can throw off pattern matching (for instance, if a comment includes text important to the pattern matching). In addition, XML entities are not expanded properly. For example, if you matched this:

```
<item num="1"> Jalape&#241;o pepper, diced </item>
```

the ñ sequence would be left unmodified.

Therefore, only consider using regular expressions if you need a quick-and-dirty hack, or if you have a simple application in which it makes sense to do this, and if your understanding of regular expressions is equal to the task. It is easier to learn how to use the XML processing modules than to learn regular expressions specifically for XML processing.

An Introduction to XML Parsing with expat

This section describes the fundamentals of XML parsing using the Python expat parsing module. expat is a freely available non-validating XML parser developed by James Clark and used in a variety of projects, including Python, Perl, and Mozilla.

It is also the only XML parser that a standard Python distribution will recognize without additionally installing another XML package such as PyXML. It is written in C, so it has the advantage of being extremely fast—which may be important if you are working with very large documents.

The primary goal of this section is to introduce simple XML processing by looking at the operation of a simple, low-level XML parser. In the next section, you learn how the techniques in this chapter extend to the more popular SAX and DOM interfaces for manipulating XML.

Python provides an interface to expat in the `xml.parsers.expat` module. For this module to be available, you may need to install the expat library on your machine and build the corresponding Python extension module. Follow the instructions in the Python distribution and the first part of this chapter for details.

The *expat* Parser Object

The `expat` module works by defining a special extension type object that is an expat parser. To control the parser, you simply set different attributes of the object, which the parser uses to perform particular actions on encountering certain document features. Listing 13.4 is a simple example that prints out all the starting tags, ending tags, and character data in a document.

Listing 13.4   *expat1.py:* **Simple XML Document Analysis**

```
 1  import sys
 2  from xml.parsers import expat
 3
 4  def start_element(name,attrs):
 5      print 'Start:', name, attrs
 6
 7  def character_data(data):
 8      print 'Data:', repr(data)
 9
10  def end_element(name):
11      print 'End: ', name
12
13  # Create an Expat parser
14  p = expat.ParserCreate()
15
16  # Attach some functions to the parser
17  p.StartElementHandler = start_element
18  p.EndElementHandler = end_element
19  p.CharacterDataHandler = character_data
20
21  # Run it on a file
22  p.ParseFile(open(sys.argv[1]))
```

When run on our example file, `expat1.py` produces the output shown in Listing 13.5.

Listing 13.5   **Running *expat1.py* on the Guacamole Recipe**

```
$ python simple.py guac.xml
Start: recipe {}
Data: u'\n'
Data: u'   '
Start: title {}
Data: u'\n'
Data: u'   Famous Guacamole'
Data: u'\n'
Data: u'   '
End:  title
Data: u'\n'
Data: u'   '
Start: description {}
Data: u'\n'
Data: u'   A southwest favorite!'
Data: u'\n'
Data: u'   '
End:  description
Data: u'\n'
Data: u'   '
Start: ingredients {}
Data: u'\n'
Data: u'       '
Start: item {u'num': u'4', u'units': u'none'}
Data: u' Large avocados, chopped '
End:  item
Data: u'\n'
Data: u'       '
Start: item {u'num': u'1', u'units': u'none'}
Data: u' Tomato, chopped '
End:  item
Data: u'\n'
Data: u'       '
Start: item {u'num': u'1/2', u'units': u'C'}
Data: u' White onion, chopped '
End:  item
Data: u'\n'
Data: u'       '
Start: item {u'num': u'2', u'units': u'tbl'}
Data: u' Fresh squeezed lemon juice '
End:  item
Data: u'\n'
Data: u'       '
Start: item {u'num': u'1', u'units': u'none'}
Data: u' Jalape'
Data: u'\xf1'
Data: u'o pepper, diced '
End:  item
```

continues

Listing 13.5 **Continued**

```
Data: u'\n'
Data: u'           '
Start: item {u'num': u'1', u'units': u'tbl'}
Data: u' Fresh cilantro, minced '
End:  item
Data: u'\n'
Data: u'           '
Start: item {u'num': u'1', u'units': u'tbl'}
Data: u' Garlic, minced '
End:  item
Data: u'\n'
Data: u'           '
Start: item {u'num': u'3', u'units': u'tsp'}
Data: u' Salt '
End:  item
Data: u'\n'
Data: u'           '
Start: item {u'num': u'12', u'units': u'bottles'}
Data: u' Ice-cold beer '
End:  item
Data: u'\n'
Data: u'     '
End:  ingredients
Data: u'\n'
Data: u'     '
Start: directions {}
Data: u'\n'
Data: u'    Combine all ingredients and hand whisk to desired consistency.  '
Data: u'\n'
Data: u'    Serve and enjoy with ice-cold beers.'
Data: u'\n'
Data: u'     '
End:  directions
Data: u'\n'
End:  recipe
```

In this example, the document is read sequentially; and functions, such as
start_element(), end_element(), and character_data(), are called as different parts
of the document are encountered. From the output, you can see how the starting and
ending tags nest. When starting tags are encountered, the attributes are conveniently
provided as a Python dictionary. For instance, the XML element

```
<item num="12" units="bottles">Ice-cold beer</item>
```

produces the following output:

```
Start: item {u'num': u'12', u'units': u'bottles'}
Data: u' Ice-cold beer '
End:  item
```

When character data is encountered, the `character_data()` function is called. In almost all cases, XML parsers return character data and attributes as Unicode strings, as denoted by the u`'...'` syntax in Listing 13.5. An important feature of receiving character data is that it is often supplied in small chunks that must be concatenated. In the example, you can see this by observing the multiple calls to the `character_data()` function that occur between certain starting and ending tags. For example, the XML element

```
<directions>
Combine all ingredients and hand whisk to desired consistency.
Serve and enjoy with ice-cold beers.
</directions>
```

produces the following sequence of calls:

```
Start: directions {}
Data: u'\n'
Data: u'   Combine all ingredients and hand whisk to desired consistency.   '
Data: u'\n'
Data: u'   Serve and enjoy with ice-cold beers.'
Data: u'\n'
Data: u'   '
End:   directions
```

Another useful feature of the parser is that special sequences, such as the entity references <, >, and ñ, are automatically expanded. For example, the element

```
<item num="1"> Jalape&#241;o pepper, diced </item>
```

is expanded as

```
Start: item {u'num': u'1', u'units': u'none'}
Data: u' Jalape'
Data: u'\xf1'
Data: u'o pepper, diced '
End:   item
```

Notice how the ñ text is replaced by the Unicode character `'\xf1'`.

Normalizing expat Parser Output

One problematic aspect of the XML parsing in our example is the handling of white space. In general, the parser does nothing to strip white space from text. Therefore, the following set of elements

```
<title>Famous Guacamole</title>
<title> Famous Guacamole </title>
<title>
Famous Guacamole
</title>
```

produce three entirely different text strings:

```
u'Famous Guacamole'
u' Famous Guacamole '
u'\nFamous Guacamole\n'
```

In many cases, you might not want the extra white space. Therefore, it is fairly common to write a normalization function to remove redundant white space. For example:

```
def normalize_whitespace(text):
    return " ".join(text.split())
```

Listing 13.6 shows a slightly different example that collects text and uses this function to normalize it.

Listing 13.6 *expat2.py:* **Normalizing Character Data Before Output**

```
1   import sys
2   from xml.parsers import expat
3
4   def normalize_whitespace(text):
5       return " ".join(text.split())
6
7   class SimpleParse:
8       def __init__(self):
9           self.parser    = expat.ParserCreate()
10          self.parser.StartElementHandler = self.start_element
11          self.parser.EndElementHandler = self.end_element
12          self.parser.CharacterDataHandler = self.character_data
13          self.cdata = [ ]
14
15      def parse(self,file):
16          self.parser.ParseFile(file)
17
18      def print_cdata(self):
19          txt = normalize_whitespace("".join(self.cdata))
20          if txt: print normalize_whitespace(txt)
21          self.cdata = [ ]
22
23      def start_element(self,name,attrs):
24          self.print_cdata()
25          print "Start:",name,attrs
26
27      def character_data(self,data):
28          self.cdata.append(data)
29
30      def end_element(self,name):
31          self.print_cdata()
32          print "End:", name
33
34  p = SimpleParse()
35  p.parse(open(sys.argv[1]))
```

The output in Listing 13.7 appears somewhat more readable.

Listing 13.7 **Running *expat2.py* to Give Normalized Output**

```
$ python simple.py guac.xml
Start: recipe {}
Start: title {}
u'Famous Guacamole'
End: title
Start: description {}
u'A southwest favorite!'
End: description
Start: ingredients {}
Start: item {u'num': u'4', u'units': u'none'}
u'Large avocados, chopped'
End: item
Start: item {u'num': u'1', u'units': u'none'}
u'Tomato, chopped'
End: item
Start: item {u'num': u'1/2', u'units': u'C'}
u'White onion, chopped'
End: item
Start: item {u'num': u'2', u'units': u'tbl'}
u'Fresh squeezed lemon juice'
End: item
Start: item {u'num': u'1', u'units': u'none'}
u'Jalape\xf1o pepper, diced'
End: item
Start: item {u'num': u'1', u'units': u'tbl'}
u'Fresh cilantro, minced'
End: item
Start: item {u'num': u'1', u'units': u'tbl'}
u'Garlic, minced'
End: item
Start: item {u'num': u'3', u'units': u'tsp'}
u'Salt'
End: item
Start: item {u'num': u'12', u'units': u'bottles'}
u'Ice-cold beer'
End: item
End: ingredients
Start: directions {}
u'Combine all ingredients and hand whisk to desired consistency. Serve and enjoy
with ice-cold beers.'
End: directions
End: recipe
```

Building a Parse Tree

The expat style of XML processing, in which special functions are invoked for differ-ent document features as the document is read, is more formally known as *event-driven parsing*. In some senses, this is the simplest way to read an XML document. However, in certain situations, it is useful to work with an entire XML document stored in a tree structure. Building a tree from an event-driven parser is usually straightforward. For example, you might start with code similar to Listing 13.8.

Listing 13.8   *expat3.py:* **Building a Document Parse Tree from XML Events**

```
1   import sys
2   from xml.parsers import expat
3
4   def normalize_whitespace(text):
5       return " ".join(text.split())
6
7   class Node:
8       def __init__(self):
9           self.nextSibling = None
10          self.prevSibling = None
11          self.parentNode  = None
12          self.firstChild  = None
13          self.lastChild   = None
14
15      def appendChild(self,c):
16          if self.firstChild:
17              c.prevSibling = self.lastChild
18              self.lastChild.nextSibling = c
19          else:
20              self.firstChild = c
21          c.parentNode = self
22          self.lastChild = c
23
24  class DocumentNode(Node):
25      def __str__(self):
26          return "DOCUMENT_NODE:"
27
28  class ElementNode(Node):
29      def __init__(self,name,attrs):
30          Node.__init__(self)
31          self.attributes = attrs
32          self.nodeName = name
33      def __str__(self):
34          return "ELEMENT_NODE: %s %s" % (self.nodeName, self.attributes)
35
36  class TextNode(Node):
37      def __init__(self,text):
38          Node.__init__(self)
39          self.nodeValue = text
```

```
40      def __str__(self):
41          return "TEXT_NODE   : %s" % repr(self.nodeValue)
42
43  class TreeParser:
44      def __init__(self):
45          self.parser   = expat.ParserCreate()
46          self.parser.StartElementHandler = self.start_element
47          self.parser.EndElementHandler = self.end_element
48          self.parser.CharacterDataHandler = self.character_data
49          self.topNode = DocumentNode()
50
51      def parse(self,file):
52          self.parser.ParseFile(file)
53          return self.topNode
54
55      def start_element(self,name,attrs):
56          n = ElementNode(name,attrs)
57          self.topNode.appendChild(n)
58          self.topNode = n
59
60      def character_data(self,data):
61          n = TextNode(data)
62          self.topNode.appendChild(n)
63
64      def end_element(self,name):
65          self.topNode = self.topNode.parentNode
66
67  p = TreeParser()
68  doc = p.parse(open(sys.argv[1]))
69
70  def print_tree(node,indent=0):
71      if not node: return
72      ispace = " "*4
73      while node:
74          print "%s%s" % (ispace*indent,node)
75          print_tree(node.firstChild,indent+1)
76          node = node.nextSibling
77
78  print_tree(doc)
```

When applied to our example, the output in Listing 13.9 shows how it has captured
the hierarchical structure of the document.

Listing 13.9   **Document Parse Tree Produced by** *expat3.py*

```
DOCUMENT_NODE:
    ELEMENT_NODE: recipe {}
        TEXT_NODE   : u'\n'
        TEXT_NODE   : u'    '
```

continues

Listing 13.9   **Continued**

```
ELEMENT_NODE: title {}
    TEXT_NODE   : u' '
    TEXT_NODE   : u'\n'
    TEXT_NODE   : u'    Famous Guacamole'
    TEXT_NODE   : u'\n'
    TEXT_NODE   : u'    '
TEXT_NODE   : u'\n'
TEXT_NODE   : u'    '
ELEMENT_NODE: description {}
    TEXT_NODE   : u'\n'
    TEXT_NODE   : u'    A southwest favorite!'
    TEXT_NODE   : u'\n'
    TEXT_NODE   : u'    '
TEXT_NODE   : u'\n'
TEXT_NODE   : u'    '
ELEMENT_NODE: ingredients {}
    TEXT_NODE   : u'\n'
    TEXT_NODE   : u'        '
    ELEMENT_NODE: item {u'num': u'4', u'units': u'none'}
        TEXT_NODE   : u' Large avocados, chopped '
    TEXT_NODE   : u'\n'
    TEXT_NODE   : u'        '
    ELEMENT_NODE: item {u'num': u'1', u'units': u'none'}
        TEXT_NODE   : u' Tomato, chopped '
    TEXT_NODE   : u'\n'
    TEXT_NODE   : u'        '
    ELEMENT_NODE: item {u'num': u'1/2', u'units': u'C'}
        TEXT_NODE   : u' White onion, chopped '
    TEXT_NODE   : u'\n'
    TEXT_NODE   : u'        '
    ELEMENT_NODE: item {u'num': u'2', u'units': u'tbl'}
        TEXT_NODE   : u' Fresh squeezed lemon juice '
    TEXT_NODE   : u'\n'
    TEXT_NODE   : u'        '
    ELEMENT_NODE: item {u'num': u'1', u'units': u'none'}
        TEXT_NODE   : u' Jalape'
        TEXT_NODE   : u'\xf1'
        TEXT_NODE   : u'o pepper, diced '
    TEXT_NODE   : u'\n'
    TEXT_NODE   : u'        '
    ELEMENT_NODE: item {u'num': u'1', u'units': u'tbl'}
        TEXT_NODE   : u' Fresh cilantro, minced '
    TEXT_NODE   : u'\n'
    TEXT_NODE   : u'        '
    ELEMENT_NODE: item {u'num': u'1', u'units': u'tbl'}
        TEXT_NODE   : u' Garlic, minced '
    TEXT_NODE   : u'\n'
    TEXT_NODE   : u'        '
    ELEMENT_NODE: item {u'num': u'3', u'units': u'tsp'}
```

```
                    TEXT_NODE    : u' Salt '
                TEXT_NODE    : u'\n'
                TEXT_NODE    : u'            '
                ELEMENT_NODE: item {u'num': u'12', u'units': u'bottles'}
                    TEXT_NODE    : u' Ice-cold beer '
                TEXT_NODE    : u'\n'
                TEXT_NODE    : u'    '
        TEXT_NODE    : u'\n'
        TEXT_NODE    : u'    '
        ELEMENT_NODE: directions {}
            TEXT_NODE    : u'\n'
            TEXT_NODE    : u'   Combine all ingredients and hand whisk to
            desired consistency.   '
            TEXT_NODE    : u'\n'
            TEXT_NODE    : u'   Serve and enjoy with ice-cold beers.'
            TEXT_NODE    : u'\n'
            TEXT_NODE    : u'    '
        TEXT_NODE    : u'\n'
```

With the tree structure in hand, it is possible to look at the document as a whole and make tree transformations (for example, nodes can be removed, moved to new locations, reordered, and so on). It is even possible to turn the tree back into XML by supplying a few additional methods to the Node class. This is done by the `generate()` method in Listing 13.10, which is an extended version of Listing 13.8. (Note that this listing shows only the differences from `expat3.py`.)

Listing 13.10 *expat4.py:* **Event-Driven XML Parsing with XML Generation**

```
class DocumentNode(Node):
    def __str__(self):
        return "DOCUMENT_NODE:"

    def generate(self,f):
        c = self.firstChild
        while c:
            c.generate(f)
            c = c.nextSibling

class ElementNode(Node):
    def __init__(self,name,attrs):
        Node.__init__(self)
        self.attributes = attrs
        self.nodeName = name

    def __str__(self):
        return "ELEMENT_NODE: %s %s" % (self.nodeName, self.attributes)

    def generate(self,f):
```

continues

Listing 13.10   **Continued**

```
            f.write('<%s ' % self.nodeName)
            for key,value in self.attributes.items():
                f.write('%s="%s" ' % (key, value.replace('"','&quot;')))
            f.write(">")
            c = self.firstChild
            while c:
                c.generate(f)
                c = c.nextSibling
            f.write("</%s>" % self.nodeName)

class TextNode(Node):
    def __init__(self,text):
        Node.__init__(self)
        self.nodeValue = text
    def __str__(self):
        return "TEXT_NODE    : %s" % repr(self.nodeValue)

    def generate(self,f):
        f.write(self.nodeValue)

...

# Read the document
p = TreeParser()
doc = p.parse(open(sys.argv[1]))

# Do something to it
...

# Write it back out
import codecs
f = codecs.open("foo.xml","w","utf-8")
doc.generate(f)
f.close()
```

Although the examples in this section focused only on parsing XML elements and text sections, parsing of other XML document features is performed in an entirely analogous manner. For example, if you wanted to capture XML comments, you would write a function like this:

```
def comment(data):
    print "Comment: ", repr(data)


...
parser.CommentHandler = comment
```

If you wanted to know where XML CDATA sections started and ended (so that you could preserve formatting), you would supply a pair of functions:

```
def start_cdata():
    print "CDATA start:"

def end_cdata():
    print "CDATA end:"

...
parser.StartCdataSectionHandler = start_cdata
parser.EndCdataSectionHandler = end_cdata
```

Similar functions can be written for capturing information from a DTD, entities, and other XML features. The following list simply itemizes all the handler methods that can be set on an expat parser object. Because you are more likely to use a high-level API such as SAX for processing XML, no further details are given here. However, more detailed information about these handlers can be found in the standard library documentation for `xml.parser.expat`.

- `XmlDeclHandler(version, encoding, standalone)`
- `StartDoctypeDeclHandler(doctypeName,systemId,publicId, has_internal_subset)`
- `EndDoctypeDeclHandler()`
- `ElementDeclHandler(name,model)`
- `AttrlistDeclHandler(elname, attname, type, default, required)`
- `StartElementHandler(name, attributes)`
- `EndElementHandler(name)`
- `ProcessingInstructionHandler(target,data)`
- `CharacterDataHandler(data)`
- `UnparsedEntityDeclHandler(entityName, base, systemId, publicId)`
- `EntityDeclHandler(entityName, is_parameter_entity, value, base, systemID, publicId, notationName)`
- `NotationDeclHandler(notationName, base, systemId, publicId)`
- `StartNamespaceDeclHandler(prefix,uri)`
- `EndNamespaceDeclHandler(prefix)`
- `CommentHandler(data)`
- `StartCdataSectionHandler()`
- `EndCdataSectionHandler()`
- `DefaultHandler(data)`
- `DefaultHandlerExpand(data)`
- `NotStandaloneHandler()`
- `ExternalEntityRefHandler(context,base,systemId,publicId)`

Although you have seen several simple examples of parsing with expat, this is rarely the approach that you would take in practice. Instead, a number of standardized high-level parsing interfaces have been developed, as discussed in the next section.

XML Processing with SAX and DOM

One issue that arises with XML processing is that there are a wide variety of parsing libraries and modules for working with XML documents. Although the previous section described the `expat` module, it is not the only XML parsing engine available for Python. If you wanted to use a different parsing module such as `xmlproc`, you would have to change your program to work with its API. Clearly this is problematic.

Two commonly used XML processing interfaces address this problem by providing standard APIs that you can use to process XML documents:

- **SAX (Simple API for XML)**—SAX is an API for event-driven XML processing.
- **DOM (Document Object Model)**—DOM is a specification for manipulating XML documents as a tree.

SAX Versus DOM

It is important to note that SAX and DOM do not refer to a specific package or library. Instead, they merely standardize the interface used to process an XML document. In fact, these interfaces are far more general than Python and extend to other languages such as Java and C++.

The two interfaces typify the two principal approaches to XML processing. Each has its adherents, and they frequently argue that their approach is the most suitable for all processing tasks. I prefer a more pragmatic approach.

The SAX interface, being event-driven, allows you to specify how your program should handle only those events significant to the task at hand. This means that you can process large documents quite efficiently, dealing only with the data that you must use for decision-making or to include in the output.

Because DOM-based parsing builds a complete representation of the parsed document, it is more appropriate when you need to completely transform the structure of the document. This may take more time than the SAX-based approach, as you first parse the whole document and then manipulate the parse tree to produce the required output.

SAX

The SAX interface is similar to the expat interface described in the previous section. To parse a document, you implement specific methods in a handler class. The methods are invoked as different parts of the document, such as elements, text, and entities, are encountered, as shown in Listing 13.11.

Listing 13.11 *sax1.py:* **SAX–Based Analysis of the Guacamole Recipe**

```
1  # Simple SAX example
2  import sys
3  from xml.sax import saxutils
4  from xml.sax import make_parser
5
6  # Define a simple SAX handler that prints elements and text
7  class SimpleHandler(saxutils.DefaultHandler):
8      def startElement(self,name,attrs):
9          print 'Start: ',name,attrs
10     def endElement(self,name):
11         print 'End: ',name
12     def characters(self,data):
13         print 'Data: ', repr(data)
14
15 # Create an XML parser object
16 parser = make_parser()
17
18 # Create a simple handler
19 sh = SimpleHandler()
20
21 # Tell the parser about it
22 parser.setContentHandler(sh)
23
24 # Parse a file
25 parser.parse(open(sys.argv[1]))
```

When run on the example file, sax1.py produces the output shown in Listing 13.12.

Listing 13.12 **Output from *sax1.py* Processing the Guacamole Recipe**

```
Start:  recipe <xml.sax.xmlreader.AttributesImpl instance at 16a59c>
Data:  u'\n'
Data:  u'   '
Start:  title <xml.sax.xmlreader.AttributesImpl instance at 16a59c>
Data:  u' '
Data:  u'\n'
Data:  u'   Famous Guacamole'
Data:  u'\n'
Data:  u'   '
End:  title
Data:  u'\n'
Data:  u'   '
Start:  description <xml.sax.xmlreader.AttributesImpl instance at 16a754>
Data:  u'\n'
Data:  u'   A southwest favorite!'
Data:  u'\n'
Data:  u'   '
End:  description
```

continues

Listing 13.12   **Continued**

```
Data:  u'\n'
Data:  u'    '
Start:  ingredients <xml.sax.xmlreader.AttributesImpl instance at 16a754>
Data:  u'\n'
Data:  u'        '
Start:  item <xml.sax.xmlreader.AttributesImpl instance at 16a59c>
Data:  u' Large avocados, chopped '
End:  item
Data:  u'\n'
Data:  u'        '
Start:  item <xml.sax.xmlreader.AttributesImpl instance at 16a59c>
Data:  u' Tomato, chopped '
End:  item
Data:  u'\n'
Data:  u'        '
Start:  item <xml.sax.xmlreader.AttributesImpl instance at 16a59c>
Data:  u' White onion, chopped '
End:  item
Data:  u'\n'
Data:  u'        '
Start:  item <xml.sax.xmlreader.AttributesImpl instance at 16a59c>
Data:  u' Fresh squeezed lemon juice '
End:  item
Data:  u'\n'
Data:  u'        '
Start:  item <xml.sax.xmlreader.AttributesImpl instance at 16a59c>
Data:  u' Jalape'
Data:  u'\xf1'
Data:  u'o pepper, diced '
End:  item
Data:  u'\n'
Data:  u'        '
Start:  item <xml.sax.xmlreader.AttributesImpl instance at 16a77c>
Data:  u' Fresh cilantro, minced '
End:  item
Data:  u'\n'
Data:  u'        '
Start:  item <xml.sax.xmlreader.AttributesImpl instance at 16a77c>
Data:  u' Garlic, minced '
End:  item
Data:  u'\n'
Data:  u'        '
Start:  item <xml.sax.xmlreader.AttributesImpl instance at 16a77c>
Data:  u' Salt '
End:  item
Data:  u'\n'
Data:  u'        '
Start:  item <xml.sax.xmlreader.AttributesImpl instance at 16a77c>
Data:  u' Ice-cold beer '
```

```
End:  item
Data:  u'\n'
Data:  u'    '
End:  ingredients
Data:  u'\n'
Data:  u'    '
Start:  directions <xml.sax.xmlreader.AttributesImpl instance at 16a77c>
Data:  u'\n'
Data:  u'    Combine all ingredients and hand whisk to desired consistency.  '
Data:  u'\n'
Data:  u'    Serve and enjoy with ice-cold beers.'
Data:  u'\n'
Data:  u'    '
End:  directions
Data:  u'\n'
End:  recipe
```

The primary difference between this and the earlier expat example is that actions
are defined as methods of a handler class, an instance of which is provided to the
SAX parser to allow it to process the events generated by particular XML features. In
addition, attributes are stored by special objects that work much like a dictionary but
provide a few additional methods for access. For example, to print the attributes, you
might change startElement() to the following:

```
def startElement(self,name,attrs):
    print 'Start: ',name
    for n in attrs.getNames():
        print "    %s = %r" % (n, attrs.getValue(n))
```

This produces output such as this:

```
Start:  item
    num = u'12'
    units = u'bottles'
Data:  u' Ice-cold beer '
End:  item
```

A further advantage of SAX is that the handler interface is relatively simple to describe
and use. The event-driven interface allows you to scan large XML documents quickly
without having to store the entire document in memory. Because the SAX interface is
one of the most common XML handling techniques, a full discussion is included in
Chapter 14.

DOM

The Document Object Model (DOM) is an interface for manipulating XML
documents as a tree. Each document is represented by a top-level Document node.
This node contains a single Element node that corresponds to the first element.

Additional subelements are then added in a way that mirrors the underlying structure of the document.

The DOM approach is useful in certain contexts because it allows you to traverse and manipulate the tree as a whole. For example, you can add new nodes, remove subtrees, or reorder the document in various ways. The DOM interface also tends to be used in interactive applications such as browsers or XML editors (in fact, much of the DOM interface was originally developed to better support the integration between JavaScript and HTML in browsers).

A full description of the DOM interface is available at `http://www.w3.org/DOM`. Because the specification is large and surprisingly readable on its own, it is not presented in detail here. However, a few simple examples are presented to illustrate its operation.

First, to work with an XML document using DOM, you have to parse it into a DOM tree. Although you could do this yourself using a program such as the tree construction code presented at the end of the last section, it is much easier to have one constructed automatically using an existing Python module. An easy way to do this is as follows:

```
# Make a DOM tree for file supplied on command line
import sys
from xml.dom import minidom
doc = minidom.parse(open(sys.argv[1]))
```

With the tree in hand, DOM defines a few standard attribute names for walking through nodes:

```
n.nextSibling
n.previousSibling
n.firstChild
n.lastChild
n.nodeParent
```

For example, the following function walks the entire DOM tree and prints out the nodes:

```
def print_tree(n,indent=0):
    while n:
        print " "*indent,n
        print_tree(n.firstChild,indent+4);
        n = n.nextSibling


print_tree(doc)
```

It produces output similar to that shown in Listing 13.13.

Listing 13.13   **The Guacamole Recipe as a Parse Tree**

```
<xml.dom.minidom.Document instance at 1cc674>
    <DOM Element: recipe at 1969980>
        <DOM Text node "\n">
```

```
<DOM Text node "    ">
<DOM Element: title at 1970220>
    <DOM Text node " ">
    <DOM Text node "\n">
    <DOM Text node "   Famous ...">
    <DOM Text node "\n">
    <DOM Text node "   ">
<DOM Text node "\n">
<DOM Text node "    ">
<DOM Element: description at 2025004>
    <DOM Text node "\n">
    <DOM Text node "   A south...">
    <DOM Text node "\n">
    <DOM Text node "   ">
<DOM Text node "\n">
<DOM Text node "    ">
<DOM Element: ingredients at 2026204>
    <DOM Text node "\n">
    <DOM Text node "         ">
    <DOM Element: item at 2030604>
        <DOM Text node " Large avo...">
    <DOM Text node "\n">
    <DOM Text node "         ">
    <DOM Element: item at 2031564>
        <DOM Text node " Tomato, c...">
    <DOM Text node "\n">
    <DOM Text node "         ">
    <DOM Element: item at 2032524>
        <DOM Text node " White oni...">
    <DOM Text node "\n">
    <DOM Text node "         ">
    <DOM Element: item at 2048412>
        <DOM Text node " Fresh squ...">
    <DOM Text node "\n">
    <DOM Text node "         ">
    <DOM Element: item at 2049372>
        <DOM Text node " Jalape">
        <DOM Text node "\xf1">
        <DOM Text node "o pepper, ...">
    <DOM Text node "\n">
    <DOM Text node "         ">
    <DOM Element: item at 2057044>
        <DOM Text node " Fresh cil...">
    <DOM Text node "\n">
    <DOM Text node "         ">
    <DOM Element: item at 2058004>
        <DOM Text node " Garlic, m...">
    <DOM Text node "\n">
    <DOM Text node "         ">
    <DOM Element: item at 2058964>
```

continues

Listing 13.13 **Continued**

```
                    <DOM Text node " Salt ">
                <DOM Text node "\n">
                <DOM Text node "        ">
                <DOM Element: item at 2066564>
                <DOM Text node " Ice-cold ...">
                <DOM Text node "\n">
                <DOM Text node "   ">
        <DOM Text node "\n">
        <DOM Text node "    ">
        <DOM Element: directions at 2068044>
            <DOM Text node "\n">
            <DOM Text node "   Combine...">
            <DOM Text node "\n">
            <DOM Text node "   Serve a...">
            <DOM Text node "\n">
            <DOM Text node "    ">
        <DOM Text node "\n">
```

Nodes in a DOM tree are classified into a few different types, the most important of which are

- **DocumentNode**—Top-level node representing entire document.
- **ElementNode**—Node representing XML elements such as `<title>...</title>`.
- **TextNode**—Raw text data (characters inside an element).

The full DOM specification details a number of other types. Typically, the type of each node is identified by a unique integer code available in the `n.nodeType` attribute. The values are set to constants such as the following:

```
xml.dom.Node.ELEMENT_NODE
xml.dom.Node.DOCUMENT_NODE
xml.dom.Node.TEXT_NODE
xml.dom.Node.ENTITY_NODE
...
```

For example, consider the program in Listing 13.14 that makes some changes to element and attribute names in a recipe and outputs a new XML file.

Listing 13.14 **_dom1.py:_ Transforming an XML Document from its Parse Tree**

```
1  import sys
2  from xml.dom.ext import PrettyPrint
3  from xml.dom import minidom
4
5  doc = minidom.parse(open(sys.argv[1]))
6
7  # Generic tree walker
8  def walk_tree(n,func):
```

```
 9     while n:
10         func(n)
11         walk_tree(n.firstChild,func)
12         n = n.nextSibling
13
14  # Fix some nodes
15  def fix_node(n):
16      if n.nodeType == n.ELEMENT_NODE:
17          if n.tagName == "ingredients":
18              n.tagName = "ingredientlist"
19          if n.tagName == "item":
20              # Change the name of "item" to "ingredient"
21              n.tagName = "ingredient"
22              # Change attribute name
23              attr = n.getAttribute("num")
24              n.setAttribute("quantity",attr)
25              n.removeAttribute("num")
26
27  walk_tree(doc,fix_node)
28  PrettyPrint(doc)
```

The output of the program might look like Listing 13.15.

Listing 13.15   **The Guacamole Recipe Transformed by *dom1.py***

```
<?xml version='1.0' encoding='UTF-8'?>
<!DOCTYPE recipe>
<recipe>
  <title>   Famous Guacamole</title>
  <description>   A southwest favorite!</description>
  <ingredientlist>
    <ingredient quantity='4' units='none'> Large avocados, chopped </ingredient>
    <ingredient quantity='1' units='none'> Tomato, chopped </ingredient>
    <ingredient quantity='1/2' units='C'> White onion, chopped </ingredient>
    <ingredient quantity='2' units='tbl'> Fresh squeezed lemon juice </ingredient>
    <ingredient quantity='1' units='none'> Jalapeno pepper, diced </ingredient>
    <ingredient quantity='1' units='tbl'> Fresh cilantro, minced </ingredient>
    <ingredient quantity='1' units='tbl'> Garlic, minced </ingredient>
    <ingredient quantity='3' units='tsp'> Salt </ingredient>
    <ingredient quantity='12' units='bottles'> Ice-cold beer </ingredient>
  </ingredientlist>
  <directions>   Combine all ingredients and hand whisk to desired consistency.
Serve and enjoy with ice-cold beers.</directions>
</recipe>
```

An even easier way to accomplish this would be to use some special methods of the Document object. A program that does this is shown in Listing 13.16.

Listing 13.16 *dom2.py:* **Transforming an XML Document Using Document Methods**

```
1   import sys
2   from xml.dom.ext import PrettyPrint
3   from xml.dom import minidom
4
5   doc = minidom.parse(open(sys.argv[1]))
6
7   for n in doc.getElementsByTagName("ingredients"):
8       n.tagName = "ingredientlist"
9
10  for n in doc.getElementsByTagName("item"):
11      n.tagName = "ingredient"
12      attr = n.getAttribute("num")
13      n.setAttribute("quantity",attr)
14      n.removeAttribute("num")
15
16  PrettyPrint(doc)
```

In all, the DOM interface contains more than a hundred functions and methods, mostly concerned with straightforward tree manipulation and data access. The details of the interface can be found in the Python library documentation for the `xml.dom` module. Because DOM is a standardized interface, even more information is available in the Document Object Model (DOM) Level-2 Specification available at `http://www.w3.org/TR/DOM-Level-2-Core`.

Other Python XML Packages

Although SAX- and DOM-based approaches tend to predominate for XML processing, a number of other techniques can be advantageous for particular problems. Although these are not treated in great depth, they are briefly described in the following sections so that you can research them as necessary.

Pyxie

Pyxie is an XML processing package developed by Sean McGrath and described in his book *XML Processing with Python*, (Prentice Hall PTR, ISBN 0-13-021119-2). Details are available at `http://pyxie.sourceforge.net`.

Pyxie works by converting XML documents into a simplified tree-encoding format known as *PYX*. A PYX representation of our earlier example (generated using the Pyxie xmln tool) looks like Listing 13.17.

Listing 13.17   **The Pyxie Form of the Famous Guacamole Recipe**

```
1   (recipe
2   -\n
```

```
 3   -
 4   (title
 5   -
 6   -\n
 7   -    Famous Guacamole
 8   -\n
 9   -
10   )title
11   -\n
12   -
13   (description
14   -\n
15   -    A southwest favorite!
16   -\n
17   -
18   )description
19   -\n
20   -
21   (ingredients
22   -\n
23   -
24   (item
25   Anum 4
26   Aunits none
27   - Large avocados, chopped
28   )item
29   -\n
30   -
31   (item
32   Anum 1
33   Aunits none
34   - Tomato, chopped
35   )item
36   -\n
37   -
38   (item
39   Anum 1/2
40   Aunits C
41   - White onion, chopped
42   )item
43   -\n
44   -
45   (item
46   Anum 2
47   Aunits tbl
48   - Fresh squeezed lemon juice
49   )item
50   -\n
51   -
52   (item
```

continues

Listing 13.17   **Continued**

```
53  Anum 1
54  Aunits none
55  - Jalape
56  -Ã±
57  -o pepper, diced
58  )item
59  -\n
60  -
61  (item
62  Anum 1
63  Aunits tbl
64  - Fresh cilantro, minced
65  )item
66  -\n
67  -
68  (item
69  Anum 1
70  Aunits tbl
71  - Garlic, minced
72  )item
73  -\n
74  -
75  (item
76  Anum 3
77  Aunits tsp
78  - Salt
79  )item
80  -\n
81  -
82  (item
83  Anum 12
84  Aunits bottles
85  - Ice-cold beer
86  )item
87  -\n
88  -
89  )ingredients
90  -\n
91  -
92  (directions
93  -\n
94  -   Combine all ingredients and hand whisk to desired consistency.
95  -\n
96  -   Serve and enjoy with ice-cold beers.
97  -\n
98  -
99  )directions
100 -\n
101 )recipe
```

Different document features are easy to parse using simple line-oriented parsers operating on PYX format data. The first character in each line determines the content: a `'('` indicates a start element, an `'A'` indicates an attribute, a `')'` indicates a closing element, and a `'-'` indicates text.

In this simplified line-oriented format, it is relatively easy to implement parsing tools without using any of the more sophisticated XML parsing modules. You can also write parsers and utilities that process data in a style not easily incorporated in SAX or DOM. For example, the script in Listing 13.18 reads a recipe in PYX format and extracts the ingredient list.

Listing 13.18   *pyx1.py:* **Extracting Ingredients from a PYX Format Recipe**

```
 1   # PYX example
 2   f = open("guac.pyx")
 3
 4   # Read an item, return as a (text,attributes) tuple
 5   def read_item(f):
 6       L = f.readline()
 7       attrs = { }
 8       text = []
 9       while L:
10           if L[0] == 'A':
11               i = L.index(' ')
12               attrs[L[1:i]] = L[i+1:-1]
13           elif L[0] == '-':
14               text.append(L[1:-1])
15           elif L[0] == ')':
16               break
17           L = f.readline()
18       return "".join(text), attrs
19
20   # Look for ingredients and print them out
21   L = f.readline()
22   while L:
23       if L[0] == '(':
24           if L[1:-1] == 'ingredients':
25               L = f.readline()
26               # Look for items list
27               while L:
28                   if L[0] == '(':
29                       if L[1:-1] == 'item':
30                           text, attrs = read_item(f)
31                           print attrs, text
32                   elif L[0] == ')':
33                       if L[1:-1] == 'ingredients': break
34                   L = f.readline()
35               break
36
```

continues

Listing 13.18   **Continued**

```
37     L = f.readline()
38
39  f.close()
```

The output of this module looks like Listing 13.19.

Listing 13.19   **Output from** *pyx1.py*

```
{'num': '4', 'units': 'none'}  Large avocados, chopped
{'num': '1', 'units': 'none'}  Tomato, chopped
{'num': '1/2', 'units': 'C'}  White onion, chopped
{'num': '2', 'units': 'tbl'}  Fresh squeezed lemon juice
{'num': '1', 'units': 'none'}  Jalapeno pepper, diced
{'num': '1', 'units': 'tbl'}  Fresh cilantro, minced
{'num': '1', 'units': 'tbl'}  Garlic, minced
{'num': '3', 'units': 'tsp'}  Salt
{'num': '12', 'units': 'bottles'}  Ice-cold beer
```

The `pyxie` module also provides a number of utilities for both event-driven and tree-based document processing as well as hooks to SAX and DOM. In addition, the PYX format is relatively easy to generate, so a program might use it as an intermediate representation (that is, a program could generate PYX and have that converted to XML using a special utility).

4Suite

4Suite is a collection of open-source XML processing applications developed by Fourthought, Inc. Portions of the 4Suite package are included in the standard PyXML distribution. However, more advanced capabilities must be downloaded separately at `http://www.fourthought.com`. The package currently includes support for the following XML-related technologies:

- XPath
- XPointer
- XSLT
- XLink
- RDF

In addition, the package includes some support for XML-database integration. Full coverage of the complete 4Suite package is impossible here. However, some of the more interesting components are the XPath and XSLT modules.

xml.xpath

The xml.xpath module can be used to easily select different parts of an XML document given a DOM tree using XPath specifiers. For instance, suppose you wanted to select all the ingredients from a recipe. Listing 13.20 shows a really easy way to do it.

Listing 13.20 *xpath1.py:* **Extracting Nodes Selected by XPath Specifiers**

```
 1   import sys
 2   from xml.dom import minidom
 3   from xml import xpath
 4
 5   # Read document into a DOM tree
 6   doc = minidom.parse(open(sys.argv[1]))
 7
 8   # Select all of the items
 9   result = xpath.Evaluate('/recipe/ingredients/item',doc)
10   print result
11
```

The result is simply a list of DOM nodes:

```
[<DOM Element: item at 136487164>, <DOM Element: item at 136557964>,
 <DOM Element: item at 136461572>, <DOM Element: item at 136589316>,
 <DOM Element: item at 136592892>, <DOM Element: item at 136597260>,
 <DOM Element: item at 136600804>, <DOM Element: item at 136604348>,
 <DOM Element: item at 136607836>]
```

To extract information, you would then walk the list and use the standard DOM API for retrieving information.

The XPath specification allows for wildcards and more advanced pattern matching similar to regular expressions. For example, if you wanted to extract an ingredient list but weren't sure about the surrounding context, you might do this:

```
result = xpath.Evaluate("/*/ingredients/item",doc)
```

If you wanted to select all items that didn't have any units specified, you might use this:

```
result = xpath.Evaluate("/recipe/ingredients/item[@units='none']",doc)
```

xml.xslt

The xml.xslt module provides support for transforming XML documents using XSLT (eXensible Stylesheet Language Transformations). XSLT is an XML-based language used to transform XML documents into other formats, such as HTML. For example, an XSLT stylesheet for our recipe might look something like Listing 13.21.

Listing 13.21 *xslt1.py:* **An XSLT Stylesheet for the Guacamole Recipe**

```
1  <?xml version="1.0"?>
2  <xsl:stylesheet version="1.0"
3  xmlns:xsl="http://www.w3.org/1999/XSL/Transform">
4
5  <xsl:template match="/recipe">
6      <HTML>
7        <HEAD>
8          <TITLE>
9          <xsl:value-of select="title"/>
10         </TITLE>
11       </HEAD>
12       <BODY>
13       <xsl:apply-templates/>
14       </BODY>
15      </HTML>
16  </xsl:template>
17
18  <xsl:template match="/recipe/title">
19      <H1>
20      <xsl:apply-templates/>
21      </H1>
22  </xsl:template>
23
24  <xsl:template match="/recipe/description">
25      <P>
26      <xsl:apply-templates/>
27      </P>
28  </xsl:template>
29
30  <xsl:template match="/recipe/ingredients">
31      <H3>Ingredients</H3>
32      <UL>
33      <xsl:apply-templates/>
34      </UL>
35  </xsl:template>
36
37  <xsl:template match="/recipe/ingredients/item[@units='none']"➡
    xml:space="preserve">
38      <LI>
39      <xsl:value-of select="@num"/> <xsl:apply-templates/>
40      </LI>
41  </xsl:template>
42
43  <xsl:template match="/recipe/ingredients/item[@units!='none']"➡
    xml:space="preserve">
44      <LI>
45      <xsl:value-of select="@num"/> <xsl:value-of select="@units"/><xsl:apply➡
        templates/>
46      </LI>
```

```
47   </xsl:template>
48
49   <xsl:template match="/recipe/directions">
50       <H3>Directions</H3>
51       <P>
52       <xsl:apply-templates/>
53       </P>
54   </xsl:template>
55
56   </xsl:stylesheet>
```

To use this stylesheet, you can put a stylesheet specifier in an XML document. For example:

```
<?xml version="1.0" encoding="iso-8859-1"?>
<?xml-stylesheet type="text/xml" href="recipe.xsl"?>
<recipe>
...
</recipe>
```

4Suite includes a tool, 4xslt, that acts as an XSLT processor, applying XSLT-specified transformations to CML documents. It would render the guacamole recipe as the HTML shown in Listing 13.22.

Listing 13.22   **The Guacamole Recipe is Transformed into HTML**

```
 1   $ 4xslt guac.xml recipe.xsl
 2   <HTML>
 3     <HEAD>
 4       <meta http-equiv='Content-Type' content='text/html; charset=iso-8859-1'>
 5       <TITLE>
 6     Famous Guacamole
 7       </TITLE>
 8     </HEAD>
 9     <BODY>
10       <H1>
11     Famous Guacamole
12       </H1>
13       <P>
14     A southwest favorite!
15       </P>
16       <H3>Ingredients</H3>
17       <UL>
18         <LI>4  Large avocados, chopped
19       </LI>
20         <LI>1  Tomato, chopped
21       </LI>
22         <LI>1/2 C White onion, chopped
23       </LI>
```

continues

Listing 13.22 **Continued**

```
24        <LI>2 tbl Fresh squeezed lemon juice
25        </LI>
26        <LI>1  Jalape&ntilde;o pepper, diced
27        </LI>
28        <LI>1 tbl Fresh cilantro, minced
29        </LI>
30        <LI>1 tbl Garlic, minced
31        </LI>
32        <LI>3 tsp Salt
33        </LI>
34        <LI>12 bottles Ice-cold beer
35        </LI>
36        </UL>
37      <H3>Directions</H3>
38      <P>
39      Combine all ingredients and hand whisk to desired consistency.
40      Serve and enjoy with ice-cold beers.
41      </P>
42    </BODY>
43  </HTML>
```

In addition, an xslt module is available that gives more control over XSLT processing.

Although some browsers can use XSLT stylesheets to render XML documents into HTML, this is a rather recent development. If you care about portability, you might not want to make such assumptions about the client's browser. A more common way to perform such transformations is to use the Cascading Style Sheet (CSS) capabilities, which are beyond the scope of this book. Even though these are more uniformly available, their implementation is still somewhat uneven across browser platforms.

Even though XSLT is a relatively simple and powerful way to specify document formatting, it is comparatively slow and requires entire XML documents to be loaded into a DOM tree to operate. If you need to turn XML into HTML quickly, it may be faster to write some special-purpose code using the SAX API or a low-level parser such as expat if the browser cannot be persuaded to perform the transformation under style sheet control.

Summary

A number of other techniques are available for XML processing, notably the xmllib and pyexpat modules, which you may encounter in existing software. Programs using older methods will usually be much easier to maintain if they are brought up-to-date with a rewrite to incorporate one of the techniques covered in this chapter.

Discussing XML at a technical level in the way that this chapter did often leaves the reader new to the subject wondering just why the information technology world seems so excited about it. Even the relatively simple processing methods you have so far encountered should have convinced you that representing data in XML allows a degree of processing flexibility not available from other representations. Elements can be represented in many ways, and it is relatively easy to automatically transform another organization's XML into the formats required by your programs.

Beyond this, XML is also being used to support more general approaches to distributed processing. The two most notable such technologies are SOAP, the Simple Object Access Protocol, and XML-RPC. Both these technologies provide a simple way to use HTTP to transmit structured request data to, and have structured data returned from, remote processes and promise to improve the flexibility of inter-communication between processes running inside the firewalls of collaborating organizations.

Chapter 14 takes a closer look at the event-driven SAX approach to processing XML documents.

14

SAX: The Simple API for XML

THIS CHAPTER PROVIDES DETAILS ON PYTHON'S support for SAX, a widely used interface specification for parsing and processing XML with which you made a first acquaintance in Chapter 13, "XML Processing." Many high-level XML processing modules use SAX for their internal processing, and there are many reasons why you might want to use it yourself. This chapter builds on the material in Chapter 13 and is intended to be more of a SAX reference.

Introduction to SAX

First, SAX is not a package that you download and install. Rather, it is a common API used to manipulate XML. SAX is based on an event model, in which XML documents are scanned sequentially, and different handler methods are invoked for different document features. This style of XML processing was illustrated in Chapter 13 in the sections describing the expat module. SAX merely generalizes that approach and makes it more widely applicable.

A detailed reference covering the entire Python SAX API is available in the standard Python library documentation. However, this documentation includes neither examples nor much of an explanation as to how the interfaces are used. The Python/XML HOWTO includes a few simple SAX examples but not a full SAX reference. Information about the SAX specification itself can be found in the web site maintained by SAX's designer at http://www.megginson.com/SAX, but even here the definition is the reference implementation in Java. Fortunately, most SAX implementations are similar enough that you can gain significant information about the Python version from almost any SAX documentation.

Effectively, SAX subdivides XML processing into a collection of different tasks, each defined by a special interface. In Python, these interfaces are implemented by a collection of classes. Figure 14.1 illustrates the different pieces.

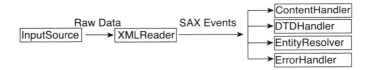

Figure 14.1   The structure of a SAX application.

At the lowest level, XML data is read from a byte stream encapsulated by a special InputSource object. This is usually just a wrapper around an ordinary file. The data read from the InputSource object is then fed into an XMLReader object. An XMLReader is just a generalized parsing interface that sits on top of a low-level XML parser such as expat or xmlproc. The XMLReader sends different events (SAX events) on to a collection of four different types of handler objects, which are used to handle different document features. For example:

- **ContentHandler**—Ordinary document text, elements, and attributes.

- **DTDHandler**—DTD declarations needed to parse the rest of the document (unparsed external entities).

- **EntityResolver**—Handling of external entities.

- **ErrorHandler**—Error handling.

In addition, SAX defines a number of miscellaneous interfaces used during processing. For instance, a special Locator object keeps track of the current parsing location, and an AttributeImpl object stores attributes.

Because SAX processing is essentially divided into two parts, parsing and handling, two different Python modules contain most of the functionality. The xml.sax.xmlreader module contains the classes pertaining to the parsing of XML and includes the XMLReader, InputSource, Locator, and AttributeImpl classes. The xml.sax.handler module contains the classes for handling different SAX events and includes the ContentHandler, DTDHandler, EntityResolver, and ErrorHandler classes. More generally, you will use the xml.sax.xmlreader module to set up a parser, and the xml.sax.handler module to implement the actions performed during parsing.

The rest of this chapter documents the different SAX interfaces and how they are used.

XML Readers

To read XML documents with SAX, you first have to instantiate a special XMLReader object. An XMLReader is really nothing more than a standardized wrapper around an existing XML parser such as expat or xmlproc. To create an XMLReader for an existing parser, use the xml.sax.make_parser() function. For example:

```
from xml.sax import make_parser
p = make_parser()       # Create default parser
```

Without any arguments, the make_parser() function consults an internal list of parsers and chooses the first one that is installed. If you must use a specific parser for some reason, you also can supply an optional argument specifying the precise parsing module. For example:

```
p = make_parser("xml.sax.drivers2.drv_xmlproc")    # Create xmlproc parser
p = make_parser("xml.sax.drivers2.drv_expat")      # Create expat parser
```

Note that the parser module name is given as a string value. Regardless of the underlying parsing engine, all XMLReader objects support a common set of methods.

```
p.parse(source)
```

starts processing SAX events for input source. source is often an open file object, but it also can be a filename, a URL, or an InputSource object (described shortly). For example:

```
p.parse("file.xml")                # Filename
p.parse(open("file.xml"))          # Open file
p.parse("http://dead.com/file.xml")  # URL
```

parse() does not return until it has processed the entire input stream. Therefore, before calling parse(), you need to set up all the handlers that will be used to process different types of SAX events. The methods shown in Table 14.1 are used to do this.

Table 14.1   **Method Handlers Used to Process SAX Events**

Method	Description
p.setContentHandler(*handler*)	Sets the current ContentHandler. A ContentHandler is used to process XML elements and text.
p.getContentHandler()	Returns the current ContentHandler.
p.setDTDHandler(*handler*)	Sets the current DTDHandler. A DTDHandler is used to process DTD declarations needed for parsing (unparsed entities and attributes).
p.getDTDHandler()	Returns the current DTDHandler.
p.setEntityResolver(*handler*)	Sets the current EntityResolver. An EntityResolver is used to handle all external entities.
p.getEntityResolver()	Returns the current EntityResolver.

continues

Table 14.1 **Continued**

Method	Description
p.setErrorHandler(*handler*)	Sets the current ErrorHandler. An ErrorHandler is used to control how parsing errors are handled.
p.getErrorHandler()	Gets the current ErrorHandler.

If you do not define a particular handler, those SAX events are usually ignored by default. For instance, if you don't define a ContentHandler, the parser won't do much at all!

In addition to setting handlers, XMLReaders provide an interface for enabling or disabling certain XML features. This is controlled by the following pair of functions:

- **p.getFeature(*featurename*)**—Returns the current setting for parsing feature *featurename*.

- **p.setFeature(*featurename*,*value*)**—Changes the value of *featurename* to *value*.

featurename is usually set to one of the constants defined in the xml.sax.handler module (see Table 14.2). *value* is set to 1 or 0 to indicate a true or false value. The default values depend on the underlying parsing engine.

Table 14.2 **Feature Name Constants Defined in the *xml.sax.handler* Module**

Value	Description
feature_namespaces	Performs namespace processing.
feature_namespace_prefixes	Uses the original prefixed names and attributes in namespace declarations. Disabled by default.
feature_string_interning	Interns element names, prefixes, attribute names, namespace URIs, and local names using the built-in intern() function. Disabled by default.
feature_validation	Reports all validation errors.
feature_external_ges	Includes all external general entities.
feature_external_pes	Includes all external parameter entities, including those defined in an external DTD.

For example:

```
from xml.sax import handler
p = make_parser()
p.setFeature(handler.feature_namespaces,1)
p.setFeature(handler.feature_validation,1)
```

Most features are read-only during parsing. Therefore, setFeature() is almost always used before calling p.parse().

In addition, `XMLReader` instances have a number of properties that control the behavior of the parser. Properties are controlled by the methods shown in Table 14.3.

Table 14.3   **Methods that Control the Properties of the Parser**

Method	Description
`p.getProperty(`*`propertyname`*`)`	Returns the current setting for property *propertyname*.
`p.setProperty(`*`propertyname,value`*`)`	Changes the value of property *propertyname* to *value*. Values for *propertyname* also are defined in `xml.sax.handler`.
`property_lexical_handler`	Optional extension handler for processing lexical events such as comments. The value is an instance of `xml.sax.saxlib.LexicalHandler`.
`property_declaration_handler`	Optional extension handler for processing DTD declarations other than those handled by the `DTDHandler`. The value is an instance of `xml.sax.saxlib.DeclHandler`.
`property_dom_node`	DOM iteration. During parsing, this is the current DOM node being visited. If not parsing, this is the root DOM node for iteration.
`property_xml_string`	The literal string of characters that was the source for the current event.

There is no guarantee that all properties will be available for a given **parser** object. Also, many properties were unsupported in earlier versions of Python, so you should upgrade to the most recent version if this is important.

```
from xml.sax import saxlib
from xml.sax import handler
class handle_comments(saxlib.LexicalHandler):
    def comment(self,text):
        print "comment :", text
ch = handle_comments()
p = make_parser()
p.setProperty(handler.property_lexical_handler, ch)
p.parse('foo.xml')
```

The `LexicalHandler` instance h used as the value for `property_lexical_handler` supports the following methods:

- `h.comment(`*`content`*`)`
- `h.startDTD(`*`name,public_id,system_id`*`)`
- `h.endDTD()`
- `h.startEntity(`*`name`*`)`

- `h.endEntity()`
- `h.startCDATA()`
- `h.endCDATA()`

The `DeclHandler` instance `d` used as the value for `property_declaration_handler` supports the following methods:

- `d.attributeDecl(`*elem_name*`,`*attr_name*`,`*type*`,`*value_def,* `value`*)*
- `d.elementDecl(`*elem_name*`,`*content_model*`)`
- `d.internalEntityDecl(`*name*`,`*value*`)`
- `d.externalEntiyDecl(`*name*`,`*public_id*`,`*system_id*`)`

Because the use of `LexicalHandler` and `DeclHandler` classes is not normally required for most typical XML processing applications, further details are not provided here. However, additional documentation can be obtained from the Python source code itself (I suggest using `pydoc xml.sax.saxlib`).

Finally, the following method is used to control locale settings of the parser:

- **`p.setLocale(locale)`**—Sets the locale for errors and warnings. This function may or may not be supported, and it is acceptable for SAX parsers to ignore locale requests.

If an error occurs in any of the SAX functions, one of the exceptions listed in Table 14.4 will be raised.

Table 14.4 **Exceptions Raised by SAX Function Errors**

Exception	Description
`SAXException(`*msg [,exception]*`)`	Base class for all other SAX exceptions. `msg` is a human readable message and `exception` optionally contains a different exception (this is used to encapsulate more specific errors).
`SAXParseException(`*msg,➡ exception, locator*`)`	Raised when a parsing error occurs. In addition to containing an error message, this exception provides information about the error location that can be obtained using the Locator interface (see the `ContentHandler` section for details).
`SAXNotRecognizedException>➡ (`*msg,exception*`)`	Raised when an `XMLReader` is asked to support 'an unrecognized feature or property.
`SAXNotSupportedException➡ (`*msg,exception*`)`	Raised when an `XMLReader` is asked to enable a feature or property that the implementation does not support.

InputSource Objects

Internally, all input to a SAX parser is supplied using a special `InputSource` object. `InputSource` really just defines a common I/O interface for a parser. An instance `i` of an `InputSource` class has the methods shown in Table 14.5.

Table 14.5   **Methods of the *InputSource* Class**

Method	Description
`i.setPublicId(id)`	Sets the public identifier.
`i.getPublicId()`	Gets the public identifier.
`i.setSystemId(id)`	Sets the system identifier.
`i.getSystemId()`	Gets the system identifier.
`i.setEncoding(encoding)`	Sets the character `encoding`. `encoding` is typically a string such as `iso-8859-1` or `utf-8` that would be acceptable in an `<?xml encoding="..."?>` declaration.
`i.getEncoding()`	Returns the character encoding.
`i.setByteStream(bytefile)`	Sets the byte stream of the object to a Python filelike object. The bytefile object should be a raw byte-oriented file and not a file that performs automatic character conversion (that is, do not pass a file that automatically decodes Unicode characters).
`i.getByteStream()`	Returns the byte stream for the input source.
`i.setCharacterStream(charfile)`	Sets the character stream. `charfile` must be a filelike object that knows how to decode bytes into characters according to the input's encoding scheme. Usually this is a Unicode file object, such as might be created by the codecs module.
`i.getCharacterStream()`	Returns the character stream.

If an application wants to supply XML data through a non-traditional mechanism, it can use the `InputSource` class directly. The corresponding `InputSource` object can then be passed to the `parse()` method directly. For example:

```
from xml.sax import xmlreader
from xml.sax import make_parser

p = make_parser()
i = xmlreader.InputSource()       # Create an InputSource instance

# XML data contained in a string
s = """<?xml version="1.0">
<recipe>
  <title>
```

```
    Famous Guacamole
    </title>
    ...
</recipe>"""

# Turn the string into a StringIO file and use as an input source
import cStringIO
f = cStringIO.StringIO(s)
i.setByteStream(f)       # Use StringIO instance as byte stream
p.parse(i)               # Parse XML using our InputSource instance
```

Content Handlers

Most of the work in a SAX parser is performed by the `ContentHandler` object. The
module `xml.sax.handler` implements a `ContentHandler` class that defines the interface.
You usually create a handler by subclassing the default implementation (see Listing
14.1).

Listing 14.1   *sax2.py:* **Subclassing the Default** *ContentHandler*

```
 1  from xml.sax import make_parser
 2  from xml.sax import saxutils
 3  # Define a simple SAX handler
 4  class SimpleHandler(saxutils.DefaultHandler):
 5      def startElement(self,name,attrs):
 6          print 'Start: ',name,attrs
 7      def endElement(self,name):
 8          print 'End: ',name
 9      def characters(self,data):
10          print 'Data: ', repr(data)
11
12  sh = SimpleHandler()
13  p = make_parser()
14  p.setContentHandler(sh)
15  file = "guac.xml"
16  p.parse(file)
```

The following methods of a `ContentHandler` are invoked during parsing.

```
c.setDocumentLocator(locator)
```

This method provides the parser with an object that it can use for location tracking.
This is especially useful for reporting error messages and knowing where different
SAX events occur. `locator` is a special `Locator` object that provides the following
methods:

- `locator.getColumnNumber()`
- `locator.getLineNumber()`
- `locator.getPublicId()`
- `locator.getSystemId()`

The getColumnNumber() and getLineNumber() methods return the approximate location within a file. The getPublicID() returns the public name of an entity (if available). The getSystemID() returns the system name being used. This is often a filename or URL.

Listing 14.2 gives a simple example of how these functions might be used.

Listing 14.2   *sax4.py:* **Simple Use of *Locator* Object Methods**

```
1   import sys
2   from xml.sax import saxutils
3   from xml.sax import make_parser
4   from xml.sax import handler
5
6   class SimpleHandler(saxutils.DefaultHandler):
7       # Obtain a locator object
8       def setDocumentLocator(self,locator):
9           self.locator = locator
10
11      def startElement(self,name,attrs):
12          col = self.locator.getColumnNumber()
13          line = self.locator.getLineNumber()
14          pubid = self.locator.getPublicId()
15          sysid = self.locator.getSystemId()
16          print 'startElement (%d,%d,%s,%s): %s' % (line,col,pubid,sysid,name)
17
18      def endElement(self,name):
19          col = self.locator.getColumnNumber()
20          line = self.locator.getLineNumber()
21          pubid = self.locator.getPublicId()
22          sysid = self.locator.getSystemId()
23          print 'endElement (%d,%d,%s,%s): %s' % (line,col,pubid,sysid,name)
24
25      def characters(self,data):
26          print 'characters: ', repr(data)
27
28  # Create a parser
29  parser = make_parser()
30
31  # Create a handler
32  sh = SimpleHandler()
33
34  # Tell the parser about it
35  parser.setContentHandler(sh)
36
37  # Parse a file
38  parser.parse(sys.argv[1])
```

Listing 14.3 shows some sample output to see what kind of values are returned.

Listing 14.3   **Sample Output Showing the Use of the *Locator* Interface**

```
startElement (16,0,None,guac.xml):  recipe
characters:  u'\n'
characters:  u'   '
startElement (17,3,None,guac.xml):  title
characters:  u' '
characters:  u'\n'
characters:  u'   Famous Guacamole'
characters:  u'\n'
characters:  u'   '
endElement (19,3,None,guac.xml):  title
characters:  u'\n'
characters:  u'   '
```

These functions are primarily intended for error recovery and reporting. Because values might be approximate, the returned locations should not be used as the basis for editing the original document.

- c.startDocument()
- c.endDocument()

The startDocument() and endDocument() methods are called to indicate the start and end of the document. They take no arguments.

- c.startPrefixMapping(*prefix,uri*)
- c.endPrefixMapping(*prefix*)

The startPrefixMapping() and endPrefixMapping() methods are used if you want to do your own tracking of XML namespaces. feature_namespaces must be enabled for this to work. If you have a namespace declaration like this:

```
<foo:bar  xmlns:foo="http://dead.com/foo">
...
</foo:bar>
```

the following calls are made:

```
startPrefixMapping("foo","http://dead.com/foo")
...
endPrefixMapping("foo")
```

Normally, it is not necessary to define these functions because XML parsers already know how to deal with namespaces.

- c.startElement(*name,attrs*)
- c.endElement(*name*)

The startElement() and endElement() methods are used to handle the start and end of XML elements. name is the element name, and attrs is a special AttributesImpl object that supports the following methods:

- **attrs.getLength()**—Returns number of attributes.

- **attrs.getNames()**—Returns attribute names.

- **attrs.getType(name)**—Returns the type of attribute name (usually '**CDATA**').

- **attrs.getValue(name)**—Returns value of attribute name.

The preceding methods are invoked only if a document is being processed without namespace support. If namespaces are enabled, the following methods are used instead:

- c.startElementNS(*name*,*qname*,*attrs*)

- c.endElementNS(*name*,*qname*)

The startElementNS() and endElementNS() methods are used to handle elements when XML namespace handling is enabled (feature_namespaces). In this case, name is a tuple (uri,localname), and qname is the fully qualified element name (which is usually None unless feature_namespace_prefixes has been enabled). attrs is a special AttributesNSImpl object that supports the normal Attribute methods (listed previously) in addition to the following:

- **attrs.getValueByQName(qname)**—Returns value for qualified name.

- **attrs.getNameByQName(qname)**—Returns (namespace,localname) pair for a name.

- **attrs.getQNameByName(name)**—Returns qualified name for a pair (*namespace*,*localname*).

- **attrs.getQNames()**—Returns qualified names of all attributes.

Listing 14.4 gives a small example. When run on the input shown in Listing 14.5, the output should be what you see in Listing 14.6.

Listing 14.4   *saxend.py:* **Identifying End Element Tags Using SAX Parsing**

```
 1   import sys
 2   from xml.sax import saxutils
 3   from xml.sax import make_parser
 4   from xml.sax import handler
 5
 6   class SimpleHandler(saxutils.DefaultHandler):
 7       def startElementNS(self,name,qname,attrs):
 8           print 'startElementNS: ', name,qname
 9           for n in attrs.getNames():
10               print "   attribute :", n, attrs.getValue(n)
11
12       def endElementNS(self,name,qname):
13           print 'endElementNS: ', name, qname
14
15   # Create a parser
16   parser = make_parser()
```

continues

Listing 14.4 **Continued**

```
17
18  # Create a handler
19  sh = SimpleHandler()
20
21  # Tell the parser about it
22  parser.setContentHandler(sh)
23  parser.setFeature(handler.feature_namespaces,1)
24
25  # Parse a file
26  parser.parse(sys.argv[1])
```

Listing 14.5 *foo.xml:* **Sample Input for** *saxend.py*

```
<?xml version="1.0"?>
<foo:bar xmlns:foo="http://dead.com">
   <foo:text foo:name="blah" type="whatever">
      Hi there
   </foo:text>
</foo:bar>
```

Listing 14.6 **Output from** *saxend.py*

```
startElementNS:  (u'http://dead.com', u'bar') None
startElementNS:  (u'http://dead.com', u'text') None
  attribute : (u'http://dead.com', u'name') blah
  attribute : (None, u'type') whatever
endElementNS:  (u'http://dead.com', u'text') None
endElementNS:  (u'http://dead.com', u'bar') None
```

c.characters(content)

The `characters()` method is used to receive raw character data.

`c.ignorableWhitespace(content)`

The `ignorableWhitespace()` method is called to supply ignorable white space in a document. This is generally invoked only if the underlying parser is running in validation mode (`feature_validation` is set). The argument is a string built by joining a contiguous sequence of all the white space characters that were ignored.

`c.processingInstruction(target,data)`

The `processingInstruction()` method is used to handle XML processing instructions. An XML processing instruction is enclosed in <? ... ?>. For example:

```
<?xml-stylesheet href="mystyle.css" type="text/css"?>
```

`target` is the type of instruction (for example, `"xml-stylesheet"`). `data` is the rest of the instruction up to the ending ?>. This method is *not* invoked for the initial <?xml ...?> declaration.

```
c.skippedEntity(name)
```

The `skippedEntity()` method is invoked for each skipped entity. Typically, a non-validating parser may skip an entity if it hasn't been declared in an external DTD and if no other information is known about it. This behavior depends on the parser and the settings of `feature_external_ges` and `feature_external_pes`.

DTDHandler

The `DTDHandler` interface is used to process DTD declarations that might be needed for parsing. Typically, this only pertains to unparsed entities and notation declarations. For example, an XML document might include declarations like that shown in Listing 14.7.

Listing 14.7   **XML Document Structure Including a DTD**

```
 1   <!DOCTYPE recipe [
 2     ...
 3     <!ELEMENT image EMPTY>
 4     <!ATTRLIST image name ENTITY #REQUIRED
 5                       alt  CDATA  #IMPLIED
 6     >
 7     <!NOTATION GIF SYSTEM "CompuServe Graphics Interchange Format 87a">
 8     <!ENTITY GuacImage SYSTEM "guac.gif" NDATA GIF>
 9     ...
10   ]>
11
12   <recipe>
13     ...
14     <image name="GuacImage"/>
15     ...
16   </recipe>
```

To capture the `NOTATION` and `ENTITY` information, you write a `DTDHandler` like the one shown in Listing 14.8.

Listing 14.8   *sax8.py:* **Structure of a Program to Process a Document with a DTD Using SAX**

```
 1   import sys
 2   from xml.sax import make_parser
 3   from xml.sax import handler
 4   class SimpleDTD(handler.DTDHandler):
 5           def notationDecl(self,name,publicid,systemid):
 6               print "notationDecl: ", name, publicid, systemid
 7           def unparsedEntityDecl(self,name,publicid,systemid,ndata):
 8               print "unparsedEntityDecl: ", name, publicid, systemid, ndata
 9
10       p = make_parser()
11       p.setDTDHandler(SimpleDTD())
12       p.parse(sys.argv[1])
```

When run on a sample file, this produces output like this:

```
notationDecl:  GIF None CompuServe Graphics Interchange Format 87a
unparsedEntityDecl:  GuacImage None guac.gif GIF
```

It is important to understand that the `notationDecl()` and `unparsedEntityDecl()` methods are only invoked for the declarations inside the DTD. They are not used when an entity actually is encountered. For example, in the element

```
<image name="GuacImage"/>
```

it would be the responsibility of the `ContentHandler` to look at the value of `name` and see whether it corresponds to a known entity (this would be done in a `startElement()` or `startElementNS()` method). If so, information received from the `notationDecl()` call can be used to take appropriate action, such as loading an image in some format or processing the file in some manner.

EntityResolver

The `EntityResolver` class is used to intercept references to external entities. For example, consider the following XML:

```
<!DOCTYPE ... [

    <!ENTITY commonheader SYSTEM "header.xml">

]>
<document>
    &commonheader;
</document>
```

In this case, the `<!ENTITY>` declaration creates an entity `commonheader` that refers to a file `"header.xml"`. Later in the document, `&commonheader;` is used to actually include the entity. Normally, the XML parser will try to load the corresponding `header.xml` file and insert it into the input stream on its own. If you want to change this behavior, you can define your own `EntityResolver` class. For example, this code catches references to `'header.xml'` and changes them to `'altheader.xml'`:

```
import sys
from xml.sax import make_parser
from xml.sax import handler
class SimpleEntity(handler.EntityResolver):
    def resolveEntity(self,publicid,systemid):
        print "resolveEntity: ",publicid,systemid

        if systemid == 'header.xml':
            return 'altheader.xml'
        else:
            return systemid

p = make_parser()
```

```
p.setEntityResolver(SimpleEntity())

p.parse(sys.argv[1])
```

Similarly, you could use an `EntityResolver` to retrieve external entities from a data-base or some other non-traditional location.

The `EntityResolver` interface only defines a single method, `resolveEntity()`, as shown previously. There are several choices for the type of the return value. If a simple string is returned, the underlying XML parser uses it as the entity name and tries to resolve it on its own. For instance, the preceding example simply changed the name of `'header.xml'` to `'altheader.xml'` by returning the string `'altheader.xml'`.

Alternatively, it is possible to return an open file object. For example:

```
import codecs
class SimpleEntity(handler.EntityResolver):
    def resolveEntity(self,publicid,systemid):
        print "resolveEntity: ",publicid,systemid
        if systemid == 'header.xml':
            return codecs.open("altheader.xml","r","utf-8")
        else:
            return systemid
```

It is also possible to return an `InputSource` object. `InputSource` is a class defined in `xml.sax.xmlreader` that can be used to define alternative input streams to the parser. For example:

```
from xml.sax import xmlreader

class SimpleEntity(handler.EntityResolver):
    def resolveEntity(self,publicid,systemid):
        print "resolveEntity: ",publicid,systemid
        if systemid == 'header.xml':
            i = InputSource()
            i..setByteStream(open("altheader.xml"))
            return i
        else:
            return systemid
```

ErrorHandler

The `ErrorHandler` class is used to intercept parsing errors and warnings. The class defines three methods.

error(exception)

This method is called when the parser encounters a recoverable error such as an undeclared attribute (for example, discovered by a validating XML parser). If this function discards the exception, parsing will continue. The only caveat is that document information may not be delivered correctly after an error has occurred. Therefore the only reason for allowing the parser to continue is to report more error messages.

fatalError(exception)

This method is invoked when the parser encounters an unrecoverable error such as a missing closing element tag or an unresolved entity. Parsing is expected to terminate when the method returns.

warning(exception)

This method is used by the parser to report minor warning information. Unless an exception is raised by this method, parsing will continue normally after return.

Here is a simple example that shows how to set up an error handler:

```
from xml.sax import handler
class SimpleError(handler.ErrorHandler):
    def error(self,exception):
        print "error: ", exception

    def fatalError(self,exception):
        print "fatalError: ", exception
        raise exception

    def warning(self,exception):
        print "warning: ", exception

p = make_parser()
...
p.setErrorHandler(SimpleError())
...
p.parse(input)
```

As input, all the `ErrorHandler` methods receive a `SAXParseException` object. If you want to propagate the error, a method can simply raise the passed argument as shown in the `fatalError()` method discussed previously.

SAX Utilities

The `xml.sax.saxutils` module contains several utility functions and classes for writing SAX processors:

- **`escape(data [,entities])`**—This function escapes special characters such as &, <, and > in a string of data. The optional entities parameter is a dictionary mapping strings to entities. For example:

```
>>> from xml.sax import saxutils
>>> saxutils.escape("<foo>")
```

```
'&lt;foo&gt;'
>>> saxutils.escape(u"Jalape\xf1o", { u'\xf1' : '&ntilde;'})
u'Jalape&ntilde;o'
```

- **XMLGenerator([out [,encoding]])**—This class implements a `ContentHandler` that converts SAX events back into an XML document. `out` is a file object, and `encoding` is the encoding of the output stream (default is `'iso-8859-1'`). You might use this class if you wanted to rewrite parts of an XML document. For example:

```
import sys
from xml.sax import saxutils
from xml.sax import make_parser

class Generator(saxutils.XMLGenerator):
    def startElement(self,name,attrs):
        if name == 'ingredients':
            name = 'ingredientlist'
        saxutils.XMLGenerator.startElement(self,name,attrs)
    def endElement(self,name):
        if name == 'ingredients':
            name = 'ingredientlist'
        saxutils.XMLGenerator.endElement(self,name)
p = make_parser()
p.setContentHandler(Generator())
p.parse(sys.argv[1])
```

- **XMLFilterBase()**—This class is used to implement a filter that sits between the `XMLReader` object and the different handler classes. Normally it doesn't do anything but pass events on unmodified. However, an application might use this if it wanted to modify SAX event processing.

- **prepare_input_source(source [,base])**—This function is used to create an `InputSource` object ready for reading by an XML parser. `source` is the name of an input source, a file object, or an `InputSource` object. `base` is an optional base URL. The `parse()` method and other parts of the XML package use this function to convert various types of input sources into an `InputSource` object that can be used by the low-level XML parser.

Summary

The SAX interface specifies a way to process XML without necessarily building a complete parse tree for the processed document, although you also can do that if you choose. The SAX approach is well-suited to extracting a limited number of features from long documents. This combines well with the creation of XML output in

Python, allowing on-the-fly transformations from one XML representation to another. It is easy to process XML with a SAX-based program, and the SAX module provides sensible default actions for the components that the program chooses not to provide.

The uses of XML for data interchange among collaborating organizations are expanding rapidly. The last three chapters should have given you enough information to be able to approach XML data interchange tasks with confidence.

V

Integrated Web Applications in Python

15

Building Small, Efficient Python Web Systems

BUILDING A WEB SYSTEM IS A COMPLICATED business. Designing any complex piece of software requires imagination and creativity as well as a solid knowledge of software engineering practice. If you are an experienced programmer, you may well possess all these things, but if not, it might be useful to get some idea of what goes on in the designer's mind while developing and building a new system. Of course I have direct access to one mind (at most), so this chapter describes my personal approach to complex web system development tasks.

Why Build It Yourself?

Web systems, and especially Internet web systems, represent quite a security threat. Many production web servers have been found to contain vulnerabilities, often in sample code distributed with the server to show how to use it. A modern web server contains tens or hundreds of thousands of lines of code and is therefore so complicated that it is impossible to satisfy yourself of its invulnerability. Not only that, but any system of sufficient generality is likely to be overweight for each individual application.

This is not an argument against the major web servers. They do have value and have focused on maintaining scalability for a wide range of loads. They also solve the problems of maintaining state across multiple browser/server interactions (either directly or indirectly using cookies to do so) and integrate many different programming frameworks. They also offer a comparatively sophisticated user authentication scheme, which is not to be sniffed at, together with address-based and domain-based security. Sometimes the price in size and complexity is worth paying, as is often the case when a program implements features you cannot easily implement for yourself.

Because Python allows you to use databases and network protocols, however, you can use it to build small, efficient frameworks for many web-based applications. Their lack of sophisticated infrastructure makes them fast, and because they are lightweight, there is no reason a single processor should not run several of them at the same time. I look forward to the day when web services are frequently provided by a number of simple servers running concurrently on the same host. The first approach to scalability then will be to move them onto different hosts. The advice in this chapter applies not just to web systems but to all systems you build, and not just in Python. Because Python has similarities with many other programming languages, it is also advice for building any systems at all.

Critical Self-Assessment

After 30 years of programming in many different languages, I have had the opportunity to observe many design and programming styles, good and bad, both in my own programming and in others'. If you are relatively new to Python, you probably will find that when you review your code after some period of time, you will find better ways to express the same algorithm. Sometimes this will improve clarity and therefore readability; sometimes it will improve execution speed. In the best of all possible worlds, it will improve both, which is a real win. So, even if you are working on your own, code reviews are an important way of consolidating your command of the language. Just because something works does not mean it cannot be improved.

At the same time, there is a trade-off here. You cannot spend all your time going back over the code you have written and polishing it to a fine gloss. Sometimes, particularly if you are faced with deadlines, you have to accept that "good enough" is good enough and move on to the next phase of a project. The more experience you gain, the better a sense you will get of that ineffable quality sometimes called "Pythonicity." An experienced programmer has a finely developed pragmatic sense of how much to polish, and how good "good enough" is. Most of all, you should never cringe when you go back to old code and see something you would not now do—not as long as the old code is working, at least.

The Significance of Style and Simplicity

Many web systems have been developed by a technique I call "programming with a trowel." This involves

- Taking several trucks full of code from similar systems (and, of course, all web systems have similarities, so almost any web system is a candidate).

- Mixing them liberally and fitting them together in an approximation to the intended system.
- Filling in the cracks with glue logic, hastily applied.

This is a long way from an engineering discipline, but it allows you to collect a fee from a customer quickly. The major disadvantage of this approach is that any change in requirements will make it obvious that the system is unable to grow organically because the coupling between the components (discussed later in the chapter) is far too tight. It is almost as though someone had poured superglue over the program after completion, so making even the slightest change can have unexpected ramifications.

Not all systems can be small, and not all systems can be efficient, but to my mind a small, simple system has a better chance of being efficient than a large one. When you build a large system such as Apache or Internet Information Server (IIS), there is a natural tendency to expect it to be able to meet a wide variety of requirements, and both these web servers do indeed behave admirably in supporting diverse systems under heavy load. For smaller systems, however, they are definitely over-engineered. Because neither carries a readily identifiable price tag, however, they are used for the smallest systems as well as the largest.

A Note on Complexity

Then there is the question of top-down versus bottom-up design. The *top-down technique* is a way of deferring having to think about the detail of a problem, whereas bottom-up builds a set of primitives, which you can then fold together with "glue" logic to solve your problem. Approaching a problem top-down gives you the ability to overlook detail, which can be merely confusing if considered too early. A good design focuses initially on the large-scale architectural features, which are easier to perceive when you know less about the problem area, as you inevitably must at the start of a project.

My own feeling is that both techniques are useful and that it is possible to work sometimes from the top down, sometimes from the bottom up. The really interesting part of a project is the meeting in the middle. Like teams building tunnels from opposite sides of a mountain whose bores do not line up, mismatches are a clear indication that the two approaches have not been working in harmony.

One technique that is very helpful with a bottom-up approach is the consistent development of unit tests for each piece of code, either before or at the same time as the code is created. The advantage this gives is the insurance that the lower-level components do indeed behave as expected. This largely avoids the need to localize the problem when you start to glue the components together: if you have confidence in the integrity of the components, then the glue logic comprising the framework is most likely to be at fault (although, of course, the testing might have been incomplete).

Modularity Really Helps: Containment in Design

Back in "the old days," when programming was a relatively new activity and there was little formal understanding of the discipline, one of the earlier approaches to controlling complexity was called *modular programming*. The primary goal of modular programming was to have programmers build code in smallish chunks, with well-defined relationships between them. The main thrust was to emphasize the interfaces between separate portions of the program and to break down the logic into functions of manageable size. Modular programming was the first programming technique to prove its value to the point of widespread adoption. This has in its turn been followed by structured programming and a long line of other styles, of which the latest is *extreme programming* (by analogy with extreme sport, whose devotees use a minimum of equipment and rely mostly on their physical skills).

Modular Programming

A modular program is composed of two types of functions: the *manager functions* use logic to determine the overall flow of control, and the *worker functions* perform the actual data manipulations. The *coupling* between modules, which is to say interactions between the logic of two different functions, should be kept loose, and one function should not need to know anything about the internal structure of others. Neither should a worker function be given a flag input, for example, which would determine which of three different types of actions it was to undertake. The flag would instead be used by a manager function, which would call one of three appropriate workers.

Logic that observes these principles is called *cohesive*, and it was soon discovered that cohesive logic was much easier to debug because of the locality of most variable references. If you ever wondered why new programmers are so frequently advised to avoid global variables where possible, it is because they represent very poor (tight) coupling between the modules that use them, leading to low cohesion. Loosely coupled systems are also desirable because they encourage code reuse. When a function uses global variables, it is much more difficult to use it in another system. Other components in the system should never have to modify their environment to pass information to the function: it is better to have all inputs to functions passed as arguments and all outputs returned as result values from a function call.

Python, of course, was designed for modular programming, and the natural unit of code is a module. There is no such thing as a truly global variable in Python except in the __built-ins__ namespace, which is very rarely modified. What is usually referred to as the global scope is actually global to a module and not to the whole program. Beginners often ask how program-global variables can be declared, and the correct answer is "Don't do that": it is much more practical to localize such variables to a module, or in class instances, which can be passed in to functions as required.

The modular nature of Python code, and its capability to pass back tuples of results that can be unpacked in a single assignment, or even an object complete with internal state and behavior, encourages clean coupling between separate functions. Python's deliberately sparse keyword set and relatively low linguistic complexity encourages a clean programming style, which in turn tends to reduce the number of intractable bugs in a program. How much easier it is to be able to write

```
filename, headers = urllib.urlretrieve("http://www.python.com")
```

than to have to return values through the argument list or in some prearranged global locations.

Modular Programming for the Web

If you look back at the wdupdt.py program from Chapter 11, "Adapting the Python Interface to Database Products," you will see that one of its inputs is indeed the value of the submit button, which is used to select whether a creation, update, or deletion operation is to be performed. You may wonder why this is so, given what you are just reading about modular programming. The reasons are simple.

First, it is difficult (though not impossible, with client-side scripting) to arrange for a form to use a different ACTION depending on which button is pressed. To keep the pages simple, the create and update cases would therefore have to be processed by the same page in any case, although it is true that the delete page could be separate.

Second, all three operations do have data in common, and if you examine the logic flow, you will see that the differences between the three cases are all isolated in the opSetup() function, which establishes the SQL statement to be executed and the data to be used. This allows the main body of the logic (effectively the manager function) to limit itself to dealing with special cases where data is illegal or not provided.

A web system depends on anchor tags (web links) and form ACTION values to determine the sequence of pages presented to the user, and there is not always as much structural flexibility as there is in a GUI-based system using a framework such as wxPython or Tkinter. You may well find that your ingenuity is sometimes taxed to the limit to provide a natural web interface to complex procedures without duplicating code or bending your logic slightly out of shape. This does not nullify the force of the arguments for modularity.

Structured Programming

Modular programming was rapidly followed by *structured programming*, which built on top of the modularity principles. In the days before object-oriented programming, programmers took a very procedure-oriented approach. Structured programming was another attempt to avoid *spaghetti* code, which had frequently been produced in languages where the flow of control could be determined by `goto` statements that arbitrarily altered the program execution sequence. Structured programming principles dictate that code should be expressed using only three basic structures:

- Sequences of operations, one performed after the other.
- Selections, where a Boolean expression is used to determine which of two sequences should be performed.

- Loops, where a sequence is performed repeatedly until some condition becomes true.

In effect, structured programming applies the tenets of modularity to the individual program statement and to sequences of statements. Today, structured programming is so firmly embedded in the group consciousness of the programming community that most newer languages, such as Python, do not even include a goto statement or its equivalent. In object-oriented programming, we tend to assume that methods are small, manageable functions. The methods of a given instance are indeed modular, and their small size usually makes it easy to ensure that they are well-structured.

You should still be aware that the instance variables, which the methods share, do represent a certain sort of global storage as far as the method logic is concerned, and you need to take care to ensure that your methods remain well-coupled. There is nothing wrong with passing an instance variable as an argument to a method even if the method could pick it up itself, and sometimes you will find that this increases the generality of your methods. It can certainly help to improve the cohesion of your large objects' internal logic.

Extreme Programming

Extreme programming (XP) is a new programming methodology that is spreading fast among developers. It is well worth examining in depth. Start at `http://c2.com/cgi/wiki?ExtremeProgramming`, or with the excellent Addison-Wesley *XP Series*, currently up to six small, readable books.

The techniques of extreme programming have been around for a few years now, and it seems no accident that the discipline emerged from an object-oriented environment. Extreme programmers show some lack of concern for a strict top-down or bottom-up approach. They also emphasize the need to *refactor* your code if it seems to be becoming too complex. Refactoring is changing the way your program is organized, and not its behavior. This is especially common when you are creating a framework (writing manager function logic intended to apply to several situations) because you can fix many reusability bugs by refactoring your framework. Some of the more notable code problems that refactoring can fix are

- **Removing code duplication**—If two different functions provide the same result, or if one function is a special case of another, then there is less code to maintain after refactoring the two functions into one.

- **Isolating existing logic from a needed change**—If you have to change certain cases currently handled by a single class, you might find it advantageous to refactor the class, turning it into two subclasses of a common base class. The changed behavior can then be implemented in just one of the subclasses.

- **Making the program run faster**—Sometimes performance becomes an issue, and it may be that your original choice of algorithm, or perhaps your choice of data structure, was inappropriate.

Extreme programming also places high value on the application of software design patterns, which can serve much the same role in program design that library modules do in program construction. The patterns community has produced several books already, and many of them are worth reading no matter what your level of programming experience.

Some extreme programmers talk about "the quality without a name," which expresses quite well the idea that code quality is hard to be objective about and that you need to learn to trust your own judgment about how good your code is, and needs to be. One of the values of experience is in helping you to develop your ability to appreciate quality and to imbue your programs with it, even if you cannot necessarily say exactly what "quality software" really is. Of course, it relates to the designed purpose of the software, but over and above that comes an aesthetic that concerns economy of structure and a sense that everything fits. Experienced programmers usually will show a degree of agreement on the quality of a given piece of software.

XP is particularly suitable for small to medium groups of developers (it needs tweaking for a lone programmer, or for a group larger than several dozens of developers) and for custom software development, whether in-house or by contractors (it needs tweaking for Net-wide open-source development, or to develop software to be sold off-the-shelf).

XP rests on the 12 core practices listed here, mostly not unique to it. The secret of XP's success is that the various practices support each other, in ways sometimes not too obvious, yielding a whole greater than the sum of its parts:

1. **Design and coding are test-driven**—Whenever you need to add functionality, you first write a test, for automatic execution, that checks whether the desired functionality is present and works well. Work in small increments; never add two features at the same time. Run the test before you add the feature: if the test works, it must show that the feature is not present. Add the feature; rerun the test. Whenever you fix defects or change details, first make sure that the tests correctly show that the defect is or isn't present, or exactly how the details are set. Test, test, and test some more! This is the key to all the rest of XP and is not really a controversial idea: everybody *preaches* it, but only XPers really *practice* it!

2. **One customer must be part of the development team**—This is the only way you can truly know that the program you are developing is really the one the customer wants. The customer develops and refines specifications by writing *user stories*, scenarios of typical interactions with the desired system. You can think of user stories as larger-scale "acceptance" tests. The customer need not be able to program; rather, he or she collaborates with developers to turn user stories into actual executable test code.

3. **Program in pairs**—Two people sitting at the same workstation write every line of code (including tests). This ensures many of the benefits of code reviews up front, and many other subtler benefits. The overall productivity boost more

than makes up for the "cost" of always taking two people at a time to code anything. Pairings must change frequently, at least once or twice a day, reinforcing team spirit and lack of individual ownership of code (see number 11).

4. **Integrate continuously—not just "at release time," not even weekly—** Each time you change or fix a module, after running its tests, integrate the module back into the system. Run the rich suite of tests and user stories; this reassures you that everything is working.

5. **Refactor mercilessly**—Whenever you notice that something is done similarly in two places, move things around so that it is done in one place and called or inherited by the "two places" previously noticed. Whenever you see violations of the coding guidelines, fix them. Whenever you notice structural defects, change the structure. At each change, rerun all tests, reassuring you that refactoring hasn't broken anything.

6. **Release often and in small granularity**—Add only a few user stories at each release. This reinforces numbers 2 and 4, further ensuring customer acceptance and avoiding the nightmare of "big bang integration."

7. **Planning and scheduling follows a careful division of responsibility—** Between developers and customers (lovingly referred to as "Gold Owners," since they pay for the project and also "Goal Donors," since they determine the project's purpose). Developers have final say on how much time each given user story will take to implement. Customers have final say on what the priorities are—that is, what is to be working soonest. These two evaluations determine the contents of each small, frequent release (see number 6).

8. **Simplicity**—"Do the simplest thing that can possibly work." Do not build in complication because it may come in handy tomorrow. Take therefore no thought for the morrow, for the morrow shall take thought for the things of itself. Sufficient unto the day is the evil thereof (Matthew 6:34). Simplicity has *many* benefits.

9. **System metaphors are preferred to describe system architecture—** Rather than detailed formal specifications, the real specs are in the tests, particularly in the user stories, and in the code that passes the tests. The only real added value documentation can give is a "unifying metaphor" to help understand the system as a whole.

10. **Standard coding methods**—The project adopts a uniform, precise set of coding conventions, and every developer follows it. This makes everybody productive in working on all different parts of the code, as required by numbers 3 and 11.

11. **No code ownership**—No piece of code must ever be "owned" by a single individual—extreme programming is a *team* effort. It is never "Joe's code" or "Jim's code," it is always our code. A programming pair therefore has no fear of

changing "somebody else's" code. Always-changing pairs, see number 3, and strong uniform coding conventions, see number 10, help with this!

12. **Use a 40-hour week**—The exact number is not crucial and depends somewhat on individuals. The key point is that overtime is counterproductive— software development requires both creativity *and* minute attention to detail. To be really productive, you need to be well-rested, relaxed, and happy.

XP, like other, "heavier" methodologies, is about how human beings organize themselves as development teams, instead of about finer details of how the code ends up— except for aspects implied by the test-first idea (number 1) and the simplicity rule (number 8). XP in particular is *not* about producing paperwork. XP minimizes deliverable artifacts from the development process down to essentials: working code, complete unit tests, all user stories, and a little narrative about the system metaphors of number 9. Anything else would be "dead weight."

Planning for Testing

One thing that a lifetime of programming has taught me, by observing both myself and others, is that the limits to human competence often appear in strange places and in unexpected ways. This is probably the reason why Murphy's Law, "if a thing can go wrong, it will," is so universally accepted. Of course it is also true that "if a thing can't go wrong, it won't," but engineering history demonstrates how difficult it is to design something that cannot go wrong. This is due partly to innate human optimism and partly to our inability to imagine the many and varied ways in which it is possible for something to go wrong.

In the case of the Tacoma Narrows bridge, which collapsed after less than a year in use, the designer failed to take into account the greater aerodynamic instability of his structure as he worked closer to the limits of the materials than previous engineers. Many software projects have failed because they were based on new technologies, for which inadequate experience was available to predict behavior in the finished system. Sometimes the vendor simply fails to deliver the new technology. Other projects fail because the development team does not properly understand the user requirements, or because the requirements change a long way down the path toward implementation.

Even if we can rule out all these factors, sometimes we programmers are our own worst enemies. One of the problems with software design is that software is so easy to change that you can easily fool yourself into thinking "I'll just make this one last little change," and thereby induce a fatal error in an otherwise almost-working piece of software. Version control systems are invaluable at times like this, with their capability to revert to a previous (working) version of your code. The fact is that it takes strong self-discipline to control that last gift from Pandora's box: the hope that things will work out, that our programs will work correctly, even when we fail to limit the opportunities for things to go wrong.

Ultimately, if each programmer is responsible for testing his own code, and especially if he is allowed to write the tests after he writes the code, preconceptions about performance will tend to make the tests inadequate. This is why the extreme programming emphasis on testing provides a more reliable product. The tests effectively define the scope of the software before the team creates the code itself, and so a mismatch between code and tests clearly appears as a defect in the software. Even if you do not adopt extreme programming practices, it has always been a good idea to specify the tests before writing the code.

Documenting and Testing Python Code

Sensible software development methodologies have for a long time now stressed the importance of specifying the tests at the same time as the software and, in large teams, having program development and test development as two different areas of responsibility. This makes sense for psychological reasons, as the person who has written code is often too close to it to determine what will test it adequately. With the introduction of release 2.1, Python has two different testing frameworks: doctest and unittest. Both these modules were available as third-party extensions for release 2.0, so you should be able to install and use them in that version if you want.

If you are already testing in other language environments, then unittest may suit you, as the module is directly based on PyUnit, which is widely available in various languages because of its simplicity and power. PyUnit was derived from Junit, which in turn, was based on the SmallTalk Sunit testing system. The doctest module, on the other hand, is designed exclusively for the Python environment. It is undoubtedly easier to set up than unittest, and so if you have no unit-testing experience, you may well prefer to use doctest, which works by embedding executable statements and their expected outcomes into the documentation strings embedded into better Python code.

The Python interpreter treats string constants in certain positions specially. If a string constant appears as the first statement in a module or as the first statement of a function, class, or method definition, it is stored as the __doc__ attribute of the object concerned (unless the interpreter has been run with the −OO option to inhibit this feature). If you include these so-called *docstrings* in your code, then users who know little about your module and the functions and classes it contains can examine the docstrings for an initial explanation of their purpose. Here is an example from standard modules imported into the interpreter interactively:

```
>>> import os.path
>>> print os.path.abspath.__doc__
Return the absolute version of a path
>>> print os.path.getmtime.__doc__
Return the last modification time of a file, reported by os.stat()
>>> import CGIHTTPServer
>>> print CGIHTTPServer.__doc__
CGI-savvy HTTP Server.
```

This module builds on SimpleHTTPServer by implementing GET and POST
requests to cgi-bin scripts.

If the os.fork() function is not present (e.g. on Windows),
os.popen2() is used as a fallback, with slightly altered semantics; if
that function is not present either (e.g. on Macintosh), only Python
scripts are supported, and they are executed by the current process.

In all cases, the implementation is intentionally naive -- all
requests are executed sychronously.

SECURITY WARNING: DON'T USE THIS CODE UNLESS YOU ARE INSIDE A FIREWALL
-- it may execute arbitrary Python code or external programs.

```
>>> print CGIHTTPServer.CGIHTTPRequestHandler.__doc__
Complete HTTP server with GET, HEAD and POST commands.

GET and HEAD also support running CGI scripts.

The POST command is *only* implemented for CGI scripts.
```

Tim Peters, now of the PythonLabs team, observed that because the docstrings are
accessible programmatically, a program could use information in the docstrings to
test the correct functioning of the code. He wrote the doctest module to analyze
docstrings, extract statements input to and output emitted from interactive Python
sessions, rerun the embedded Python statements, and verify the output.

Listing 15.1 shows the code of a module, tested.py, which is designed for testing
by doctest. This is typical of a testable module in the early stages of construction, and
it includes just one function. Observe that the docstring for the slen() function contains several lines from an interactive session, both input and output, including one
example where the function is deliberately called with incorrect arguments and raises
an exception.

Listing 15.1   *tested.py:* **A Module Designed to Be Tested with** *doctest*

```
 1   """Demonstrates the doctest module in action."""
 2
 3   def slen(s, tlen=8):
 4       """Returns effective length of string,
 5       allowing for tabs of given length.
 6
 7       >>> slen(" ")
 8       1
 9       >>> slen("\t"), slen(" \t")
10       (8, 8)
11       >>> [slen(" "*i+"\t") for i in range(16)]
```

continues

Listing 15.1 **Continued**

```
12      [8, 8, 8, 8, 8, 8, 8, 8, 16, 16, 16, 16, 16, 16, 16, 16]
13      >>> [slen(" "*i+"\t", 3) for i in range(16)]
14      [3, 3, 3, 6, 6, 6, 9, 9, 9, 12, 12, 12, 15, 15, 15, 18]
15      >>> [slen(" \t"*i) for i in range(10)]
16      [0, 8, 16, 24, 32, 40, 48, 56, 64, 72]
17      >>> [slen("\t"*i+" ") for i in range(12)]
18      [1, 9, 17, 25, 33, 41, 49, 57, 65, 73, 81, 89]
19      >>> slen("Hello")
20      Traceback (innermost last):
21        ...
22      ValueError: Illegal white space character
23      """
24      r = 0
25      for c in s:
26          if c == " ": r = r+1
27          elif c == "\t": r = ((r+tlen)/tlen)*tlen
28          else: raise ValueError, "Illegal white space character"
29      return r
30
31  def _test():
32      import doctest, tested
33      return doctest.testmod(tested)
34
35  if __name__ == "__main__":
36      _test()
```

When you run this module as a main program, what will you see? Well, that depends on whether your code works. When the module is the main program, the last two lines make it call the _test() function, which imports both doctest and the module itself and then runs the testmod() function on the module. By default, the testmod() function runs silently, so if you see no output, then testmod() has verified the same results that you pasted in from your interactive testing. If you prefer to see the output from your testing, simply add the −v option to the command line, and doctest becomes rather chatty, as Listing 15.2 shows.

Listing 15.2 **Output from Testing of** *tested.py* **with Verbose Output**

```
Running tested.__doc__
0 of 0 examples failed in tested.__doc__
Running tested.slen.__doc__
Trying: slen(" ")
Expecting: 1
ok
Trying: slen("    "), slen("    ")
Expecting: (8, 8)
ok
Trying: [slen(" "*i+"    ") for i in range(16)]
```

```
Expecting: [8, 8, 8, 8, 8, 8, 8, 8, 16, 16, 16, 16, 16, 16, 16, 16]
ok
Trying: [slen(" "*i+"    ", 3) for i in range(16)]
Expecting: [3, 3, 3, 6, 6, 6, 9, 9, 9, 12, 12, 12, 15, 15, 15, 18]
ok
Trying: [slen("     "*i) for i in range(10)]
Expecting: [0, 8, 16, 24, 32, 40, 48, 56, 64, 72]
ok
Trying: [slen("    "*i+" ") for i in range(12)]
Expecting: [1, 9, 17, 25, 33, 41, 49, 57, 65, 73, 81, 89]
ok
Trying: slen("Hello")
Expecting:
Traceback (innermost last):
...
ValueError: Illegal white space character
ok
0 of 7 examples failed in tested.slen.__doc__
1 items had no tests:
  tested
1 items passed all tests:
  7 tests in tested.slen
7 tests in 2 items.
7 passed and 0 failed.
Test passed.
```

Tim Peters makes the point in doctest's own documentation that your testing in the interactive shell will probably be verifying the limiting cases of your code (if it is not, it should be). Using doctest and capturing the output of your interactive tests ensures that the documentation of your module corresponds with the output it produces, and that if you change your code later it is easy to ensure that nothing has broken.

Remember that doctest is subtler than this short presentation allows for, so you should read its documentation to find out the many possibilities. Although a part of the standard distribution only from release 2.1, doctest is backward-compatible with release 2.0 (in fact Listing 15.2 was produced from release 2.0).

Lessons from Stonehenge

Every project has its requirements for durability. Some programs are built to run once. Some such programs survive, evolving into something that becomes a frequently run and indispensable utility. Others originally intended to run daily or weekly wither and die if their output is not useful, as no maintenance effort is justified unless the organization sees benefit from the information that the program produces. Most production programs and web pages are intended to be available all the time. I have worked with teams building systems for an operational lifetime of 30 years (you cannot call a space probe back for repairs). In the scale of things, this isn't much when you consider that

Stonehenge in England is (allegedly) an astronomical calculation algorithm with graphical output that has existed, without need for debugging, for almost 5,000 years.

Imagine the budget overrun if, three months before the opening ceremony, the site foreman reported that all slabs were a foot too long, and the circle had to be moved 20 feet to the north. In software, of course, it is much easier to change things, to the extent that sometimes it is difficult, when faced with a multitude of architectural possibilities, to select the one you will actually use. However, it really is worth knowing when a change breaks your components' behavior. By building the testing into the software, you create a much greater chance that induced errors will be picked up as a part of the regular testing process.

If you know how to use a version control system such as Microsoft's Visual SourceSafe, or CVS, this can be an invaluable aid in tracking the maturity of your coding style as well as the evolution of your design. After you learn to walk in Python, you soon find yourself breaking into a run from time to time, and the disciplined user of version control can much more easily avoid the "what did I change since this worked?" syndrome. Not only that, but the mistaken structure you discarded two months ago on your last project can sometimes turn out to be the very thing you need as the development base for a part of your next project. Having ready access to the history of your source code means you do not need to rewrite the code, simply extract it from the last project's history.

If we all assume that the code we write has to work in 5,000 years, we might well write less code, which need not be an altogether bad thing. Of course, Stonehenge has not survived intact, and this tells us something about the ravages our systems are likely to be subjected to by environmental influences entirely beyond our control. I would not be entirely surprised if a thorough excavation revealed a list of inadequacies with an annotation that, when translated, reads "fixed in next release."

Planning Interactive Web Systems

A web system is effectively a programmed method for generation of linked content, usually (but not necessarily) presented with some degree of structural uniformity. For web pages, the unifying theme is usually the page layout but in XML could be the presentation style, possibly selected from a number of styles defined in cascading style sheets.

The structure of web pages is often hierarchical, with a group of pages embellishing a style inherited from the pages above it in the conceptual hierarchy. One of the features of Zope is its capability to inherit page structure, overriding as necessary within a tree-structured hierarchy; and you will learn a little more about Zope and other frameworks in the next chapter. For now, though, suppose you need to put a site together that has such an implied hierarchy (remembering that this is a stylistic rather than a technical decision).

Overall Architecture

You have by now seen enough Python code that one more HTTP server would be neither here nor there. It may be that your current web services run external programs as CGIs as a matter of policy. In that case, you must be prepared to write your systems as CGI scripts, which will make them slower and perhaps more complex.

Generally, it is best to try to separate the HTTP service from the content generation. The architecture of web systems is such that HTTP carries HTML, XML, and so on, and so the two are at different layers in the software architecture.

You may need to understand your server environment quite closely if you want to use techniques like *persistent CGI*, which can improve performance. However, just as in databases, the early stages of design are too soon to start considering physical models; it is often better to design the system in a simple way and then look at how to improve performance if that proves necessary. Because you now know you can write web servers in pure Python, thanks to the socket library, you need not fear the artificial constraints of a server framework.

Determining Page Structure

Some sort of plan is required. This is a good time for what the extreme programming community calls a *spike solution*. This is essentially "producing the simplest thing that can possibly work," usually without frills of any kind, to determine what sort of architecture might best match the problem requirements. Any attempt to produce something that will be incorporated into the finished product should, however, be firmly resisted. Whatever your instincts tell you, it is foolish to do too much coding until you have some idea of how the basic components are going to fit together, and so you should build prototypes to be discarded.

You have to present content inside a structure, which you might think of as layout if you are primarily aiming at human-readable webs. Spend some time considering structure without worrying too much about content, and decide how the different required layouts relate to each other. Usually some form of nested layout will be appropriate, with an overall "site look-and-feel" providing the outer style elements, with different variations (sometimes on content, sometimes on layout, sometimes both) filling in the gaps.

At this point in a web design, I tend to think mostly about the variable elements— the items of content that will vary from page to page. These variable elements are those that are ultimately going to be filled with information—from databases, from other sources on the network (for example, your server could be a network news client, or a client of other web servers from which it extracts XML content), or from files whose paths may be selected using computations on inputs.

An important structural aspect of many webs is the hierarchy of the pages. Some pages will share common top-level features but differ at lower levels. There may be several different versions of a high-level page, which differ primarily in content rather than structure. Look for the common structural features and abstract them from the content. You can often map the page hierarchy onto an object hierarchy, using a top-level page as a template for lower-level pages, and so on down a tree. As long as you can parameterize the page designs according to content, a graphic designer can take the parameterized design and modify the site look and feel.

My most rewarding web work has always involved working with a designer or design team with good visual creative skills, which I do not myself possess. They provide the eye candy (and, coincidentally, also structure the information to enhance its readability and usefulness), and I build the engine room that drives it. Ultimately, it becomes a matter of slotting (appropriately formatted) variable segments, incorporating content provided by the customer, into what the designers have produced.

Suppose you want your web site to have two basically orthogonal sets of content: some parts of the content are to be available everywhere, whereas others are clustered around a category such as "topic." You might determine that your overall look-and-feel should be as in Figure 15.1, with the same site banner and graphic on every page. The top and bottom navigation bars are to be used for the links to invariant pages, and the left-hand navigation bar will contain links that depend on the particular topic covered in the page.

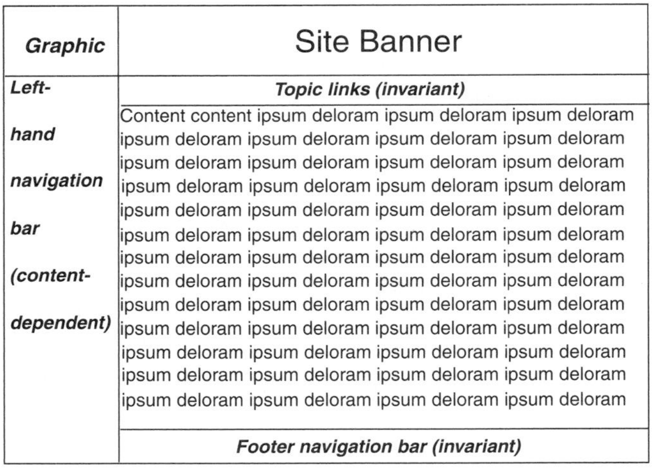

Graphic	Site Banner
Left-	***Topic links (invariant)***
hand	Content content ipsum deloram
navigation	
bar	
(content-	
dependent)	
	Footer navigation bar (invariant)

Figure 15.1   Outline of a web site's page structure.

Supposing you choose to represent each page style as an object, you have four variable areas whose content will need to be determined on a page-by-page basis. If you then want certain topics to allow the reader to navigate among subtopics, you might then choose to impose a finer-grained structure on the main portion of the page. These subtopic pages will (since they all refer to the same major topic) effectively have the same structure as the topic page to which they relate, but they might (for example) have a navigation bar at the top of the content area, which allows the user to navigate between different subtopics.

So you could use a subclass of the topic page routine, in which the main content window method first generates a subtopic navigation bar, to generate these pages. The topic page methods will still be parameterized by the topic, but the subtopic pages will be parameterized by the subtopic in addition.

It might be that you have subtopics common to all topics. In this case, the same object inheritance structures will serve for both types of subpage, but the data relationships might be different. You need to spend some time thinking about these relationships before you start to determine what structure you want your code to have. Even then you will be wrong about the code structure; you will just be less wrong!

Web Inputs

The potential sources of input to a web-based service are

- The URI's path
- The URI's query string, with any fragment
- The HTTP headers
- For certain HTTP transactions (usually those involving the POST protocol method), standard input

A web server typically will treat the request's path as a directory path in a virtual file-store called a web, and select either a piece of static content or a CGI script to be run on arguments specified in the query portion of the URI. Although this interpretation is conventional in traditional web servers, it is quite possible to split up the path into components and use them as database keys, for example. Servers such as Apache offer the capability to perform complex remapping on the path to transform incoming URIs into others, precisely to adapt the classical model into something more flexible. The output from the web server is a function of the inputs, and from one point of view, changes in the site's database are merely side effects of producing the output! By writing your own server, you make it much easier to perform the mappings directly and minimize the overhead involved in setting up the service.

Think back to the database mini-web server of Chapter 10, "The Python Database Interface," (see Listing 10.1, "*dbwebsrv.py:* A Simple Data-Driven Asynchronous Web Server"). This server has about the simplest possible interface to its web clients: it gets the operation (HTTP protocol method) and the path (which, technically, includes any query and fragment as well). The server engine to drive that simple content generation scheme created a new object, a dbpage, whenever it received a request and generated its output using the call

```
self.obuffer = dbsource.page(op, path)
```

Because the creation of a dbpage does not read standard input, the CGI data stream is available to any pages prepared to accept POST method calls, which in practice none of them did. The `cgi` library module is useful in this context even when a classical web server does not trigger the scripts.

Maintaining State

The most difficult thing about web systems is the inherently stateless nature of the HTTP protocol used to communicate between client and server. Netscape designed the cookie mechanism as a way around this problem. Each cookie is associated with a domain and a path and is stored on the client rather than the server. When the client makes any web request, it first searches its cookies and returns any that match both the domain and the path as a part of a request. By serving up appropriate cookies, a server can ensure that a browser identifies itself in such a way that a request can be associated with previous requests.

If properly implemented, cookies can actually assist users in maintaining their privacy, by storing confidential data (or keys that allow the server to retrieve it from a local database) on the client side. Unfortunately, cookies have received bad press, largely due to their capability to track users through several sites where the same advertiser serves up advertising impressions. Because the advertiser can serve up cookies related to the advertising content, and because HTTP requests often include a reference to the URL in which they were embedded, it is possible to track a set of visits to pages from unrelated sites both using the same advertiser. What is more, too many naïve cookie implementations fail under "replay" attacks, where someone who can snoop the network traffic can forge a client's identity simply by using the same data again.

If you plan to maintain state using cookies, you should satisfy yourself (if necessary by hiring somebody who understands the problems in sufficient depth) that your implementation is reasonably secure. Most of all, do not assume that, because the details of your scheme are undisclosed, that will make it any harder to break—a scheme often referred to as "security by obscurity." Companies as large as Lotus Corporation have made this mistake and learned that cryptanalysis can lay such schemes bare in short order. My own personal approach to security might be summed up as "security by total insignificance": I have little information anyone would want to steal that I am not already giving away. Such is the world of open-source.

Determining Interaction Sequences

Some web sites are so difficult to use that they have to offer something quite valuable for users to be prepared to tolerate the pain of driving their interfaces. If you want a web site to be used, it is worth considerable effort to ensure that the users can quickly navigate to the areas they are interested in and that they find it easy to interact with the site. This is especially important if the user has to fill out forms, because forms in web-based interfaces are much less flexible in their interactions than their windowed counterparts, unless the web system also uses extensive client-side programming to manage interactions.

Try to arrange your logic so that when you validate a form's input you can present the form again, with messages about fields in error and the original form content still available. If you present an error message and ask the user to use her browser's "Back" button to correct the input, you are making it unnecessarily difficult to interact with your system. The only mandatory fields should be those that are truly indispensable to the operation of the system, and it is often a good idea to include a catch-all "other comments" text area to allow free-form user input.

The primary lack in the web development world of the end of last century was simple, uniform ways of undertaking common tasks. There were a million snippets of HTML, JavaScript, Perl, and VBScript, very few of which were actually designed to be used as components in general systems. Many web interfaces have never met an interface designer, and it shows both visually and ergonomically. It is very important to examine the sequences of pages that users must navigate through to accomplish higher-level tasks like "sign up for mailing list" or "submit question of the day." Can they go back at any stage? Do they get sensible warning messages, with forms repeated so that it is easy to change the unacceptable elements and resubmit? Experienced web designers have often grappled with these interface questions and may be able to speed you through to a practical interface design. I hate clunky interfaces, but that's the kind I often design.

Data Analysis

Instead of focusing entirely on architectural issues at this stage, it offers a refreshing perspective to be able to look at the data. Ask the customer (even if you are your own customer) about the information content of each page. When is *this* different, does *this* change at the same time as *that*, where does this input come from? This lets you ask yourself what entities you must therefore store as relational data. When you start to get a picture of the data, you can ask yourself where and how it is going to be processed.

There can also be structural data, of course. If the organization needs to represent its departments on the web, each department has certain things in common. The techniques of normalization can help here to avoid falling too early into the trap of over-complicated design and to suggest lines along which the software might be partitioned. Suppose you have a department entity: how should the department's data appear to the users? Will every department use the same page template or will there be a need to vary the presentation? Does the department determine the page style? Which classes of users will be putting in what type of data? Sometimes it is useful to be able to offer drill-down, expanding the detail of summarized figures with pages lower down the hierarchy. Where in the web would this be useful? The operational data may live in an entirely different database from the structural information. There is no reason that web processes cannot use multiple data sources.

This initial uncertainty about how well it will be possible to fulfill the users' expectations can add pressure, but it is important to have considered more than one alternative for as many aspects of the system as possible. The whole exercise is a little like fitting a jigsaw puzzle together. The earlier pieces are more difficult to fit together because there is less context in which to determine their overall and relative positions. At this stage of a design, I find myself doing a lot of wondering—will this entity relate to that, will separate activities share data, which pages will use which parts of the database, and so on. It is almost as useful to find something that *won't* work, and understand the reasons why, as it is to find something that will work.

Brainstorming techniques also can be very useful during the early stages of design. If you have not come across the technique before, it is a small-group activity in which ideas are generated with no "that could never work" censors in place. Participants are encouraged to free-associate, and to propose even the most outrageous and impossible ideas. After the idea-generation period is over, critical evaluation is used to examine the ideas for any useful germ of relevance. Surprisingly often, brainstorming can produce innovative design ideas. If you have never considered using this technique, you might be interested in a visit to `http://www.brainstorming.co.uk/`.

Finally, you have to decide what framework you are going to use to support the structures you are imagining. That is the subject of the next chapter. However, you will have begun to realize that compared with the classic web servers, very little has been done so far with their lightweight counterparts.

Summary

This chapter has been something of a ramble, trying to draw together all the various threads that careful design work entails as well as a little methodology. Eventually, you will arrive at a first design, probably with an incomplete architecture and incomplete functionality, and you will want to start trying things out. To do so, you will need tools at your disposal, both to handle the HTTP communications (about which you should now be fairly confident) and to generate the content. This latter topic can be difficult because Python is such a versatile language, it has led to many different attempts to provide support. In Chapter 16, "Web Application Frameworks," you will take a look at some of the existing frameworks that can help with this.

The complexity of software design is such that it helps to approach the problem from several different angles to more fully consider what might go wrong. I mentioned Murphy's Law in passing. Apparently, Murphy had a colleague, Dr. Stapp, who gave birth to Stapp's Ironical Paradox. This should stand as a testament to the accomplishments of software engineering: "The universal aptitude for ineptitude makes any human accomplishment an incredible miracle."

16

Web Application Frameworks

IF YOU DON'T LIKE TO DO YOUR OWN PLUMBING, you send for a plumber. If you don't like building web systems from the ground up, you use frameworks. Python's natural affinity for the web has been exploited many times to build web-system frameworks, with varying degrees of success, and the results are often freely available through the generosity of their authors. Some frameworks assume that you are working with a classic web server. Others give you more freedom by concentrating mostly on HTML generation, but even these tools often include the capability to intermingle Python and output text for more flexibility in content generation.

In this chapter, you will review the classic web server architecture, and the roles that Python can play under such a regime. Next you will go on to look at some of the possible pure Python architectures for web systems. Finally, you will meet Xitami, a lightweight web server with the capability to interact with long-running processes. Although this may not cover the whole range of server architectures available, it is a sufficiently diverse range to give you a good idea of the possibilities.

Along the way, you will learn some things that will help in many different architectural contexts. The task of interacting with web clients has many common features no matter what the eventual architecture. You also will learn an easy way to integrate databases with Python, allowing you to address all database columns as attributes of the rows that contain them. The chapter concludes with a look at HTML generation and a glance at intercomponent communications. At that stage, you will be ready to tackle the kind of problem that webs are being built to solve every day.

Information Sources

It is difficult to keep track of Python web toolkits. Cameron Laird maintains useful information on web uses of Python at `http://starbase.neosoft.com/ ~claird/comp.lang.python/web_python.html/`, and Paul Boddie makes a good survey of the field at `http://www.paul.boddie.net/Python/web_modules.html`. Both of these resources appear to be actively maintained at the time of writing.

Most publicly available web servers come with copious documentation. The Python code you will find comes with documentation of varying quality, ranging from "thin" to "excellent," but sadly the former tends to outweigh the latter. One of the current shortcomings of the open-source world is that more people want to write code than document it. This is a real pity, when you consider that good documentation usually increases the likelihood of software being reused by others.

The software world has always undervalued documentation (at least from the pragmatic point of view of not producing enough). The Python language is a model of its type, and although the documentation may not be perfect, Fred Drake does a very good job of ensuring that it is both useful and consistent, as anyone can see at `http://www.python.org/doc/current/`. Ka–Ping Yee presents another model site at `http://web.pydoc.org/` and simultaneously manages to demonstrate the value of his `pydoc` module. What follows is an eclectic summary of available web frameworks of various types, all of which accommodate Python somehow. The exclusion of a particular framework from this chapter does not imply a value judgment about that framework. There really are far too many Python web frameworks for a single chapter, so I have tried to choose a representative sample that gives a flavor of the current state of the art.

Web Server Architectures

If you are already familiar with how web servers are put together, feel free to skip this whole section, in which we break down the server into its component parts and discuss how these parts fit together to act as a coherent whole, meeting all the requirements for a web service. Most web servers look like Figure 16.1.

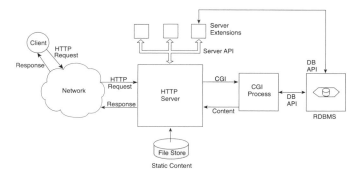

Figure 16.1   The classical web server architecture.

The process of serving *static content* is the easiest to understand. The client makes an HTTP request, the URI identifies a file in the web's virtual filestore, and the server returns the content of that file preceded by an appropriate set of HTTP response headers, including a Content-Type header that tells the client the MIME type of the output. Many things can go wrong along the way, but the process is normally a simple one. You are also familiar with the concept that although the client is often a browser, it might equally be any HTTP client program, possibly one of your own manufacture.

In Chapter 6, "A Server Framework Library," you received a simple introduction to the operation of the CGI mechanism, a time-honored way to activate *dynamic content*, which is to say content that is computed rather than simply retrieved and served up. The important elements are that the protocol method used by the browser can either be GET or POST. When POST is used, the standard input is the form content, encoded as a set of *name=value* pairs separated by ampersands, with the data appropriately escaped to make its interpretation unambiguous.

If a CGI routine has to use a database, then it can be a lengthy process because the following has to happen (here we consider a Python CGI, but the process is much the same with any interpreted language). First the server must locate the CGI script and verify that it is executable. Then it has to trigger the Python interpreter to read and execute the script (here Python at least precompiles modules as it imports them, although the main program would require precompilation—for example, by the compile program in Python's tools directory—to be run from its compiled form). The interpreter will then run the program, using standard input and/or the query string and/or the HTTP headers for inputs, and reading and writing files or relational databases as necessary.

This means that each CGI script carries the overhead of creating a new process, starting up the Python interpreter, and creating any required database connections or opening required files before it can start to process the inputs from the client. No wonder that various solutions exist for the elimination of the CGI script!

The real issue is therefore application scalability: if dynamic content can be created with lower overhead, then more web pages can be produced in a given period of time. If your server is lightly loaded, process startup overhead might be a complete non-problem. As with network bandwidth, the situation deteriorates rapidly when the demand outstrips the supply and the server becomes a saturated resource. Just the same, it is comforting to remember that CGI scripting is compatible with almost all web servers and is easily achieved in Python.

One of the most popular early ways of omitting the overhead was for a server to define an extension API. Server extensions use the API to use server functionality and are loaded into memory as the server starts. When a request is associated with a server extension, the server can simply call the extension code directly, with no need to create a separate process. Of course, the server may or may not be threaded: if it is, then several threaded copies of it may be executing concurrently on separate requests, and if extensions are written in a thread-safe way, it is much easier for the server to scale up by adding threads as it gets busier. Your choices here depend on the relative costs of process and thread creation in the operating system platform that supports your server.

Another advantage of the server extension is that if database connections are required, they can be created on demand (or when the server starts) and pooled among the various pages that use them. Effectively, the extension can implement persistent storage on behalf of any web application because it is a part of a permanent process, which continues to exist between requests. For this reason, server extensions such as ColdFusion have been very popular, not only offering a useful increment in performance over traditional CGIs but also automatically implementing easy-to-use state-maintenance mechanisms.

Different servers have defined different extension APIs, and one of the problems of providing functionality as server extensions is the nonportable nature of the solution. The technique has therefore been much more popular with the more widely used servers such as Apache and Internet Information Server. Although it comprises less than 1 percent of the Internet web server population, the open-source AOLserver has a loyal following among sites generating a lot of traffic, and it too has received attention from the Python community.

CGI remains the baseline (or lowest common denominator, depending on your point of view). It is almost universally available, with only the Medusa server standing out as one that eschews the CGI function. It does so primarily because the process creation required by CGI conflict's with Medusa's design goals, which favor a small footprint and fast response.

Apache Integration with Python

The Apache server is a development of the earlier NCSA server, and is an open-source product, just approaching a major second release. Apache is the favored web server in the UNIX environment, and it continues in its long-time position as the most popular web server on the Internet (you can check the usage statistics at `http://www.netcraft.com/survey/`). It provides a module API, which has been used to implement many server extensions. Apache processes each request in a number of phases, and each phase may call a number of handler functions. Handler functions from optional modules can be invoked at certain points in each phase if they are correctly installed and described in the Apache configuration file.

Apache was originally implemented under UNIX, but it is now also available for Windows NT and 2000, with an experimental version available for Windows 9X. This latter version appears to be relatively stable and supports standard Python CGI scripts quite well, albeit slowly because of the overhead of starting up the Python interpreter for each request. Apache is therefore a good choice if you might want to migrate from one OS platform to another. It also supports a number of Python-oriented extensions of varying levels of sophistication. The three best known, in order of increasing complexity, are PyApache, `mod_python`, and `mod_snake`. All are open source, giving you complete freedom to change what you do not like.

PyApache

PyApache by Lele Gaifax has a well-run resource center web site (`http://bel-epa.com/pyapache/`) maintained by Graham Higgins. PyApache embeds the Python interpreter into Apache as an extension module. Effectively, the server loads the Python interpreter when it starts and then initializes it for each script it must execute, making the language readily available for CGI scripting without the interpreter having to be loaded for each script. PyApache has reasonably good documentation about how to use it, with excellent advice on modifying your web server configuration file and some lively CGI examples surrounded by common-sense advice on defensive programming techniques in a web environment.

Although using PyApache overcomes the problem of process creation for CGI scripts, clearly each script is run as a standalone object, and therefore must create its own database connections and so on, which will be released when the script ends. The nice part about PyApache is that absolutely any standard CGI script will work with it. You can easily port webs that already work using Python CGI to the PyApache environment, or simply install PyApache in your existing Apache server and thereby gain a useful performance increment.

mod_python

This module, maintained by Gregory Trubetskoy at `http://www.modpython.org`, is much broader in initial concept than PyApache, allowing you to define your own handler module functions in Python. You effectively nominate a Python module as a handler for certain classes of URL. The handler module is registered in the Apache configuration file using a structure like the following:

```
<Directory /pscripts>
    AddHandler python-program .py
    PythonHandler myscript
</Directory>
```

The argument to the `<Directory>` directive is a physical directory, and this configuration specifies that any request for a `*.py` file from the `/pscripts` directory should be handled by the script `/pscripts/myscript.py`. In this particular case, `PythonHandler` is the generic handler, which handles the phase during which content is generated (the authentication handler would be `PythonAuthenHandler`, for example). When `mod_python` arrives at the generic handler phase, it does the following:

1. Inserts the directory to which the Python Handler directive applies at the start of `sys.path` (unless this has already been done).

2. Attempts to import the handler module (in this case, `myscript`) by name.

3. Calls the script's `handle()` function, passing it a `Request` object (which encodes details of the current request and which the handler can use to set response attributes such as the MIME type of the returned content).

Here is a suitable handler, which would be located at `/pscripts/myscript.py`:

```
from mod_python import apache

def handler(request):
    req.content_type = "text/plain"    # establish content type
    req.send_http_header()             # send headers to client
    req.write("Hello, Python users!")  # send output
    return apache.OK                   # inform server no errors
```

The particular handler directive shown previously, which installed this handler, specifies that the script be called for *any* URL ending in `.py`. The handler you see simply ignores the URL and sends the same output. A more adventurous handler might return `Content-Type: text/html` and send back an HTML version of the Python code indicated by the URL path with appropriate syntax coloring. Another handler might simply treat the Python script named in the URL as a CGI script and attempt to execute it.

Clearly, `mod_python` is more intimately integrated with Apache than PyApache is, and this gives it more flexibility—at the usual cost of additional complexity, though if you are running Apache and you program in Python there is nothing to fear. `mod_python` does not integrate fully with the server, however. It does not allow the use of embedded Python in content, for example. Also, at the time of writing, `mod_python` was only available for the Apache 1.3 implementation. There is no indication of how likely it is to be available for the forthcoming Apache 2.0 release, in which the internals have changed somewhat.

mod_snake

This interesting extension, maintained by Jon Travis at `http://modsnake.sourceforge.net/`, is designed to interoperate with both the Apache 1.3 and 2.0 architectures. It integrates with Apache to give Python modules the capability to do anything that a module coded in the C language could do. Because the majority of users want to create simple modules, accelerate CGI scripts, or embed Python in their web pages, `mod_snake` also provides specialized (and simpler) APIs to perform these common tasks.

CGI script acceleration is provided by `mod_snake_cgi`, which requires the following line in the `httpd.conf` Apache configuration file:

```
SnakeModule      mod_snake_cgi.SnakeCGI
```

Notice that in `mod_snake`, you can define new modules as well as new handlers. You also have to associate particular paths with the module to ensure that scripts in certain areas of your web are run as Python CGIs. A typical configuration entry for this purpose follows:

```
Alias /pythoncgi/ ''/home/httpd/apache/cgipy/''
<Directory ''/home/httpd/apache/cgipy''>
    SetHandler snakecgi
    AllowOverride None
    Options ExecCGI
    Order allow,deny
    Allow from all
</Directory>
```

When Apache now sees a request of the form `http://your.host.com/pythoncgi/foo.py`, it will run it via `mod_snake_cgi`, looking for the script in the aliased directory `/home/httpd/apache/cgipy`. Before running a Python CGI script, `mod_snake_cgi` checks an internal cache of already-loaded modules. If the script is not yet loaded, then it is imported and added to the list of loaded modules. Otherwise, its modification time is checked, and if this is later than the last load, the Python module is reloaded to ensure that the new version will be run. The compiled code then runs in its entirety.

To allow embedded Python in your web pages, in a similar (but more advanced) way to ASP processing under IIS, you would need to add the following directives to your main Apache configuration file:

```
SnakeModule mod_snake_epy.SnakeEPy
AddType application/x-httpd-epy .epy
```

This tells Apache that scripts whose names end in `.epy` should be processed as extended Python scripts. There are configuration options you can use to

- Set processing of embedded Python code on or off.
- Send errors to the client instead of the log file (useful when you are debugging a new set of scripts because you no longer have to continually review the error file).
- Log extended Python errors somewhere other than the standard error log file.

Within an extended Python script, there are three delimiters you can use to indicate the inclusion of Python code. They are distinguished by different escape sequences for the three different purposes to which code might be put. Table 16.1 lists these delimiters.

Table 16.1   *mod_snake* **Python Markup and Its Interpretation**

Delimiters	Purpose of Code
`<+ ... +>`	Initialization code that should run only the first time the script executes. This can be used to open database connections, read in data files, and so on.
`<| ... |>`	To be executed with return value discarded.
`<: ... :>`	To be executed with the return value replacing the bracketed expression in the content sent to the client.

The CGI code modules have a global object `EPY` made available in their namespace before execution, which has several useful methods. A CGI script can use `EPY` to

- Set a script to be persistent, in which case global objects created during execution will be available during subsequent requests.
- Set output headers to be returned to the client.
- Write data to the remote client.

Here is a simple example from the `mod_snake` documentation to show the code in use:

```
<+
import time

EPY.set_persist(1)
HitCount = 1
+>

The current time is: <:time.ctime(time.time()):><BR>
This page has been hit <:HitCount:> times.
<|HitCount = HitCount + 1|>
```

This module sets itself persistent the first time it is run, so the hit count is only initialized once, and the variable will be available to successive invocations of this script (as will module time). The content returned to the client will contain interpolated output of the two Python expressions, which give the time and the hit count, respectively. Finally, the hit count is incremented, but nothing further is inserted into the output stream.

mod_fastcgi

FastCGI is a general mechanism described at `http://www.fastcgi.com/` and intended to be applicable without limitations as to language or web server architecture. FastCGI processes persist across requests, solving the interpreter startup problem. By multiplexing standard input, standard output, and standard error over a single pipe or network connection, it allows web processes to run remotely from the server.

FastCGI modules can be any of the following:

- *Responders*, which play the traditional role of CGI functionality.

- *Filters*, which apply computation to a resource identified by the web server and can achieve performance improvements by caching, for example.

- *Authorizers*, which receive the same information as a CI script would, but are only required to return an HTTP response indicating whether the request is acceptable.

Robin Dunn provides one implementation of FastCGI for Python, tested with both the Apache and Stronghold web servers, at `http://alldunn.com/python/`. FastCGI can speed up CGI performance significantly without unduly complicating your scripts and is worth a look if other techniques are unavailable or do not yield good enough performance.

AOLserver Integration with Python

AOLserver is maintained on SourceForge (at `http://sourceforge.net/projects/aolserver/`) by Kris Rehberg and Jim Davidson with the help of many other AOL staff members. It is an open-source, enterprise-level web server, which differs from Apache in some fundamental ways. It is a multithreaded application, whereas Apache runs client processes to handle requests (although multithreading is to be added in Apache's 2.0 release). This does not imply deficiencies in the Apache architecture, which by choice prefers flexibility to efficiency.

AOLserver also has its own database-independent API, which allows the server to establish a pool of database connections and then share them among the various worker threads as necessary—an ODBC interface has recently been added. Finally, AOLserver includes a complete implementation of the Tcl language along with many Tcl routines designed to assist with common tasks, such as retrieving connection information and handling forms.

Python access to many of AOLserver's functions is available through the PyWX module maintained by C. Titus Brown, Brent A. Fulgham, and Michael R. Haggerty at `http://pywx.idyll.org/`. This module's major attractions are

- Support for threaded execution, with the option to reuse the same interpreter on multiple threads or invoke a separate one.

- Access to AOLserver's internal C API, as well as the Tcl language implementation.

- Persistent database connections via the AOLserver internal implementation.

- An optional CGI-compatible environment with compiled script caching similar to `mod_snake`.

The configuration information available is complete, but it assumes a reasonable familiarity with the structure of AOLserver, so there is little point repeating it here. The AOLserver/PyWX combination seems to be powerful, but at the same time some of the demonstration scripts available on the web site note that "if you get strange results, it could be that someone else is running the scripts at the same time." One might hope that this is because the scripts are deliberately simplified.

Internet Information Server Integration with Python

Microsoft's IIS is widely used on intranets, and on the Internet to a lesser degree, by organizations whose standard server platform is Windows NT or Windows 2000. This includes some major web hosting corporations. IIS can use Active Scripting, and the usual solution is to run VBScript pages with an `.asp` extension, thereby invoking the VBScript interpreter for blocks enclosed in `<% ... %>` delimiter pairs. Microsoft also supplies Personal Web Server (PWS), which offers an ASP scripting environment sufficiently close to IIS for testing purposes.

Active Scripting, however, is not limited to just VBScript. By default, the engine will also allow you to interpret server-side JavaScript (or Microsoft's implementation of it) for scripts characterized as follows:

```
<SCRIPT LANGUAGE="JScript" RUNAT="Server">
```

If you install the Python win32all extensions, Python also is installed as an Active Scripting language, and you can use `LANGUAGE="Python"` to trigger it. However, all is not sweetness and light, for a number of reasons:

- Indentation is a big problem if you try to intermingle HTML and program code as is common in VBScript. The best workaround for this problem is "don't do that!"—use programming to create HTML from Python as discussed later in this chapter, and output it only when you have generated it all.

- Do not try to be too literal in your translations because VBScript syntax takes a number of liberties (such as allowing function calls with no parentheses or arguments), which Python does not.

- You need some insight into the ASP object model to know exactly how to refer to each object type. Many ASP objects make information available as *collections*, which are ASP's equivalent of the Python dictionary. However, a collection can have a default item, which the collection returns when its name is not qualified by an attribute name.

You also need to be careful to ensure that your Python pages are named with the `.asp` extension; otherwise, they will not be treated as Active Server Pages at all, much to your chagrin. This probably trips up 50 percent of those who start down the Python/ASP road (including your author).

One of the features of Active Server Pages is the object hierarchy it makes available to you. This includes session and application objects, which if carefully used allow automatic maintenance of data storage between successive interactions with a particular browser, or for all browsers accessing a subset of the virtual web defined at the server as an application. This feature is useful, but storing randomly created COM objects in session or application space is not a good idea. After initially promoting the session object as a suitable way to maintain state, Microsoft later backpedaled when users began storing large record sets in the session to save repetitious database access.

The ASP environment automatically makes available several useful objects:

- **Application**—ASP defines an application as a directory in the web's virtual filestore, plus all its subdirectories that are not themselves applications. You can use the application object to store data that all pages need to share, avoiding the overhead of creating them on a page-by-page basis. Offers `Lock()` and `Unlock()` methods to avoid synchronization problems on multisession access.

- **ASPError**—Various properties of this object can be read to determine information about an error.

- **ObjectContext**—Used to control interactions with Microsoft Transaction Server.

- **Request**—Used to access the data that characterize the client's request. Properties include `Certificates`, `Cookies`, `Form`, `QueryString`, and `ServerVariables`.

- **Response**—By far the most complex of these objects, `Response` has many attributes and methods, of which the most important are `Cookies` (an attribute that returns cookies to the client), `Write` (used to send output to the client), and `AddHeader` (which adds an HTTP header to the response seen by the client).

- **Server**—The `CreateObject()` method can be used to create an arbitrary COM object. Python can use COM objects almost as easily as native Python objects, thanks to Mark Hammond's win32 extensions. The `HTMLEncode()` and `URLEncode()` methods offer features that would otherwise require additional Python modules to be loaded, and the `GetLastError()` method returns an `ASPError` object detailing the last ASP error that occurred.

- **Session**—The major use of the `Session` object is for storage of data that need to persist at the server between successive client interactions. It also has a number of useful methods, including `Abandon()` to terminate the session unilaterally and `Contents.Remove()` to remove a named item from session storage.

The `Request` object will actually search a number of collections for an attribute, so if you know the attributes you want, they will be retrieved from *either* the `Form` or the `QueryString` collection as necessary. Some software authors use this technique to produce ASP scripts that will work with either `GET` or `POST` methods.

Listing 16.1 shows a simple ASP page, which shows how you can use the `QueryString` attribute of the `Request` object. `QueryString` is a collection of the names and values from the URL's query string. As you can see from line 12, Python sees the default value as a list of the keys. In line 13, dictionary access is used to retrieve the values of individual values. Figure 16.2 shows the output of this page when run on my IIS server. The `Form` object, filled from the script's standard input when first accessed, provides similar access for method `POST` calls. The method of HTML production is typical of Python ASP programs because it avoids the need to intermingle Python and HTML.

Listing 16.1 *cgitest.asp:* **A Simple CGI Test Script from the ASP Environment**

```
1  <%@ LANGUAGE="PYTHON" %>
2  <%
3  def _test():
4      import os, sys, os, string
5
6      eol = "\r\n"
7      doc = ['<HTML><HEAD><TITLE>CGI Test App</TITLE></HEAD>\r\n<BODY>']
8      doc.append('<H2>CGI test app</H2><P>')
9      if hasattr(os, 'getpid'):
10         doc.append('<b>pid</b> = %s<br>' % os.getpid())
11     doc.append('<br><b>Query String Data:</b><BR>')
12     for ff in Request.QueryString:
13         doc.append(ff + " : " + Request.QueryString[ff] + "<BR>")
14     doc.append('<HR><P><pre>')
15     keys = os.environ.keys()
16     keys.sort()
17     for k in keys:
18         doc.append('<b>%-20s :</b>  %s' % (k, os.environ[k]))
19     doc.append('\n</pre><HR>')
20     doc.append('</BODY></HTML>')
21
22
23     Response.Write(string.join(doc, '\r\n'))
24
25
26  _test()
27  %>
```

Figure 16.2   Output from `cgitest.asp` running on IIS 4.0 on Windows NT.

The COM objects you can create using `Server.CreateObject()` include ActiveX Data Objects (ADO), now Microsoft's preferred way to access ODBC- and OLEDB-accessible databases. This is a useful way of accessing the ADO model, which some people find more natural than the Python DB API. Because it was designed to integrate into Microsoft operating systems, the ADO model offers features that cannot be made available via ODBC, for example, but that come "out of the box" when using the more advanced OLE drivers.

The three main objects in the ADO object model are `Connection`, `RecordSet`, and `Command`. These can combine together in a confusing number of ways, so most programmers tend to find the way that works most easily for them and stick with that. RecordSets are interesting objects because they can be detached from their data source, modified, and then later reattached and used to update the database. Listing 16.2 shows a simple use of the ADO primitives to retrieve two columns from a table.

Listing 16.2   *adotest.asp:* **Using ADO Objects from Python**

```
 1  <%@ LANGUAGE="PYTHON" %>
 2  <%
 3  def _test():
 4      import os, sys, os, string
 5
 6      eol = "\r\n"
 7      doc = ['<HTML><HEAD><TITLE>ADO Test App</TITLE></HEAD>\r\n<BODY>']
 8      doc.append('<H2>ADO test app</H2><P>')
 9      oConn = Server.CreateObject("ADODB.Connection")
10      oConn.open("prom20", "promuser", "promuser")
11      rs = Server.CreateObject("ADODB.Recordset")
12      rs.Open("SELECT DptCode, DptName FROM department ORDER BY DptName", oConn)
13      rs.MoveFirst()
14      doc.append("<TABLE>")
15      doc.append("<TR><TD><B>Code</B></TD><TD><B>Name</B></TD></TR>")
16      while not rs.EOF:
17          doc.append("<TR><TD>%s</TD><TD>%s</TD></TR>" %
18              (rs.Fields.Item("DptCode"), rs.Fields.Item(1).Value))
19          rs.MoveNext()
20      doc.append('</TABLE>')
21      doc.append('</BODY></HTML>')
22      rs.Close()
23      oConn.Close()
24
25      Response.Write(string.join(doc, eol))
26
27  _test()
28  %>
```

Note that on line 18, two alternative ways are shown to access a field's value. The first uses the field's name as an argument to a call of the record set's Item attribute and relies on the fact that Value is the default attribute. The second uses an explicit numeric argument to specify its position and explicitly requests the Value attribute. The output is shown in a browser window in Figure 16.3.

As I write, Microsoft is enthusiastically promoting its .NET framework, which includes an ADO.NET enhancement to its Active Data Objects technology. It appears that even Microsoft felt that there were too many ways to achieve the same end in ADO because it has rationalized the object model somewhat and removed some of the redundancy. The Visual Basic.NET language, an update to Visual Basic with many backward incompatibilities, removes the idea of default attributes for objects.

Figure 16.3   Output from `adotest.asp` running on the author's NT system.

Xitami Integration with Python

Xitami (`http://www.xitami.com`) is an open-source server, intriguing to those inter-ested in lightweight web processing. Not only does it support web operations, it also includes an FTP server so that you can easily manage your web content remotely. Its design philosophy is to keep the server as small and fast as possible, and to give it as many interesting ways as possible to interact with other components. Xitami is based on SMT multithreading software from iMatix Corporation and has been ported to an amazing number of platforms. As well as supporting UNIX of various flavors, Xitami also runs on Windows NT, 2000, and 9X as well as OS/2 and OpenVMS.

Xitami is an easily maintained product; most operator actions can be performed through the administrative web pages, which are unusually well composed. It handles virtual hosting to serve several web sites from the same IP address and port number, it supports persistent CGI, you can write your own modules using iMatix's libraries, and it also supports the *long-running web process* (LRWP), which gives the server a huge increase in versatility and performance.

Xitami Architecture and Long-Running Web Processes

The basic architecture appears in Figure 16.4. It is quite similar to the standard web server, except that as well as a standard extension API (the ISAPI interface offered by Microsoft's IIS, only available in Xitami on Windows platforms) there is a socket interface to LRWPs. These processes connect and register to serve an application by name with the server. Xitami associates application names with particular paths. If the application name and the path differ, you have to configure the paths in Xitami's configuration file.

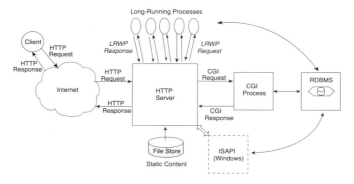

Figure 16.4 Xitami architecture showing long-running web processes.

The parallel FTP server not shown in Figure 16.4 is handy for updating web content, for example, and downloading statistics (yes, Xitami does keep statistics, in several standard and therefore easily analyzed formats).

When the server receives a request for a path matching a registered application, if one or more registered processes is ready, then the request is encoded and passed across the socket connection to a free LRWP serving that application. The process decodes the transmission, computes its result, and sends it back across the socket interface to the Xitami server, which relays it back to the web client. The LRWP then waits for its next request.

The beauty of this scheme is its scalability. Each LRWP can create its own database connections and perform any necessary initialization before it even connects to Xitami to register its availability. Because Xitami is multithreaded, if several LRWPs are registered for the same application, Xitami sends out requests to as many concurrent LRWPs as are currently registered, allowing parallelism at the process level with no per-call startup penalty. Requests that Xitami cannot handle immediately (because all LRWP server processes are busy) sit in a queue, and Xitami passes them out to LRWPs as they become available.

In the absence of a registered process for an application, Xitami simply treats requests as normal and looks for a document in the web filestore in the traditional way. This is useful if you only want to process a given number of requests. If the processing LRWP terminates when it has processed the required number of requests, further clients simply see an HTML or CGI script announcement (whose path is the same as the application's) that the server will accept no further requests. It is also possible to start LRWPs automatically under the control of a CGI script.

The CGI interface is standard, and you should expect a script that runs under Apache to run under Xitami without modification. The core Python `cgi` library module allows you to process the query string or the form contents as necessary. Xitami uses the first line of the CGI script to determine which processor will process it, so on Windows 98, my Xitami CGI scripts all begin with the following line, although you can probably understand that the path can be omitted on a correctly configured server:

```
#! D:/Python20/python
```

You may be wondering about the LRWP interface. This is the wonderful part: a Python LRWP interface module is available as a part of Xitami, and it makes the task of registering a Python process with Xitami and accepting requests very straight-forward. The whole module contains fewer than 300 lines of code (including test code), and after it has registered with Xitami, the LRWP requests look like CGI requests as far as the LRWP process is concerned. It is easy to turn a standard CGI script into an LRWP.

Experiments with Xitami

Xitami is an extremely interesting model for lightweight webs built of cooperating processes. A major example in this chapter is based on Xitami's LRWP model as a typical web speedup technique. To get the most from the example, you would be well-advised to download Xitami and run the code with it. The download is a relatively small one, and Xitami's capability to run on Windows 9X as well as many other platforms makes this a worthwhile exercise for you.

You might find that the `lrwplib.py` module needs editing. In the version I downloaded, line 104 reads

```
self.sock.connect(self.host, self.port)
```

when it should have read

```
self.sock.connect((self.host, self.port))
```

This minor edit reflects a common usage bug in socket connections, where the host and port are separate arguments rather than the elements of a tuple. The socket libraries only stopped accepting these erroneous calls after release 1.5.2. The `lrwplib` module is exceptionally clear code. You should have no trouble understanding it, and I encourage you to read it.

Each copy of Xitami (and many may run on a single host) is configured with a "base port" number. If this is zero, then FTP service appears on port 21, web service on port 80, and LRWP processes connect to port 81. The base port number is added to each of these port numbers, so it is the easy way to adjust your port numbers to avoid conflict with any services you may already have running. You can also configure Xitami to run several virtual hosts and distinguish between requests to the same IP address by the symbolic (DNS) hostname to which they were directed. Finally, different Xitami servers can be attached to different IP addresses on the same machine.

Listing 16.3 shows a simple LRWP program, using the standard lrwplib module to communicate with the local Xitami server whose port base is zero. The URL to access this process will be something like

```
http://hostname/lrtest/
```

If you have chosen some other port base, then you will need to adjust the port number on line 16 and modify the URL to access port 80+ (Xitami base port).

Using Python LRWP Programs with Xitami

When running with a zero port base to give HTTP service on port 80, the Xitami server makes non-standard use of port 81 to listen for connecting long-running web processes. This normally will not matter because the service associated with port 81 is rarely used.

For your LRWP services to be available through Xitami, you must take the following steps:

1. Configure and run the Xitami server.

2. Run one or more copies of the LRWP code, checking that each one successfully attaches to the Xitami server.

3. Access the correct service URL with a suitable web client.

Because they connect to a network socket, the LRWP programs do not need to be installed in any particular directory.

Listing 16.3   *lrwpskel.py:* **A Simple Xitami Long-Running Web Process**

```
1   """A small long-running web process for Xitami.
2
3   Takes a run-time argument and returns this plus a call count
4   each time it is called, terminating after ten calls."""
5
6   import sys
7   myname = sys.argv[1]
8   callcount = 0
9
10  import lrwplib
```

```
11  #
12  # One-time LRWP startup logic: connect to local Xitami
13  # to serve a fixed number of application "lrtest" requests
14  #
15  try:
16      lrwp = lrwplib.LRWP("lrtest", '127.0.0.1', 81, '')
17      lrwp.connect()
18      print "Connected to Xitami"
19      sys.stdout.flush()
20  except:
21      raise # comment this out when connection works
22      sys.exit("Could not start long-running web process.")
23
24  while 1:
25      #
26      # Per-request code
27      #
28      request = lrwp.acceptRequest()      # blocks until server has work
29      query = request.getFieldStorage()   # retrieve task as a CGI call
30      callcount += 1
31      #
32      # Page generation logic
33      #
34      #request.out.write("""Content-Type: text/html\n\n""")
35      request.out.write("""<!DOCTYPE HTML PUBLIC "-//W3C//DTD HTML 3.2➥
        Final//EN">
36      <html>
37      <head>
38      <title>LONG-RUNNING WEB PROCESS %s</title>
39      </head>
40      <body>
41      """ % myname)
42      request.out.write("""<H1>Process %s, call %d</H1>""" % (myname,➥
        callcount))
43      request.out.write("""
44  </body>
45  </html>
46  """)
47      request.finish()
48      if callcount == 10:
49          break
50
51  #
52  # LRWP Process termination
53  #
54  lrwp.close()
```

Connection to the Xitami server is extremely straightforward: create an `lrwplib.LRWP` object, passing it the name (web path) of the application you want to serve and the IP address and port of the server you want to connect to. You should clearly understand that *a Xitami LRWP need not run on the same host as the Xitami server it serves*. This gives additional scalability by allowing application servers to be LAN hosts whose processes do not compete for resources with the web server.

The remainder of the program is a simple loop in which the process waits for a request from Xitami, puts it into a `FieldStorage` object (just like a regular CGI call would do), and produces an HTML response, which in this case is very simple. The server process and its run number are identified to make it easy for a client or clients to know which process is responding.

Initial experiments showed that it was difficult to drive a set of browsers with the mouse in a way that would give meaningful loads on the server and allow you to see the action of Xitami distributing work among a number of LRWPs. You probably will find the client program shown in Listing 16.4 useful for testing: it is a modification of Chapter 6's asynchronous web client. `lrwpcli.py` makes 10 concurrent calls to the same URL and only prints lines coming back from the server that contain `<H1>` HTML tags.

Listing 16.4   *lrwpcli.py:* **An Asynchronous Client for** *lrwpskel.py*

```
 1   import syncope
 2   import socket
 3
 4   class http_client (asyncore.dispatcher):
 5
 6       def __init__ (self, host, path, cnum):
 7           asyncore.dispatcher.__init__ (self)
 8           self.path = path
 9           self.cnum = cnum
10           self.host = host
11           self.wflag = 1
12           self.create_socket (socket.AF_INET, socket.SOCK_STREAM)
13           self.connect ((self.host, 80))
14
15       def handle_connect (self):
16           self.send ('GET %s HTTP/1.0\r\n\r\n' % self.path)
17           self.wflag = 0
18
19       def handle_read (self):
20           data = self.recv (8192)
21           if not data:
22               return ""
23           lines = data.split("\n")
24           for line in lines:
25               if line.find("<H1>") >= 0:
```

```
26                    print "Channel:", self.cnum, ">>>", line
27
28      def handle_close(self):
29          self.close()
30
31      def handle_write (self):
32          return
33
34      def writable(self):
35          return self.wflag
36
37  import sys
38  import urlparse
39  cnum = 0
40  for url in ["http://127.0.0.1/lrtest/"]*10: # or as you please ...
41      parts = urlparse.urlparse (url)
42      if parts[0] != 'http':
43          raise ValueError, "HTTP URL's only, please"
44      else:
45          cnum += 1
46          host = parts[1]
47          path = parts[2]
48          http_client (host, path, cnum)
49  asyncore.loop()
```

You have seen a similar program earlier in the book, when you were studying asynchronous server processes. Line 40 begins a loop that submits 10 requests from the web server and processes the responses from them.

You can vary this script easily for your own testing purposes. Listing 16.5 shows the output from the program when three lrwpskel.py LRWP processes were running.

Listing 16.5 **Output from a Run of** *lrwpcli.py* **with Three Active** *lrwpskel* **Processes**

```
D:\Book1\Code\Ch16>python ashttpcli.py
Channel: 2 >>>       <H1>Process ONE, call 5</H1>
Channel: 5 >>>       <H1>Process TWO, call 4</H1>
Channel: 6 >>>       <H1>Process THREE, call 4</H1>
Channel: 8 >>>       <H1>Process ONE, call 6</H1>
Channel: 4 >>>       <H1>Process TWO, call 5</H1>
Channel: 10 >>>       <H1>Process THREE, call 5</H1>
Channel: 3 >>>       <H1>Process ONE, call 7</H1>
Channel: 7 >>>       <H1>Process TWO, call 6</H1>
Channel: 9 >>>       <H1>Process THREE, call 6</H1>
Channel: 1 >>>       <H1>Process ONE, call 8</H1>
```

Significance of Xitami and Long-Running Web Processes

A Xitami server process accepts registrations from long-running web processes on port 81. Each LRWP registration provides the web path it will serve; this is the first argument to the `lrwplib.LRWP()` call, which parameterizes the connection between the LRWP and the Xitami server. When Xitami receives a request from a web client for a web path served by an LRWP, it passes the request data out to the appropriate LRWP. If the LRWP is busy, then Xitami holds the request in a queue until it can be served.

There is nothing, however, to stop multiple LRWPs registering *to serve the same web path*. In this case, the Xitami server treats the LRWPs serving the same path as a pool: when a request arrives for the path, it need not be queued in Xitami if there is an inactive LRWP available to serve it. Each web path served by LRWPs is therefore scalable, simply by running multiple copies of the LRWP and letting Xitami act as a queuing request multiplexer.

You can think of a group of LRWPs serving the same application as an application group. Each application can be served by as many LRWPs as are required for adequate performance. Different servers can serve the same application group if one or more LRWPs register for the application with each web server. This is not the limit of Xitami's scalability, however. One host can run several instances of Xitami, each using a different base port number. Because the architecture is lean and multithreaded, this does not impose a heavy load on the host processor under quiescent conditions. Each Xitami server can accept registrations from LRWP application servers, so the same application can be served at many different HTTP ports, each by a Xitami server that is time-sharing with the other Xitami servers and the LRWPs.

A host running several copies of Xitami might be represented by the diagram in Figure 16.5: each circle represents a single Xitami server process; the ellipses are LRWPs, labeled with the name of the application they are serving; and a dotted line surrounds the host. This makes it easy to serve the same applications at different ports—and your LRWPs can serve the same or different data sources on different ports or IP addresses. That is just a matter of the initialization code. This gives you a single-host architecture in which you can apply parallelism at the web level (by replicating servers), and at the application level (by replicating LRWPs) to scale up to the level of performance you need. The different server instances can serve webs with different structures, allowing a single computer to host several web sites with a degree of flexibility.

Even this is not the end of the scalability, however: Xitami allows you further room to grow when you have exhausted the resources of a single host. All intercomponent communications in Figure 16.5 (ISAPI extensions, limited to local access, are ignored in the diagram) are network sockets. This means that they could just as easily be running over a LAN, communicating between independent hosts. So a further level of scalability and flexibility can be achieved by extending the architecture to span several machines. In this case, LRWPs can be either local or remote.

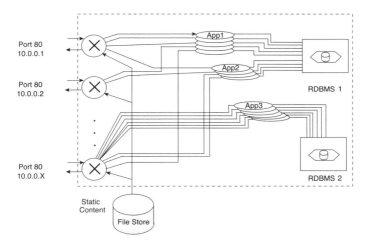

Figure 16.5 Several Xitami servers running on different IP addresses on a single host.

As Figure 16.6 shows, you could then locate your LRWPs where you want them—for example, because they accessed a database for which you had no network drivers—but serve them from any of the machines running Xitami. This multihost architecture is almost frightening in its simplicity and economy. Of course the best part from our point of view is that all the serious application work can now be performed in Python-based CGI scripts and LRWPs. Although Figure 16.6 shows a separate host for each web, application, and database, there is no reason why you cannot partition the tasks for best use of any particular hardware combination. Putting each process on a separate host would probably be a wasteful strategy.

A Simple, Flexible LRWP-Based Application

To give you the flavor of writing database code behind LRWPs, I have put together an example that runs nicely with Xitami. It uses a database to store most of the content, although text templates determine the look-and-feel. This is a slightly error-prone method of generating HTML, but it shows how you can easily achieve stylistic uniformity. You will learn about more structured methods of content generation later in the chapter.

Database Structure

The database structure used is simple: there is one table called `StdPage`, and each row in the table represents a page in the database. The pages are presented as a linked set on the home page and as links in the left-hand navigation bar on the standard page layout. Table 16.2 illustrates the structure.

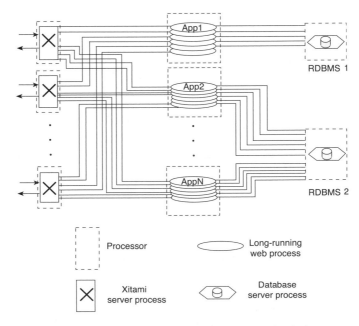

Figure 16.6   Xitami architecture with functions on individual processors.

Table 16.2   **Layout of the *StdPage* Table That Drives the *Xitami1* Database**

Field Name	Data Type	Description
Name	Text	Code used as primary key.
CrDT	Date/Time	Creation timestamp.
MoDT	Date/Time	Modification timestamp.
Num	Number	Defines the ordering of the pages.
PageSet	Text	We are only interested in type Std.
LinkText	Text	Text used in linking and titling the page.
Template	Text	None, or alternative page style.
Content	Long Text	What the user actually sees.

To make the project a little more interesting, you can edit the pages of this web (in other words, the content of the database that generates them) by clicking on a link at the bottom of each of its pages. Only the home page is fixed in content. To run this server, you must have a functioning copy of Xitami running, and you will need to register the HoldenWebSQL data source (if you are using ODBC) or modify the database access code (if you want to use some other module for database access). The book's web site contains a copy of the database used in testing, which you can either use with the Jet driver on Windows or migrate to the engine of your choice on your preferred platform.

The architecture of this application repays some study, and you can run several copies of the LRWP against a single Xitami server to determine whether this improves the application's performance. A modified version of the client program from Listing 16.4 might be helpful in load testing but is left as an exercise.

Application Server Module (appsrv.py)

This section presents the code of the long-running web process that implements the basic service I call a *mini-web server*. For each request it receives, this LRWP calls a page generation routine selected according to the page argument in the URL query string. The page generation logic, being contained in other modules, is described in later sections.

```
 1  #! D:/Python20/python
 2
 3  import mx.ODBC.Windows, cgi, sys
 4  import lrwplib as web
 5  import stdpage
 6  import frmpage
 7
```

This module (which lives with the other code in the xitami1 subdirectory of the web site Chapter 16 code) uses a database and the CGI interface. It is a long-running web process, and it uses two local modules to generate standard and forms-based pages for the web client.

```
 8  #
 9  # One-time LRWP startup logic
10  #
11  try:
12      db = mx.ODBC.Windows.Connect("HoldenWebSQL")
13      CR = db.cursor()
14      print "Connected to database"
15  except:
16      sys.exit("Could not connect to database.")
17  try:
18      lrwp = web.LRWP("xitami1", '127.0.0.1', 81, '')
19      lrwp.connect()
20      print "Connected to Xitami"
21      sys.stdout.flush()
22  except:
23      sys.exit("Could not start long-running web process.")
24
```

Lines 8 through 24 are standard LRWP startup logic, connecting to the database and the Xitami server. Remember that you need to change the port number if you configured Xitami with a port base number other than zero. The LRWP seems to work well with several DB API-compliant driver module and engine combinations.

```
25  while 1:
26      #
27      # Per-request code
28      #
29      request = lrwp.acceptRequest()
30      query = request.getFieldStorage()
31
```

The application server then begins an infinite loop, which starts by getting a request from Xitami and building a `FieldStorage` structure from the query string.

```
32      #
33      # Page generation logic
34      #
35      request.out.write("""<!DOCTYPE HTML PUBLIC "-//W3C//DTD HTML 3.2➥
        Final//EN">
36      <html>
37      <head>
38      <title>Xitami LRWP: Simple Sample App Server</title>
39      </head>
40      <body>
41      """)
42
43      try:
44          PageName = query["page"].value
45      except KeyError:
46          PageName = "default
```

With an unsophisticated approach to content generation, the application simply assumes that all output will be HTML pages with the same title. This is not a brilliant practice, especially since it will confuse people trying to use their browser history when they see a list of pages all called "Xitami LRWP: Simple Sample App Server"! The LRWP retrieves the name of the page from an argument to the URL, so it can generate the required content. If it finds no page name, it reverts to its default page, a generic home page with links to each standard page in the table.

```
47  #
48  # XXX This should really be done by some more elegant
49  # technique, but we are in hack mode just now...
50  #
51      if PageName == "default":
52          r = stdpage.default(query, request, CR)
53      elif PageName == "StdPage":
54          r = stdpage.StdPage(query, request, CR)
55      elif PageName == "FormStdPage":
56          r = frmpage.FormStdPage(query, request, CR)
57      elif PageName == "NewStdPage":
58          r = frmpage.NewStdPage(query, request, CR, db)
59      elif PageName == "UpdateStdPage":
60          r = frmpage.UpdateStdPage(query, request, CR, db)
61      else:
```

```
62              r = "<h2>Page '%s' not found...</h2>" % (PageName, )
63          request.out.write(r)
64          request.out.write("""
65  </body>
66  </html>
67  """)
68          request.finish()
69          if PageName == "Finish":
70              break
71
```

Calling the appropriate page function generates the content. The preceding code is
a straightforward and inelegant way of calling the right function for a particular page
type. Note that the server passes the query and the request through to the page content generator functions: it has no idea which page is to be produced, and it does not
care. There is a "back door" to allow easy termination of the LRWP by setting the
Page argument to Finish. It should be eliminated from a production server because
the last thing you want to do is stop the server on the instructions of J. Random User.

```
72  #
73  # LRWP Process termination
74  #
75  db.close()
76  lrwp.close()
```

If a URL containing Page=Finish as an argument arrives, the server tidies itself up
and terminates. Of course the logic you have just seen implements only the main
application's flow of control. It uses the page generation modules to build the HTML
content that the user sees rendered in the browser window. The annotated source from
the stdpage module follows.

Standard Pages Module (stdpage.py)

Standard pages are those containing only simple HTML content. These pages are conveniently generated by functions defined in the same module because that allows them
to easily share a common look-and-feel, implemented by module-level functions.

```
1  import urllib
2  from dtuple import TupleDescriptor, DatabaseTuple
3
4  StdPageBody = open("text/StdPageBody.txt").read()
5  DefaultBody = open("text/DefaultBody.txt").read()
6
```

The code uses the dtuple module to make it easier to refer to database fields by name
in the code. It reads in the standard page body templates from a text file. You can use
a graphical editor such as FrontPage to generate the look-and-feel if you want, just
dropping in %s strings where the LRWP should insert particular pieces of content
retrieved from the database.

```
 7  #
 8  # Left-Hand Navigation Bar
 9  #
10  def LHNav(ThisPage, CR):
11      dt = TupleDescriptor([["Name"], ["LinkText"], ["Template"]])
12      CR.execute("""SELECT Name, LinkText, Template FROM StdPage
13                      WHERE PageSet='Std' ORDER BY Num""")
14      SP = CR.fetchall()
15      LHNavBar = []
16      for sp in SP:
17          sp = DatabaseTuple(dt, sp)
18          if sp.Template == "None":
19              tname = "StdPage"
20          else:
21              tname = sp.Template
22          if sp.Name != ThisPage:
23              mgtext = """<img src="/HWimages/cblob.gif" border=0 alt=""➡
                width=10 height=8>
24                          <a href="/xitami1/?page=%s&Name=%s">%s</a>""" %➡
                (tname, urllib.quote(sp.Name), sp.LinkText)
25          else:
26              mgtext = """<img src="/HWimages/rblob.gif" width=10 height=8➡
                border=0 alt="">""" + str(sp.LinkText)
27          LHNavBar.append("<nobr>%s</nobr><br><br>" % (mgtext,))
28      LHNavBar = "".join(LHNavBar)
29      return LHNavBar
30
```

The left-hand navigation bar function retrieves three fields for each of the standard pages in the database. It iterates over the retrieved rows, generating a suitable hypertext link for each (except the current page: in this case, a visual flag is used to indicate that it *is* the current page). If a particular page requires a non-standard page style, this can be flagged in the Template column for the page. This feature is not currently used and is not yet implemented elsewhere in the code. It is, however, a convenient way of introducing variety in the appearance of pages generated from a common database.

```
31  #
32  # Default site page
33  #
34  def default(form, req, CR):
35      CR.execute("""SELECT Name, LinkText, Template FROM StdPage
36              WHERE PageSet='Std' ORDER BY Num""")
37      SP = CR.fetchall()
38      ct = 0
39      FtrNavBar = []
40      for sp in SP:
41          template = sp[2]
42          if template == "None": template = "StdPage"
43          FtrNavBar.append("""<nobr>
```

```
44            <img src="/HWimages/cblob.gif"><a➡
              href="/xitami1/?page=%s&Name=%s">\%s</a></nobr> """ %➡
45                (template, urllib.quote(sp[0]), sp[1]))
46        ct = ct + 1
47        if ct == 8:
48            ct = 0
49            FtrNavBar.append("<BR>")
50     return DefaultBody % ("".join(FtrNavBar), )
51
```

The home page for the site uses the `DefaultBody` template, read when the module was initialized. Because it needs to refer to each page, it again uses the database to retrieve the required information. The link generation here is not so smart and needs updating to use the `Template` column in the same way as the left-hand navigation bar. It also would be aesthetically more pleasing to distribute the links evenly across the lines instead of simply breaking after every eight links.

```
52  #
53  # Page Body Builder (XXX UNSOPHISTICATED)
54  #
55  def PageBody(LinkText, LHNav, Content, EditLink=None):
56      if EditLink:
57          Link = """<font size="-3"><center><A HREF="?page=%s">EDIT
58          THIS PAGE</a></center></font>""" % (EditLink, )
59      else:
60          Link = ""
61      return StdPageBody % (LinkText, LHNav, Content, Link)
62
```

All standard page routines call the `PageBody()` function to generate the content they return. Up to four variable elements are passed as arguments. Certain pages are generated "on-the-fly," and these do not provide an `EditLink` argument (since they cannot be edited).

```
63  #
64  # Standard Page
65  #
66  def StdPage(form, req, CR):
67      try:
68          StdPageName = form["Name"].value
69      except KeyError:
70          return "<h2>Name not given for standard page display</h2>"
71      # XXX lines below should be replaced with DatabaseTuple
72      FldList = (['Name'], ['LinkText'], ['PageSet'], ['Num'], ['Content'])
73      dt = TupleDescriptor(FldList)
74      CR.execute("""SELECT Name, LinkText, PageSet, Num, Content
75              FROM StdPage WHERE  Name=? AND PageSet='Std'""",
76                          (StdPageName, ))
77      TP = CR.fetchone()
78      if TP == None:        # Use a page which should always exist
79          CR.execute("""SELECT Name, LinkText, PageSet, Num, Content
```

```
80                    FROM StdPage WHERE Name='ERROR'""")
81        CR.fetchone()
82     rec = DatabaseTuple(dt, TP)
83     LHNavBar = LHNav(StdPageName, CR)
84     return PageBody(rec.LinkText, LHNavBar, rec.Content,↪
       "FormStdPage&Key="+StdPageName)
```

Finally comes the function to generate standard page contents. It extracts the name of the page from the URL if one was given (if not, it simply returns a message to the user, who will doubtless be perplexed). The page name is used to pull the required content from the database, and if the specified page is not found, then a standard ERROR page is pulled from the database instead. If this page is missing, the logic fails horribly. The database fields are then used to generate the page content, which is returned to the application server. Figure 16.7 shows a browser window with a page from the database displayed.

Although the screen dump for Figure 16.7 omitted the cursor, it was actually positioned over the EDIT THIS PAGE link at the foot of the page. You can see in the status bar that this is a hypertext link to the following URL:

```
http://127.0.0.1/xitami1/?page=FormStdPage&Key=hardware
```

If you click on this link, then you start to invoke pages from the frmpage module, whose listing you will find in the next section.

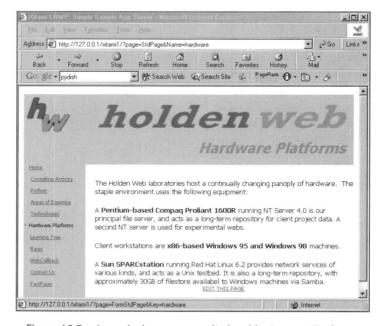

Figure 16.7 A standard appsvr page displayed by Internet Explorer.

Form Pages Module (**frmpage.py**)

```
1   from dtuple import TupleDescriptor, DatabaseTuple
2   import pyforms
3   import pySQL
4   import stdpage
5
```

This module in turn uses two others, pyforms and pysql, for which there is no
detailed discussion in this chapter. You covered the basics of form generation in
Chapter 11, "Adapting the Python Interface to Database Products," and the generation
of SQL statements is rather unsophisticated. If you have any questions, use the source,
Luke! Bear in mind as you do so that these were early implementation prototypes,
so I do not recommend them as examples of best practice. They do perform as
required, however, and you might find them useful (if a little inflexible) in other
contexts. Functions from the stdpage module generate simple "on-the-fly" pages
for error messages.

The first function in this module uses a form generator driven by a form description to build the page content. The form is populated from the database or with blank
data depending on the URL that triggered it.

```
6   #
7   # Form for Standard Page Update
8   #
9   def FormStdPage(form, req, CR):
10      result = [ """
11      <h4>Edit or Show Any Standard Page</h4>
12      <table cellpadding="2">
13
14      """]
15
16      try:
17          KeyVal = form["Key"].value
18      except KeyError:
19          KeyVal = None
20      if KeyVal == None:     # Bare call to page gets list of pages
21          Stmt = "SELECT Name, LinkText, Num from StdPage WHERE PageSet =➥
                'Std' ORDER BY Num"
22          CR.execute(Stmt)
23          records = CR.fetchall()
24          dt = TupleDescriptor(([ 'Name'],['LinkText'],['Num']))
25          for r in records:
26              RS = DatabaseTuple(dt, r)
27              result.append('<tr><td>%s</td> <td>%s</td><td>%d</td><td><a➥
                href="?page=FormStdPage&Key=%s"> Edit</a></td><td><a➥
                href="?page=StdPage&Name=%s"> Show</a></td></tr>\r\n'➥
28                              % (RS.LinkText, RS.Name, RS.Num, RS.Name,➥
                                RS.Name))
29          result.append("""
30          </table>
```

```
31              <BR><a href="?page=FormStdPage&Key=*CREATE*"> ***CREATE NEW➡
                RECORD***</a><BR>\r\n""")
32      else:
33          if KeyVal == "*CREATE*":
34              RS = None
35          else:
36              Stmt = "SELECT Name, PageSet, Num, LinkText, Template, Content➡
                FROM StdPage WHERE name=?"
37              CR.execute(Stmt, (KeyVal, ))
38              record = CR.fetchone()
39              dt = TupleDescriptor((['Name'],['PageSet'],['Num'],➡
                ['LinkText'],['Template'],['Content']))
40              RS = DatabaseTuple(dt, record)
41          Flist = (
42              # Note options MUST now be a string, not None
43              ["Comment1", "Web Page Details", "REM", "+2", ""],
44              ["Name", "Page Name", "KSA", 20, "R"],
45              ["PageSet", "Page Set Name", "T", 20, "R"],
46              ["Num", "Page Number", "N", 5, ""],
47              ["LinkText", "Link Text", "T", 30, ""],
48              ["Template", "Template Name", "T", 30, ""],
49              ["Content", "Page Content", "M", (10, 60), "R"]
50          )
51          result.append(pyforms.FormBuild(Flist, "StdPage", "name",➡
                str(KeyVal), RS))
52      return "".join(result)
53
```

This is a multifunction page. If it is called without specifying the page to be edited (that is, the URL contains no Key argument), then lines 21 through 31 generate a list of the pages in the database, each linked with the Page and Key arguments to edit that page. A link to display each page's content also is included, to allow users to check what they are going to edit and to return easily to the main web content.

If the URL included a Key argument, then lines 33 through 51 generate a form, populated with the contents of the specified database record. The argument value "*CREATE*" is an instruction to display an empty form instead. Here most of the work is done by the pyforms.FormBuild() routine, driven by the form description bound to the Flist variable. Figure 16.8 shows a browser displaying a form, after I clicked on the EDIT THIS PAGE link in Figure 16.7. The form page itself could have conformed to the look-and-feel of the other pages, but this seemed unnecessary.

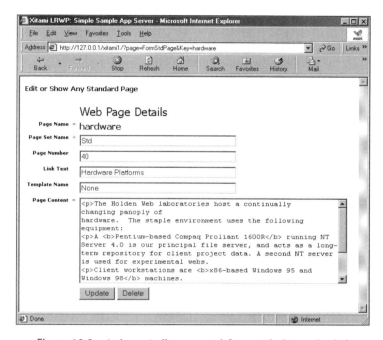

Figure 16.8   A dynamically generated form with data preloaded.

The form that is generated uses different actions according to its function. The form's action attribute is not specified in the <FORM> tag because all pages in this web have the same URL and simply differ in their `Page` and `Name` argument values. The form therefore contains a hidden field that sets the `Page` argument to `NewStdPage`. The `lrwplib getFieldStorage()` method generates the `FieldStorage` from the query string for a `GET` method call and from the standard input for a `POST`. When acting on an existing record (whether update or deletion is being requested), the form's `Page` input will contain `UpdateStdPage`, which can handle both updates and deletions (according to which Submit button was clicked). This effectively selects one action routine for page creation and a different one for update and delete.

```
54   #
55   # New Standard Page
56   #
57   def NewStdPage(form, req, CR, db):
58       try:
```

```
59          Flist = eval(form["#Flist#"].value)
60          KeyVal = form["#KeyVals#"].value
61      except KeyError:
62          return "<H4>Could not access #Flist# or #KeyVals#</H4>"
63      if KeyVal != "*CREATE*":
64          return """<H4>ERROR: New Called with Key Value!</h4>"""
65      else:
66          Stmt = pySQL.SQLInsert(form, "StdPage", Flist, "" ,"", "")
67      result = ["<BR>SQL IS: %s" % (Stmt, )]
68      try:
69          CR.execute(Stmt)
70          db.commit()
71      except:
72          db.rollback()
73          return stdpage.PageBody("Database Operation Error",
74                          stdpage.LHNav(KeyVal, CR),
75                          "Sorry, unable to create this page")
76      result.append("""
77      <h2>StdPage %s Created</h2>
78      <BR>
79      <A HREF="?page=%s">Back to Page List</A>
80      """ % (form["Name"].value, "FormStdPage"))
81      return "".join(result)
82
```

The pyforms module actually cheats a little bit. It passes the form description (which it received as an argument) across to the processing page as a hidden field of the form, as it does with the key value. This technique is not recommended for public use. A malevolent user would be able to decode all this and modify the form description. You might improve the security by encrypting these values using a key known only to the program, or by retaining this value on the server using some kind of session-state mechanism. It would be even better practice to store the forms descriptions as a part of the database and simply pass database key values between successive pages.

Further, pyforms relies on the form field value to be a Python expression, which it evaluates to recover the form description. This practice is even more dangerous because the aforementioned malevolent user would be able to spoof an HTTP request that caused the server to execute arbitrary Python code!

The mechanism is convenient, of course. However, in an environment where your network's security is potentially at risk, convenience should not be a factor. If you are worried about the security implications of this code, note that you will learn solutions to these problems in Chapter 17, "AWeFUL: An Object-Oriented Web Site Framework," and Chapter 18, "A Web Application—PythonTeach.com."

The NewStdPage function generates a SQL INSERT statement using the pySQL library and executes it. It generates a failure page and rolls back the current transaction if the execution raises any exceptions. If it succeeds, then you can see the SQL statement in the HTML output for debug purposes. A final link allows the user to navigate back to the list of pages for more editing work or to return to page viewing.

```
83  #
84  # Update Standard Page
85  #
86  def UpdateStdPage(form, req, CR, db):
87      Operation = str(form["Submit"].value)
88      Flist = eval(str(form["#Flist#"].value))
89      KeyVal = str(form["#KeyVals#"].value)
90      if Operation == "Update":
91          Stmt = pySQL.SQLUpdate(form, "StdPage", (("Name","S"),), (KeyVal,),➥
                Flist, "")
92          which = "StdPage&Name=" + KeyVal
93          pp = "Updated Page"
94      elif Operation == "Delete":
95          Stmt = pySQL.SQLDelete("StdPage", (("Name","S"),), (KeyVal,))
96          which = "default"
97          pp = "Home Page"
98      try:
99          CR.execute(Stmt)
100         db.commit()
101     except:
102         db.rollback()
103         return stdpage.PageBody("Database Operation Error",
104                     stdpage.LHNav(KeyVal, CR),
105                     "Sorry, unable to update this page's details")
106     return stdpage.PageBody("%s Completed" % (Operation, ),
107                 stdpage.LHNav(KeyVal, CR),
108                     """
109     <h2>Page %s %sd</h2>
110     <!-- <BR>SQL IS: %s<BR> -->
111     <BR>
112     <A HREF="?page=%s">Show %s Page</A>
113     """ % (KeyVal, Operation, Stmt, which, pp),
114                         None)
```

The UpdateStdPage function handles both updates and deletions, and deduces the required function from the value of the Submit button the user pressed. The routine generates the correct SQL statement (look in PySQL.py if you want to know how) and runs it to update the database. Finally, it generates a page that informs the user that it has made the requested update and offers a link to the updated page.

Forms and SQL Generation Modules (pyforms.py *and* pySQL.py)

The only routine intended for public consumption in the pyforms module is FormBuild, which has a long list of arguments, some of which are complex in structure. When you call

```
FormBuild (List, Action, KeyNames, KeyVals, R=None
```

FormBuild() should return a complete HTML form. The first argument is a form description of the sort you saw in the frmpage module: a tuple holding a name, a description, a field type, a size, and some options represents each field in the form.

The `Action` argument is appended to either `New` or `Update` and used as the value of the form's `ACTION` attribute. This will select the appropriate processing function as described previously. `KeyNames` and `KeyVals` are two lists of equal length, passed in the form as hidden fields to allow the required database update to take place after the form is filled out (another security risk). Finally, `R` is a data row, which might have been read in from a database or pulled from a form currently being processed. For new data, you should use the default value rather than passing a data row.

The `pySQL` module defines three functions: `SQLInsert`, `SQLUpdate`, and `SQLDelete`. The argument lists for these functions are long, possibly longer than strictly necessary.

```
SQLInsert(Form, TableName, Fields, iFlds, iVals, Prefix)
```

Here the `Form` argument is the form data, which should be a `DatabaseTuple`, generated from either a `FieldStorage` object containing forms input from a web client, or from a database row.

The individual fields need only be accessible using subscripting by name, so you could use a dictionary if you chose. `TableName` is, as you would expect, the name of the database table on which to operate. The `Fields` argument is the form description as used by the forms pages: the first item of each tuple is used as a field name; other elements determine whether the field is included in the SQL statement and, if so, how it is processed.

The `iFlds` and `iVals` arguments hold the names and values of any other fields that need to be included in the `INSERT` statement, and the `Prefix` argument is a simple string you can use to select processing of only a subset of the data in the form whose names all begin with the prefix.

```
def SQLUpdate(Form, TableName, KeyNames, KeyVals, Fields, Prefix
```

This function uses the same `Form` and `TableName` arguments as `SQLInsert()`, but these are followed by a list of key names and values (which together should uniquely specify a single row of the table if just one row is to be updated, as is normally the case). The `Fields` and `Prefix` arguments again describe the form contents and determine which fields should be processed.

```
def SQLDelete(table, KeyNames, KeyVals)
```

This function generates a SQL `DELETE` statement, using arguments described previously. Again, the key names and values should ideally specify a unique row in the table, but if you know what you are doing (and if you are careful), you can use `SQLDelete` and `SQLUpdate` in other contexts to generate statements affecting multiple rows.

Architectural Weaknesses of the Xitami Sample

Probably the most obvious, and perhaps the most disappointing, thing about this server is its failure to use the object-oriented parts of Python. It defines no classes and creates relatively few objects. The procedural style of the code is easy to understand, but the execution sequence for any given page request is linear. There may be other, more efficient ways to organize this or similar code.

Because the LRWPs are not maintaining state, they are simple, and any LRWP in a set can handle any incoming request for any page in an application. When the LRWPs need a context for a particular set of page accesses, then the state data has to be stored somewhere all the processes can access it because Xitami takes no notice of state when handing out work to a set of LRWPs all registered for the same application.

The best way to manage web session-state information is for the server to return a cookie, whose value represents a session-specific key value, to the browser. When the browser sends further requests, it returns the cookie, and the server can use it to locate the state data for the browser's session. It is *not* appropriate to use cookies for large quantities of data for three reasons: first, because this will use unnecessary network bandwidth; second, because browsers place limits on the number and size of cookies they will store; and third, because the information is much less secure when transmitted over the network than when it is stored on the server.

Much of the data retrieved from the database is purely structural: it appears in navigation bars, lists of links, and so on. In most sites, this type of data is unlikely to change with any frequency, so it would make sense for the application server to cache a copy, refreshing it infrequently. No such sophistication appears here, however. To keep the code simple, everything is read from the database as it is needed.

Zope Integration with Python

Zope (www.zope.org) is probably the closest thing there currently is to the Python "killer app." The question of Python integration is almost trivial because Zope itself is written entirely in Python. Whenever someone asks for a list of large Python applications, Zope is always among the first to be mentioned. Zope is an object-oriented web framework whose ZServer core server module is built on the Medusa architecture you looked at in Chapter 7, "Asynchronous Services," but there is a huge amount more to the system. The Python integration is therefore a given, and Zope (formerly Digital Creations) employs the team who maintains the Python core.

You maintain and administer Zope content using web and/or FTP access, so you can perform these tasks as easily from a remote location as locally. It is an open-source product, so after you master its complexities, it is extremely cost-effective, and of course if you are even more ambitious, then you can extend it with your own custom code. Indeed, several books either newly published or shortly to appear, will help you make sense of this complex software. Here I will only try to sketch the briefest outline, to try to show you what Zope can do in broad terms. If you need more in-depth understanding, try *The Zope Book* by Amos Latteier and Michael Pellatier (© 2002 New Riders).

Zope is based around a transactional object database, ZODB, maintained by Andrew Kuchling. This database allows you to specify a set of changes as a single transaction and to undo them all as a whole rather than individually. Each object in the database maps to a URL, and vice versa, reflecting the underlying philosophy that the web is object-oriented.

You specify the content of a Zope site largely in DTML, an HTML-like tagged markup language. DTML allows you to safely script your content based on the Zope objects available in the context of the current URL. Because the content is in a hierarchy, it is possible to write a DTML description of your site's look-and-feel at the top of the tree and have it cascade down to affect all pages that do not explicitly override it. Security of a fine-grained nature applies to all Zope objects, and again a security setting established at the top of the tree will cascade downward unless over-ridden. This general capability to build the environment from the top down is called *acquisition* in Zope terminology.

Acquisition is similar in principle to the concept of inheritance as implemented in object-oriented systems but rather different in practice. The relationship between a class and its subclasses is statically determined, whereas acquisition relationships are determined by containment. Zope objects can implement services, and when objects are placed inside a folder, the folder acquires the capability to provide the services implemented by the objects, and the objects acquire all the services of the folder. Because folders are also Zope objects, they acquire services from their containing folders, in the same way as subclasses inherit methods and attributes from their base classes.

Other objects in the Zope object tree can be SQL methods, which specify sets of relational data. These too can be used in DTML, giving good integration with external data sources. You can also drop `Zcatalog` objects into the object tree, which enable indexing of arbitrary content underneath the object whether it is relational data, DTML, email messages, or LDAP data.

To facilitate development, there can be several *Versions* of a given Zope system, which are independently maintained in the object database. This means that several developers can each be working on their own Version without affecting other developers or the user community. The Version can thus be debugged and tested for stability in isolation from other changes that may be taking place. When everything is approved, the Version can be checked in, making it visible to the user community at large.

Webware

Webware (`http://webware.sourceforge.net/`) is a Python web application suite designed by Chuck Esterbrook and others to help produce web applications that are object-oriented, cached, and multithreaded. The components are designed to work together, although some of them can be used independently, and the package typically uses standard technologies such as servlets and server pages, which are already familiar to many web developers. All components are open-source, and the project has spent a lot of time ensuring that the documentation is helpful and to the point. The installation was simple (after a fight with a recalcitrant path setting), and using Xitami as the base web server, I soon saw the WebKit page shown in Figure 16.9.

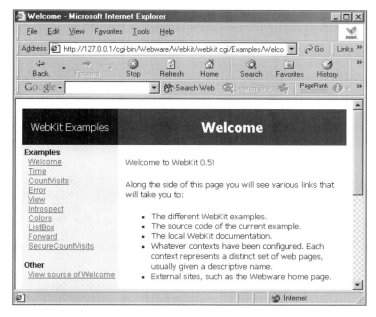

Figure 16.9   A WebKit page soon after Webware installation.

Among the nicer features of the online documentation is the object hierarchy listing, which contains links to a summary of, and to the complete source for, each class.

WebKit is the central component of Webware, and it allows the Python programmer to work with applications, servlets, requests, responses, and transactions. The application is a server-side entity, which receives incoming requests and delivers them to servlets. The servlets in turn produce responses, which the server returns to the client. Transactions hold references to all the other types of objects and are accessible to them all. The application therefore bears some resemblance to a Xitami long-running web process. After you have installed Webware, you must run the application server before the Webware components can be activated.

In the simplest installations, and for testing, your requests are passed to the application server by the `webkit.cgi` script. As well as the standard CGI adapter, which is the easiest way to get Webware started, there are also adapters for FastCGI, `mod_python`, and `mod_snake` as well as a native `mod_webkit` for Apache. Unlike CGI scripts, these adapters stay resident in memory, providing a significant performance increment. There is currently no LRWP adapter, which would be a nice enhancement for Xitami users.

To give you the flavor of Webware pages, Listing 16.6 shows you the source of a secure page counter. This defines a subclass of `SecurePage`, which requires only the `writeContent()` method to complete its functionality.

Listing 16.6 **A Secure Page Counter in Webware**

```
 1 from SecurePage import SecurePage
 2
 3 class SecureCountVisits(SecurePage):
 4     def writeContent(self):
 5         count = self.session().value('num_visits', 0)+1
 6         self.session().setValue('num_visits', count)
 7         if count>1:
 8             plural = 's'
 9         else:
10             plural = ''
11         self.writeln("<p> You've been here %d time%s." % (count, plural))
12         self.writeln('<p> This page records your visits using a session➧
           object. Every time you RELOAD or revisit this page, the counter will➧
           increase. If you close your browser, then your session  will end and➧
           you will see the counter go back to 1 on your next visit.')
13         self.writeln('<p> Try hitting RELOAD now.')
14         user = self.getLoggedInUser()
15         if user:
16             self.writeln('<p> Authenticated user is %s.' % user)
17         self.writeln('<p> <a href="SecureCountVisits">Revisit this page</a>➧
                    <a href="SecureCountVisits?logout=1">Logout</a>')
18
```

Among other components included with Webware are

- **PSP (Python Server Pages)**—Allows you to use an ASP-like syntax to mingle Python code and HTML. (PSP is described later in this chapter.)

- **ComKit**—Lets you use COM objects in a multithreaded web context, giving access to a wide range of ActiveX components.

- **TaskKit**—Gives you tools to schedule tasks at repeated intervals, or at specific times.

- **MiddleKit**—For building the "middle tier" (the application-specific objects implementing business rules) of multitier applications, which communicates with both the web front end and a back-end data repository.

- **UserKit**—Handles the management of a user base, including their passwords and related data.

- **CGI Wrapper**—Allows you to easily import "legacy" CGI code into your Webware environment.

- **WebUtils**—Includes common functions for a variety of web-related tasks.

The major feature of the Webware application server is its capability to dispatch web requests to be handled by Python objects. In this respect, it closely parallels the Zope architecture; although it is more lightweight, the coupling between its components is looser, and it is therefore easier for Python programmers to dip into.

More advanced developers may enjoy Webware's "plug-in" architecture and servlet factories, which make extending Webware feasible. An increasing number of plug-ins and patches, accessible via the Webware home page and mailing list, have sprung up over time. There is also built-in support for servlets that handle XML-RPC, and the design allows for the addition of protocols besides HTTP. The product is supported by an active developer group and has been used to support a number of professional intranet and public web sites already. It is one of the more hopeful signs in the current Python web server world.

HTML (and XML) Generation

There are as many ways to generate HTML in Python as there are to persuade Python scripts to interact with a web server. Some approaches are more complete, some better known, than others. A first stopping point might be `http://www.python.org/topics/web/HTML.html`, which lists some possibilities but by no means all.

The Python world is full of projects that start, show promising results, and then run out of steam before all the loose ends are tied up and the whole packaged up for convenient use. When it comes to HTML generation, the situation is no different, with some initially promising packages still in alpha after two years lying fallow and release numbers between 0.1 and 0.5 quite common. I suspect that sometimes this is due to the 80/20 rule, which suggests that you can get 80 percent of the return on a project for 20 percent of the investment. When you are writing open-source code, the last 20 percent can seem not worth four times the effort to date, particularly if other projects are further along.

Whether there is any way to stop such duplication of effort is another question. Web sites such as SourceForge and FreshMeat do a good job of publicizing projects in need of assistance, but many other projects are undertaken independently. At least those who start a project but do not complete it have learned a lot about writing software, besides picking up some programming technique. It takes more than just a good programmer to bring a project to completion.

Despite these gloomy ponderings, there are some exceptionally bright spots in the HTML landscape and some approaches you should know about whether you intend to adopt them or choose a "roll-out-your-own" approach. Because of their diversity it is only possible to pick a representative sample. You will find many other tools on the web that do similar things, and the ones you read about here are simply the best-known.

Programmed Techniques

The most flexible way to generate HTML is by writing code (Python, naturally), so this first section outlines the most popular way of doing that. These systems are equally suitable for producing static content but are not limited to that role.

HTMLgen

This module (found at
`http://starship.python.net/crew/friedrich/HTMLgen/html/main.html`) is probably
the best-known way of generating HTML. It defines an object hierarchy that closely
parallels the hierarchy of HTML elements. Each object is capable of rendering itself in
HTML, which it does when you call its __str__() method. Because the print statement also calls this method, you can generate a whole document by assembling components, appending the components to the document, and printing the document.
This outputs the required HTML. Here is a simple interactive example:

```
>>> import HTMLgen
>>> lst = HTMLgen.List()
>>> lst.append("hello")
>>> lst.append("everybody run!")
>>> lst.append("goodbye")
>>> print lst
<UL>
<LI>hello
<LI>everybody run!
<LI>goodbye
</UL>
```

The general approach is to create some sort of document and then append content to
it until you have assembled the whole page. You can build the content in chunks, in
the same way as the preceding list. HTMLgen also allows you to use several different
base objects for your document, including a SeriesDocument. This last is an interesting
object because you can parameterize the characteristics of a whole series of documents
in an initialization file and even link the set with pointers to "up," "previous," "next,"
and "home" documents of every page. This makes it easy to build coherent document
sets composed of static content.

Albatross

Albatross (`http://www.object-craft.com.au/projects/albatross`) is a small open-
source toolkit for constructing highly stateful web applications. The toolkit includes an
extensible HTML templating system similar to Zope DTML. Although templates can
be used standalone, Albatross also provides an application framework. A number of different mixin classes enable applications to be deployed either as CGI programs or, to
improve efficiency, via mod_python. Application state can be stored either at the server
or client. Albatross uses distutils for installation and provides a reasonably complete
programming guide that covers all toolkit features.

Listing 16.7 is a simple CGI program that uses Albatross templates to display the
CGI process environment. It creates a SimpleContext object in line 5 and on line 8
makes the os.environ dictionary available to the template under the name environ.

Listing 16.7   **A Simple Albatross CGI Script**

```
 1  #!/usr/bin/python
 2  import os
 3  import albatross
 4
 5  ctx = albatross.SimpleContext('.')
 6  templ = ctx.load_template('showenv.html')
 7
 8  ctx.locals.environ = os.environ
 9
10  templ.to_html(ctx)
11  print 'Content-Type: text/html'
12  print
13  ctx.flush_html()
```

The templating system uses the `locals` member of the execution context as the local namespace for evaluating Python expressions. You can see in Listing 16.8 that the template iterates over the `os.environ` dictionary, which is accessible inside the template as a result of line 8 of Listing 16.7.

Listing 16.8   **Accessing Execution Context in an Albatross Template**

```
 1  <html>
 2   <head>
 3    <title>The CGI environment</title>
 4   </head>
 5   <body>
 6    <table>
 7     <al-exec expr="keys = environ.keys(); keys.sort()">
 8     <al-for iter="name" expr="keys">
 9      <tr>
10       <td><al-value expr="name.value()"></td>
11       <td><al-value expr="environ[name.value()]"></td>
12      <tr>
13     </al-for>
14    </table>
15   </body>
16  </html>
```

When you use Albatross to build an application, the execution context becomes the session object, and each page is implemented by a Python page module (or object) plus one or more template files. Each page module contains a `page_process()` function to handle browser requests and a `page_display()` function to generate the response. Listing 16.9 is the `login.py` page module from the Albatross `popview` example application.

Listing 16.9 *login.py* **from Albatross's** *popview* **Example**

```
1 import poplib
2
3 def page_process(self, ctx):
4     if ctx.req_equals('login'):
5         if ctx.locals.username and ctx.locals.passwd:
6             try:
7                 ctx.open_mbox()
8                 ctx.add_session_vars('username', 'passwd')
9             except poplib.error_proto:
10                return
11            ctx.set_page('list')
12
13 def page_display(self, ctx):
14    ctx.run_template('login.html')
```

Ad Hoc Methods

If you do not have too much HTML to generate, and it is not important to be able to update the style of a set of pages with a single change, the techniques used in previous web examples in the book might be acceptable. Just parameterize HTML snippets with Python formatting symbols and use the string formatting (%) operator to insert the variable content you need. This technique certainly works for small webs, but the larger the web and the greater the amount of content, the more difficult this approach is to maintain. You need to be systematic if your approach is to scale up to large webs, so you should usually reserve *ad hoc* methods for experimentation, or for smaller systems where the work does not become too tedious.

Templating Tools

Sometimes there is simply too much detail in the HTML of a site to program it directly. This certainly applies when you want to take advantage of the visual effects of the newest WYSIWYG HTML generators but insert your own content inside the frameworks they produce. For these and other reasons the technique of filling in a template with variable content is a popular one, and many authors have produced useful results this way.

Cheetah

Cheetah (`http://www.cheetahtemplate.org/`) is an interesting template utility that can be used with equal facility to generate HTML, XML, PostScript, and any number of other formats. Four main principles guide its design:

- Easy *separation* of content, code, and graphic design
- Easy *integration* of content, code, and graphic design

- Limit complexity, and use programming for difficult cases
- Easily understood by non-programmers

The simple example from the Cheetah documentation shown in Listing 16.10 gives you the idea.

Listing 16.10 **A Simple Cheetah HTML Definition**

```
 1 <HTML>
 2 <HEAD><TITLE>$title</TITLE></HEAD>
 3 <BODY>
 4
 5 <TABLE>
 6 #for $client in $clients
 7 <TR>
 8 <TD>$client.surname, $client.firstname</TD>
 9 <TD><A HREF="mailto:$client.email">$client.email</A></TD>
10 </TR>
11 #end for
12 </TABLE>
13
14 </BODY>
15 </HTML>
```

You can see that the dollar sign triggers variable substitution. Cheetah calls strings with these leading dollar signs *placeholders*. The placeholders are arbitrary Python expressions (with some syntax modifications to adapt to non-programmer use), which Cheetah evaluates when it renders the template. In very broad terms, a Cheetah template takes a definition such as the one in Listing 16.10 and a namespace (which is a Python dictionary). When you tell the template to render, it uses the namespace as the evaluation context for any placeholders it comes across in the definition. As with the UNIX shell, the placeholder following the dollar sign can be surrounded by braces to separate it from surrounding text if no spaces can be inserted.

An interesting design decision, based on the requirement that Cheetah be comprehensible to non-programmers, was to represent dictionary lookup by name qualification. Thus, if the namespace contained a variable client, which was bound to a dictionary such as {"firstname": "Steve", "surname": "Holden", "email": "sholden@holdenweb.com"}, then the previous example would access the elements of the dictionary. You can still use subscripting if you want, but most non-programmers find the qualified name notation much easier to work with.

For more complex data structures, the namespace used in a template can actually be a *search list*, which is a sequence of namespaces that Cheetah searches in turn until the required definition is found. This simple technique allows the creation of templates with a hierarchy of namespaces. Further, a placeholder can evaluate to another template, which is then itself evaluated, allowing Cheetah templates to be easily nested inside one another.

As you can observe in Listing 16.10, you can also include *directives* preceded by a pound sign. Some of these are Python statement constructs, interpreted much as you would expect. Others are specific constructs not related to Python. There are also macro definition facilities, which are beyond the scope of this short description. These features give you access to Python for anything that is too complex to perform using the standard placeholder features.

The Webware project has adopted Cheetah as its standard for template substitution of content. Although the software is still in beta at the time of writing, it is already stable and easy to use either with or without Webware. It looks as though Cheetah will be useful to many web projects, as well as any others that need flexible template substitution of a general nature.

Python Server Pages (PSP)

Confusingly, there are at least two systems going by the name of *Python Server Pages*, which should be no surprise. The version by Kirby Angell at `http://www.ciobriefings.com/psp/` comes with a long license I did not have time to read and appears to combine Jython (or is it *really* JPython) with a servlet engine.

The *PSP for Webware* engine at `http://writewithme.com/Webware/PSP/Documentation/PSP.html`, whose primary author is Jay Love, declares itself on its home page to be open-source and therefore commanded attention rather more immediately. From now on, this is what I refer to when I mention PSP, but I cannot determine whether the name has any trademark status.

PSP processes three special constructs:

- `<%@ ... %>`—**Directives**   `import` allows you to import other Python modules. `extends` defines the base class of the current page, in the spirit of Java. `method` is used to define new methods of the class being defined by the current file. Various other directives are concerned with Webware organization, and, finally, `include` is pretty obvious.

- `<%= ... %>`—**Expressions**   In a similar vein to ASP, the engine replaces such constructs with the value of the bracketed expression.

- `<% ... %>`—**Script blocks**   These can span several lines, and three reserved variables are defined for use inside the blocks: `res` the response object, including a `write()` method; `req` the request object, containing web inputs; `trans` the transaction object, which provides a context for successive Webware page inter-actions handled by the same servlets.

Because PSP actually generates a Webware method body, normal text (not a directive, expression, or script block) gets wrapped in code that sends it out through the server. The code in script blocks is copied verbatim into the method. There is a special `<end>` tag you can use to close an indented Python suite that spans multiple script blocks.

Yaptu

Yaptu, by Alex Martelli, (available at URL
`http://aspn.activestate.com/ASPN/Cookbook/Python/Recipe/52305`) stands for
"Yet Another Python Templating Utility." Like Cheetah, it is not specifically geared
to HTML, but rather suited to any kind of text-based document (for example, RTF,
LaTeX, even plain text, as well as HTML and so on). Unlike Cheetah, Yaptu does
not alter Python syntax. Yaptu lets the user define which specific regular expressions
denote a placeholder (an arbitrary Python expression) and the beginning, continuation, and end of arbitrary Python statements. This ensures that Yaptu markup can
indeed be used for any kind of document, since the regular expressions can be chosen
to avoid any conflict with the syntax of the language of that document.

Yaptu's main claim to fame is that, despite its generality, net of comments, and
docstrings, it comprises just 50 lines of code—lightweight enough to carry around
wherever needed. This requires a compromise: if a Python clause to be embedded as
Yaptu markup ends with a colon (such as an `if condition:`, for example), it must
not be followed by a comment; if a clause does not end with a colon (such as a `break`
statement, for example), it *must* be followed by a comment. If such restrictions, or
some aspect of Python syntax, should prove unacceptable for a given application, Yaptu
supplies two "hooks" making it easy for the application programmer to tailor things
further. The application programmer can pass a "preprocessor" routine that gets a
chance to manipulate all Yaptu-markup strings (expressions and statements) before
Python sees them; and, for expressions only, a "handler" routine, that gets a chance
to return a result and continue the templating process if an exception is raised while
evaluating an expression.

Together with the capability to supply Yaptu with an arbitrary mapping to be
used for "variable values" and arbitrary objects playing the roles of "input" (sources)
and "output" (targets), Yaptu packs quite a punch for such a small and simple utility.
It is instructive to examine the richly commented and documented source, and the
internals-oriented discussion, at the previously mentioned "Python Cookbook" URL.

User Interaction Control

An important requirement is to be able to define interactions with the user in much
the same way that you define interactions between software components. You have to
be more careful with users, of course, since their behaviors are not programmed, and
you can therefore expect them to provide dangerous operating systems commands
as first and last names simply in the hope of seeing what they can provoke. If you
examined the `pyforms` form handling module and the `pySQL` module for the Xitami
example earlier in this chapter, you are now aware of a number of data-driven
approaches to forms handling (and of some of the attendant risks).

If a forms handling machine is sufficiently flexible, then all it really needs is an
adequate description of the form contents and a knowledge of its place in a workflow
that specifies how each form is processed and what interactions take place with

databases along the way. The work I have described in this area should have led you to expect a movement toward storing forms descriptions as relational data. To date, I have not found an existing package that does this. Others have developed libraries of varying degrees of sophistication, but nothing that would persuade me to leave the homegrown system I find so easy to use. Perhaps I will be able to incorporate database-driven forms handling in later versions.

One technology I *am* keeping an eye on, though, is *XML Forms for Webware*, a package under construction by Paul Boddie, whose name you read at the start of the chapter as the compiler of a web technology list. The package can be downloaded from `http://thor.prohosting.com/~pboddie/`. The documentation is much more detailed than most treatments of user interaction and addresses issues of state management as well as other development and maintenance techniques. Because Webware servlets are persistent, a servlet can include a description of the form it is processing as a part of its state. This makes it simpler to repeat the form with selective error messages if some inputs do not meet verification or validation criteria. That Paul chose Webware as his platform underlines the architecture's flexibility.

Component Interaction: Choose Your Model

Finally, you should consider how the various components of your web framework are going to interact. Some frameworks, such as Webware and Xitami, include facilities for interaction between their components. You can always use socket programming for such interactions, but this has two potential disadvantages. The first is simply the amount of programming required, and the second is the lack of generality.

If your components need to communicate with others, there are two systems in general use that are designed to facilitate such interactions, and another two newer ones that focus on the use of a combination of XML and HTTP. Because they are all complex, it is only possible to give the briefest of outline to close this chapter.

The Common Object Request Broker Architecture (CORBA)

CORBA is a heterogeneous system for locating and using services in a networked environment. It is an open standard maintained by the Object Management Group (OMG), whose web site (`http://www.omg.org`) prominently features CORBA. The site also describes UML, the Unified Modeling Language used to describe services, and CWM, the Common Warehouse MetaModel, which describes complex data structures for interchange between structured repositories. These last two topics are not considered here.

You describe a CORBA service interface in the OMG Interface Definition Language (IDL). This allows you to specify the data to be passed between objects in a platform-independent manner. Python CORBA interfaces can parse IDL to allow CORBA-mediated interactions between arbitrary system components using the features of Xerox PARC's ILU project, for which Python provides the reference

implementation. For a full description see
`ftp://ftp.parc.xerox.com/pub/ilu/ilu.html`. ILU is a free, CORBA-compliant, object request broker (ORB) that supplies distributed object connectivity to myriad platforms using a variety of programming languages.

The CORBA architecture is designed to allow clients and servers of particular services to locate each other on the Net and interact by means of what CORBA calls transactions. These are simply programmed interactions rather than the database transactions discussed in earlier chapters.

Microsoft's Distributed Common Object Model (DCOM)

Mark Hammond, Greg Stein, and others have interfaced Python to Microsoft's COM, Distributed COM, and ActiveX architectures. This means, among other things, that you can use Python in ASP or as a COM controller (for example, to automatically extract from or insert information into Excel, Access, or any other COM-aware application). Python can even be an Active Scripting host (which means you could embed JScript inside a Python application, if you had a strange sense of humor).

Python support for many Microsoft Foundation Classes (MFC), COM, DCOM, and Active Scripting is integrated into the ActivePython distribution available from `www.activestate.com`. You can also download the win32all extension package separately if you already have Python installed on your Windows computer.

The major disadvantage of DCOM when compared with CORBA is its restriction to Microsoft-supported environments. DCOM is not an open system because Microsoft controls the standards. This might not matter if you work exclusively with Windows anyway. There has been some work to bridge the CORBA and DCOM worlds using IIOP, the Internet Inter-ORB Protocol, but this has not so far led to massive integration between the Microsoft world and everything else.

DCOM has also proved to be difficult to scale to larger systems without explicit use of MTS. Although this is an acceptable overhead for large-scale projects, it appears to require disproportionate effort for small- and medium-sized developments. A good description of DCOM technology, along with many examples of how Python can be integrated into the DCOM environment, is available in *Programming Python on Win32* (Mark Hammond and Andy Robinson, O'Reilly).

XML-Based Interactions

Various communication schemes are current that use XML to encode remote requests and responses between system components, the two best known being XML-RPC and SOAP. *SOAP* is of interest to web developers because it uses HTTP as the request/response transmission protocol and so is available wherever web services can operate. Microsoft has built its BizTalk services around SOAP, carving out an early market share in distributed services. The XML-RPC camp promotes technologies that allow a similar style of interactions, with all data interchanged using XML.

It will be interesting to see whether BizTalk is operated as a closed framework: if third parties do not run BizTalk servers, then even Microsoft may not be able to provide a large enough infrastructure to win out over an open systems protocol. SOAP itself is receiving broad support across the industry, by companies as large as IBM, so its future seems assured independently of BizTalk.

One of the "features" used to promote SOAP and similar techniques is that it uses HTTP, which corporate firewalls already accommodate. What this really means, however, is that any server that can be accessed for web services can also be accessed for remote procedure calls after it becomes SOAP-capable. This would seem to be a somewhat specious argument in favor of SOAP because opening firewalls to other RPC protocols like IIOP would only involve substantially the same risks. Whether the managers of corporate firewalls will want to allow SOAP traffic to continue to pass unhindered after they appreciate its implications remains to be seen.

Summary

Python can play a role in most areas of the web, as can be clearly seen from a review of existing and developing technologies. The availability of this object-oriented, high-level scripting language has the potential to allow the experimental development of new and different web architectures that can be successfully deployed in production environments on the Internet.

17

AWeFUL: An Object-Oriented Web Site Framework

YOU HAVE SEEN A NUMBER OF PYTHON web server examples in the course of reading so far, and some of them (built using existing web libraries) have been surprisingly small. Each has its advantages and disadvantages, but they have been valuable principally for learning purposes. None of them has really been fully effective to the point where you would be comfortable using it for production sites.

Although some of the frameworks you read about in Chapter 16, "Web Application Frameworks," are in daily use to support production web sites, it would be unfortunate if you finished the book with the impression that you do not know enough to produce your own framework for production-quality sites. In this chapter, therefore, you will read about a small, self-contained framework that does not rely on an external web server but is written entirely in Python. The framework is called AWeFUL—Another Web Framework, Useful but Lightweight. At the time of this writing, AWeFUL has held up interestingly well in live, albeit low-volume, testing on the Internet.

Why Another Framework?

The traditional approach to building web sites has been to write the content as static HTML files and CGI scripts and use a conventional server such as Apache to handle the task of serving the content and running the CGI scripts on demand. This is a heavyweight approach, however: it means having the server do many things on every request that are strictly necessary only for a very limited subset of the requests. In turn, this means that the traditional approach can be inefficient, although modern computers are speedy enough that you need not usually worry too much about that unless your site is heavily loaded.

This is not to say that traditional servers are a bad idea. They provide a lot of infrastructure, and so you can build a site with minimal attention to all the detail, which the server takes care of automatically. What is more, a traditional server should be able to handle everything that the web environment throws at it and still produce correct results. As your sites become more complex, you might well be glad of this assistance because it means that you can often avoid having to think about details like content caching and proxy server interactions.

From an educational point of view, though, the server-based approach hides a lot of detail. A pure Python framework gives you a chance to see how to handle details that it would be interesting to understand. You can observe code using direct access to HTTP protocol elements, for example, the details of which are otherwise hidden in large amounts of heavyweight server code, usually in C. An industrial-strength web server has to be "all things to all systems." A framework, unlike a web server, only needs to implement the features required by the underlying applications. A lightweight framework, although a little more detailed than anything presented so far, should be relatively easy for you to understand. In turn, this will increase your knowledge of web architectures generally.

This last one is not a trivial point. Until I had to write code to handle HTTP authentication, for example, I was a little hazy about some of the details. Producing working code has forced me to clarify my understanding (by reading the RFC document that specifies it). While writing Chapter 15, "Building Small, Efficient Python Web Systems," I was mulling over the structures (both logic and data) that would be necessary to support an application you will read about in Chapter 18, "A Web Application—PythonTeach.com." AWeFUL embodies many of the design considerations from Chapter 15, and during development, it was encouraging to see how naturally new features fit into the design. The code grew in a fairly monolithic way until most of the functionality was in place, and I then spent a couple of days refactoring for better modularity, looser coupling between the components, and easy comprehension. This also made it easier to add the final portions of the required functionality. If you have read the whole book up to this point, there should be nothing in AWeFUL's design to frighten or intimidate you. If you are browsing this book, you will find most of the material you do not understand covered in earlier chapters.

Framework Requirements

I would not claim that the AWeFUL framework is sufficiently comprehensive to replace a production web server for all uses. The main intention has been to produce something to support Python web applications in a way that allows you to build some interesting experimental web sites without having to build them from scratch. AWeFUL accommodates session state maintenance and user authentication to make it suitable as a platform for real-world applications. You have not yet read about these features, so this section discusses the necessary details.

Session State Maintenance

A major problem for web site builders, given the stateless nature of HTTP, is that of associating successive requests from a particular client with each other to allow continuity across a sequence of client/server interactions. This is unimportant when the content is purely static, but with dynamic (program-generated) content, it becomes much more significant. Traditional CGI-based approaches required the use of cookies generated by the CGI code. Nowadays, server environments such as IIS and ColdFusion perform the session management automatically, providing the application programmer with a storage area that holds data between interactions.

The AWeFUL server provides each request handler with a `Session` object containing data stored by previous session scripts. It identifies a particular session by issuing a cookie (built using the standard `Cookie` module) and creates new sessions as requests come in without such a cookie. The session is a Python object, so the code can use the public nature of Python's class attributes to store data with arbitrary names in the `Session` objects.

The server has to maintain a set of `Session` objects between requests, so it holds them all in a dictionary and passes the appropriate `Session` object through to the handler it creates for each request. To avoid the size of this dictionary growing without bounds, the server timestamps each session when client interactions occur and periodically purges sessions that have not been accessed within a particular amount of time. The parameters for `Session` time-out are global to the server, and you can easily configure both the examination periodicity and the length of the time-out period. The server itself does store a few values, in attributes whose names begin with a single underscore, in the `Session` object. Application code can avoid these server attributes by not using leading underscores for `Session` attribute names.

User Authentication

Some parts of many applications require users to validate their identity. Users may have to sign in to gain access to personal data, and staff members may need to validate their identity to use areas of the site not intended for public use. Such areas of the site are known as *authentication realms*, and a site may need to maintain several realms for different classes of users. When a browser makes a request to the server for a page from inside an authentication realm, the server looks in the HTTP request for an `Authorization:` header containing an authentication token for the realm (there are several authentication schemes, but AWeFUL uses only the Basic scheme, which all browsers implement).

If there is no token, or if the username and password do not validate for the realm, the server returns a 401-error response, challenging the browser with a `WWW-Authenticate`: header to provide authentication for the realm. On receiving such a response, most browsers require the user to enter a username and password in a dialog box and then repeat the request to the server with an `Authorization`: header containing a token representing the authentication data entered by the user. If the user fails to authenticate within a given number of attempts (usually three), the browser finally displays whatever content the server returns in the 401-error response. The server cannot therefore simply add authentication error responses to normal content for the requested URI. If it did, the content would be visible in the browser window after an authentication failure.

Hierarchical Content, Function, and Layout

The web appears to its users as a virtual filestore. The server must therefore map all requests to make the content appear hierarchical, as though it were the content of such a filestore. It does this by using a data structure to map the leading elements of the URI path to the class that implements the functionality of that subtree. This gives a very loose coupling between the structure of the virtual web filestore and the object-oriented structure of the application code. The same code can appear at several places in the web, even in different realms, and any residual path elements are available for use as arguments to the application process.

Objects produce the content generated within the framework. Python's object orientation makes it natural to provide a functional hierarchy of objects for dynamic content generation, and one particular object is used to retrieve static content from the filestore. The looseness of the coupling between the web hierarchy and the functional hierarchy means that they need not be exactly parallel.

The third hierarchical aspect of a well-designed web site is in layout. Pages with similar functions should have a similar look-and-feel, and pages lower in the content hierarchy should reflect the layout of the pages above them, although perhaps with more refinements at the lower structural levels. The layout hierarchy will probably have some parallels with the web and functional hierarchies, but branching will likely be less frequent because the layout will often not change at several web or functional levels.

The AWeFUL Framework Structure

AWeFUL uses a server based on the `asyncore` module described in Chapter 7, "Asynchronous Services," and is similar to the mini-web server presented in that chapter. Slight modifications allow the creation and maintenance of the session dictionary and timing out of entries with no interaction within a time-out period that is set as an installation parameter. The server creates an `HTTP` handler object, a subclass of the `asynchat` class discussed in Chapter 7, for each request it receives.

A handler receives the socket for the connection, the address of the connecting client, and the dictionary of Session objects from the server. The handler regards the blank line at the end of the HTTP headers as a terminator, so if the request contains data, the page's code can read and interpret it as appropriate. The handler locates, or creates, the session instance for the connection and updates the session access time. It then splits out the operation and the URI from the HTTP command, and splits the URI into path and query components.

The handler then calls a factory function, which creates and returns an object of the appropriate type to handle requests for the URI as determined by the site structure map. Next it tells that object to generate its HTTP response, which it stores in the socket's output buffer for outward transmission by the asynchronous dispatcher. Finally, the handler checks to see whether the session's housekeeping timer has timed out, and if so, it prunes the dictionary by deleting any sessions not accessed within their time-out period. The site structure map, and the functions associated with it, give the required loose coupling between the server framework and the modules responsible for generating content.

All content is generated by subclasses of a top-level class called Web.Page. If you understand software design patterns, it might help to realize that content generators use the Template pattern. The top-level Web.Page object defines a method, Generate(), which produces page content by calling the object's other methods. The subclasses override these methods to determine the content that the Generate() method produces.

Producing a functioning web then means writing Web.Page subclasses to produce the appropriate web content and a site mapping to specify which objects are created for which URI paths.

The Framework Code

You should now know everything you need to make sense of the code of the AWeFUL framework, which you will read in this section.

The Server

Listing 17.1 shows the server. The only difference between this server and others based on asyncore is the creation of a dictionary on line 15. This dictionary is passed through to the handler objects created on line 35. The dictionary is seeded with a key of "NEXT" to make the generation of new session keys easier. The main portion of the program accepts an argument, to override the default TCP port number of 8080.

Listing 17.1   *Server.py:* **The AWeFUL Server**

```
1  #!/c/python20/python
2  # $Workfile: Server.py $ $Revision: 6 $
```

continues

Listing 17.1 **Continued**

```
 3  # $Date: 10/04/01 6:39p $ $Author: Sholden $
 4  #
 5  import asyncore, socket, sys
 6  import Handler
 7
 8  class http_server(asyncore.dispatcher):
 9      """Simple asynchronous HTTP server."""
10
11      def __init__(self, ip, port):
12          """Create a handler for each incoming client connection."""
13          self.ip= ip
14          self.port = port
15          self.sessions = {"NEXT": 0L}
16          asyncore.dispatcher.__init__(self)
17          self.create_socket(socket.AF_INET, socket.SOCK_STREAM)
18          self.bind((ip, port))
19          self.listen(5)
20
21      def readable(self):
22          """Stop dispatcher from reading the socket until it can accept➥
            connections."""
23          return self.accepting
24
25      def handle_accept(self):
26          """Create a handler for each client connection."""
27          try:
28              conn, addr = self.accept()
29          except socket.error: # rare Linux error
30              print "Socket error on server accept()"
31              return
32          except TypeError: # rare FreeBSD3 error
33              print "EWOULDBLOCK exception on server accept()"
34              return
35          Handler.HTTP(conn, addr, self.sessions)
36
37  def serve():
38
39      port = 8080
40
41      if len(sys.argv) >1:
42          try:
43              port = int(sys.argv[1])
44          except:
45              sys.exit("Illegal port number")
46
47      server = http_server('', port)
48      try:
49          asyncore.loop(1.0) # Frequent checks for interrupt
50      except KeyboardInterrupt:
```

```
51          print "Completed"  # on console
52
53  if __name__ == "__main__":
54      serve()
```

Running the AWeFUL Server

If you downloaded the code for this book from the associated web site, you need to set up your database source to access the data, which is a Jet database in the file Ch17.mdb. The default in the dbsource module is to use the mx.ODBC.Windows module to access an ODBC source whose name is preset in the Params module to be "Ch17". If you have architectural variations, you might need to change this part of the source.

I hope to provide a sample database in other formats to make the sample code as usable as possible. Please check on the web site to find out what is currently available and report any new successes of your own.

After your data source can be connected to Python programs, you simply need to run Server.py. You can give a port number as a command-line argument, but by default the server serves port 8080.

If your server is running on the same machine as your browser, you should then be able to see its home page by navigating to http://127.0.0.1:8080/.

The HTTP Handler

The HTTP handler objects created by the server are subclassed from the asynchat.asynchat object you learned about in Chapter 7. Carriage returns are stripped as the HTTP request is collected in the input buffer. As usual, the main business takes place in the found_terminator() method, which is considerably more complex than any you have previously come across. All of Handler.py is shown in Listing 17.2.

Listing 17.2   *Handler.py:* **The HTTP Request Handler**

```
1   #
2   # $Workfile: Handler.py $ $Revision: 8 $
3   # $Date: 10/05/01 12:35a $ $Author: Sholden $
4   #
5   import Cookie
6   import Session
7   import MapSite
8   from Params import STIMEOUT_INTERVAL, SCHECK_INTERVAL
9   import asynchat, cgi, rfc822, cStringIO, time, sys
10
11  lastflushtime = 0    # session flushing clock
```

continues

Listing 17.2   **Continued**

```
12
13  class HTTP(asynchat.async_chat):
14
15      def __init__(self, conn, addr, sessions):
16          asynchat.async_chat.__init__(self, conn=conn)
17          self.addr = addr
18          self.sessions = sessions
19          self.ibuffer = []
20          self.obuffer = ""
21          self.set_terminator("\r\n\r\n")
22
23      def collect_incoming_data(self, data):
24          """Buffer the data, removing carriage returns."""
25          self.ibuffer.append(data.replace('\r', ''))
26
27      def found_terminator(self):
28          """Parse headers as rfc822, authenticate as necessary and generate➥
            content.
29
30          Note that the standard input remains unread, to allow appropriate
31          handling (such as CGI dictionary creation) from the page code."""
32
33          global lastflushtime
34          buffer = "".join(self.ibuffer)
35          linebreak = buffer.find("\n")
36          request = buffer[:linebreak]
37          headers = rfc822.Message(cStringIO.StringIO(buffer[linebreak+1:]))
38          cookies = Cookie.SimpleCookie()
39          chdr = headers.getheader("cookie")
40          if chdr:
41              cookies.load(chdr)
42          try:
43              now = time.time()
44              self.sessid = cookies["session"].value
45              self.session = self.sessions[self.sessid]
46              if now - self.session._atime > STIMEOUT_INTERVAL:
47                  del self.sessions[self.sessid]
48                  raise KeyError
49              self.session._atime = now
50          except KeyError:
51              # New session required because no cookie or session timed out
52              self.sessions["NEXT"] += 1
53              self.sessid = str(self.sessions["NEXT"])
54              self.session = self.sessions[self.sessid] = ➥
55                                  Session.Session(self.sessid)
56          op, path, protocol = request.split()
57          if len(path) > 1:
58              path = path[1:]
59          self.ibuffer = []
```

```
60              if "?" not in path:
61                  query = ""
62              else:
63                  path, query = path.split("?", 1)
64              path = path.split("/")
65              query = cgi.parse_qs(query, 1)
66              # Assume argument names appear only once, so no need for lists
67              for k, v in query.items():
68                  query[k] = v[0]
69              generator = MapSite.PageSpec(op, path, query, self.session, headers)
70              self.obuffer = generator.Generate()
71              if now - lastflushtime > SCHECK_INTERVAL:
72                  lastflushtime = now
73                  for k in self.sessions.keys():
74                      if k != "NEXT" and➡
75                          (now - self.sessions[k]._atime) > STIMEOUT_INTERVAL:
76                          del self.sessions[k]
77              sys.stdout.flush()
78
79      def writable(self):
80          return len(self.obuffer) > 0
81
82      def handle_write(self):
83          sent = self.send(self.obuffer)
84          self.obuffer = self.obuffer[sent:]
85          if len(self.obuffer) == 0:
86              self.close()
87
88
```

The found_terminator() method first splits the request line from the front of the
incoming request. Next it parses the lines of header data using the rfc822 module. It
then looks in the headers for a session cookie. If such a cookie is present in the headers, the browser has visited this server before. The session number extracted from the
cookie is used to retrieve the appropriate session state dictionary entry. If this session
has timed out, then the session entry is deleted; otherwise, its access time is updated to
delay time-out again.

If no session exists, or if the session has just been deleted because it timed out, the
handler creates a new session object. The key used is one higher than the current maximum session number. This is a simplistic algorithm, which does not guarantee that a
browser will not come back with an old session number and pick up a new session
issued under the old number if the server has been restarted and is counting up from
session 1 again. It will suffice for present purposes, however.

A more secure method would avoid such "session hijacks" by appending some
unrelated data item (for example, the session creation time) to the session identifier as
a *verifier*, and then validating it each time the client presented the session cookie. Two

different sessions with the same identifier would then have different verifiers, and the old session would fail to validate. You will see this technique in use in Chapter 18.

The handler splits the path and the query string that form the request and, in turn, splits up the path into individual components and generates a `CGI.FieldStorage` object from the query string. It then calls `SiteSpec.PageSpec`, a factory function that returns a `Web.Page` subclass object, which generates the content that is ultimately sent back to the client.

Finally, the handler places the output from the object's `Generate()` method into its output buffer, from whence the asynchronous dispatcher sends it back to the client. If the handler has not scanned the session dictionary for a certain period, it flushes any sessions that have not been active in the required time-out period. The purpose of flushing the standard output is to ensure that any output appears in the console terminal window if you inserted any debugging print statements. Another option would be to run the standard output stream unbuffered by starting the interpreter with the –u option.

Session Objects

The `Session` objects are simple from the framework's point of view, as you can see from Listing 17.3. They come into existence with only four attributes: the session identifier, a dictionary to hold authentication data (whose keys are the realms to which the authentication data belongs), a creation time, and an access time. Of course the application code is free to store whatever it wants as `Session` object attributes.

Listing 17.3   *Session.py:* **The Session Object**

```
 1  #
 2  # $Workfile: Session.py $ $Revision: 2 $
 3  # $Date: 8/27/01 11:24p $ $Author: Sholden $
 4  #
 5  import time
 6
 7  class Session:
 8      """Session object, for use by server and application code.
 9
10      Server uses only names beginning with an underscore."""
11
12      def __init__(self, sessid):
13          self._id = sessid
14          self._auth = {}                # Authentication details, one per realm
15          self._ctime = time.time()      # Creation time
16          self._atime = self._ctime      # Access time
```

Site Specification Data

The specification of a web site is a complex matter, as anybody who has had to perform surgery on an Apache configuration file can testify. The SiteSpec module provides data about how URIs are mapped to page generator objects, and about how to authenticate realms. Because each site is different, the module shown in Listing 17.4 is an example from a small but usable database-driven site. You have to write your own SiteSpec to define the mapping you need between paths and content generators. As you can see, SiteSpec simply defines two data structures.

Listing 17.4   **A Sample *SiteSpec.py* from a Small Site**

```
 1  """Map path prefixes to page classes, and realms to authentication tables."""
 2  #
 3  # $Workfile: SiteSpec.py $ $Revision: 5 $
 4  # $Date: 8/28/01 11:56p $ $Author: Sholden $
 5  #
 6
 7  import Static, HomePage, Auth, DeptPages, ErrorPages
 8
 9  PageMap = {
10      "":             (HomePage.Home, None),
11      "Auth": ({
12          "Secret":       (Auth.Secret,   "PythonTeach"),
13          "Secret2":      (Auth.Secret2,  "Staff")
14      }, None),
15      "Image":        ("images",          None),
16      "Text":         ("text",            "Staff"),
17      "DeptHome":     (DeptPages.Home,    None),
18      "DeptLinks":    (DeptPages.Links,   None),
19      "DeptNews":     (DeptPages.News,    None),
20      "DeptNewsItem": (DeptPages.NewsItem, None),
21      "DeptQod":      (DeptPages.Qod,     None),
22      "DeptQodAns":   (DeptPages.QodAns,  None),
23      "DeptPgPage":   (DeptPages.PgPage,  None),
24      "Error":        (ErrorPages.ErrorPage, None)
25      }
26
27  RealmAuth = {
28      "PythonTeach":  ("Student", "StdEmail", "StdPasswd"),
29      "Staff":        ("Staff", "StfUserName", "StfPasswd")
30  }
```

PageMap is a dictionary mapping first-level path elements to two-element tuples. The second item in each tuple is the authentication realm for the content. A value of None specifies that no authentication is required for that content. The first element of the tuple can be one of three types of objects:

- **string**—The content is static, and the string is the path relative to the server root where the resource (named by any remaining path elements) can be found.

- **dictionary**—Specifies the mapping of next-level path elements, recursively.

- **class**—The class that should be instantiated to generate the content.

The RealmAuth dictionary simply maps from authentication realms to authentication parameters, which are three-element tuples. The Web module currently assumes that authentication data are in a database table, so the tuple elements are a table name, the name of the column holding usernames, and the name of the column holding passwords.

Object Selection Logic

When the handler has performed the session selection, it uses the PageSpec() function from the MapSite module to determine (from leading elements of the path) which class is required and instantiate that class with appropriate arguments. The PageSpec() function in turn uses data from the SiteSpec.PageMap dictionary, which you will notice in Listing 17.5 is its default Map argument.

Listing 17.5 *MapSite.py:* **Site Mapping Logic**

```
 1  """Used to instantiate required page generators, and look up realm➡
    authentication data."""
 2
 3  import urllib
 4  import SiteSpec, Static, ErrorPages
 5  from types import ClassType, DictType, StringType
 6
 7  def PageSpec(op, path, query, session, headers,
 8      Map=SiteSpec.PageMap, Realm=None, PathFound=None):
 9      """Return the page processor and authentication realm corresponding➡
        to  path."""
10      if not path:
11          return ErrorPages.Error404Page(op, PathFound, query, session,➡
            headers, Realm=None)
12      pathel = path[0]
13      if not PathFound:
14          PathFound = [pathel]
15      else:
16          PathFound.append(pathel)
17      del path[0]
18      try:
19          item, realm = Map[pathel]
```

```
20          if not realm:
21              realm = Realm # Inherit realm from containing tree
22          itemtype = type(item)
23          if itemtype == DictType:
24              return PageSpec(op, path, query, session, headers,
25                              Map=item, Realm=realm, PathFound=PathFound)
26          elif len(PathFound) and not len(path): # A mapped element was not➥
            followed by a "/"
27              URI = "/".join([""]+PathFound+path+[""])
28              if query:
29                  URI += "?" + urllib.urlencode(query)
30              return ErrorPages.Error301Page(op, path, query, session,➥
                headers, Realm=realm,
31                              oHeaders=["Location: %s" % URI])
32          if itemtype == StringType:
33              return Static.Page(op, path, query, session, headers,
34                              Realm=realm, Initpath=item.split("/"))
35          elif itemtype == ClassType:
36              if path[-1] == "": # remove evidence of trailing slash
37                  del path[-1]
38              return item(op, path, query, session, headers,
39                              Realm=realm, Initpath=PathFound)
40          else:
41              raise KeyError
42      except KeyError:
43          return ErrorPages.Error404Page(op, path, query, session, headers,➥
            Realm=None)
44
45  def RealmData(realm):
46      try:
47          return SiteSpec.RealmAuth[realm]
48      except KeyError:
49          return None
```

If the path is empty, PageSpec instantiates an error page that returns a 404 Not Found error to the user. The PageSpec routine looks in its Map argument for an element corresponding to the first path item. Otherwise, it adds the path element to a list of elements already found and looks to see what kind of item it has found.

For another dictionary, it recursively calls itself to look up the next path item. For a string item, it instantiates a Static.Page object (passing it the directory in which to start searching) that locates the content in the filestore and returns it to the server. For a class, it calls the class to instantiate an object that generates the content programmatically.

There is one somewhat subtle point in this process. When a browser requests a resource (such as a directory in a conventional static web) without including a trailing slash, the server has a slight problem. The browser, from the URI it sends, cannot tell that it has been asked to request a directory resource, and so if it already has authentication data for the realm of the containing directory, it presents the data as an `Authorization:` header in its HTTP request. Because the directory requested without a trailing slash may actually be the root of a contained realm, a well-behaved server returns a `301 Permanently moved` response, with a `Location:` header containing the URI including the trailing slash. In turn, the well-behaved browser then repeats its request; but because it can now see from the path that it is requesting a directory, it includes the correct authentication data (if it has it) in the HTTP request headers.

The `RealmData` function will be a relief after that lengthy security digression. It simply looks up the authentication data in the `SiteSpec.RealmAuth` dictionary, returning the appropriate tuple or `None`.

Content Generator Abstract Class

The `Web` module defines a `Page` class that classes in other modules can use as a template, overriding its methods as needed to specialize the output they produce. The two methods that only very specialized subclasses override are `Generate()`, which is the coordinator for all the others, and `Authenticate()`, which ensures that a user can only access pages for which they have presented credentials. This module handles request authentication as well as determines the basic look-and-feel of almost all pages in your site. As you can see from Listing 17.6, it is by far the largest single module in the framework.

Listing 17.6   *Web.py:* **The Root Class for Page Generation**

```
 1  #
 2  # $Workfile: Web.py $ $Revision: 14 $
 3  # $Date: 8/29/01 12:54a $ $Author: Sholden $
 4  #
 5  import os, base64
 6  import cgi
 7  import mx.DateTime
 8  import Cookie
 9  import MapSite
10  from dbsource import dbsource
11
12  conn = dbsource("prom2000").conn
13  cursor = conn.cursor()
14
15  class Page:
16      """Implement common page behavior, with only the most basic➥
          look-and-feel.
17
18      This is the ultimate ancestor class for all dynamic pages."""
19
20      def __init__(self, op, path, query, session, headers,
21                   oHeaders=None, Realm=None, Initpath=""):
22          """Build the page to prepare for content generation."""
```

```
23          self.op = op
24          self.path = path
25          self.query = query
26          self.session = session
27          self.headers = headers
28          if oHeaders:
29              self.oheaders = oHeaders
30          else:
31              self.oheaders = []
32          self.realm = Realm
33          self.initpath = Initpath
34
35      def Generate(self):
36          auth = self.Authenticate()
37          if auth:
38              return auth
39          else:
40              return self.PageContent()
41
42      def Authenticate(self):
43          if not self.Realm():    # no authentication required
44              return
45          else:                   # verify authentication
46              try:
47                  passwd = self.session._auth[self.Realm()]["password"]
48                  # Already authenticated for the realm
49                  return
50              except KeyError:
51                  # Check authentication credentials in HTTP headers
52                  auth = self.headers.getheader("authorization")
53                  if auth:
54                      auth = auth.split()
55                      if auth[0].lower() == "basic": # username:password
56                          auth = base64.decodestring(auth[1]).split(":")
57                          self.session._auth[self.Realm()] = {"email":➥
                          auth[0].lower()}
58                          # Retrieve authentication data from realm table
59                          a = MapSite.RealmData(self.Realm())
60                          if a: # Always fail if no data for the realm
61                              stmt ="SELECT %s FROM %s WHERE %s = ?" % (a[2],➥
                              a[0], a[1])
62                              cursor.execute(stmt, (auth[0].lower(), ))
63                              pw = cursor.fetchall()
64                              if pw and pw[0][0].lower()  == auth[1].lower():
65                                  self.session._auth[self.Realm()]➥
                                  ["password"] = pw[0][0]
66                                  # This realm is authenticated for the➥
                                  first time
67                                  return
68          # No credential is present for this realm, so we require
```

continues

Listing 17.6 **Continued**

```
69                # authentication. If the browser stops trying, the content
70                # we return instead of the page offers the password via
71                # email. Email is only sent to users in the database!
72                return Error401Page(self.op, self.path, self.query,➥
                 self.session, self.headers,
73                               oHeaders=["WWW-Authenticate: Basic realm=%s" %➥
                                 self.Realm()],
74                               Realm=None).Generate()
75
76        def PageContent(self):
77            """Return content when authentication not required or known good."""
78            content =➥
79    """<HTML>
80    <HEAD>
81        <TITLE>%s [Session %s]</TITLE>
82    </HEAD>
83    <BODY BGCOLOR="#ffffff">
84    <TABLE>
85      <tr>
86        <td VALIGN="TOP"><IMG SRC="/Image/py.gif"></td>
87        <td VALIGN="TOP"><H3><font color="red">
88            Web/Database Technology Demonstrator</font></H3></td>
89      </tr>
90      <tr><td colspan="2"><hr></td></tr>
91      <tr>
92        <td valign="TOP" width="80">%s</td>
93        <td valign="TOP" width="250">%s</td>
94      </tr>
95    </TABLE>
96    </BODY>
97    """ % (self.Title(), self.session._id, self.NavBar(), self.Body())
98            return➥
99    """HTTP/1.0 %d OK Content Follows
100   Content-Type: text/html
101   Content-Length: %d
102   Cache-Control: no-cache
103   %s
104   %s
105
106   %s""" % (self.ReturnCode(), len(content), self.Cookie(), self.Headers(),➥
      content)
107
108
109        def Body(self):
110            return "Error: Page subclass requires Body() method"
111
112        def Cookie(self):
113            cookie = Cookie.SimpleCookie()
114            cookie["session"] = self.session._id
```

```
115          cookie["session"]["path"] = "/"
116          #cookie["session"]["expires"] = "31 Dec 2002" # Seems to make it➡
             permanent
117          return cookie
118
119      def NavBar(self):
120          return "Error: Page subclass requires NavBar() method"
121
122      def Headers(self):
123          return "\r\n".join(self.oheaders)
124
125      def Realm(self):
126          """Return the authentication realm, if any."""
127          return self.realm
128
129      def ReturnCode(self):
130          return 200
131
132      def Title(self):
133          return "Error: Page subclass requires Title() method"
134
135
136  class Error401Page(Page):
137      """Error 401 is directly declared here to avoid circular imports."""
138
139      def Body(self):
140          return➡
141  """<P><FONT COLOR="RED" SIZE="+1"><B>Authentication Required</B></FONT></P>
142  <P>If you would like us to remind you of your password by
143  email please <A HREF="/MailPass/%s">click here</A>[sr]
144  """ % self.Realm()
145
146      def Message(self):
147          return "Authentication Required"
148
149      def NavBar(self):
150          return """<A HREF="/">HOME</A>"""
151
152      def ReturnCode(self):
153          return 401
154
155      def Title(self):
156          return "Authentication Required"
```

The module creates a database connection to use in case it has to perform authentication. You may decide this is unnecessary and simply use a dictionary instead. A database is very convenient if you want your web users to be able to sign up online, however.

__init__()

The __init__() method takes many arguments, which Table 17.1 summarizes. When the PageSpec() factory routine instantiates the object, it extracts the additional data for the initialization arguments from the data structure used to analyze the URI path.

Table 17.1   __init__() **Arguments**

Argument	Type	Description
op	string	HTTP method from the request.
path	list	List of path elements from the URI, without the leading elements used to determine which object to instantiate.
query	CGI.FieldStorage	Query string data transformed into a CGI.FieldStorage object.
session	Session	Session object selected (or created) by the handler.
headers	rfc822.Message	Message object encapsulating the data from the HTTP request headers.
oHeaders	list	List of output headers that must be added to the generated output.
Realm	string	Authentication realm name.
initpath	list	List of path elements, if any, that should replace the initial elements removed before object instantiation. This argument is only used in static content generation.

Generate()

The central method is Generate(), the method called by the handler after it instantiates the object with the MapSite() factory method. Generate() simply calls the Authenticate() method, which returns a false result if authentication is not required or is acceptable. If authentication succeeds, then Generate() returns the result of the PageContent() method. If authentication fails, then Authenticate() instantiates an Error401Page and returns the content the error page generates. This tells the browser to request authentication data for the realm from the user and to repeat its request. If the next request fails to authenticate, then the process repeats until the browser tires of it, at which point it displays the error page.

Authenticate()

The Authenticate() method is tricky. An immediate return handles the trivial case where the content is not in any realm. Otherwise, the server looks in the Session object to see whether the browser previously presented a correct password for this realm and returns immediately if this is so. If no password has yet been recorded, the server has to check the request's `Authorization:` header, because this request might be the browser's response to an earlier 401 error. The Basic authentication mode contains the username and password, separated by a colon, encoded in base 64.

Be aware that the Basic authentication mode allows easy decoding of usernames and passwords. Therefore, do not rely on it to provide secure authentication where network traffic might be intercepted. For better security, use some sort of encrypted channel, such as the Secure Socket Layer used by the HTTPS protocol, or an encrypted tunnel between the hosts.

If `Authenticate()` finds the header, it extracts the username and password, stores the username in the `Session` object (in case authentication fails), and retrieves the realm details from the database. Supposing they are present, `Authenticate()` looks up the password in the appropriate database table. If a result comes back from the query, and if that result matches the password that the browser submitted, finally `Authenticate()` adds a password to the authentication item for the realm in the `Session` object and returns success. Thereafter, the `Session` object authenticates any further accesses to the realm.

If `Authenticate()` falls at any of the hurdles described previously, the nested conditional logic drops through to the final statement in the method, which instantiates an `Error401Page` you read about earlier and returns the content that the error page generates.

PageContent()

This method is responsible for creating the HTTP response normally expected. It builds the HTML content, and thereby determines the site's central look-and-feel, because most dynamically generated pages simply inherit this method from `Web.Page`. The session identifier is included in the title for testing purposes, and the default layout is a simple two row-by-two column table with a graphic in the top-left-hand corner, a standard title at top right, a navigation bar in the bottom-left cell, and the main body of the content in the bottom-right cell. You saw this layout in earlier mini-webs. Not being a graphic designer, I do not feel obliged to be especially creative in this area! Notice that all the interesting parts of the content are actually produced by method calls.

The HTML thus developed is then inserted into an HTTP response, in which methods are again used to insert the more interesting portions.

Body()

This method produces the content for the bottom-right cell of the generated HTML. Your subclasses definitely need to override this method. Of course `Web.Page` is an *abstract class*, which means that it should not be instantiated directly. Normally, you would not include this class in your `SiteSpec`, but to show you that it does generate real output, Figure 17.1 shows a browser displaying such a page. `Body()`, and the other abstract methods try to return an indication that something is wrong and tell the programmer which class should be corrected.

Figure 17.1 Web.Page's generated output displayed in Internet Explorer.

Cookie()

Every request should receive session identification, and so the Cookie() method always returns a cookie containing that data. (You will remember that the handler looks for this cookie to identify the session.) If your own classes override Cookie(), they should probably start by calling Web.Page.Cookie(self) to ensure that session state is correctly maintained. This creates an object to which you can add your own cookies.

The comment shows you one way to make a cookie permanent, although there are others. Session state maintenance specifically requires cookies that expire when the browser is terminated. The nice part about the Cookie core library module is that you can build several cookies into the same object by dictionary assignment to multiple keys.

NavBar()

This method should return HTML, which links to various other portions of the site. Again the abstract method returns nothing useful.

Headers()

Occasionally, you might want to add HTTP header lines to the HTTP response. You can do this in two ways. The first technique is to write a `Headers()` method that returns one or more valid RFC822 headers, and this is what you will mostly do.

Another possibility is to provide a list of strings (or other objects whose `__str__()` method renders them as valid RFC822 headers) as the `oHeaders` argument when you create the page object. The error page created at line 72 of Listing 17.6 adds the necessary authentication request for the browser using this second technique. Most pages, of course, are created by the `MapSite()` function, so you do not have this choice unless you create a page dynamically.

Realm()

This method returns the authentication realm for the page. It rarely needs to be overridden.

ReturnCode()

When everything works well, web pages almost invariably return an error code of 200, indicating success. This means that you will almost never need to override `ReturnCode()`. If you want to generate your own error pages, you might choose to override it, however.

Title()

Here you get to specify what the user sees in the title bar of his browser window, courtesy of the `<TITLE>` HTML tag. The abstract method again simply attempts to make you aware of the problem if you forget to override the method in your own page objects.

Generating Error Pages

As a first simple subclass of `Page`, look at the `Error401Page` class defined in the remainder of the module. This class is defined separately from the other error pages because they are in a separate module that imports this one. Rather than struggle with circular imports, where one module imports a second which in turn imports the first, the pragmatic solution is to define the one error page class that `Web.Page` relies on locally. The remainder of the framework's error pages, to preserve modularity, are generated in the `Error` module described in a later section.

Serving Static Content

The `Static` module declares a `Page` class responsible for serving all static content from the site. You may remember that the `MapSite()` function instantiates a `Static.Page` directly when the `PageMap` contains a string value, and that the string value is the path stub for the file lookup. Listing 17.7 shows the module, which is neither lengthy nor complicated.

Listing 17.7   *Static.py:* **The Static Content Page Generator**

```
 1  #
 2  # $Workfile: Static.py $ $Revision: 6 $
 3  # $Date: 8/29/01 4:28a $ $Author: Sholden $
 4  #
 5  import Web
 6  import os
 7  from mimetypes import guess_type
 8  from ErrorPages import Error404Page, Error405Page, Error415Page
 9
10
11  class Page(Web.Page):
12      """Handle content present as a file in the virtual web filestore.
13
14      Note that a whole passel of stuff is inherited, from Web.Page,
15      much of which is neither required nor used because the content
16      is simply dragged from a file and squirted down to the client.
17      """
18
19      def Generate(self):
20          """Generate static content by squirting file content."""
21          if self.op.upper() != "GET":
22              return Error405Page(self.op, self.path, self.query,
23                       self.session, self.headers,
24                       oHeaders=self.Headers(), Realm=self.Realm()).Generate()
25          else:
26              auth = self.Authenticate()
27              if auth:
28                  return auth
29              fname = self.path[-1]
30              ext = os.path.splitext(fname)[1]
31              mimetype, encoding = guess_type(fname)
32              if encoding:
33                  enchdr = "Content-Encoding: %s\r\n" % encoding
34              else:
35                  enchdr = ""
36              if not mimetype:
37                  return Error415Page(self.op, self.path,
38                           self.query, self.session, self.headers,
39                           oHeaders=self.Headers(),➥
                            Realm=self.Realm()).Generate()
40              try:
41                  filepath = os.sep.join(self.initpath + self.path)
42                  f = open(filepath, "rb")
43                  img = f.read()
```

```
44                      return➡
45   """HTTP/1.0 200 OK Content as requested
46   Content-Type: %s
47   Content-Length: %s
48   %s
49   %s""" % (mimetype, len(img), enchdr, img)
50              except IOError:
51                  return Error404Page(self.op, self.path,
52                      self.query, self.session, self.headers,
53                      oHeaders=self.Headers(),➡
                        Realm=self.Realm()).Generate()
```

The only special method for static content is `Generate()`. Anything else required is simply inherited from `Web.Page`, although as the comment notes, many of the superclass's methods are not required. The method checks that the request is a `GET` (you might have noticed that AWeFUL does not handle `HEAD` requests), returning an error page content otherwise.

Static content is also authenticated using the `Authenticate()` inherited from `Web.Page`. Then the method uses the `mimetypes.guess_type` function to try to guess the MIME type and content encoding of the file. If no content encoding can be divined, it is simply omitted, but `Generate()` refuses to handle content of unknown types and instead returns a 415 error. It opens and sends the file whose path is the lookup value from the `PageMap` with whatever remains of the URI path appended. If the file cannot be found, then the classic 404 error is returned instead.

Error Pages

This module should not be hard to understand if you have been paying attention up to now. Error pages (see Listing 17.8) are similar to any other, but their content is simple. The important thing is that by inheriting from `Web.Page`, all error pages adopt the standard look-and-feel of the site they are a part of.

Listing 17.8   *ErrorPages.py:* **Generating HTTP Error Reports**

```
1    #
2    # $Workfile: ErrorPages.py $ $Revision: 3 $
3    # $Date: 8/27/01 11:21p $ $Author: Sholden $
4    #
5    import Web
6
7    class ErrorPage(Web.Page):
8
9        def Title(self):
10           return "Program Error"
11
12       def Realm(self):
```

continues

Listing 17.8   **Continued**

```
13              """Return null realm to ensure no authentication requested."""
14              return ""
15
16      def NavBar(self):
17              return """<A HREF="/">HOME</A>"""
18
19      def Body(self):
20              return """<FONT COLOR="RED" SIZE="+1"><P><B><I>Error %d:<BR>
21              %s</FONT></I></B></P>""" % (self.ReturnCode(), self.Message())
22
23      def Message(self):
24              return "Unspecified problem"
25
26  class Error301Page(ErrorPage):
27
28      def Message(self):
29              return "Permanently Moved"
30
31      def ReturnCode(self):
32              return 301
33
34  class Error404Page(ErrorPage):
35
36      def Message(self):
37              return "Page Not Found"
38
39      def ReturnCode(self):
40              return 404
41
42  class Error405Page(ErrorPage):
43
44      def Message(self):
45              return """Illegal Operation"""
46
47      def ReturnCode(self):
48              return 401
49
50  class Error415Page(ErrorPage):
51
52      def Message(self):
53              return """Unknown content type"""
54
55      def ReturnCode(self):
56              return 415
```

Site Parameters

At present there are few parameters for the site. They are the data source name, the checking interval for session time-out, and the session time-out limit itself. It might be easier to store these in the `SiteSpec` module along with the other data, but a small parameter file is adequate. Listing 17.9 is presented mostly for completeness.

Listing 17.9 *Params.py:* **Site Parameters**

```
1  #
2  # $Workfile: Params.py $ $Revision: 3 $
3  # $Date: 10/04/01 6:38p $ $Author: Sholden $
4  #
5  DBSOURCE = "Ch17"
6  STIMEOUT_INTERVAL = 1200    # 20-minute session timeout
7  SCHECK_INTERVAL = 60        # check every minute
```

Summary

You should have learned something about Python's power in this chapter even though you have not really seen the framework in serious action yet. The structure of the framework gives a loose coupling between the framework and the content it serves. Control over look-and-feel is centralized in the abstract class from which most content generators should be subclassed, with the result that a complete site will have a nice consistency and can be changed across the board by editing a single file.

AWeFUL has its deficiencies, and it is likely that there are bugs lurking and still to be pulled out. Its approach to error handling is at times a little cavalier, and the lack of `try ... except` protection around the page generation routines in the handler makes the server a little fragile under development at times. Considering the whole thing comes in at a little under 500 lines of code, however, it seems to support the Python community's assessment of its favorite language in terms of productivity and flexibility.

If you understood the code of the framework, then the applications will seem positively simple by comparison. In Chapter 18, you are going to see an application that makes use of the framework, somewhat hardened for production use, to perform typical everyday tasks that web users tend to take for granted.

18

A Web Application—
PythonTeach.com

THROUGH THE LAST 17 CHAPTERS, YOU have learned a lot about the technologies underlying web systems and how to program them in Python. To tie all this knowledge together you need to see it in a system that, although perhaps smaller in scale, solves many of the problems faced by real-world web designers. This is the purpose of PythonTeach.com, a mythical small company that uses the web as a part of its business infrastructure.

In this final chapter, you will learn about the PythonTeach business environment and the database intended to meet its applications' needs. You also see the framework of the web portions of the company's applications. The example code is intended to bring you face to face with the real problems you will have to solve to build web systems, and to encourage you to do it in Python.

Because PythonTeach is a training company, you must distinguish between the classes that PythonTeach offers (which are training sessions in classrooms) and the classes implemented in the web application. I hope that the distinction will usually be clear from the context!

The Company Mission

PythonTeach provides the finest Python learning available anywhere in the galaxy (or so the company mission statement says). It specializes in one-day classes and keeps attendance low to ensure that each student receives personal attention as she learns. Classes can be public (usually at a hotel venue: PythonTeach does not maintain its own education center) or on-site.

A customer can make a request for an on-site training session. Such a requests can specify up to three classes, to run on consecutive days at the same location, and up to three starting dates for the first class. Instructors can offer to fill these requirements (fully or partially). The company reviews these offers, chooses the instructor or instructors, and then issues a quotation, which the customer may choose to accept. If the quotation is accepted, then the company allocates a class number and records the instructor details.

Students enroll for public and on-site classes via the web site; the on-site classes are not listed on the site, but the customer is provided with a URL that he can pass on to students for registration purposes. A booking is tentative until payment confirms it. Students for public courses can pay by providing their credit card details in a follow-up telephone call, or by sending payment in the mail. They receive an invoice by email at the close of any business day in which they place orders—secure web payments are on the feature list for the next release. If an invoice remains unpaid a month before the class commences, the sales manager has the option to cancel the booking. Students can call to cancel their own bookings (paid or unpaid). They may also elect to join the wait list for a full class, and as cancellations occur, wait-listed students are informed by email or by telephone if the date is close.

Structure of the Application

PythonTeach has decided to use a hardened version of the AWeFUL framework to build its web site. Having experienced Python programmers at its disposal, PythonTeach had no problem modifying the code, and in the open-source tradition, they fed back changes to the original implementor in case they might be useful to other users. One major modification allows content generation code to raise exceptions when the server should make an error response of some sort to the client. You review some of the more significant changes later.

PythonTeach decided to put most of the site content into a database. This provides increased content flexibility, and PythonTeach needs a database anyway to record the course enrollments and related information. As well as handling the mechanics of class enrollment, PythonTeach wants the site to present a set of pages containing general information about the various technical areas of interest to site visitors, with links to the appropriate classes. These pages are organized as departments similarly to the web you saw in Chapter 17, "AWeFUL: An Object-Oriented Web Site Framework."

To ensure a degree of security in the system, students (or anyone else who wants to make reservations) must be authenticated to the system. To create an account, a user fills out a form, whose details go in the Wannabe table, along with any pending order. The system then sends the user a mail message containing a URL that confirms the reservation. When the user follows that link, the system moves the user's details into the Student table, and he can authenticate himself to the site thereafter. The user can confirm the pending order by following a link from the confirmation page.

Course information is presented in several ways. A page listing all courses allows users to click and see the basic information about a course. From the basic information page, they can click on a link to see when and where the class is running. They can also select class listings by location or by course. Whenever a class schedule is presented, a user can click to either book a place or (if the class is already full) to add himself to the wait list for the class. When the user takes such actions, a "shopping cart" link appears on every successive page allowing him to review his requests. Because a user can enter booking or wait-list requests without authentication, the user must either authenticate himself to use the ultimate confirmation page or sign up for a new account. In the latter case, the reservations are pending until the account is confirmed.

A final "members only" section allows students to update their details and will be expanded as time goes by to offer materials to encourage prospective and former students to visit regularly.

Request-Handling Logic

Several changes have been made to the request-handling framework of Chapter 17. None of them are major, but several are significant because they increase the robustness of the server, or make writing applications simpler.

Dealing with *POST* Requests

Although the initial AWeFUL implementation was sufficient to handle GET HTTP protocol requests, handling POST requests requires the server to read additional input after the headers are parsed. The asynchat library module on which the handler is based is flexible enough to do this because it allows the programmer to set three different terminator types. You have already seen it handling string terminators to mark the end of the HTTP headers on encountering a "\r\n\r\n" string.

You can also set an integer terminator, in which case the asynchronous handler calls found_terminator() after the given number of bytes has been read from the socket. A terminator of None reads the socket without ever encountering a terminator. Listing 18.1 shows the updated found_terminator() method.

Listing 18.1 **Updated *Handler.found_terminator()* Method**

```
def found_terminator(self):
    if self.reading_headers:
        self.reading_headers = 0
        self.parse_headers()
        if self.op.upper() == "POST":
            clen = self.headers.getheader("content-length")
            self.set_terminator(int(clen))
```

continues

Listing 18.1 **Continued**

```
        else:
            self.handle_request()
    elif not self.handling:
        self.set_terminator(None) # browsers sometimes over-send
        self.cgi_data = parse(self.headers, self.ibuffer)
        self.handling = 1
        self.ibuffer = []
        self.handle_request()
```

The handler starts out using a terminator of "\r\n\r\n" as before and now maintains state to determine whether it is reading headers. If it is, finding a terminator causes it to parse the headers. If the request is a POST, the handler sets the terminator to read the correct number of bytes in the input stream. Otherwise, it assumes that the request is a GET and handles the request immediately.

In the POST case, found_terminator() is called a second time after the entity content has been read. The terminator is changed yet again—this time to None, to avoid a looping condition in the asynchronous event handler. found_terminator() then parses the CGI data into a dictionary, and finally the request is handled.

The handle_request() method maps the URI path on to the appropriate resource as usual and calls its Generate() method to perform authentication (if required) and content generation. The handler also uses additional data passed in by the server to log all requests it processes, although not in a standard form.

Content Generation Logic

The PythonTeach home page (in an early version) appears in Figure 18.1. The navigation bar at the left of the page distinguishes between the three major areas of the site and allows the user to reach the site home page from anywhere. Navigation features are determined for each page; and because the web is object-oriented, a page requiring the same navigation features as its superclass can simply inherit the navigation routines.

Figure 18.1 The (experimental) PythonTeach.com home page.

The *Generate()* Method

The `Web.py` module determines the overall look-and-feel of the site as the ultimate ancestor of all content generation pages. The structure is a little more complex than that of the AWeFUL framework discussed in Chapter 17, to accommodate the increased content complexity. Overall, the pages are still generated by the `Generate()` method, whose updated code appears in Listing 18.2.

Listing 18.2 **The Enhanced *Web.Page.Generate()* Method**

```
def Generate(self, Input=None):
    self.input = Input
    try:
        self.Authenticate()
        return self.HTTP(self.Content())
    except Error, error:
        self.returncode, self.message, self.realm, self.oheaders, self.errmsg, \
        self.errcontent = error()
        self.mimetype = "text/html"
        return self.HTTP(self.Content())
```

Handling Authentication Failures More Effectively

The method still proceeds to authenticate the page if required, but a custom-defined exception (Error) is raised in the event of problems that do not allow content generation to proceed. The exception takes several arguments, allowing the raising code to pass values (including a server response code) back to the Generate() method, which will modify the generated content. Calling the Error instance retrieves the arguments to the exception class, using its __call__() special method. In this version of the code, even the Authenticate() method signals inability to authenticate by raising an error with a response code of 401, as shown in Listing 18.3.

Listing 18.3   **Raising an Error Exception to Signal Authentication Failure**

```
raise Error(401, "Authentication required", self.Realm(),
            oheaders=['WWW-Authenticate: Basic realm="%s"' % self.Realm()],
            errmsg="""Authentication Required<BR><BR>
            Would you like an <BR>
            <A HREF="/MailPass/%s/"> email password reminder</A>?<BR><BR>
            Or do you want to <BR>
            <A HREF="/NewAccount/%s/">open a new account</A>?
            """ % (self.Realm(), self.Realm())))
```

As you can see from this example, the content generation code gets a chance to ask the framework to include particular headers in the HTTP output. It can also set either a message (as in Listing 18.2) for presentation inside the standard layout, or error content to completely replace the standard page layout, which is unnecessarily heavyweight for some purposes.

Creating Content and Accommodating Errors

The PageContent() method has been renamed Content() and appears in Listing 18.4.

Listing 18.4   **Generating Web Content According to Error Status**

```
def Content(self):
    """Return content when authentication not required or known good.

    If error occurred, generate standard or abbreviated page depending
    on whether the error overrode the errcontent argument."""
    if self.returncode == 200:
        return pageformat % (self.Title(), self.session._id,
                             self.NavBar(), self.Body())
    elif self.errcontent is None:
        return pageformat % (self.Title(), self.session._id,
                             self.NavBar(), self.ErrMsg())
    else:
        return self.errcontent
```

You can see that if the exception sets the `errcontent` instance variable, then no fancy content generation is attempted; whereas if `errcontent` is unset, a normal page is generated using the `ErrMsg()` method to provide the content. This is why Listing 18.2 results in a page with the site's standard look-and-feel if the browser gives up on authentication.

Improved Navigation Features

The navigation bar of Chapter 17's framework was fine when all content was undifferentiated, but many sites have a sectional nature. The updated top-level navigation bar reflects the fact that the PythonTeach web site comprises three main sections (see Listing 18.5).

Listing 18.5 **The Top-Level Navigation Bar**

```python
def NavBar(self, Home=0):
    try:
        name = "%s %s<BR>" % (self.session._udata.StdFirstName,
                              self.session._udata.StdLastName)
    except AttributeError:
        name = ""
    if self.session._bookings:
        checkout = """<A HREF="/CourseViewCart/">Shopping Cart</A><BR>"""
    else:
        checkout = ""
    return """
            <table border="0" cellpadding="0
                            cellspacing="0" width="158">
              <tr>
                <td width="10" valign="top">
                <img src="/images/spacer.gif"
                    width="10" height="5" border="0"></td>
                <td class="navtext" width="148">
                <img src="/images/spacer.gif"
                    width="5" height="5" border="0"><br>
<b>%s%s</b></td>
              </tr>
            </table>
%s
%s
%s
%s
""" % (name, checkout, self.NavSection("/", "home"),
       self.NavSection("/DeptStart/", "departments", self.DeptNav()),
       self.NavSection("/CourseStart/", "courses", self.CourseNav()),
       self.NavSection("/Auth/Usrs/", "PythonTeach", self.PTNav()))
```

The NavBar() method, shown in Listing 18.5, has two optional features at the start. The first displays the user's name if this information exists in the session data. This will be the case if the user authenticated herself in the PythonTeach realm. The second is a link allowing the user to review her shopping cart, which is only displayed if the cart is not empty.

The method calls the NavSection method four times, once to create a simple link to the Home button and three more times with a third argument that calls the different sectional navigation methods—DeptNav(), CourseNav(), and PTNav(). The base implementations of these three methods in Web.py simply return the null string, so the home page contains only the buttons for the sectional start pages. This behavior is modified by descendants to ensure that the user can always see appropriate navigation features for the particular type of page being presented. This gives much more flexibility than a constant navigation bar, with little additional code complexity.

Additional Forms Convenience Methods

The only two other methods of significance are at the top level for convenience because they handle forms input, even though they do not appear in the home page.

The getValidForm() method retrieves a form descriptor from the session (stored there by the page that presented the form) and, if so requested, verifies that the form contains a hidden identification field that holds the id() value of the form descriptor (or raises an Error exception). It also raises an exception if the session form description identifier has been reset to None because the session timed out, and a new one was created. This makes it possible to prohibit users from submitting the same form twice with a high degree of certainty. The ChkReqd() method checks that all fields marked as "required" in the form descriptor are in fact present in the input, returning a list of error messages if not.

Although this increases the security of the system against events such as the user moving backward and resubmitting a form, form fields of type HIDDEN can be clearly seen by any browser user who uses the View Source option. Hidden fields should not be used to transmit values that need to remain hidden from users and casual network snoopers.

HTTP Generation from Content

The page content finally generated is folded up inside HTTP headers using the HTTP() method. This is a more flexible way of allowing various additional headers to be included in the response as necessary. As you can see in Listing 18.6, most of the HTTP is provided by methods, which retains the flexibility for subclasses to override the standard variants, most of which simply return the value of an instance variable. The content passed in has usually been generated by the Content() method.

Listing 18.6 **HTTP Generation Method**

```
    def HTTP(self, content):
        return """HTTP/1.0 %d %s
Content-Type: %s
Content-Length: %d
Date: %s
%s
%s
%s""" % (self.ReturnCode(), self.Message(), self.MIMEtype(), len(content),
            arpa.str(mxdt.now()),  self.Cookie(), self.Headers(), content)
```

Database Content Caching

Unlike the production data, such as course booking information, the tables containing the navigational structure information do not change frequently. It does not therefore make sense to read them every time they are required when they could be cached instead, and only re-read at intervals. Such caching minimizes the database bandwidth required for navigational features and improves site responsiveness. The `cachequery` module implements a simple technique to speed up single-table queries using column-equality selection criteria. Although you cannot use such a technique with *all* queries, it helps with a substantial majority of the queries used to determine the site's departmental navigation.

You can read the code in Listing 18.7. Each query holds a table name, a sequence of names of columns to be retrieved, a sequence of names of columns that will be used as keys, a database connection, and an optional caching refresh interval. The default value for this last argument is zero, which disables caching (the rows have a zero-length lifetime in the cache). You also can add a list of extra conditions using a WHERE argument and a sequencing clause using a list of column names.

Listing 18.7 *cachequery.py:* **Caching Non-Critical Queries to Reduce Database Load**

```
 1  #
 2  # $Workfile: cachequery.py $ $Revision: 5 $
 3  # $Date: 9/12/01 11:26p $ $Author: Sholden $
 4  #
 5  import mx.DateTime
 6  import dtuple
 7
 8  QueryCount = 0  # we identify queries by serial numbering them
 9
10  class CacheQuery:
11
12      """Defines a database query that caches single-table row sets.
```

continues

Listing 18.7 **Continued**

```
13
14      This object is initialized with
15
16      tbl         table name in the database
17      colnames    list of field names retrieved
18      keynames    list of keys used for retrieval
19      conn        database connection
20      refresh     caching refresh interval
21
22      Individual results are read by calling the object with a
23      tuple of key values as an argument. If the row set associated
24      with this particular set of keys is not present, or was read
25      longer than the refresh interval ago, it is re-read from the
26      database and stored in the content table as a list of database
27      tuples, which allow columns to be accessed by name.
28
29      Otherwise the already-cached database tuple set is returned.
30
31      Refinements might be added, such as registering with an
32      observer that might clear down all cache entries periodically
33      to force a global database refresh, and using a second SQL query
34      on row-modified timestamps to determine whether a refresh is
35      really required (which may or may not be a win for a given set
36      of columns).
37      """
38
39      def __init__(self, tbl, colnames, keynames, conn,
40                   refresh=0, WHERE=[], ORDER=None, debug=0):
41          """Create a caching data set for the given table, columns and keys."""
42          global QueryCount
43          QueryCount += 1
44          self.qnum = QueryCount
45          self._flush()
46          self.tbl = tbl
47          self.keynames = keynames
48          self.refresh = refresh
49          self.cursor = conn.cursor()
50          self.debug = debug
51          self.flushtime = mx.DateTime.now()
52          self.sql = "SELECT %s FROM %s" % (",".join(colnames), tbl)
53          if WHERE:
54              WHERE = [WHERE]
55          if keynames or WHERE:
56              condition = " AND ".join(["%s=?" % f for f in keynames] + WHERE)
57              self.sql += " WHERE %s" % condition
58          if ORDER:
59              self.sql += " ORDER BY " + ", ".join(ORDER)
60          self.desc = dtuple.TupleDescriptor([[n, ] for n in colnames])
```

```
61          if self.debug:
62              print "Descriptor:", self.desc
63              print QueryCount, "SQL:", self.sql
64
65      def _flush(self):
66          """Remove all trace of previous caching."""
67          self.recs = {}
68          self.when = {}
69
70      def __call__(self, keyvals=(), debug=0):
71          """Return the data set associated with given key values."""
72          if len(self.keynames) == 1 and type(keyvals) != type(()):
73              keyvals = (keyvals, ) # convenience
74          assert len(keyvals) == len(self.keynames)
75          now = mx.DateTime.now()
76          # flush the cache if it's time to do so
77          if now - self.flushtime >= self.refresh:
78              for k in self.when.keys():
79                  if now - self.when[k] >= self.refresh:
80                      del self.when[k]
81                      del self.recs[k]
82                      if self.debug or debug:
83                          print "Flushed", self.qnum, self.tbl, k, " at", now
84              self.flushtime = now
85          if self.recs.has_key(keyvals) and self.refresh and (now - ➥
            self.when[keyvals] < self.refresh):
86              if self.debug or debug:
87                  print "Used:", self.qnum, keyvals, "after", now - ➥
                    self.when[keyvals]
88              result = self.recs[keyvals]
89          else:
90              self.cursor.execute(self.sql, keyvals)
91              if self.debug or debug:
92                  print "Retrieving", self.qnum
93              rows = self.cursor.fetchall()
94              result = [dtuple.DatabaseTuple(self.desc, row) for row in rows]
95              if self.refresh:
96                  if self.debug or debug:
97                      print "Caching", self.qnum, self.tbl, keyvals, " at", now
98                  self.recs[keyvals] = result
99                  self.when[keyvals] = now
100         return result
101
102     def close(self):
103         self.recs = None
104         self.when = None
105         self.cursor.close()
106
107
108 if __name__ == "__main__":
```

continues

Listing 18.7   **Continued**

```
109    #
110    # Sorry, you'll need your own database details in here
111    #
112    import mx.ODBC.Windows as odbc
113    conn = odbc.connect("Ch18")
114    s1 = CacheQuery("department",                          # table
115                    "DptName DptWelcome DptLnksTxt".split(),  # columns
116                    ("DptCode",),                          # key columns
117                    conn, refresh=0)                       # other stuff
118    while 1:
119        dc = raw_input("Department Code: ")
120        if not dc:
121            break
122        rows = s1((dc, ), debug=1)
123        if len(rows) == 0:
124            print "No such department"
125        else:
126            for row in rows:
127                print """
128 Department: %s Full Name: %s
129 Welcome Text:
130 %s
131 Links Text:
132 %s
133 """ % (dc, row.DptName, row.DptWelcome, row.DptLnksTxt)
134    s1.close()
135    conn.close()
```

The __init__() method spends most of its time building the query it is eventually going to be issuing across the database connection, but it also creates two empty dictionaries, recs and when. The recs dictionary is used to hold the cached records, and the when dictionary associates an origination time with each record.

To use the query object, you call it, passing a tuple of values (or a single value, which as a kindness the __call__() method converts into a single-element tuple for you, to simplify calling sequences). You must use a tuple of key values because the argument becomes a dictionary key and must therefore be immutable. The query first checks whether it is time to flush its cache, and if so, it deletes all expired entries. It next examines its cache to see whether a nonexpired entry exists and if so, sets the result. Otherwise, it retrieves the required data from the database and caches it unless the refresh time is zero.

The result for a given set of key values is all rows from the named table that match the criteria in the constructed WHERE condition. For example, suppose you wanted to know when a particular course was running. Assuming the database structure discussed later, in the "Courses Database Structure" section, and given the following CacheQuery creation call:

```
c = CacheQuery("Class", ("ClsNum", "ClsDate", "ClsPublic"), ("CrsNum", ), conn, ➥
refresh=30, debug=1)
```

the constructed SQL statement (which you will see printed, because debugging is on) will be

```
SELECT ClsNum,ClsDate,ClsPublic FROM Class WHERE CrsNum=?
```

Calling the query object `c` with an appropriate course number argument returns a list of rows, each containing the class number, class date, and public flag for a class that teaches the given course number. The rows are `DatabaseTuple` objects, so you can use either the column names or numeric indexes to retrieve the values from each row.

This technique would also work with more complex queries, but column naming could be a problem if it were extended to multiple tables. Furthermore, there will always be some queries that do not lend themselves to it. For example, the `Qod` table is queried to see whether the current date and time is between the `QodDate` field and one day after the `QodDate`. Because the key to this query is the date and time of the query, the same key will never be used more than once, and caching will actually consume resources without giving any speedup. Just the same, for nonvolatile data, the `CacheQuery` object offers considerable benefits.

The Site Structure

The site functionality appears as three main sections: Departments, Courses, and PythonTeach. Each has an associated button that always appears in the navigation bar, allowing the user to select that area of site functionality. Different links can appear under the buttons according to the subpage displayed. The link sets are constant for all pages in Courses and PythonTeach. For Departments, the start page displays a list of available departments, and the user selects a particular department by using these links. The Departments navigation area then changes to allow selection of appropriate departmental features.

The Departments Section

The departmental pages present information of a general nature to the user, organized into sections each relating to a particular technology. Many organizations have similar needs, and so the code does not assume any particular set of departments will be present in the database. The departmental content comes almost entirely from a relational database, and it is an easy matter to delete the existing information and substitute your own should your interests lie somewhere besides selling Python classes.

The Departmental Database Structure

Because the Departments content is driven by content from the database, the code to generate the second-level navigation bars uses database queries to determine whether particular features should appear—there is no point generating links to empty features!

Figure 18.2 shows the structure of the departmental content as depicted in a Microsoft Access relationships diagram.

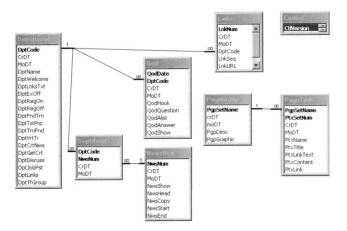

Figure 18.2   Structure of the data tables for departmental content.

The Department table contains the basic attributes describing a department. The existing code does not use all columns because the table was "inherited" from a previous design and still requires trimming of the excess columns. The DPTLnks column holds text that, if non–NULL, will be included in the navigation bar. This allows free-form entry of any desired editorial or linking content on a department-by-department basis.

Department is in a many-to-many relationship with the News entity through a linking entity called DeptNews. News items are topical snippets that might apply to several departments. Their content is dated for topicality by a start and end date, which indicates their currency. The many-to-many requirement arises because not only may the same news appear under different departments, but also any given department might display several news items. If relevant news items are found, the second-level navigation bar contains a News link.

There is also a one-to-many relationship between Department and Links. This allows details of large numbers of relevant web pages to be entered into the database rather than maintained as static content. If a department has related links, then a Links link appears in the second-level navigation bar.

The last direct relationship is one-to-many from Department to Qod (an abbreviation for questions of the day). Each Qod occurrence is relevant to a single day whose date is held in the QodDate column. The idea is that if there is a question for the current date, then its QodHook value appears as a "teaser" link in the navigation bar, and clicking on that link then displays the question in the main content area, with a further link to see the answer.

The `PageGroup` and `PageText` tables are there to store sets of pages that can be used to present related material. They have no direct relationship with the `Department` table, but the `DeptWelcome` and `DeptLinks` columns, which hold free-form HTML, can include links to pages that refer to these page sets. This allows a great deal of content flexibility, particularly because the same page set can be displayed in various different contexts if required.

Departmental Start Page

When the user clicks on the Departments button, the user sees the departmental start page, a generic welcome to the PythonTeach Departments section. The code for the start page class is surprisingly short, until you remember how much of its behavior it inherits from `Web.Page`. The code is shown in Listing 18.8. The module creates a private connection to the database with its own cursor and builds a `CacheQuery` to retrieve the codes and names of all departments. This query uses an empty key set, so only one entry can ever be cached.

Listing 18.8   *DeptStart.py:* **The Departmental Start Page**

```
 1  #
 2  # $Workfile: DeptStart.py $ $Revision: 1 $
 3  # $Date: 9/12/01 11:09a $ $Author: Sholden $
 4  #
 5  import Web
 6  from Error import Error
 7  from cachequery import CacheQuery
 8  from dtuple import TupleDescriptor, DatabaseTuple
 9  from dbsource import dbsource
10  import mx.DateTime
11
12  DptNames = ["DptCode", "DptName"]
13  conn = dbsource(").conn
14  cursor = conn.cursor()
15  qDept = CacheQuery("department", DptNames, (), conn, ORDER=(("DptName", )),➝
    refresh=30)
16
17  class Page(Web.Page):
18      """Abstract page implementing departmental look and feel."""
19
20      def Body(self):
21          return """<H2>Departments</H2>
22          <P>Welcome to the PythonTeach.com departments.
23          Many people with an interest in Python also need technical
24          resources to assist them in their research and development
25          work. These departments are intended to assist you in finding
26          useful information.</P>
27          <P>These areas of the site are maintained in a database, so
28          we can update them in a timely fashion. We hope you will make
```

continues

Listing 18.8   **Continued**

```
29          use of them on a regular basis, and
30          <HREF="mailto:Departments@holdenweb.com">assist us</A> by
31          suggesting other useful links, news items and questions of
32          interest.
33
34          """
35
36      def Title(self):
37          """Title is generic for departments."""
38          return "PythonTeach Departments"
39
40      def DeptNav(self):
41          """Generate navigation bar for departments start page."""
42          return "\n".join([self.NavLink(➡
                            ("/DeptHome/%s/" % p.DptCode, p.DptName)➡
                                         ) for p in qDept()])
```

The DeptNav() method returns a set of navigation links, one for each department in the database. The output of this method is the list of departments shown in Figure 18.3. The list is composed from the database, and each department name is linked to the standard departmental home page, personalized by adding the department code to the path of the URL.

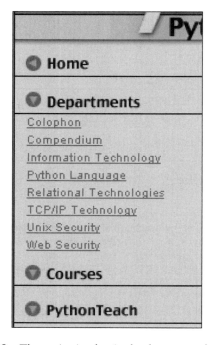

Figure 18.3   The navigation bar in the departmental start page.

Features Common to Other Department Pages

The remaining department pages have several features in common. They all expect the department code to appear on the URI path following the elements used to select the appropriate generator page. This is one difference between AWeFUL and many other web frameworks, where such parametric information must be included in the query string. AWeFUL effectively maps a parameterized set of object instances onto the virtual web. The departmental pages all use the same navigation structure. Consequently, they are all subclasses of an abstract (not meant to be instantiated) `Dept.Page` class, which extends the `Web.Page.__init__()` method by querying the database for relevant data and provides a tailored `DeptNav()` method, as you can see from Listing 18.9.

Listing 18.9 *Dept.py:* **The Abstract Departmental Page Definition**

```
 1  #
 2  # $Workfile: Dept.py $ $Revision: 5 $
 3  # $Date: 9/07/01 3:06p $ $Author: Sholden $
 4  #
 5  import Web
 6  from Error import Error
 7  from cachequery import CacheQuery
 8  from dtuple import TupleDescriptor, DatabaseTuple
 9  from dbsource import dbsource
10  import mx.DateTime
11
12  DptNames = ["DptCode", "DptName", "DptWelcome", "DptLinks", "DptLnksTxt"]
13  conn = dbsource().conn
14  cursor = conn.cursor()
15  qDept = CacheQuery("department", DptNames, ("DptCode", ),
16                     conn,  refresh=30)
17  qLnks = CacheQuery("links", ("LnkURL", "LnkText"), ("DptCode", ),
18                     conn,  refresh=30)
19  TD = TupleDescriptor([[d] for d in DptNames])
20
21  class Page(Web.Page):
22      """Abstract page implementing departmental look and feel."""
23
24      def __init__(self, *args, **kw):
25          Web.Page.__init__(self, *args, **kw)
26          try:
27              if len(self.path) == 0:
28                  raise ValueError
29              else:
30                  self.DptCode = self.path[0]
31              self.path = self.path[1:]
32              self.dpt = qDept(self.DptCode)
33              if not self.dpt:
34                  raise ValueError
35              self.dpt = self.dpt[0]
36          except ValueError:
```

continues

Listing 18.9   **Continued**

```
37                  self.DptCode = "Missing"
38                  self.dpt = DatabaseTuple(TD, ("Missing", "Missing Department",➡
                    "Welcome", "", ""))
39          now = mx.DateTime.today()
40          stmt = """SELECT DptCode, newsitem.NwsNum, NwsHead FROM newsitem,➡
            deptnews
41                      WHERE DptCode=?
42                      AND deptnews.NwsNum=newsitem.NwsNum
43                      AND ? BETWEEN NewsItem.NwsStart AND NewsItem.NwsEnd"""
44          cursor.execute(stmt, (self.dpt.DptCode, now))
45          self.Nws = cursor.fetchall()
46          self.lnk = qLnks((self.dpt.DptCode, ))
47          stmt = """SELECT QodHook, QodQuestion, QodAlist, QodAnswer
48                      FROM Qod WHERE ? BETWEEN QodDate AND QodDate+1
49                      AND DptCode = ?
50                      AND QodShow"""
51          cursor.execute(stmt, (now, self.dpt.DptCode))
52          self.qod = cursor.fetchall()
53          if self.qod:
54              self.qod = self.qod[0]
55          # There *SHOULD* be at most one ... but we use the first to be safe!
56
57
58  def Title(self):
59          """Title is department name."""
60          return self.dpt.DptName
61
62      def DeptHeader(self):
63          """Page starts with the department name."""
64          if self.DptCode:
65              text = self.dpt.DptName
66          else:
67              text = "No Department Name"
68          return """<H2>%s</FONT></H2>""" % text
69
70      def DeptNav(self):
71          """Generate navigation bar for any department page."""
72          result = []
73          if self.DptCode:
74              result.append("""<BR><A HREF="/DeptHome/%s/">Department➡
                Home</A><BR><BR>""" %
75                      self.dpt.DptCode)
76              if len(self.Nws):
77                  result.append("""<A HREF="/DeptNews/%s/">News</A><BR><BR➡
                    """ % self.dpt.DptCode)
78              if self.dpt.DptLnksTxt:
79                  result.append("%s<BR><BR>" % self.dpt.DptLnksTxt)
80              if len(self.lnk):
```

```
81                   result.append("""<A HREF="/DeptLinks/%s/">More➡
                     Links</A><BR><BR>""" % self.dpt.DptCode)
82             if len(self.qod):
83                 # Departmental question of the day
84                 result.append("""<B>Today's question:</B><BR>
85                 <A HREF="/DeptQod/%s/">%s ...</A><BR><BR>""" %➡
                   (self.dpt.DptCode, self.qod[0]))
86   return "\n".join(result)
```

The __init__() method retrieves the appropriate row from the Department table with
a CacheQuery. If the department name given is not found in the database, rather than
raise an exception when no department data are found, the method fictionalizes to
provide a usable DatabaseTuple. It fetches appropriate news item data, uses another
CacheQuery to retrieve any Links data that may exist, and retrieves any question of
the day for this department and today's date. This information is all stored in instance
variables and is available to any subclass's methods.

The DeptNav() method builds a list of HTML chunks, most of them optional
according to the content of the database retrieved by the __init__() method. The
result of DeptNav() is the concatenation of all the individual chunks. This code is
somewhat intricate, but you should remember here that we are coding for many
classes that will inherit this behavior rather than just one, so the effort is justified. This
is a major benefit of programming in object-oriented languages: copy-and-paste of
code, with its consequent maintenance problems, is less likely when inheritance provides subclasses with access to the superclass's code. You will see what the rendered
navigation bars look like in the next section.

The Department Home Page

Each department in the database uses the same home page, whose appearance the
content of the database configures appropriately. Given the advantages of object-
orientation mentioned at the end of the last section, you should not be surprised to
find from Listing 18.10 that the code for the department home page is pleasantly short.

Listing 18.10   *DeptHome.py:* **The Department Home Page**

```
1  #
2  # $Workfile: DeptHome.py $ $Revision: 2 $
3  # $Date: 9/13/01 12:47a $ $Author: Sholden $
4  #
5  import Dept
6  from Error import Error
7
8  class Page(Dept.Page):
9
10     def Body(self):
11 return self.DeptHeader() + self.dpt.DptWelcome
```

All the class needs to do is declare a `Body()` method that adds the departmental welcome message, read from the database by the `Dept.__init__()` method, to the standard department header, generated in `Dept.DeptHeader()`.

Figure 18.4 shows the home page of a full-featured department, with many navigation bar features present.

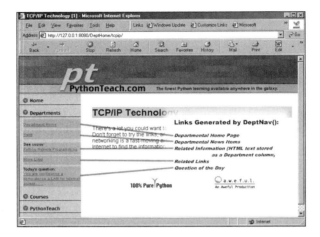

Figure 18.4   A full-featured department home page with many navigation features.

By contrast, Figure 18.5 shows a department with very little ancillary navigational content. The only additional feature generated from the database is the "related course" link, generated from the Department's `DptLnks` column.

Figure 18.5   A department home page with few navigational features.

The capability of programmed sites to change their behavior in this way makes them much easier to maintain. The site content is largely stored in the database, and the site reacts to any changes in the data by adjusting the linkages automatically, without any need to edit HTML.

It would, of course, be much more convenient for the graphic designers to be able to edit the HTML without having to tread all over delicate code. One advantage of the templating approaches you saw in Chapter 16, "Web Application Frameworks," is that many of them do indeed implement such a separation. The overall look-and-feel of the site is determined by a separate file, which is read by the Web module when the server starts. More could be done to separate content from logic, however, and this would improve the overall maintainability of the site. This is another enhancement the company is thinking about for Release 2.

Departmental News Pages

The News link, when present, indicates that a list of departmental news items can be viewed by clicking the link. Each news item is presented as a linked headline, which brings up the appropriate news item. Again these pages are relatively small due to inheritance from the Dept.Page class. Listing 18.11 shows the news listing page.

Listing 18.11 *DeptNews.py:* **Listing the News Items for a Department**

```
 1  #
 2  # $Workfile: DeptNews.py $ $Revision: 2 $
 3  # $Date: 9/13/01 8:04a $ $Author: Sholden $
 4  #
 5  import Dept
 6  from Error import Error
 7
 8
 9  class Page(Dept.Page):
10
11      def News(self):
12          result = ["""<BR><P>"""]
13          for row in self.Nws:
14              result.append("""<A HREF="/DeptNewsItem/%s/%s">%s</A> <BR><BR>"""➡
                    % row)
15          result.append("""<FONT></P>""")
16          return "\n".join(result)
17
18      def Body(self):
19          return self.DeptHeader()+"<B>%s</B><BR>%s" % ("News", self.News())
```

The Body() method simply returns the departmental header, followed by a subpage title and a list of news items. Note that the self.Nws instance variable was set by the query defined by the Dept.Page.__init__() method, at line 40 of Listing 18.9. Each row contains the department code, news item number, and headline, in exactly the sequence required by the string format used in line 14. The order of the fields is guaranteed by the field order of the SELECT statement; so in this case, the additional work of creating a database tuple is unnecessary. This generates a link such as

```
<A HREF="/DeptNewsItem/tcpip/1">News Item Number 1</A>
```

for each row retrieved from the database.

This might be an appropriate point to expand on one disadvantage of using inheritance so heavily. Inheritance brings many benefits, but you may remember I suggested in Chapter 16 that the instance variables of an object related to the methods somewhat as global variables relate to the regular functions. Because instances save state between method invocations, it can be difficult when you read the code for an object-oriented system to determine how, when, and where particular instance variables are set. These problems can be eased by the use of advanced IDE software tools incorporating class browsers. As the Python user base grows, you can expect to see such tools emerging, but at the time of this writing they are few and far between.

Each news item is displayed by the class associated in the site map with the /DeptNewsItem/ path. The code of this class is shown in Listing 18.12. The only method required is a simple Body() to display the requested item in the context of the current department, and most of the code is concerned with establishing a CacheQuery to retrieve the news items (because these also do not change on a minute-to-minute basis).

Listing 18.12 *DeptNewsItem.py:* **Here Is the News**

```
 1  #
 2  # $Workfile: DeptNewsItem.py $ $Revision: 4 $
 3  # $Date: 9/12/01 10:47a $ $Author: Sholden $
 4  #
 5  import Dept
 6
 7  from cachequery import CacheQuery
 8  from dbsource import dbsource
 9  from Error import Error
10
11  conn = dbsource().conn
12  cursor = conn.cursor()
13
14  qNitm = CacheQuery("NewsItem", ("NwsHead", "NwsCopy"), ("NwsNum", ), conn,�
    refresh = 30)
15
16  class Page(Dept.Page):
17
18      def Body(self):
19          if not self.path:
20              raise Error(400, "Bad Request", errmsg="No news item number➥
                given")
```

```
21          item = qNitm(self.path[0])[0]
22          return self.DeptHeader()+"<B><I>%s</I></B><br>%s" % (item.NwsHead,➥
            item.NwsCopy)
```

The returned page body shows the news item's headline in boldface after the
department heading, followed by the content of the news item. Of course, with
a suitable information source such as O'Reily's Meerkat
(`http://www.oreillynet.com/meerkat/`), you could use XML–based technologies
to extract live feeds from the Internet. A good starting point for looking at such
techniques is `http://www.oreillynet.com/pub/a/rss/2000/12/08/lightweight.html`.
You will find that support code in Python is readily available.

Departmental Links

The links page is simply a list of the external links related to the current department.
The `Dept.__init__()` method retrieves the list of links (refer to line 46 of Listing
18.9), and the `Dept.NavBar()` method includes a `More Links` link if the set is not
empty. Following this link causes the handler to generate content using a
`DeptLinks.Page` object, whose code appears in Listing 18.13.

Listing 18.13 *DeptLinks.py:* **Displaying Departmental Links**

```
 1  #
 2  # $Workfile: DeptLinks.py $ $Revision: 2 $
 3  # $Date: 9/13/01 9:51a $ $Author: Sholden $
 4  #
 5  import Dept
 6
 7  from dbsource import dbsource
 8
 9  conn = dbsource().conn
10  cursor = conn.cursor()
11
12
13  class Page(Dept.Page):
14
15      def Links(self):
16          result = ["""<BR><P><FONT SIZE="-1">"""]
17          for row in self.lnk:
18              result.append("""<A HREF="http://%s">%s</A><HR>""" %➥
                (row.LnkURL, row.LnkText))
19          result.append("""</FONT></P>""")
20          return "\n".join(result)
21
22      def Body(self):
23          return "%s<B>%s</B></P>%s" % (self.DeptHeader(), "Additional Links",➥
            self.Links())
```

The `Body()` method uses the `Links()` method to generate a list of hypertext links and returns the list preceded by the departmental header and an Additional Links subheader.

Departmental Question (and Answer) of the Day

The final optional navigation feature for departmental pages is the Question of the Day. A set of questions and answers is held in the `Qod` database table under a composite primary key of department and date. If the `Dept.Page.__init__()` method finds an appropriate question, then the `QodHook` column value appears as a navigation feature, linked to a page that displays the full question and a set of possible answers. Note that the complexity of determining the right question is such that the required results are retrieved in the `__init__()` method to avoid using two similar queries, the first of which simply establishes the presence of the question.

A `DeptQod.Page` object displays the question followed by the answer list, and a `DeptQodAns.Page` object displays the answer. Listings 18.14 and 18.15 show the code for these pages, respectively.

Listing 18.14 *DeptQod.py:* **Displaying the Question of the Day**

```
 1  #
 2  # $Workfile: DeptQod.py $ $Revision: 1 $
 3  # $Date: 9/03/01 12:01p $ $Author: Sholden $
 4  #
 5  import Dept
 6
 7
 8  class Page(Dept.Page):
 9
10      def Body(self):
11          result = [self.DeptHeader(),
12                      """<B><I>Question of the Day</I></B>➠
                        <BR><BR>%s<BR><BR>%s<BR><BR>""" %
13                          self.qod[1:3]]
14          result.append("""<A HREF="/DeptQodAns/%s">Click for the➠
            answer</A>""" % self.dpt.DptCode)
15          return "\n".join(result)
```

Listing 18.15 *DeptQodAns.py:* **Displaying the Answer of the Day**

```
 1  #
 2  # $Workfile: DeptQodAns.py $ $Revision: 1 $
 3  # $Date: 9/03/01 12:02p $ $Author: Sholden $
 4  #
 5  import Dept
 6
 7
```

```
 8  class Page(Dept.Page):
 9
10      def Body(self):
11          return """%s<B><I>Answer of the Day</I></B><BR><BR>%s<BR><BR>""" % ➥
12                      (self.DeptHeader(), self.qod[3])
```

Due to the groundwork laid by the `Dept` superclass, both classes are about as simple as you have any right to expect a web page's code to be.

Using Departmental Page Groups

You will remember from reading about the departmental database structure seeing a one-to-many relationship from the `PageGroup` table to the `PageText`, even though these tables had no relationships to any other database content. Every page group has a unique name (the `PgpName` field, which is the primary key for the `PageGroup` table). The member pages of a page group use a composite primary key whose first attribute is the `PgpName` of the page group and whose second item is numeric.

The idea behind page groups is to allow presentation of related pieces of information without having to define Python classes to present the individual member pages. This feature is integrated into the departments section through the `DeptPg.Page` class and could easily be added in a similar way to any other section of the site. It might even be possible to define a `mixin` class that could be added to any standard page generator's base classes. The code of the page generator class appears in Listing 18.16, and a sample page is shown in Figure 18.6.

Listing 18.16   *DeptPg.py:* **The Departmental Page Group Member Page Generator**

```
 1  #
 2  # $Workfile: DeptPg.py $ $Revision: 3 $
 3  # $Date: 9/12/01 10:48a $ $Author: Sholden $
 4  #
 5  import Dept
 6
 7  from cachequery import CacheQuery
 8  from dbsource import dbsource
 9  from Error import Error
10
11  conn = dbsource().conn
12  cursor = conn.cursor()
13
14
15  qPlnk = CacheQuery("PageText",
16                      ("PtxLinkText", "PtxSetNum", "PtxLink"),
17                      ("PgpSetName", ),
18                      conn, refresh=30)
19  qPttl = CacheQuery("PageText",
20                      ("PtxTitle", "PtxContent"),
```

continues

Listing 18.16 **Continued**

```
21                          ("PgpSetName", "PtxSetNum"),
22                          conn, ORDER=("PtxSetNum", ), refresh=30)
23
24  class Page(Dept.Page):
25
26      def Body(self):
27
28          if len(self.path) >= 2:
29              self.PgpSetName = self.path[0]
30              self.PtxSetNum = self.path[1]
31              self.path = self.path[2:]
32              linkdata = qPlnk((self.PgpSetName, ))
33              pttl = qPttl((self.PgpSetName, self.PtxSetNum))
34              if not pttl:
35                  raise Error(404, "Not Found", errmsg="No such page group➥
                    page")
36              self.pttl = pttl[0]
37              result = [self.DeptHeader(), '<font size="-2"><center>']
38              links = []
39              for PtxLinkText, PtxSetNum, PtxLink in linkdata:
40                  if not PtxLink:
41                      PtxLink = "DeptPgPage"
42                  if str(PtxSetNum) != self.PtxSetNum:
43                      links.append('<A HREF="/%s/%s/%s/%s">%s</A>' % (PtxLink,➥
                        self.DptCode, self.PgpSetName, PtxSetNum, PtxLinkText))
44                  else:
45                      links.append(PtxLinkText)
46              result.append(" | ".join(links)) # XXX need sensible multiline➥
                behavior here
47              result.append('</center></font>')
48              result.append("<BR><HR>%s" % (self.pttl.PtxContent))
49              return "\n".join(result)
50          else:
51              raise Error(400, "Bad request", errmsg="Need a page group and➥
                group number")
```

The generator uses two CacheQueries. The first, qPlnk, retrieves link information for every page in a set. This is used in the Body() method to generate a set of links at the top of the page, allowing the user to easily switch to any page in the set by clicking on the link. It is also easy to make pages refer to each other, using an HREF attribute of "../N" where N is the page number to link to: because the page group and page number are the last two items in the path, a page group looks like a directory in the virtual web! The second CacheQuery, qPttl, retrieves the information from the particular member page of interest for display as the page content.

Lines 39 through 47 generate the page header links. You can see that the code is careful not to make the member page being displayed a hypertext link. The comment reminds the author to try later to ensure that a single link does not unnecessarily appear as an orphaned item on a line by itself, although this will be a refinement. The method ends by appending the member page's content to the generated link headers and returning its result.

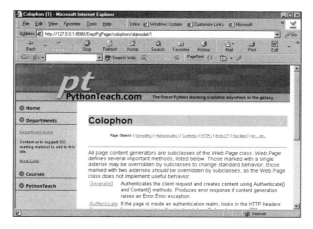

Figure 18.6 A departmental page group page.

The Courses Section

The PythonTeach web site is a commercial vehicle for the courses offered by the company. To sell courses, the site has to make information about them available in easy-to-find ways, and it has to make it easy for the site visitor to enter orders, without prior administrative work such as creating an account. Ultimately, the users must identify themselves to place orders, but a site that requires them to enter their details before shopping turns off many people. After they decide that they want something, they are much more likely to fill out a simple form to identify themselves.

For this reason, the pages that display course details and accept requests for bookings are outside any authentication realm and can be used by any visitor. The only protected page related to ordering is the one in which the user confirms that he wants to proceed with an order. Of course, this raises a few logistical problems because PythonTeach wants to be sure that it has at least some likelihood of collecting the money for ordered places, and this requirement will only be satisfied if PythonTeach can establish communication of some sort with the user.

PythonTeach has therefore opted for a system that asks the users to identify themselves using their email address. After the user's details are captured, the system sends her an email as described in "Structure of the Application" at the start of this chapter. The PythonTeach marketing staff therefore feel there is at least some probability that the user will be genuine if she is prepared to reveal her email address. Unfortunately, this means that the user's order must somehow be held in abeyance until the account is activated by use of the confirmation URL.

Fortunately, Python has a solution: the `pickle` module allows arbitrarily complex data structures to be rendered into text format and reloaded at a future time. As you will see, the booking information is pickled into a database field and stored awaiting the user's sign-up confirmation, at which time it is unpickled back into the new session state.

When new users follow the link to place an order, they are shown a page with two possible exits. The first asks them to place their order using an existing account, whereas the second allows them to create a new account. If they choose the first option but fail to authenticate themselves, they see the standard authentication failure page, which gives them the option to receive a password reminder by email (which happens only if they entered an email address that occurs in the authentication table), or to create a new account.

Here you see another advantage of close integration between the server and the application code. A standard web server, such as Apache, requests browser authentication whenever the user attempts to access an authenticated page. If users fail to authenticate themselves, no information is available to the application code, which therefore finds it difficult to know how to proceed.

The Courses Database Structure

The database structure that supports the course-ordering process appears in Figure 18.7. Try not to let the number of tables and relationships confuse you; it is a straightforward design when explained. Some features of the database support requirements not implemented by web functionality in the current design. In the interests of pragmatism and a fast startup, PythonTeach is currently implementing these features by either entering data directly into tables or using a graphical front-end tool such as Access to create the necessary entry forms. By the time you reach the end of the book, you should have all the necessary skills to implement such additional functions yourself should you so require. Perhaps you should check to see whether PythonTeach have added a Recruitment department because they still have some way to go in building their systems.

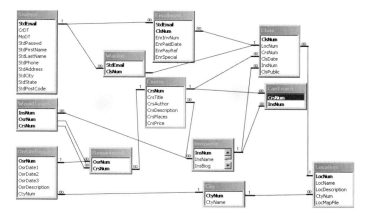

Figure 18.7   Structure of the data tables for course ordering.

The most important tables in the design are `Student`, `Class`, and `Course`. Without recording student details, there would be little point in the rest of the system. Figure 18.7 shows that students can either be enrolled or wait-listed for a class, so there are two independent many-to-many relationships between `Student` and `Class`, each implemented by separate linking entities. Classes may be public or on-site, but the course-ordering pages only list public classes. Relational integrity cannot ensure, however, that a student enrolled for a class is not also wait-listed for it. This is a semantic integrity constraint, which the application code rather than the RDBMS should handle.

A relatively simple change to the database schema would allow referential constraints to suffice, though. Rather than enrollments and wait-list places being separate entities, they could be a single entity, implementing a many-to-many relationship between `Student` and `Class`, with an attribute indicating which type of booking was involved. In this case, there could only *either* be a booking or a wait-list entry, due to the uniqueness constraint on the primary key. This simplification will probably also be introduced into PythonTeach's next release.

There is a complex set of relationships between `Instructor`, `Course`, and `Class`. Each class presents a particular course, giving a one-to-many relationship from `Course` to `Class` (the same course can be taught in many classes). A particular instructor presents each course, giving a one-to-many relationship from `Instructor` to `Class`. The classes that a particular instructor can teach (in other words, for which the instructor has relevant technical skills and training) appear in `CanTeach`, which implements a many-to-many relationship between `Instructor` and `Course`. Again, the need for instructors to present only courses they are trained to teach is a little too complex for relational integrity constraints and requires application code to enforce it during the scheduling process.

Courses are presented at particular venues whose details appear in the `Location` table, and each location is hosted in a particular city. Both relationships are one-to-many: a city may host several locations, and a location may be the venue for several classes.

The final part of the puzzle is the section pertaining to on-site class requirements, not currently implemented as web code. An `OnSiteRequirement` has up to three possible start dates and requests a number of courses at the nearest available city. There is therefore a many-to-many relationship between on-site requirements and courses, implemented by the `Requirement` table, as well as a many-to-one relationship between on-site requirements and cities. Eventually, software will be provided to allow instructors to examine on-site requirements for classes they can teach and express a willingness to teach particular sessions. The `Requirement` table is therefore in a many-to-many relationship with `Instructor`.

Ultimately someone will make the decision as to whether an on-site requirement can be filled, and by which instructors, and issue a quotation to the customer (Student) making the enquiry. If the quotation is accepted, then the classes are entered into the `Class` table but not as public classes. A similar registration mechanism to the one used for public courses then allows students to register in advance for the on-site classes.

As you can see, the PythonTeach programmers have their work cut out for them. They have made a good start, though, and do not anticipate any major difficulties in implementing the rest of the system.

The Courses Start Page

When a web site visitor clicks on the Courses navigation button, he sees a page generated by a `Courses.Page` object. This object generates a canned piece of HTML content in its `Body()` method and implements a `CourseNav()` method that is inherited by all other courses page objects. As Listing 18.17 shows, it also implements a `ListCourses()` method, which it does not use—again this is intended to be used by descendant classes.

Another advantage of keeping site content in a database is that the display language can be a parameter to the retrieval, allowing the construction of multilingual web sites.

My limited experience in designing such sites suggests that, although this does complicate the database design somewhat, it is simpler than hard-coding the multilingual features in the HTML generation code.

Listing 18.17   *Courses.py:* **The Course Start Page**

```
1  #
2  # $Workfile: Courses.py $ $Revision: 5 $
3  # $Date: 9/12/01 12:38p $ $Author: Sholden $
4  #
5  import Web
6  from Error import Error
7  from cachequery import CacheQuery
8  from dtuple import TupleDescriptor, DatabaseTuple
9  from dbsource import dbsource
10 import pyforms
11
12 import mx.DateTime as mxdt
13
14 CrsNames = ["CrsNum", "CrsTitle", "CrsAuthor", "CrsDescription",➥
   "CrsPlaces", "CrsPrice"]
15 InsNames = ["InsName"]
16
17 conn = dbsource().conn
18 cursor = conn.cursor()
19 qCrss = CacheQuery("Course", CrsNames, (),
20                    conn, ORDER=("CrsNum",), refresh=30)
21 qIns = CacheQuery("Instructor", InsNames, ("InsNum", ),
22                    conn, refresh=30)
23
24 class Page(Web.Page):
25
26     def Body(self):
27         return """
28         <h3>PythonTeach Courses</H3>
29         <P>We specialise in one-day training courses covering➥
           [ ... HTML text omitted ... ]
46         object-oriented scripting language.
47         """
48
49     def Title(self):
50         return "PythonTeach: Course Information"
51
52     def CourseNav(self):
53         links = [
54             ("/AllCourses/", "Current Courses"),
55             ("/CourseCity/", "Classes by Location"),
56             ("/CourseNum/", "Classes by Course")
57             ]
58         return "\n".join([self.NavLink(p) for p in links])
```

continues

Listing 18.17   **Continued**

```
59
60      def ListCourses(self, r, heading):
61          color = 0
62          result = ["""
63          <h3>%s</h3>
64          <P>
65          <table cellpadding="2">
66          <tr>
67          <td>Date</td>
68          <td>Class Title and Location</td>
69          <td>Price</td>
70          <td> </td>
71          </tr>
72          """ % heading]
73          for c in r:
74              color = 1-color
75              city, locn, date, titl, cnum, plcs, price = c
76              cursor.execute("SELECT COUNT(*) FROM Enrollment WHERE ClsNum=?",➡
                (cnum, ))
77              enrl = cursor.fetchall()[0][0]
78              if enrl >= plcs:
79                  ltxt = "WaitList Me"
80                  lhref = "/CourseWaitList/%s/" % cnum
81              else:
82                  ltxt = "Enroll Me"
83                  lhref = "/CourseEnroll/%s/" % cnum
84              result.append("""
85              <tr bgcolor="%s">
86              <td valign="top"><b>%s</b></td>
87              <td valign="top"><b>%s</b><br><font size="-2">%s</font></td>
88              <td valign="top"><b>$%d</b></td>
89              <td valign="top"><a href="%s"><b>%s</b></a></td>
90              </tr>""" % (
91                  ("#ccffff", "#33ffff")[color], date.strftime("%b %d"),
92                  titl, locn, price, lhref, ltxt))
93          result.append("""
94          </table>
95          </P>""")
96          return "\n".join(result)
```

The `CourseNav()` method is a straightforward use of `NavLink()` to provide links to access course details and class lists by city and by course. The navigation bar it produces is shown in Figure 18.8, which displays the courses start page.

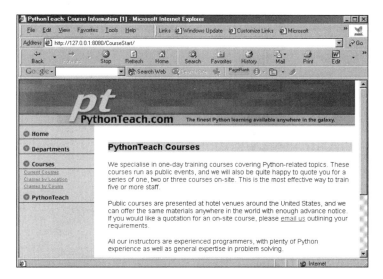

Figure 18.8   The courses navigation feature in the site navigation bar.

The `ListCourses()` method produces an HTML table from a list of rows, each of which is a seven-tuple containing information about a class and a heading. You can see how the table renders in Internet Explorer—for complex reasons, in Netscape Navigator 4.x the shaded backgrounds do not appear—in the section on "Selecting Courses by City."

Basic Course Information

Clicking on the `Current Courses` link triggers a page generated by a `CourseAll.Page` object. The code is a simple HTML generator that iterates over the course rows retrieved by the `qCrss` `CacheQuery` defined in the `Courses` module. It uses a further `CacheQuery`, `qIns`, from that module to retrieve the instructor names. The generated HTML includes anchor tags to link each course title to a page that displays full details. The instructor name is also a hypertext link, but at present PythonTeach has not implemented the code, so clicking the link results in a 404-error response from the server. The code for the `CourseAll` module appears in Listing 18.18.

Listing 18.18   *CourseAll.py:* **Listing the Courses**

```
1  #
2  # $Workfile: CourseAll.py $ $Revision: 2 $
3  # $Date: 9/12/01 1:01p $ $Author: Sholden $
4  #
5  import Courses
6
```

continues

Listing 18.18 *Continued*

```
 7
 8  class Page(Courses.Page):
 9
10      def Body(self):
11          result = ["""<H3>PythonTeach Course Offerings</H3>
12          <P>This lists all our current classes. Please click on the course ➡
            title
13          for more information.</P><TABLE>"""]
14          crslst = Courses.qCrss()
15          for c in crslst:
16              a = Courses.qIns(c.CrsAuthor)[0]
17              result.append("""
18  <TR><TD VALIGN="TOP">%d</TD>
19      <TD VALIGN="TOP"><A HREF="/Course/%d/">%s</A><BR>
20          <FONT SIZE="-2"><i>by</I> <A➡
            HREF="/Instructor/%d/">%s</A></FONT></TD>
21      <TD VALIGN="TOP">$%d</TD>
22  </TR>""" % (c.CrsNum, c.CrsNum, c.CrsTitle, c.CrsAuthor, a.InsName,➡
    c.CrsPrice))
23          result.append("</TABLE>")
24          return "\r\n".join(result)
```

Clicking on a course title drills down to the more complete information on that particular class. The database content here is somewhat sparse at present, but the CourseShow.Page object displays whatever is there. As you can see from Listing 18.19, the object uses a module-level CacheQuery to retrieve the course data. A Schedule link, visible at the top of Figure 18.9, allows the user to see which classes are currently scheduled to present the course.

Listing 18.19 *CourseShow.py:* **Listing the Information About a Single Course**

```
 1  #
 2  # $Workfile: CourseShow.py $ $Revision: 2 $
 3  # $Date: 9/12/01 1:01p $ $Author: Sholden $
 4  #
 5  import Courses
 6  from Error import Error
 7  from cachequery import CacheQuery
 8  from dbsource import dbsource
 9
10  conn = dbsource().conn
11  cursor = conn.cursor()
12
13  qCrs = CacheQuery("Course", Courses.CrsNames, ("CrsNum", ),
14                    conn, refresh=30)
15
16  class Page(Courses.Page):
```

```
17
18      def Body(self):
19          if not self.path:
20              raise Error(404, "Not Found", errmsg="No course number")
21          crsNum = self.path[0]
22          c = qCrs(crsNum)[0]
23          a = Courses.qIns(c.CrsAuthor)[0]
24          return """
25  <P>Course %d : %s : $%d [<A HREF="/CourseByNum/%s/">Schedule</A>]</P>
26  <P>%s</P>
27  <P><FONT SIZE="-2">This course, written by <A➥
    HREF="/Instructor/%d/">%s</a>, can
28      accommodate a maximum of %d students.</P>""" % ➥
29              (c.CrsNum, c.CrsTitle, c.CrsPrice, c.CrsNum, c.CrsDescription,
30                      c.CrsAuthor, a.InsName, c.CrsPlaces)
```

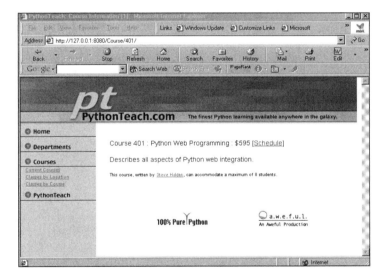

Figure 18.9   Display of course detail from `CourseShow.py`.

Selecting Classes by City and by Course

Inevitably, when users have to make inputs to web systems, they end up filling
out forms. You have read about code to generate forms automatically, but the user
experience can be less than satisfactory if the feedback from the form handling code is
inadequate. Ideally, if the form input is inadequate in some way, then the user should
receive back a copy of the form, *with valid inputs still present* and one or more messages
indicating how the input should be changed to make it acceptable.

As you will see in "The User Section" later in this chapter, the techniques adopted by PythonTeach within the AWeFUL framework allow it to provide just such helpfully explicit feedback to its users and would-be users. The code uses a still-further enhanced version of the `pyforms` module, which now includes the capability to build pull-down selection items from database tables. This is the feature used to select classes to be listed in the PythonTeach web site.

PythonTeach wants class details to be easily available. The marketing staff says that there are two primary search vectors that prospective students will use above all others:

- What classes are running (and when) in a particular city
- When (and where) a particular class is running

This is why the second and third links appear in the courses navigation feature: they bring up forms that allow the user to select a city or a course and receive a listing of classes from which they can select those they want to reserve. The (Python) classes that provide these listings are extremely small and appear in Listings 18.20 (classes by city) and 18.21 (classes by course).

Listing 18.20   *CourseCtForm.py:* **Select a City for a Class Listing**

```
 1   #
 2   # $Workfile: CourseCtForm.py $ $Revision: 3 $
 3   # $Date: 9/13/01 11:23p $ $Author: Sholden $
 4   #
 5   import Courses
 6   import pyforms
 7
 8
 9   class Page(Courses.Page):
10
11       def Body(self):
12           FD = (
13                   ["CityNum","Location","DDA","City:CtyNum:CtyName",""],
14               )
15           self.session._fd = FD
16           self.session._secureform = 0
17           return pyforms.FormBuild(FD, "Search", "/CourseByCity/",
18                           cursor=Courses.cursor, Buttons=(("LIST", 0), ))
```

Listing 18.21   *CourseNmForm.py:* **Select a Course for a Class Listing**

```
 1   #
 2   # $Workfile: CourseNmForm.py $ $Revision: 3 $
 3   # $Date: 9/13/01 11:25p $ $Author: Sholden $
 4   #
```

```
 5   import Courses
 6   import pyforms
 7
 8   class Page(Courses.Page):
 9
10       def Body(self):
11           FD = (
12                   ["CrsNum","Course","DDA","Course:CrsNum:CrsTitle",""],
13               )
14           self.session._fd = FD
15           self.session._secureform = 0
16           return pyforms.FormBuild(FD, "Search", "/CourseByNum/",
17                           cursor=Courses.cursor, Buttons=(("LIST", 0), ))
```

Both page classes create a form description, which is in the conventional `pyforms` format: quintuples of data. The third element in these particular tuples is `"DDA"`, which stands for "DropDown (autosubmitting)." The fourth element in the tuple gives a colon-separated list consisting of the table name to read when generating the drop-down, the name of the column to supply the values to be transmitted in the form, and the name of the column to supply the values seen by the user. These last two column names may be the same if required, although they are not in these examples.

The form description is stored in session state: the page that processes the form content will extract the description and use it to analyze the user's input. The `self.session._secureform` variable indicates that there is no need for security on these forms. A further enhancement comes into action if `self.session._secureform` is true: the forms contain a hidden field that holds the `id()` value of the form description, and this is checked for a match with the `id()` description being used to process it.

This makes it much less likely that a user will be able to request one form and then go back through his browser's history to another form, which he then submits for processing, because the probability of the two form descriptions being generated with the same `id()` value is vanishingly low. However, in this case, all the forms do is select from class lists, and we are happy to have users go back and change their selection to generate a new list, so security is unnecessary.

The forms generated are simple, each comprising one drop-down and one Submit button. Because the auto-submit drop-downs use a client-side JavaScript trick to automatically submit the form when a value is selected, the button is only required by older browsers. The forms are shown in Figures 18.10 and 18.11.

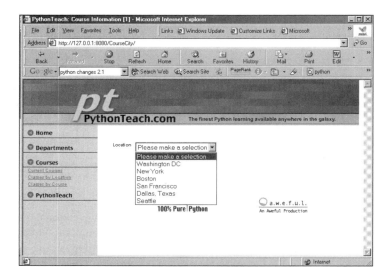

Figure 18.10   Selecting classes by city.

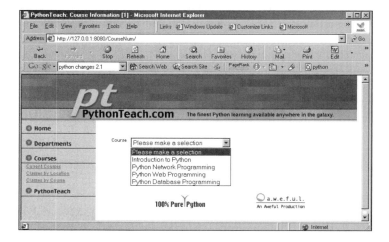

Figure 18.11   Selecting classes by course.

Displaying Classes by City and Course

The forms presented in the previous section have to be processed to produce an appropriate class listing. You have already seen a method to list classes, introduced higher up the inheritance tree as the `Courses.Page.ListCourses()` method (see Listing 18.17). This method is used to generate content in both the form-processing pages, whose code is therefore reasonably short and comprehensible.

The forms are so simple that no reference to the form description is required in the code. Listing 18.22 shows the generation of the courses for a particular city. There is only one value of interest (the "CityNum" field), so it is extracted directly from the CGI input held in the self.input instance variable and used as an argument to an appropriate SQL statement.

Listing 18.22 *CourseByCity.py:* **Listing All Classes in a Specified City**

```
 1  #
 2  # $Workfile: CourseByCity.py $ $Revision: 2 $
 3  # $Date: 9/12/01 1:01p $ $Author: Sholden $
 4  #
 5  import Courses
 6  from dbsource import dbsource
 7
 8  conn = dbsource().conn
 9  cursor = conn.cursor()
10
11  class Page(Courses.Page):
12
13      def Body(self):
14          FD = self.getValidForm()
15          city = self.input["CityNum"]
16          if not city:
17              raise Error(404, "Not Found", errmsg="No city selected")
18          sql = """
19          SELECT CtyName, LocName, ClsDate, CrsTitle, ClsNum, CrsPlaces,➥
          CrsPrice
20          FROM City, Location, Course, Class
21          WHERE City.CtyNum = Location.CtyNum
22              AND Course.CrsNum = Class.CrsNum
23              AND Location.LocNum = Class.LocNum
24              AND City.CtyNum=?
25              AND Class.ClsPublic
26              ORDER BY ClsDate"""
27          cursor.execute(sql, (city, ))
28          r = cursor.fetchall()
29          if not r:
30              cursor.execute("SELECT CtyName FROM City WHERE CtyNum=?",➥
              (city, ))
31              r = cursor.fetchall()
32              return "<H3>No classes are currently scheduled for %s</H3>" %➥
              r[0][0]
33          else:
34              return self.ListCourses(r, "Upcoming %s Classes" % r[0][0])
```

The query joins four tables across their relationships to produce all the information that the user will need to see in the listing. You can see a sample in Figure 18.12. Notice that the table row for each class ends with a link that allows the user to enroll for the class (or, if the class is full, to join the wait list for the class). These links implement the shopping functions of the site discussed in "Shopping the Site" later in the chapter.

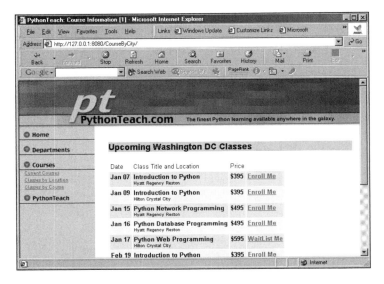

Figure 18.12   A listing of classes at all venues in Washington, DC.

The code to list the presentations of a particular course, shown in Listing 18.23, serves a dual purpose. Not only does the form trigger this page, but so do the [Schedule] links on the course information pages (refer to Figure 18.8). The code therefore examines the HTTP method and takes its input from an appropriate source depending on whether the request is a POST or a GET. The SQL query is almost the same, joining the same four tables and producing exactly the same result columns, and the Courses.Page.ListCourses() method is again used to present the results to the user, so the output is very similar to Figure 18.12 with the exception that the course is always the same but the locations differ.

Listing 18.23   *CourseByNum.py:* Displaying the Classes Presenting a Given Course

```
1  #
2  # $Workfile: CourseByNum.py $ $Revision: 2 $
3  # $Date: 9/12/01 1:01p $ $Author: Sholden $
4  #
5  import Courses
6  from Error import Error
7  from dbsource import dbsource
8
9  conn = dbsource().conn
```

```
10   cursor = conn.cursor()
11
12
13   class Page(Courses.Page):
14
15       def Body(self):
16           crsnum = None
17           if self.op == "POST":
18               FD = self.getValidForm()
19               crsnum = self.input["CrsNum"]
20           elif self.path:
21               crsnum = self.path[0]
22           if not crsnum:
23               raise Error(404, "Not Found", errmsg="No class number selected")
24           sql = """
25           SELECT CtyName, LocName, ClsDate, CrsTitle, ClsNum, CrsPlaces,➥
           CrsPrice
26           FROM City, Location, Course, Class
27           WHERE City.CtyNum = Location.CtyNum
28               AND Course.CrsNum = Class.CrsNum
29               AND Location.LocNum = Class.LocNum
30               AND Course.CrsNum=?
31               AND Class.ClsPublic
32               ORDER BY ClsDate"""
33           cursor.execute(sql, (crsnum, ))
34           r = cursor.fetchall()
35           if not r:
36               return "<H3>No %s classes are currently scheduled.</H3>" % crsnum
37           else:
38               return self.ListCourses(r, "Upcoming %s Classes" % crsnum)
```

Shopping the Site

Now that you know how the courses database is presented to users, how do they actually enroll for classes? The answer is in the Enroll Me and Waitlist Me links on the class listings pages. The CourseShop module contains four page definitions that manipulate a "shopping cart" held in the _bookings list in the session object. When the user follows one of the shopping links, the site uses either a CourseShop.Enroll or CourseShop.WtLst object, which makes the necessary adjustments to the shopping cart and produces a listing of the current cart contents. This listing displays all classes currently held in the cart, with a Remove link in the right-hand column that creates a CourseShop.DlBk object to remove the relevant line. Finally, when users click the Check Out link, they activate a CourseShop.ChkOut object, which shows them instructions for confirming the order.

All these page object classes are defined in the same module, but the classes actually share a common base class, CourseBook.Page, which is defined in a separate module. Listing 18.24 shows the CourseBook.py module.

Listing 18.24   *CourseBook.py:* **The Shopping Cart Common Base Class Definition**

```
 1   #
 2   # $Workfile: CourseBook.py $ $Revision: 2 $
 3   # $Date: 9/12/01 1:01p $ $Author: Sholden $
 4   #
 5   import Courses
 6   from Error import Error
 7   from dbsource import dbsource
 8
 9   conn = dbsource().conn
10   cursor = conn.cursor()
11
12   class Page(Courses.Page):
13
14       def Book(self, btype):
15           if not self.path:
16               raise Error(400, "Bad Request", errmsg="Class number required")
17           if self.path[0] not in [b[0] for b in self.session._bookings]:
18               # cannot check database as may not have an email address yet
19               request = self.path[0], btype
20               self.session._bookings.append(request)
21               msg = """
22                   <P><B>Your reservation has been entered into your shopping➡
                         cart.</B>
23                   Please remember to check out before leaving the site!</P>
24                   """
25           else:
26               msg = """
27               <P><B>You have already reserved a place on this class.</B>
28               Please do not attempt multiple reservations: each student
29               must make their own bookings, although you can pay for several
30               students with a single payment.</P>
31               """
32           return msg+self.ViewCart(self.session._bookings)
33
34       def Reservation(self, eml, clsnum, tblname):
35           cursor.execute("""
36               SELECT CrsTitle, LocName
37               FROM %s, Class, Location, Course
38               WHERE %s.ClsNum=Class.ClsNum
39                 AND Class.CrsNum=Course.CrsNum
40                 AND Location.LocNum=Class.LocNum
41                 AND StdEmail=? AND Class.ClsNum=?""" % (tblname, tblname),
42                         (eml, clsnum))
43           return cursor.fetchall()
44
45       def Enrollment(self, eml, clsnum):
46           return self.Reservation(eml, clsnum, "Enrollment")
47
48       def WaitList(self, eml, clsnum):
```

```
49            return self.Reservation(eml, clsnum, "Waitlist")
50
51    def ViewCart(self, bookings, final=0):
52        result = []
53        if bookings:
54            result.append("""
55            <table cellpadding="2">
56              <tr>
57                <td>Date</td>
58                <td>Class</td>
59                <td align="right">Price</td>
60                <td>Request</td>""")
61            if not final:
62                result.append("""
63                <td> </td>""")
64            result.append("""
65              </tr>""")
66            total = 0
67            color = 0
68            for clsnum, btp in bookings:
69                color = 1-color
70                cursor.execute("""
71                    SELECT ClsDate, CrsTitle, CrsPrice, LocName
72                    FROM Class, Course, Location
73                    WHERE Class.CrsNum=Course.CrsNum
74                      AND Class.LocNum=Location.LocNum
75                      AND ClsNum=?""", (clsnum, ))
76                dt, ttl, prc, loc = cursor.fetchall()[0]
77                if btp == "E":
78                    b = "Enrol"
79                    total += prc
80                    prc = "$%d" % prc
81                else:
82                    b = "Wait"
83                    prc = "N/A"
84                result.append("""
85                <tr bgcolor=%s>
86                  <td valign="top">%s</td>
87                  <td valign="top">%s<br><font size="-2">%s</font></td>
88                  <td valign="top" align="right">%s</td>
89                  <td valign="top">%s</td>""" % (("#ccffff", ➥
                    "#33ffff")[color],
90                         dt.strftime("%b %d, %Y"),
91                         ttl, loc, prc, b))
92                if not final:
93                    result.append("""
94                    <td valign="top"><a href="/CourseDelBook/%s/"➥
                    >Remove</a></td>
95                    """ % clsnum)
96                result.append("""
```

continues

Listing 18.24   **Continued**

```
97                      </tr>
98                      """)
99
100          if not final:
101              brh = """<a href="/CourseChkOut/">Check Out</a>"""
102          else:
103              brh = " "
104          result.append("""
105              <tr>
106                <td> </td>
107                <td>TOTAL COST</td>
108                <td align="right">$%d</td>
109                <td> </td>
110                <td>%s</td>
111              </tr>
112            </table>""" % (total, brh))
113       else:
114          result.append("""
115              <P><B>Your shopping cart is currently empty.</B></P>""")
116       return "\n".join(result)
```

The *CourseBook.Page* Common Base Class

CourseBook.Page is an abstract class and defines features required by all shopping pages.

The Book() method takes a booking type argument and expects to see a class number on the path. It searches the current bookings to ensure that no reservation is currently held for that class and returns an appropriate message. The Reservation() method is used by the Enrollment() and WaitList() methods to fetch the course title and location name for a booking of a particular student (identified, remember, by email address) and class number. Because these two elements are the composite primary keys for both the Enrollment and the WaitList tables, they can return at most one row. The ViewCart() method is similar to ListCourses(), but it uses a bookings array passed as an argument, and it modifies its output, if the final argument is set, to exclude the usual Remove links on the course rows and the final Check Out link on the final (totals) row.

You can see all these methods in use in Listing 18.25, the source for the CourseShop module.

Listing 18.25   *CourseShop.py:* **The Shopping Cart Manipulation Pages**

```
1  #
2  # $Workfile: CourseShop.py $ $Revision: 1 $
3  # $Date: 9/12/01 12:39p $ $Author: Sholden $
4  #
```

```
 5   import CourseBook
 6   from Error import Error
 7
 8   class Enroll(CourseBook.Page):
 9
10       def Body(self):
11           return self.Book("E")
12
13   class WtLst(CourseBook.Page):
14
15       def Body(self):
16           return self.Book("W")
17
18   class VwCrt(CourseBook.Page):
19
20       def Body(self):
21           return """
22           <P>Your shopping cart currently holds
23           the following items:<br>""" + ➥
24                       self.ViewCart(self.session._bookings)
25
26   class DlBk(CourseBook.Page):
27
28       def Body(self):
29           if not self.path:
30               raise Error(400, "Bad Request", errmsg="Class number required")
31           if self.path[0] not in [b[0] for b in self.session._bookings]:
32               raise Error(400, "Bad Request", errmsg="Class not found in ➥
                 shopping cart.")
33           self.session._bookings = ➥
34               [(b[0], b[1]) for b in self.session._bookings ➥
35                           if b[0] != self.path[0]]
36           msg = """
37               <P><B>Your reservation has been deleted from your shopping ➥
                 cart.</B>
38               Please remember to check out before leaving the site!</P>
39               """
40           return msg+self.ViewCart(self.session._bookings)
```

The CourseShop.Enroll and CourseShop.WtLst object definitions differ in precisely
one character: one's Body() method calls the inherited Book() method with a booking
type of "E"; the other with a type of "W". The CourseShop.VwCrt object simply uses
the ViewCart() method also inherited from CourseBook.Page. The final page definition is for the DlBk page object that deletes a booking from the shopping cart. It
returns an error message if the requested class cannot be found in the cart; otherwise,
it replaces the shopping cart with a copy that excludes the class taken from the
URI path.

All methods return the current contents of the shopping cart as their HTML content, so after any change to the shopping cart, the user immediately sees its updated content. This type of direct feedback is important to users shopping for high-priced items. There is nothing so annoying as clicking on a "do something to shopping cart" link and then having to click on View Shopping Cart to verify your changes.

Because all these pages have `Courses.Page` as an ancestor, they all show the class listing links in the left-hand navigation bar, making it easy for a user to either use the Back button or select a new set of class data after reserving a place in a class. The navigation structure is simple and direct, and it is easy to fill the cart with the classes you want. Figure 18.13 shows a typical shopping cart display.

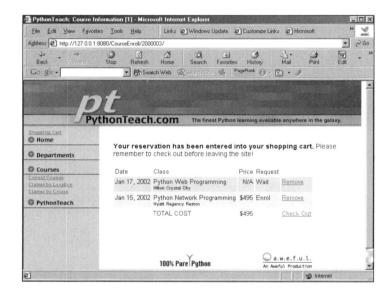

Figure 18.13 The shopping cart contents after adding a class.

Of course until now the bookings have not made any changes to the database at all; they are bound to the `self.session._bookings` session variable as a list of (`ClsNum`, `Type`) tuples. Ultimately, PythonTeach wants the user to buy something, and so every time they display the shopping cart, they include the `Check Out` link that allows them to do it. The final question is, how does the site handle the checkout process? For this, you need to study the last courses module, `CourseOrd`, which defines a `ChkOut` and an `Order` page class, and is shown in Listing 18.26.

Listing 18.26 **CourseOrd.py: Handling Checkout and Ordering**

```
1  #
2  # $Workfile: CourseOrd.py $ $Revision: 2 $
```

```
 3  # $Date: 9/12/01 1:01p $ $Author: Sholden $
 4  #
 5  import CourseBook
 6  from dbsource import dbsource
 7
 8  conn = dbsource().conn
 9  cursor = conn.cursor()
10
11
12  class ChkOut(CourseBook.Page):
13
14      def Body(self):
15          msg = """
16          <P>If you already have an account you may
17          proceed to <a href="/CrsOrder/">place your order.</A></P>
18          <P>If you are not currently an account holder
19          then you may
20          <a href="/NewAccount/PythonTeach/">create one now</a>.
21          <B>If you need to open an account, your order
22          will NOT be lost.</B></P>
23          <P>You will receive an email, confirming your account
24          details and explaining how to finalize the order.</P>
25          """
26          return msg+self.ViewCart(self.session._bookings, final=1)
27
28  class Order(CourseBook.Page):
29
30      def Body(self):
31          if not self.session._bookings:
32              return """
33              <P>No order details can be found to enter.</P>
34              """
35          eml = self.session._udata.StdEmail
36          result = []
37          booking = []
38          invoice = 0
39          for clsnum, typ in self.session._bookings:
40              if self.Enrollment(eml, clsnum) or �
41                  self.WaitList(eml, clsnum):            # already subscribed
42                  cursor.execute("""
43                      SELECT CrsTitle, LocName, ClsDate
44                      FROM Course, Location, Class
45                      WHERE Location.LocNum=Class.Locnum
46                        AND Course.CrsNum=Class.CrsNum
47                        AND Class.ClsNum=?""", (clsnum, ))
48                  r = cursor.fetchall()
49                  CrsTitle, LocName, ClsDate = r[0]
50                  result.append("""
51                  <P><font size="-2">You are already
52                  waitlisted or enrolled for the %s
```

continues

Listing 18.26   **Continued**

```
53                class in %s on %s. No additional
54                reservation was made.</font></P>
55                """ % (CrsTitle, LocName, ClsDate.strftime("%b %d")))
56            else:
57                if typ == "E":
58                    tblname = "Enrollment"
59                    invoice = 1
60                else:
61                    tblname = "Waitlist"
62                cursor.execute("""
63                    INSERT INTO %s (StdEmail, ClsNum)
64                    VALUES(?, ?)""" % tblname,
65                    (eml, clsnum))
66                booking.append((clsnum, typ))
67        conn.commit()
68        if booking:
69            result.append("""
70            <P>The following places have been reserved for you:""")
71            result.append(self.ViewCart(booking, final=1))
72        if invoice:
73            result.append("""
74            <P>An invoice will be emailed to you
75            at the end of our business day.</P>""")
76        result.append("""
77            <P>Thank you very much for your business.</P>""")
78        self.session._bookings = [] # empty the cart
79        return "\n".join(result)
```

The ChkOut page is really quite simple. It uses the inherited ViewCart() method to display the cart, this time providing a true value for the final argument so that the user has no chance to change things. The link to /CrsOrder/ finally takes the user into the PythonTeach authentication realm, so if a click on this link succeeds, the CourseOrd.Order object will have the user's email address and the shopping cart available in session state memory to complete the order. If it fails, then the Authenticate() method provides hypertext links allowing the user to either open a new account or request an email reminder of his password.

As you will see in the next section, which completes the discussion of site structure by explaining the user maintenance pages, if the user has to create a new account, the code takes care to ensure that the order need not be re-entered (another web site turn-off responsible for the loss of much business).

Up to this stage, the database has not been checked for bookings under the user's email address because most users will not bother to authenticate themselves before commencing the ordering process. When the user finally clicks to place his order on the link produced by the CourseOrd.ChkOut object, these checks are made for each reservation request in the shopping cart. Most of the logic is handled by the methods inherited from the `CourseBook.Page`, and some database code is needed to provide a meaningful error message if the checks fail.

If there is no prior reservation in the database, line 62 makes an entry into the appropriate table. At the same time, a fresh shopping cart, containing only the successful entries, is built up in a local variable. The user is warned that she will be receiving an invoice if any new `Enrollment` rows have been entered, and the list of successful reservations made is added to the HTML content. The cart is then emptied, and the user can continue to browse the site. Figure 18.14 shows a sample order confirmation page.

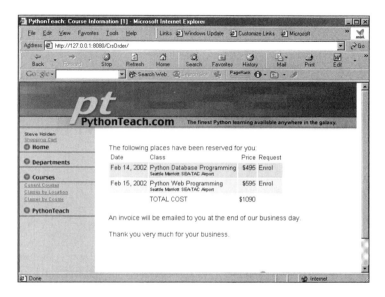

Figure 18.14   The final result: Your order is confirmed!

Because only the email address and the class number are stored in the `Enrollment` table, it is relatively easy for a batch job to scan the table and produce invoices for the enrollments that have a null invoice number, print the invoice, mail it to the student, and then update the `Enrollment` rows. The database can also record payment details, but this functionality is not yet included in the web-based system.

Serving Static Content

Most web sites, no matter how dynamic, expect to serve some of their content from the filestore. PythonTeach is no exception: it expects it will make software available for download, for example. Serving such content over the web is a straightforward process if you do not mind re-sending the content every time a user requests it. This works perfectly well, but given that the AWeFUL framework uses HTTP 1.0, and makes no attempt to reuse connections to the client, this can lengthen response times and certainly use up unnecessary bandwidth.

The `Static.Page` object therefore returns a `"Last-Modified:"` header with each piece of content it serves, and a well-behaved web client sends future requests for the same content with an `"If-Modified-Since:"` header echoing the `"Last-Modified:"` date it received from the server. If the requested resource has not been modified since the `"If-Modified-Since:"` header date, then it is allowed to return a `"304 Not Modified"` response, which the client takes to mean that there is no need to actually download the object again. The `Static` module shown in Listing 18.27 uses this approach, despite its added complexity, to improve network performance and site responsiveness.

Listing 18.27   *Static.py:* **Serving Content from the Filestore**

```
1   #
2   # $Workfile: Static.py $ $Revision: 8 $
3   # $Date: 9/12/01 10:54a $ $Author: Sholden $
4   #
5   import Web
6   from Error import Error
7   import os
8   from mimetypes import guess_type
9   import mx.DateTime as mxdt
10  import mx.DateTime.ARPA as arpa
11
12
13  class Page(Web.Page):
14      """Handle content present as a file in the virtual web filestore.
15
16      Note that a whole passel of stuff is inherited, from Web.Page,
17      much of which is neither required nor used because the content
18      is simply dragged from a file and squirted down to the client.
19      """
20
21      def Content(self):
22          """Generate static content by squirting file content."""
23          if self.ReturnCode() == 200:    # No error raised
24              if self.op.upper() != "GET":
25                  raise Error(405, "Method Not Allowed", errmsg="Illegal➡
                        Operation")
26              else:
27                  if not self.path:
28                      raise Error(400, "Bad Request", errmsg="Missing file➡
                            path")
29                  fname = self.path[-1]
30                  ext = os.path.splitext(fname)[1]
31                  mimetype, encoding = guess_type(fname)
32                  if not mimetype:
```

```
33                          raise Error(415, "Unsupported Media Type",➡
                            errmsg="Content type not recognised")
34                  try:
35                      filepath = os.sep.join(self.initpath + self.path)
36                      ims = self.headers.getheader("if-modified-since")
37                      s = os.stat(filepath)
38                      mdt = mxdt.local2gm(mxdt.DateTimeFromTicks(s[8]))
39                      if ims:              # optimize if file not modified
40                          sdt = arpa.ParseDateTime(ims.split(";")[0])
41                          # print "If-mod-since:", ims, "Last-mod:", mdt
42                          if mdt <= sdt:
43                              raise Error(304, "Not modified",
44                                      errcontent="Not modified")
45                      self.oheaders.append("Last-Modified: %s" %➡
                        arpa.str(mxdt.DateTimeFromTicks(mdt)))
46                      if encoding:
47                          enchdr = "Content-Encoding: %s\n" % encoding
48                      else:
49                          enchdr = ""
50                      f = open(filepath, "rb")
51                      img = f.read()
52                      return img
53                  except (IOError, OSError):
54                      raise Error(404, "Not Found", errmsg="Content Not Found")
55          else:
56              return Web.Page.Content(self) # standard method has smarts we➡
                do not
```

The `Static.Page` object defines only one method, `Content()`. Most other objects are happy to use the standard `Content()` method and implement a `Body()` method whose output is wrapped inside the site look-and-feel before being encapsulated in HTTP headers and sent to the client. This would not do for static content such as graphics, for example, because the entity sent to the client should be exactly the contents of the specified file. The `Content()` method can sometimes be called twice (when the content generation code raises an `Error` exception the first time through), and such second calls are detected by the presence of a return code other than 200. In this case, `Static.Page` simply delegates the second `Content()` call to `Web.Page` to avoid duplicating the required error handling logic.

By the time the `Content()` method is called, some elements will have been removed from the URI path held in the list bound to the path instance variable. In the case of static content, the virtual path represented by the removed elements has been mapped to the `initpath` argument of the `__init__()` method and is stored in the `initpath` instance variable. The code makes a guess at the MIME type implied by the file's extension; and if that succeeds, it creates a filename from the mapped initial path and the residual elements of the URI path.

Next the method looks up the modification timestamp of the file and checks for an `"If-Modified-Since:"` header in the request. If the header is found, then the file time-stamp is compared with the `"If-Modified-Since:"` timestamp; and if the file has not changed since that date and time, it raises a `"304 Not Modified"` error. It sets the `errcontent` argument to `Error()` rather than the `errmsg`, to avoid having the response wrapped up in standard site look-and-feel.

Eventually, this results in a second call to `Content()`, but because the return code is now 304, the `Web.Page.Content()` method is invoked to produce the output.

The User Section

Every web site with registered users needs some way to allow account creation, user sign-on, and data maintenance at the very minimum. If registration is integrated with HTTP authentication, it can lead to a much more pleasant experience for the user. The PythonTeach web site allows users to sign up over the web and to maintain their personal information to accommodate changes in address and telephone number. Because a user's email address becomes her primary identifier to the site, she is not allowed to change it herself.

Of course, you could argue about the reasonableness of this. The main problem occurs when a registered user changes her Internet service provider and then forgets the password on the web account. In such a case, the user can only receive email to the old address, effectively locking her out of the account. The no-change restriction on the user's email address is not strictly necessary in the present design; and in a production system, such a rigid design might lose customers. A better technique, for example, would be to repeat the email address verification process after a change (although this would still allow "account hijacking" if a user logged in to the site and someone else then used the user's browser to access the authenticated session).

The User Start Page

The pages that handle user sign-up and account data maintenance are all based on the `User.Page` class, which is also used to welcome users to the PythonTeach area of the site. The `User` module is shown in Listing 18.28, and you can see it defines a `BuildFD` function as well as the expected `Title()`, `Body()`, and `PTNav()` methods. It also provides a `GetFormData` method that can be used to create a `DatabaseTuple` from the CGI data, to make handling form data easier. The module finally contains a tiny test page class, `Secret`, used to verify the authentication features during testing.

The `BuildFD` function is used to create a form description from a number of arguments. However the form is intended to be used, most of its content is the same. The commentary will need to differ, though, among other things to allow error messages to be inserted when corrections are required. Also certain fields have different functions to update an existing account: when a user record is being edited, the email address, which is the user's primary key, cannot be changed, and the password should be preset in both the entry and confirmation boxes. When an account is being created, the email address is a standard entry field, and the password entry is not preset.

Listing 18.28   *User.py:* **The User Module and User Start Page**

```
 1  #! Python
 2  #
 3  # $Workfile: User.py $ $Revision: 13 $
 4  # $Date: 9/14/01 5:54p $ $Author: Sholden $
 5  #
 6  """Collect details of new account, and allow changes on existing accounts.
 7
 8  NOTE: THIS CODE ASSUMES that it is in the PythonTeach realm or outside any
 9  realm requiring authentication. The latter location is used to enter new
10  details. It doesn't make sense to use this for other realms unless they use
11  the same authentication base as PythonTeach, since we are handling user data!
12  """
13
14  #
15  # XXX Note that some of this code might migrate into the pyforms module
16  #
17
18  import pyforms
19  import Web
20  import HomePage
21  from cachequery import CacheQuery
22  from dtuple import TupleDescriptor, DatabaseTuple
23  from dbsource import dbsource
24  from Error import Error
25  from Params import WEBMASTER
26
27  conn = dbsource().conn
28  cursor = conn.cursor()
29
30
31  def buildFD(comment1, comment2, newkey=1):
32      if newkey:
33          emtype = "T"
34          pwtype = "PP"
35      else:
36          emtype = "H"
37          pwtype = "PPP"
38      Fdescription = (
39              ["Comment1",      comment1,       "REM", "+2", ""],
40              ["Comment2",      comment2,       "REM", "-2", ""],
41              ["StdEmail",      "Email",        emtype, 50, "R"],
42              ["StdFirstName",  "First Name",   "T",    25, "R"],
43              ["StdLastName",   "Last Name",    "T",    25, "R"],
44              ["StdPhone",      "Telephone",    "T",    25, "R"],
45              ["Comment3",      "Remember to set <B>both</B> password fields",
```

continues

Listing 18.28 **Continued**

```
46                                              "REM",    "-2",  ""],
47             ["StdPasswd",    "Password",     pwtype, 12, "R"],
48             ["StdAddress",   "Address",      "T",    40, ""],
49             ["StdCity",      "City",         "T",    25, ""],
50             ["StdState",     "State/Province", "T",  15, ""],
51             ["StdPostCode",  "Zip/Post Code","T",    10, ""]
52         )
53     return Fdescription
54
55 StdNames = Web.StdNames
56 StdNokey = [x for x in StdNames if x != "StdEmail"]
57 TD = TupleDescriptor([[x] for x in StdNames])
58 qStud = CacheQuery("Student", StdNames, ("StdEmail", ), conn)
59
60
61 class Page(HomePage.Home):
62
63     def Title(self):
64         return "My PythonTeach"
65
66     def Body(self):
67         udata = self.session._udata
68         return """
69         <H3>Welcome back, %s %s</H3>
70         <P>We are glad to see that you are using the
71         features of our site. If you need any special
72         help, please <A HREF="mailto:%s">mail us</A>
73         to let us know what you want.</P>
74         """ % (udata.StdFirstName, udata.StdLastName, WEBMASTER)
75
76     def PTNav(self):
77         links = [
78             ("/Auth/UserCheck/", "My Account"),
79             ("/Auth/Secret/", "Members Only")
80             ]
81         return "\n".join([self.NavLink(p) for p in links])
82
83     def getFormData(self):
84         udata = tuple([self.input[x] for x in StdNames])
85         udata = DatabaseTuple(TD, udata)
86         return udata
87
88     def RedText(self, t):
89         return """<FONT COLOR="RED">%s</FONT>""" % t
90
91
92 class Secret(Page):
93
94     def Title(self):
```

```
95          return "PythonTeach Authenticated Page"
96
97      def Body(self):
98          return """<P>This page can only be seen by authenticated
99          members of the PythonTeach realm.</P>"""
```

Figure 18.15 shows the user start page the user sees after authenticating his account to the server. Note that the navigation bar shows detail only under the PythonTeach button, and that the user's name appears at the top of the navigation bar as well as being a part of the page header. This is because when the server authenticates a user in the PythonTeach realm, it automatically retrieves the user's details from the `Student` table and stores them in the session. The standard navigation bar code detects this and verifies the user identity in this way so that users can see they are logged in.

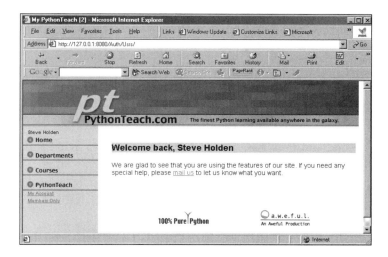

Figure 18.15   The user start page of a site that likes to be friendly.

The AWeFUL framework is perfectly capable of handling multiple authentication realms in the same site. Students and other customers authenticate themselves using their email address as their username, and the server integrates the `Student` table into the authentication of the PythonTeach realm. For new users, there has to be a non-authenticated page for account data entry; otherwise there would be no way for them to create their accounts without already being account holders! The `UserEntry.Page` object is mapped into the site's virtual address space twice: it is used outside any authenticated realm for initial account entry and inside the PythonTeach realm to allow users to update their personal information. Listing 18.29 shows the code for this class.

Listing 18.29   *UserEntry.py:* **Entry and Update of User Details**

```
1   #! Python
2   #
3   # $Workfile: UserEntry.py $ $Revision: 5 $
4   # $Date: 9/14/01 6:26p $ $Author: Sholden $
5   #
6   import User
7   import pyforms
8   from Error import Error
9   from Params import WEBMASTER
10
11  class Page(User.Page):
12      """Accept account details from user to create or update database entry.
13
14      This code only handles new accounts for the PythonTeach realm. If a
15      user hits some other protected area by accident we politely solicit
16      an email request.
17      """
18      def Body(self):
19          if not self.Realm():    # new user: check realm
20              if not self.path:
21                  return ➡
22                  """<P>Sorry, I have to know what type of account
23                  you want me to create.</P>"""
24              if self.path[0] != "PythonTeach":
25                  return ➡
26                  """<P>Sorry. Accounts for the '%s' area of the site can
27                  only be created by email. You can send your request
28                  in by <A HREF="mailto:newaccount@holdenweb.com">
29                  clicking here</A>.""" % self.path[0]
30              udata = None
31              action = "/UserSignUp/"
32              FD = User.buildFD("Please Enter Your Details",
33                      "Use the CREATE button to create your account")
34              buttons = (("CREATE", 0), )
35          else:                       # existing, authenticated PythonTeach user
36              action = "/Auth/UserChange/"
37              FD = User.buildFD("Current User Details",
38                      "Use the CHANGE button to update this data",
39                      newkey=0)
40              buttons = (("CHANGE", 0), )
```

```
41            if self.Realm() != "PythonTeach":
42                raise Error(500, "Server Error", "", [],
43                    errmsg="""Program error: this page should be in the
44                        'PythonTeach' realm - please report this to our
45                        <A HREF="mailto:%s>webmaster</A>.""" % WEBMASTER)
46            try:
47                udata = self.session._udata
48            except AttributeError:
49                username = self.session._auth["PythonTeach"]["email"]
50                # must have accessed this row to authenticate for the realm
51                # now read it all in and stash it in the session
52                udata = User.qStud(username)[0]
53                self.session._udata = udata
54        self.session._fd = FD
55        self.session._secureform = 1
56        form = pyforms.FormBuild(FD, "UserForm",
57                    action, Width=25,
58                    Buttons=buttons,
59                    R=udata)
60        return form
```

When the `UserEntry` page is mapped outside the PythonTeach realm, its `Body()`
method verifies that a PythonTeach account is being requested. At present, the Staff
realm is not used, but this is an obvious area for update as the web expands its application's scope. The `Body()` method then builds a form with appropriate comments and
buttons for the creation of a new account, and sets the user data to `None` to ensure that
the `FormBuild()` routine creates a form with no content.

Inside the PythonTeach realm, the `Body()` method assumes that it is dealing with
an existing user. The form description created has slightly different comments and is
created with the `newkey` argument false so that the email address is fixed and the password entry boxes are filled out. The user's data are retrieved from the session or, if
something has caused them to be deleted, from the database.

In either case, the form description is stored in the session along with a secure indication to avoid multiple submissions. A form is built from the description and the user
data and an appropriate action URL—very different objects handle the user sign-up
and the modification of existing account data—and the form is returned as the page's
body. Figure 18.16 shows an existing user detail change form.

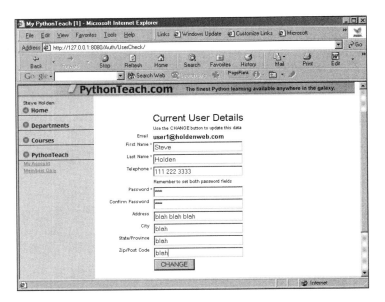

Figure 18.16 Users can alter their account details with this sign-up page.

The `UserSignUp.Page` object (see listing 18.30) must again live outside the PythonTeach realm because it processes the account data but does not immediately turn the applicant into a valid user. The sign-up process is a little involved because PythonTeach requires its users to respond to an email to validate their account applications. This is a common requirement and has the merit of confirming that at least the person who applied for the account has access to the email address used to sign up!

Listing 18.30 *UserSignup.py:* **Accepting New User Data, but Deferring Final Registration**

```
 1  #! Python
 2  #
 3  # $Workfile: UserSignUp.py $ $Revision: 4 $
 4  # $Date: 9/12/01 7:59p $ $Author: Sholden $
 5  #
 6  import User
 7  import pyforms
 8
 9  from Params import SITENAME, MAILHOST, WEBMASTER
10  from Error import Error
11  import whrandom
12  import smtplib
13  import mx.DateTime as mxdt
14  import mx.DateTime.ARPA as arpa
```

```
15  import pickle
16
17  class Page(User.Page):
18      """Accept new account details posted by EntryForm.
19
20      We record the user details in the Wannabe table, using a
21      six-digit random number as a confirmation key. We then
22      send an email to their address containing a URL with the
23      confirmation key masked by twelve other digits to discourage
24      exhaustive searches. We assume that the user will only get to
25      the URL if they see the email. Accessing the URL will use the
26      Activate class to move the details from Wannabe to Student.
27      """
28      def Body(self):
29          if self.op != "POST":
30              raise Error(405, "Method Not Allowed", errmsg="You can only➡
                    POST to this page")
31          FD = self.getValidForm()
32          udata = self.getFormData()
33          errors = self.ChkReqd(FD, udata)
34          if not errors:
35              # Do the expensive stuff only if the data is OK
36              User.cursor.execute(
37                      "SELECT count(*) FROM student WHERE StdEmail=?",
38                      (self.input["StdEmail"], ))
39              r1 = User.cursor.fetchall()[0][0]
40              User.cursor.execute(
41                      "SELECT count(*) FROM wannabe WHERE StdEmail=?",
42                      (self.input["StdEmail"], ))
43              r2 = User.cursor.fetchall()[0][0]
44              if r1+r2:
45                  errors.append("Email address in use")
46          if errors:
47              errors = self.RedText("<BR>\r\n".join(errors))
48              FD = User.buildFD(self.RedText("Please Correct"), errors)
49              form = pyforms.FormBuild(FD, "UserForm",
50                          "/UsrSignUp/", Width=25,
51                          Buttons=(("CREATE", 0), ),
52                          R=udata)
53              self.session._fd = FD
54              self.session._secureform = 1
55              return form
56          # Generate random number for email authentication URL
57          count = 0
58          sql = "SELECT count(*) FROM Wannabe WHERE Stdconf=?"
59          while count < 1000: # We should find one quickly
60              conf = whrandom.randint(1000000, 9999999)
61              User.cursor.execute(sql, (conf, ))
62              if User.cursor.fetchall() == [(0,)]:
63                  break
```

continues

Listing 18.30 **Continued**

```
64          else:
65              raise Error(500, "Internal Server Error",
66                      errmsg="Could not generate confirmation number after➡
                        1,000 tries!")
67          sql = "INSERT INTO Wannabe (%s) VALUES (%s)" % ➡
68                      (", ".join(User.StdNames+["StdConf", "StdOrder"]),
69                       ", ".join(["?" for x in User.StdNames+[1, 1]]))
70          data = [self.input[x] for x in User.StdNames] + ➡
71                  [conf, pickle.dumps(self.session._bookings)]
72          User.cursor.execute(sql, tuple(data))
73          User.conn.commit()
74          # Send confirmation email to our wannabe
75          # If they have an order pending, tell them how to proceed
76          dt = arpa.str(mxdt.now())
77          # hide the real confirmation number
78          c1 = whrandom.randint(1000000, 9999999)
79          c2 = whrandom.randint(1000000, 9999999)
80          conf = "%d%d%d" % (c1, conf, c2)
81          if self.session._bookings:
82              orderp = """
83 Your order can be confirmed as soon as you have activated
84 your new account.
85 """
86          else:
87              orderp = ""
88          msg = """Date: %s
89 Subject: Your PythonTeach Account Activation Code
90 From: %s
91 To: %s
92
93 Thank you for enrolling with PythonTeach. We very much hope you
94 will find our services valuable, and that we can help you for
95 many years to come.
96
97 All you need to do to activate the account and enable login is
98 to visit the following URL:
99
100    http://%s/Activate/%s/
101
102 You will then be able to log in as follows:
103
104    Username: %s
105    Password: %s
106
107 Please make a record of these details.
108 %s
109 Sincerely
110 PythonTeach
111 """ % (dt, WEBMASTER, udata.StdEmail, SITENAME, conf, udata.StdEmail,➡
    udata.StdPasswd, orderp)
```

```
112            try:
113                smtp = smtplib.SMTP(MAILHOST)
114                result = smtp.sendmail(WEBMASTER, [udata.StdEmail], msg)
115                smtp.quit()
116                return """<H3>Welcome to PythonTeach!</H3>
117                <P>Thank you for entering your details,
118                which have been recorded.</P>
119                <P>You should shortly receive an email
120                containing a confirmation URL. Your account
121                will be activated once you have visited this URL.
122                If you were processing an order when you signed
123                up, the email will include details of how to
124                confirm that order.</P>
125                <P>You will not be able to submit any further
126                orders until you have completed sign-up.
127                In the meantime please feel free to browse
128                the remainder of the site.</P>
129                """
130            except smtplib.SMTPException:
131                return """<P>Sorry, our outgoing mail service
132                is temporarily disabled.</P>
133                <P>Please <A HREF="mailto:%s">email us</A>
134                explaining the situation, and we will
135                send your activation code by hand</P>
136                <P>If you do not receive a reply, you should
137                try other means of contact listed elsewhere
138                on this site.
139                """ % WEBMASTER
```

The Body() method retrieves the form description from the session. Because the form was marked as secure when it was stored in the session, an exception is raised if the id() of the stored description does not match the identifier built into the form when it was created. It next sucks the data out of the form as a DatabaseTuple and checks for the presence of all required fields, using the method inherited from User.Page. If there are errors at this stage, it skips the database checks, which verify that the email address is not already in use or pending. If errors have been discovered, then a new form description is created, incorporating error messages passed from the validation routines, and that form (conditioned to return to the same URL) is returned as the page body.

If all checks are passed, then the Body() method generates a six-digit confirmation number, which it verifies is not in use for some other application. After it generates this number, Body() computes a SQL statement to store the application details, the verification number, and any pending order data in the database. The confirmation number and the pickled order are added to the user data on line 70, and line 72 writes the Wannabe entry to the database.

This particular method uses the `pickle` module in text mode. There is a compatible module, `cPickle`, which handles a narrower range of object types, and this should really be used whenever possible. Because it is an extension module, it cannot be sub-classed like pickle, but it is much faster. It would also be more efficient to use `pickle`'s (or `cPickle`'s) binary mode, which uses more compact data descriptions.

If order data is found, a reassuring sentence is generated for the email message to ease any concern the user might have about lost data. An `rfc822` message is formulated containing a URL that includes the verification number, masked by 12 other random digits. This message is transmitted via SMTP, and the method returns a message explaining the situation. Should the SMTP transmission fail, a rather less reassuring message is generated, asking the user to take action to confirm his account.

User Activation Page

After entering their details, users must wait to receive their confirmation email, this being the only way they can access the activation page with a correct verifier. Fortunately, the email service is usually both speedy and reliable, so before long they should see something like Figure 18.17 in their mailbox.

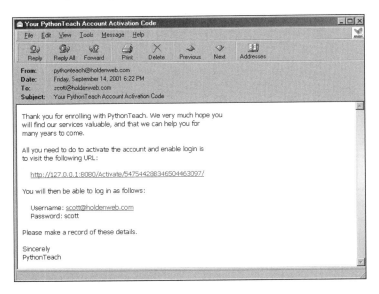

Figure 18.17 You've got mail: the PythonTeach account verifier arrives.

Modern mail user-agents display a URL inside the message window as a hypertext link and start the browser automatically when the user clicks the link. This triggers the server to create a `UserActivate.Page` object, which performs the final registration step by using the verifier to extract the `Wannabe` data and storing it as a new entry in the

Student table. The code in Listing 18.31 shows the `Body()` method removing the user data from the `Wannabe` table and storing it in the `Student` table. After changes to the database are committed, the method checks to see whether the `Wannabe` had an order in progress when making the application. It does so simply, by unpickling the value of the last column of the `Wannabe` row into the `_bookings` session value.

If the retrieved shopping cart is not empty, the method adds a link to the output so that the user can check out—or continue to add to the shopping cart if she wants.

Listing 18.31 *UserActivate.py:* **How Users Confirm Their Account Sign-up**

```
 1  #! Python
 2  #
 3  # $Workfile: UserActivate.py $ $Revision: 4 $
 4  # $Date: 9/12/01 7:59p $ $Author: Sholden $
 5  #
 6  import User
 7
 8  from Params import WEBMASTER
 9  from Error import Error
10  import whrandom
11  import smtplib
12  import mx.DateTime as mxdt
13  import mx.DateTime.ARPA as arpa
14  import pickle
15
16  class Page(User.Page):
17
18      def Body(self):
19          if not self.path or len(self.path[0]) != 21:
20              raise Error(400, "Bad Request", errmsg="A confirmation number➡
                  is required.")
21          conf = int(self.path[0][7:14])
22          sql = "SELECT %s FROM Wannabe WHERE StdConf=?" % ",➡
                  ".join(User.StdNames+["StdOrder"])
23          User.cursor.execute(sql, (conf, ))
24          r = User.cursor.fetchall()
25          if not r:
26              return """<P>Unable to find confirmation number %s.</P>
27                  <P>Either you have already confirmed your membership,
28                  or you confirmation number is incorrect.</P>
29                  <P>Please <A HREF="mailto:%s">email us</A> and
30                  we will try to resolve the problem.</P>""" % ➡
31                          (self.path[0], WEBMASTER)
32          sql = "INSERT INTO Student (%s) VALUES (%s)" % (
33                          ", ".join(["CrDT"] + User.StdNames),
34                          ", ".join("?"*(len(User.StdNames)+1)))
35          User.cursor.execute(sql, ➡
                      (mxdt.DateTimeFromTicks(int(mxdt.now())), )+r[0][:-1])
36          User.cursor.execute("DELETE FROM Wannabe WHERE StdConf=?", (conf, ))
```

continues

Listing 18.31   **Continued**

```
37          User.conn.commit()
38          self.session._bookings = pickle.loads(r[0][-1])
39          if self.session._bookings:
40              orderp = """
41                  <P><B>Click here to <A HREF="/CourseChkOut/">verify your➥
                    order</A>
42                  and proceed with confirmation.</B></P>
43                  """
44          else:
45              orderp =""
46
47          return """
48              <H3>User Account Created</H3>
49              <P>Thank you. By using this link you have allowed
50              us to verify your email address. You can now use
51              the restricted functions of the site by logging
52              as outlined in your confirmatory email.</P>
53              """ + orderp
```

User Update Page

After a user activates his account, he may want to make changes from time to time. At present, the data stored against the user's email address is very limited, but PythonTeach plans to expand it to allow users to determine which departments they want to see on the site, whether they receive email notification of content changes and special course offers, and a number of other marketing and informational channels that can be user-selected.

The logic of the update is simple: check the form and, if it contains errors, redisplay it with error messages. Otherwise, update the database and thank the user for her input. The code is equally direct and to the point, as Listing 18.32 shows.

Listing 18.32   *UserUpdate.py:* **Updating the User's Details**

```
1  #! Python
2  #
3  # $Workfile: UserUpdate.py $ $Revision: 5 $
4  # $Date: 9/12/01 7:59p $ $Author: Sholden $
5  #
6  import User
7  from Error import Error
8
9  class Page(User.Page):
10     """Accept updated user details and update database.
11
12     Allows change of any field except the email address, which is used as
13     the primary key and the student identifier -- too many downstream
```

```
14      problems, so at present this requires manual attention to maintain
15      any database relationships.
16      """
17      def Body(self):
18          if self.op != "POST":
19              raise Error(405, "Method Not Allowed", errmsg="You can only POST➧
                to this page")
20          FD = self.getValidForm()
21          udata = self.getFormData()
22          errors = self.ChkReqd(FD, udata)
23          if errors:
24              errors = self.RedText("<BR>\r\n".join(errors))
25              FD = User.buildFD(self.RedText("Please Correct"), errors,➧
                newkey=0)
26              form = pyforms.FormBuild(FD, "UserForm",
27                          "/SignUp/", Width=25,
28                          Buttons=(("UPDATE", 0), ),
29                          R=udata)
30              self.session._fd = FD
31              self.session._secureform = 1
32              return form
33          sql = "UPDATE Student SET  %s WHERE StdEmail=?" % ➧
34                  ", ".join(["%s=?" % x for x in User.StdNokey])
35          User.cursor.execute(sql, tuple([udata[x] for x in➧
            User.StdNokey+["StdEmail"]]))
36          User.conn.commit()
37          self.session._udata = User.qStud((udata["StdEmail"], ))[0]
38          return "<P>We have amended your details. Thank You!</P>"
```

Overall Site Specifications

Sometimes you can increase the flexibility of your code by using data to drive its
logic, and two modules exist primarily to define data that describe the structure of the
site. The Params module contains individual pieces of data (such as the appropriate
SMTP hosts name or IP address) that will need to be different from one implementation to another. It also contains the mapping from authentication realms to database
columns, which is a simple table. The SiteSpec module defines a single dictionary,
which maps path prefixes to content generator objects.

In a more comprehensive implementation, these values might be available for modification through the medium of a GUI (or possibly a web page). For the present,
however, PythonTeach is more focused on the task of generating revenues than on
developing its framework to meet gold-plated requirements. This fits in well with the
typical Pythonista philosophy, which we might sum up as "First, make it work. Then,
leave it alone." Without a purpose, there can be little justification for making the code
more capable than it already is, and the development staff's time would be better spent
ironing out residual bugs in what is still pretty new code.

The modules are shown, for completeness, in Listings 18.33 and 18.34.

Listing 18.33   *Params.py:* **Basic Site Parameters**

```
1  #
2  # $Workfile: Params.py $ $Revision: 4 $
3  # $Date: 9/01/01 5:14a $ $Author: Sholden $
4  #
5  DBSOURCE = "Ch18"
6  STIMEOUT_INTERVAL = 1200    # 20-minute session timeout
7  SCHECK_INTERVAL = 60        # check every minute
8  SITENAME = "127.0.0.1:8080"
9  MAILHOST = "mail.holdenweb.com"
10 WEBMASTER = pythonteach@holdenweb.com
11 LOGFILE = "aweful.log"
12
13 RealmAuth = {
14     "PythonTeach":  ("Student", "StdEmail", "StdPasswd"),
15     "Staff":        ("Staff", "StfUserName", "StfPasswd")
16 }
```

Listing 18.34   *SiteSpec.py:* **Mapping the Web Space to the Object Space**

```
1  #
2  # $Workfile: SiteSpec.py $ $Revision: 13 $
3  # $Date: 9/12/01 1:01p $ $Author: Sholden $
4  #
5  """Map path prefixes to page classes, and realms to authentication tables."""
6
7  import HomePage, Auth, HTML
8  import User, UserActivate, UserEntry, UserMailPass, UserSignUp, UserUpdate
9  import DeptStart, Dept, DeptHome, DeptNews, DeptNewsItem, ➥
10         DeptLinks, DeptQod, DeptQodAns, DeptPg
11 import Courses, CourseAll, CourseShow, CourseCtForm, CourseByCity, ➥
12         CourseNmForm, CourseByNum, CourseShop, CourseOrd
13
14 import Web
15
16 PageMap = {
17     "":             (HomePage.Home, None),
18     "Auth": ({
19         "Usrs":        (User.Page,        None),
20         "Secret":      (User.Secret,      None),
21         "UserCheck":   (UserEntry.Page,   None),
22         "UserChange":  (UserUpdate.Page,  None)
23     }, "PythonTeach"),
24
25     "Staff": ({
```

```
26            "Secret2":        (Auth.Secret2,        None)
27        }, "Staff"),
28
29        "Image":           ("images",            None),
30        "images":          ("images",            None),
31        "Text":            ("text",              "Staff"),
32        "html":            (HTML.Page,           None),
33        "Demo":            ("Demo",              None),
34        "DeptStart":       (DeptStart.Page,      None),
35        "DeptHome":        (DeptHome.Page,       None),
36        "DeptLinks":       (DeptLinks.Page,      None),
37        "DeptNews":        (DeptNews.Page,       None),
38        "DeptNewsItem":    (DeptNewsItem.Page,   None),
39        "DeptQod":         (DeptQod.Page,        None),
40        "DeptQodAns":      (DeptQodAns.Page,     None),
41        "DeptPgPage":      (DeptPg.Page,         None),
42        "CourseStart":     (Courses.Page,        None),
43        "AllCourses":      (CourseAll.Page,      None),
44        "Course":          (CourseShow.Page,     None),
45        "CourseCity":      (CourseCtForm.Page,   None),
46        "CourseByCity":    (CourseByCity.Page,   None),
47        "CourseNum":       (CourseNmForm.Page,   None),
48        "CourseByNum":     (CourseByNum.Page,    None),
49        "CourseEnroll":    (CourseShop.Enroll,   None),
50        "CourseWaitList":  (CourseShop.WtLst,    None),
51        "CourseViewCart":  (CourseShop.VwCrt,    None),
52        "CourseDelBook":   (CourseShop.DlBk,     None),
53        "CourseChkOut":    (CourseOrd.ChkOut,    None),
54        "CrsOrder":        (CourseOrd.Order,     "PythonTeach"),
55        "NewAccount":      (UserEntry.Page,      None),
56        "MailPass":        (UserMailPass.Page,   None),
57        "UserSignUp":      (UserSignUp.Page,     None),
58        "Activate":        (UserActivate.Page,   None)
59        }
```

There is little to say about the data. There may be better ways to structure it and store it, but almost every web framework (except the simplest) has some way to describe the mapping between the virtual web space and the real space of the implementation. In the case of static content (those values for which the translation dictionary yields a string), the mapping is from virtual directories to real ones, and you can see that the same real directory (images) is mapped on to several virtual existences.

The mapping from virtual directories to object classes has also proved to be of value. For example, the capability to link between different members of a page set by using relative links was unforeseen at design time and allowed the same page set to be mapped onto multiple virtual destinations in a way that increased the utility of the feature at no extra cost in programming.

Summary

This very long chapter documents a substantial piece of software that implements a flexible framework for many kinds of web development. As with any piece of software, there will be bugs and inconsistencies, but the purpose of the chapter was twofold. First, I wanted to try and convince the skeptical reader (as well as the skeptical bookstore browser) that Python is a suitable vehicle for development of web systems without relying on any external server software. Second, I wanted to try to provide you, the loyal reader, with something you might feel like experimenting with the next time you need a web-based solution that does not seem like a good fit with traditional (heavyweight) web server technology.

How well the first goal has been met you can measure for yourself by looking at Table 18.1, which contains a snapshot of code sizes for the various modules you have read about in this chapter. The Source line count column *includes* blank lines, documentation strings and comment, and the Code column counts just the Python code, which still includes docstrings.

Table 18.1 **PythonTeach Web Site Module Code and Source Sizes**

Module	Code	Source
Auth.py	7	18
CourseAll.py	17	26
CourseBook.py	105	117
CourseByCity.py	27	37
CourseByNum.py	30	41
CourseCtForm.py	11	21
CourseNmForm.py	11	18
CourseOrd.py	69	80
CourseShop.py	28	42
CourseShow.py	22	33
Courses.py	84	97
Dept.py	75	87
DeptHome.py	5	13
DeptLinks.py	13	25
DeptNews.py	11	20
DeptNewsItem.py	13	25
DeptPg.py	40	52
DeptQod.py	8	17
DeptQodAns.py	5	14
DeptStart.py	33	43

Module	Code	Source
Error.py	14	21
HTML.py	15	25
Handler.py	199	230
HomePage.py	17	25
MapSite.py	40	48
Params.py	11	17
Server.py	45	59
Session.py	13	20
SiteSpec.py	52	60
Static.py	59	68
User.py	73	102
UserActivate.py	45	56
UserEntry.py	53	63
UserMailPass.py	64	77
UserSignUp.py	125	142
UserUpdate.py	31	41
Web.py	239	275
cachequery.py	118	136
dbsource.py	19	26
dtuple.py	190	233
pyforms.py	200	227
total	2236	2777

With 41 modules, almost 6 percent of the source lines are version control header commentary! Offhand, I cannot think of any language other than Python in which I would have attempted a project of this magnitude without expecting lengthy development times. As always, the development time was longer than I anticipated, but an eXtreme Programming "velocity" of roughly 0.35 would account for the discrepancy (that is, I was actually able to spend about one-third of my time actually developing—designing, coding, testing—rather than doing all the many other things one has to do in life, including staring into a blank screen for a while in "programmer's block" and writing this text, as well as stuff not related to the project). Overall, 0.35 is not a bad velocity to achieve, and it is typical of projects born under a reasonably good star.

The functionality implemented by less than 3,000 lines of Python is impressive when you review the code this chapter has covered. The PythonTeach web site may not be up to commercial standards, but it is a usable system, which clearly proves the feasibility of the framework. It is certainly not a "heavyweight" web server, in terms of implementing all recommendations of all appropriate standards, but it copes well with interactions from common browsers. I therefore hope that the PythonTeach application is small enough and general enough to be adapted for many other web-based applications, including yours.

The code listed in this chapter, along with all other code in the book, is available from the web site, which will also link to a live version of the current PythonTeach code. I plan to continue developing AWeFUL, and the PythonTeach site, as an open-source application. If you want to help, or have suggestions, keep your eye on the web site for developments in that area, or send email to `pythonteach@holdenweb.com`.

There is some evidence that the Python community is not receptive to commercial course offerings of long duration, and this concurs with my own judgment that Python is best absorbed in small bites, with practice between training sessions. Although PythonTeach is a mythical company, it may even end up existing if enough Python users want professional training.

This book has been an attempt to explain all the important technologies on which web-based systems rely, to a sufficient depth that an intelligent reader will be able to implement suitable code, in Python, for any task to be accomplished. All such grandiose schemes are inevitably going to succeed only partially at best, but I hope you feel better-informed for having read *Python Web Programming*.

VI

Appendixes

Changes Since Python 2.0

THIS BOOK WAS ORIGINALLY BASED ON THE Python 2.0 release, but Python is a fast-changing language; so by the time you read this, it is likely that 2.2 or higher will be the current release. The good news is that the developers have made every effort to retain backward compatibility with previous versions. Some changes might affect your code, however, and you might like to use some of the new features in your programs.

I am grateful to Andrew Kuchling, who graciously gave permission to extract this material from his web documents. Most of the material omitted is relevant only to those who write C extensions for the Python language. Because release 2.2 was not finalized at the time of this writing, you might want to confirm the later material about the 2.2 release by visiting `http://www.amk.ca/python/2.2/`.

Notice that many headings refer to numbered PEPs, which are Python Enhancement Proposals. Changes to the language are now preceded by a formal proposal, which is discussed and refined before being submitted to a vote by the development team (Guido having an absolute veto). To find out more about the process, and to see current, rejected, and proposed PEPs, go to `http://python.sourceforge.net/peps/`.

Introduction to Changes in Python 2.1

It's that time again…time for a new Python release, Python 2.1. One recent goal of the Python development team has been to accelerate the pace of new releases, with a new release coming every six to nine months. Python 2.1 is the first release to come out at this faster pace, with the first alpha appearing in January, three months after the final version of 2.0 was released.

This appendix explains the new features in 2.1. Although there aren't as many changes in 2.1 as there were in Python 2.0, there are still some pleasant surprises in store. Python 2.1 is the first release to be steered through the use of PEPs, so most of the sizable changes have accompanying PEPs that provide more complete documentation and a design rationale for the change. This appendix doesn't attempt to document the new features completely but simply provides an overview of the new features for Python programmers. Refer to the Python 2.1 documentation, or to the specific PEP, for more details about any new feature that particularly interests you.

The final release of Python 2.1 was made on April 17, 2001.

PEP 227: Nested Scopes

The largest change in Python 2.1 is to Python's scoping rules. In Python 2.0, at any given time there are at most three namespaces used to look up variable names: local, module-level, and the built-in namespace. This often surprised people because it didn't match their intuitive expectations. For example, a nested recursive function definition doesn't work:

```
def f():
    ...
    def g(value):
        ...
        return g(value-1) + 1
    ...
```

The function g() will always raise a `NameError` exception, because the binding of the name g isn't in either its local namespace or in the module-level namespace. This isn't much of a problem in practice (how often do you recursively define interior functions like this?), but this also made using the `lambda` statement clumsier, and this was a problem in practice. In code that uses `lambda`, you can often find local variables being copied by passing them as the default values of arguments:

```
def find(self, name):
    "Return list of any entries equal to 'name'"
    L = filter(lambda x, name=name: x == name,
               self.list_attribute)
    return L
```

The readability of Python code written in a strongly functional style suffers greatly as a result.

The most significant change to Python 2.1 is that static scoping has been added to the language to fix this problem. As a first effect, the `name=name` default argument is now unnecessary in the preceding example. Put simply, when a given variable name is not assigned a value within a function (by an assignment, or the `def`, `class`, or `import` statements), references to the variable will be looked up in the local namespace of the enclosing scope. A more detailed explanation of the rules, and a dissection of the implementation, can be found in the PEP.

This change may cause some compatibility problems for code where the same variable name is used both at the module level and as a local variable within a function that contains further function definitions. This seems rather unlikely though, since such code would have been pretty confusing to read in the first place.

One side effect of the change is that the `from module import *` and `exec` statements have been made illegal inside a function scope under certain conditions. The Python reference manual has said all along that `from module import *` is only legal at the top level of a module, but the CPython interpreter has never enforced this before. As part of the implementation of nested scopes, the compiler that turns Python source into bytecodes has to generate different code to access variables in a containing scope. `from module import *` and `exec` make it impossible for the compiler to figure this out because they add names to the local namespace that are unknowable at compile time. Therefore, if a function contains function definitions or `lambda` expressions with free variables, the compiler will flag this by raising a `SyntaxError` exception.

To make the preceding explanation a bit clearer, here's an example:

```
x = 1
def f():
    # The next line is a syntax error
    exec 'x=2'
    def g():
        return x
```

Line 4 containing the `exec` statement is a syntax error, since `exec` would define a new local variable named `"x"` whose value should be accessed by `g()`.

This shouldn't be much of a limitation, since `exec` is rarely used in most Python code (and when it is used, it's often a sign of a poor design anyway).

Compatibility concerns have led to nested scopes being introduced gradually; in Python 2.1, they aren't enabled by default but can be turned on within a module by using a future statement as described in PEP 236. (See the following section for further discussion of PEP 236.) In Python 2.2, nested scopes will become the default, and there will be no way to turn them off, but users will have had all of 2.1's lifetime to fix any breakage resulting from their introduction.

For more information, see PEP 227, "Statically Nested Scopes," written and implemented by Jeremy Hylton.

PEP 236: __future__ Directives

The reaction to nested scopes was widespread concern about the dangers of breaking code with the 2.1 release, and it was strong enough to make the Pythoneers take a more conservative approach. This approach consists of introducing a convention for enabling optional functionality in release N that will become compulsory in release N+1.

The syntax uses a `from...import` statement using the reserved module name `__future__`. Nested scopes can be enabled by the following statement:

```
from __future__ import nested_scopes
```

Although it looks like a normal `import` statement, it's not; there are strict rules on where such a `future` statement can be put. They can be only at the top of a module and must precede any Python code or regular `import` statements. This is because such statements can affect how the Python bytecode compiler parses code and generates bytecode, so they must precede any statement that will result in byte-codes being produced.

For more information, see PEP 236, "Back to the __future__," implemented primarily by Jeremy Hylton.

PEP 207: Rich Comparisons

In earlier versions, Python's support for implementing comparisons on user-defined classes and extension types was simple. Classes could implement a `__cmp__` method that was given two instances of a class and could only return 0 if they were equal, or +1 or –1 if they weren't; the method couldn't raise an exception or return anything other than a Boolean value. Users of Numeric Python often found this model too weak and restrictive because, in the number-crunching programs that numeric Python is used for, it would be more useful to be able to perform element-wise comparisons of two matrices, returning a matrix containing the results of a given comparison for each element. If the two matrices are of different sizes, then the compare has to be able to raise an exception to signal the error.

In Python 2.1, rich comparisons were added to support this need. Python classes can now individually overload each of the <, <=, >, >=, ==, and != operations. The new magic method names are as follows:

Operation	Method Name
<	__lt__
<=	__le__
>	__gt__
>=	__ge__
==	__eq__
!=	__ne__

(The magic methods are named after the corresponding Fortran operators .LT., .LE., &c. Numeric programmers are almost certainly familiar with these names and will find them easy to remember.)

Each of these magic methods is of the form method(*self, other*), where *self* is the object on the left-hand side of the operator, and *other* is the object on the right-hand side. For example, the expression A < B causes A.__lt__(B) to be called.

Each of these magic methods can return anything at all: a Boolean, a matrix, a list, or any other Python object. Alternatively, they can raise an exception if the comparison is impossible, inconsistent, or otherwise meaningless.

The built-in cmp(A,B) function can use the rich comparison machinery and now accepts an optional argument specifying which comparison operation to use; this is given as one of the strings "<", "<=", ">", ">=", "==", or "!=". If called without the optional third argument, cmp() will only return -1, 0, or +1 as in previous versions of Python; otherwise, it will call the appropriate method and can return any Python object.

There are also corresponding changes of interest to C programmers. There's a new slot tp_richcmp in type objects and an API for performing a given rich comparison. I won't cover the C API here but will refer you to PEP 207, or to 2.1's C API documentation, for the full list of related functions.

For more information, see PEP 207, "Rich Comparisons," written by Guido van Rossum, heavily based on earlier work by David Ascher, and implemented by Guido van Rossum.

PEP 230: Warning Framework

Over its 10 years of existence, Python has accumulated a certain number of obsolete modules and features along the way. It's difficult to know when a feature is safe to remove, since there's no way of knowing how much code uses it—perhaps no programs depend on the feature, or perhaps many do. To enable removing old features in a more structured way, a warning framework was added. When Python developers want to get rid of a feature, it will first trigger a warning in the next version of Python. The following Python version can then drop the feature, and users will have had a full release cycle to remove uses of the old feature.

Python 2.1 adds the warning framework to be used in this scheme. It adds a warnings module that provides functions to issue warnings and to filter out warnings that you don't want to be displayed. Third-party modules can also use this framework to deprecate old features that they no longer want to support.

For example, in Python 2.1 the regex module is deprecated, so importing it causes a warning to be printed:

```
>>> import regex
__main__:1: DeprecationWarning: the regex module
          is deprecated; please use the re module
>>>
```

Warnings can be issued by calling the `warnings.warn` function:

```
warnings.warn("feature X no longer supported")
```

The first parameter is the warning message; an additional optional parameter can be used to specify a particular warning category.

Filters can be added to disable certain warnings; a regular expression pattern can be applied to the message or to the module name to suppress a warning. For example, you may have a program that uses the `regex` module and not want to spare the time to convert it to use the `re` module right now. The warning can be suppressed by calling

```
import warnings
warnings.filterwarnings(action = 'ignore',
                        message='.*regex module is deprecated',
                        category=DeprecationWarning,
                        module = '__main__')
```

This adds a filter that will apply only to warnings of the class `DeprecationWarning` triggered in the _main_ module. It also applies a regular expression to match only the message about the `regex` module being deprecated and will cause such warnings to be ignored. Warnings can also be printed only once, printed every time the offending code is executed, or turned into exceptions that will cause the program to stop (unless the exceptions are caught in the usual way, of course).

Functions were also added to Python's C API for issuing warnings; refer to PEP 230 or to Python's API documentation for the details.

For more information, see PEP 5, "Guidelines for Language Evolution," written by Paul Prescod to specify procedures to be followed when removing old features from Python. The policy described in this PEP hasn't been officially adopted, but the eventual policy probably won't be too different from Prescod's proposal. Also, refer to PEP 230, "Warning Framework," written and implemented by Guido van Rossum.

PEP 229: New Build System

When compiling Python, the user had to go in and edit the `Modules/Setup` file to enable various additional modules; the default set is relatively small and limited to modules that compile on most UNIX platforms. This means that on UNIX platforms with many more features, most notably Linux, Python installations often don't contain all the useful modules they could.

Python 2.0 added the Distutils, a set of modules for distributing and installing extensions. In Python 2.1, the Distutils are used to compile much of the standard library of extension modules, autodetecting which ones are supported on the current machine. It's hoped that this will make Python installations easier and more feature-ful.

Instead of having to edit the `Modules/Setup` file to enable modules, a `setup.py` script in the top directory of the Python source distribution is run at build time and attempts to discover which modules can be enabled by examining the modules and header files on the system. If a module is configured in `Modules/Setup`, the `setup.py` script won't attempt to compile that module and will defer to the Modules/Setup file's contents. This provides a way to specific any strange command-line flags or libraries required for a specific platform.

In another far-reaching change to the build mechanism, Neil Schemenauer restructured things so that Python now uses a single makefile that isn't recursive rather than makefiles in the top directory and in each of the Python/, Parser/, Objects/, and Modules/ subdirectories. This makes building Python faster and also makes hacking the makefiles clearer and simpler.

For more information, see PEP 229, "Using Distutils to Build Python," written and implemented by A.M. Kuchling.

PEP 205: Weak References

Weak references, available through the weakref module, are a minor but useful new data type in the Python programmer's toolbox.

Storing a reference to an object (say, in a dictionary or a list) has the side effect of keeping that object alive forever. There are a few specific cases where this behavior is undesirable, object caches being the most common one, and another being circular references in data structures such as trees.

For example, consider a memoizing function that caches the results of another function f(x) by storing the function's argument and its result in a dictionary:

```
_cache = {}
def memoize(x):
    if _cache.has_key(x):
        return _cache[x]

    retval = f(x)

    # Cache the returned object
    _cache[x] = retval

    return retval
```

This version works for simple things such as integers, but it has a side effect; the _cache dictionary holds a reference to the return values, so they'll never be de-allocated until the Python process exits and cleans up. This isn't noticeable for integers, but if f() returns an object, or a data structure that takes up a lot of memory, this can be a problem.

Weak references provide a way to implement a cache that won't keep objects alive beyond their time. If an object is only accessible through weak references, the object will be deallocated, and the weak references will now indicate that the object it referred to no longer exists. A weak reference to an object *obj* is created by calling wr = weakref.ref(*obj*). The object being referred to is returned by calling the weak reference as if it were a function: wr(). It will return the referenced object, or None if the object no longer exists.

This makes it possible to write a `memoize()` function whose cache doesn't keep objects alive, by storing weak references in the cache:

```
_cache = {}
def memoize(x):
    if _cache.has_key(x):
        obj = _cache[x]()
        # If weak reference object still exists,
        # return it
        if obj is not None: return obj

    retval = f(x)

    # Cache a weak reference
    _cache[x] = weakref.ref(retval)

    return retval
```

The `weakref` module also allows creating proxy objects that behave like weak references—an object referenced only by proxy objects is deallocated—but instead of requiring an explicit call to retrieve the object, the proxy transparently forwards all operations to the object as long as the object still exists. If the object is deallocated, attempting to use a proxy will cause a `weakref.ReferenceError` exception to be raised:

```
proxy = weakref.proxy(obj)
proxy.attr   # Equivalent to obj.attr
proxy.meth() # Equivalent to obj.meth()
del obj
proxy.attr   # raises weakref.ReferenceError
```

For more information, see PEP 205, "Weak References," written and implemented by Fred L. Drake, Jr.

PEP 232: Function Attributes

In Python 2.1, functions can now have arbitrary information attached to them. People were often using docstrings to hold information about functions and methods, because the __doc__ attribute was the only way of attaching any information to a function. For example, in the Zope web application server, functions are marked as safe for public access by having a docstring; and in John Aycock's SPARK parsing framework, docstrings hold parts of the BNF grammar to be parsed. This overloading is unfortunate, since docstrings are really intended to hold a function's documentation; for example, it means you can't properly document functions intended for private use in Zope.

Arbitrary attributes can now be set and retrieved on functions using the regular Python syntax:

```
def f(): pass

f.publish = 1
f.secure = 1
f.grammar = "A ::= B (C D)*"
```

The dictionary containing attributes can be accessed as the function's _dict_. Unlike the _dict_ attribute of class instances, in functions you can actually assign a new dictionary to _dict_, though the new value is restricted to a regular Python dictionary. You *can't* be tricky and set it to a UserDict instance or any other random object that behaves like a mapping.

For more information, see PEP 232, "Function Attributes," written and implemented by Barry Warsaw.

PEP 235: Case-Insensitive Platforms and *import*

Some operating systems have filesystems that are case-insensitive, MacOS and Windows being the primary examples. On these systems, it's impossible to distinguish the filenames FILE.PY and file.py, even though they do store the file's name in its original case (they're case-preserving, too).

In Python 2.1, the import statement will work to simulate case sensitivity on case-insensitive platforms. Python will now search for the first case-sensitive match by default, raising an ImportError if no such file is found, so import file will not import a module named FILE.PY. Case-insensitive matching can be requested by setting the PYTHONCASEOK environment variable before starting the Python interpreter.

PEP 217: Interactive Display Hook

When using the Python interpreter interactively, the output of commands is displayed using the built-in repr() function. In Python 2.1, the variable sys.displayhook can be set to a callable object that will be called instead of repr(). For example, you can set it to a special pretty-printing function:

```
>>> # Create a recursive data structure
... L = [1,2,3]
>>> L.append(L)
>>> L # Show Python's default output
[1, 2, 3, [...]]
>>> # Use pprint.pprint() as the display function
... import sys, pprint
>>> sys.displayhook = pprint.pprint
>>> L
[1, 2, 3,  <Recursion on list with id=135143996>]
>>>
```

For more information, see PEP 217, "Display Hook for Interactive Use," written and implemented by Moshe Zadka.

PEP 241: Metadata in Python Packages

A common complaint from Python users is that there's no single catalog of all the Python modules in existence. T. Middleton's Vaults of Parnassus at `http://www.vex.net/parnassus` are the largest catalog of Python modules, but registering software at the Vaults is optional, and many people don't bother.

As a first small step toward fixing the problem, Python software packaged using the Distutils `sdist` command will include a file named `PKG-INFO` containing information about the package such as its name, version, and author (*metadata*, in cataloguing terminology). PEP 241 contains the full list of fields that can be present in the `PKG-INFO` file. As people begin to package their software using Python 2.1, more packages will include metadata, making it possible to build automated cataloguing systems and experiment with them. With the resulting experience, perhaps it'll be possible to design a really good catalog and then build support for it into Python 2.2. For example, the Distutils `sdist` and `bdist_*` commands could support an `upload` option that would automatically upload your package to a catalog server.

You can start creating packages containing `PKG-INFO` even if you're not using Python 2.1, since a new release of the Distutils will be made for users of earlier Python versions. Version 1.0.2 of the Distutils includes the changes described in PEP 241, as well as various bug fixes and enhancements. It will be available from the Distutils SIG at `http://www.python.org/sigs/distutils-sig`.

For more information, see PEP 241, "Metadata for Python Software Packages," written and implemented by A.M. Kuchling. Also refer to PEP 243, "Module Repository Upload Mechanism," written by Sean Reifschneider. This draft PEP describes a proposed mechanism for uploading Python packages to a central server.

New and Improved Modules

Ka-Ping Yee contributed two new modules: `inspect.py`, a module for getting information about live Python code, and `pydoc.py`, a module for interactively converting docstrings to HTML or text. As a bonus, `Tools/scripts/pydoc`, which is now automatically installed, uses `pydoc.py` to display documentation given a Python module, package, or class name. For example, `pydoc xml.dom` displays the following:

```
Python Library Documentation: package xml.dom in xml

NAME
    xml.dom - W3C Document Object Model implementation for Python.

FILE
    /usr/local/lib/python2.1/xml/dom/__init__.pyc

DESCRIPTION
    The Python mapping of the Document Object Model is documented in the
    Python Library Reference in the section on the xml.dom package.
```

```
This package contains the following modules:
   ...
```

`pydoc` also includes a Tk-based interactive help browser. `pydoc` quickly becomes addictive; try it out!

Two different modules for unit testing were added to the standard library. The `doctest` module, contributed by Tim Peters, provides a testing framework based on running embedded examples in docstrings and comparing the results against the expected output. PyUnit, contributed by Steve Purcell, is a unit testing framework inspired by JUnit, which was in turn an adaptation of Kent Beck's Smalltalk testing framework. See `http://pyunit.sourceforge.net/` for more information about PyUnit.

The `difflib` module contains a class, `SequenceMatcher`, which compares two sequences and computes the changes required to transform one sequence into the other. For example, this module can be used to write a tool similar to the UNIX `diff` program, and in fact the sample program `Tools/scripts/ndiff.py` demonstrates how to write such a script.

`curses.panel`, a wrapper for the panel library, part of ncurses and of SYSV curses, was contributed by Thomas Gellekum. The panel library provides windows with the additional feature of depth. Windows can be moved higher or lower in the depth ordering, and the panel library figures out where panels overlap and which sections are visible.

The PyXML package has gone through a few releases since Python 2.0, and Python 2.1 includes an updated version of the `xml` package. Some noteworthy changes include support for expat 1.2 and later versions, the capability for expat parsers to handle files in any encoding supported by Python, and various bug fixes for SAX, DOM, and the `minidom` module.

Ping also contributed another hook for handling uncaught exceptions. `sys.excepthook` can be set to a callable object. When an exception isn't caught by any `try...except` blocks, the exception will be passed to `sys.excepthook`, which can then do whatever it likes. At the Ninth Python Conference, Ping demonstrated an application for this hook: printing an extended traceback that not only lists the stack frames but also lists the function arguments and the local variables for each frame.

Various functions in the `time` module, such as `asctime()` and `localtime()`, require a floating-point argument containing the time in seconds since the epoch. The most common use of these functions is to work with the current time, so the floating-point argument has been made optional; when a value isn't provided, the current time will be used. For example, log file entries usually need a string containing the current time; in Python 2.1, `time.asctime()` can be used, instead of the lengthier `time.asctime(time.localtime(time.time()))` that was previously required.

This change was proposed and implemented by Thomas Wouters.

The `ftplib` module now defaults to retrieving files in passive mode, because passive mode is more likely to work from behind a firewall. This request came from the

Debian bug tracking system, since other Debian packages use `ftplib` to retrieve files and then don't work from behind a firewall. It's deemed unlikely that this will cause problems for anyone, because Netscape defaults to passive mode and few people complain; but if passive mode is unsuitable for your application or network setup, call `set_pasv(0)` on FTP objects to disable passive mode.

Support for raw socket access has been added to the `socket` module, contributed by Grant Edwards.

The `pstats` module now contains a simple interactive statistics browser for displaying timing profiles for Python programs, invoked when the module is run as a script. Contributed by Eric S. Raymond.

A new implementation-dependent function, `sys._getframe([depth])`, has been added to return a given frame object from the current call stack. `sys._getframe()` returns the frame at the top of the call stack; if the optional integer argument *depth* is supplied, the function returns the frame that is *depth* calls below the top of the stack. For example, `sys._getframe(1)` returns the caller's frame object.

This function is only present in CPython, not in Jython or the .NET implementation. Use it for debugging, and resist the temptation to put it into production code.

Introduction to Changes in Python 2.2

This document is a draft and is subject to change until the final version of Python 2.2 is released. Currently it's up to date for Python 2.2 alpha 1. Please send any comments, bug reports, or questions, no matter how minor, to akuchlin@mems-exchange.org.

This appendix explains the new features in Python 2.2. Python 2.2 includes some significant changes that go far toward cleaning up the language's darkest corners, and some exciting new features.

This appendix doesn't attempt to provide a complete specification for the new features but instead provides a convenient overview of the new features. For full details, refer to 2.2 documentation such as the *Python Library Reference* and the *Python Reference Manual*, or to the PEP for a particular new feature.

The final release of Python 2.2 was scheduled, at the time of this writing, for December, 2001.

PEP 234: Iterators

A significant addition to 2.2 is an iteration interface at both the C and Python levels. Objects can define how they can be looped over by callers.

In Python versions up to 2.1, the usual way to make `for item in obj` work is to define a `__getitem__()` method that looks something like this:

```
def __getitem__(self, index):
    return <next item>
```

`__getitem__()` is more properly used to define an indexing operation on an object so that you can write `obj[5]` to retrieve the sixth element. It's a bit misleading when you're using this only to support `for` loops. Consider some file-like object that wants to be looped over; the *index* parameter is essentially meaningless, as the class probably assumes that a series of __getitem__() calls will be made, with *index* incrementing by one each time. In other words, the presence of the __getitem__() method doesn't mean that `file[5]` will work, though it really should.

In Python 2.2, iteration can be implemented separately, and __getitem__() methods can be limited to classes that really do support random access. The basic idea of iterators is simple. A new built-in function, `iter(obj)`, returns an iterator for the object *obj*. (It can also take two arguments: `iter(C, sentinel)` will call the callable *C*, until it returns *sentinel*, which will signal that the iterator is done. This form probably won't be used often.)

Python classes can define an __iter__() method, which should create and return a new iterator for the object; if the object is its own iterator, this method can just return `self`. In particular, iterators will usually be their own iterators. Extension types implemented in C can implement a `tp_iter` function to return an iterator, and extension types that want to behave as iterators can define a `tp_iternext` function.

So what do iterators do? They have one required method, `next()`, which takes no arguments and returns the next value. When there are no more values to be returned, calling `next()` should raise the `StopIteration` exception:

```
>>> L = [1,2,3]
>>> i = iter(L)
>>> print i
<iterator object at 0x8116870>
>>> i.next()
1
>>> i.next()
2
>>> i.next()
3
>>> i.next()
Traceback (most recent call last):
    File "<stdin>", line 1, in ?
StopIteration
>>>
```

In 2.2, Python's `for` statement no longer expects a sequence; it expects something for which `iter()` will return something. For backward compatibility, and convenience, an iterator is automatically constructed for sequences that don't implement __iter__() or a `tp_iter` slot, so `for i in [1,2,3]` will still work. Wherever the Python interpreter loops over a sequence, it's been changed to use the iterator protocol. This means you can do things like this:

```
>>> i = iter(L)
>>> a,b,c = i
>>> a,b,c
(1, 2, 3)
>>>
```

Iterator support has been added to some of Python's basic types. Calling `iter()` on a dictionary will return an iterator that loops over its keys:

```
>>> m = {'Jan': 1, 'Feb': 2, 'Mar': 3, 'Apr': 4, 'May': 5, 'Jun': 6,
...      'Jul': 7, 'Aug': 8, 'Sep': 9, 'Oct': 10, 'Nov': 11, 'Dec': 12}
>>> for key in m: print key, m[key]
...
Mar 3
Feb 2
Aug 8
Sep 9
May 5
Jun 6
Jul 7
Jan 1
Apr 4
Nov 11
Dec 12
Oct 10
>>>
```

That's just the default behavior. If you want to iterate over keys, values, or key/value pairs, you can explicitly call the `iterkeys()`, `itervalues()`, or `iteritems()` methods to get an appropriate iterator. In a minor related change, the `in` operator now works on dictionaries, so *key* `in` `dict` is now equivalent to `dict.has_key(`*key*`)`.

Files also provide an iterator, which calls the `readline()` method until there are no more lines in the file. This means you can now read each line of a file using code like this:

```
for line in file:
    # do something for each line
```

Note that you can only go forward in an iterator; there's no way to get the previous element, reset the iterator, or make a copy of it. An iterator object could provide such additional capabilities, but the iterator protocol only requires a `next()` method.

For more information, see PEP 234, "Iterators," written by Ka-Ping Yee and GvR; implemented by the PythonLabs crew, mostly by GvR and Tim Peters.

PEP 255: Simple Generators

Generators are another new feature, one that interacts with the introduction of iterators.

You're doubtless familiar with how function calls work in Python or C. When you call a function, it gets a private area where its local variables are created. When the function reaches a `return` statement, the local variables are destroyed, and the resulting value is returned to the caller. A later call to the same function will get a fresh new set of local variables. But what if the local variables weren't destroyed on exiting a function? What if you could later resume the function where it left off? This is what generators provide; they can be thought of as resumable functions.

Here's the simplest example of a generator function:

```
def generate_ints(N):
    for i in range(N):
        yield i
```

A new keyword, `yield`, was introduced for generators. Any function containing a `yield` statement is a generator function; this is detected by Python's bytecode compiler, which compiles the function specially. Because a new keyword was introduced, generators must be explicitly enabled in a module by including a `from __future__ import generators` statement near the top of the module's source code. In Python 2.3, this statement will become unnecessary.

When you call a generator function, it doesn't return a single value; instead it returns a generator object that supports the iterator interface. On executing the `yield` statement, the generator outputs the value of `i`, similar to a `return` statement. The big difference between `yield` and a `return` statement is that, on reaching a `yield`, the generator's state of execution is suspended, and local variables are preserved. On the next call to the generator's `.next()` method, the function will resume executing immediately after the `yield` statement. (For complicated reasons, the `yield` statement isn't allowed inside the `try` block of a `try...finally` statement; read PEP 255 for a full explanation of the interaction between `yield` and exceptions.)

Here's a sample usage of the `generate__ints` generator:

```
>>> gen = generate_ints(3)
>>> gen
<generator object at 0x8117f90>
>>> gen.next()
0
>>> gen.next()
1
>>> gen.next()
2
>>> gen.next()
Traceback (most recent call last):
    File "<stdin>", line 1, in ?
    File "<stdin>", line 2, in generate_ints
StopIteration
>>>
```

You could equally write `for i in generate__ints(5)`, or `a,b,c = generate__ints(3)`.

Inside a generator function, the `return` statement can only be used without a value and signals the end of the procession of values; afterward, the generator cannot return any further values. `return` with a value, such as `return 5`, is a syntax error inside a generator function. The end of the generator's results can also be indicated by raising `StopIteration` manually, or by just letting the flow of execution fall off the bottom of the function.

You could achieve the effect of generators manually by writing your own class and storing all the local variables of the generator as instance variables. For example, returning a list of integers could be done by setting `self.count` to 0, and having the `next()` method increment `self.count` and return it. However, for a moderately complicated generator, writing a corresponding class would be much messier. `Lib/test/test_generators.py` contains a number of more interesting examples. The simplest one implements an in-order traversal of a tree using generators recursively:

```
# A recursive generator that generates Tree leaves in in-order.
def inorder(t):
    if t:
        for x in inorder(t.left):
            yield x
        yield t.label
        for x in inorder(t.right):
            yield x
```

Two other examples in `Lib/test/test_generators.py` produce solutions for the N-Queens problem (placing N queens on an NxN chessboard so that no queen threatens another) and the Knight's Tour (a route that takes a knight to every square of an NxN chessboard without visiting any square twice).

The idea of generators comes from other programming languages, especially Icon (`http://www.cs.arizona.edu/icon/`), where the idea of generators is central to the language. In Icon, every expression and function call behaves like a generator. One example from "An Overview of the Icon Programming Language" at `http://www.cs.arizona.edu/icon/docs/ipd266.htm` gives an idea of what this looks like:

```
sentence := "Store it in the neighboring harbor"
if (i := find("or", sentence)) > 5 then write(i)
```

The `find()` function returns the indexes at which the substring `"or"` is found: 3, 23, 33. In the `if` statement, `i` is first assigned a value of 3, but 3 is less than 5, so the comparison fails. Icon retries it with the second value of 23, which is greater than 5, so the comparison now succeeds, and the code prints the value 23 to the screen.

Python doesn't go nearly as far as Icon in adopting generators as a central concept. Generators are considered a new part of the core Python language, but learning or using them isn't compulsory; if they don't solve any problems that you have, feel free to ignore them. This is different from Icon, where the idea of generators is a basic concept. One novel feature of Python's interface as compared to Icon's is that a generator's state is represented as a concrete object that can be passed around to other functions or stored in a data structure.

For more information, see PEP 255, "Simple Generators," written by Neil Schemenauer, Tim Peters, and Magnus Lie Hetland; implemented mostly by Neil Schemenauer and Tim Peters, with other fixes from the PythonLabs crew.

PEP 238: Changing the Division Operator

The most controversial change in Python 2.2 is the start of an effort to fix an old design flaw that's been in Python from the beginning. Currently Python's division operator, /, behaves like C's division operator when presented with two integer arguments. It returns an integer result that's truncated down when there would be fractional part. For example, 3/2 is 1, not 1.5, and (-1)/2 is -1, not -0.5. This means that the results of division can vary unexpectedly depending on the type of the two operands, and because Python is dynamically typed, it can be difficult to determine the possible types of the operands.

(The controversy is over whether this is *really* a design flaw, and whether it's worth breaking existing code to fix this. It has caused endless discussions on python-dev, and in July erupted into an storm of acidly sarcastic postings on `comp.lang.python`. I won't argue for either side here; read PEP 238 for a summary of arguments and counter-arguments.)

Because this change might break code, it's being introduced gradually. Python 2.2 begins the transition, but the switch won't be complete until Python 3.0.

First, some terminology from PEP 238. *True division* is the division that most non-programmers are familiar with: 3/2 is 1.5, 1/4 is 0.25, and so forth. *Floor division* is what Python's / operator currently does when given integer operands; the result is the floor of the value returned by true division. *Classic division* is the current mixed behavior of /; it returns the result of floor division when the operands are integers and returns the result of true division when one of the operands is a floating-point number.

Here are the changes 2.2 introduces:

- A new operator, //, is the floor division operator. (Yes, we know it looks like C++'s comment symbol.) // *always* returns the floor divison no matter what the types of its operands are, so 1 // 2 is 0 and 1.0 // 2.0 is also 0.0.

  // is always available in Python 2.2; you don't need to enable it using a __future__ statement.

- By including a from __future__ import true_division in a module, the / operator will be changed to return the result of true division, so 1/2 is 0.5. Without the __future__ statement, / still means classic division. The default meaning of / will not change until Python 3.0.

- Classes can define methods called __truediv__ and __floordiv__ to overload the two division operators. At the C level, there are also slots in the PyNumberMethods structure so that extension types can define the two operators.

For more information, see PEP 238, "Changing the Division Operator," written by Moshe Zadka and Guido van Rossum; implemented by Guido van Rossum.

Unicode Changes

Python's Unicode support has been enhanced a bit in 2.2. Unicode strings are usually stored as UCS-2, as 16-bit unsigned integers. Python 2.2 can also be compiled to use UCS-4, 32-bit unsigned integers, as its internal encoding by supplying `--enable-unicode=ucs4` to the configure script. When built to use UCS-4 (a *wide Python*), the interpreter can natively handle Unicode characters from U+000000 to U+110000, so the range of legal values for the `unichr()` function is expanded accordingly. Using an interpreter compiled to use UCS-2 (a *narrow Python*), values greater than 65535 will still cause `unichr()` to raise a `ValueError` exception.

All this is the province of the still-unimplemented PEP 261, "Support for 'wide' Unicode characters"; consult it for further details, and please offer comments on the PEP and on your experiences with the 2.2 alpha releases.

Another change is much simpler to explain. Since their introduction, Unicode strings have supported an `encode()` method to convert the string to a selected encoding such as UTF-8 or Latin-1. A symmetric `decode([encoding])` method has been added to 8-bit strings (though not to Unicode strings) in 2.2. `decode()` assumes that the string is in the specified encoding and decodes it, returning whatever is returned by the codec.

Using this new feature, codecs have been added for tasks not directly related to Unicode. For example, codecs have been added for uu-encoding, MIME's base64 encoding, and compression with the `zlib` module:

```
>>> s = """Here is a lengthy piece of redundant, overly verbose,
... and repetitive text.
... """
>>> data = s.encode('zlib')
>>> data
'x\x9c\r\xc9\xc1\r\x80 \x10\x04\xc0?Ul...'
>>> data.decode('zlib')
'Here is a lengthy piece of redundant, overly verbose,\nand repetitive text.\n'
>>> print s.encode('uu')
begin 666 <data>
M2&5R92!I<R!A(&QE;F=T:'D<<&EE8V4@;V8@<F5D=6YD86YT+"!O=F5R;'D@
>=F5R8F]S92P*86YD('-E<&5T:71I=F4@=&5X="X*
 
end
>>> "sheesh".encode('rot-13')
'furrfu'
```

`encode()` and `decode()` were implemented by Marc-André Lemburg. The changes to support using UCS-4 internally were implemented by Fredrik Lundh and Martin von Löwis.

For more information, see PEP 261, "Support for 'wide' Unicode Characters," written by Paul Prescod; not yet accepted or fully implemented.

PEP 227: Nested Scopes

In Python 2.1, statically nested scopes were added as an optional feature, to be enabled by a `from __future__ import nested_scopes` directive. In 2.2, nested scopes no longer need to be specially enabled but are always enabled.

[Note to the reader from author: This information is omitted because it has already been presented in the previous material that addresses Python 2.1 changes.]

New and Improved Modules

The `xmlrpclib` module was contributed to the standard library by Fredrik Lundh. It provides support for writing XML-RPC clients; XML-RPC is a simple remote procedure call protocol built on top of HTTP and XML. For example, the following snippet retrieves a list of RSS channels from the O'Reilly Network and then retrieves a list of the recent headlines for one channel:

```
import xmlrpclib
s = xmlrpclib.Server(
        'http://www.oreillynet.com/meerkat/xml-rpc/server.php')
channels = s.meerkat.getChannels()
# channels is a list of dictionaries, like this:
# [{'id': 4, 'title': 'Freshmeat Daily News'}
#  {'id': 190, 'title': '32Bits Online'},
#  {'id': 4549, 'title': '3DGamers'}, ... ]

# Get the items for one channel
items = s.meerkat.getItems( {'channel': 4} )

# 'items' is another list of dictionaries, like this:
# [{'link': 'http://freshmeat.net/releases/52719/',
#   'description': 'A utility which converts HTML to XSL FO.',
#   'title': 'html2fo 0.3 (Default)'}, ... ]
```

See `http://www.xmlrpc.com/` for more information about XML-RPC.

- The socket module can be compiled to support IPv6; specify the `--enable-ipv6` option to Python's configure script. (Contributed by Jun-ichiro "itojun" Hagino.)

- Two new format characters were added to the `struct` module for 64-bit integers on platforms that support the C `long long` type. "q" is for a signed 64-bit integer, and "Q" is for an unsigned one. The value is returned in Python's long integer type. (Contributed by Tim Peters.)

- In the interpreter's interactive mode, there's a new built-in function `help()` that uses the `pydoc` module introduced in Python 2.1 to provide interactive help documentation. `help(object)` displays any available help text about *object*. `help()` with no argument puts you in an online help utility, where you can enter the names of functions, classes, or modules to read their help text. (Contributed by Guido van Rossum, using Ka-Ping Yee's `pydoc` module.)

- Various bug fixes and performance improvements have been made to the SRE engine underlying the `re` module. For example, `re.sub()` will now use `string.replace()` automatically when the pattern and its replacement are both just literal strings without `regex` metacharacters. Another contributed patch speeds up certain Unicode character ranges by a factor of two. (SRE is maintained by Fredrik Lundh. The `BIGCHARSET` patch was contributed by Martin von Löwis.)

- The `imaplib` module, maintained by Piers Lauder, has support for several new extensions: the `NAMESPACE` extension defined in RFC 2342, `SORT`, `GETACL`, and `SETACL`. (Contributed by Anthony Baxter and Michel Pelletier.)

- The rfc822 module's parsing of email addresses is now compliant with RFC 2822, an update to RFC 822. The module's name is not going to be changed to "rfc2822". (Contributed by Barry Warsaw.)

- New constants `ascii_letters`, `ascii_lowercase`, and `ascii_uppercase` were added to the string module. There were several modules in the standard library that used `string.letters` to mean the ranges A-Za-z, but that assumption is incorrect when locales are in use because `string.letters` varies depending on the set of legal characters defined by the current locale. The buggy modules have all been fixed to use `ascii_letters` instead. (Reported by an unknown person; fixed by Fred L. Drake, Jr.)

- The `mimetypes` module now makes it easier to use alternative MIME-type databases by the addition of a `MimeTypes` class, which takes a list of filenames to be parsed. (Contributed by Fred L. Drake, Jr.)

Other Changes and Fixes

As usual there were a bunch of other improvements and bug fixes scattered throughout the source tree. A search through the CVS change logs finds there were 43 patches applied, and 77 bugs fixed; both figures are likely to be underestimates. Some of the more notable changes are

- Keyword arguments passed to built-in functions that don't take them now cause a `TypeError` exception to be raised, with the message `"function takes no keyword arguments"`.

- The code for the Mac OS port for Python, maintained by Jack Jansen, is now kept in the main Python CVS tree.

- A new script, `Tools/scripts/cleanfuture.py` by Tim Peters, automatically removes obsolete `__future__` statements from Python source code.

- The new license introduced with Python 1.6 wasn't GPL compatible. This is fixed by some minor textual changes to the 2.2 license, so Python can now be embedded inside a GPLed program again. The license changes were also applied to the Python 2.0.1 and 2.1.1 releases.

- When presented with a Unicode filename on Windows, Python will now convert it to an MBCS encoded string, as used by the Microsoft file APIs. As MBCS is explicitly used by the file APIs, Python's choice of ASCII as the default encoding turns out to be an annoyance. (Contributed by Mark Hammond with assistance from Marc-André Lemburg.)

- The `Tools/scripts/ftpmirror.py` script now parses a `.netrc` file, if you have one. (Contributed by Mike Romberg.)

- Some features of the object returned by the `xrange()` function are now deprecated, and trigger warnings when they're accessed; they'll disappear in Python 2.3. `xrange` objects tried to pretend they were full sequence types by supporting slicing, sequence multiplication, and the `in` operator, but these features were rarely used and therefore buggy. The `tolist()` method and the `start`, `stop`, and `step` attributes are also being deprecated. At the C level, the fourth argument to the `PyRange_New()` function, `"repeat"`, has also been deprecated.

- There were a bunch of patches to the dictionary implementation, mostly to fix potential core dumps if a dictionary contains objects that sneakily changed their hash value or mutated the dictionary they were contained in. For a while, `python-dev` fell into a gentle rhythm of Michael Hudson finding a case that dumped core, Tim Peters fixing it, Michael finding another case, and round and round it went.

- On Windows, Python can now be compiled with Borland C thanks to a number of patches contributed by Stephen Hansen.

- Another Windows enhancement: Wise Solutions generously offered PythonLabs use of its InstallerMaster 8.1 system. Earlier PythonLabs Windows installers used Wise 5.0a, which was beginning to show its age. (Packaged up by Tim Peters.)

- Files ending in `.pyw` can now be imported on Windows. `.pyw` is a Windows-only thing, used to indicate that a script needs to be run using `PYTHONW.EXE` instead of `PYTHON.EXE` to prevent a DOS console from popping up to display the output. This patch makes it possible to import such scripts, in case they're also usable as modules. (Implemented by David Bolen.)

- On platforms where Python uses the C `dlopen()` function to load extension modules, it's now possible to set the flags used by `dlopen()` using the `sys.getdlopenflags()` and `sys.setdlopenflags()` functions. (Contributed by Bram Stolk.)

B

Glossary

4Suite A collection of open–source XML processing applications developed by Fourthought, Inc. Portions of the 4Suite package are included in the standard PyXML distribution. However, more advanced capabilities must be downloaded separately at `http://www.fourthought.com`.

abstract class A class defined for use as a *base class*, and not intended to be instantiated.

abstract method A method not implemented by a class, even though it may be used by other defined methods. Normally you use abstract methods in an abstract class's method implementations, with the expectation that the concrete subclasses will define their own implementations of the abstract methods.

ActivePython A Python distribution that currently includes the Python core libraries; commonly used external modules, including *expat* for XML processing; *zlib* for data compression; a suite of Windows tools developed by Mark Hammond, including the *PythonWin* IDE; the *PythonCOM* system; and more. ActivePython is available for Windows, Linux, and Solaris, and can be freely used for commercial and noncommercial purposes but may not be redistributed without permission from ActiveState Corporation (`http://www.activestate.com/`).

API Application Programming Interface: specifies which routines must be called, and in what sequence, to use the features of a particular program component.

associative entity   Sometimes also called a *linking entity*. An entity defined to denote a many-to-many relationship between two other entities. The primary key of the associative entity is the composite of the primary keys of the related entities.

attribute   A data value associated with a class, an instance, a module, or, in relational databases, an entity. In various contexts, you might also see attributes referred to as properties or *members*.

base class   A class used as the basis for a subclass definition, and from which the subclass will inherit methods and other attributes.

binding   The act of attaching a value to a name, also sometimes used to describe the value bound to a name. The most common way to bind a value to a name in Python uses the assignment statement, but other ways exist. For example, the class statement binds the class definition to the class name.

bound method   A method invoked by qualifying an instance rather than the class is automatically bound to the instance, which is provided as a first argument to the method call. A method can also be pre-associated with an instance, and such a *bound method* can therefore be used similarly to a standard function. Contrast with *unbound method*. For example, you can bind a name to a bound method of a particular dictionary with the statement

```
isfood = {'eggs': 'yes', 'dirt':➥
'no', 'spam': 'maybe'}.get
```

The name `isfood` is now bound to the `get()` method of the given dictionary, and so the expression

```
isfood('spam')
```

has the value

```
'maybe'
```

business object   Often used to refer to an object that implements a *business rule* [q.v.]. This usage has become more common as distributed systems have adopted *multitier* architectures. In such systems, the middle tier is often focused on maintaining the *business rules*, and such policy is implemented by the methods of the appropriate business objects.

business rule   Also known as a *semantic integrity constraint*. In relational systems, the simplest structural requirements of the database can be implemented by *declarative constraints*, but the application may have more complex requirements such as "the sum of all account balances should equal the balance of the control account," which must be maintained as system invariants (they must always be true). These more complex constraints, specific to a particular system, and requiring application logic to ensure that they are maintained, are often called business rules.

C++   A fully compiled language with relatively strong static typing. Although derived from the C language, of which it is almost a syntactic superset, C++ includes full-featured object-orientation. It supports encapsulation by enabling the programmer to declare exactly which portions of objects are accessible outside the interface and which are available only to the implementation. C++'s templates give the language's power a substantial boost, enabling (albeit only at compile time, and with cluttered syntax) the signature-based polymorphism, which is such a big part of Python's own power, but (potentially) without any penalty in terms of program performance. C++ excels at fully exploiting a machine's potential, but only at the cost of enormous complexity.

call level interface (CLI) An *API* used by programmers to pass requests to a database engine.

callable Any Python object that can be the subject of a function-like call is a callable. Besides functions, classes are also callables—you call the class to create an instance. Instances with a __call__() special method are also callables, as are methods. In most contexts where the Python documentation says a function is required, any callable will suffice.

callback (1) In event-driven processes, a function provided as an argument to a *callable*, with the express intention that the called code will (at some unspecified point in the future) call the callback routine when a certain event occurs. (2) A function provided as an argument to a routine that traverses some data structure, and called by the traversal routine to take action on encountering specified nodes.

candidate key An attribute, or set of attributes, of a relation whose value is unique for each tuple in the relation, and which might therefore be used as the *primary key* of the table that implements the relation.

cardinality (1) The number of rows in a table. (2) A definition of the number of tuples in one relation that can be related to tuples in another relation. The possible relationship cardinalities are

one-to-one (1:1), one-to-many (1:M) and many-to-many (M:N).

Channel A dispatcher object serviced by the asynchronous loop in the asyncore module.

Cheetah A template utility that can be used with equal facility to generate HTML, XML, PostScript, and any number of other formats.

class attribute A value associated with the class rather than with a particular instance. Because the attribute is bound to the class rather than an instance, the mechanics of name lookup make it appear as common to all instances of the class.

classes The definitions of new types of objects.

client (1) In distributed computing, the software component that requests service, usually by establishing a network connection to the *server* (in TCP-based protocols) or sending a request to the server (in UDP-based protocols). (2) In object-oriented programming, an object that uses the services of other objects by calling their methods.

cohesion A measure of how well the elements of the code focus on a single objective, and how many details of the code's structure must be known by other components wanting to use it. Cohesive code generally is self-contained and used entirely by calling its functionality through published interfaces such as the methods of a class.

commit To make changes to a database permanent. A set of changes is normally treated as a *transaction*, and either all changes should be committed, or (in the event that this is impossible for application or system reasons) any partial changes should be discarded by *rollback*.

Common Gateway Interface (CGI) A standardized way of having the web server present request data, plus additional information that provides a context to the request, to whatever script or program is run as a result of the request.

complex numbers Represented as the sum of a real and an imaginary number. Complex numbers are Python's widest built-in numeric type.

conceptual entity An entity in a database design that represents something intangible (such as an account or a purchase), about which information must nevertheless be recorded.

concrete entity An entity in a database design that describes something tangible (such as a part or a person) about which information must be recorded.

coupling The manner in which information is passed between system components. A loosely coupled system uses information passed only across defined interfaces, allowing implementation changes in components without requiring changes in their clients. Tightly coupled software might, for example, pass arguments through global variables. If the name of the global were to be changed, then the implementations of all callers would also have to be changed, making the maintenance of the software a difficult and error-prone task.

cursor Sometimes held to be an abbreviation for "current set of records," an object used to interface to a relational database. Generally, a program creates a connection to a database and then creates one or more cursors on that connection to perform the necessary database operations, which the program achieves by executing SQL statements on the cursor. For insert, update, and delete operations, the set of records associated with a cursor will be empty. For retrieval operations, the set of records will be those retrieved by a SQL SELECT statement, and the program can then process the records by manipulating the cursor interface.

Data Definition Language (DDL) A subset of SQL that allows you to maintain the schema by changing its structure and tuning it as requirements and usage changes.

data dictionary Predefined system tables that describe the structure of the application data (the user tables, the attributes of each table, the primary and foreign key constraints, and so on).

data structures The simplest objects that you can create in Python. They are collections of data items often called *members*, *fields*, or *attributes*. Python has several built-in data structures.

database A collection of related data, designed for a known group of users, to be used in particular applications.

declarative constraint A limitation on the contents of a database's application tables that can be enforced automatically by the RDBMS. Usually limited to *entity integrity*, *referential integrity*, and simple check constraints to limit the range of values for a specific attribute.

delegation A technique by which one object passes method calls to the methods of another object. Delegation can be explicit for each delegated method, as in this case:

```
def write(self, string):
    return self.file.write(self,➡
    string.upper())
```

Here we assume that some class is being defined. Objects of this class implement their `write()` method by explicit delegation to the `write()` method of their file attribute. Delegation can be more general, however, as in the following example:

```
def __getattr__(self, attr):
    return getattr(self.file, attr)
```

In this case, sometimes called "blind delegation," the interpreter invokes the object's `__getattr__()` method when it cannot locate the attribute it has been told to look for. The object responds with a general delegation, effectively telling the interpreter to use the corresponding attribute of the object's file attribute. This technique works not only for methods but also for data attributes (in a read-only sense; adding `__setattr__` allows delegating attribute binding and rebinding, and `__delattr__` lets you delegate the unbinding of attributes).

dictionary An associative array, which holds values stored against keys.

DOM Document Object Model: a specification of the structure of XML and HTML documents as a tree. A top-level Document node represents each document. This node contains a single Element node that corresponds to the first element. Additional subelements are then added in a way that mirrors the underlying structure of the document.

domain name system (DNS) A hierarchical, distributed database, which often operates over UDP (although the protocol can use either TCP or UDP). The nature of the application protocol is such that several servers are often identified that might answer a particular query, so if no reply is received from one due to traffic loss, the answer will usually be obtained from another source.

DTD Document Type Definition: a formal specification that enumerates all the allowable elements, attributes, and values that may appear in an XML or SGML document. Not only that, a DTD precisely defines the structure of how these elements are supposed to be used in relation to each other within the document tree.

dynamic content Content in a web system that is computed rather than simply retrieved from filestore and served up.

encapsulation A property of program systems whereby the algorithms are treated as "black boxes," and no internal details are available to the clients of the system. In object-oriented systems, objects have both state (expressed as the object's attribute values) and behavior (expressed as the methods implemented and inherited by the class's implementation). In a fully encapsulated implementation, an object's state is only accessed and/or modified through method calls. Python does not enforce encapsulation, but it does allow you to use it.

entity (1) Any distinguishable object or concept that must be represented in a database. In relational implementations, each entity type is represented by a table, and each row in a table represents an occurrence of the defined entity type. (2) What the HTTP protocol transfers between client and server in non-empty requests and responses. (3) An XML language element reference introduced by an ampersand and terminated by a semicolon (for example, `&foo;`).

entity integrity Requires that no part of the primary key may be NULL.

entity set A collection of things all of the same type.

ephemeral port Contrast with *well-known port*. When a network client needs to communicate with the server, it requests an ephemeral port, whose number is above 1023 but otherwise cannot be predicted. The transport layer guarantees not to give the same port number on the same transport-layer protocol to any other program while it remains in use.

escape sequences In Python string literal representations, a sequence of characters beginning with a backslash, used to represent a character that would otherwise be difficult to include in the string value.

event-driven parsing A style of XML processing in which special functions are invoked for different document features encountered as the document is read.

event entity *Conceptual entities* that record interactions taking place at a specific point in time. For example, when a shipment of stock is consigned to a customer, a delivery takes place at the point when the carrier hands the shipment to the customer and gets a signature for it. A carrier such as UPS or FedEx needs to record relevant attributes of the delivery entity—for example, the date and time, the name of the recipient, and the identity of the courier's representative —to be able to prove it has met its service obligations to its customers.

extreme programming (XP) An "agile programming" discipline emerged from an object-oriented environment. Extreme programmers show total lack of concern for strict top-down or bottom-up approaches and focus instead on implementing system features that have direct business value, in the priority order negotiated (and continuously renegotiated: system specification is an ongoing process, not a state) with the customer.

FIFO First-in first-out queue.

field An attribute of an object, a component of a record from a file, or a particular column of a database row.

foreign key An attribute of an entity occurrence that identifies an occurrence of some related entity type by the primary key value of the related occurrence.

formal public identifier (FPI) Most commonly used when referring to entities that are highly standardized or in wide public use.

FTP File Transfer Protocol: a stream-oriented bidirectional platform-independent system for transferring both text and binary files between the client and the server. It uses a control connection to allow the client to send commands to the server and dynamically creates additional connections for data transfer as required. Error detection and recovery are essential to the protocol, which is complex enough without adding such features to it. Old-time network users swear by FTP; security experts swear at it. It's a security nightmare (passwords traveling over the Net in the clear, data connections opened on-the-fly needing to be passed through firewalls, total vulnerability to man-in-the-middle attacks, and so forth).

global   In general terms, a value from the surrounding context of an object or module. In Python, global values are held in the namespace associated with the module that contains a function or class's definition.

horizontal fragmentation   Takes a table from the normalized design and splits it into a number of tables, each containing some rows from the original table.

identifier   A legal Python name that is made up of letters of either case, digits, and the underscore character. The first character of an identifier may not be a digit.

IDLE   Integrated DeveLopment Environment for Python: a part of the standard Python distribution, which works on any platform that supports the Tkinter GUI.

imaginary numbers   Similar to floating-point numbers but followed by "j" or "J."

IMAP4   An Internet mailbox-protocol that allows users to adopt either an online or an offline model: they may transfer messages down to their personal computer if they want, but they may equally retain messages in folders on the server.

immutable   Types whose instances cannot be changed. The built-in Python immutable types are the numeric types,

None, strings, and tuples. Only immutable values can be used as dictionary keys.

inheritance   The means by which subclasses acquire the method and attribute definitions of the base class(es) on which they are defined unless they provide specific overriding definitions. Python supports *multiple inheritance*, allowing several base classes to provide inherited definitions.

instance   An object created by calling a class definition and hence in Python implicitly calling its _init_() special method if such a method exists. In general, each instance maintains its own attribute values and uses the method definitions of its base class(es) by *inheritance*.

introspection   The capability of a programmed system to examine its own internal structure.

join   In relational systems, the operation of combining the values in two tables by concatenating the rows of the first table with the rows of the second. If no conditions are used to select a subset of the joined rows, the result of a join operation is the Cartesian product of the two tables, which joins each row of the first table with every row of the second and is frequently meaningless. This is why SQL SELECT statements frequently include join conditions that join two tables across the relationship between them. The SQL syntax allows several tables to be joined in a single SELECT statement. An *inner join* omits rows from either table with no joinable rows in the other table; an *outer join* includes such rows from one table or the other (depending on whether it is a *left outer join* or a *right outer join*), replacing the nonexistent row from the other table with NULLs.

latent typing   Dynamically typing variables (by name binding, or assignment) rather than statically typing by declaring the data type associated with a particular name.

list   Represented as a number of expressions separated by commas and surrounded by brackets. A *tuple* is similar but uses parentheses, which in many cases are optional.

logical design   (1) A conceptual representation of the way data is represented in your system. (2) The process of designing something strictly according to user requirements rather than in terms of the technologies that will be used to implement the eventual solution.

long integers   Integer values whose size is limited only by available memory. Long integer constants are indicated by ending the integer literal value with a letter "L"—experienced programmers tend to use uppercase rather than lower- because a lowercase "l" is far too easily confused with the digit "1."

loopback interface   In TCP/IP (version 4) stacks, network 127.0.0.0 is by convention and standard reserved for communication between processes on the same host. It uses a network-layer driver in which the transmission process simply copies data from the transmit buffer to a local receive buffer, from where it makes its way back up the receiving side of the stack.

mail transfer agent (MTA)   Tries to deliver messages across the Internet autonomously, possibly over multiple hops.

mail user agent (MUA)   The software responsible for showing users the contents of their mailbox, allowing them to compose messages, and so on: the user interface to the email system. The MUA (a program such as Netscape Messenger or Microsoft Outlook Express) will typically pass outgoing messages to a local or remote MTA for delivery.

manager function   A function whose purpose is primarily to direct the actions of a program according to the values of option or flag settings, choosing different courses of action under different circumstances.

metadata   Data stored in the data dictionary *about* the structure of the user data.

method   An operation that should be performed in the context of, and particularly using the namespace of, some object representing an instance of a particular class. The methods of a class are normally defined as a part of the class definition, and common to all instances of that class.

Microsoft Database Engine (MSDE)   A freely available database engine, 100 percent compatible with SQL Server's Transact-SQL and, according to Microsoft's literature, "optimized for up to five simultaneous users." MSDE comes as a part of certain Microsoft products and can be downloaded from its web site by those who have not purchased the relevant products. (Without a product purchase, you have no rights to redistribute the software.)

The only difference between the redistributable MSDE and the small-scale SQL Server delivered as part of such products as Office Small Business Edition appears to be the lack of many GUI-based tools.

mixin class   A class in Python (and other languages implementing *multiple inheritance*) designed to provide additional behaviors desirable for a wide range of classes by being included as a base class in those classes' definitions.

modular programming   One of the earlier approaches to controlling complexity. The primary goal of modular programming was to have programmers build code in small chunks, with well-defined relationships between them. The main thrust was to emphasize the interfaces between separate portions of the program and to break down the logic into functions of manageable size. Modular programming improves both the *coupling* and the *cohesion* of program code.

mutable   Able to change, or to be changed. Lists and dictionaries, for example, are mutable types because the values of individual entries can be changed, and the values seen by all references to the object change. Contrast with *immutable*.

namespace   (1) In Python, a place in which the interpreter can look up the value associated with a particular name. (2) In XML, an external definition whose elements are referred to by the use of name prefixes. (3) In general, a set of defined names that are legal in some particular context.

non-validating parsers   Require that an XML document be well-formed.

normalization   The process of transforming a relational structure into a form that is not subject to update anomalies; you can normalize by examining functional dependencies or by the application of Codd's rules.

occurrence   In relational systems, an object in the modeled system with an identifiable *entity* type. In the relational data model, each occurrence of a given entity type is modeled by a row in the table that models the entity type. Contrast with an instance in an object-oriented system.

online analytical processing (OLAP)   Processing typically used on the high-volume read-only databases known as data warehouses. Although OLAP systems have much in common with standard relational databases, there is a much stronger emphasis on de-normalization to achieve high performance levels on queries over huge volumes of data.

Open Database Connectivity (ODBC) interface   A widely adopted database interface standard. ODBC provides a standard set of functions by which the database programmer can interact with any database system with an ODBC-compliant driver.

operator precedence   The way languages specify the order of evaluation of expressions with no parentheses in them: higher-precedence operations are performed first.

Oracle RDBMS   One of the most widely used database management systems in the world. Python users can use Oracle with an ODBC interface, or they can use the `DCOracle2` module built and maintained by Zope Corporation, or the newer `cx_Oracle` module from Computronix.

OSI seven-layer model
International Standard Organization specified an idealized model of networking systems. The model was intended to encourage open systems interconnection (refer to Table 4.1).

persistence   Persistent data continues to exist in, and can be retrieved from, a storage medium even after a particular process terminates. Data that exists only for the duration of a particular program's execution would be transient, and could not be retrieved by subsequent processes. A relational database is one form of storage for persistent data; files are another.

physical design   (1) An implementation of the logical design in some relational database management system. (2) A design that takes into account the properties of the system on or in which it will be implemented. Contrast with *logical design*. Generally, we tend to produce logical designs that we then implement according to some physical design scheme. Logical designs that take physical design considerations into account are sometimes said to exhibit "implementation bias," normally considered to be a bad thing.

polymorphism   Literally "of multiple shapes" or "of many forms." The property of a set of classes that, although defining different types of objects, implement a set of operations common to all types. The advantage of polymor-

phic representations is that a program can be written to be independent of the object type it is dealing with because operations can be performed on any type.

POP3   An older Internet mailbox protocol, less capable than IMAP4 but also simpler to program. It uses an offline mail reading model, where the client system connects to the server and downloads messages to the user's personal machine for reading and possible reply.

port number   A software identifier that identifies the sending and receiving processes; both TCP and UDP use 16-bit port numbers.

primary key   The set of one or more attributes that uniquely determine a single row in a relational table, mapping the unique identifier of the *entity* type implemented by the table.

PROM   Programmable Read-Only Memory: memory whose content is determined by a programming process during hardware manufacture. Unlike other forms of memory, the content of the PROM is available as soon as the computer is switched on, so PROM is frequently used to hold code executed during the bootstrap loading process.

protocol   Generally, a formula for interactions of any kind. By extension, the rules by which two processes or pieces of hardware can communicate.

Python 3000   Intended as something of a joke about the long-range aspirations of the project because when it was first envisaged, the computer applications world was going through the tribulations of Y2K adjustment. The intention is to produce a new, Python-like language that addresses some of the more fundamental issues of efficiency in current implementations (without taking 1,000 years about it). Nowadays, when Guido talks about language changes incompatible with existing versions, he generally refers to Python 3.0.

Python Enhancement Proposal (PEP)   A process used as a means of controlling discussions about the future of the language. PEPs can be informational, intended to shed light on some of the more obscure areas of the language, or they can be standards-track. This latter class of document is usually created as a result of discussions on the `python-dev` mailing list, and each one starts as a draft. After a suitable discussion period, Guido or his delegates review the draft and either reject or accept it. After acceptance, a PEP must be implemented in the development environment on SourceForge before it is accorded active status, thereby becoming a part of the language.

Python Software Foundation   A body that ensures Python remains open-source, in which the copyrights in the language and its implementations will be vested.

PythonWin   An interactive development environment available under Microsoft Windows as a part of the *ActivePython* distribution. PythonWin offers a simple interface to most of the important Microsoft Foundation Classes (MFC). PythonWin interacts with you in much the same way as the interpreter but also has great debugging and analysis features.

Pyxie   An XML processing package developed by Sean McGrath. Details are available at `http://pyxie.source-forge.net`. Pyxie works by converting XML documents to a simplified tree-encoding format known as PYX.

qualified name   A sequence of dot-separated names.

raw string   A string literal representation that does not use the normal backslash escaping conventions. Raw strings allow the programmer to represent strings containing backslashes more easily and therefore are frequently used for Windows file paths and regular expressions, for example. A raw string's representation precedes the opening string quote with an upper- or lowercase letter "r," as in

```
r"C:\Temp\downloads\myfile.txt"
```

The same string would conventionally be represented as

```
"C:\\Temp\\downloads\\myfile.txt"
```

recursive relationship   Sometimes also known as a "reflexive relationship": a relationship among two sets of occurrences in the same relation. For example, in a human resources system, each employee may have a "manager" attribute to define the employee to whom he reports. Because managers are also employees, "Employee [as subordinate] reports-to employee [as manager]" is a recursive relationship on employee.

refactoring   The process of reorganizing the structure of code to make it easier to understand, maintain, and/or extend while not affecting its function. This is especially common when you are creating a framework (writing manager function logic intended to apply to several situations) because a lot of reusability bugs can be fixed by refactoring your framework.

referential integrity   Requires that in each occurrence of every entity, foreign key attribute values *must* either be NULL, indicating that this particular occurrence does not take part in the relationship, or occur as a primary key value in the related table, specifying the occurrence in the related table to which the occurrence holding the foreign key value is related.

relation   A set of tuples representing the occurrences of an entity, with the properties that

- No duplicate tuples exist within the set.
- The elements in the tuples are identified by name, and the order of the elements is not significant.
- The order of tuples in the set is not significant.

Mathematically speaking, a relation is a mapping, or function, from a set of key values to a set of *tuples*.

relationship   Formally, a mapping between two relations. In a relational database system, a relationship is implemented using *foreign keys* to specify the mapping. Informally, a relationship is a significant association between two entities.

rollback   An action taken by an application or database management system to reverse the effects of a partial transaction that cannot be completed.

SAX   A widely used interface specification for parsing and processing XML and a common API used to manipulate XML. SAX is based on an event model in which XML documents are scanned sequentially and different handler

methods are invoked for different document features.

secondary key   A set of one or more attributes in a relation that identifies a set of occurrences sharing common characteristics. Also sometimes used to describe any attribute or set of attributes on which an index (a secondary index) is defined.

semantic integrity constraint   See *business rule*.

server   A process that offers service to *clients*, which connect to a network port on which the server listens, and transmits requests over the connection. The requests are processed by the server, which returns its results over the same network connection. Also used to describe a computer whose primary purpose is to offer services to other computers.

signature   The number and types of a function's arguments and its return value.

slicing notation   An extension of the idea of array subscripting common to many programming languages, slicing uses brackets containing two numeric or empty expressions separated by a colon to generate a consecutive subsequence of the elements of a sequence.

SMTP   Simple Mail Transfer Protocol: a protocol used to pass electronic mail messages across the Internet. For email to be effective, its users must be confident in the integrity of the transmissions, so SMTP is TCP-based, ensuring messages are neither lost nor modified in transmission. However, SMTP's integrity is only meant against accidental damage: the protocol's security characteristics are very weak.

socket API Specifies a way for programmers to create a network connection and to transmit information across it.

spike solution In extreme programming, a test implementation producing "the simplest thing that can possibly work," usually without frills of any kind, to determine what sort of architecture might best match the problem requirements. By analogy, extreme programmers also run "performance spikes," "process spikes," and so on, when temporarily concentrating on an implementation aspect not directly connected to making a business-valued feature work (but, rather, to making it work fast, smoothing development process kinks, evaluating technology alternatives, and so on).

stored procedure A named module of code, stored in the database, that can be invoked by a client call or from within another stored procedure.

string A sequence of characters.

suite A block of statements that, by virtue of their increased indentation level, are all subsidiary to single compound statement header clause.

TCP Transmission Control Protocol: the reliable transport-layer protocol used on the Internet. TCP creates a virtual circuit between two processes, and uses synchronized sequence numbering with retransmission to ensure that all errors are detected and corrected.

thick client architectures A system in which the logic on the client side contains significant assumptions about, and knowledge of, the structure of the database, embedded in application-specific coding. If the structures or

business rules are changed, new versions of the client-side applications are required for the desktop machines, leading to complex system maintenance problems.

thin client architectures A system in which the desktop code is either minimal and/or dynamically updateable, avoiding the maintenance problems so prevalent on *thick client architectures*.

thread Similar to a lightweight process: a threaded model tracks several concurrent execution paths within a single address space. The key difference between processes and threads is that the operating system provides no intrinsic protection between threads of the same process.

three tier architectures A system in which the desktop computer handles the user interaction and possibly some of the application logic. A middle tier, running *business objects*, interacts with the desktop client and applies business rules. The middle tier communicates with the back-end database engine, which continues to handle data management tasks. Often generalized in theory to "N-tier" systems but generally only implemented as three-level, except on the largest, most complex distributed systems.

Tkinter A Python-specific interface to the Tk toolkit, which provides a range of graphical interface components.

transaction A set of operations on a relational database that should be treated as a unit, all occurring if any of them do. A transaction is normally a sequence of operations performed over the same connection to an RDBMS. Changes made by transactions on one connection should be invisible to other connections unless and until the transaction is *committed*.

transport layer　Whether TCP, UDP, or some other protocol, allows simultaneous communications between multiple processes on the same pair of hosts to take place without confusion. The transport layer acts as a multiplexing and demultiplexing mechanism, and also provides error detection and correction in reliable transport layers such as TCP.

trigger　A stored procedure run automatically by the RDBMS when certain changes occur. The changes that fire the trigger are specified when the trigger is installed.

Trivial File Transfer Protocol (TFTP)　A simplistic, block-oriented file transfer scheme with application-level, end-to-end acknowledgments. It is implemented over UDP principally because it is often used in an environment where no operating system support is available (for example, at bootstrap time).

UDP　User Datagram Protocol: the unreliable transport-layer protocol used on the Internet. UDP is not connection-oriented, and the protocol simply makes a "best efforts" attempt to deliver each packet, independent of any others.

unbound method　A method of an object class not associated with any particular instance. Contrast with *bound method*. A class name qualified by the name of one of its methods specifies an unbound method. An unbound method call *must* provide an instance object of the right class (or a subclass thereof) as an explicit first argument.

Unicode strings　Use standard string notation preceded by a letter "U" in upper- or lowercase. Unicode is a 16-bit character scheme with a number of different possible encodings. Unicode makes practical the handling of large character sets, such as those needed for Asian languages, which cannot easily be represented using 8-bit codes such as the ASCII code or the various ISO 8859-x encodings.

Unix-to-Unix copy program (uucp)　A utility used for file transfer over serial lines since before local area networks were available.

validating parser　Requires that a document not only be well-formed but also that it conforms to a DTD. This means that all elements, attributes, and entities must be formally defined in the DTD. It also means that document elements must be properly structured according to the DTD specification.

vertical fragmentation　Useful if the majority of programs using a particular database table only need access to a limited set of attributes for that entity. The designer will split up the relevant table into a set of frequently accessed columns and a set of less frequently accessed columns. The original entity effectively becomes two entities with a *one-to-one* relationship between them, and the primary key field is the same in both.

virtual circuit　A network connection between two processes that persists across several interactions.

Webware　A Python web application suite designed by Chuck Esterbrook and others to help produce web applications that are object-oriented, cached, and multithreaded (`http://webware.source-forge.net/`).

well-known ports Fixed *port numbers*, originally all privileged ports under 1024 but nowadays from outside this range as well, which are associated with particular network protocols and services by an Internet standard.

widening If a numeric operation is performed on two numbers of different types, the "narrower" type will be converted to the "wider" type first, and the result of the expression will be of the wider type. Complex is the widest type, then floating-point, then long integer, and finally integer.

worker function In modular programming, a function that performs data transformations. Contrast with *manager function*.

wrapper class Wraps the behavior of a Python type inside a user-defined class that your own classes can then inherit from. Efforts are under way to unify the Python types and user-defined classes, ultimately reducing or eliminating the need for wrapper classes when it becomes possible to use Python types directly as the base for *inheritance*.

wxPython A user interface toolkit, which is a Python wrapper over the wxWindows toolkit. This toolkit is multiplatform and conforms closely to the look-and-feel of the underlying platform.

XML eXtensible Markup Language: an increasingly popular document and data-encoding standard used on the Internet and in many other areas of computation.

XMLReader A standardized wrapper around an existing XML parser such as expat or xmlproc.

Zope An open-source web application server that makes it easy for groups of programmers to collaborate in producing highly dynamic web sites. Zope is the product of Zope Corporation (formerly Digital Creations), for whom the Python development team now works, so it has a high degree of Python expertise at its disposal.

Index

Symbols

B

H

M

P

X

VOICES THAT MATTER

HOW TO CONTACT US

VISIT OUR WEB SITE

WWW.NEWRIDERS.COM

On our web site, you'll find information about our other books, authors, tables of contents, and book errata. You will also find information about book registration and how to purchase our books, both domestically and internationally.

EMAIL US

Contact us at: **nrfeedback@newriders.com**

- If you have comments or questions about this book
- To report errors that you have found in this book
- If you have a book proposal to submit or are interested in writing for New Riders
- If you are an expert in a computer topic or technology and are interested in being a technical editor who reviews manuscripts for technical accuracy

Contact us at: **nreducation@newriders.com**

- If you are an instructor from an educational institution who wants to preview New Riders books for classroom use. Email should include your name, title, school, department, address, phone number, office days/hours, text in use, and enrollment, along with your request for desk/examination copies and/or additional information.

Contact us at: **nrmedia@newriders.com**

- If you are a member of the media who is interested in reviewing copies of New Riders books. Send your name, mailing address, and email address, along with the name of the publication or web site you work for.

BULK PURCHASES/CORPORATE SALES

If you are interested in buying 10 or more copies of a title or want to set up an account for your company to purchase directly from the publisher at a substantial discount, contact us at 800-382-3419 or email your contact information to corpsales@pearsontechgroup.com. A sales representative will contact you with more information.

WRITE TO US

New Riders Publishing
201 W. 103rd St.
Indianapolis, IN 46290-1097

CALL/FAX US

Toll-free (800) 571-5840
If outside U.S. (317) 581-3500
Ask for New Riders
FAX: (317) 581-4663

New
Riders

WWW.NEWRIDERS.COM

RELATED NEW RIDERS TITLES

ISBN: 0735709211
800 pages
US$49.99

MySQL

Paul DuBois

MySQL teaches you how to use the tools provided by the MySQL distribution, by covering installation, setup, daily use, security, optimization, maintenance, and trouble-shooting. It also discusses important third-party tools, such as the Perl DBI and Apache/PHP interfaces that provide access to MySQL.

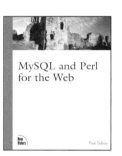

ISBN: 0735710546
500 pages
US$44.99

MySQL and Perl for the Web

Paul Dubois

Paul DuBois does it again with *MySQL and Perl for the Web*. This time he tells you how to bring your web site to life by using the powerful combination of Perl and MySQL.

ISBN: 0735711100
475 pages
US$49.99

Zope

Steve Spicklemire, Kevin Friedly, Jerry Spicklemire, Kim Brand

This book will change the way you develop web sites by teaching you the key concepts behind Zope programming. After giving you a solid foundation in Zope fundamentals, the authors describe the latest Zope technologies (using detailed examples and plenty of source code).

ISBN: 0735711119
500 pages
US$49.99

Jython for Java Programme

Robert W. Bill

Delve into the new and exciting world of Jython, a speedy and efficient scripting language written in Java. After a brief introduction the book utilizes examples to ens that you increase your programmi productivity and get the most fror Jython.

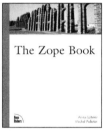

ISBN: 0735711372
350 pages
US$39.99

The Zope Book

Amos Latteier, Michel Pelletier

The much-anticipated first book on Zope from the creators themselves! This book teaches you to efficiently create and manage web sites using the leading Open Source web application server.

ISBN: 0735710910
400 pages
US$34.99

Python Essential Reference Second Edition

David Beazley

"This excellent reference concisely covers the Python 2.1 language and libraries. It is a model of what a reference should be: well-produced, tightly written, comprehensive without covering the obsolete or arcane."

—An online reviewer

Solutions from experts you know and trust.

www.informit.com

New Riders has partnered with **InformIT.com** to bring technical information to your desktop. Drawing on New Riders authors and reviewers to provide additional information on topics you're interested in, **InformIT.com** has free, in-depth information you won't find anywhere else.

- **Master the skills you need, when you need them**

- **Call on resources from some of the best minds in the industry**

- **Get answers when you need them, using InformIT's comprehensive library or live experts online**

- **Go above and beyond what you find in New Riders books, extending your knowledge**

As an **InformIT** partner, **New Riders** has shared the wisdom and knowledge of our authors with you online. Visit **InformIT.com** to see what you're missing.

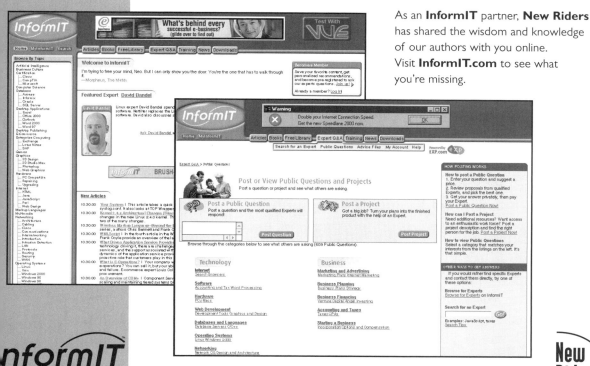

www.informit.com ■ www.newriders.com

New Riders

Publishing
the Voices
that Matter

Colophon

The cover on the front of this book is of the Wat Phra Sri Sanphet Temple in Ayutthaya, Thailand. Wat Phra Sri Sanphet, built in 1491, was at the command of King Borom Trilokkanatin in the grounds of Wang Luang. Two of the now-restored Ceylonese-style chedis were built during the reign of King Rama Thi Badee II to enshrine the relics of his father, King Trillokanatin, and brother. The third was added later, by his own son King Borom Racha, to enshrine the relic of his father.

The temple also once housed a 16m-high, gold-covered Buddha image that was cast by King Ramahatibodhi II in 1500. Unfortunately, the image was destroyed by the rampaging Burmese, who stripped it of its gold.

This book was written using Microsoft Word and laid out in QuarkXPress. The font used for the body text is Bembo and MCPdigital. It was printed on 50# Husky Offset Smooth paper at R.R. Donnelley & Sons in Crawfordsville, Indiana. Prepress consisted of PostScript computer-to-plate technology (filmless process). The cover was printed at Moore Langen Printing in Terre Haute, Indiana, on 12pt, coated on one side.